FRESCOES FROM TANJORE

A HISTORY OF SOUTH INDIA

A History of SOUTH INDIA

from Prehistoric Times to the Fall of Vijayanagar

K. A. NILAKANTA SASTRI, M.A.

THIRD EDITION

OXFORD UNIVERSITY PRESS
1966

Oxford University Press, Ely House, London W. 1

GLASGOW NEW YORK TORONTO MELBOURNE WELLINGTON
CAPE TOWN SALISBURY IBADAN NAIROBI LUSAKA ADDIS ABABA
BOMBAY CALCUTTA MADRAS KARACHI LAHORE DACCA
KUALA LUMPUR HONG KONG

Bharat Insurance Building, Mount Road, Madras 2

Kallidaikurichi Aiyah Aiyar NILAKANTA SASTRI 1892

First published 1955
Second edition 1958
Third edition 1966

PRINTED IN INDIA BY K. A. KORULA AT THE WESLEY PRESS, MYSORE
AND PUBLISHED BY JOHN BROWN, OXFORD UNIVERSITY PRESS, MADRAS 2

DEDICATED

BY HIS GRACIOUS PERMISSION

TO

HIS HIGHNESS

SRI JAYACHAMARAJA WADIYAR BAHADUR

G.C.B., G.C.S.I.

MAHARAJA OF MYSORE

PATRON OF ARTS AND LETTERS

FOUNDER OF THE CHAIR OF INDOLOGY

IN THE UNIVERSITY OF MYSORE

PREFACE TO THE THIRD EDITION

THIS edition differs from its predecessor in the main in two respects. The chapter (III) on Earliest People and Cultures has again come in for much close attention and revision, evidence of the progress of prehistory in the interval since 1958. In the revision of this chapter I have received invaluable help from Mr S. R. Rao, the excavator of Lothal and now Superintendent of Archaeology in Madras, and from my friend and former colleague Dr M. Seshadri of Mysore University. The history and chronology of the Pallavas and the Pāndyas of the ninth and early tenth centuries have been altered considerably. This part of the work was aided greatly by Dr T. V. Mahalingam, Professor of Archaeology in the University of Madras, willingly placing at my disposal his manuscript of the Meyer Lectures he delivered for 1962 on the subject. A transcript of the Dalavayagraharam plates of Vīranārāyana was kindly furnished to me by Dr G. S. Gai, Government Epigraphist for India; Sri K. R. Srinivasan, till recently in charge of the Temple Survey Project in South India and now Deputy Director-General of Archaeology in New Delhi made valuable suggestions for the revision of the chapter on Art and Architecture and permitted the use of the proofs of his monograph on the Cave Temples of the Pallavas. I am very grateful to all these friends for their generous help. Minor revisions have been effected throughout the book where necessary.

K. A. N.

PREFACE TO THE SECOND EDITION

This edition has been carefully revised in the light of suggestions made by many reviewers who have generally given a warm reception to it in the learned periodicals. The Chapter (III) on the Earliest Peoples and Cultures has been rewritten in part in the light of recent advances in the knowledge of the prehistory of South India due particularly to the excavations of the Archaeological Department of India. Rather more attention has been given to the history and culture of Kerala than in the first edition. Some of the illustrations which figured in it have been dropped and a few new ones added. My thanks are due to Dr M. Seshadri of Mysore University and Messrs K. R. Srinivasan and N. R. Banerjee of the Indian Archaeological Department for much valuable help in the revision of the chapter on prehistory. Professor K. K. Pillai of the Madras University and Mr G. Harihara Sastri gave much help in the revision of the sections on Kerala history and culture. Prof. Mariappa Bhat helped in the revision of the section on Kannada literature.

Diacritical marks and transliteration always present problems in books of this kind, and compromises were followed in both instances in the first edition with a view to minimize the marks which embarrass the general reader for whom the book is particularly meant and in order to retain familiar forms of the names of persons, rivers, and places even at the sacrifice of a consistent adherence to strict rules of transliteration. The reader will thus find both *c* and *ch* used for च, and ṣ and sh for ष in different contexts.

Dr T. V. Mahalingam made a number of valuable suggestions as the book was being printed and Mr S. Krishnamurti prepared the Index; I am grateful to them for their help.

K. A. N.

PREFACE TO THE FIRST EDITION

THE aim, scope and plan of the book are explained in the introductory part of Chapter I, and this Preface is meant primarily to be an acknowledgement of the assistance I have received in the preparation of the book. It was not, however, till I began to plan the chapters of the book and the details of their sections that I came to realize how little equipped I was for the task and how much I had to depend on the co-operation of others for its fulfilment. But the help I so much needed was forthcoming in ample measure, particularly from my colleagues in the allied departments of study in the University, and this enabled me to press on with the work in spite of difficulties and complete it in a little over a year from its commencement.

Chapter II on the geography of South India in relation to its history owes a great deal to the invaluable aid of Mr V. Kalyanasundaram of the Geography Department, who, in addition, drew all the maps accompanying the book, with the assistance of Mr R. Tirumalai (Research Scholar) on the historical side. In writing Chapter III on the prehistory of South India Professor T. Balakrishnan Nayar of Presidency College gave me aid of no less importance. Chapters IV-XIII, comprising the core of political history and a sketch of social and economic conditions, and Chapter XV on Religion and Philosophy, are based primarily on published sources and the work of earlier authors in the field to which references are given at the end of every chapter; but they incorporate also the results of much unpublished work, my students' as well as my own, carried on in the University for over seventeen years, and this must be taken into account for any differences from current views that the reader may notice. Chapter XIV on Literature covers very wide ground and indebtedness to my friends is correspondingly heavy: to the late Dr T. R. Chintamani and to Dr V. Raghavan, both of the Sanskrit Department, for the section on Sanskrit; to Mr. S. Vaiyapuri Pillai for that on Tamil; to Mr M. Mariappa Bhat for Kannada; to Mr S. Kameswara Rao (Research Scholar) and Dr N. Venkataramanayya for Telugu; and lastly, to Mr K. Kanakasabhapati Pillai (Research Fellow) and Mr P. Krishnan Nayar of the Malayalam Department for

Malayalam. I must not omit to make special mention of the fact that the task of sketching the history of South Indian architecture and art was rendered particularly easy by the excellent guidance furnished by Percy Brown's monumental survey of the subject which leaves all the older work on the subject at a great distance.

I wish to make it clear that though I have availed myself of the co-operation, very willingly given, of so many scholars, they are in no way responsible for the views that find expression in this book.

The sources of the various illustrations are indicated in the list of Plates and our thanks are due to the authorities concerned for permission to reproduce them here.

UNIVERSITY OF MADRAS K. A. N.
10 *August* 1947

CONTENTS

ILLUSTRATIONS

MAPS

CHAPTER I

SURVEY OF THE SOURCES

1. *Scope:* Neglect of South Indian history—its interest and general trends—no thesis to maintain or lessons to draw—main approach still necessarily from the North—political and cultural history: their relation.
2. *Sources:* Inscriptions: stone, copper—coins—literature: Indian, foreign.

OUR aim in this book is to present a brief general survey of the ancient history of South India to the middle of the seventeenth century A.D. Then began a new epoch with the downfall of the empire of Vijayanagar, its partition between the sultanates of Bijapur and Golconda, and the establishment of the English East India Company at several points on the coast of peninsular India. We mean by South India all the land lying south of the Vindhyas—Dakshiṇa (the Deccan) in the widest sense of the term. Our knowledge of the history of this region has been greatly advanced during the last sixty years by many important discoveries, archaeological and literary. Much of this new source-material lies embedded in the inaccessible periodical reports of the different branches of the Archaeological Survey of India, and of the more important 'Indian states', such as Hyderabad, Mysore and Travancore. Scholars, none too many, have addressed themselves to the task of interpreting the data and have written learned monographs mostly confined to particular dynasties, areas, or topics; these are very helpful as far as they go, but by their very nature cannot give a general idea of the main lines of movement in the history of politics and culture. Sir R. G. Bhandarkar's *Early History of the Dekkan* (1895) is the nearest approach to a general history; but that brilliant sketch is now outdated and does not deal with the history of the extreme South. Dr S. K. Aiyangar wrote several papers and books elucidating many aspects, but they fall far short of being a regular history of the country. P. T. Srinivasa Iyengar's *History of the Tamils* (1929) deals only with the early history of the extreme South.

In general histories of India, the part of the country with which we are concerned figures only in a small way. Vincent

Smith rightly observed: 'Hitherto most historians of ancient India have written as if the South did not exist', and explained this neglect of the South in two ways. 'The historian of India,' he said, 'is bound by the nature of things to direct his attention primarily to the North, and is able to give only a secondary place to the story of the Deccan plateau and the far South.' Again, 'the northern record is far less imperfect than that of the peninsula. Very little is known definitely concerning the southern kingdoms before A.D. 600, whereas the history of Hindustan may be carried back twelve centuries earlier. The extreme deficiency of really ancient records concerning the peninsula leaves an immense gap in the history of India which cannot be filled.' Scanty as our information is on the earliest phase of the history of the South, the situation is not so hopeless as Smith depicts it, and this will become clear as we proceed.

On any view the history of South India is an integral and not the least interesting part of the history of India. The Deccan is one of the oldest inhabited regions of the world and its prehistoric archaeology and contacts with neighbouring lands, so far as they are traceable, constitute an important chapter in the history of the world's civilizations. All over India the foundations of Indian culture were laid by the fusion of Indo-Aryan and pre-Aryan elements in varying conditions and proportions; and in the languages, literatures and institutions of the South there has survived much more of pre-Aryan India than anywhere else. The Marathas of the western Deccan are the southernmost of the Indo-Aryan-speaking peoples of India, and all the country to the east and south of them speaks languages that fall into a single group, the Dravidian, of which Tamil is the oldest surviving literary idiom. And the earliest strata of Tamil literature take us back at least to the early centuries of the Christian era. A picture of politics and society drawn on the basis of this early literature must be interesting in itself and go some way to help unravel problems of early culture-contacts between Aryan and pre-Aryan. The rise of Hindu kingdoms in the eastern lands across the Bay of Bengal is but an expansion and continuation of the process by which South India and Ceylon were colonized and aryanized; and beyond doubt the Deccan and the far South formed the advanced bases from which this transmarine movement started in the early centuries before and after the Christian era: in Indonesia and Indo-China emigrants from India met the same problems as in India south of the Vindhyas and solved them in more or less the same manner. A detailed study of the many interesting analogies between the results of these early culture-contacts in these different lands has not yet been attempted and lies beyond the scope of this book; but we should do well to remember that the history of India has been too long studied more or less exclusively in isolation and from the continental point of view, little regard being paid to the maritime side of the story. The Sātavāhanas were described as 'lords of the three oceans' and promoted overseas colonization and trade. Under them Buddhist art attained the superb forms of beauty and elegance preserved to this day in the cave-temples of western India and the survivals from the stupas of Amarāvatī, Goli, Nāgārjunikonda and other places in the Krishna valley; and the tradition was continued long after the Sātavāhanas by their successors both in the eastern and western Deccan. The latter half of Sātavāhana rule in the Deccan coincides with the age of the literature of the Śangam in Tamil and of active trade between India and the Roman empire in the west, and there is good reason to believe that the plastic arts of the Deccan in this period and the succeeding one owed something to Græco-Roman models and artists.

After the close of the Śangam epoch, from about A.D. 300 to A.D. 600, there is an almost total lack of information regarding occurrences in the Tamil land. Some time about A.D. 300 or a little later the whole country was upset by the predatory activities of the Kalabhras who are described as evil rulers who overthrew numberless kings (*adhirājar*) of the land and got a stranglehold on the country. With the overthrow of the Kalabhras opens the new era of Pāndya-Pallava achievements from the close of the sixth century A.D. This obscure period of Tamil history was marked in the Deccan proper by the rise into prominence of several dynasties of kings who divided among themselves the heritage of the Sātavāhana empire, kept up its administrative and political system, and carried forward its artistic and cultural traditions. The Ābhīras and Traikūṭakas in the north-west, the Vākāṭakas in Berar, the Ikshvākus, Sālankāyanas and Vishnukundins in the eastern Deccan, and the Chutus, Kadambas, Gangas and Pallavas in the south Deccan are the most notable among these dynasties. Buddhism and Jainism made considerable progress in this period, the former inspiring the art of Ajantā, the Andhra country, and Sigiriya in Ceylon, the latter finding widespread acceptance among the kings of the western Deccan and the Tamil country and possibly also among considerable sections of their subjects. To this period also belong the earliest extant inscriptions from Burma, Malaya, Java, Borneo and Indo-China that furnish unmistakable evidence of the important part played by the Deccan and South India in the colonization and aryanization of these lands.

The next period (*c.* A.D. 600-950) is one of relatively large states each with a notable record of its own in war and peace. In the Deccan at first the Chālukyas of Bādāmi rise and spread their power over the entire country between the two seas, though the Telugu country along the east coast and the province of Lāṭa in the north-west develop into virtually independent kingdoms under collateral branches of the royal line. The Chālukyas hold their own against Harshavardhana and confine his empire to the north of the Vindhyas; they wage successful war against other neighbours in the North, and the Pallavas in the South, and the many fine stone temples, rock-cut and structural, found at Aihole, Bādāmi and Pattadakal attest their devotion to religion and architecture; doubtless some of the additions to the caves and paintings at Ajantā must also be ascribed to this period. By the middle of the eighth century, the power of the Chālukyas declines, and from among their numerous feudatories the Rāshtrakūtas rise into eminence and establish a new empire with Mānyakheta (Malkhed) as its centre. In administration, and in its relations with its neighbours in the north and south, this empire generally continues the tradition of the Chālukyas of Bādāmi, except for the fact that it keeps up an almost perpetual feud with the Chālukyas of Vengi, the rulers of the eastern Deccan. The splendid rock-cut temple of Kailāsa at Ellora is perhaps the most remarkable monument of the Rāshtrakūtas.

In the South the Pallavas and the Pāndyas share the country, and the frontier between their territories is shifting about the line of the Kaveri as a result of repeated warfare; the Pallavas in particular have a strenuous time as they have to fight all the while on two fronts. The name of the Cholas, who were so prominent in the Śangam Age and were again to raise in the succeeding epoch one of the most splendid empires known to history, almost disappears from the political map of the Tamil country; and it is not known what relation, if any, the Telugu-Chodas of the Renādu country in the Ceded Districts, one of the minor dynasties of this epoch, bore to their namesakes of the Tamil land, though they claimed descent from Karikāla, the most celebrated of the early Chola monarchs of the Śangam Age. The Pāndya-Pallava period was marked by striking developments in religion, literature and art. Sanskrit held an honoured place as the language of higher literature and culture, and the Ganga monarch Durvinīta had claims to authorship both in Sanskrit and in Kannada. The Pallava king, Mahendravarman I, aptly styled *vicitra-citta*—'wonderful-mind'—was author, architect, musician and painter. In his time or very soon after there arose a strong reaction against the growing influence of Jainism and Buddhism, which found expression in a widespread *bhakti* movement among the worshippers of Śiva and Vishnu; the leaders of this movement were known as Nāyanārs and Āḻvārs, and their exuberant devotional songs, gathered later in the collections known as the *Dēvāram* and the *Divyaprabandham*, celebrate every orthodox shrine they visited many times over in the course of their propagandist peregrinations, and constitute the most priceless treasure in all Tamil literature. The great Kumārila and the still greater Śankara also lived and taught in the same age, the former restating the principles of Vedic exegesis and upholding the religion of sacrifice, the latter expounding the fundamentals of monistic vedānta with unsurpassed power and brilliance. The temples and sculptures of the period register the highest perfection of form that their arts attained in the South. Māmallapuram (Mahābalipuram) and Kānchīpuram (Conjeevaram) are the best museums of this art even now.

The rise of the imperial Cholas of the line of Vijayālaya may be dated from the middle of the ninth century A.D. As they emerged from their obscurity, they soon displaced the remnants of Pallava power to the north of their capital Tanjore, and subdued the Pāndya and Chera countries in the south and west and invaded Ceylon. The hostility of the Rāshtrakūtas, particularly of Krishna III, threatened to wreck the Chola empire at its birth (*c.* 950), but the Karnātaka power was operating too far from its base to achieve permanent results; and Krishna's wars, while putting a temporary check on the rising imperialism of the Cholas, spelled disaster to his own empire which was easily overthrown under his successors by the Chālukya Taila II. The Chola power recovered soon after the withdrawal of Krishna's arms, and swept on to its meridian in the first part of the eleventh century under Rājarāja I and his even greater son Rājendra I. At a time when Northern India was divided into a number of weak and warring states, some of which began to stagger under repeated Islamic inroads, these two great monarchs gave political unity to the whole of Southern India for the first time and established it as a respected sea-power controlling the highways of the Indian Ocean and effectively regulating the affairs of the empire of Śrī Vijaya by invasion and diplomacy. They perfected a highly organized administrative system of central control and fostered the autonomy of village assemblies as none had done before; the father constructed the Great Temple of Tanjore, the purest and most magnificent gem of South Indian architecture; and the son created its replica in the wilds of the Trichinopoly district and called up a new city to surround it. The name of the city, Gangaikondaśōḻapuram—'the town of the Chola who took the Ganges'—was an advertisement of the new power of South India to the rest of the country. This was the silver age of the religious revival which had begun under the Pallavas; a fresh commentary on the Rig-Veda was composed by Venkaṭa Mādhava who lived in a village on the banks of the Kaveri in the reign of Parāntaka I; the Tamil hymns, Śaiva and Vaishṇava, of the last epoch, were gathered together and grouped into canonical books, a form which they have retained to this day; the glorious conception of the form of the Dancing Lord Naṭarāja found embodiment in many monumental bronze images which, alike for the technical skill they imply and the artistic perfection they exhibit, have few rivals in the history of the world's art.

The Chālukyas of Kalyāṇi who built up their power on the ruins of the Rāshtrakūta empire were the contemporaries and opponents of the Cholas during the eleventh and twelfth centuries A.D. The frontier between their kingdoms fluctuated about the line of the Tungabhadra as the result of many wars, some of which were fought with unusual bitterness. The Eastern Chālukya kingdom of Vengi was the bone of contention throughout; its rulers were allied to the Kalyāṇi Chālukyas by descent; but they were also beholden to the Cholas who had restored them to their throne whence they had been driven into exile as the result of a civil war (at the end of the tenth century), and several dynastic alliances followed and brought the lines closer together until, in A.D. 1070, when succession failed in the Chola male line, the ruler of Vengi himself succeeded to the Chola throne. This was Kulottunga I.

His great Chālukya opponent was Vikramāditya VI. Their rivalry filled the annals of South India for about half a century and made for the weakening of their respective empires under their less competent successors. The Hoysalas of Dvā(ō)rasamudra, the Yādavas of Devagiri and the Kākatīyas of Wārangal, all feudatory powers nurtured on the breast of the Chalukyan empire of Kalyāṇi, come up in the latter half of the twelfth century and partition among themselves the territories of the parent empire. Ruling territory contiguous to the Chola empire, the Hoysalas not only aggrandize themselves partly at its expense, but intercede with effect in the politics of the far South; they protect the Chola monarchs from the aggressions of their overgrown vassals. At the beginning of the thirteenth century the Pāndya line begins to throw up a succession of able and powerful monarchs, and the northern half of the Chola empire is dominated by the ambition and turbulence of Kōpperunjinga, a chieftain who claimed descent from the Pallavas. The help of the Hoysalas secures a brief respite for the Chola kingdom, but the inevitable end soon overtakes it and by the middle of the century the whole of the Tamil country and the east coast right up to Nellore passes under the Pāndyas. Hoysala efforts to check the growth of Pāndyan power were not attended by any conspicuous success, nor did the Telugu-Chodas fare better in the enterprise.

Sanskrit learning and literature found patronage everywhere, while the study and cultivation of the languages of the people received encouragement each in its own place—Kannada under the Chālukyas and Hoysalas; Telugu under the eastern Chālukyas, Rāshtrakūtas, Kākatīyas and Telugu-Chodas; and Tamil under the Cholas and Pandyas. The *Rāmāyana* and *Mahābhārata* were rendered into all these languages by celebrated poets, and a large volume of devotional and polemical literature in religion began to grow. The practice of entertaining a poet-laureate at each important court came into vogue and gave birth to many secular literary works of a quasi-historical nature. Political and juristic thinking made considerable progress and expressed itself in the form of commentaries on old law books like that of Yājnavalkya or in independent treatises on polity. In religious philosophy Rāmānuja systematized the doctrines of Viśishta-Advaita and sought to reconcile the Upanishadic doctrine of the Absolute with the theistic predilections of the great Vaishnava Āḻvārs and Āchāryas who had preceded him. Close to Rāmānuja's system, but still differing from it in some important respects, was that of Nimbārka in whose theology Krishna and Rādhā take the place of Nārāyaṇa and Lakshmī, and claim the exclusive devotion of their followers. The construction of large stone temples was undertaken everywhere in the land by all the dynasties, and architecture, sculpture and allied arts found extensive patronage and achieved new forms of beauty and splendour. In many ways the age of the Cholas and Chālukyas (900-1200) was the grandest epoch in the history of South India.

The thirteenth century was the age of the four Hindu kingdoms which inherited the territories and traditions of the two large empires that had preceded them. The Pāndyas and Hoysalas in the south, and the Yādavas and Kākatīyas in the north are the chief powers, and as usual a number of local feudatory dynasties flourished under the suzerainty of each. This state-system experienced a shock from outside at the end of the thirteenth century and the beginning of the fourteenth. The Khilji sultans of Delhi after consolidating their power in North India began to cast their covetous eyes on the South; and the Khiljis were followed by the Tughlaks. At first the motive was only plunder and spoil; but soon the spread of Islam and territorial conquest became the objectives. Considerable parts of the country passed under the nominal sway of Delhi; and Madura, at first the seat of a Muslim governor from Delhi, grew by the rebellion of the governor into an independent sultanate. Colonies of Muslim soldiers and generals found lodgement in several parts of the country and began to control the administration of the land; temples were plundered and demolished, and mosques came to be erected. Hindu society faced a new peril; but the crisis was of relatively short duration; the distance from Delhi, the inherent weakness of a far-flung military imperialism, and the spirit of resistance in the people saved the Hindu faith in the South. Out of the numerous revolts that disrupted the empire of Muhammad bin Tughlak there arose two kingdoms in the Deccan, with centres in Vijayanagar and Gulbarga, in the first half of the fourteenth century.

The Bāhmanī kingdom of Gulbarga was a Muslim state which spread its sway from sea to sea in the northern Deccan, and was no less opposed to its Muslim neighbours in the north than to the Hindu empire to its south. The annals of the Bāhmanī kings make no pleasant reading; fourteen sultans occupied the throne between 1347 and 1518; of these, four were murdered, two others were deposed and blinded, and all were cruel and bloodthirsty fanatics addicted to drink and debauchery. 'It would be difficult,' says a modern historian, 'to specify any definite benefit conferred upon India by the dynasty.' This harsh, but not altogether unjust, judgement may be mitigated by the recollection of the patronage extended by the rulers to authors and architects from Persia, and of their particular regard on some occasions, as in time of famine, for the well-being of their Muslim subjects. In the sixteenth century the Bāhmanī kingdom split up into five separate sultanates which kept up the feud with Vijayanagar though they quarrelled not less among themselves. Bijapur and Golconda were the most prominent among them; all were absorbed in the Mogul empire at different dates in the seventeenth century.

Starting on its career a decade earlier than the Bāhmanī kingdom, that of Vijayanagar became the focus of resurgent Hindu culture which offered a more successful resistance to Islam in this part of the country than anywhere else. But it was a long military vigil; the polity had to be organized on a warlike footing, and there was no room for weak or incompetent monarchs on the throne; whenever the hereditary claimants were found wanting, they were displaced by the ablest among their lieutenants. The empire is best looked upon as a military confederacy of many chieftains co-operating under the leadership of the biggest among them. Even so, the exigencies of the struggle compelled the rulers of Vijayanagar to resort to the employment of foreigners and even Muslims in the artillery and cavalry sections of their armies to make them adequate for the defence of their country and religion. This course had its obvious disadvantages. The fact, however, remains that Vijayanagar kept up the fight, with not inconspicuous success, for the best part of three centuries before it succumbed to the forces it had struggled against so long; but, by then, other and in the long run more decisive factors had put in their appearance in the form of European trading companies, and a new epoch begins. The Portuguese indeed had built up their short-lived and predatory maritime empire much earlier—from the first half of the sixteenth century; but their activities never counted as a serious menace to the Hindu empire with which they took care to be on friendly terms though they quarrelled often enough with its feudatories on the coast, especially in the west. Their attempts to plunder rich Hindu temples, and the conversions to Christianity procured by the Jesuits and other orders of monks in the 'pearl fishery coast' and elsewhere, constituted a threat to Hinduism from another side; but it was soon controlled and checked by the monarchs of Vijayanagar and their agents.

The task of Vijayanagar was thus to conserve Hindu society and save it from the dissolution which threatened it from several directions. Little wonder therefore that during this period the outlook of the Hindus of the South developed new standards of a narrow and rigid orthodoxy in social and religious matters which persist to this day in great force and render a widespread reform at once necessary and difficult. Literature and the arts subserved this rising tide of orthodox feeling and strengthened it in every way. The work of Sāyaṇa, Mādhava and others, resulting in the great commentaries on the Vedas and on the *Smriti* of Parāśara and in a new codification of the philosophical systems in the *Sarvadarśana-sangraha* ('Digest of all systems of philosophy'), may be said to have laid the foundations of this development. The erection of new *maṇḍapas*, pavilions and colonnades, as well as *gōpuras*, in all the important shrines of the country, and the innumerable gifts to temples and learned men for the promotion of religious worship, education and learning that are found recorded in copper-plate grants and stone inscriptions all over the country attest the large material support given to the movement by the monarchs and the nobles of the court. Painting, music, drama, indeed all fine arts, gathered round the court and the temple and found liberal support from both.

In one important respect, however, there was a setback. In the villages the people seem to have lost a good deal of their initiative and come to depend more and more on the tender mercies of petty officials appointed and controlled by the central government or its representatives. The admirable system of autonomous village rule that had been established under the Cholas, and that survived intact for several generations after them, now fell into neglect and all but disappeared in this period, thanks to the pressure of military needs on the emperors and the feudatory *nāyakas*. The militarization of the empire proved disastrous to some of its most valued civil institutions.

In narrating briefly the history of the political and cultural movements in ancient South India in the following pages, the present writer has no thesis to maintain, and any lessons that the story may suggest he is well content to let the reader draw for himself. His endeavour will be to present as simply and clearly as possible a connected narrative of ascertained facts with the minimum of comment necessary to make the story intelligible. Attention will be confined to facts, persons and tendencies of outstanding importance—minor details being everywhere eschewed in order not to distract the attention of the reader by an array of names and details that often serve only to obscure the main trends.

The study of the subject is still in its initial stages and there is scope for widely different views and interpretations at almost every stage of the story. The plan of this book does not allow of elaborate discussions of rival authorities or citations from them, and to this reason and to no other must be ascribed the apparently summary and even dogmatic treatment of controversial topics. Care has always been taken, however, to choose the most reasonable reconstructions for presentation; but it is too much to expect that all of them will satisfy every reader. Several of the conclusions set forth will be found argued at some length in the works to which reference is made at the end of each chapter.

'Attention has been concentrated too long on the North, on Sanskrit books, and on Indo-Aryan notions,' said Vincent Smith. 'It is time,' he added, 'that due regard should be paid to the non-Aryan element.' And, before Smith, an Indian scholar, Professor Sundaram Pillai, had remarked: 'The scientific historian of India ought to begin his study with the basin of the Krishna, of the Kaveri, of the Vaigai, rather than with the Gangetic plain, as has been now long, too long, the fashion.'

But this cannot yet be done, and it is doubtful if it will ever be possible to undertake such a revolutionary, though undoubtedly logical, treatment of the subject. This is due to no reluctance on the part of historians to recognize the influence of pre-Aryan elements on the formation and growth of Indian culture, but to a very real difficulty which was recognized by Professor Sundaram Pillai himself. For after affirming that India south of the Vindhyas was India proper, where the bulk of the people still continue distinctly to retain their pre-Aryan features, their pre-Aryan languages and their pre-Aryan social institutions, he took care to add: 'Even here, the process of aryanization has gone indeed too far to leave it easy for the historian to distinguish the native warp from the foreign woof. But if there is anywhere any chance of such successful disentanglement, it is in the South; and the farther south we go the larger does the chance grow.' The difficulty of distinguishing the Aryan from pre-Aryan elements in Indian culture has continued to baffle the skill of modern scholarship to this day, and forced efforts to discover 'Dravidian' elements has sometimes led to curious results like the attempt to derive the name Hanumān from *āṉ mandi*—an impossible contradiction in terms unknown to Tamil—or to connect the Sanskrit word *pūjā* (worship) with the Tamil words *pū* (flower) and *śey* (do), on the one hand, or *pūśu* (smear, with unguents or the blood of sacrificed animals), on the other. The Indus valley excavations have raised more problems than they have solved, and until the writing on the numerous seals has been satisfactorily deciphered, it will not be easy to decide the relation of this culture to that of the Indo-Aryans or of the 'Dravidians' so called. Some attempt will be made in the third chapter to give a brief tentative account of the earliest inhabitants of the land and of their culture, as far as the evidence of prehistoric archæology and of probable survivals in later times at present enables us to do so; but it must be recognized clearly that the systematic study of the prehistory of South India has just begun, and that our main approach to the historical growth of South Indian culture must for the present still continue to be made from the North.

The complaint is often heard that history generally, and that of India in particular, tends to be a chronicle of dynasties of kings and the endless wars they waged, and devotes little attention to the common people and the cultural movements that influenced their daily life in a profound manner. The fact is that in recent times the conception of history has become much wider than it used to be, and changes in polity and administration, the development of social and economic institutions, and developments in the spheres of religion and art claim the attention of the historian much more today than ever before. But chronology is the skeleton of history, and for the most part the establishment of a dependable chronology necessarily rests on an adequate study of political history; and when large sections of that history are still in the process of being studied and there remains scope for differences of opinion on a number of unsettled questions, the historian is obliged to devote rather more attention to the political side if he is to make his narrative intelligible. Further, the kings and chieftains who so much attract our attention were often splendid promoters of culture and the arts besides being the upholders of society and the protectors of the people. Their history, if pursued on a proper scale and with a full knowledge of the sources, will often be seen to verge on that true history of the life of the people which the critics of dry-as-dust history pine for.

The ancient history of South India is still a relatively new subject of study, and the workers in the field are few; there is no dearth of source material, but the progress in its elucidation and interpretation has not been as great as one would wish. In this book we must pass by all unsettled questions and confine ourselves to the more or less established facts; but even the general outlines of South Indian history are so little known that they deserve to be set forth at some length before we proceed to sketch the main lines of cultural movements in the land.

Inscriptions are the most copious and authentic source of Indian history, particularly of South Indian history. The earliest are in the Brāhmī script and constitute the southern versions of the Aśokan edicts found in Siddāpura, Jaṭinga-Rāmeśvara, and Brahmagiri in Mysore state, Maski in Raichur district, and Yeṟṟaguḍi and Rajula-Mandagiri in Kurnool district. They show the extent of the Mauryan empire in the South, but their contents belong to the general history of India and have little particular bearing on conditions in the South. Not so the short inscriptions found in natural caves in the Tamil districts which seem to record the names of the carvers of the rock-cut beds they contain or of their occupants; though their script is Aśokan Brāhmī with modifications, the language employed in them seems to be the most ancient form of Tamil so far known to epigraphy. These records number only twenty or thirty in all, though many more cf a similar nature are found in the island of Ceylon. These brief records which still continue to be enigmatic in some measure are evidence of the spread of ascetic orders, probably Jain but also Buddhist, in the early centuries before the beginning of the Christian era. To the same epoch belong the inscribed relic casket from Bhaṭṭiprolu in the Krishna valley, an early witness to the stronghold of Buddhism in that region, and the early inscriptions of the Sātavāhana dynasty found engraved on the walls and pillars of the exquisite cave temples at Kanheri, Karle, Nasik and other places in the western Deccan. The language of these records is generally a local variety of Prākrit which is the generic name for all popular tongues with Sanskritic affiliations; the script is Brāhmī with variations due to locality and time; all are engraved on stone.

In addition to stone inscriptions, copper-plate grants come into vogue under the successors of the Sātavāhanas, and some dynasties among them like the Brihatphalāyanas are known only by a single copper plate. Prākrit continues to be the language of the inscriptions till about the fourth century A.D., and then Sanskrit comes to be preferred as the sole language of official documents by the Kadambas, Gangas and Pallavas for a period of two or three centuries. Later inscriptions become bilingual, employing Sanskrit generally at the beginning and the end, and the local speech of the people—Kannada, Telugu or Tamil—in the body of the document, particularly when describing in detail the gifts made and the boundaries of land given to temples, learned men, and so on. From about the tenth century A.D. inscriptions composed altogether in the popular speech become very common, though Sanskrit continues to be employed wholly or in part in other records and holds an honoured place everywhere as the best medium of cultural intercourse. The script undergoes many changes and evolves, in the Deccan, into the ancestor of the modern Telugu and Kannada scripts while farther south its evolution first assumes the early form of Grantha known from the Pallava inscriptions of the seventh and eighth centuries, and then undergoes modifications under the influence of the Tamil alphabet in its two forms—Tamil properly so called and Vaṭṭeḻuttu or round hand. The origin of these two scripts is by no means definitely settled yet. It may be noted, however, that Bühler held it probable that the Tamil alphabet was derived from a northern alphabet of the fourth or fifth century which in course of time was strongly influenced by the Grantha used in the Tamil districts for writing Sanskrit. He also pointed out that 'the Vaṭṭeḻuttu may be described as a cursive script, which bears the same relation to the Tamil as the modern northern alphabets of the clerks and merchants to their originals, e.g., the Modi of the Marathas to the Bālbodh and the Ṭākari of the Dogras to the Śārada'. The Vaṭṭeḻuttu went out of use in the Tamil country about the tenth century A.D. though it continued in use till much later on the west coast.

The early Pallava-Grantha script in the stage when it is yet little differentiated from the ancestor of Telugu-Kannada was carried by Hindu colonists across the seas to west Java, Borneo and Indo-China. the earliest stone inscriptions in this script from these places dating from about A.D. 300. The language of these early colonial inscriptions is Sanskrit.

Stone inscriptions begin to increase in number steadily from the sixth century onwards, but copper-plate records continue to be the mainstay of the historian for some centuries more, and at no time can they be left out of the reckoning. The history of the early Pāndyas from the seventh to the tenth century A.D. rests very largely on two long copper-plate records which are both bilingual and employ the Grantha script for the Sanskrit and the Vaṭṭeḻuttu for the Tamil parts; so also the history of the contemporary Pallava line of Simhavishnu is derived more from copper plates than from stone inscriptions. Almost the whole Eastern Chālukyan history, and much of that of the Chālukyas of Bādāmi are also based on copper-plate charters. Some of the Chola charters on copper plates attained enormous length, being engraved on a large number of good-sized, well-turned-out plates strung together on huge rings with a big circular seal soldered on them; the most conspicuous examples are the Leyden grant of Rājarāja (21st year)—so called because it happened to fall into the hands of the Dutch and pass into the custody of the Leyden museum—the Tiruvālangādu and the Karandai plates of Rājendra I, and the Chāralā plates of Vīrarājendra (7th year), the long Sanskrit *praśasti* of which is a copy of the Kanyākumārī stone inscription of the same monarch. The copper plates of the Vijayanagar rulers often employ a variety of the Nāgarī script, known as Nandi Nāgarī, for Sanskrit. Sometimes, but very rarely and only in recent centuries, the charters were inscribed on more precious material than copper; a charter granted by Vijayarāghava Nāyaka of Tanjore to the Dutch in 1658, and another to the same power by Ekoji in 1676, the former in Telugu and the latter in Tamil, are both engraved on silver plates now in the Jakarta (formerly Batavia) museum. But copper is the metal prescribed in the law books and the most powerful rulers of the land did not employ any other metal.

Copper plates, however, are apt to be fabricated either to establish titles to property or from other motives. Such spurious records betray themselves in one way or other, and the expert epigraphist generally experiences little difficulty in separating the genuine from the false. An exceptionally large number of spurious copper plates brought confusion and obscurity into the early history of the Gangas of the Mysore country, which is beginning to clear up with the discovery of more genuine records.

While copper-plate inscriptions number all together only a few hundreds, stone inscriptions amount to several tens of thousands. Most of them are records of small gifts of lamps, sheep, land, and so on, to temples, and are of little historical value. Records of larger gifts, especially when they are made by the ruling monarchs, are sometimes of exceptional interest as they record details of taxes remitted in favour of donees and privileges conferred on them, and furnish other details of administrative organization and policy. The Tamil inscriptions of Chola Rājarāja I on the walls of the Tanjore temple deserve special mention for the technical perfection of their engraving and the complete and detailed picture they give of the entire economy of the Great Temple—a creation of Rājarāja calculated to symbolize all the glory and grandeur of the empire he had built up. Quite a number of other fairly long inscriptions give interesting information on the constitution and functions of village assemblies, the part played by craft and trade guilds in the economic and artistic life of the country, the courses of study and the numbers of pupils and teachers in important educational centres, and so on. The Tirumukkūdal inscription of Vīrarājendra is unique in the list it furnishes of the stock of medicines maintained in a hospital in the locality; and the Motupalli inscription of Kākatīya Gaṇapati is one of the very few records which give some idea of the conditions of maritime trade.

Almost every inscription on stone or copper, unless it is the very brief record of a mere name or small gift, is seen to follow a definite order. The opening is generally an invocation, either a brief formula in prose, a verse or sometimes a number of verses invoking either one deity or several deities one after another. Then follows a preamble, the *praśasti*, in which the names and achievements of the ruler and his ancestors are narrated, sometimes in a set form which is common to several records of the reign; it is this part which is generally most valuable to the student of political history. After this comes a description of the actual donor, if he happens to be other than the king, together with details of his achievements and those of his ancestors, with a similar but generally briefer description of the donee and his ancestry where he is an individual. If the gift is made to a group or an institution, that is described in some detail. Next there is a description of the object given—money, cattle, taxes, and so on; often it is land, and then the boundaries of the land are carefully specified. Then comes the formula of gift which usually says that it is given with water poured out from the hand of the donor into that of the donee for his perpetual and undisturbed enjoyment. The record concludes with an imprecation on anyone who may terminate the charity or otherwise disturb it, and praise of those who will maintain and protect it in the future. This analysis of the different parts of a typical inscription indicates roughly their relative value to the historian.

Some of the longer inscriptions are dedicatory and commemorative and often contain valuable *praśastis* of long lines of rulers; the Aihole inscription of the reign of Pulakeśin II and the Tālagunda pillar inscription of the Kadambas are the most conspicuous examples of this class. But few are so purely historical in their contents as the Tiruvendipuram inscription of the reign of Chola Rājarāja III which gives an unvarnished account of the troubles of this ruler and of the manner in which he got relief from the intervention of the Hoysalas. Two other inscriptions deserve particular mention. One is the fairly long Kuḍumiyāmalai inscription from Pudukōṭṭai region, beautifully engraved in the ornate Pallava Grantha of the seventh or eighth century on a wide rock face and containing groups of musical notes arranged for the benefit of his pupils by a king, who was a *māheśvara* (worshipper of Śiva) and a pupil of a certain Rudrāchārya. The other inscription comes from Tiruviḍaivāyil in the Tanjore district and contains an entire hymn, otherwise unknown, composed by Ñānasambandar to the local deity and bearing all the marks of a genuine composition of the great saint.

All the early inscriptions are dated in the regnal years of kings, and often there is no guide to absolute chronology except the palæography of the inscriptions; synchronisms are rare, but very decisive where they clearly occur. The first mention of the Śaka era by name is found in the Bādāmi rock inscription of Pulakeśin I, dated Śaka 465 (A.D. 543), recording the fortification of the hill of Vātāpi by that monarch; the existence of this record was brought to light only in 1941. Later inscriptions, whether they bear Śaka dates or not, often contain astronomical details which do not always work out satisfactorily; in some cases, there is no way of reconciling all the data given in the inscriptions, and our choice must depend on the probabilities and remain to some extent arbitrary. One inscription in the reign of the Chola Parāntaka I from South Arcot is dated by counting the number of days that had elapsed since the commencement of the Kaliyuga and the date arrived at supplies satisfactory verification of the other details recorded. In giving the regnal years of kings, the Pāndyan inscriptions often mention one year opposite another; the exact significance of this has not been understood, and epigraphists are agreed in adding up the figures and treating the total as the year of the reign when the inscription was issued.

Inscriptions can by no means be said always to speak the truth, much less the whole truth: legends and exaggeration are often found, and easily recognized as such; more difficult is the task of detecting the truth behind partisan statements made by the composers of records of different dynasties engaged in constant warfare. The instances are not few in which both parties claim victory in a war, and there is often some kind of justification for the claim. And much work still remains to be done in the study and interpretation of the social and economic information contained in the inscriptions—work that has been delayed mainly by the slackness of the Epigraphical Department in publishing the texts.

Closely allied to the evidence of inscriptions on stone and copper is that of the shorter legends on coins. But the coinage of South India 'presents greater difficulties to the student and offers less reward for his labours than that of the North'. Really ancient coins are rare and contain no dates and few intelligible legends, often only the ruler's name or title; also, the devices upon them are often crude and indistinct. The rectangular pieces of impure silver bearing several punch-marks, the *purāṇas* (eldlings) of the law books, were common to both Northern and Southern India and certainly belong to the centuries before Christ; copper punch-marked coins were also known, and this type of coinage may be taken to have gone out of circulation about A.D. 200. In later times the principal coinage of the South was struck in gold, not silver; copper was used for smaller denominations. Of gold coins there were generally two denominations: the *varāha*—perhaps deriving its name from the Chālukya crest of a boar; also called *pon*, *hun*, pagoda (from *bhagavati*?) and *pardaos* (Portuguese)—usually weighing a *kaḻañju* (Molucca bean), or 50 to 60 grains; and the *fanam*, being a tenth of the *varāha*, its weight, 5 to 6 grains, conforming to the *mañjāḍi*. The earliest gold coins are spherules of plain gold bearing a minute punch-mark; a little later came the *padma-ṭankas* which were thin cup-shaped pieces stamped with punches, at first on one side only and then on both; the gold coins of Rājēndra I and Rājādhirāja I Chola, and of Rājarāja I E. Chālukya, discovered at Dowleśvaram in 1946, are marked and inscribed on one side only; and finally came the die-struck pieces of which the thick, small Vijayanagar pagodas are the best surviving specimens. There was a general preference for small coins and the silver *tāres* of Calicut, only one or two grains in weight, furnish some of the smallest specimens of coins known.

During the early centuries of the Christian era Roman imperial coins of gold and silver were imported in considerable quantity in the course of trade and circulated freely in the country;

the small copper coins bearing Roman devices and legends might have been locally produced by foreign settlers. The Sātavāhanas used lead for many of their issues, and their coins bear legends of the names of kings which confirm the Purāṇic lists of these names. One of the most interesting types of these coins is that bearing a two-masted ship on the obverse, an indication of the maritime power and activity of the Andhras; the same design is found on some copper coins of about the same date or a little later from farther south.

The earliest *padma-ṭankas* were perhaps struck by the Kadambas; but one of the coins that can be most satisfactorily dated is a base silver piece with a lion device and the title Vishamasiddhi on the obverse which clearly belongs to Vishnuvardhana (615-33), the founder of the long line of Eastern Chālukya rulers. The practice of punch-marking on the gold coinage lingered long after its disuse on silver and copper, and a large hoard of coins struck by the Telugu-Chodas of Nellore in the thirteenth century, found in 1913 at Kodur, shows that the *padma-ṭanka* type had a long history and wide ramifications. Nāgarī legends, generally incomplete, appear on Kākatīya coins and continue in those of Vijayanagar; they are also found on the coins of some other dynasties like the Kadambas of Goa and the Cholas. The legends on coins of other dynasties are in Kannada, Telugu or Tamil according to the locality in which they were struck.

Conquests are often indicated by designs on coins; thus the Chola coins portray a tiger seated under a canopy in the centre of the field, with the Pāndya fish on one side and the Chera bow at the bottom, the latter symbols being smaller and less prominent than the tiger.

The pagodas of many Vijayanagar kings are known; they are small and dumpy, and were issued also in their half and quarter divisions. Their legends were at first either in Kannada or Nāgarī, while later kings used Nāgarī exclusively.

The coinage of the short-lived sultanate of Madura, usually in billon and copper, follows the contemporary Delhi models and is hardly distinguishable from Delhi issues except by its southern type of calligraphy. The gold and silver coins of the Bāhmanī sultans also followed the Delhi patterns on a more generous scale. In those of earlier reigns there is some variety in arrangement and design, but later a single design was adopted for both metals. The earliest copper closely followed that of Delhi, but innovations soon appeared, and the copper standard underwent many and frequent changes. The five sultanates that succeeded the Bāhmanī kingdom had their own separate issues, though not so well turned out.

Literary evidence is the next important source of knowledge. It is both indigenous and foreign. In all Indian literature there are few professedly historical works. There are indeed some temple chronicles like the *Maduraittala-varalāṟu*, and the *Śrīrangam-kōyil-oḷugu*. While furnishing valuable hints on comparatively recent times, say from 1200 onward, they are nothing more than a farrago of legends for the earlier period and contain too many inaccuracies and distortions to be used by themselves without the testimony of other more trustworthy sources. The semi-historical works that were produced at the beginning of the nineteenth century to the orders of Col. Colin Mackenzie do not concern us as they deal with recent events outside the scope of this book. The *Kongu-deśa-rājākkaḷ caritram* and the *Kēralōtpatti* in its various recensions have often been overrated and are in fact of very little value; so too are the numberless *sthalapurāṇas*, mostly recent redactions of popular legends. Ballads like the *Rāmappayyan-ammānai* are in a somewhat better class, but no early specimens of such popular quasi-historical material have survived.

While the direct contribution to history from literary sources is thus seen to be of little importance, the indirect value to the historian of a study of the literatures of the country can hardly be overrated. Not only do they enable him to picture the social and religious milieu in which the characters of history lived and moved and acted, but the prologues, epilogues and colophons of different works often embody valuable data on the lineage and achievements of the authors of the works and their royal patrons, and these often eke out the scrappy information drawn from inscriptions. The history of South Indian literatures in Sanskrit, Tamil, Telugu and Kannada will be briefly reviewed in the chapter on literature, and mention need be made here only of some outstanding facts of general interest.

The later Vedic literature and the epics, though composed in the North and mainly preoccupied with that country, contain unmistakable hints of the progressive penetration of North Indian influences in the southern lands, and these constitute almost the only source of our knowledge about this important movement of culture. The earliest extant stratum of Tamil literature, that of the Śangam Age, exhibits clearly the results of this movement. It reveals to us a fairly well-developed civilization evolved out of the harmonious blending of much that was borrowed from the incoming northern culture with that already in existence. The details of this most interesting chapter of human history are here as elsewhere hidden from our view. But none can miss the significance of the facts that early Tamil literature, the earliest to which we have access, is already fully charged with words, conceptions and institutions of Sanskritic and northern origin, while it is characterized by a direct and forceful expression and an unrivalled vividness and realism all its own. The independence of the framework of the language and a good part of its vocabulary, and of many of the social institutions and conventions reflected in this literature, is also very clearly seen. Legends bearing on this blend of cultures are preserved both in the northern and southern literatures; though legend is not history, the historian can never afford altogether to neglect the memory of races which often takes these fascinating if enigmatic shapes.

Some types of the *prabandha* class of literature in Tamil, such as the *kalambakam*, *ulā*, *paraṇi* and *kōvai*, narrate much history by the way, especially if they happen to be the compositions of court poets who chose their royal patrons as the heroes of their poems. A *Pāṇḍik-kōvai* is cited extensively in an ancient commentary on the celebrated *Iṟaiyanār Agapporuḷ*; though the verses of the *kōvai* mention the names of several battles fought by the Pāndya rulers of the line of Kaḍungōn, yet the hero of the poem seems to have been not any single king of the line, but a composite figure to whom the poet attributes the achievements of the entire dynasty; the adoption of such literary conventions was quite common, and without great caution one is apt to be easily misled by them. The *Nandik-kalambakam*, which has Pallava Nandivarman III for hero, is much more trustworthy and of real value on the history of the time. Somewhat richer in historical content are a few works of a quasi-historical nature that belong to the imperial Chola period; prominent among them are the *Kalingattup-paraṇi* of Jayangoṇḍār, treating of the invasion of Kalinga by the Chola forces in the reign of Kulottunga I, and the three *ulās* of Oṭṭakkūttan on three successive monarchs —Vikrama Chola, Kulottunga II and Rājarāja II. In Kannada, the *Pampa-bhārata* and Ranna's *Gadāyuddha*, though mainly devoted to themes from the Great Epic, shed much welcome light on contemporary Rāshtrakūta and Chālukya history because the authors have chosen to identify their patrons with some of the epic characters and find occasion to introduce into their narrative several historical incidents very well known to them. Bilhaṇa's *Vikramānkadeva-carita*, a Sanskrit *kāvya* not devoid of poetic quality, is not nearly so useful to history as some of the Tamil and Kannada works just mentioned.

For the history of Vijayanagar, Indian literary evidence becomes very voluminous. Much of this has become accessible in two handy collections of select sources brought out by the University of Madras. Though the class of works known as *Kālajñānas*, purporting to be prophecies of the future by seers, are not as helpful as one would expect, the value of this literature as a whole lies in the necessary corrective it furnishes to biased accounts written by the Muslim historians of the Bāhmanī kingdom and its succession states.

The Muslims gave themselves much more to genuine historical writing than the Hindus, and a number of historical works were composed in Persian under the patronage of Muslim monarchs in the Deccan. Many, however, have either perished or are still to see the light of day; Ferishta mentions several works which he used in the composition of his great history but they are no longer accessible. The most important among those that survive and bear on the period covered by this book may be briefly noticed here. The *Futuh-us-salatin* by Isāmy is the only extant contemporary work on the history of the Bāhmanī kingdom. The author was the grandson of an old Sipah Salar Isāmy who was compelled by Sultan Muhammad bin Tughlak to leave Delhi for Daulatabad in A.D. 1327; the grandfather died on the way, but young Isāmy made his home there. He attached himself to the first Bāhmanī sultan, began to write his work in 1358 and completed it the next year. Modelled on the *Shāh Nāmā* of Firdausi, the work is written in limpid verse and narrates the history of the sultanate of Delhi to the time of Muhammad bin Tughlak. It then gives a vivid picture of the years of political turmoil in the Deccan which preceded the foundation of the Bāhmanī kingdom besides much valuable and accurate information on the Muslim conquest of the Deccan and South India and on the reign and character of the first Bāhmanī sultan. Other works on the Bāhmanī kingdom were late compositions written long after the extinction of the sultanate and from the particular standpoint of one or other of the succession states. Notable among them is the *Burhan-i-maasir* of Ali bin Aziz-ullah Taba Tabaī of Simmīn (Persia)—a contemporary of the more famous Ferishta, and like him at first a courtier of the Nizam Shahi kingdom of Ahmadnagar. Little is known of the life and activities of Taba Tabaī; he began his history in 1591 and completed it in the next five years. It is a history of the Nizam Shahis to which is prefixed an account of the Bāhmanī sultans as an introduction. His bias in favour of his patrons is evident throughout his narrative; but in some respects his statements seem to be more authentic than those of Ferishta and better in accord with the evidence from coins. But beyond a shadow of doubt Ferishta is the prince of Muslim historians of the period. The wide range and sweep of his work which forms a general history of Muslim rule in India, the number of authorities he consulted, and the general sense of perspective that dominates the entire narration impart a monumental character to his history. Covering wide ground, and often at second hand, he is sometimes inaccurate in detail: writing in the court of the Adil Shahis of Bijapur at the instance of Ibrahim II, he narrates Deccan affairs in a way that puts his patrons in the most favourable light. There is no doubt that this history, finished in 1606, is the most comprehensive and readable account of Indian Islam. A Persian by birth, Muhammad Kasim Hindu Shah Ferishta came to Ahmadnagar with his father at the age of twelve in 1582. The father became tutor to a Nizam Shahi prince, but died soon after. Young Ferishta took to a military career, but a palace revolution deprived him of his position as captain of the king's guard. Being a Shiah and having few friends at Ahmadnagar, he migrated to Bijapur where he obtained an appointment in the army. We do not know how and when he changed the sword for the pen and found his true vocation.

Another work, also written from the standpoint of Bijapur, is the *Tazkirat-ul-muluk* by a Persian merchant from Shiraz, known as Shirāzī on that account. His business brought him to Sagar on the Krishna in 1560, and he entered Adil Shahi service in 1574. He wrote his work between the years 1608 and 1610; apparently of not much value for Bāhmanī affairs, it is a contemporary account of some aspects of Bijapur history giving many details not otherwise known. Of the four historians noticed here, three came directly from Persia and all of them wrote in Persian, signal proof of the great influence of Persia on Indo-Muslim culture. 'Abd Allāh Shirāzī Wassaf, a Persian writing in Persia early in the fourteenth century, had access to information on contemporary occurrences in the Tamil country, and he gives some valuable data on the civil war in the Pandyan country and conditions of trade prevalent at that time.

Notices of Southern India by foreign writers are often both instructive and interesting. Speaking generally, the earliest accounts are those of the Greek and Roman writers whose references to India gain in extent and accuracy to the end of the second century A.D. Then we have the Chinese travellers and annalists, the subjects of researches that are still in progress. From the eighth century the writings of Arab merchants and travellers, historians and geographers begin to be important, and the Chinese sources become more copious and definite than before. We also have occasional notices by European travellers like Benjamin of Tudela and Marco Polo. After the end of the fourteenth century the number of foreign travellers and writers increases greatly; at first Portuguese and Italians predominate, but soon Dutchmen, Englishmen and others join in.

Among classical writers, the first direct notice of South India occurs in Megasthenes who gives a quaint account of the Pāndyan kingdom ruled over by Pandaia, a daughter of Herakles to 'whom he assigned that portion of India which lies southward and extends to the sea'. The kingdom was organized into 365 villages; one village had to bring the royal tribute to the treasury every day and, if necessary, assist the queen in collecting it from defaulters. Trade between South India and Egypt was carried on in the Hellenistic period and continued more actively under the Roman empire. Strabo records the increase in the knowledge of India among the Romans of his day and the success of the expedition under Gallus, sent by Augustus (25 B.C.) to secure for the empire the command of Aden and the Red Sea route to India which was becoming increasingly popular among the merchants of the empire. Pliny the Elder (*c.* A.D. 75), the anonymous author of the *Periplus of the Erythraean Sea*, and Ptolemy (A.D. 130) represent the further stages in that increasing acquaintance of the Romans with the countries of the east of which we get the first hints in Strabo. While Pliny and Ptolemy derived their information from other writers, the author of the *Periplus* certainly visited many of the ports of western India and had a direct knowledge of the conditions of trade that prevailed there. However, he seems to have had little knowledge of the east coast. Ptolemy's geography, on the other hand, takes account of the east coast of India and of much of Farther India as well. Recent excavations at Arikamedu near Pondicherry and at Oc-Eo in the delta of the Mekong in Indo-China have furnished striking confirmation of the statements in the classical sources on Roman trade in the Indian Ocean. The most notable name after Ptolemy is that of the crotchety Byzantine monk Cosmas (*c.* A.D. 550) called Indikopleustes ('the man who sailed to India'). A merchant in his early life, he visited many places on the Persian Gulf, on the west coast of India and as far east as Ceylon. His *Christian Topography* has been characterized, not very unjustly, as 'a continent of mud' from which we may extract, however, 'a few geographical fossils of considerable interest'.

Intercourse between China and South India by sea as early as the second century B.C. is attested to by the record of a Chinese embassy to Kānchī ('Houang-tche') and the discovery of a Chinese coin of about the same date from Chandravalli in Mysore. Entries in the Chinese annals of the third, fourth, and fifth centuries A.D. show clearly that the Hindu kingdoms of Indo-China and the archipelago were in active touch with South India on the one side and China on the other: they are said to have sent to the Chinese court on many occasions presents of *vaiḍūrya* (the semi-precious 'cat's eye'), sandalwood and pearls which are specifically South Indian products. Fa-hien did not visit the mainland of South India: he took ship from Tamluk to Ceylon, and his account of the Deccan and the 'pigeon monastery' is just edifying gossip. Many Buddhist monks went from

South India and Ceylon to China by sea and settled there, helping to spread Buddhism in that land and to translate Buddhist scriptures into Chinese. Cosmas mentions the arrival of Chinese ships bringing silk to Ceylon. The celebrated Yuan Chwang, Master of the Law (of Buddhism), travelled much more extensively in India than any of his compatriots who came on similar missions, and on the whole he was much less of a recluse than they. He spent a number of months in the states of the Deccan and South India (A.D. 641-2) and has left behind interesting observations on the religious and social conditions that prevailed in these lands in his day; but even he does not completely satisfy the curiosity of modern students, and it has been said of him: 'He was not a good observer, a careful investigator, or a satisfactory recorder, and consequently he left very much untold which he would have done well to tell.' I-tsing who spent many years in India in the last quarter of the seventh century did not visit South India and has nothing directly to tell us about it. But his works are valuable for the itineraries they contain, for their notices of differences in doctrine and practice among the Buddhists of different lands and, above all, for the brief biographies of about sixty eminent monks who visited India at the same time as he. There are records in the Chinese annals of embassies exchanged between China and the Pallava court of Kānchī in the eighth century and the Chola court in the eleventh. A fair amount of trade was carried on between China and South India in the following centuries and Chinese junks visited Indian waters pretty freely. One of the most valuable notices of the Kingdoms of South India in the Middle Ages is that of Chau Ju-Kua, the Chinese inspector of foreign trade who compiled his work called *Chu-fan-chi* about A.D. 1225. The great Mongol emperor Kublai Khan sent a number of embassies to South Indian states and some of them even sought to influence the course of local politics; with what results we are not in a position to judge. A Chinese merchant, Wang Ta-yüan, visited a number of foreign countries for purposes of trade between the years 1330 and 1349, and wrote the *Tao-i-chi-lio* (*Description of the Barbarians of the Isles*). This work, poor in style but marked by the wide learning and philosophic turn of the author's mind, describes no fewer than ninety-nine countries, ports and noteworthy localities, and is valuable as the account of an eye-witness. Colombo, the Maldives, Kāyangulam, Eli and Calicut are among the places he described. In the first quarter of the fifteenth century A.D., the third emperor of the Ming dynasty sent out a series of stupendous naval expeditions calculated to establish the fame and supremacy of the dynasty over many lands; this prompted a number of foreign rulers in their turn to send embassies to the Chinese court. No fewer than seven of these expeditions reached South India under the command of the famous Cheng Ho. He was accompanied on these expeditions by Fei Hsin and Ma Huan who have left behind accounts of the different countries they visited. Fei Hsin's *Hsing-cha-sheng-lan* or *Description of the Star Raft* (1436) and Ma Huan's *Ying-yai-sheng-lan* (*Description of the coasts of the Ocean*, 1451) are particularly valuable for their notices of Ceylon, Cochin and Calicut in the interval between Ibn Batuta's travels and the arrival of the Portuguese.

Arab travellers and geographers begin to be a valuable source from the ninth century A.D. Much of the trade of the Indian Ocean was in the hands of Arabs from very early times, and with the rise of Islam there came a sudden expansion, the effects of which were not confined to religion and politics but spread to commerce and science. Muslim merchants enjoyed great prestige as the Prophet himself had been one of them. Before the end of the seventh century a colony of Muslim merchants had established themselves in Ceylon, and in 758 the Arabs and Persians settled in Canton were sufficiently numerous for them to be able to raise a tumult in the city and profit by the resulting confusion. Ibn Khurdadbeh, a Persian Muslim of Magian descent, is the first writer who claims mention here; his *Book of Routes and Kingdoms*, composed between 844 and 848 and still being revised in 885, covers wide ground but presents facts in a dry and often incomplete manner. Then, Abu Zaid Hassan of Siraf on the Persian Gulf, no great traveller himself, had many opportunities of meeting much-travelled merchants and scholars, the celebrated Masūdī among them. Abu Zaid declares (916) that his object was to supplement an earlier work on India and China with data drawn from his own studies and talks with persons who had travelled in the eastern countries. Abu Zaid's predecessor who wrote his work in 851 has often been identified with the merchant Suleiman who seems, however, to have been only one of the sources of information commanded by that unknown writer. Ibn al-Fakīh, another writer of the early tenth century who slightly preceded Abu Zaid and Masūdī, also drew largely upon this anonymous writer; in fact it is a common trait of Arab writers to copy one another extensively and this absolves us from noticing in any detail many other authors of the tenth century. The illustrious Alberuni (1030) has little on South India and the celebrated historian and geographer Abulfeda (1273-1331) marks no great advance in knowledge relating to India. His notices of South India are brief, vague and second-hand, though he cites quite often the inveterate traveller and geographer Ibn Said (1214-86). The last and perhaps the most important Arab writer we must notice is the indefatigable Moorish explorer Ibn Batuta. Born in Tangier about 1300, he left his native place at the age of twenty-two, and continued to travel incessantly for the next thirty years. He died at Fez in 1377. He spent many years in India during the time when the mad tyranny of Muhammad bin Tughlak drove all the governors of provinces into open revolt, and led to the rise of independent kingdoms in different parts of the empire. By profession a doctor of the Muhammadan law and traditions, he was a good liver and keen observer of men and affairs. A good part of his work is devoted to an account of his travels and experiences in South India, and contains much accurate information on the state of politics, religion and society at the time.

To turn lastly to the European travellers in India after Cosmas, it has been doubted if the Jewish traveller from Spain, Benjamin of Tudela (*c.* 1170), ever visited India, though he has some interesting remarks to offer on Quilon and its trade. With Marco Polo, the 'prince of medieval travellers', begins a new epoch in the direct contacts between Europe and the East. He reached the court of Kublai Khan after a hazardous journey of three and a half years across Asia. He spent seventeen years in the Mongol court where he became a great favourite of the Khan and was employed on many important missions. Finally he was chosen to escort a princess of the Khan's family on her bridal journey to the ruler of Persia. He left China in 1292 and his voyage to Persia through the Indian seas lasted about a year and a half. Thence he travelled to Constantinople and returned to Venice finally in 1295. He was only passing through some parts of South India on his way to Persia, but the amount of information he was able to collect is indeed surprising. His veracity and justness of observation were doubted for a long time, but this is no longer so. He has much to tell on the manners, beliefs, and practices of the people of South India, and on their maritime trade. 'The commerce of India he found stretching, like an immense chain, from the territories of Kublai Khan to the shores of the Persian Gulf and of the Red Sea. He found the shores and the islands of the Indian Sea luxuriantly covered with nature's choicest products. . . He tells us of the topaz, the amethyst, and the emerald, of the sapphires of Ceylon, and the diamonds of Golconda.'

If the Venetian merchant represents one side of the culture-contacts between the West and East, the three monks who visited South India soon after Marco Polo represent another. First among them was the Franciscan friar, John of Monte Corvino, who travelled in 1292-3 by way of India to China to preach the gospel in that vast land of paganism and, what he considered little better, Nestorianism. This lonely monk was out of sympathy with much that met his eye in India, and with him may be said to begin the stream of Christian missionary criticism of Indian life and habits which has not always been either intelligent or charitable. Nearly 30 years later came Friar Odoric of Pordenone who reached India soon after 1321. He travelled along the west coast, visited Ceylon and went up to the shrine of St Thomas in 'Mailāpūr'. His account of some Hindu customs and practices is obviously that of an eye-witness. Lastly we have Friar Jordanus who may have reached India a little before Odoric. Two of his letters are dated from India in 1321 and 1324; in both, he holds out to his brother friars in Europe the prospect of extensive missionary work in the East. His mention of the Parsis and their mode of exposing the dead is among the earliest notices of this community in India. He was appointed Bishop of Columbum (Quilon) in 1328, but it is not known if he actually took charge of the office. Yet another monk, John of Marignolli, a native of Florence, deserves a passing mention; he went out to China by land, like Marco Polo, as papal legate to the court of the Great Khan; he left China by sea from the celebrated port of Zayton in 1346 and reached Quilon where he spent some time before setting sail for the Coromandel Coast to visit the shrine of St Thomas. He also spent some time in Ceylon and gives an interesting account of the Buddhist monks of the Island.

The rise of Vijayanagar in the fourteenth century and of the Portuguese power in the East a little later attracted many foreigners to India, and as a consequence foreign evidence on South India increases vastly in volume, variety and interest. We cannot possibly go over all this evidence here, but must confine our attention to those sections of it which are of particular value to us. The earliest European visitor to Vijayanagar whose account has come down to us is the Italian Nicolo Conti who came to the city in 1420 or 1421; he wrote nothing himself, but narrated his experiences to a papal secretary who wrote them down in Latin for his master's information; this was translated into Portuguese and from Portuguese into Italian. The original Latin version is not extant. Conti gives a description of the Vijayanagar court and its festivals, its currency and other matters. At about the same time, there came to Vijayanagar the Persian ambassador Abdur Razzak, sent on an important mission to the Zamorin by Shah Rukh. He sailed to Calicut from Ormuz in 1442, and did not much like that city. His stay there was cut short by a message from the Rājā of Vijayanagar asking that he should be sent on to the capital without delay. Abdur Razzak went to Vijayanagar by way of Mangalore, was well received and witnessed the *Mahānavami* festival. Later some jealous merchants from Ormuz cast doubts on his credentials with the result that the ambassador came to be treated with less consideration than before: he left Vijayanagar for Mangalore towards the end of 1443, and Mangalore for Persia early in 1444. The record of his mission is the testimony of a trained official on the state of administration and society at the time.

The Russian trader Athanasius Nikitin spent some years in the Deccan round about 1470 and travelled in the Bāhmanī kingdom which he entered by way of Chaul. His observations give details of the court, the army, and the condition of the people under Bāhmanī rule. Ludovico di Varthema of Bologna, an Italian gentleman and soldier who was eventually knighted by the Portuguese, travelled in India during the years 1502-8 and has left behind a vivid record of his experiences. His credibility was doubted for a long time, but wrongly. His account of Goa and Calicut and other ports of the west coast and of the effects on them of the advent of the Portuguese, and his description of the city and empire of Vijayanagar, contain much that is interesting and valuable. The Portuguese Duarte Barbosa served the government of his country in India from 1500 to about 1516; he knew the Malayalam language very well and 'spoke it better than the natives of his country'. He was *feitor* (factor) in Cannanore in 1502, and acted as interpreter between Francisco Albuquerque and the king of Cannanore in 1503. He was valued as a writer by Gaspar Correa, and was employed by Alfonso D'Albuquerque for his ability, though he did not support the policy of developing Goa at the expense of Cochin and Cannanore. Barbosa returned to Portugal between 1517 and 1518 and then gave the final touches to his narrative which covers much wider ground than the sphere of his official activities and includes a full description of Vijayanagar. The value of other Portuguese writers for the history of the sixteenth century has been sufficiently recognized since Sewell emphasized it generally in *A Forgotten Empire* (1900) which included translations of the chronicles of Domingos Paes (*c.* 1520-2) and of Fernao Nuniz, a horse-dealer who spent three years in Vijayanagar (1535-7), besides part of a letter written from Cochin by Manuel Barradas (12 December 1616) giving an account of the origin and course of the civil war then in progress in the kingdom of Vijayanagar. Caesar Frederick, who visited Vijayanagar a couple of years after the battle of Talikota (Rakshasi-Tangadi), Ralph Fitch who spent the years 1583-91 in India, Nicolas Pimenta, Visitor of the Jesuits in India at the close of the sixteenth century, the Dutch traveller John Huighen van Linschoten (1583) are other writers who have their own contribution to make to our knowledge of South India in their day. The contemporary Jesuit letters from South India often embody passing, but vivid, references to political events of the early seventeenth century. The affairs and trade of the kingdom of Golconda and the port of Masulipatam at that time receive much elucidation from the writings of the Dutch factor Schorer (1615) and the English factor William Methwold (1618-22), which have been edited by Moreland together with another Dutch account, anonymous, dating from about the same time.

This sketch of our foreign sources may be closed with the mention of Pietro della Valle who has been described as the most eminent among those who travelled for pleasure, with no motive of trade or service, 'the most intelligent in apprehension and the most accurate in description'. He was born in Rome in 1586 and sailed for India from Bandar Abbas in January 1623. He visited Cambay, Ahmadabad, Chaul, Goa, Ikkeri, Mangalore and Calicut, and sailed back from Goa to Muscat in November 1624. His letters 'bring before the mind's eye a vivid and life-like representation of men and manners as they existed in the early part of the seventeenth century in the Portuguese settlements in the coast and in the native territories adjacent to them'.

BIBLIOGRAPHY

C. J. Brown: *The Coins of India* (London, 1922)

Sir T. Desikachari: *South Indian Coins* (Trichinopoly, 1933)

K. A. N. Sastri: *Foreign Notices of South India* (Madras, 1939)

—and H. S. Ramanna: *Historical Method in relation to Indian History* (Madras, 1956)

V. A. Smith: *Oxford History of India* (Oxford, 1923)

CHAPTER II

THE LAND IN RELATION TO HISTORY

North and South—the peninsula—the Western Ghats—passes and trade routes—the Eastern Ghats—the Deccan plateau—rainfall and vegetation—changes in coast level—drainage—the Godāvari—the Krishna, Bhima and Tungabhadra—the Kaveri—the Narmada—the Tapti—ports—western coast strip—the east coast—river deltas—Coromandel coast.

In this chapter we shall attempt to give a general description of the geography of the country to serve as the foundation for the historical chapters which follow. Our concern is primarily with the land lying to the south of the Vindhyas, that rugged mountainous tract varying much in width and elevation and stretching almost east to west along the Tropic of Cancer. On the northern side of the Vindhyas the slope is gentle and there are no well-marked spurs or steep valleys; on the southern side, however, there is a steep fall from the crest to the valley of the Narmada, and we have a mountain wall buttressed by several forest-clad spurs overlooking the deep, narrow trough of the river bounded on the south by the Satpura-Mahadeo-Maikal range. From the southern slopes of the Satpuras the Tapti flows parallel to the Narmada to the west and the Mahanadi to the Bay of Bengal in the east. This double wall effectively divides the peninsular South from the plains of North India, but not in a manner that hinders seriously the intercommunication between the two regions. From prehistorical times to the present day there has been no period when the two regions did not influence each other politically and culturally, and on at least three occasions before the advent of British rule both the North and the South formed parts of a single empire embracing nearly the whole of India.

The peninsula juts out into the Indian Ocean between the Arabian Sea and the Bay of Bengal and narrows to a point at Cape Comorin. From Cape Comorin the Malabar and Coromandel coasts extend for a thousand miles, the one to the north-west, and the other at first northward and then to the north-east. There are few good natural harbours along either coast, though the west coast is a little better than the Coromandel coast in

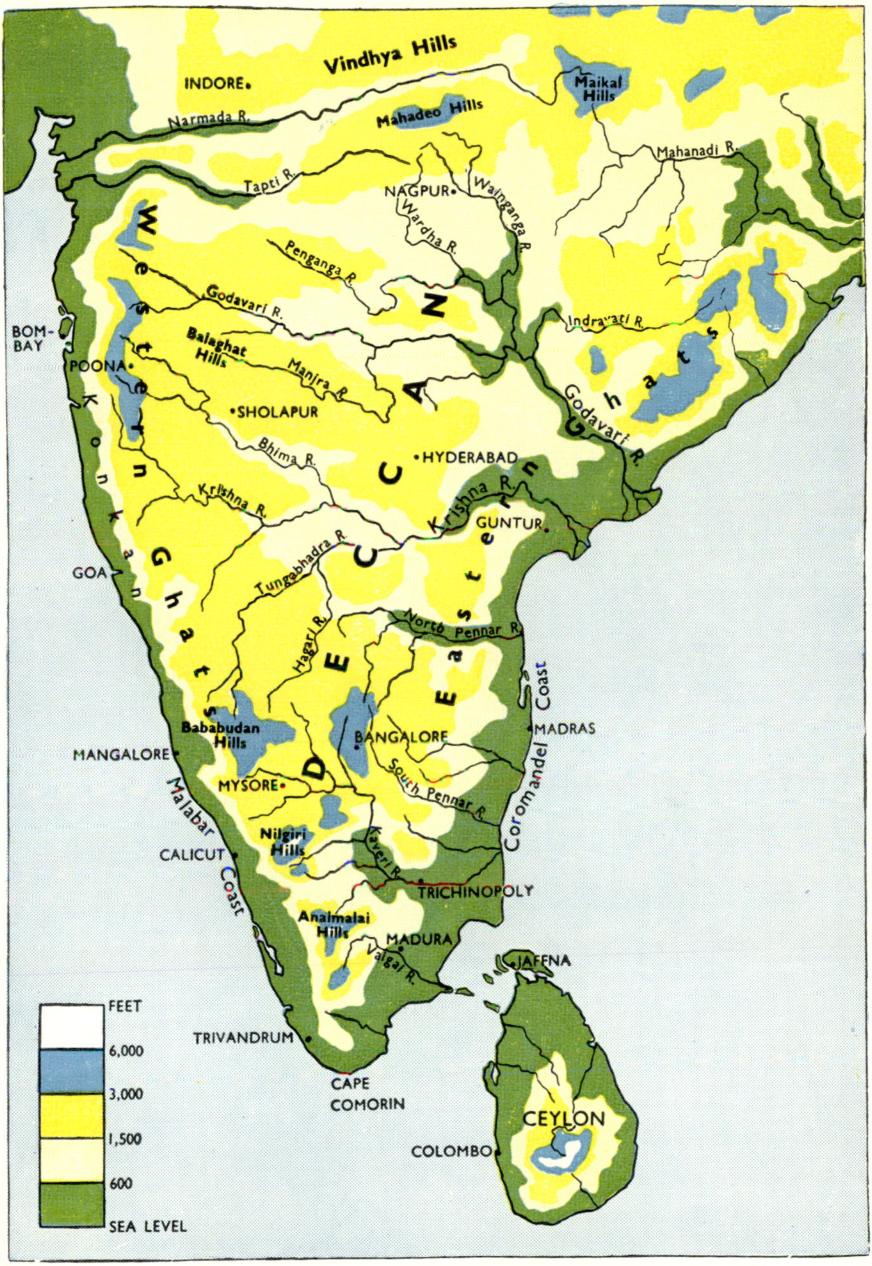

SOUTH INDIA (PHYSICAL)

this respect, as places like Cochin, Goa and Bombay offer fairly safe anchorages for ships. Located half-way on the maritime routes from the Mediterranean and Africa to China, peninsular India developed and maintained a fairly brisk maritime trade with the nations on either side, and had a large share in the colonization of the eastern lands across the Bay of Bengal. And its rulers, at least some of them like the Sātavāhanas, Pallavas and Cholas, are known to have devoted particular care to the maintenance of a strong navy. The Malabar coast retained for many centuries an unenviable reputation for the piratical activity of its sailors, while the mariners of the Chola country came to be looked upon as authorities on sailing conditions in the Indian Ocean and were cited by the Arab geographers of the Middle Ages. An early account of the ports of peninsular India and the conditions of maritime trade is found in the *Periplus of the Erythraean Sea*.

The nucleus of the peninsula is a triangular block of very old rocks that covers its greater part from the Satmala-Ajanta ranges to the Nilgiris. This has a typical plateau relief: its western edge is a steep brink, the Western Ghats, overlooking the west coast formed by a narrow strip of rough, wet lowland; its surface has a gentle fall to a lower brink in the east, the Eastern Ghats. Between the Eastern Ghats and the Coromandel coast is a belt of lowland, the Carnatic, much wider, smoother and relatively drier than the western strip.

Seen from the west the Western Ghats present the appearance of a gigantic sea-wall, often rising in steps from the shore-line—hence the name 'ghats'. They are a steep and rugged mass of hills, little more than 2,000 feet above sea-level at the northern end, rising to more than 4,000 about the latitude of Bombay, generally increasing in altitude towards the south and culminating in the Nilgiris with Dodabetta at a height of 8,760 feet where the Eastern Ghats meet the Western after making a sweep from the other side of the peninsula. Immediately south of the Nilgiri plateau lies the only break in the continuity of the Western Ghats, the Palghat or Coimbatore gap, which is about twenty miles from north to south and affords lowland access from the Carnatic to the Malabar coast at a level of about a thousand feet above the sea. This easy road into the Carnatic from Cochin and Calicut and other ports on the west has played an important role all through history. South of the gap, the ghats reach an even greater height in Anaimudi peak (8,841 ft.) and strike SSE., terminating at the extremity of the peninsula in Cape Comorin. The crest line of the ghats is generally at a distance of from fifty to one hundred miles from the Arabian Sea although in places it approaches so close to the shore as to restrict the width of the coastal plain to no more than five miles, and it is not uncommon for spurs and ridges to end as cliffs along the coast.

North of Goa the surface of the ghats is largely covered by an immense thickness of basaltic lava-flows—the Deccan trap of Indian geology. They reach their maximum thickness about the latitude of Bombay. ‘ The weathering action of ages has shaped the trap formation into natural citadels and fortresses which dominate the crest of the hills, and were found most useful as military positions in the wild days of Maratha supremacy.’ The uplands round Poona being clothed with the volcanic cotton soil are quite as fertile as the alluvial valleys of the Narmada and Tapti rivers. South of Goa, however, the ghats become a series of gneisses and schists, much more resistant than the lava-capped belt.

‘ South of Bombay the seaward face of the hills is clothed with dense forest, and passes inland from the coast are few. But in the north the interior plateau is approached by several roads, famous in history, from the level coast strip on the western side.’ Notable among these is Trimbak Pass at the source of the Godāvari. Vaitarna, the only considerable river draining into the Arabian Sea across northern Konkan, issues from a point almost opposite to the source of the Godāvari. The sacredness of its source and the importance of its valley made it one of the earliest trade routes between the sea and the north Deccan, and the beauty of the lower reaches of the river attracted to its banks some of the earliest Aryan settlements. The Thal Ghat is another historic pass carrying the road from Bombay to Agra and now the northern branch of the Western railway. Then we have the Pimpri Pass bearing an old route from Sopara and Kalyan to Nasik, and the Nana Pass between Junnar and the Konkan, guarded by Shivner, the fort of Junnar. Bhimsankar at the source of the Bhima river, and Chakan are important historic strongholds in this region. Perhaps the best known of the passes is the Bhor Ghat or Khandala Pass (about 2,000 feet) by which the Bombay-Poona road and the southern branch of the Western railway enter the Deccan; this ancient military road 'has ever been regarded as the key to the Deccan' and on or near it lie the historic caves of Kondane, Karle, Bhāja and Bedsa. The Amba Pass carrying the road from Ratnagiri to Kolhapur, and the passes providing less important routes from Vengurla to Belgaum, Karwar to Dharwar, and so on, need not be mentioned. The Shencottah Ghat and the Aramboli Pass form the two southernmost passes providing routes between Travancore and the Pāndya country.

'The precipitous square-cut peaks, which give such a fantastic appearance to the scenery of the Western Ghats, are to be found wherever horizontal strata of varying degrees of resistance are subject to sub-aerial denudation. They repeat themselves in the droogs of Deccan scenery.'

In South India the Anaimalai hills form the most striking range; the higher range consists of a series of plateaux 7,000 feet in elevation running up to peaks of over 8,000. They are covered with rolling downs and dark evergreen forests, cut off from one another by deep valleys characterized by magnificent scenery. The lower range which lies to the west has an average elevation of 3-4,000 feet, and thousands of acres of this area are now under coffee. It contains the teak belt and also produces most of the timber usual in deciduous forest belts of the same elevation; much valuable game, including elephant which gives its name to the range, are also found there. It is inhabited by hill tribes like the Kāḍan, Muduvan and Pulaiyan.

The Eastern Ghats possess little of the magnificence gained by the regular structure but irregular outlines of the ghats of the west. They are scattered, broken, and of much lower altitude, though geologically they seem to be distinctly older than the Western Ghats. Beginning in Orissa, they pass into Andhra state keeping parallel to the coast, generally at a distance of fifty miles as far south as latitude 16°N. They then recede from the coast, follow a north to south course till the latitude of Madras where they strike south-westwards to form the southern edge of the Deccan plateau in its wider sense and meet the Western Ghats in the Nilgiris. Because of their lower elevation and their broken character, the Eastern Ghats have not been as great an obstacle to intercourse between the plateau and the coastal plain as the Western Ghats; and the fact that the major rivers rise on the crest of the Western Ghats and course down all the way to the Bay of Bengal, cutting across the Eastern Ghats, has also helped freedom of movement.

The Deccan plateau has a general elevation of 2,000 feet, but tends to become higher and more rugged as the ghats are approached on the east and west, and attains its highest elevation at the southern end, in the Nilgiris formed by the convergence of the two ghats; the Mysore plateau in consequence has a higher average elevation than the rest of the Deccan. The general slope of the whole is towards the south-east as indicated by the course of the major rivers of the peninsula, the Godāvari, Krishna (Kistna) and Kaveri (Cauvery). The monotony of the plateau surface is broken by a number of spurs from the Western Ghats and other mountain features. Among these, two may be noted in particular: the two ranges enclosing the triangular plateau on which Ahmadnagar stands, the watershed between the Godāvari and the Bhima; and the Mahadeo range forming the watershed between the Bhima and the Krishna. Closely associated with the Eastern Ghats are a range of hills with different local names. The Nallamalais extend north to south from the banks of the Krishna to the Penner valley and are made up of Cuddapah quartzite overlaid by Cuddapah slate; their average height is less than 2,000 feet, but the maximum elevation reached is over 3,000; they contain several plateaux but scarcity of water has foiled attempts at habitation there. Śrīśailam was apparently inhabited of old, and the remains of ancient towns, forts, temples, reservoirs and wells testify to the prosperity of the settlements. Only Chenchus inhabit the region today. The forests are neither dense nor large as the rainfall is poor and the rocks are deeply fissured and fail to retain enough moisture on the surface for large trees to grow. The Erramalais to the west of the Nallamalais in the Kurnool district, and other minor ranges, do not call for detailed notice.

The south-eastern and the relatively higher southern Mysore portion of the plateau is a granitoid and gneissic country strikingly different from the trap region. The extensive vista of level-topped, square-crested, nearly horizontal lava-capped hills gives place to more rounded and graceful dome-capped hills and knolls in the south. Many of these circular or nearly circular hills rise precipitously from the surrounding gneissic plain and their strategic value was appreciated by successive rulers of the land who erected extensive and sometimes impregnable fortifications on them.

Lying athwart the course of the Arabian Sea branch of the south-west monsoon, the Western Ghats bring about a striking difference in rainfall between the regions on either side of them; west of the ghats, the steep edge receives the bulk of the moisture carried by the monsoon, while to the east on the leeward side is the rain-shadow region where the rainfall is not only scanty but highly variable in character. The monsoon literally pours on the west, the annual average being 80 inches on the coastal plain increasing in the higher regions to more than 300 in some stations like Mahabaleshwar. On the eastern side of the ghats the rainfall in most cases is less than 40 inches. This difference in rainfall is naturally reflected in the vegetation. The copious summer rainfall of the coastal plain and the windward slopes of the ghats clothes them with dense vegetation of the evergreen-forest type. The forests contain many kinds of trees of great size and much economic value. Bamboos are plentiful and associated with them locally are to be found teak in abundance, rosewood, and ironwood. The shore is skirted with coconuts and the villages surrounded with groves of betel-nut palm and talipot. Cassia and cardamom flourish wild in the jungles, and the fact that pepper can be cultivated without the screens used in other parts of India to preserve the humidity conveys an idea of how naturally moist the coastal region is.

In the Deccan plateau where the rainfall is not enough to support a vegetation of tall evergreen trees, deciduous forests form the most conspicuous feature of the flora. Teak is found at intervals in relatively well-watered areas over the whole region, though it is economically cultivated under plantation conditions only in certain places. Forests of odoriferous sandalwood abound in Mysore and the adjoining districts. The steep slopes of the Eastern Ghats also have an evergreen type of vegetation, though owing to the lighter rainfall the trees are shorter than those of the Malabar area.

Changes in the level of the Coromandel coast in historical times are attested to in different ways; the once wealthy commercial cities of Koṟkai and Kāyal on the Tinnevelly coast, which were flourishing in the thirteenth century, are now buried under sand dunes miles from the sea; on the other hand in some places not very distant from those named above the sea has encroached on the land, and large parts of once-flourishing ports like Kāvēri-paṭṭinam and Māmallapuram (Mahābalipuram) seem to have disappeared under the waves. In some instances, particularly Kāvēripaṭṭinam, popular tradition preserves the memory of the occurrence though with no clue to its date. Similar changes have occurred in the Gulf of Cambay and its neighbourhood.

The Narmada and Tapti in the north are the two remarkable exceptions to the generally eastward drainage of the peninsula; they flow westwards in comparatively deep and narrow valleys into the rapidly shallowing Gulf of Cambay. The Western Ghats form the water-parting between the easterly and westerly drainage of the plateau; the crest line of the water-parting is at no great distance from the west coast, but the main rivers of the peninsula which have their sources in these heavily forested ghats course right across the peninsula and drain into the Bay of Bengal. This is thought to be the relic of a relatively ancient geographical feature, a view which finds support in the sluggish nature of the rivers which flow along fairly broad and flat-bottomed valleys across a wide and nearly level or gently undulating tract of country in striking contrast to the short swift-flowing rapids that drain the western face of the ghats into the Arabian Sea. The steep-sided valleys of the streams and their tendency to deepen and reach backward at their sources seem to testify to a yet unadjusted gradient.

The three great rivers of the plateau proper are the Godāvari, the Krishna and the Kaveri; and to these may be added the Mahanadi. Among the minor rivers, the Penner, Palar, Pennar and the Vaigai and Tambraparni are important. In the early part of their courses these rivers seem rather to drain the country than water it as they flow rapidly in deep rocky valleys, but as they approach the more level ground of the coastal plain, dams have been thrown across all of them and their waters turned to account for irrigation. The deltas of the Godāvari, Krishna and Kaveri are covered with wide expanses of irrigated crops.

The Godāvari is surpassed in India only by the Ganges and the Indus for its sanctity, the picturesque scenery of its course, and its utility to man. Rising in the hills behind Trimbak in the Nasik district, within fifty miles of the Arabian Sea, it runs a course of 900 miles before reaching the Bay of Bengal and drains an area of 1,12,000 square miles. Above Nasik it flows along a narrow rocky bed, but farther east the banks are lower and more earthy. Below Sironcha it is joined on its left by the Pranhita, carrying the combined waters of the Wardha and the Wainganga which drain the whole of the Satpura and Nagpur plains. A few miles farther down it receives the Indravati which drains the wild and thickly forested areas of the Eastern Ghats in Bastar and its neighbours. Below this confluence the river strikes a predominantly south-easterly course till it joins the sea. Half-way in its course, after it enters Andhra Pradesh, the bed of the river is broad and sandy, from one to two miles in width, and interrupted by rocks in only two places. After running placidly through this flat and monotonous country, it begins to force its way across the Eastern Ghats by a deep and narrow gorge barely 200 yards wide, on either side of which the picturesque wooded slopes of the hills rise almost sheer from the dark waters of the river. Once across the ghats, the river opens out again and forms a series of broad reaches dotted with low alluvial islands—the *lankas*. Below Rajahmundry it forks into two—the Gautami Godāvari on the east and the Vasistha Godāvari on the west which with their distributaries flow down the fan-shaped delta formed in the course of ages by the silt the river has deposited. Below Rajahmundry the river has been dammed at Dowleśvaram from where high-level channels take the water for irrigating an enormous area of the country. The main canals are also used as lines of communication.

Shorter by a hundred miles in its course than the Godāvari, and perhaps less sacred in popular estimation than either the Godāvari or Kaveri, the Krishna is the largest of the three in the area of its drainage basin. Rising just north of Mahabaleshwar, within forty miles of the Arabian Sea, it flows southwards skirting the eastern spurs of the Western Ghats and receiving a number of tributaries mostly from the west. Below Kurundvad it turns eastwards to pass through the south Maratha country into Mysore and Andhra Pradesh. Near the hills the channel is rocky and the stream too rapid for navigation, but it is used largely for irrigation in the Satara district and the more open country to the south-east. In the Belgaum and Bijapur districts its banks of black soil and laterite are high (between 20 and 50 feet) especially on the southern side. On entering Mysore it drops down from the tableland of the Deccan proper to the alluvial doab of Raichur by crossing a succession of lofty ledges of granite that stretch across the river. The stream is very swift here with a fall of over 400 feet in three miles. It receives first the waters of the Bhima draining the Ahmadnagar, Poona and Sholapur districts, and later the Tungabhadra draining the northern part of the Mysore plateau and the districts of Bellary and Kurnool. Then for a considerable distance its bed is deep and rocky, its channel has a rapid fall, and then its course winds in a north-easterly direction across the Nallamalai range. On reaching the Eastern Ghats, it turns sharply south-eastwards and flows directly to the sea which it enters by two mouths. At Vijayavada, forty-five miles from the sea as the crow flies, it runs through a gap barely 1,300 yards wide in a range of gneissic hills and just below this point the river has been dammed for irrigation purposes. Below the dam the channel of the river is at a somewhat higher level than the surrounding plain.

The Tungabhadra is the chief tributary of the Krishna formed by the union, near Kudali, of the two streams Tunga and Bhadra which rise near the Bababudan hills in the western marches of Mysore. The united stream strikes in a north-easterly direction through Mysore and skirts the Ceded Districts till it reaches its confluence with the Krishna a little beyond Kurnool town after a total run of 400 miles. The bed of both the headstreams of the Tungabhadra is rocky, and the country along the course of the united stream rises rapidly away from the river rendering difficult the use of its waters for irrigation. The river is perennial in character and comes down in frequent heavy rushes during the rains. It was dammed by the rulers of Vijayanagar near Hampi for watering the palaces and gardens of that great city.

The Tungabhadra has served as a historic natural frontier right through the centuries; the Chālukyas of Bādāmi, the Rāshtrakūtas, and the Chālukyas of Kalyāṇi to its north, and the Pallavas and Cholas to its south, not to speak of the Gangas who were mostly subordinate to one or other of these powers, made several attempts to extend their sway across the river and only met with indifferent success. The historic city of Vijayanagar and its predecessor Kampili rose on the southern bank of the Tungabhadra. And the Raichur doab between the Tungabhadra and Krishna might well be called ' the cockpit of the Deccan '.

The Kaveri, known as the southern Ganges, has a course of 475 miles and is equally famous for its sanctity, its picturesque scenery and its usefulness for irrigation. Tamil literature cherishes many traditions of its origin and is replete with expressions of pious and fervent admiration for the life-giving properties of its water. It rises in the Brahmagiri, near Talakaveri in Coorg, and flows generally south-eastwards across the plateau, making great falls as it descends the Eastern Ghats, and traverses the Carnatic lowland past Trichinopoly and Tanjore to the Bay which it enters by a number of distributaries in the district of Tanjore. After a tortuous course in Coorg over a rocky bed bordered by high banks covered with luxuriant vegetation, it enters Mysore state and passes through a narrow gorge with a fall of 60 to 80 feet in the rapids of Chunchankatte, after which it widens out. The river twice forks into two streams, only to reunite a few miles farther on, thus forming two islands —Seringapatam and Śivasamudram—fifty miles apart. The celebrated falls of Śivasamudram have been harnessed to supply electrical power to the Kolar Gold Fields over a hundred miles distant. The enterprise was the first of its kind in India and, at the time of its inception (1903), involved one of the longest lines of high tension electric transmission in the world. The Kaveri receives a number of tributaries in its course across Mysore, the most important being the Kabbani, the Hemavati and the Arkavati. In the plain, the course of the river is strongly controlled by the structure of the country as is well shown by its straight course and acute bends. After the confluence of the Bhavani, it changes its southern for a south-eastern direction and then takes an east-south-easterly course before forking a third time to form the island of Śrīrangam. Immediately below Śrīrangam, the river divides into two, the Coleroon and the Kaveri, the latter repeatedly branching and thus ramifying over the entire surface of the Tanjore delta. The waters of the Kaveri are used extensively for irrigation in Mysore state and Coimbatore and Trichinopoly districts, but it is in Tanjore that they are used to the fullest. The problem of utilizing the flood waters of the Kaveri for irrigation was tackled from very early times by successive Chola monarchs though not with the efficiency commanded by modern engineering.

Passing over less important rivers, we may note that the Tambraparni, rising amongst the wooded hills of the southern ghats and benefiting from both the monsoons, forms a life-line for agriculture in the Tinnevelly district. At its mouth in the Gulf of Mannar are the famous pearl fisheries often described by travellers from other countries.

Turning now to the rivers draining on the west, the remarkably straight trend of the valleys and the precipitous rise of the banks of Narmada and Tapti as well as the exceptional course of their drainage are the results of a geological accident.

The Narmada (Namnadios in the *Periplus* and Namados to Ptolemy) is one of the seven sacred rivers of India and rises on the summit of the plateau of Amarkantak at the north-eastern apex of the Satpura range in Rewah in Central India. It runs a course of 801 miles before entering the Gulf of Cambay by a wide estuary 17 miles across below Broach, the Bharukaccha of ancient fame. The river is estimated to drain an area of about 36,000 square miles lying principally to the south of it and comprising the northern portion of the Satpura plateau. Its rocky bed and liability to rapid floods render the river useless for navigation, and its high banks are an obstacle to irrigation. It can be used by small craft up to Broach, 30 miles from its mouth, though the influence of the tide reaches up to 55 miles.

The Tapti (436 miles in length), rising on the Satpura plateau near Multai, flows through a straight and steep-sided valley, locally opening out to form wide alluvial plains, to the Gulf of Cambay which it joins by an estuary. Its banks are too high (30 to 60 feet) for the water to be used for irrigation while the frequent rocky ridges crossing the river render navigation impossible except for the last 20 miles of its course. The Khandesh plain in the middle Tapti valley is the most northern section of the Deccan; stretching for 150 miles east to west it is an extensive area of rich alluvial black soil, a land of large and prosperous towns. Physically it merges eastward into the Nagpur plain characterized by the same type of land use. The rugged hilly and forested regions adjoining the river were breeding-grounds for wild elephants until about the seventeenth century.

The Gulf of Cambay was once frequented by Arab mariners,

and in the early days Broach was more prominent than the better port of Surat which rose only after the silting up of the Narmada estuary and the advent of the European traders who first came to India round the Cape of Good Hope. Besides the estuarine mouths of the rivers, there are a number of real island harbours—Diu, Daman, Bombay. The west coast of the peninsula from Daman southwards to Trivandrum possesses a unity of structure, relief, and climate. On details of relief it can be divided into two halves—the northern half being the Konkan coast and the southern the Malabar coast. The term Konkan is now applied to the strip of country below the ghats south of the Damanganga river up to North Kanara. It varies from 20 to 50 miles in width and is intercepted by hills and cliffs jutting into the sea from the ghats, and numbers of little streams forming rapid torrents during the rains but dwindling to insignificant dimensions in the dry weather. Annual floods have carved deep tidal creeks in their mouths which form valuable highways for traffic. These westward-flowing streams become larger in the extreme south, and one of them, the Sharavati, plunges 850 feet downward from the mountains to form the celebrated Gersoppa falls. The coastal plain is thus altogether a difficult country to traverse; where flat it is fertile and capable of yielding valuable crops of rice.

The Malabar coast differs from the Konkan in many ways. The ghats recede much farther from the sea and the coastal strip is broader, and the Palghat gap relieves the country from the more or less complete isolation of the Konkan tracts and makes for easy communication with the Carnatic plain. The long, firm coastline of Bombay is lost here and replaced by inlets and backwaters that break across the dividing line of sea and shore creating the beautiful, and also typical, coastal scenery of Malabar. The backwaters, which are elongated parallel to the coast, provide easy and natural communication from north to south. The seaward scarp of the ghats has been opened up for the cultivation of tea, coffee, cardamom and cinchona; and natural forests of great commercial value containing bamboos, blackwood and teak grow with special luxuriance.

'The low-lying plains bordering the sea throughout the whole length of western India from Kathiawar promontory to Cape Comorin represented in medieval ages most of the wealth and strength of India, and are still noted for their great fertility. Ancient ports and factories (Arab, Portuguese, and Dutch) are to be found scattered along the coastline, and amid the palm groves of Malabar are many relics of the days when the commerce of the East centred on this coast.' Historically, there has been a striking contrast between the relative political isolation of this coastal country from the rest of India and its generally active contact by sea with the nations of the outside world —the Roman empire, Arabs, Chinese, Portuguese and the rest.

The lowland that interposes between the Eastern Ghats and the shore of the Bay of Bengal extends with little variation from the Mahanadi to Cape Comorin. The maritime strip varies at first from 50 to 100 miles in width, but becomes broader as the ghats recede from the coast about 16°N. Everywhere there is the same narrow strip of sandy foreshore leading to a wide vista of green rice-crops and palm growth, the same background of forest-clad hills now receding into misty distance, now breaking the dead monotony of the surf-beaten coast with bold, bleak headlands, with large lagoons here and there, not unlike the backwaters of the Malabar coast, with wide expanses of sandbanks and shallows opposite the deltaic mouths of rivers which render close approach to the ports impossible to ships of any size. Where no such silt formations exist, the open roadsteads usually afford fair and close anchorage as at Cuddalore and Cocanada and, until they were developed recently into artificial harbours, at Madras and Vizagapatam.

The coast of the Northern Circars, the historic Golconda coast, recalls in a measure some of the features of the west coast —the parallelism between the ghats and the coastline, the nearness of the edge of the ghats to the sea which restricts the coastal lowland to a narrow elongated strip, with spurs from the ghats descending the scarp face and jutting out to sea to end in headlands like the Dolphin's Nose. The ghats are fairly densely clothed with forest while the flat lowland is covered with scrub jungle. A succession of short streams descend the ghats and run directly out to sea. Important features of this region are the Chilka lake and the double delta of the Godāvari and Krishna embracing the Colair lake.

Except in the immediate neighbourhood of the short rivers, the coastal strip is for the most part covered with low-level laterite, red gravel, and clay, and is therefore not very productive. But the conditions change thoroughly when the deltas of the Godāvari and Krishna are reached. With their immense quantities of water and of rich black mud drawn largely from the fertile lava of the trap area, they have created a double delta extending over a million acres round the 300 square miles of the Colair depression. The delta country is a regular granary of rice and produces many other valuable crops like tobacco, cotton and sugarcane. The coast of the delta was the site of some of the earliest settlements of Europeans in India, the Dutch, French and English having all established factories there; the channels of the rivers which led to these have since largely silted up.

Half lake, half swamp, Lake Colair is the only large natural freshwater lake in coastal Andhra. Originally a part of the Bay it has been cut off from it by the growth of the two river deltas which, growing year after year, pushed out farther and farther into the sea until the northern end of the one joined the southern extremity of the other. Lake Colair is known to history as Kolanu, and its chieftains, the Sarōnāthas, played a fairly prominent part in the history of the Andhra country.

In the Coromandel area the ghats, as noted already, turn away from the coast to converge with the Western Ghats in the Nilgiris. There are offshoots like the Javadi, Shevaroy, Pachaimalai, and so on, which retain something of the plateau aspect; but the Carnatic or the Tamil plain increases in width steadily southwards until in the Kaveri basin it stretches for about 170 miles. This plain presents a great contrast to the other parts of the coastal plains and to the Deccan plateau in topography, in climate and in history. This is the real old India of the South, the land where all the great historical kingdoms of South India fixed their capitals, 'the land of unnumbered temples, of indigenous arts and of almost prehistoric industries'. Here artificial irrigation was practised from remote antiquity, and the irrigation system of the fertile river belt between Karūr and Tanjore must be almost as old as agriculture itself.

BIBLIOGRAPHY

S. L. HORA: *Outlines of Field Sciences of India* (Science Congress Association)
The Imperial Gazetteer of India, Vols. I-IV (Oxford, 1909)
L. W. LYDE: *The Continent of Asia* (Macmillan)
SIR J. H. MACKINDER: 'The Sub-Continent of India' (*Cambridge History of India*, Vol. I)
D. N. WADIA: *Geology of India* (Macmillan)

CHAPTER III

THE EARLIEST PEOPLES AND CULTURES

Nature of the subject and evidence—Paleolithic Stage—Upper Paleolithic—Mesolithic Stage and Microliths—Neolithic Stage—rock-paintings—Megaliths and their date—Ādichanallur—Nilgiris—race-types: negrito; proto-Australoid; proto-Mediterranean; Mediterranean; Alpine-Armenoid; Nordic—Languages: Indo-Aryan; Dravidian; Austro-Asiatic—linguistic affinities of Dravidian in western Asia—cultural affinities between western Asia and South India—Haimendorf's view of the Dravidian problem.

THE people of South India cannot be said to have any well-marked racial characteristics. They are 'a miscellany of differing physical types', most clearly the product of a mixture from immemorial antiquity of many different strains, and modern attempts to distinguish these strains are matters of opinion based on the appraisal of obscure and intricate evidence along several lines. The subject-matter of this chapter affords therefore little scope for confident assertions of a categorical nature.

The evidence bearing on the cultural and racial problems of the prehistoric period is threefold. First, there is the actual distribution of physical characteristics among the population of the country today which may, when carefully related to similar characteristics of peoples elsewhere, furnish clues to the early origins and movements of peoples. Secondly, there is the distribution of language-groups and the interrelations among them. It is now well recognized that language has no definite relation to race, but the value of good linguistic evidence for the study of cultural history can be very great. Lastly, archæological excavation brings to light the tools and utensils used by men in different places and times, and comparison of their types and designs, particularly in pottery, as also of the different levels at which they are found in the earth's surface, often gives clues to the movements and relative ages of the cultures of these localities. The remains of human skeletons found in ancient graves sometimes throw light on the probable racial elements in the population. Clearly each of these lines of evidence is difficult to study and interpret properly, and the co-ordination of results reached along the different lines is much more so.

Such study and co-ordination has hardly yet begun, and without going into details we can only set forth the broad conclusions so far reached by scholars.

When did man begin to inhabit South India? The answer is suggested by the examination of fossil remains of fauna found along with primitive stone tools in the terraces of river valleys like the Godāvari and the Narmada, and of mountain ranges like the Siwaliks. The antiquity of human life in these regions goes back about 300,000 years; but for quite a long time man lived at what is known as the 'Old Stone' (Paleolithic) Stage, using only crude stone implements and able only to gather his food as he found it instead of growing it according to his needs. His tools were simple hand-axes and cleavers. Clactonian or Levalloisian flakes at first, but later blades and burins came into use. The paleolithic industries of India can be grouped as follows: (1) the 'Chopper' industries of the North (Sohan); (2) the Abbevillo-Acheulian hand-axes of the South (Madras); and (3) a mixture of both prevailing. This cannot, however, be a hard and fast rule, and the Singrauli basin near Mirzapur (U.P.), Deogarh in Jhansi district (U.P.) in the basin of the Betwa, Chitorgarh and Kotah districts in the Chambal valley of Rajasthan, the Mayurbhanj region, Mahi and Sabarmati valleys in Gujarat, and Krishna and Tungabhadra valleys in the south have been found to furnish meeting points of the two tool traditions of Sohan and Madras. The Kurnool and Nāgārjunakonda bifacial hand-axe industries which manifest a pebble tool facies are believed to be earlier than the Sohan industry with its Levallois flake facies and it seems likely that the former had greater force in diffusion over larger areas than the latter.

The Paleolithic Stage is generally divided into Early or Lower Paleolithic and Later or Upper Paleolithic. We cannot be sure if India had an Upper Paleolithic Stage. According to Movius its presence is suggested by the 'evolved Sohan'; on the other hand the microlithic industries of South India are not linked up with the Upper Paleolithic, and Seshadri derives them from a hypothetical Levalloisian flake industry and this excludes the Upper Paleolithic from the succession of the Stone Stage cultures of India. Further exploration and the study of the *tēri* industries of the south-east littoral and Bruce Foote's finds of the Kurnool caves may throw light on this question.

Whereas in Europe Upper Paleolithic tools consist of fine blades struck off by pressure flaking or with the help of a punch and burins used for engraving on bones etc., no such clear-cut assemblage of tools is noticeable anywhere in India. The recent exploration of the sandstone caves and rock-shelters of Itar Pahar in Rewa district of Madhya Pradesh by S. R. Rao has brought to light several factory sites yielding a large number of blades, blade-points, scrapers, borers and occasionally arrowheads in fine-grained material such as chalcedony, agate, jasper and chert similar in shape and function to those found in Maharashtra, Malwa, and Andhra where the tool-bearing stratified deposits rest against the earlier implementiferous deposits. The new industry has been variously named by the discoverers as 'Newasian', 'Series II', 'Middle Paleolithic', etc. Recently archaeologists have agreed to call it the Middle Stone Age. Distinguished from the paleolithic industries of the Early Stone Age on the one hand, and the microliths of the Late Stone Age on the other, the term 'Middle Paleolithic' cannot be applied to it in the absence of any clear evidence of the Upper Paleolithic Stage in India. The people of the Middle Stone Age lived on river banks and in rock shelters where they could find the raw material for tools. They continued to be hunters, using more advanced equipment such as the bow and arrow and the javelin as indicated by the tanged arrow-heads etc. The country was less wooded owing to less rainfall.

In India the Mesolithic Stage is not so well defined as in Europe. Microliths, now called Late Stone Age tools, have a very wide distribution extending from Jamalgarhi (Peshawar district) in the North-west Frontier to Sawyerpuram (Tinnevelly district) in the extreme south, and from Karachi in Sind on the west to Serai Kala in Bihar on the east. They cannot be said to be truly Mesolithic in stage as they overlap with the Neolithic and the Metal Stages. However, V. D. Krishnaswami opines that in their typology they exhibit a striking similarity with the Western Capsian of the Mesolithic Stage. It may, in all probability, be derived from the western Mesolithic, inasmuch as the Mesolithic has not yet been found in Burma. The material employed in their preparation consists of jasper, agate, carnelian, flint, chert, chalcedony, quartz and other semi-precious stones. The main types are the blade, crescent, trapeze, triangle point, beaked engraver and side-and-end scraper. These tiny tools must have been attached singly or collectively to a handle made of wood or bone for effective use as arrow heads, sickles, etc.

Foote observed that the Tinnevelly microliths lay embedded in the fossil sand-dunes (*tēris*) and were stained red by their long contact with the ferruginous soil; in 1949 Zeuner found microliths near Tuticorin in a geological section which suggests that some of them may be of considerable antiquity. These facts and similar evidence from Nandi Kanama and Khandivli have led to the supposition that the first appearance of microliths may be placed some time between 8000 and 6000 B.C.

The microlithic industries of India may be divided roughly into two classes: (1) pre-pottery industries and (2) those associated with pottery. Gordon has given an elaborate list of the microlithic sites of India, and the discovery of a large number of sites subsequently in recent years will have to be added to the list. Special studies of the microlithic industries of Gujarat, particularly Langhnaj, have been made by Zeuner and Sankalia, and of the Mysore ones by Seshadri. It is now fairly certain from the evidence from Mysore and elsewhere that some of the microlithic industries are contemporaneous with metal industries. The problem of similarities of the Indian microliths with those of South Africa and Palestine is a fascinating but unexplored field as yet. Attempts have been made to differentiate the microliths as coastal and inland groups; the former are perhaps older, simpler and cruder than those found inland, but their range of types is different and rather larger, though the only type that they may possess which the inland ones definitely do not is the burin. From the functional point of view it may be well to classify these industries into (*a*) hunting group and (*b*) peasant group.

The excavations at Rangpur in Kathiawar by S. R. Rao in 1954-55 have for the first time fixed the lower limit of the pre-pottery microlithic industry. Triangle, trapeze, borer, scraper and arrow-head in jasper and agate were the main types found in a gravel lens below a barren layer of silt which in turn was capped by the occupational deposits of the Harappan period. On stratigraphic evidence the Rangpur microlithic industry is assigned to 3000 B.C. On this basis we may say that the date of the pre-pottery microlithic industry ranges between 6000 and 3000 B.C.

The evidence from Langhnaj suggests that the microlith-using people occupied elevated sand-dunes overlooking inundation lakes. The climate was more wet than at present and the sand-dunes were formed during the previous dry phase. Hunting and fishing were the main occupations of the people. They used cattle, nīlgai, deer, rhinoceros, mongoose, pig, mice and fish for their food and made use of blades, burins and points either singly or in composite tools for hunting, fishing and cutting up animals. The long slender legs of the human skeleton unearthed at Langhnaj suggest that the people belonged to a hunter-fisher group. The dead were buried in a highly flexed posture usually in a north-south direction. Physically or racially they were fairly tall, with a long head and slightly protruding lower lip, and recall the Hamitic people of Egypt. Pottery was known to them but there is no evidence of grains being used, even if collected wild. The microlithic industry is assigned to the Late Stone Age.

It is noteworthy that microliths are associated with polished stone celts. This has been proved from a carefully conducted excavation at Brahmagiri in Mysore State. This site is remarkable for its culture continuity extending from the polished stone axe culture to early historic cultures. Whether, in India, there was any break or not in this continuity from Paleolithic through the so-called Mesolithic to Neolithic requires more careful investigation. In Europe and elsewhere this continuity prevailed, the Mesolithic merging into the Neolithic when the art of grinding and polishing stone tools became generally known together with domestication of animals and plants. The great revolution from food-gathering to food-producing, typical of the Neolithic, had a long transition. In Palestine have been discovered mounted on bone handles microlithic sickle blades with that peculiar gloss consequent on cutting grass and plants.

In India it is exceedingly difficult to reconstruct the Neolithic complex. This difficulty has been pertinently pointed out by Zeuner. Not much evidence is available for the domestication of plants from our sites. The study of skeletal material with a view to differentiating wild species from domesticated ones should go a long way to throw light on the problem. But large quantities of polished stone axes, adzes and chisels come from all our so-called Neolithic sites in Bellary, Mysore, 'Hyderabad' and other parts of the Deccan. Since the material for these tools came from trap dykes, the sites and settlements of these people are situated in the neighbourhood of these dykes. As yet excavation has been confined to a few important sites. Sanganakallu, Maski and Brahmagiri in North Mysore, T. Narsipur in South Mysore, Utnur, Piklihal and Nāgārjunakonda in Andhra and Burzahom in Kashmir. At Brahmagiri two phases of the polished stone axe culture have been distinguished on the basis of pottery and also by the presence of a sterile layer. The authors of this culture, besides using Neolithic celts and microliths, had knowledge of the working of copper and bronze though in a restricted degree. The pottery study at Brahmagiri and Sanganakallu relating to this culture is of great value to the student of the prehistoric cultures of India. Sanganakallu has yielded evidence of fresh stone axes, a fine microlithic industry, and pale grey ceramic ware decidedly earlier than, though apparently of the same culture complex as, Brahmagiri, and going back to 1000 B.C. or beyond, dubbed, 'True Neolithic' by Subba Rao.

The Nāgārjunakonda valley harboured a Neolithic community which appears to have known a primitive mode of agriculture as indicated by the axe-types and other evidences. The Neolithic culture of the site was coeval with the upper levels of Sanganakallu (II, 1) and Brahmagiri I (A and B). The tool-types found by K. V. Soundararajan in the excavation and on the surface included axes, shoe-last hoe, wedge, adze, pick, chisel and hammer, the most predominant type being the pick-hoe or pick-chisel with a twin working edge. Although it is not possible to assess the duration of the Neolithic culture in the valley, the occurrence of iron slag with the neoliths in the late levels suggests the intrusion of a new culture which on the analogy of Brahmagiri may be said to be the megalithic culture.

The excavation at T. Narsipur in Mysore district has revealed a neolithic deposit noted for a thick burnished grey ware and polished stone axes made of trap rock with a flat cutting edge at one end and a butt at the other. An intrusion of the chalcolithic element from western India is suggested by the occurrence of neoliths along with a thin burnished grey ware painted on the tip in red ochre, as in Bahal, and channel-spouted vases similar to those found at Nevasa. It must however be added that there was no trace of copper. A remarkable feature of the site is a burial. The body was placed in an east-west direction with the hands placed on the abdomen. Grave furniture consisted of hand-made cream-coloured pots and a shallow bowl with a channel spout. The so-called neck-rest was found to be a pottery rest.

The most important evidence about the habitation of the Neolithic people in the north-west comes from Burzahom in Kashmir. Khazanchi has distinguished two periods of neolithic occupation. The dwelling pits of period I, narrow at the top and wide at the bottom, had landing steps. Perhaps ladders were occasionally used as the steps reached only to a part of the depth. The floor was flat and the walls plastered with mud. During sunny days the pit-dwellers lived in the open air, as indicated by hearths and storage-pits at ground level. Sometimes a superstructure of perishable material covered the pits. In period II the pits were covered and used as floors. The post-holes indicate erection of superstructures of perishable material. Besides polished axes, harvesters, polishers, pounders, chisels and mace-heads of stone, dagger-points, awls, chisels, needles and harpoons of bone and antler were noticed in periods I and II. The neolithic culture was succeeded by an intrusive megalithic culture in period III.

The Carbon-14 date for the Neolithic deposits at Utnur is 2000 B.C. while those of Burzahom have been dated 1700 B.C. On this basis the Brahmagiri Stone Axe Culture should be considered as earlier than 1000 B.C. It is also certain that the Neolithic people had contacts with the post-Harappan chalcolithic people of the northern Deccan.

The problem of the 'shouldered celt' is not to be mixed up with the 'pointed butt' type; very probably it was confined to an Austric people who had more affinities with the peoples and cultures of Indo-China and Malay Peninsula.

The date of the rock-paintings of Peninsular India was at one time thought to go back to the Stone Age. But recent studies assign them to a later period when iron had come into common use. A considerable number of paintings have been found in the Mahadeo Hills from Tamia on the east to just south of Seoni-Malwa in the west; the latest of them are believed to be of the tenth century A.D. and it is held unlikely that any are earlier than the seventh century B.C. It must however be noted that from the undisturbed occupational deposits in three out of ten rock-shelters of Itar Pahar in Rewa district S. R. Rao collected several fluted cores, parallel-sided blades, a point and an arrowhead, all in jasper or chalcedony. The animals seen in the paintings are the wild ass, wild buffalo, horse, rhinoceros, nīlgai, dog and deer. Some of the men depicted are found to be wearing half-skirts of skin. From the primitive dress and weapons and the occurrence of microliths in the deposits accumulated on the floor of the caves Rao is inclined to attribute the paintings to the microlith-using folk who lived in the caves. The rock-paintings of Singhanpur and Kābrā Pahār, 'Raigarh State' (Madhya Pradesh), have been connected with the earlier paintings of the Mahadeo Hills; they are probably contemporary with some of the microliths found in their immediate vicinity and this applies also to the shelters, paintings and microliths of the Son Valley.

Both at T. Narsipur and Piklihal (Andhra) an intrusive chalcolithic element noted for its black or pin-on-red painted ceramic ware is evident. The home of this new industry, greatly influenced by the degenerate Harappa wares noticed at Lothal and Rangpur in Gujarat, appears to be the Narmada, Tapti and Godāvari valleys. The use of the stone axe and furnished grey ware was still in vogue in the Neolithic settlements of the south in spite of the infiltration of copper and painted ware.

Lastly, the megaliths of South India present a series of questions that have found no satisfactory answer as yet. Their existence has been noticed for well over a century, and some investigations were made in the early years of this century at Ādichanallur (Tinnevelly district), Perumbair and the Nilgiris. But the work was not followed up. It is only since 1945 that the Indian Archæological Department has resumed systematic work on these monuments. A detailed ground survey has been conducted in the Chingleput district and adjoining areas, Pudukkottai, and Cochin; and a few monuments have been excavated. The monuments of each of these areas apparently belong to a common megalithic complex; the dead were exposed for excarnation, and the bones were collected in part and interred in different ways—in sarcophagi with legs, in urns, in pits or dolmenoid cists with port-holes, besides circular rock-cut underground vaults with or without a central pillar (typical of the West Coast).

Without stopping to note these differences in detail, we may observe that iron implements and polished black-and-red ware pottery are generally found all over. 'These monuments have invariably been found to occur on rocky high grounds which are themselves unfit for cultivation, in close juxtaposition to a hillock and an irrigation-tank, but in very close proximity to arable land' (Srinivasan and Banerjee). This was perhaps the beginning of irrigated rice-cultivation in South India.

On the data obtained at Brahmagiri in Mysore, Maski in Raichur district and Porkaḷam in Kerala, Sanur, Amritamangalam and Kunrattūr in Chingleput, this culture is thought to have been introduced by an iron-using people from the south some time between 300 B.C. and the middle of the first century A.D.; and 800 B.C. has been suggested as the earliest possible date for the first occupation of Brahmagiri. The date suggested for the commencement of megalithic culture appears, however, to be rather too late; Gordon's date some time between 700 and 400 B.C. sounds better, but it may go still further back.

Many of the South Indian megaliths show a similarity, seemingly amounting to kinship, with megaliths in other parts of the world—in the lands bordering upon the Mediterranean and the Atlantic, in the Caucasus, in Iran. The monuments in Europe have yielded Stone Stage implements on the basis of which they have been dated to about 2000 B.C. and the dolmens in the Caucasus area are assigned to a somewhat later date, 1500 B.C. Between Iran and India lies a vast expanse of space without any known trace of megalithic monuments. While the distribution of megaliths in the West is coastal, elsewhere, particularly in India, this culture penetrated far into the interior, and they generally contain iron implements. In spite of these rather wide gaps, spatial and chronological, Gordon Childe has suggested that 'Sialk B (graves in Iran) might be used to link with the west, with the Caucasus or Palestine, the celebrated Indian dolmens; for these too may at least be entered through port-hole slabs.' He adds: 'But they are concentrated in the south of the Peninsula in areas not likely to be affected by land borne impulses from Iran, but exposed rather to maritime influences. If their distribution does suggest inspiration from the West, that must surely have come by sea.'

The most interesting evidence of the megalith-builders influencing even those who believed in cremating the dead is seen at Amreli in Kathiawar. During the excavations at Amreli in 1953 S. R. Rao found several post-cremation burials surrounded by circles with a tumulus of rubble as in the pit-circles of South India. Thus we find here for the first time the megalithic monument being adapted for preserving remains in the second and third century A.D. Whether the Amreli people borrowed the idea from the cairn-building iron-users of the Indo-Iranian borderland or the megalith-builders of the south it is difficult to say at present. The Amreli pit-circles contained red-polished ware, iron arrowheads and knives besides shell bangles and small quantities of charred human bones.

At Ādichanallur in Tinnevelly district another class of interments, urn-burials without any megalithic appendage in the form of a bounding circle or otherwise, has been found in large numbers; though they cannot be brought strictly into the orbit of megalithic monuments, they seem to be somehow related to them as iron implements, black-and-red ware, and fragmentary burials are common to both. There are other notable differences also. The pottery of Ādichanallur is more primitive than the megalithic pottery of the other sites. There is found here also a quantity of bronze ware and gold diadems or mouth pieces not found elsewhere in South India but having typological parallels in Palestine about 1200 B.C. as also in Syria and Cyprus. Among the tombs of the early Iron-Age of the time of Solomon in Palestine an outstanding find was a remarkable three-pronged iron fork or trident similar to the Ādichanallur tridents in the same metal. And the eastern Mediterranean has been suggested by Childe as the region where the megalithic complex originated, presuming that it had a single origin at all. But it is difficult as yet to say exactly when and in what order the urn-burials and the dolmen and port-hole slab reached the Indian peninsula. It seems to be clear that this iron-using culture did not grow out of the earlier Neolithic culture.

The evidence from Ādichanallur also appears to suggest that the worship of Murugan or Velan, a popular deity with the Tamils from very early times, was known at the time. The god's favourite weapon was the *vēl* (trident) and his banner carried a wild fowl as his emblem. Besides iron tridents, there have been found at Ādichanallur iron banner-bases and representations of fowls in bronze. The practice of wearing mouth pieces, still maintained by devotees carrying *Kāvadi* to the shrine of Murugan in the Paḷni Hills, may well be a survival from prehistoric times.

The people of Ādichanallur cultivated rice; several earthenware bowls containing the husk of paddy and bronze bowls with grains of rice in them have been found.

The Nilgiri cairns and barrows are different from the megaliths of the plain in their structural details and pottery. The bronze vases and bowls found there were thought by Richards to have a philogenetic connexion with a gold bowl from Ur discovered by Woolley. Other likenesses were also discovered by the earlier archæologists, but until their work is checked again and confirmed by fresh studies, no conclusions can be drawn from such vague and stray data.

We turn now to a brief consideration of the racial composition of the population. We do not know to which stock the men of the Paleolithic Stage in South India belonged, as no human skeleton associated with this culture has yet been discovered in peninsular India, apart from a tibia at Attirampākkam (Chingleput). At Vadnagar in Baroda a fossil skeleton of a Pygmy man, thirty inches in height, was discovered in 1935; in this skeleton we probably have the earliest representative of the negrito in India. The negrito is a diminutive type of negro which, rising in Africa like the negro, passed through India eastward, and is found in the Andamans associated with a pre-lithic stage of culture. There is reason to hold that a large part of peninsular India was inhabited by this type for a considerable period of the Old Stone Stage. The occurrence of dwarfish woolly-haired individuals with more or less round heads among the Kādars of Parambikkuḷam and the Pulaiyans of the adjoining Ānaimalai hills in the extreme south of the peninsula may be taken to attest the influence of this early negrito type. Designs on the bamboo combs of the Semangs, a negrito people of Malaya, seem to be identical with those on the combs used by Kādar women, a fact suggesting that originally the Kādars and the Semangs shared the same culture and possibly even belonged to the same ethnic group which underwent a change in India in consequence of the later advent of long-headed peoples.

The Brahmagiri megaliths reveal a predominantly autochthonous Australoid type and a more or less medium-statured, meso-cephalic, medium-vaulted, flat-nosed type with a robust constitution and powerful upper and lower jaws, probably of Scytho-Iranian stock. The single child skull from the Stone-Axe culture appears to be of the autochthonous Australoid type.

There is a mixed population of the Australoid as well as the Armenoid elements at Lothal. Hence it is difficult to say who were the real authors of the Indus civilization in Kathiawar.

Next must be mentioned the proto-Australoid element with long heads, protruding faces, broad flat noses and pronounced brow-ridges. There is no early evidence from India supporting the presence of this element; but evidence from neighbouring lands, too complicated to be set out here, strongly supports the assumption of its presence in India. There is no doubt that the bronze figure of a dancing girl from Mohenjo-Daro has unmistakable proto-Australoid features; her coiffure is strongly reminiscent of the coiffure of the present-day proto-Australoid jungle-folk of Central and Southern India. In South India this element generally entered into the composition of the so-called exterior castes and forms the basis of jungle-folk like the Chenchus, Malayans, Kādars, Kurumbas, and Yeruvas.

A third element is furnished by the proto-Mediterranean type with its long narrow head and face, nose of medium length and straight or aquiline shape, and dark brown hair. This is the dominant type among the Dravidian-speaking peoples of South India at the present day.

As there was perhaps no break in continuity between the Mesolithic and Neolithic Stages, it seems safe to conclude that the people of the Neolithic Stage were the descendants of the proto-Mediterranean stock. Proto-Mediterranean was also the prevailing type at Ādichanallur and in the iron-age cairns of the Deccan.

Another racial element that is traceable has been called Mediterranean and seems to have been the major element among the mixed population of the Indus valley. Slender build, short to medium height, a long head, small brow-ridge, an oval face and, usually, a pointed chin are its dominant characteristics. Typical examples of this stock occur most frequently today among the Telugu Brahmins, and the Kaḷḷars. If the Mediterranean type was not evolved from the proto-Mediterranean in India, but represented an imported strain as it seems to have done, then its arrival in India has to be placed in late Neolithic times.

In certain parts of South India the basic long-headed element represented by the proto-Mediterranean and Mediterranean has been overlaid by a short-headed element. Its occurrence is greatest in Mahārāshtra and can be traced through the Mysore plateau into Tamilnad beyond. It has affected Andhradeśa slightly but has left Keraḷa untouched. This short-headed element is of two main types, the Alpine and the Armenoid which is a specialized variety of the Alpine. The Alpines are concave or straight-nosed, square-jawed people with globular heads. They were in evidence in the Indus valley during chalcolithic times, and are now traceable in Gujarat, Mahārāshtra, Coorg and Karnātaka.

The Armenoid type is short-headed with a markedly convex high-bridged nose, and a high-vaulted head rising steeply from the nape of the neck. This type seems to have been evolved in south-west Asia. These characteristics are now found, though both seldom occur together in the same individual, among peoples inhabiting the mountainous tract extending from the Pamirs and the western flanks of the Himalayas to the mountains of Anatolia.

In South India the Armenoid type is found especially among the Tamil-speaking people. But this type could not have arisen in South India. The present home of this type—the wide tract of Asia stretching from the Pamirs to the Levant—must also have been its original home, that is to say the area of its characterization. According to Keith, the Armenoid in India is the result of an early trade migration from Persia (Iran) or an adjacent country along the Persian Gulf. Round-headedness among the Tamils can be traced through the Deccan, Gujarat and Sind into the eastern portions of the Iranian plateau where there is a striking group of round-heads. In Iran they are more numerous in the uplands than in the plains. Some writers postulate a connexion between these round-heads of the Iranian plateau and uplands and the Dravidian-speakers of India, a connexion borne out by resemblances between the culture of the Caspians, the earliest inhabitants of the highlands of Iran, and the Dravidian-speakers.

The fact that Andhradeśa and Keraḷa—Andhradeśa to a lesser degree than Keraḷa—are free from the round-headed (Alpine-Armenoid) element, shows that it came in by way of Sind, Gujarat and Mahārāshtra, and broke into Tamilnad over south-eastern Mysore. If numbers be any criterion, the round-heads who constitute a small percentage when compared with the basic long-heads (proto-Mediterranean and Mediterranean) are later arrivals in India—a conclusion supported by the evidence on the succession of race strata elsewhere.

Lastly, there remains to be noticed another progressive long-headed element, the Nordic, which entered South India in late prehistoric or proto-historic times. Deriving from the same original stock, the Mediterranean and the Nordic show resemblances in the shape of their heads; but whereas the Mediterranean head is small, the Nordic is massive. The largest percentage of this element in South India is found among the Chitpavan or Konkanastha Brahmins. Its presence among Tamil Brahmins is not entirely unknown.

It remains to add that another type of round-headedness, different from that of Alpine-Armenoid and akin to the Mongolian, has also been noticed in South India, though only in a very slight degree, from Orissa in the east to Malabar in the west; this is supposed to be the result of an oceanic migration in prehistoric times.

The languages of South India fall into three main groups—the Indo-Aryan represented by Marāthi, the Dravidian represented by Tamil, Telugu, Kannada and Malayāḷam besides Gondi and other minor dialects, and the Austro-Asiatic by the Munda languages including Kharia, Juang, Savara and Gadaba of the north-eastern portions of the Deccan, the Kurku of the north-western districts of Madhya Pradesh. Though the Indo-Aryan vocabulary shows traces of Munda influence, the number of Dravidian loan-words in it is much larger and the conclusion seems inevitable that the Dravidian group of languages is more recent than the Austro-Asiatic which is usually recognized as pre-Dravidian. There is no doubt that at one time the Munda languages spread over the whole of North India, for they form the basis of a number of mixed languages along the Himalayan fringe from the Punjab to Bengal. But the Dravidian languages have also left survivals in north-western India, including the islet of Brahui in Baluchistan in an ocean of Indo-Aryan. Hence this group of languages may have prevailed in the north-west at the time the Indo-Aryans arrived. If this view is correct, throughout the bulk of India, Dravidian speech was preceded by Austro-Asiatic and followed by Indo-Aryan. Fuerer-Haimendorf, however, has, with good reason, questioned the correctness of this view, and held that the Dravidian speech never prevailed in India outside its present area. Brahui in Baluchistan, he thinks, can be explained by a migration of Dravidian speakers on land or by sea along the coast from more western lands.

Munda languages now survive also in the Mahadeo Hills of Madhya Pradesh and are found as far south as the Godāvari; they must have prevailed at one time over the whole of the Deccan, for Bhili shows Munda affinities. Whether they extended farther south cannot be determined at present; a few tribes in the extreme south like the Kakkalans of Travancore are said to possess languages peculiar to themselves, but how far, if at all, they include Munda elements is not known.

There is a divergence of opinion among scholars as to which particular race was responsible for the introduction of the Austro-Asiatic languages into India. The proto-Australoid, the Mongolian and the proto-Mediterranean have all been suggested by different writers. Racial prehistory when correlated with linguistic prehistory seems to suggest the following provisional general conclusions. Indo-Aryan was the latest language family to reach India, and it seems reasonable to ascribe it to the Nordics, the last ethnic element to arrive. But the Nordics were by no means a pure stock when they entered India; on their way they must have absorbed much of the Alpine element of the Pamirs and their neighbourhood. For a similar reason, Dravidian must have been the speech of the round-heads, particularly the Armenoids who represent the earlier amongst the two strata of round-heads in India, and Austric the language of the Mediterraneans. About the language of the other ethnic elements noted above we have no knowledge.

Dravidian language and culture hark back to the highlands of Anatolia, Armenia and Iran, the area of characterization of the Armenoid type. The script of the Indus valley seals has not yet been satisfactorily deciphered, and this casts a shadow of doubt over all the problems of pre-Aryan Indian culture. Yet there are not wanting many indications that point to some connexion between the great culture-complex that spread from the Mediterranean to the Indus valley in the third and second millennia B.C. and the prehistoric culture of South India. The name Trimmlai by which the Lycians of Asia Minor called themselves in their inscriptions is a very close approach to Dramila (Tamil). Caldwell indicated a connexion between Susian and Dravidian as regards structure. A large number of ancient place-names in Afghanistan, the highlands of Iran, the plains of the Euphrates and the Tigris, and Mesopotamia generally, have been shown to conform to Dravidian forms, and the non-Semitic, non-Aryan pre-historic peoples of this region have been held to have been Dravidian-speaking. The Hurrian and Kassite languages possess a clearly demonstrable affinity with Dravidian. One writer has connected Elamite and Brahui. The conclusion seems unavoidable that there is some genetic connexion between all these languages. Western Asia being the home of Elamite, it seems not unlikely that the Dravidian or rather proto-Dravidian language and its speakers also reached India from this part of the world.

A number of cultural affinities enforce this conclusion suggested by linguistic data. Inheritance through women which still survives in Dravidian India was in vogue among the Elamites, the earliest branch of the 'Caspian' to emerge into history. There is evidence of the prevalence of the snake-cult in the earliest pre-historic stratum at Persepolis; Dravidian-speaking India is the stronghold of snake worship at the present day. The worship of the Mother-goddess under the name 'Lady of the Mountain' and the annual celebration of her nuptials with the Moon-god of Ur closely resemble the Indian worship of Pārvatī in her various forms and the annual celebration of the *tirukkalyāṇam* (divine marriage) in South Indian Śiva temples; in fact the resemblance is so close that, in spite of the absence of any direct proof of connexion, it is difficult to believe that it is accidental. Again, the nature of the worship offered in the temples of ancient Sumeria and the organization and even the structure of the temple itself have much in common with what has prevailed in South India to this day, allowance being made for the changes that naturally flowed from the increasing aversion to meat-eating among the higher classes of India. 'The essence of worship,' says Leonard Woolley, of ancient Sumer, 'was sacrifice, and by the ritual of sacrifice the cooked flesh of the animal was shared between the god, his priests and the worshipper; the kitchen was therefore not the least important part of the temple, and at all times of the day the fires would be burning and the priests would be overseeing the slaves who carried on the work of butchers, bakers, scullions and cooks.' Numerous medieval inscriptions of southern India bear abundant testimony to the readiness of the people to enrol themselves as the slaves of a neighbouring temple and bind their descendants also to the same status. The institution of *devadāsis* common in South India was well known in ancient Sumer. Again, what can be more accurate as a description of the form and spirit of worship in the Indian temple of today, of the *rājopacāra* offered to the image of God, than this account given by Woolley of worship in the Sumerian temple: 'Where the God was also the King, where church and state were so nearly synonymous, material efficiency was only too likely to get the better of faith. Long life and well-being in this world was the reward men asked in return for formal service such as they might have rendered to a human overlord, and they regarded the wealth and prosperity of the Moon-god as a pledge for the welfare of the city.' The temple and the palace are both indicated by one word *kōyil* in Tamil, and *prāsāda* in Sanskrit, and it is universally recognized that temple-worship was not part of the original Vedic religion.

It must be admitted that much of this evidence on which the old approach to the Dravidian problem was based is vague and circumstantial, and furnishes no reliable chronological frame-work. Not so the recent and very plausible attempt of Fuerer-Haimendorf to equate the Dravidian-speakers with the iron-using megalithic folk who came to South India from the west by sea, perhaps leaving colonies along the coast in the course of their migration—which may account for the megaliths near Karachi and Brahui in Baluchistan. He thinks that an immigration of Dravidian speakers about 500 B.C. would allow sufficient time for the development of the early Tamil literature of the Śangam; but this may well be doubted and the mention of four well-ordered Tamil kingdoms in the Aśoka inscriptions may also indicate the need for postulating an earlier date. This view suggests that the Dravidian civilization of South India is much younger than has been supposed, and that the Aryan occupation of the North and the Dravidian occupation of the South were more or less contemporary. Haimendorf writes: 'It is in Mahārāshtra that the megalithic iron-age civilization must have clashed with the southward movements of the first Aryan people to invade the Deccan'; this suggestion gains some support from the Agastya legends centering round Vātāpi (Bādāmi) as will be seen in the next chapter. But the whole question needs further study and it is too early yet to decide if the postulate of Haimendorf should be accepted as it is or should be modified suitably to take into account the other racial and cultural data briefly reviewed above.

BIBLIOGRAPHY

A. AIYAPPAN: 'Mesolithic Artefacts from Sawyerpuram in Tinnevelly Dt., S. India' (*Spolia Zeylania*, Vol. 24, Pt. 2, 1945)

B. ALCHIN: 'The Indian Middle Stone Age' (*Bulletin of the Institute of Archaeology, University of London*, No. 11, 1959)

F. R. ALCHIN: 'The Neolithic Stone Industry of North Karnataka Region' (*Bulletin of the School of Oriental and African Studies*, Vol. XIX, No. 2, 1957)

—: *Excavations at Piklihal* (Hyderabad, 1960)

—: *Utnoor Excavations* (Hyderabad, 1961)

J. C. BROWN: *Catalogue of Prehistoric Antiquities in the Indian Museum, Calcutta* (Simla, 1917)

BP. CALDWELL: *Comparative Grammar of the Dravidian Languages* (London, 1913)

L. A. CAMMIADE: 'Pygmy Implements of the Lower Godavari' (*Man in India*, IV)

—: 'Prehistoric Man in India and the Karnul Bone Caves' (*Man in India*, VII, Nos. 1-12)

L. A. CAMMIADE AND M. G. BURKITT: 'Fresh Light on the Stone Ages in South-east India' (*Antiquity*, Vol. IV, 1930)

S. N. CHAKRAVARTI: 'The Prehistoric Periods in India' (*Journal of the University of Bombay*, Vol. X, Pt. I, July 1941)

—: 'An Outline of the Stone Age in India' (*JRASB* Letters, Vol. X, Pt. I, 1944)

V. GORDON CHILDE: 'Megaliths' (*Ancient India*, No. 4, July 1947-January 1948)

H. DE TERRA AND T. T. PATTERSON: *Studies in the Ice Age in India and Associated Human Cultures* (Carnegie Institute of Washington, Pub. No. 493, Washington, 1939)

—: 'The Siwaliks of India and Early Man' (*Early Man*, 1939)

R. B. FOOTE: *The Foote Collection of India, Prehistoric and Protohistoric Antiquities*, Catalogue Raisonné (Govt. Museum, Madras, 1914)

—: 'Notes on Their Ages and Distribution' (Govt. Museum, Madras, 1916)

D. H. GORDON: 'Early Use of Metals in India and Pakistan' (*Journal of the Royal Anthropological Institute*, 1952)

—: 'The Stone Industries of the Holocene in India and Pakistan' (*Ancient India*, No. 6, Jan. 1950)

—: *The Prehistoric Background of Indian Culture* (Bombay, 1958)

B. S. GUHA: *Racial Elements in the Population* (Bombay, 1944)

CHRISTOPHER VON FUERER-HAIMENDORF: 'When, How and From Where Did the Dravidians Come to India?' (*The Indo-Asian Culture*, Vol. II, No. 3, January 1954, pp. 238-47)

—: 'New Aspects of the Dravidian Problem' (*Tamil Culture*, Vol. II, No. 2, 1953)

E. HERZFELD AND A. B. KEITH: 'Iran as a Prehistoric Centre' in A. U. Pope's *Survey of Persian Art*, Vol. I, Ch. II (Oxford)

J. H. HUTTON: *Census of India*, 1931, Vol. I, Pt. I

R. V. JOSHI: *Pleistocene Studies in the Malaprabha Basin* (Poona, 1955)

V. D. KRISHNASWAMI: 'Megalithic Types of South India' (*Ancient India*, No. 5, Jan. 1949)

—: 'Progress in Pre-history' (*Ancient India*, Special Jubilee Number 9, 1953)

—: 'Environmental and Cultural Changes of Prehistoric Man near Madras' (*Journal of the Madras Geographical Association*, Vol. XIII, pp. 58-90, 1938)

—: 'Prehistoric Man round Madras' (*Indian Academy of Sciences*, Madras Meeting, 1938)

—: 'The Neolithic Pattern in India' (Presidential address of the Anthropology section of the Indian Science Congress, 1956)

B. B. LAL: 'Protohistoric Investigation' (*Ancient India*, No. 9, 1953)

H. L. MOVIUS (JR.): 'Early Man and Pleistocene Stratigraphy in Southern and Eastern Asia' (*Peabody Museum Paper* XIX, No. 3, 1-25)

STUART PIGGOTT: *Prehistoric India to 1000 B.C.* (London, 1950)

L. V. RAMASWAMI AIYAR: 'Dravidic Place-names in the Plateau of Persia' (*QJMS*, Vol. XX, Bangalore, 1929-30)

S. R. RAO: 'Excavations at Lothal' (*Lalit Kala* Nos. 3 & 4, Bombay, 1956-57)

H. D. SANKALIA: *Investigations into the Prehistoric Archaeology of Gujarat* (Sri Pratapa Simha Maharaj Rajyabhisheka Grantha Mala, Memoir IV, Baroda State Press, 1946)

—: *History of Prehistory at Nevasa* (Poona, 1960)

—: *Indian Archaeology Today* (Bombay, 1962)

H. D. SANKALIA AND S. B. DEV: *Excavations at Nasik and Jorwe* (Poona, 1955)

H. D. SANKALIA AND I. KARVE: 'The Second Gujarat Prehistoric Expedition' (*New Indian Antiquary*, Vol. IV, No. 4)

—: '*Preliminary Report on the Third Gujarat Prehistoric Expedition and Human Remains Discovered So Far*' (Times of India Press, 1945)

H. D. SANKALIA, B. SUBBA RAO AND S. B. DEV: *Excavations at Maheshwar and Navdatoli* (Poona and Baroda, 1958)

Y. D. SARMA: 'Rock Cut Caves of Cochin' (*Ancient India*, No. 12, 1956)

—: 'Exploration of Historical Sites' (*Ancient India*, No. 9, 1953)

K. A. N. SASTRI: 'Southern India, Arabia and Africa' (*New Indian Antiquary*, Vol. I, 1938)

M. SESHADRI: 'Microlithic Industries of Mysore' (*Annual Report of the Institute of Archaeology*, London, 1953)

—: 'New Light on Megalithic Dating in India' (*Journal of the Mysore University* [Arts] 1956)

—: *Prehistoric and Protohistoric Mysore* (London, 1956)

—: 'The Paleolithic Industry of Kibbanahalli' (Mysore State) (*Artibus Asiae*, 1955, xviii, pp. 271-87)

—: *Megalithic Excavations at Jadigenahalli* (Mysore, 1960)

K. R. SRINIVASAN: 'The Megalithic Burials and Urn Fields of South India in the light of Tamil Literature and Tradition' (*Ancient India*, No. 2, 1946)

K. R. SRINIVASAN AND N. R. BANERJEE: 'Survey of South Indian Megaliths' (*Ancient India*, No. 9, 1953)

B. SUBBA RAO: *The Personality of India* (Baroda, 1958)

B. K. THAPAR: 'Porkaḷam 1948: Excavation of a Megalithic Urn-burial' (*Ancient India*, No. 8, 1952)

—: 'Maski 1954—A Chalcolithic Site of the Southern Deccan' (*Ancient India*, No. 13, Jan. 1957)

K. R. U. TODD: 'Prehistoric Man round Bombay' (*Proceedings of the Prehistoric Society of East Anglia*, Vol. VII, Ipswich, 1932)

—: 'Paleolithic Industries of Bombay' (*Journal of the Royal Anthropological Institute*, Vol. LXIX, London, 1939)

—: 'The Microlithic Industries of Bombay' (*Ancient India*, No. 6, Jan. 1950)

R. E. M. WHEELER: 'Brahmagiri and Chandravalli, 1947' (*Ancient India*, No. 4, July 1947-January 1948)

—: *Early India and Pakistan* (London, 1959)

F. E. ZEUNER: 'The Microlithic Industry of Langhnaj, Gujarat' (*Man*, article No. 182, September 1952)

F. E. ZEUNER AND BRIDGET ALCHIN: 'The Microlithic Sites of Tinnevelly District, Madras State' (*Ancient India*, No. 12, 1956)

Indian Archaeology—A Review: Annual Publication of the Archaeological Survey of India, New Delhi, 1953-54 onwards

CHAPTER IV

THE DAWN OF HISTORY: ARYANIZATION

Evidence—Āryāvarta—Vindhya and Pāriyātra—Vidarbha—Growing knowledge of the South in North Indian literature—Pānini—Kātyāyana—Kauṭilya—Greek accounts—Baudhāyana—Aśokan edicts.

Agastya legends and their significance—Paraśurāma and the west coast—nature of aryanization—evidence of language—later reactions and theories—routes from north to south—contact with lands in the west—and in the east.

HISTORY begins in the South of India as in the North with the advent of the Aryans. The progress of the aryanization of the South is reflected in literature and legend. Until about 600 B.C., works composed in the North exhibit little knowledge of India south of the Vindhyas, but acquaintance increased with the progress of the centuries. Legends centering round the name of Agastya found in the epics and the Purānas appear in their own quaint way to preserve the memory of this vast and important cultural movement. Another clearly later cycle of legends has Paraśurāma for hero and seeks particularly to account for the peculiarities of the Kerala country and its institutions.

The Vindhya range was the recognized southern limit of the Aryan land. Manu states distinctly that the country between the Himalayas and the Vindhyas and between the eastern and western oceans comprised Āryāvarta, the abode of the Aryas. 'The name Pāriyātra', says Bhandarkar, 'was given to the more northern and western portion of the (Vindhya) range from which the rivers Chambal and Betva take their rise, probably because it was situated on the boundary of their *yātrā* or range of communication'. A comparatively late hymn of the Rig-Veda mentions that one expelled from the Aryan fold betook himself to the South and turned his feet in that direction (*dakshiṇāpada*). The *Aitareya Brāhmaṇa* mentions the kingdom of Vidarbha (Berar) and its king Bhīma. The same *Brāhmaṇa* and the *Śānkhāyana Śrautasūtra* state that the sage Viśvāmitra condemned his fifty sons who were jealous of Sunahśepha Devarāta to live on the borders of Āryāvarta, and that their descendants were the Dasyus, like the Andhras, Pundras, Śabaras, Pulindas and Mūtibas. Clearly, in the period of these books, while the aryanization of Northern India had become complete, little progress had been made beyond the Vindhyas; only one settled Aryan kingdom was known, Vidarbha, and the rest of the South was peopled by pre-Aryan inhabitants. Possibly some of the more enterprising Aryans ventured into their midst, married their women and raised families of mixed descent who were looked down upon by the 'purer' Aryans of the north, as may be inferred from the story of the sons of Viśvāmitra. It is difficult to fix any definite date for this stage of affairs, but round about 1000 B.C. may well be suggested.

The next stage is marked by the mention of Cherapādāh, the Cheras, in the *Aitareya Āraṇyaka*, as one of the three peoples who transgressed certain ancient injunctions; but the text is obscure and its meaning is by no means clearly settled. However, if we accepted it as a reference to the Cheras, it would be proof that the customs and habits of Malabar began very early to diverge from those of the rest of the South. But of this we have no other early evidence.

The grammarian Pānini, who may be taken to have lived more or less about 600 B.C., mentions only Kalinga in the east and knows nothing south of the Narmada on the west except the country of Aśmaka, near the headwaters of the Godāvari. The *Sutta Nipāta* of the Buddhist canon records that a teacher Bāvari left Kosala and settled in a village on the Godāvari in the Assaka country in Dakshiṇāpatha. His pupils are said to have gone north to meet the Buddha and their route lay through Patitthāna (Paithan) in the Mulaka country, Māhishmatī (Māndhāta) on the Narmada, and Ujjain. Bāvari is said to have been learned in the Vedas and performed Vedic sacrifices. Probably we have in him the type of many a teacher who took part in the task of colonizing and aryanizing the southern lands by a process of slow and peaceful permeation. The descriptions of *āśramas*, abodes of ascetics situated in the Dandaka forest, which are found in the *Rāmāyana* of Vālmīki confirm the impression derived from the story of the teacher Bāvari.

Kātyāyana, the grammarian of the fourth century B.C., who was probably a southerner and who supplemented the aphorisms of Pānini to bring his grammatical system up to date, makes mention of the countries of the extreme South, Pāndya, Chola and Kerala. These countries were well known to Kauṭilya and the Aśokan edicts, which last mention Ceylon also under the name Tambapanni. Kauṭilya speaks of the pearls and muslins of the Pāndyan country. The name of the Pāndyan capital Madhurā recalls Mathurā of the North, and Greek accounts, as we have seen, narrate the story of Herakles (in the context, Krishna) setting his daughter Pandaia to rule over the kingdom bordering on the southern sea. Other Mathurās are known in Ceylon and near Java, and they suggest the continuity of the movement from North India to the South, and farther across the seas. Baudhāyana, one of the earliest lawgivers, notices in his *Dharmasūtra* five customs as peculiar to the people of the Deccan, viz. dining with one who is not initiated (*anupeta*), dining with women, eating food kept overnight, marrying the daughter of one's maternal uncle, and marrying the daughter of one's paternal aunt. We know that the last two customs mentioned here, cross-cousin marriages, are practised conspicuously to this day in South India among all classes of the people. And Baudhāyana's notice must really belong to a very early period; for he also states that travel by sea to other lands was permissible only to North Indians—a statement which ceased to be true at least at the dawn of the Christian era if not earlier.

Thus it is evident that starting somewhere about 1000 B.C. the movement of the Aryans into the South proceeded more or less steadily and peacefully, and had reached its completion some time before the establishment of the Mauryan empire which included in its fold all India except the extreme South. The fact that the edicts of Aśoka were engraved in places as far south as Mysore and Kurnool shows that there must have been present in these places people to whom the Brāhmī script and the Prākrit idiom were nothing strange; also that Aśoka had political and diplomatic relations with the southern countries that lay outside his empire.

Even the slightest consideration shows that it is this large movement of the aryanization and civilization of the South that provides the historical basis for the Agastya legends which figure prominently in the epics and the Purānas as well as in Tamil literature. In the Rig-Veda there occurs a brief reference to his miraculous birth from a pitcher (*kumbha*), but otherwise he is a real historical person who composes hymns, has a wife and sister and perhaps also a son; and he is applauded for combining domesticity with a life of austerity. In the *Mahābhārata* the story is more fully developed, and Agastya's connexion with the South comes into prominence. His marriage with Lopāmudrā, a princess of Vidarbha, is mentioned together with her demand that, before claiming the exercise of his marital rights, he should provide her with costly jewellery and all the luxuries she was used to in her father's house, without in any manner impairing his asceticism. The only way in which Agastya could meet his wife's wish was by seeking a large gift of wealth. He approached three Aryan kings one after another, but in vain, so they all went to Ilvala, the *daitya* king of Manimati. Ilvala, however, was no friend of the Brahmins, because one of them had refused to grant him a son equal to Indra. His vengeance took a queer form. He used to transform his younger brother Vātāpi 'into a ram and offer his flesh to Brahmins as food, and then to recall him to life (whomsoever Ilvala summoned with his voice would come back even from the abode of Yama), and Vātāpi, ripping the flanks of the Brahmins, would come out laughing'. The two brothers thus killed many Brahmins and, on the occasion of the visit of Agastya and the three kings, Ilvala wanted to play the same game. 'He prepared the flesh of Vātāpi in order to entertain them, at which the kings became sad, but Agastya ate it all, and when Ilvala summoned Vātāpi there came only air out of Agastya's stomach, Vātāpi having already been digested. Then Ilvala, becoming sad, promised to give him wealth, if Agastya could tell him what he intended to give.' Agastya was able to give the right answer and he and the kings returned with the wealth they needed. Vātāpi, as is well known, is the name of the fortified city in the western Deccan which was the capital of the early Chālukyas; it is now called Bādāmi. And if, as seems probable, the abode of the two *daitya* kings is to be sought in this region, this story may be taken to mark the beginning of Agastya's connexion with the South.

The *Mahābhārata* also records the story of Agastya drinking up the waters of the ocean to enable the Devas to dispose of their enemies who had taken refuge under the sea, and of his journey to the South on some unspecified business—when he prevailed upon the Vindhyas to stop growing until he returned, which, however, he never did. In later Tamil tradition, Agastya's southerly march is accounted for by the interesting legend that on the occasion of Śiva's marriage with Pārvatī, Agastya had to be sent to the South to redress the balance of the earth which had been rudely disturbed by the assemblage of all the gods and sages in the North.

The pact with the Vindhya mountains and the drinking of the waters of the ocean have been generally accepted as allegorical representations of the spread of Aryan culture first to India south of the Vindhyas, and then across the seas to the islands of the archipelago and to Indo-China—an interpretation not only intrinsically quite plausible, but supported by other facts relating to Agastya and his abode.

In the *Rāmāyana*, as they are on their way to Agastya's *āśrama*, Rāma tells his brother Lakshmana how Agastya, intent upon the good of the world, overpowered a deadly demon and thereby rendered the earth habitable. He goes on to narrate the story of the death of Vātāpi in a form which differs from that of the *Mahābhārata* in some ways, though the deviations are of no significance. What deserves particular notice is the idea that the Dandakāranya was first made fit for human (Aryan) occupation by the success of Agastya against the *asuras*. Agastya's conflict with the *asuras* and *rākshasas* is also hinted at elsewhere in the *Rāmāyana*. The sage Viśvāmitra, for instance, explains to Rāma the reason for Tātakā's depredations against Aryan settlers. Agastya had destroyed Tātakā's husband Sunda, and was consequently attacked by Tātakā and her son Mārīca. Agastya cursed them both, turning Mārīca into a *rākshasa* and his mother into an ugly ogress. From that time to the moment when Rāma did away with her, she maintained a war of revenge.

'It is very clear,' observes a modern student of the Agastya legends, 'that the stories of Agastya were based on historical memories. Agastya is typical of the early fighters among the Aryans in the South of India. In the Deccan, he is even now one of the most famous of holy men and is considered the oldest teacher of ancient times. A later age has transformed this first apostle of Aryan culture into a *tapasvin* and a holy man. But he must have been a brave and doughty man, a hard fighter and a keen hunter, who triumphed in the midst of barbarous enemies. And the same Agastya, the famous hunter and archer, whom, like Hercules, none could approach in eating and drinking and whose inner essence is yet traceable behind the distortions of old sagas, was a holy man somewhat of the brand of Friar Tuck in *Ivanhoe*.'

The site of Agastya's *āśrama* has been located in many places from the Himalayas to Cape Comorin, as well as outside India —that in the Malaya mountains, the southernmost section of the Western Ghats, being perhaps the most famous. This multiplicity of Agastya *āśramas* and *bhavanas* has been taken to imply either that he is a purely mythical figure or that a whole clan of Agastyas spread to all the places mentioned, though it is admitted that there is nothing to show when or how the clan arose. It seems better to suppose that round the one historical Agastya, the author of the Vedic hymns and husband of Lopāmudrā, who played an important role in his time in furthering the aryanization of the South, there naturally gathered in course of time a number of stories representing the further stages of the movement he started.

One of the latest accretions to the cycle is the following story which, in some versions of the *Rāmāyana*, Agastya himself narrates to Rāma. The great forest of Dandaka had become unfit for human habitation because Bhārgava had cursed it. From the foot of the Vindhyas to the far South, the land remained a howling wilderness for a thousand *yojanas*. Agastya, however, happening to go there from the white peaks of the Himalayas, caused rain to fall, restoring fertility to the soil, and making it a fit dwelling-place for several groups of Aryan sages (*rishis*).

This narrative is not found in any early manuscript of the *Rāmāyana* and is not annotated by any of the commentators. It is obviously a late and clumsy invention. Its account of Agastya's reclamation of desert land and its reference to Bhārgava's curse nevertheless seem to bring it into some relation with the following legend of Paraśurāma's creation of the Kerala country, which is also of relatively recent origin and finds no place in the genuine Purānas.

Paraśurāma slew his mother Renukā at the command of his father Jamadagni, and had to expiate this sin by undertaking to exterminate the Kshatriyas, enemies of the Brahmins. This he did in twenty-one expeditions, and then, at the instance of

Viśvāmitra, gave the whole earth to the Brahmins. As he was thus left with nowhere to call his own where he could live, he sought Subrahmanya's assistance and, by penance, obtained from Varuna, the god of the seas, some land to dwell on. Its extent was to be determined by a throw of his *paraśu* (axe). He threw it from Kanyākumārī to Gokarnam, which became the chief place in the land won from the sea, the land of Paraśurāma. To people this land, he imported Brahmins from abroad, settling them in sixty-four *grāmas*, and making laws and institutions for them and for other settlers who came at the same time. It may be noted that Kannada inscriptions of the early twelfth century A.D. outline the Paraśurāma story in relation to the creation of Konkan, the coastal strip to the north of Kerala.

A rough idea of the process and results of the aryanization of the South may be formed by a study of the linguistic map of India as it is today, always remembering that difference in language is by no means indicative of difference in race, but only in culture. The languages of Northern India and Mahārāshtra in the Deccan are clearly dialects of Sanskrit, or some idiom closely akin to it, formed in the process of its being spoken by different classes of people whose original language it was not. Sounds and words unknown to Sanskrit are found in considerable numbers in these popular dialects, and they are doubtless derived from the original languages of the pre-Aryan inhabitants which, in general, were killed by the speech of the more masterful incoming culture. But while this was the course of events in Northern India and the western Deccan, it was quite different on the eastern coast and farther south. Here too the Aryans penetrated in sufficient numbers to communicate their own civilization to the local inhibitants; but they 'were not able to incorporate them thoroughly into their own society and to root out their languages and their peculiar civilization'. The bulk of the population in these parts retained their own speech and customs, and both were enriched and refined by contact with the northern culture. On the other hand, the incoming Aryans had to learn the language of the people of the South in addition to cultivating their own Sanskrit idiom, to accept local customs and incorporate them as part of the new composite social order they evolved, and to find more or less suitable places in their elastic pantheon for the many godlings and goddesses cherished by the pre-Aryan peoples. We shall never know the exact details of the process; but a study of early Tamil literature, the oldest evidence from the southern side to which we have access, produces the definite impression that the new influences were everywhere welcomed and embraced with alacrity, and that the changes were effected peacefully and in an orderly manner. This impression may be due to Tamil literature being relatively late in its development, and by no means contemporary with the first Aryan impact on the South—the product, perhaps, of an age of peace and harmony that followed a period of initial struggles. But the little we know of the history of Indo-Aryan civilization in North India and the eastern colonies renders such a supposition unnecessary. Nevertheless, the *Rāmāyana* lays stress on the hostility of the *rākshasas* to the sacrificial religion of the Aryan sages, on their repeated incursions into halls of sacrifice where they created much confusion and disorder, and on the great need that existed for Rāma to curb the excesses of these inimical folk in order to secure the safety and peace of the *āśramas*. If this part of the story has any historical basis (it is indeed very doubtful if it has), it would provide some evidence of initial opposition to the incoming culture on the part of the older inhabitants of the land.

Tradition makes Agastya the father of Tamil, the author of the first grammar of that language, and the royal chaplain (*kulaguru*) of the divine line of Pāndyan rulers, the descendants of Śiva and Pārvatī who condescended to become the first king and queen of this celebrated line.

There is no clear and specific reference to Agastya, the sage, much less to his exploits, in any of the early Tamil works now known—the anthologies of the Śangam Age; once indeed the phrase ' Sage of Podiyil ' (Podiyil being the southernmost section of the Western Ghats, the Bettigo of Ptolemy) is applied to the star Canopus—an indication that the legends relating to Agastya were not unknown in the Tamil land at the time. His miraculous birth and his relation to Vasishṭha were known to the author of the poem *Maṇimekalai*. The same work also says that Agastya was a friend of the Chola king Kānta at whose request he released the Kāveri from his water pot, that Agastya's abode was in the Malaya mountains, and that he advised another legendary Chola monarch—he who overthrew the hanging castle (*tūngeyil*)—to institute at Puhār an annual festival in honour of Indra. Another story narrated by Naccinārkkiniyar (*c.* A.D. 1400), a commentator of the Middle Ages, on the authority of a more ancient writer, is that Rāvana who tyrannized over the extreme South was persuaded by Agastya when the latter came to Podiya hill to leave that land alone and betake himself to Lankā.

References to Agastya's work on Tamil grammar make their appearance rather late. The first occurs in the amazing legend of the three Śangams narrated in the *Iṟaiyanār Agapporuḷ Urai*, a work of the eighth or ninth century A.D. Here Agastya is counted as a member of the first and second Śangams which lasted for 4,440 years and 3,700 years respectively. His work *Agattiyam* is said to have been the grammar (*nūl*) for the first Śangam, while that work together with the *Tolkāppiyam* and three other works formed the *nūl* for the second Śangam.

Whether Agastya wrote a treatise on Tamil grammar, and if so in what relation that work stood to the *Tolkāppiyam*, the oldest extant work on the subject, has been discussed by all the great annotators of the Tamil country. Pērāśiriyar (*c.* A.D. 1300) says that in his day some scholars held that Tolkāppiyan, the author of the grammar named after him, composed his work on principles other than those of the *Agattiyam*, following in this other grammars no longer extant. He refutes this theory by an appeal to tradition and authority, the *Iṟaiyanār Agapporuḷ Urai* being the chief. He maintains, with support from more ancient writings, that Agastya was the founder of the Tamil language and grammar, that Tolkāppiyan was the most celebrated of the twelve pupils of the great sage, that the *Agattiyam* was the original grammar, that Tolkāppiyan must be held to have followed its teachings in his new work, and that Agastya's work must have been composed before the Tamil country was confined, by an inundation of the sea, to the limits indicated by Panambāranār in his preface to the *Tolkāppiyam*—i.e. from Vengadam hill to Cape Comorin. The opposite party that denied Tolkāppiyan's indebtedness to Agastya did not give up its position. The general belief that Tolkāppiyan was a disciple of Agastya was too strong for them to deny, so they postulated hostility between teacher and pupil arising out of Agastya's jealousy and hot temper. Naccinārkkiniyar records the story that after his migration to the South, Agastya sent his pupil Triṇadhūmāgni (Tolkāppiyan) to fetch his wife Lopāmudrā from the North. Agastya prescribed that a certain distance should be maintained between the pupil and the lady during their journey, but when the rising of the Vaigai threatened to drown Lopāmudrā, Tolkāppiyan approached too close in holding out to her a bamboo pole with the aid of which she reached the shore in safety. Agastya cursed them for violating his instructions saying that they would never enter heaven; to which Tolkāppiyan replied with a similar curse on his master. This silly legend represents the last phase of a controversy, longstanding, significant, and by no means near its end even in our own time.

The affirmation and denial of Agastya's fathership of Tamil and of his work being the source of the *Tolkāppiyam* are both symbolic of an attitude to the incoming northern Sanskritic influences. As a matter of fact there is no mention of Agastya either in the *Tolkāppiyam* or in the preface to it by Panambāranār. The earliest reference to the *Agattiyam* occurs only in the eighth or ninth century A.D., as we have seen, and that is also the time when the Pāndyan charters begin to proclaim the preceptorship of Agastya to the Pāndyas, the patrons of Tamil literature and the Śangam, and the first genuine Tamil power to achieve political expansion and establish an empire in the full light of history. Almost all the stories meant to support Agastya's connexion with Tamil and Tolkāppiyan must have been elaborated in subsequent ages; but the attempt to give Agastya the dominant position in the evolution of Tamil culture evoked a challenge. Things went on smoothly so long as Aryan influence, the influence of the 'Northern' speech and culture, was content to penetrate the Tamil land quietly and by imperceptible stages, and effect a silent transformation of the native elements. This process began very early and was accepted by the Tamils to an extent that has rendered it all but impossible to differentiate the elements that have gone to make up the composite culture. But when a theory was put forward, that is when a legend was invented to show that Tamil as a spoken language and with it the entire culture of the Tamil country was derived from a Vedic seer, this was met, naturally, by a counter-assertion and the elaboration of legends in the opposite sense. And then, as with some even now, legends were arguments.

The aryanization of the South was doubtless a slow process spread over several centuries. Beginning probably about 1000 B.C., it had reached its completion before the time of Kātyāyana, the grammarian of the fourth century B.C., who mentions the names of the Tamil countries of the extreme South. What were the routes followed by the colonists who moved into the South? Arguing *a priori*, some scholars have held that the hills and forests of the Vindhya and the Satpura ranges and the Narmada river formed an effective barrier to movement towards the South, and that consequently the chief line of communication must have lain along the eastern coast. But the Aryan expansion started from the north-west and proceeded towards the east and south. The eastern parts of North India came under Aryan influences at a relatively late period, and even then were not as completely aryanized as the western half. Though Kalinga is indeed mentioned by Pānini, it still appears extremely unlikely that the main route of Aryan advance to the South lay along the east coast. The evidence of the Brāhmanas, of the *Rāmāyana* and of the Buddhist canon indicates clearly that the barrier of the Vindhyas was negotiated at convenient points and that the chief routes lay right across them, the Narmada and the Satpuras. Vidarbha is one of the earliest kingdoms to be mentioned and no one has sought to locate any place connected with Rāma's exile anywhere to the east of Nagpur, while many would locate them all in the western Deccan, Nasik and its neighbourhood having the best claims. The route taken by the pupils of Bāvari from Aśmaka to Magadha must have been the reverse of the usual Aryan route to the South, which must have passed through the Avanti country to Māndhāta on the Narmada, whence it crossed the river and mountains into the South. The Mulaka country with Paithan as its principal city must have been among the earliest colonies after Vidarbha, and then Aśmaka might have followed. The route farther South cannot be traced with any certainty. It has been suggested that the name of one section of South Indian Brahmins, Brihaccarana, 'the great migration', preserves the memory of a great movement towards the South; and if this view is correct, the fact that a section of this group, the Maḻanādu, is further subdivided into the Kandra-Mānikkam, Māngudi and Satya-mangalam—all names of villages along the Western

Ghats—may be taken to indicate that the immigrants hugged the line of the adjacent highlands and peopled the skirts of Mysore and the Coimbatore and Madura districts before they spread elsewhere. But all this is too speculative, and there is no direct evidence worth the name. Other routes than across the Vindhyas might have been followed; there is, for example, the sea-route from the mouths of the Indus to Gujarat and the north Bombay coast; or, at a relatively later date, the eastern route by Kalinga. Ceylon, perhaps, was aryanized by immigrants who followed the sea-route from North India, as evidenced by their language, Sinhalese, which is Indo-Aryan.

During the long period of seven or eight centuries when South India was being progressively aryanized and a new culture was being evolved, the ancient maritime contacts of the country with the lands to the west and east were still maintained, the tangible evidence of which, literary and archaeological, deserves the following brief notice.

The queen of Sheba visited Solomon at Jerusalem 'with a very great train, with camels that bare spices, and very much gold, and precious stones'. Again, the navy of Hiram 'that brought gold from Ophir, brought in from Ophir great plenty of almug trees, and precious stones'. King Solomon made 'a great throne of ivory, and overlaid it with the best gold'. Lastly, 'the king had at sea a navy of Tharshish with the navy of Hiram: once in three years came the navy of Tharshish, bringing gold, and silver, ivory, and apes, and peacocks'. Hiram was the Phoenician king of Tyre and Solomon's alliance with him was an essential element in the prosperity of Jerusalem in his time. Hiram used Solomon's kingdom as a high road to the Red Sea where he built shipping which greatly promoted trade and led to an accumulation of great wealth in Jerusalem. Ophir may well be the Ābhīra country, and its twin Tharshish may also be sought there. The peacocks and sandalwood (almug) Solomon obtained are both South Indian in name as well as in origin. Though silver was not an Indian product some of the ivory might have been, especially as the Hebrew, Egyptian and Greek names for the elephant are derived ultimately from the Sanskrit *ibha*. Ebony was another Indian article conveyed to Palestine in this period by the merchants of Dedan on the south shore of the Persian Gulf. The Assyrian and Babylonian empires traded with India by sea from their ports on the Persian Gulf and continued to receive gold, spices and fragrant woods from India. It has been pointed out rightly that 'rice, peacocks, sandalwood, every unknown article which we find imported by sea into Babylon before the fifth century B.C., brought with it a Dravidian, not a Sanskrit, designation'. In the seventh century B.C. traders from the west introduced into southern China a system of inscribed coinage based on a Babylonian standard, and a sea-trade between Babylon and China necessarily includes India. A beam of Indian cedar found in the palace of Nebuchadnezzar (604—562 B.C.), the teak logs found in the temple of the Moon-god at Ur at levels belonging to about the same age or a little later, and the Bāveru Jātaka which relates the adventures of certain Indian merchants who took the first peacock by sea to Babylon, all confirm the existence of active maritime intercourse between South India and its western neighbours. In the seventh and sixth centuries B.C., Babylon was at the height of its splendour, the greatest commercial mart of the world; men of many nations frequented its bazaars, and we may well assume that among them were merchants from South India. When Babylon fell, the trade passed into the hands of the Arab merchants of Mouza, Aden and Kane. The author of the *Periplus* says that the voyage to India was made along the shore and in small ships until Hippalus discovered the monsoon; but the normal trade route from the Persian Gulf to India can never have lain along the inhospitable shores of Gedrosia, and 'the exploring expeditions despatched by Darius in 512 B.C. from the mouth of the Indus, and nearly two centuries later by Alexander the Great, show the difficulties and dangers of the route, the time it occupied, and the ignorance of the pilots'. The knowledge of the monsoons must have been very common among the sailors of India, Arabia and Persia from early times, and the mariners who reached China in the seventh century B.C. could not have feared sailing on the open seas. Hippalus' discovery (*c.* A.D. 45), if it was a fact, must have been of value to the Roman and Greek traders of his time.

In Chinese historical sources occur references to maritime traders bringing typical Indian products to China as far back as the seventh century B.C. Generally regarded with incredulity, these accounts receive striking confirmation by the discovery in the Philippines of a number of Iron-Age finds bearing close resemblance to objects found in South India of about the same age—the first millennium B.C. These comprise iron implements and weapons such as knives, axes, daggers and spear-points; glass beads and bangles, both green and blue; and finally beads of semi-precious stones such as agate, cornelian, amethyst, and rock-crystal. In the earlier Iron-Age strata only green glass, whose colour is due to iron, occurs; in the later, a blue glass, whose colour is due to copper, also occurs. 'Both the iron and glass objects are similar to and in some cases identical with the prehistoric glass and iron finds in the South of India. These occur in the dolmen tombs and in burials which are found by the hundreds of thousands, and which almost certainly antedate the historic Chera, Chola and Pāndyan kingdom, whose history goes back to the beginning of the Christian era or before. As finds of similar glass beads and bangles have recently been made in the Malay Peninsula, in dolmen tombs in Java, and in North Borneo, the inference is inescapable that we have clear evidence of a trade contact between the northern Philippines and Southern India running well back into the first millennium B.C. The extensive trade and colonization and later conquests of the South Indian kingdoms, in Sumatra and Java as well as in Indo-China in the early centuries of the Christian era, are of course well known. The new material, however, seems to make it clear that this was far from being the beginning of such contacts, but rather the last stages in an association reaching as far as the northern Philippines, which had begun many centuries before.'

BIBLIOGRAPHY

D. R. BHANDARKAR: *Lectures on the Ancient History of India from 650 to 325 B.C.* (Calcutta, 1919)

R. G. BHANDARKAR: *Early History of the Dekkan* (Bombay, 1895)

R. B. DIXON: 'Recent Archaeological Discoveries in the Philippines' (*Proceedings of the American Philosophical Society*, Vol. 69, 1930)

P. T. SRINIVASA IYENGAR: *History of the Tamils* (Madras, 1929)

J. KENNEDY: 'The Early Commerce of Babylon with India' (*JRAS*, 1898)

W. LOGAN: *Malabar*, Vol. I (Madras, 1887)

W. H. SCHOFF (ed.): *The Periplus of the Erythraean Sea* (New York, 1912)

CHAPTER V

THE AGE OF THE MAURYAN EMPIRE

Nanda rule in the South—Jain accounts of the end of Chandragupta Maurya—inscriptions—*Arthaśāstra* on trade between North and South India—Megasthenes on Pāndya—Tamil kingdoms in the edicts of Aśoka—Satiyaputa—Aśoka's empire in the Deccan—confederacy of Tamil states—Mauryan interest in the politics of the South—Brāhmī inscriptions in caverns and their import.

IN the fourth century B.C., the empire of Magadha was greatly expanded under the powerful, though unpopular, dynasty of the Nandas who, according to purānic accounts, conquered all rival monarchs and became sole emperors of the whole of India. How far their sway extended into the South, it is by no means easy to determine. That it included Kalinga seems to be confirmed by the famous Hāthīgumpha inscription of Khāravela who ruled over Kalinga in the second century B.C. This inscription mentions a Nanda raja in connexion with the construction of an aqueduct, and states elsewhere that King Nanda carried away as trophies of war a statue of Jina and other heirlooms of the rulers of Kalinga. Kannada inscriptions from Mysore of the tenth and eleventh centuries A.D. preserve faint memories of the rule of the Nandas in the Kuntala country; but there is little confirmation of this tradition. Nander on the upper reaches of the Godāvari has sometimes been taken to be the survival of an ancient name like Nau-Nandadhera and as indicating the extent of Nanda power into the Deccan. Indeed, punch-marked Purāna coins, which are found all over the Deccan, South India, and Ceylon as well as in North India, are clear witnesses of ancient contacts between the North and South whose details are now lost; but while they enable us to infer the existence of trade connexions, they are of no avail in fixing the southern limit of the Nanda empire. The inclusion of Kuntala in that empire conforms to the limits of the Mauryan empire under Aśoka as determined by the existence of his inscriptions in the South, and there is no clear evidence of the Mauryan emperors having undertaken wars of conquest in the South. It may, after all, be that the Kannada inscriptions mentioned above preserve a correct tradition—that the Mauryas came by their Southern possessions as a matter of course by overthrowing the imperial dynasty of the Nandas. The enormous wealth accumulated by the Nandas was well known to the ancient Tamils, and became proverbial. Māmūlanār, one of the poets of the Śangam Age, puts these words into the mouth of a love-lorn lady: 'What is it that has attracted my lover more than my charms and kept him away from me so long? Can it be the treasure accumulated in prosperous Pātaliputra and hidden in the waters of the Ganges by the great Nandas victorious in war?'

Jain tradition affirms that when Bhadrabāhu, the last of the saints called *śrutakevalins*, foretold a famine of twelve years' duration, the Mauryan emperor Chandragupta abdicated the throne and migrated to the South with the saint and his pupils. The emperor is said to have lived for many years as a Jain ascetic in Śravana Belgola in Mysore, and ultimately committed suicide by *sallekhana*, or starvation, surviving his teacher by twelve years. Inscriptions from Śravana Belgola and its neighbourhood mention Bhadrabāhu and Chandragupta *munīndra*; one inscription, which may be as old as A.D. 600, mentions the pair (*yugma*) and says that theirs was the safe faith (*dharma*); and another of even earlier date, probably not later than the fifth century, contains all the elements of the story given above. Bhadrabāhu, according to this account, foretold at Ujjain a period of twelve years of dire famine, and the whole of the Jain *sangha* thereupon migrated from the North to the South under his leadership. When they arrived at a mountain named Katavapra (that is, Chandragiri) in a populous and prosperous country (Mysore), an Āchārya (Prabhāchandra by name), knowing he had but a short time to live, sent away the entire *sangha* and, with only one disciple attending on him, performed penance and gained emancipation from his body. Two inscriptions of about A.D. 900 from the neighbourhood of Seringapatam describe the summit of the lower hill Chandragiri at Śravana Belgola as marked by the footprints of both Bhadrabāhu and Chandragupta *munipati*. Later inscriptions at Śravana Belgola bearing dates in the twelfth and fifteenth centuries repeat this tradition with variations. Similar attestation also comes from literary sources, of which the earliest seems to be the *Brihatkathākośa* of Harishena (A.D. 931). The absence of any clear evidence about the actual end of Chandragupta

Maurya lends some plausibility to this legend; but it is improbable in itself, and the identity of the Chandragupta *muni* of the inscriptions is by no means beyond doubt.

The *Arthaśāstra* of Kauṭilya gives some information of value about the trade between the North and the South in the age of the early Mauryan empire. ' Among land routes,' says Kauṭilya, ' my teacher considers that leading to the Himalaya superior to the one leading to Dakshiṇāpatha, because of the elephants, horses, spices, ivory, hides, silver and gold articles, all very valuable (to be had there).' He then expounds his own quite different view as follows: ' No,' says Kauṭilya. ' Although it is deficient in woollen cloth, hides and horses, the Dakshiṇāpatha abounds in conch-shells, diamonds, precious stones of other kinds, pearls, and articles of gold. Moreover, the southern trade route across Dakshiṇāpatha traverses a territory rich in mines and valuable merchandise, is frequented by many (traders) and easy to travel by. That is the superior route.' This passage almost brings before our eyes the large-scale opening-up of trade with the South which the foundation of the Nanda and Mauryan empires brought about. The view represented by Kauṭilya's teacher (*āchārya*) was becoming rapidly out of date as a result of new conditions, and the pupil affirms that there were in his day more wealth and larger possibilities of trade in the South than ever before. The mention of gold, diamonds and other precious stones and pearls, and of the easy conditions of travel along the much frequented routes, deserves to be particularly noted. Again, in his account of the articles that entered the royal treasury, Kauṭilya includes varieties of pearls from the Tambraparni river in the Pāndyan country, from Pāndyakavāta (which is explained in the commentary as the Malayakōti mountain in the same area), and from the Chūrnā river in Kerala. He also mentions fine cotton fabrics from Madura, as well as *vaiḍūrya* (beryl) of various colours, and varieties of sandalwood which must also have come from South India.

The legendary account given by Megasthenes of the rule of the Pāndyan kingdom by Pandaia, a daughter of Herakles, has been noticed already; it must be understood as recounting the origin of the kingdom rather than as describing contemporary conditions. Megasthenes says that each day one village brought its due tribute to the royal treasury, this tribute being, perhaps, a payment in kind calculated to ensure a regular supply of provisions for the daily consumption of the royal household. There is a similar statement in the *Śilappadikāram* (*c.* A.D. 600) that on a particular day a certain cowherd family in a suburb of Madura took its turn to supply ghee to the royal palace.

The kingdoms of South India, together with Ceylon, are mentioned in the second and thirteenth rock-edicts of Aśoka. The list in the second edict is the more complete and includes the names of Chola, Pāndya, Satiyaputa, Keralaputa and Tambapanni (Ceylon). All these lands are distinctly stated to have lain outside the empire of Aśoka; but the great emperor was on such friendly terms with them that he undertook to arrange for the proper medical care of men and animals in all of them, and for the importation and planting of useful medicinal herbs and roots wherever they were needed. He also sent missionaries to preach the *dhamma*, the essentials of Buddhism, among the people of these countries, thus evincing a keen interest in their spiritual and moral well-being no less than in their physical fitness. The mere mention of such facts is enough to indicate a certain level of general culture and progress in the arts of civilization among the people of the South. The Tamils and the Sinhalese must have had a settled polity and lived in well-ordered states for some time before Aśoka could think of starting his friendly intercourse with them.

The identification of the Satiyaputa kingdom is not easy and has long been a subject of controversy. The name was, till recently, recognized as a tribal name which may be Sanskritized into Satyaputras, 'members of the fraternity of truth', and the only tribe answering to this description known to early Tamil literature is held to be the Kōśar, celebrated for their unswerving fidelity to the plighted word as well as for their heroism in war. Their home is said to have been in the Kongu country—roughly the modern districts of Salem and Coimbatore—and they overran the Tulu country on the west coast in the early centuries of the Christian era. They occupy a considerable place in the literature of the Śangam period, and it seemed highly probable that they should find a place in the earliest enumeration of the political divisions of the Tamil country next to the three main kingdoms of the South. Scholars therefore tentatively accepted the identity of the Satiyaputa with the Kōśar and their country with Kongu. The Satputes among modern Marathas were taken to be descendants of emigrants to Mahārāshtra from the South. A more satisfactory equation is that of Satiyaputa with Adiyamān (also Adigamān or Adigaimān), first suggested by K. G. Sesha Aiyar and supported on good linguistic grounds by T. Burrow.[1]

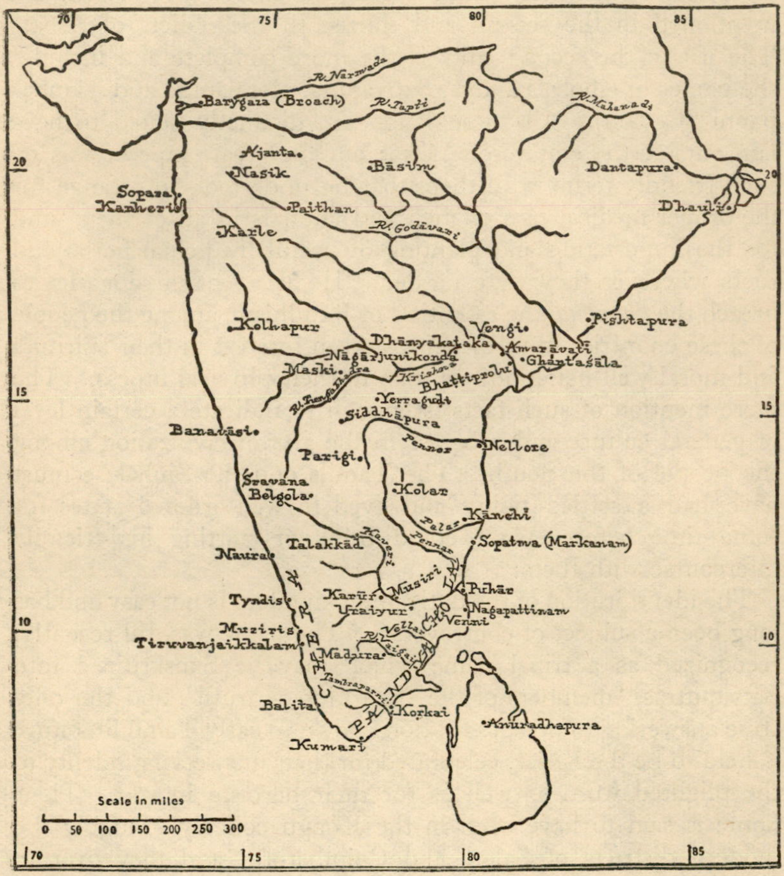

SOUTH INDIA: 300 B.C.-A.D. 500

The conquest of Kalinga by Aśoka (*c.* 260 B.C.) is one of the best-known events of his reign and formed the turning-point in his spiritual career. No wonder his edicts are found in Dhauli in the delta of the Mahanadi, and at Jaugada in the Ganjam

[1] See *Bulletin of the School of Oriental and African Studies* (London), XII (1948), pp. 136-37 and 146-47.

district, then certainly part of Kalinga. Dhauli was perhaps the same as Tosali, the capital of Kalinga in those days. A fragment of one of the edicts of Aśoka discovered at Sopara near Bombay proves the inclusion within the Mauryan empire of the north-west as well as the north-east of the Deccan. Farther south Aśokan inscriptions have been found in the Raichur and Chitaldrug districts in Mysore, and in the Kurnool district of Andhra. How much farther south the empire of the Mauryas extended can only be conjectured; it seems not unlikely that a part of the Tondaimandalam was included in it; at any rate, a Pallava inscription of the ninth century A.D. (the Velūrpālaiyam plates) mentions an Aśokavarman among the earliest rulers of Kānchipuram. The countries of the Deccan are very well represented in the account given by the Ceylonese chronicle *Mahāvamsa* of the missions sent after the third Buddhist council at Pātaliputra for the propagation of the *dhamma* in different countries. We learn that a certain Mahādeva was sent to Mahishamandala (Mysore) and one Rakkhita to Vanavāsi (afterwards the centre of the Kadamba kingdom), a Yona Dhammarakkhita, possibly a Greek monk, was deputed to Aparantaka (the northern half of the 'Bombay' coast) and Mahārakkhita to the Maratha country. Mahinda, the son of Aśoka, who was responsible for the conversion of Ceylon, also finds a place in the list along with four others who share with him the honour of carrying the gospel to Lankā. Though this account is seven or eight centuries later than the time to which it relates, there is good reason to believe that it preserves a fairly correct tradition quite in conformity with the evidence of the Aśokan inscriptions. All the Deccan states mentioned were of course within the empire of Aśoka.

The Rathikas and Bhojas of the western and northern Deccan as well as the Andhras and Paradas of the eastern Deccan and the Pitenikas who have not yet been localized seem to have enjoyed a considerable measure of autonomy in their government. They could not have been independent as they are definitely described in Aśoka's inscriptions as peoples in the king's territory. The Deccan was an important part of the Mauryan empire and contained the seats of two viceroyalties—Tosali (Dhauli), and Suvarnagiri, now called Kanakagiri, between Hampi and Maski in Andhra Pradesh. The land was placed under *mahāmātras*, some assisting viceroys, others in charge of districts and others dispensing justice in the cities. *Antamahāmātras* were charged with defence and missionary work among backward peoples.

The characters of the Aśokan inscriptions in Mysore and Kurnool vary in several respects from those of the northern edicts and have been recognized as a special southern variety of the Brāhmī script. This shows that writing must have been in use in the South for some time before to allow of such variations being developed, and that the southerners understood the language and were the equals of their North Indian contemporaries in their culture and outlook.

Inscriptions on stone relic caskets found in the stupa at Bhaṭṭiprolu near the mouth of the Krishna river are probably only a few decades later than Aśoka's edicts; they are engraved in the same southern variety of the Brāhmī script, and their language obviously reflects many peculiarities of local speech. These inscriptions mention a king Kubiraka and his father whose name is lost.

The famous Hāthīgumpha inscription of Khāravela (first half of the second century B.C.) mentions a league of Tamil states that was 113 years old at the date of the inscription and had been for some time a source of danger to the Kalinga kingdom. This shows that the different states of the Tamil country were, even at that early age, capable of entering into enduring diplomatic relations and pursuing a steady policy towards neighbouring states, near and far.

The poet Māmūlanār, whose reference to the hoarded wealth of the Nandas has been cited above, says that the Kōśar started operations against their foes and gained successes against many of them; but as the chief of Mōhūr did not submit, the Mōriyar, who had a large army of which the war-like Vaḍugar formed the vanguard, sent an expedition to the South to assist them. Māmūlanār wrote about four centuries later than the fall of the Mauryan empire, and if his expression '*vamba mōriyar*' is taken to refer to the newly-risen Mōriyas, the dispatch of assistance to the Kōśar to help them in their conquests must have occurred when the Mauryan empire was still strong and powerful. This active intervention of the Mauryas in the politics of the Tamil country has so far escaped notice, but the lines of Māmūlanār are clear in their import. The political unification of

India under the Mauryas was then very real, and the court of Pātaliputra was interested in occurrences in the extreme south of the peninsula. ' Vaḍugar ' literally means ' northerners ', and was the name applied in Śangam literature to the ancestors of the Telugu-Kannada people living in the Deccan, immediately to the north of the Tamil country whose northern limit was Vengadam, the Tirupati Hill. The Deccan was a part of the Mauryan empire, and that Deccani troops formed the vanguard of the Mauryan army is quite intelligible.

Māmūlanār himself and other poets make further references to the Mauryas strongly tinged with the mythology of the concept of Chakravarti—the wheel-emperor; but these need not detain us or detract from the value of the specific historical references in Māmūlanār cited above. Let us note further that the poems contain no basis for the view often expressed that the Mauryas invaded South India and reached the Podiya mountain in the extreme South.

The short Brāhmī inscriptions found in natural rock caverns in the hills of the South have many features in common with the similar, but more numerous, records of Ceylon, and are among the earliest monuments of the Tamil country to which we may assign a date with some confidence. The script employed resembles that of the inscriptions from Bhaṭṭiprolu and may well be assigned to the second century B.C. The later inscriptions may be taken to be of the third century A.D. like the one at the Ariccalur Cave in Coimbatore district. The Brāhmī graffiti found on the pottery from Arikamedu excavations may be taken also to belong to this class of inscriptions. They are definitely datable to about A.D. 50 and fall chronologically about the middle of the period covered by these records. These inscriptions have not yet been fully elucidated; but clearly they are mostly either brief donative records or the names of the monks who once lived there. One of the places where the caverns are found bears the name Kaḻugumalai, ' vulture's hill ', Tamil for Gridhrakūṭa, a name hallowed in the annals of early Buddhism. From this fact it has been deduced that these monuments were all of them of Buddhist origin; but it is premature to formulate final conclusions on this matter. New caves and inscriptions are still being discovered, such as the inscribed natural cave at Malakonda in Nellore district and the one at Ariccalur just mentioned. And tradition is strong, as we have seen, that Jainism came into South India about the same time as Buddhism, if not earlier. It is not possible to assert that these monuments owe their origin exclusively to Buddhists or Jains; it is probable that some may be attributed to the one and some to the other.

Though the script of these inscriptions is Brāhmī of the southern variety, the language employed in them is Tamil in its formative stages except in two graffiti from Arikamedu in Prākrit. The writing was alphabetic, and already included signs for peculiarly Dravidian sounds, ḻ, ḷ, ṟ and ṉ. Soft consonants are totally absent, and aspirated ones virtually so but for *dha* and *tha*. There are two other notable features in the earlier records: the absence of the doubling of consonants, and the lengthening of *a* before the unvoiced consonant, e.g., *tāndai* for *tandai*. These developments (and others not detailed here) must have resulted from a process of trial and error extending perhaps over several generations.

The exact contents of these inscriptions still remain obscure, but a few facts emerge from tentative studies of them. We can say, for instance, that among the cities named are 'Maturai' (Madura) and 'Karu-ūr' (Karur), that among the donors of monuments were a husbandman (*kuṭumbika*) of Ceylon (Īḻa), besides a woman, merchants (*vaṇikar*), and members of the Karani caste. The professions of *pon-vāṇikan* (gold merchant), *kūla-vāṇikan* (grain merchant), and *kaikkōḷan* (weaver ?) are mentioned. The term *nikāmattār* (members of a guild) occurs twice, once as donor, and again as donees. The word *kōn* (chief or king) also occurs. Some words of religious import are: *atittānam* (abode), *dhamam* (dharma), *aṟattār* (followers of dharma), *tāna* (gift), *upāsa-a* (lay worshipper), *pāḻiy* (paḻḷi, a Jaina or Buddhist place of worship), and *yakaru* (yakshas) and Kuvira (Kubera). These brief inscriptions are thus seen to bear testimony to the support commanded from all classes of the laity by the ascetics who pursued their spiritual life in the solitudes of mountains and forests. Yet it seems easy to exaggerate their social and religious significance; there is no evidence that the Tamil people in general had accepted Jainism or Buddhism in this early period; and the evidence from the literature of the succeeding age, that of the Śangam, shows the Vedic religion of sacrifice and some forms of popular Hinduism entrenched in the affections of the people and their rulers.

BIBLIOGRAPHY

K. GOPALACHARI: *Early History of the Andhra Country* (Madras, 1941)
G. JOUVEAU-DUBREUIL: *Ancient History of the Deccan* (Pondicherry, 1920)
Proceedings of the Third All-India Oriental Conference (1924), pp. 275 ff.
B. L. RICE: *Mysore and Coorg from Inscriptions* (London, 1909)
R. SHAMA SASTRI (ed.): *Arthaśāstra of Kauṭilya* (Mysore, 1909)
P. T. SRINIVASA IYENGAR: *History of the Tamils* (Madras, 1929)

CHAPTER VI

THE SĀTAVĀHANAS AND THEIR SUCCESSORS

Duration and area of Sātavāhana rule—Sātavāhanas and Andhras—rise and expansion of the Sātavāhana power—Hāla—Śaka conquests—Sātavāhana revival under Gautamiputra Śātakarni and his son—Yajna Śātakarni—later Sātavāhanas—Sātavāhana polity—society—cities—ports—trade—religion.

Successors of the Sātavāhanas—Ābhīras—Chutus—Ikshvākus and their administration—Brihatphalāyanas—Pallavas and their administrative system.

The Sālankāyanas—Māṭharas of Kalinga—Vishnukundins—kings of the Ānanda *gōtra.*

The Vākāṭakas of Berar—the Kadambas of Banavāsi—the Gangas of Gangavādi.

In the Deccan, the Mauryan empire was followed by the rule of the Sātavāhanas, which lasted for four and a half centuries from about 230 B.C. At its greatest extent the Sātavāhana empire covered the whole of the Deccan and spread far into Northern India, perhaps even as far as Magadha. Its collapse followed ultimately upon long wars against the Śakas of Gujarat in the first and second centuries A.D. By the beginning of the third century the empire had virtually disappeared, giving place to a number of minor independent dynasties.

The dynasty (*kula*) of the Sātavāhanas is doubtless identical with the Andhras or Andhrabhrityas in the purānic lists of kings. They were called Andhras because they were of Andhra origin (*jāti*) and their rule was probably confined to the Andhra country at the time the purānic lists were compiled. The other name, Andhrabhrityas ('Andhra servants'), may imply that the ancestors of the royal Sātavāhanas were employed in the service of the Mauryan empire and thus moved into the western Deccan where they set up an independent state when that empire declined after Aśoka. Pliny mentions the Andhra territory in the eastern Deccan as including thirty walled towns, besides numerous villages, and as maintaining an army of 100,000 infantry, 2,000 cavalry, and 1,000 elephants. Though the Purānas list thirty kings of the dynasty ruling altogether over 460 years, it is very difficult, in the present state of our knowledge, to narrate their history in a connected form. The names of the earliest kings in the purānic lists figure also in inscriptions and on coins found in the western Deccan at Nasik, Karle and Naneghat. There is no trace of these early monarchs in the Andhra country on the east coast. Again, Khāravela of Kalinga states clearly that the territory of the Sātavāhana king Śātakarni lay to the west of his kingdom. From these facts we may conclude that the Sātavāhanas rose to power in the western Deccan, in the region round about Paithan (Pratishthāna) traditionally associated with them, and thence spread their empire in all directions. In the first instance they conquered north and south Mahārāshtra, eastern and western Malwa, and what is now Madhya Pradesh. In this task they were helped by the Rathikas and Bhojas who were duly rewarded with offices, titles and matrimonial alliances.

The exact date of the foundation of Sātavāhana power cannot be determined, but the purānic lists suggest that the first king, Simuka, probably began to reign about 230 B.C. This suggestion is confirmed by the script of the Nasik inscription of the second king Kanha (Krishna) which has been assigned by Bühler to 'the times of the last Mauryas or the earliest Śungas, in the beginning of the second century B.C.' According to Jain accounts Simuka (who ruled for 23 years) grew so wicked towards the end of his reign that he was dethroned and killed. He was succeeded by his brother Kanha (207-189 B.C.) who extended his kingdom to the west as far as Nasik if not farther. The third king was Śrī Śātakarni I, whose figure was sculptured *in rilievo* at Naneghat along with the figures of his father Simuka, his queen Nāganikā, a Mahārathi, and three princes. He conquered western Malwa, and an inscription of his queen records his performance of certain great sacrifices and the fees paid to the officiating priests, including tens of thousands of cows, thousands of horses, numbers of elephants, whole villages and huge sums of money (tens of thousands of *kārshāpanas*). Twice it appears that Śātakarni proclaimed his suzerainty by performing the horse-sacrifice, and the victory thus celebrated must have been at the expense of the Śungas, the imperial power of the North. In the drama *Mālavikāgnimitra*, Kālidāsa mentions a victory of the Śungas over the Andhras, which was doubtless an episode in the struggle which ended with the final victory of the Andhras. Coins and inscriptions indicate the progress of Sātavāhana power, first from Pratishthāna to Ujjain and then to Vidiśā.

Śātakarni I is described in the inscription of his queen as 'the Lord of Dakshiṇāpatha' and as 'the wielder of the unchecked wheel' (*apratihata-chakra*). Śātakarni II (*acc.* 166), the sixth king, enjoyed the longest reign, 56 years, and wrested Malwa from the Śungas. He was most probably the Śātakarni whom Khāravela of Kalinga defied in the second year of his reign by sending a large army of horse, elephant, foot-soldiers and chariots to the west. Two years later Khāravela claims to have humbled the Rathikas of the Maratha country and the Bhojas of Berar, both feudatories of the Andhra ruler of Pratishthāna. This challenge to the predominant power of the Deccan was apparently not pursued beyond the limit of safety. Śātakarni II may have extended his empire to Madhya Pradesh, as a coin of his successor Āpīlaka has been found in the eastern half of that state. Hāla, the seventeenth Sātavāhana king (*c.* A.D. 20-24), is famous in literature as the compiler of *Sattaśaī* (*Saptaśatī*), a collection of 700 erotic *gāthas* in the Āryā metre in Mahārāshtrī Prākrit. In its present form the work contains linguistic features of the second or third century A.D. or even later.

The expansion of the Sātavāhanas received a check from a new power from the west. About 75 B.C., the Śakas of Seistan had occupied the Indus delta, known thereafter as Śākadvīpa to Indian writers and as Indo-Scythia to Greek geographers. A legendary episode in the history of Ujjain may be taken to mark the beginnings of the long struggle between the Śakas and the Andhras, the varying fortunes of which can be traced clearly in the inscriptions of a slightly later time. The story is that the Jain saint Kālaka was insulted by King Gardabhilla of Ujjain and persuaded the Śakas to invade Ujjain and avenge his wrong. Gardabhilla was thus overthrown, but some years later his son Vikramāditya (' Sun of Valour ') issued from Pratishthāna, repelled the invaders and founded an era in 57 B.C. to commemorate his victory. It is not improbable that these traditions have an historical basis connected with the history of the Andhras. But it is certain that the Śaka power in the west was finally destroyed by the Gupta ruler Chandragupta II (A.D. 380-414), also a Vikramāditya, and that legend has failed to distinguish the later Vikramāditya from his earlier namesake.

The four immediate successors of Hāla had short reigns totalling less than a dozen years altogether, an indication of a troubled time. About the same time the 'western satraps' (Śakas) came into prominence. Bhūmaka is the earliest of them, and Nahapāna the greatest conqueror. His rule extended over Gujarat, Kathiawar, northern Mahārāshtra, Konkan, and even parts of southern Mahārāshtra for a time. The *Periplus* states that the kingdom of Mambanus (Nahapāna) began with Ariake (Āryaka of Varāhamihira), and that the Greek ships coming into the Sātavāhana port of Kalyan were diverted to Barygaza (Broach). Nahapāna's capital was Minnagara, perhaps Dohad, half-way between Ujjain and Broach. The expansion of Śaka power at the expense of the Śatavāhanas probably occurred in the period A.D. 40-80, about the time of the *Periplus*.

Under Gautamīputra Śātakarni (*c.* A.D. 80-104), the Sātavāhana power revived. He is described as the destroyer of the Śakas, Pahlavas and Yavanas. He overthrew Nahapāna and restruck large numbers of his silver coins. From the Śakas he recovered northern Mahārāshtra and the Konkan, the Narmada valley and Saurāshtra, besides Malwa and western Rajputana. His empire extended to Vidarbha (Berar) and to Banavāsi in the south. There is no evidence of his rule in Andhradeśa, though it may have touched Kalinga. His achievements are recorded in glowing terms by his mother, Gautamī Balaśrī, in an inscription at Nasik engraved after his death and in the nineteenth year of his son and successor Pulumāyi II. This shows that the Śakas did not regain their lost possessions for some time. Coins of Pulumāyi II who reigned for at least 24 years have been found in the Godāvari and Guntur districts and on the Coromandel coast as far south as Cuddalore. His preoccupations in the east gave the Śakas an opportunity to regain some of their lost territory in western Rajputana and Malwa (*c.* A.D. 126-31). In an effort to stay this reconquest Pulumāyi's successor, a Śātakarni, married the daughter of Mahākshatrapa Rudradāman. But this Śaka king defeated the next Sātavāhana ruler twice in 'fair fight' and took from him Aparānta (north Konkan) and Anūpa (the Narmada valley).

Perhaps the best known Sātavāhana ruler is Śrī Yajna Śātakarni (*c.* A.D. 170-99). He must have renewed the struggle with the Śakas and recovered some of the provinces lost by his predecessors. His rare silver coins imitating the satrap coinage must have been struck for circulation in the newly-conquered western districts. Some of the potin coins he issued have been found in the Chanda district (Madhya Pradesh), while many of bronze and lead have come to light in the eastern provinces. Others, bearing the figure of a ship, should also be referred to his reign and indicate that his power was not confined to the land. Also belonging to his reign are inscriptions found at Kanheri and Nasik in the west and at Chinna Ganjam in the east. As far as we know, Śrī Yajna was the last king to retain control of both the western and the eastern provinces.

His successors were Vijaya, whose coins have been found in Akola in Maharashtra, Śrī Chandra, one of whose inscriptions is in Kalinga and whose coins have been picked up in the Godāvari and Krishna districts, and finally a Pulumāyi one of whose inscriptions has been found in Bellary district.

The names of other Sātavāhana kings—Karna, Kumbha and Rudra Śātakarni who ruled over the eastern Deccan and Madhya Pradesh—are known from coins but are not included in the purānic list which was presumably compiled before their reigns began. Other princes of Sātavāhana extraction governed minor kingdoms in different parts of the Deccan, but nothing is known of the causes that brought about the downfall of the main dynasty.

Despite the vast extent of the Sātavāhana empire its polity was simple and local administration was left largely to feudatories subject to the general control of royal officials. Kingship was hereditary in the male line though matronymics were freely prefixed to the names of kings and nobles. The king was the guardian of the established social order and was expected to raise taxes justly and to further the prosperity of the poor equally with the rich. Feudatories were of three grades: Rājas who struck coins in their own names; Mahābhojas and Mahārathis who were confined to a few families in the western Deccan—the latter being connected with the Sātavāhanas by marriage; and relatively late in the history of the empire was created the office of *mahāsenāpati* which continued under later dynasties. Some *mahāsenāpatis* were in charge of outlying provinces while others controlled departments at the centre. The state was divided into *āharas* (administrative divisions) each under a minister (*amātya*). Below these came the villages, each with its own headman (*grāmika*). Other officials named in the inscriptions are treasurers and stewards, goldsmiths and coiners, administrators (*mahāmātras*), record keepers, ushers, and ambassadors.

In society new sub-castes were forming on an occupational basis, such as shepherds (*golikas*) and ploughmen (*hālikas*). More interesting is the total assimilation of foreigners, Śakas and Yavanas, either as Buddhists or as degraded Kshatriyas, many of them bearing such thoroughly Indian names as Dharmadeva, Rishabhadatta and Agnivarman. The Śaka Rishabhadatta, we read, made a pilgrimage to Pushkara on the river Barnāsa and presented cows and villages to Brahmins; but we do not hear of foreigners following Hindu practices in the western Deccan after the second century A.D. Gautamīputra, who is said to have destroyed the Śakas, Yavanas and Pahlavas, was evidently thorough in his work. Though nothing is said of the Yavanas in the eastern Deccan, it is certain that Graeco-Roman influences had a great share in fashioning the stupas at Amarāvatī and other places in the Krishna valley, and Greek (*yonaka*) lamps are mentioned in an inscription from Allūru.

That women were prominent in social life and held property in their own right is seen from records of their lavish charity mentioned in inscriptions. In sculptures we see them worshipping Buddhist emblems, taking part in assemblies and entertaining guests alongside of their husbands. Men vied with women in the scantiness of their dress and in the profusion of their ornaments. Even the cottage had its share of such comparative luxuries as jugs, jars, chairs, tables, stools, beds and other household furnishings of attractive design.

Cities were protected by high walls, ramparts and gates which were often built of brick and mortar, gateways being surmounted by *tōraṇas* as at Sānchī. Armies were led into battle by foot-soldiers who carried short swords for offence, and projected themselves from the enemy's weapons with circular shields and bandages wound round their stomachs. The infantry was flanked by the cavalry and elephants, with bowmen in the rear. Long spears, battle-axes and mallets were also used. Cavalrymen and elephant-drivers, but not the foot-soldiers, wore turbans.

The western and eastern coasts were studded with ports throbbing with trade. Ptolemy names several in 'Maisolia', the region between the deltas of the Godāvari and Krishna, and states that one of them was the starting-point of ships bound for 'Golden Chryse'—the Malay peninsula and the eastern archipelago. In the western Deccan, Barygaza (Broach) was the most northern port, Sopara the most ancient, and Kalyan the largest. The market-towns of the interior, besides Paithan and Tagara, were Junnar, Karahātaka, Nasik and Vaijayantī; those of the eastern Deccan were less important: Dhānyakataka, Vijayapura and Narasela. Each group of traders—corn-dealers, braziers, weavers, florists, ironmongers and scribes—was organized into a guild. Each guild had an alderman (*seṭhi*) and its own office or guildhall (*nigamasabhā*), and acted as a bank, receiving deposits and lending out money. Imports included luxuries like wine, cloth of the finest texture, choice unguents, glass, storax and sweet clover. Exports were common cloth, cornelian, muslins and mallow cloth. The absence of roads hindered commerce as much as it was helped by the plentiful currency towards the end of the first century A.D. The eastern Deccan seems to have entered at this time upon a period of great industrial and commercial activity which reached its climax towards the end of the second century.

Buddhism was well established by the third century B.C. and continued to flourish throughout the Sātavāhana period; indeed, the first two centuries of the Christian era constitute the most glorious epoch of Buddhism in the Deccan. The stupa of Amarāvatī was enlarged and embellished, and at Allūru, Gummadiduru, Ghantaśāla, Gudivāda and Goli new stupas were built or old ones enlarged. New caves were cut and additional benefactions made at Nasik, Karle, and Kanheri. In the inscriptions of the time appear the names of a number of sects as well as of monks of various grades of learning and eminence engaged in enlightening the faithful in the Law of the Master. Stupas, the sacred tree, the footprints of the Master, the *triśūla* emblem, the *dharmachakra*, relics and statues of the Buddha and other great teachers and of the Nāgarājas were all objects of worship. The sculptures of this time show men and women in states of ecstatic devotion rather than merely kneeling or perhaps prostrating themselves with joined hands before the objects of their devotion.

Brahminism also flourished and most of the Sātavāhana rulers were devoted to it. The third king of the line performed a number of Vedic sacrifices and even named one of his sons Vediśrī. Hāla's *Saptaśatī* opens with a passage in adoration of Śiva. Gautamīputra Śātakarni was a great supporter of the Brahmins and tried to emulate the epic heroes Rāma, Keśava and Arjuna. The pantheon of Hinduism in this period included Indra, Vāsudeva, the sun and the moon, Śiva, Vishnu, Krishna, Ganeśa and Paśupati. Temples to Gaurī are mentioned in the *Saptaśatī* as also the *vrata* of fire and water.

After its fall, the Sātavāhana empire was partitioned among the Ābhīras in the north-west, who also make their appearance in the lower Krishna valley (Nāgārjunikonda) at the close of the third century A.D., the Chutus in the South and the Ikshvākus in Andhradeśa. In Madhya Pradesh, descendants of the Sātavāhanas themselves continued to rule and the Pallavas rose to power in the south-east. Thus was broken the political unity of the Deccan which had lasted for about six centuries from the time of the Nandas.

The Ābhīras were certainly foreigners and are mentioned in the *Mahābhāshya.* In the second century A.D., they figure as generals under the Śaka satraps of western India. The Purānas state that ten Ābhīras succeeded the Sātavāhanas and ruled for 67 years. An inscription from Nasik speaks of king Mādharīputa Īśvarasena, the Ābhīra, and a son of Śivadatta. The record has much in common with Sātavāhana inscriptions, including the manner of its dating. Īśvarasena was perhaps the founder of the dynasty about which nothing more is known than that in A.D. 248-49 it originated an era called Kalachuri or Chedi in later times. An inscription dated in the thirtieth year of Ābhīra Vasushena (A.D. 279) has been found recently at Nāgārjunikonda.

As little is known of the Chutus who ruled in Mahārāshtra and Kuntala. The names of certain kings of the line are known from coins found in the North Kanara and Chitaldrug districts of Mysore, and from inscriptions in Kanheri, Banavāsi and Malavalli. Lead coins with the horse device and inscribed with the name Hārīti (a part of the name of the Chutus) have come from the Anantapur and Cuddapah districts. Some historians consider the Chutus to be a branch of the Sātavāhanas, while others postulate a Nāga origin for them. They were supplanted by the Kadambas.

The Ikshvākus ruled over the Krishna-Guntur region. The Purānas call them Śrīpārvatīyas—rulers of Śrīparvata and Andhrabhrityas ('Servants of the Andhras'). Though seven kings are said to have ruled for 57 years in all, only a few are known by name from inscriptions. Originally they were feudatories of the Sātavāhanas and bore the title *mahātalavara*. Vāsiṭhīputa Siri Chāntamūla, the founder of the line, performed the *aśvamedha* and *vājapeya* sacrifices. The reign of his son Vīrapurisadāta (*c.* A.D. 275) formed a glorious epoch in the history of Buddhism and in diplomatic relations. He took a queen from the Śaka family of Ujjain and gave his daughter in marriage to a Chutu prince. Almost all the royal ladies were Buddhists: an aunt of Vīrapurisadāta built a big stupa at Nāgārjunikonda for the relics of the great teacher, besides apsidal temples, *vihāras* and *maṇḍapas*. Her example was followed by other women of the royal family and by women generally as we know from a reference to one Bodhisiri, a woman citizen. The next member of the line, son of Vīrapurisadāta, is Ehuvula Chāntamūla, who came after a short Ābhīra interregnum (A.D. 275-80) and whose reign witnessed the completion of a *devīvihāra*, a stupa and two apsidal temples. We hear also of a *Sīhala vihāra*, a convent founded either by a Sinhalese, or, more probably, for the accommodation of Sinhalese monks; and a *Chaitya-ghara* (Chaitya hall) was dedicated to the fraternities (*theriyas*) of Tambapanni (Ceylon). Ceylonese Buddhism was thus in close touch with that of the Andhra country. Ehuvala had a Śaka queen of the Brihatphalāyana gotra; his son by another queen, a Vāsishṭhi, was Rudrapurushadatta who ruled at least eleven years. The sculptures of Nāgārjunikonda, which include large figures of the Buddha, show decided traces of Greek influence and Mahāyāna tendencies, but do not depict the crowds of devotees that characterized the monuments of the preceding century.

In administration and social life, the Sātavāhana tradition was continued, although signs of change are not wanting. The titles of officials, for example, continued to be the same as in the Sātavāhana period, but the duties of several were often combined in one individual; and while matronymics continued to be employed, patronymics are also mentioned. The slightly later Kadamba practice of bearing matronymics and the patronymic *gōtra* is in the line of development from Sātavāhana to Pallava practice. *Āharas* came to be called *rāshtras*, and the title Rāja gave place to the more impressive Mahārāja.

In the Andhra country the Ikshvākus were followed by kings of the Brihatphalāyana *gōtra*, only one of whom—Jayavarman—is known by name, from the solitary surviving copper-plate grant of the line. His kingdom was divided into *āharas*, each under an executive officer, *vāpatam* (*vyāprita*). This grant may be said to start the series of *brahmadeyas*, or gifts to Brahmins, which increase in number and importance through the centuries and confirm the decline of both Buddhism and Jainism.

The Pallavas, in the south-east of the former Sātavāhana empire, made Kānchipuram their capital. A foreign, Pahlava, origin has often been postulated for them, and this seems to gain some support from the crown, recalling that of the Indo-Greek king Demetrius, in the shape of an elephant's scalp, offered to Nandivarman II on the occasion of his being chosen for the throne; but on a broad view they appear—like the Kadambas and even the Chutus before them—to have been a dynasty of North Indian origin which moved to the South and there adapted local traditions to their own use. Thus Śātakarni of the Chutu dynasty, ruler of Banavāsi, worshipped at and endowed the shrine of the god of Malavalli, and the Kadamba king who succeeded him did likewise. A little later the Kadamba line began to declare its devotion to the *kadamba* tree and to Svāmi Mahāsena (i.e. Subrahmanya) whom Tamil tradition regarded as dwelling in the *kadamba* tree. In the same manner, Pallava, as the name of the dynasty of Kānchipuram, must be taken to be the Prākrit-Sanskrit rendering of *toṇḍai*, the name of the land and its rulers as well as of a creeper.

Pallava history opens with three copper-plate grants, all in Prākrit and all dating from the time of Skandavarman, the earliest when he was *yuvarāja*, the others after he had become king. He belonged to the Bhāradvāja *gōtra*, performed the *agnishtōma*, *vājapeya* and *aśvamedha* sacrifices and bore the title 'Supreme King of Kings devoted to *dharma*'. In his time Kānchipuram was the capital and his kingdom extended up to the Krishna in the north and the Arabian Sea in the west. The steps by which this empire was built up cannot now be traced. A ninth-century tradition, recorded in the Vēlūrpālaiyam plates of the sixth year of Nandivarman III, affirms that Vīrakūrcha, an early Pallava king of great fame, seized the insignia of royalty together with the daughter of the Nāga king. This may be an echo of the Pallava conquest of the Chutus who, as we have seen, ruled the west for a time after the dissolution of the Sātavāhana empire. Vīrakūrcha is said to have had a son Skandaśishya, who captured the *ghaṭikā* of the Brahmins from king Satyasena—an incident of which no elucidation seems possible now. And Skandaśishya's son Kumāravishnu is described as a victor in battles who seized the city of Kānchī, it is not stated from whom. To turn back to the early Prākrit charters: we do not know the name of Skandavarman's father but obviously Skandavarman was not the first Pallava ruler of Kānchī. The title *yuvarāja* makes that clear enough; his father was, perhaps, Simhavarman, a king mentioned in a Prākrit stone inscription recently discovered in the Guntur district. His successors were a son, Buddhavarman, who was *yuvarāja* and his son Buddhyankura by his queen Chārudevī. All the three charters of Skandavarman's time may be taken to belong to the first half of the fourth century A.D. In this period other princes of the royal family besides the *yuvarāja* took an active part in the administration, in which many officials with specific duties in different territorial divisions or state departments were employed. The designations of these officials, and other administrative details, can all be gathered from inscriptions.

The Pallavas were followers of the Brahminical religion and made gifts of land to gods and Brahmins in the belief that they would thereby secure health, prosperity and victory in war.

The total darkness that follows the records of Skandavarman's time is broken only by a streak of light in the account of Samudragupta's invasion of the South, given in his Allahabad pillar inscription of about the middle of the fourth century A.D. From this it is evident that he did battle with his opponent Vishnugopa, the ruler of Kānchī, somewhere north of this city and never, in fact, reached the Pallava capital. Another of his opponents, Ugrasena of Palakka ruling somewhere in the Nellore district, was probably a feudatory of Vishnugopa.

The next stage in the annals of Pallava rule is represented by a dozen copper-plate charters and a fragment of another charter, all of them in Sanskrit; some of them, however, are suspect. They are all dated in the regnal years of the kings. For absolute chronology, therefore, we depend on a Śaka date in the Jain manuscript *Lokavibhāga.* This work on cosmology was finished on the equivalent of the 25th of August 458 in the twenty-second year of Simhavarman's reign. This date receives confirmation from the Ganga charters and enables us to construct the following genealogical table for the Pallavas.

(1) *Prākrit charters*

Simhavarman I A.D. 275-300
- (Śiva) Skandavarman
  - Buddhavarman
    - Buddyankura

(2) *Sanskrit charters*

Kumāravishnu I (350-70)
- Skandavarman (370-85)
  - Vīravarman (385-400)
    - Skandavarman II (400-36)
      - Simhavarman I (436-60)
        - Skandavarman III (460-80)
          - Nandivarman (480-510)
          - Kumāravishnu II (510-30)
            - Buddhavarman (530-40)
              - Kumāravishnu III (540-50)
      - *Yuvamahārāja* Vishnugopavarman
        - Simhavarman II
          - Vishnugopavarman II

The charters on which this table is based only record grants, so that the political history of the Pallavas from 350-500 is almost a blank. All we can deduce, therefore, is that Vishnugopa, the opponent of Samudragupta, was a contemporary and perhaps brother of Kumāravishnu I, while *Yuvamahārāja* Vishnugopavarman I probably did not live to reign as king, and Simhavarman II must have had a very prosperous reign as he is known to have issued a large number of grants; but what happened after his death is by no means clear. Possibly the Pallavas were engaged in conflicts with the southern Tamil powers in their efforts to extend their territory in that direction. The Vēlūrpālaiyam plates describe Buddhavarman, for instance, as 'the submarine fire to the ocean of the Chola army'. Simhavarman, the father of Simhavishnu, who started the best-known line of Pallava rulers towards the end of the sixth century A.D., finds no place in this genealogy and thus leaves another gap in the line of succession which cannot be bridged.

We can say, however, that the Pallava administrative system made a further advance at this time. The king adopted the additional title of *bhaṭṭāraka*, the heir-apparent had a recognized position, as *yuvamahārāja*, and the other princes continued to be employed on state affairs. Different classes of district officers are listed, though the exact nature of their functions is not known. There is evidence of strong military and police organizations and labour may have been conscripted by force. The manufacture of salt, and sometimes of sugar, was a royal monopoly, and villages were expected to maintain the king's officers free of charge when they were on tour. On the other hand, exemption of taxation was allowed on all gifts of land to Brahmins who were held, in theory at any rate, to be entitled to a total of eighteen such immunities. This is a continuation and development of Sātavāhana practice for the Pallava kings also followed the Brahminical religion, worshipped Śiva and Vishnu and performed sacrifices.

The obscure but extensive political revolution in which the Kalabhras overthrew all the established dynasties of Southern India affected the Pallava kingdom also. The next stage of Pallava history therefore opens with the subjugation of the Kalabhras by Simhavishnu, son of a Simhavarman, at the close of the sixth century.

At this point, however, we shall go back to the Andhra country. Another opponent of Samudragupta was Hastivarman (*c.* 350), ruler of Vengi which may be identified with Peddavegi, near Ellore, in the Krishna district. Hastivarman's family, known to historians as the Sālankāyanas from the *gōtra* to which it belonged, must have risen to power at the expense of the Brihatphalāyanas and possibly also of the Pallavas. The earliest known member of the dynasty is Devavarman whose father was evidently an independent king as he was given the title *bhaṭṭāraka*. Devavarman certainly ruled before Hastivarman, but the relationship between the two princes is not known. His only extant inscription is dated by the month and *tithi* (lunar day), a practice followed by later dynasties but different from the older Sātavāhana method of mentioning the particular fortnight of one of the three seasons into which the year was divided.

Hastivarman was not much affected when Samudragupta invaded his territory. At the time the eastern Deccan was cut up into a number of minor kingdoms, among them Kosala, comprising the modern districts of Bilaspur, Raipur, Sambalpur and part of Ganjam; Kurāla, the region around lake Colair; two small kingdoms in the Ganjam district with capitals at Koṭṭūra and Erandapalla; two more in the Godāvari district with Pishtapura and Avamukta as capitals; Devarāshtra (i.e., Elamanchili) in the Viśākhapatnam district, and kingdoms with Palakka and Kusthalapura as capitals. We have little definite knowledge of the political position of these Southern states or of their relations with one another.

Hastivarman was succeeded by his son Nandivarman I (*c.* 375). His kingdom included the *vishaya* of Kudrahāra on both sides of the Krishna river. The part that lay to the south was subsequently conquered by the Pallavas who named it Vengirāshtra. Nandivarman I was followed on the throne by his son Hastivarman II; then came Skandavarman son of Hastivarman II; Skanda was followed by Chandavarman, the second son of Nandivarman I, and the latter by his son Nandivarman II (*c.* 430), the last known king of the line.

Like the Pallavas the Sālankāyanas had the bull crest, but there is little else to show definitely that the two dynasties were closely related or that on that account the Sālankāyanas were left unmolested by their more powerful neighbours in the South. The Sālankāyana administrative system had much in common with that of the contemporary Pallavas. The village headman was called *mutuḍa*, or alderman, a title that does not occur elsewhere. The tutelary deity of the dynasty was the sun god and they worshipped Śiva or Vishnu in addition. Their charters bear a close resemblance in their script to the earliest inscriptions of the Hindu colonies of Indo-China and Malaysia, and there is good reason to hold that the Telugu country took a prominent part in the movement of colonization abroad.

In Kalinga the period following Samudragupta's invasion is taken up by the rule of a line of kings who belonged to the Māṭhara *kula.* Seven kings bearing names ending with *varman* are known, from their copper-plate grants, although their genealogy is not forthcoming. Pishtapura, Simhapura, and Vardhamānapura are among the places from which grants were issued. Though some of the kings used matronymics and adopted the antique Sātavāhana mode of dating their records, in other respects they clearly mark a transition to the records of a later time. The language of the inscriptions is Sanskrit and the kings called themselves Kalingādhipatis and Paramamāheśvaras. Roughly, the period of their rule extended from 375 to 500 when they were succeeded by the Gangas in north Kalinga, south Kalinga becoming part of Vengi.

In Vengi the Sālankāyanas were followed by the Vishnukundins who had Śrīparvatasvāmi ('Lord of Śrīparvata') for their family deity. The genealogy of this line has been the subject of much difference of opinion but without entering into details the best view of the whole matter may be presented as follows:

Mādhavavarman I (440-60)
- Devavarman
  - Mādhavavarman (48 years)
- Vikramendravarman I (460-80)
  - Indra-bhaṭṭāraka (480-515)
    - Vikramendra II (515-35)
      - Govindavarman (535-56)
        - Mādhavavarman II (556-616)
          - Manchana-bhaṭṭāraka

Mādhavavarman I is reputed to have performed eleven *aśvamedhas* and countless *agnishtōmas*, but we need not take this literally for the same is also said of Mādhavavarman II (556-616). Mādhavavarman I's queen must have been a Vākāṭaka princess for we read that his son Vikramendra I belonged to the families of Vishnukundi and Vākāṭaka. Indra-bhaṭṭāraka was victor in many fights, on one occasion overwhelming a kinsman—probably Mādhavavarman of the collateral line, lord of Trikūta. He also came into conflict with the eastern Ganga Indravarman and enlarged his kingdom at his expense. Govindavarman had the title Vikramāśraya ('Refuge of Valour'), and his son Mādhavavarman II was probably the greatest monarch of his line and became the centre of many popular legends in later times. He had the title Janāśraya ('Refuge of the People') and performed a *hiranyagarbha*. Hostilities with the Gangas seem to have continued throughout his reign and he is said to have crossed the Godāvari to conquer the eastern region. The Vishnukundins were still ruling the Vengi country and its neighbourhood at the time of the invasion of the eastern Deccan, at the beginning of the seventh century, by the Chālukya ruler of Bādāmi, Pulakeśin II.

Between the kingdom of the Vishnukundins in the north and that of the Pallavas in the south there rose, early in the sixth century, a small kingdom ruled by kings of the Ānanda *gōtra*. The first of the line was Kandara who gave his daughter in marriage to a Pallava prince and who, after sharp battles with the Vishnukundins on the banks of the Krishna, wrested from them the title 'Lord of Trikūtaparvata'. His kingdom was nevertheless small, probably comprising no more than the modern taluks of Guntur and Tenali. Other kings of the line were Dāmodaravarman, whose father performed many sacrifices, Attivarman and Kandara's grandson whose name is not known but who has left at Chezarla a stone inscription which may be assigned to the last quarter of the sixth century. The capital of the kingdom, Kandarapura, is mentioned in inscriptions and must have been founded by king Kandara. The kings of this house were generally Śaivites, though Dāmodaravarman was a Buddhist; and whatever their own predilections may have been they patronized all sects impartially.

The Vākāṭakas of Madhya Pradesh held an important place in the politics and culture of the land in the fourth and fifth centuries A.D. They had notable diplomatic and matrimonial relationships with all the great contemporary royal families like the imperial Guptas, the Vishnukundins and the Kadambas. They made substantial additions to the famous gallery of cave temples and paintings at Ajanta.

The name of the Vākāṭakas has been connected by some historians with the little village of Bagat in Bundelkhand, while others are inclined to treat it as of Andhra origin. They rose to power at a time when the last of the Sātavāhanas had ceased to rule in Madhya Pradesh and the Śaka satraps had exhausted themselves by their long struggles with the Sātavāhanas. The Purānas mention Vindhyaśakti as their founder and Purikā in ' Berar ' as their early capital, and also testify to the expansion of their power north of the Vindhyas as far as Vidiśā. This rise of the Vākāṭakas may be placed in the last quarter of the third century A.D.

The son and successor of Vindhyaśakti was Pravarasena I (*c.* 280-340) who made extensive conquests in all directions and was the only king of the dynasty to bear the title *samrāt* (emperor). He had four sons whom he set over the newly conquered provinces. The eldest, Gautamīputra, died before his father. Another, Sarvasena, ruled over southern Berar and the north-western part of ' Hyderabad '. In the west the absence of the title of Mahākshatrapa among the Śaka rulers between 304 and 345, and the total cessation of coinage between 332 and 348, suggest the extension of Vākāṭaka power over the Śaka dominions. Pravarasena I celebrated his victories by performing several sacrifices—four *aśvamedhas* and a *vājapeya.* When Rudrasena I (340-65), son of Gautamīputra, succeeded his grandfather, his uncles, who were viceroys, proclaimed their independence. He overcame two of them with the help of his maternal grandfather Bhavanāga of the Bhāraśiva family ruling in Padmāvati in central India, but the house of Sarvasena continued its independent rule.

Rudrasena was more fortunate in his relations with the Guptas and the conquests of Samudragupta did not affect him. The Śakas succeeded in improving their position and reviving the title of Mahākshatrapa from 346. Rudrasena's son, Prithvīshena I (365-90), assisted the house of Sarvasena in its conquest of a part of Kuntala or southern Mahārāshtra. A greater event of his reign was the marriage of his son Rudrasena II with Prabhāvatī-guptā, daughter of Chandragupta II. The alliance was probably meant to strengthen the position of the Guptas in the execution of their plans against the Śakas; but Rudrasena II died prematurely after a reign of five years leaving two minor sons. The widowed Gupta princess became regent, and uncles of the collateral branch ruling at Bāsim did not venture to oppose the arrangement. It was during her regency that Gujarat and Kathiawar were conquered by Chandragupta II, Prabhāvatī-guptā offering considerable help to her father. After she had been regent for 13 years, her elder son Divākarasena died and she held the regency on behalf of the younger son Dāmodarasena (later Pravarasena II) till 410. Pravarasena II (410-45) was a man of peace, more devoted to literature and the arts than to war. A worshipper of Vishnu, he composed the Prākrit poem *Setubandha*, said to have been revised by Kālidāsa, describing the most famous exploits of Rāma. He also founded a new capital at Pravarapura to which he moved in the second half of his reign. The crown prince, Narendrasena, married a Kadamba princess—the daughter of Kakusthavarman.

Narendrasena (445-65) was beset by difficulties at the beginning of his reign. The Nala king Bhavadattavarman ruling in 'Bastar state' invaded the Vākāṭaka kingdom and for a time his victory seemed to be complete. Narendrasena, however, soon recovered his strength and turned the tables on the enemy, even though his grand-uncle Kumāragupta was in no position to help him on account of the danger to his own empire from the Hūnas. Malwa, Mekalā and Kosala also passed under the rule of Narendrasena for a time. His son, Prithvīsheṇa II, the last known king of the main line, had to retrieve the fortunes of his family twice. His opponents were very probably the Nalas, and possibly the Traikūṭakas of southern Gujarat.

The history of the collateral Bāsim branch may now be briefly noticed. Sarvasena was succeeded by his son Vindhyasena or Vindhyaśakti who conquered southern Mahārāshtra with the aid of Prithvīsheṇa I of the main line. His son was Pravarasena II who, after a reign of fifteen years, left on the throne a minor son of eight who had a long and peaceful reign. His son Devasena (*c.* 460-80) was a pleasure-seeker who left the government of the state to a minister named Hastibhoja, and was succeeded by his son Harisheṇa (*c.* 480-515). He was the most powerful ruler of the line and succeeded Prithvīsheṇa II in the main kingdom as well. His Ajanta record shows that he extended his rule over Gujarat, Malwa, southern Kosala and the Kuntala provinces, thus extending the boundaries of the empire wider even than under Pravarasena I. The fall of the Vākāṭakas occurred between 515 and 550, during which period Chhattisgarh was lost to the Somavamśis, southern Mahārāshtra to the Kadambas, northern Mahārāshtra to the Kalachuris, and Malwa and the northern part of Madhya Pradesh to Yaśodharman. Finally the Chālukyas of Bādāmi completed their overthrow (*c.* 550).

From the middle of the fourth century, the Kadambas rose to power in the south-west Deccan as a result of the Pallavas' weakened position after Samudragupta's invasion of the South. The earliest Kadamba inscription is in the Prākrit language and is found engraved on a pillar below a shorter record of the Chutus. The Kadambas were a Brahmin family which derived its descent from Hārīti and belonged to the Mānavya *gōtra.* They were devoted to the study of the Vedas and the performance of Vedic sacrifices. The Kadamba king Mayūraśarman entered the *ghatikā* (college) at Kānchipuram with the intention of studying the entire Veda; but a fierce quarrel with a mounted Pallava guard encouraged him to forsake the scholar's cell for the battlefield. He overpowered the Pallava frontier-officials and entrenched himself in the dense forests round about Śrīparvata after levying tribute from the Brihadbāṇas and other subordinates of the Pallavas. He continually harassed the Pallava forces sent against him and peace only came when they recognized his sovereignty over all land between 'the western sea and Preharā' (by which, perhaps, is meant the Tungabhadra or Malaprabha). A short stone inscription in Prākrit from Chandravalli mentions in relation to Mayūraśarman a tank, and the names of Ābhīra, Sakasthāna, Sayindaka, Punnāṭa and Mokari, among others; the import of the record is by no means clear.

The genealogy of the Kadambas of this period with an approximate indication of chronology is given opposite.

Later legend credited Mayūravarman, as he then came to be called, with the performance of eighteen horse-sacrifices and the distribution of many villages among Brahmins, but the early inscriptions of the dynasty say nothing about this. Vākāṭaka Vindhyasena of the Bāsim branch is said to have conquered Kuntala, and his invasion was resisted with a fair measure of success by Kangavarman. Vaijayantī (Banavāsi) was the capital of the Kadambas, and Pālāsikā (Hālsi) a secondary capital.

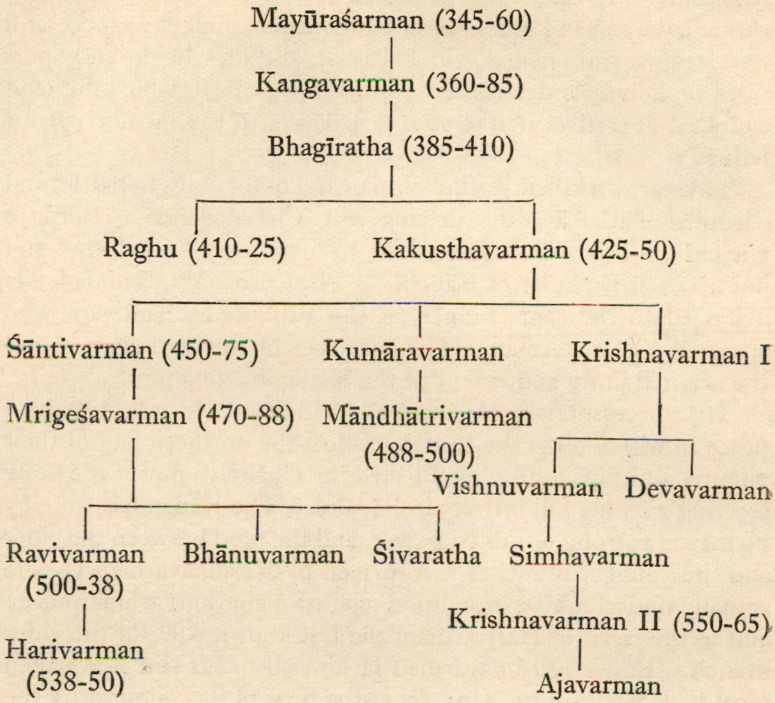

THE KADAMBAS

Kakusthavarman was one of the great rulers of the line. He had a prosperous reign and his daughters married into many important royal families, including the Guptas. His son Śāntivarman was a ruler of great fame and much personal charm. He is said to have worn three crowns and 'attracted to himself the prosperity of his enemies'. During his reign danger threatened from the Pallavas; and the situation was met by transferring control in the southern districts to his younger brother, Krishnavarman. This amounted to a virtual division of the kingdom, as is seen from the latter's performance of a horse-sacrifice—never undertaken by a subordinate ruler. The war with the Pallavas cost Krishnavarman his life, besides ruining the principality of the Kekayas, the homeland of his queen. His son Vishnuvarman had to accept investiture from the Pallavas. The Pallava rulers concerned were

Nānakkāsa and Śāntivara, names otherwise unknown. Mrigeśavarman, the son and successor of Śāntivarman, fought unsuccessful wars against the Gangas and Pallavas. Besides being an expert rider of horses and elephants, he was a scholar who built and endowed liberally a Jain temple in Pālāsikā to the memory of his father.

Ravivarman killed Vishnuvarman and other kings in battle, and occupied Pālāsikā after driving out Chandadanda, 'Lord of Kānchī', a title which here seems to mean only 'a Pallava' and not necessarily 'ruler of Kānchī'. Most probably Chandadanda belonged to the same branch of the Pallavas as Śāntivara who anointed Vishnuvarman. The successes of Ravivarman restored the original unity and extent of the Kadamba kingdom.

His successor was Harivarman (538-50). He was a man of peace in whose reign the Kadambas lost the northern half of their empire, and Pulakeśin I established the Chālukya power is 545 by erecting a strong hill fortress in Bādāmi. The Kadambas were by no means a strong or united power, and the feud between the elder and the younger branches was revived by Krishnavarman II who actually undertook an expedition against Vaijayantī which put an end to the reign of Harivarman, the last known ruler of the elder branch. Either Krishnavarman II himself or his son Ajavarman must have been ruling Banavāsi at the time of its conquest by the Chālukya Kīrtivarman, son of Pulakeśin I.

In between the territory of the Kadambas in the west and the Pallavas in the east lay the kingdom of the Gangas in the southern part of the modern Mysore territory which came to be known as Gangavādi by its long association with Ganga rule. Early Ganga history has been much obscured by legend and by an unusually large number of spurious copper-plate grants. According to the authentic contemporary inscriptions, the first ruler, Konganivarman, belonged to the Jāhnaveya *kula*, the family of the Gangas, and the Kāṇvāyana *gōtra*. He distinguished himself in many battles and carved out a prosperous kingdom for himself. His title 'Dharma Mahādhirāja' implies independent status in the beginning, but the Gangas soon lost their position and throughout their long history were compelled to acknowledge the suzerainty of one or other of the greater dynasties of South India. Konganivarma may be placed about 400. The name of his capital is not given in the inscriptions, though later tradition first locates it at Kuvalāla, modern Kolar, and afterwards at Talakād, nearer the hostile frontier of the Kadambas against whom, in company with the Pallavas, he waged war at this date.

Konganivarman's son and successor was Mahādhirāja Mādhava I (*c.* 425). He was a clever politician to whom later tradition attributes the authorship of a commentary on the *Dattakasūtra*, a treatise on erotics. The next ruler was his son Āyyavarman (*c.* 450), a great warrior who was also proficient in the *śāstras*, *itihāsas* and Purānas. He was anointed by the Pallava Simhavarman I of Kānchī, possibly because he sought support from the Pallava ruler in a dispute for the throne with his younger brother, Krishnavarman. He is called Harivarman in later inscriptions which credit him with the removal of the capital to Talakād. The disputed succession was evidently settled by a virtual division of the kingdom between the two brothers, both of whom named their sons Simhavarman in recognition of their political relation to the Pallava ruler. This division seems to have continued under their sons and successors Mādhava II, *alias* Simhavarman, and another Simhavarman. The former was anointed by Pallava Skandavarman and married a sister of Kadamba Krishnavarman I. According to later grants, Avinīta, the child of this union, was anointed successor to the throne while still a baby (*c.* 500). The genealogy of the Gangas may then be represented as follows:

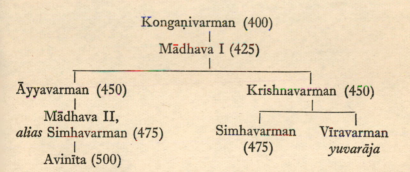

- Konganivarman (400)
  - Mādhava I (425)
    - Āyyavarman (450)
      - Mādhava II, *alias* Simhavarman (475)
        - Avinīta (500)
    - Krishnavarman (450)
      - Simhavarman (475)
      - Vīravarman *yuvarāja*

The social, administrative and religious conditions that prevailed in the Kadamba and Ganga kingdoms were very much the same as those in the contemporary Pallava kingdom.

BIBLIOGRAPHY

Epigraphia Indica, Vols. 20, 21, 29, 33 and 34 for Ikshvāku inscriptions

K. Gopalachari: *Early History of the Andhra Country* (Madras, 1941)

G. Jouveau-Dubreuil: *Ancient History of the Deccan* (Pondicherry, 1920)

T. V. Mahalingam: *Kānchipuram in Early South Indian History* (Meyer lectures, 1963 Ms.)

K. A. N. Sastri: *The New History of the Indian People*, Vol. VI, Ch. 12, 'South India' (Lahore, 1946; Banaras, 1954)

D. C. Sircar: *Successors of the Sātavāhanas* (Calcutta, 1939)

CHAPTER VII

THE AGE OF THE ŚANGAM AND AFTER

Kalinga and the Tamil states—Śangam literature—its age—The Cheras—Āy and Pāri—Adigaimān Anji—the Cholas, Karikāla—Ilandiraiyan—the Pāndyas—Neduñjeḻiyan of Talaiyālangānam—his ancestors—civil war in the Chola kingdom—end of the Śangam age, political changes.

Social life—composite culture—land—people—monarchy—*sabhā* and *manram*—revenue—army—war—royal patronage of arts and letters—poetry, music and dance—pastimes—houses—popular beliefs and customs—trade, foreign and internal—religion and ethics—dark age after the Śangam, Kalabhras.

THE inscription of Khāravela briefly mentioned in an earlier chapter contains the only early epigraphic reference to the kingdoms of the Tamil country after the Aśoka inscriptions. Khāravela ruled in Kalinga in the first half of the second century B.C., and in the eleventh year of his reign (*c.* 155 B.C.) is said to have destroyed a confederacy of Tamil states—*Tramiradeśasanghātam*—which was 113 years old at the time, and had long been a source of danger. The same inscription records that Khāravela caused 'numerous pearls in hundreds' to be brought from the Pāndya to Kalinga, and perhaps also horses, elephants, jewels and rubies. In itself a difficult document, the gaps in the inscription and its extremely worn-out condition render its meaning very uncertain. Of the Tamil confederacy and its aims, of how it became a danger to Kalinga, and of the measures taken by Khāravela to avert the danger and the new relations he established with the Pāndyan kings we hear nothing more from any other source.

The first well-lighted epoch in the history of the Tamil land is that reflected in the literature of Śangam (i.e. the first three or four centuries A.D.)—the earliest stratum of Tamil literature now available. This is found grouped in eight more or less schematic anthologies, viz., (1) *Naṟṟiṇai*, (2) *Kuṟundogai*, (3) *Ainguṟunūṟu*, (4) *Padiṟṟuppattu*, (5) *Paripāḍal*, (6) *Kalittogai*, (7) *Ahanānūṟu* and (8) *Puṟanānūṟu*; a ninth group *Pattuppaṭṭu* ('Ten Idylls') completes the tale. The entire collection includes 2,279 poems of lengths varying from three lines to over eight hundred, by 473 poets (including some women) besides 102 anonymous pieces. At the end of each poem are notes giving the name of its author, the occasion of its composition and other details. These notes, probably the work of the editors, must be taken generally to represent a correct tradition though there are difficulties about doing so.

The *Tolkāppiyam*, a comprehensive work on Tamil grammar, is also of the same age.

Doubtless what has survived is only a part of the much vaster literature of these remote times. An inscription of the early tenth century A.D. mentions among the achievements of the early Pāndyas the translation of the *Mahābhārata* into Tamil and the establishment of a Śangam at Madura. This translation has been lost, though poems composed by 'Perundēvanār who sang the *Bhāratam*' form the invocations placed at the beginning of six out of the eight anthologies named above. Parts of a Tamil *Bhāratam* by a Perundēvanār have come down to us, but the author was a contemporary of Nandivarman III Pallava (ninth century A.D.) and probably different from his namesake of the Śangam anthologies.

That a college (Śangam) of Tamil poets flourished for a time under royal patronage in Madura may well be a fact. But the earliest account of it, which occurs in the introduction to the commentary on the *Iṟaiyanār Agapporuḷ* (*c.* A.D. 750), is enveloped in legend. It refers to three Śangams which lasted, at long intervals, for 9,990 years altogether and counted 8,598 poets (including a few gods of the Śaiva persuasion) as members, and 197 Pāndyan kings as patrons. Some of the names of the kings and poets—such as Kaḍungōn and Ugrapperuvaḻudi—are found in inscriptions and other authentic records, showing that some facts have got mixed up with much fiction, so that no conclusions of value can be based on it.

A careful study of the synchronisms between the kings, chieftains and poets suggested by the notes at the end of the poems indicates that this body of literature reflects occurrences within a period of four or five continuous generations at the most, say a period of 120 or 150 years. It is only for the Chera line of rulers that we can construct anything like a continuous genealogy, and this shows the existence of two lines of rulers, either connected by marriage or otherwise, each extending over three or four generations at the most. In all other instances we only have unrelated names which render a regular history of the period impossible.

We must therefore rest content with the outstanding figures and their achievements reported by the poets.

The land was divided among the three ' crowned kings ' of the Chera, Chola and Pāndya lines, and a number of minor chieftains, who according to the political conditions of the time either owned allegiance to or fought for one or other of these monarchs, or else led an independent existence. Seven of these chieftains gained particular recognition from the poets for their liberal patronage of literature and the arts and were described as *vaḷḷaḷs* (patrons).

We have seen that the language of the short Brāhmī inscriptions of the second century B.C. was Tamil, still in its formative stages, with an admixture of words of clearly Sanskritic origin. In the poems of the Śangam anthologies, the Tamil language has reached maturity and begun to serve as a powerful and elegant medium of literary expression, and has already received and assimilated many words and ideas from Sanskrit sources. It also reflects the existence of a fairly elaborate code of conventions governing the portrayal of social life in literature. This must clearly have been the result of a long course of development spread over some generations.

Another indication of the date of this literature is furnished by the synchronism of Gajabāhu I of Ceylon with Śenguṭṭuvan, one of the Chera monarchs celebrated in the *Padiṟṟuppattu*, the anthology exclusively devoted to the Cheras. The date of Gajabāhu's reign has been fixed at about 173-95, and this may well be the period when Śenguṭṭuvan flourished. On this basis, the Śangam age may be taken to have extended from say A.D. 100 to 250.

But this synchronism is found not in any of the Śangam anthologies, but in the *Śilappadikāram* which presents with great literary charm the popular legend of Kōvalan and Kaṇṇagi, and relates the institution of the Kaṇṇagi cult in South India and Ceylon. In its present form this work cannot be placed earlier than the fifth century; some would place it much later, but considering the quasi-religious nature of the story and the institution of the cult, it is not unlikely that the legend preserved the memory of a historically correct synchronism.

The third and strongest line of argument in support of this suggested chronology for the Śangam is to be found in the striking correspondence between the evidence of the poems on the trade and other relations of the Tamil states with the Yavanas (Greeks and Romans) in this period and that of the classical writers on the same subject, particularly Strabo, the anonymous author of the *Periplus of the Erythraean Sea*, Pliny, and Ptolemy. The details are set forth later in the chapter, and they show beyond a shadow of doubt that this stratum of Tamil literature must have belonged to the age of the classical writers mentioned above.

Archaeology confirms the evidence of literature. The numerous discoveries throughout South India of gold and silver coins of the Roman emperors of the first two centuries A.D. and the evidence recently unearthed of the presence of a 'Roman factory' at Arikamedu (Aruhan mēḍu, Jaina mound) in the neighbourhood of Pondicherry in the first century go far to confirm the correctness of the date suggested for the Śangam age.

We may now set forth the salient facts of the politics of the period before proceeding to give an account of its social life. The monarchies of the Cheras, Cholas and Pāndyas were believed, at least in subsequent ages, to be of immemorial antiquity; and the poems of the Śangam attest the anxiety of all of them to connect themselves with the events of the Great War between the Kauravas and the Pāndavas. The first Chera monarch we hear of, Udiyanjēral (*c.* A.D. 130) is said to have fed sumptuously both the armies of Kurukshetra, and thereby earned for himself the title 'Udiyanjēral of the great feeding'. Perhaps it is best to look upon this as a conventional attribution to him of an achievement of some remote ancestor. The same honour is also claimed in other poems for the Pāndyas and Cholas.

The son of Udiyanjēral was Nedunjēral Ādan who won a naval victory against some local enemy on the Malabar coast, and took captive several Yavana traders whom for some time he subjected to harsh treatment, for reasons that are not clear, but subsequently released after obtaining a heavy ransom. He is said to have fought many wars and spent many years in camp with his armies. He won victories against seven crowned kings, and thus reached the superior rank of an *adhirāja*. He was called *Imayavaramban*—'He who had the Himālaya for his boundary'—a title explained by the claim that he conquered all India and carved the Chera emblem of the bow on the face of the great mountain—an instance of poetic exaggeration not uncommon in these poems. His capital is called Marandai. He fought a war with the contemporary

Chola king in which both the monarchs lost their lives and their queens performed *satī*.

Ādan's younger brother was 'Kuṭṭuvan of many elephants' who conquered Kongu and apparently extended the Chera power from the western to the eastern sea for a time. Ādan had two sons by different queens. One of them was known as 'the Chera with the *kaḷangāy* festoon and the fibre crown'; the crown he wore at his coronation is said to have been made of palmyra fibre and the festoon on it contained *kaḷangāy*, a small black berry. It was not altogether to be despised for the crown had a golden frame and festoons of precious pearls; but why the king had to wear such an extraordinary tiara is not explained anywhere. He is said to have won successes against the contemporary Adigaimān chieftain Anji of Tagaḍūr and to have led an expedition against Nannan whose territory lay to the north of Malabar, in the Tulu country. He too was an *adhirāja* wearing a garland of seven crowns.

The other son of Ādan was Śenguṭṭuvan, 'the Righteous Kuṭṭuva' (*c.* 180), celebrated in song by Paraṇar, one of the most famous and longest-lived of the poets of the Śangam age. Śenguṭṭuvan's life and achievements have been embellished by legends of a later time of which there are no traces in the two strictly contemporary poems, both by Paraṇar—the decad on the king in the 'Ten Tens', and a song in the *Puṟanāṉūṟu*. The only martial achievement they celebrate is a victorious war against the chieftain of Mōhūr. Paraṇar also says that Śenguṭṭuvan exerted himself greatly on the sea, but gives no details. He was given a title for driving back the sea, and this is taken to mean that he destroyed the efficiency of the sea as a protection to his enemies who relied on it. If this is correct he must have maintained a fleet. For the rest, we only learn that he was a skilled rider on horse and elephant, wore a garland of seven crowns as *adhirāja*, and was adept in besieging fortresses, besides being a great warrior and a liberal patron of the arts.

The epilogue to the decad adds a number of new particulars, the most important bearing on the establishment of the Pattini cult, i.e., the worship of Kaṇṇagi as the ideal wife. Others refer to an attack on Viyalur in Nannan's country (perhaps to suppress a rebellion), the overthrow of the fortress of Koḍukūr in the Kongu country, and intervention in a Chola war of succession resulting in that throne being secured to one prince at the cost of the lives of nine others. The stone for making the image of Pattini, the Divine Chaste Wife, was obtained after a fight with an Aryan chieftain and bathed in the Ganges before being brought to the Chera country. All these events are narrated with numerous embellishments and in epic detail in the *Śilappadikāram*, though whether this poem derives from the epilogue to the decad, or the epilogue from the epic, is more than we can say. The antiquity and popularity of the story of Kaṇṇagi and Kōvalan and the probable existence of other and earlier versions of the Kaṇṇagi saga which preceded the *Śilappadikāram* are fairly well attested, and it is not unlikely that Śenguṭṭuvan took the lead in organizing the cult of Pattini, and was supported in his effort by the contemporary rulers of the Pāndya and Chola countries and of Ceylon as the *Śilappadikāram* says.

Altogether five monarchs of the line of Udiyanjēral belonging to three generations are mentioned in the *Padirruppattu*. The number of years they are said to have ruled totals 201, while another three monarchs of the collateral line are said to have reigned for a further 58 years in all. Their reigns surely cannot have been successive, and we must therefore postulate a very considerable degree of overlapping. The Chera kingdom must have been a sort of family estate in which all the grown-up males had a share and interest—what Kautilya calls a *kula-sangha*, a family group, and considers a very efficient form of state organization. A similar clan-rule might also have prevailed in the Chola and Pāndya kingdoms in this period. Such an assumption for the Cholas would be the best means of explaining Śenguṭṭuvan's interference in a war of succession in which nine Chola princes lost their lives; it would also furnish a natural explanation for the occurrence in the Śangam poems of so many royal names, all to be accommodated within four or five generations.

The heroes of the last three decads of the 'Ten Tens' and their ancestors must be taken to have ruled contemporaneously with the kings of the house of Udiyanjēral. The first to be heard of among them are Anduvan and his son Śelvakkaḍungō Vāḻi Ādan, both praised by the poets in general terms for their valour and liberality; the father is said to have been a well-read scholar and the son performed many Vedic sacrifices. Famous among the minor chieftains who were their contemporaries were Āy and Pāri, both celebrated in several poems by a number of poets. Āy was the patron of a Brahmin poet from Uṟaiyūr, and Pāri befriended and patronized another Brahmin, Kapilar, who repaired to the Chera court only after Pāri's death. There he was welcomed by Anduvan's son whom he praised in the seventh decad of the 'Ten Tens'.

Āy was one of the many *vēḷ* chieftains ruling in several parts of the Tamil country. The *vēḷs* claimed to have issued from the sacrificial fire-pit of a northern sage and cherished other legends of their connexion with Vishnu and Agastya, and of one of their ancestors having shot down a tiger which was about to attack a sage in the midst of his penance—legends very similar to those of the Hoysalas in later times. The country he ruled lay round about the Podiya hill, the southernmost section of the Western Ghats; and the Greek geographer Ptolemy says that one 'Aioi' was ruling in the country which included Cape Comorin and Mount Bettigo. Āy seems to have been a dynastic name borne by all the kings of the line as a prefix to their personal names. The patron of the Brahmin poet of Uṟaiyūr was also called Aṇḍiran, a Sanskrit word meaning hero. His country is described as fertile and teeming with elephants which he presented liberally to his favourites. He is said to have presented the God Śiva with a cloth of very fine texture given to him by a *nāga* chieftain Nīla.

Aṇḍiran seems to have been a man of peace; while the excellence of his country and his liberality form the theme of a large number of poems, there is only one casual reference to his success in the battle-field when he is said to have once pursued the Kongar to the western sea. On his death, the poet says, Aṇḍiran was welcomed in the abode of the gods and the drum in Indra's palace reverberated at his arrival.

Pāri, the lifelong friend and patron of Kapilar, was another *vēḷ* chieftain also noted for heroism and generosity. His principality lay in the Pāndya country round the hillock known as Koḍungunṟam or Pirānmalai. The fame of Pāri's liberality was echoed in a later age in the Śaiva saint Sundaramūrti's lament: 'There is no one ready to give, even if an illiberal patron is exalted in song to the level of Pāri'. Pāri's country is said to have comprised three hundred villages round the fortified hill at the centre. The fertility of the land, the strength of the fortress on the hill, and the ruler's liberality are praised in many charming poems, not only by Kapilar. Kapilar stood by Pāri through thick and thin when his hillock was closely invested by the three crowned kings of the Tamil land. Kapilar's intelligence went far to aid Pāri's heroism in prolonging the resistance; for instance, several other poets say that Kapilar trained a large number of birds (parrots according to one) to fly out from Pāri's beleaguered fortress into the open country behind the enemy's lines and bring in corn to feed the city and the army for several months! But the inevitable end came, and in a short poem Pāri's two daughters thus bewailed the occurrence: 'In those days we enjoyed the moonlight happily with father, and our enemies could not take our hill. Now, this day, in this bright moonlight, kings with victorious war-drums have captured the hill, and we have lost our father.' The reference to the victorious drum is ironical as Pāri was not killed in open fight but by treachery.

After Pāri's death Kapilar took charge of his two unmarried daughters and tried without success to get them suitably married. Of what happened subsequently there are different accounts. A note at the end of one of the poems in the *Puṟanāṉūṟu* records that Kapilar, after the death of Pāri, left his daughters in the charge of Brahmins and committed suicide by starvation. The tradition recorded in a Chola inscription of the eleventh century, however, is very different; it mentions only one daughter whom Kapilar had given in marriage to the Malaiyamān before the former entered the fire to attain heaven. And there exist many songs by Kapilar on Malaiyāmān Tirumuḍik-Kāri of Muḷḷur, the excellence and easy defensibility of his country, and his liberal patronage of poets and minstrels. Kapilar also states that Kāri killed in battle another chieftain called Ōri and transferred his mountain, Kolli-malai, to the Cheras.

Whatever may be the truth about the marriage of Pāri's daughter or daughters, it is certain that Kapilar neither committed suicide by starvation nor by entering fire soon after the death of his friend and patron. In fact, he repaired to the court of the Chera prince Śelvakkaḍungō Vāḷi Ādan, the son of Anduvan, because he was reputed to possess all the great qualities of Pāri. Kapilar celebrated Ādan in song and was sumptuously rewarded for his effort.

Ādan's son was Perunjēral Irumpoṟai (*c.* 190) renowned for his overthrow of the stronghold of Tagaḍūr (Dharmapuri in Salem district), the seat of the power of the Adigaimān chieftains. He is also said to have subjugated a rebellious shepherd leader named Kaḻuvuḷ and captured his fortress. He was learned, performed many sacrifices and begat heroic sons worthy of succeeding him. His wise and righteous conduct was such as to induce his *purohit* to renounce the things of the world and retire to a life of asceticism.

Adigaimān, also called Neḍumān Anji, the opponent of Irumpoṟai and lord of Tagaḍūr, was one of the 'seven patrons' and the supporter of the celebrated poetess Auvaiyār who has left many songs about him and some about his son Poguṭṭeḻini. Evidently patron and poetess did not get on well at first start, for one poem gives expression to Auvaiyār's vexation at having waited a long time for a present. Soon, however, a perfect understanding grew up between them; the poetess is all praise for the hero and his achievements in the field, and undertakes a diplomatic mission to the Tondaimān on his account. On his side Anji showed his devotion by many valuable presents including a rare myrobalan fruit believed to prevent the ailments of old age and to assure longevity. According to Auvaiyār, Adigaimān was born of a family which honoured the gods by *pūjā* and by sacrifices, which introduced into the world the sweet sugar-cane from heaven, and ruled the world with great ability for a very long time. Adigaimān fought with success against seven opposing princes and destroyed amongst other rebellious strongholds that of Kōvalūr. The Chera invasion of Tagaḍūr, however, is not mentioned by Auvaiyār in her poems, evidently because she did not like to advert to the misfortunes that befell her patron; the event formed the theme of a poem of later times, the *Tagaḍūr Yāttirai*, now known only from quotation in other works. Adigaimān was aided by the Pāndya and Chola monarchs against the Chera, but their help made no difference to the result. The war led to Adigaimān's acknowledgement of the suzerainty of the Chera on whose behalf he subsequently led an expedition against Pāḻi, the capital of Nannan, where, after inflicting great losses on Nannan's forces, he was killed in battle along with Āy Eyinan, another Chera feudatory, by the intrepid general of Nannan, known as Ñimili or Miñili. Auvaiyār laments his death without mentioning its occasion, and bewails the desolation of the days that remained to her after Adigaimān had earned his title to a hero-stone, a clear statement that he fell on the battle-field.

The last Chera prince mentioned in the extant portions of the 'Ten Tens' is Kuḍakko Iḷanjēral Irumpoṟai (*c.* A.D. 190), a cousin of the victor of Tagaḍūr. He is said to have fought a battle against 'the two big kings' (Pāndya and Chola) and Vicci, to have captured five stone fortresses, to have defeated the big Chola who ruled at Potti and the young Paḷaiyan Māṟan, and to have brought to the ancient city of Vanji much booty from these campaigns.

The mention of the Vāni river flowing near the Chera capital shows that Karuvūr was in fact Vanji. The discovery of numerous Roman coins in the neighbourhood, and Ptolemy's statement that the inland city of Korura was the Chera capital, also point to the same conclusion. The location of Vanji has been much debated in recent years however, and some historians hold strongly, though with few tangible reasons, to the view that it is to be sought on the west coast at Tiruvanjaikkaḷam in Kerala State (Cochin).

Another Chera prince deserving mention is 'Śēy of the elephant eye' who had also the title Māndaranjēral Irumpoṟai (*c.* A.D. 210). After one battle, he was captured by his Pāndya contemporary Neḍunjeḻiyan, victor of Talaiyālangānam, but regained his freedom in time to prevent his enemies at home from deposing him.

Among the Cholas, Karikāla (*c.* A.D. 190) stands out pre-eminent. He is described in a poem as the descendant of a king (not named) who compelled the wind to serve his purposes when he sailed his ships on the wide ocean—possibly a reference to the early maritime enterprise of the Cholas. Karikāla's father was Iḷanjēṭcenni 'of many beautiful chariots', a brave king and a hard fighter. Karikāla means 'the man with the charred leg', a reference to an accident by fire which befell the prince early in life. Other explanations for the name were invented in later times, however, and it has also been taken to be a compound word in Sanskrit meaning either 'death to Kali' or 'death to (enemy) elephants'. Early in life he was deposed and imprisoned. The plucky way in which he escaped and re-established himself on the throne is well portrayed by the author of *Paṭṭinappālai*, a long poem on the Chola capital Kāvēri-paṭṭinam in the *Pattuppāṭṭu* ('Ten Idylls'). One of his early achievements was the victory in a great battle at Veṇṇi, modern Kōvil Veṇṇi, 15 miles to the east of Tanjore. This battle is referred to in many poems by different authors. Eleven rulers, *vēḷir* and kings, lost their drums in the field; the Pāndya and the Chera lost their glory, and the latter sustained the last disgrace that could befall a warrior—a wound on his back—and from a sense of profound shame he sat facing north, sword in hand, and starved himself to death. Veṇṇi thus marked a turning point in the career of Karikāla; his victory meant the breaking-up of a widespread confederacy that had been formed against him. Another important battle he fought was at Vāhaipparandalai, 'the field of *vāhai* trees', where nine minor enemy chieftains lost their umbrellas and had to submit. As a result of his victorious campaigns, says the poet of *Paṭṭinappālai*, 'the numerous Oḷiyar submitted to him, the ancient Aruvāḷar carried out his behests, the Northerners lost splendour, and the Westerners were depressed; conscious of the might of his large army ready to shatter the fortresses of enemy kings, Karikāla turned his flushed look of anger against the Pāndya, whose strength gave way; the line of low herdsmen was brought to an end, and the family of Irungōvēḷ was uprooted.' The Aruvāḷar were the people of Aruvānāḍ, the lower valley of the Pennār, to the north of the Kaveri delta. Karikāla is said to have prevented the migration of people from his land to other regions evidently by offering them inducements to stay.

Karikāla's wars thus resulted in his establishing a sort of hegemony among the 'crowned kings' of the Tamil country and in some extension of the territory under his direct rule. The description of Kāvēri-paṭṭinam and its foreshore, which takes up so much of the *Paṭṭinappālai*, gives a vivid idea of the state of industry and commerce at this time. Karikāla also promoted the reclamation and settlement of forest land, and added to the prosperity of the country by multiplying its irrigation tanks. The poems also bear evidence that the king, who was a follower of the Vedic religion, performed sacrifices and lived well, enjoying life to the full.

In later times Karikāla became the centre of many legends found in the *Śilappadikāram* and in inscriptions and literary works of the eleventh and twelfth centuries. They attribute to him the conquest of the whole of India up to the Himālayas and the construction with the aid of his feudatories of the flood-banks of the Kaveri. The famous scholar Naccinārkkiniyar probably follows a correct tradition when he says that Karikāla married a *vēḷir* girl from *Nāngūr*, a place celebrated in the hymns of Tirumangai Āḻvār for the heroism of its warriors. More open to suspicion is the story in the *Śilappadikāram* about a supposed daughter of Karikāla's, named Ādi Mandi, and her husband, a Chera prince called Āṭṭan Atti. Earlier poems which mention their names and some of the incidents attest only the relation between Ādi Mandi and Atti, but not that between her and Karikāla, nor the Chera descent of Atti. Both husband and wife were, according to the early testimony, professional dancers—*āṭṭan* means dancer.

Tondaimān Iḷandiraiyan, who ruled at Kānchipuram, was a contemporary of Karikāla and is also celebrated by the poet of the *Paṭṭinappālai* in another poem in the 'Ten Idylls'. Iḷandiraiyan is said to have been a descendant of Vishnu and belonged to the family of Tiraiyar given by the waves of the sea. There is no hint anywhere of his being related to Karikāla or of his political subordination to the Chola power. Nor is it clear whether it was to him or to some other member of his line that Auvaiyār went as Adigaimān's ambassador. Iḷandiraiyan was himself a poet, and there are four extant songs by him, one of them on the importance of the personal character of the monarch in the promotion of good rule.

The Pāndya king Neḍunjeḻiyan distinguished by the title 'he who won the battle at Talaiyālangānam' may be taken to have ruled about A.D. 210. This ruler was celebrated by two great poets, Māngudi Marudan *alias* Mānguḍi Kiḻār, and Nakkīrar, each contributing a poem on the monarch to the 'Ten Idylls' (*Pattuppāṭṭu*) besides minor pieces in the *Puṟam* and *Aham* collections.

From the *Maduraikkānji* of Mānguḍi Marudan and elsewhere, we learn something of three of Neḍunjeḻiyan's predecessors on the Pāndyan throne. The first is an almost mythical figure called Neḍiyōn ('the tall one'), whose achievements find a place in the 'Sacred Sports' of Śiva at Madura and among the traditions of the Pāndyas enumerated in the Vēḷvikuḍi and Śinnamanūr plates. He is said to have brought the Pahruli river into existence and organized the worship of the sea. The next is Palśālai Mudukuḍumi, doubtless the same as the earliest Pāndya king named in the Vēḷvikuḍi grant and about whom there are several poems. He is a more life-like figure than Neḍiyōn, and is said to have treated conquered territory harshly. He also performed many sacrifices, whence he derived his title *palśālai* meaning 'of the many (sacrificial) halls'. It is not possible to say what distance in time separated these two kings from each other or from their successors. The third ruler mentioned in the *Maduraikkānji* was another Neḍunjeḻiyan, distinguished by the title 'he who won a victory against an Aryan (i.e., North Indian) army'. The tragedy of Kovalan's death at Madura occurred in his reign, which according to the *Śilappadikāram* caused the king to die of a broken heart. A short poem ascribed to this king puts learning above birth and caste.

Neḍunjeḻiyan of Talaiyālangānam came to the throne as a youth and soon after his accession, he proved himself more than equal to a hostile combination of his two neighbouring monarchs and five minor chieftains. There exists a simple poem of great force and beauty in which the youthful monarch swears an oath of heroism and victory in the ensuing fight. Despising his tender years and hoping for an easy victory and large booty, his enemies invaded the kingdom and penetrated to the heart of it; but, nothing daunted, Neḍunjeḻiyan readily took the field, pursued the invading forces across his frontier into the Chola country and inflicted a crushing defeat on them at Talaiyālangānam, about eight miles north-west of Tiruvālūr in the Tanjore district. It was in this battle that the Chera king 'Śey of the elephant eye' was taken captive and thrown into a Pāndyan prison. By his victory Neḍunjeḻiyan not only made himself secure on his ancestral throne, but gained a primacy over the entire state system of the Tamil country. He also conquered the two divisions (*kūṟṟam*) of Miḻalai and Muttūṟu from Evvi and a *vēḻir* chieftain and annexed them to his kingdom. The *Maduraikkānji* contains a full-length description of Madura and the Pāndyan country under Neḍunjeḻiyan's rule. The poet gives expression to his wish that his patron should spread the benefits of his good rule all over India. He makes particular mention of the farmers and traders of a place called Muduveḻḻilai (unidentified) as among his most loyal subjects for many generations. He also refers to the battle of Ālangānam, calls his patron lord of Koṟkai and the warlord of the southern Paradavar—hinting that the people of the pearl-fishery coast formed an important section of his army.

Passing over the many contemporaries of Neḍunjeḻiyan—Pāndya and Chola princes and the poets who mention them and their achievements—we must now notice a rather protracted civil war in the Chola kingdom mentioned by Kōvūr Kiḻār and other poets. This war was between Nalangiḷḷi (also called Śēṭcenni) and Neḍungiḷḷi. The latter shut himself up at Āvūr which was being besieged by Māvaḷattān, the younger brother of Nalangiḷḷi. In one poem Kōvūr Kiḻār says that if he claimed to be virtuous, Neḍungiḷḷi should open the gates of the fort, or if he claimed to be brave he should come into the open and fight. He did neither, but caused untold misery to the people of his beleaguered city by shutting himself up in a cowardly manner. Another poem dealing with the siege of Uṟaiyūr by Nalangiḷḷi himself, once more Neḍungiḷḷi being the besieged, is more considerate and impartial; it is addressed to both princes and exhorts them to stop the destructive war, as whoever loses would be a Chola, and a war to the finish must necessarily end in the defeat of one party. A third poem relates to a somewhat piquant situation. A poet, Iḷandattan by name, who went into Uṟaiyūr from Nalangiḷḷi, was suspected by Neḍungiḷḷi of spying. As he was about to be killed, Kōvūr Kiḻār interceded with his song on the harmless and upright nature of poets and thus saved him. Another poem hints at internal dissensions in the royal family at Uṟaiyūr, which induced Nalangiḷḷi's soldiers to rush to war in utter disregard of omens. Civil war seems, indeed, to have been the bane of the Chola kingdom in this age; Śenguṭṭuvan, as we have seen, was called upon to intervene in another war at an earlier time.

This sketch of the political conditions of the Śangam age may be closed with the mention of two other Chola rulers, both opponents of the Cheras in war. Iḷanjēṭcenni of Neydalangānal captured two fortresses from the Cheras known by the names of Śeruppāḻi and Pāmaḷūr. Śengaṇān, the Chola monarch famed in legend for his devotion to Śiva, figures as the victor in the battle of Pōr against the Chera Kaṇaikkāl Irumpoṟai. The Chera was taken prisoner, asked for drinking water when he was in prison, got it rather late, and then, without drinking it, confessed the shame of his position in a song. Subsequently, Poygaiyār, a friend of the Chera monarch, is said to have secured his release from the Chola prison by celebrating the victory of Śengaṇān in a poem of forty stanzas—the *Kaḷavaḻi*. According to this poem, the battle was fought at Kaḻumalam, near Karuvūr, the Chera capital. Śengaṇān became the subject of many pious legends in later times. It is possible that this monarch who, according to

Tirumangai, built 70 fine temples of Śiva, lived somewhat later, say in the fourth or fifth century A.D.

A thorough change in the political map of South India and the definite close of an epoch seem to be clearly implied in the *Śiṟupāṇ-āṟṟuppaḍai* by Nattattanār, one of the *Pattupāṭṭu* ('Ten Idylls'). The poem has Nalliyakkōḍan for its hero and he may be taken to stand right at the end of the Śangam age. He ruled a territory which included Gidangil, a village near Tindivanam, Eyiṟpaṭṭanam—modern Markanam, and Āmūr and Vēlūr, all places in the South Arcot district. We may assign to him a date about A.D. 275, and in his day the poet says that charity had dried up in the capitals of the three Tamil kingdoms, and all ancient patrons of learning and the arts were no more! There may well be some exaggeration here; but clearly Vanji, Uṟaiyūr and Madura must have passed the meridian of their prosperity and entered on a period of decline.

Of the social and economic conditions of the age, the cultural ideas and ideals accepted and cherished by the people, of the institutions and activities which embodied and sustained them, the literature of the Śangam gives an unusually complete and true picture. The most striking feature in the picture is its composite character; it is the unmistakable result of the blend of two originally distinct cultures, best described as Tamilian and Aryan; but it is by no means easy now to distinguish the original elements in their purity. Some of them may be recognized, however, to have clearly originated in Northern India and made their way into the South during the period of its aryanization and later. The stories of the *Mahābhārata* and *Rāmāyana* were well known to the Tamil poets, and episodes from them are frequently mentioned. The claim of each of the three Tamil kings to have fed the opposing forces on the eve of the Great Battle has been noted already. The destruction of the three metallic forts of the Asuras (*Tripura*) by Śiva, king Śibi giving away the flesh of his body to save a dove that was pursued by a vulture, and the struggle between Krishna and the Asuras for the possession of the sun, are among other legends alluded to by the authors. The presence of a great fire underneath the ocean, Uttara-kuru (the northern country) as a land of perpetual enjoyment, Arundhati as the ideal of chastity, the conception of the threefold debt (*riṇatraya*) with which every man is born, the beliefs that the *cakora* bird feeds only on raindrops, and that raindrops turn into pearls in particular circumstances, are instances of other Sanskritic ideas taken over bodily into the literature of the Śangam period. The *Tolkāppiyam* is said to have been modelled on the Sanskrit grammar of the Aindra school.

The *Tolkāppiyam* states definitely that marriage as a sacrament attended with ritual was established in the Tamil country by the Aryas. It is well known that the earliest Dharmaśāstras mention eight forms of marriage as part of the Aryan code—itself the result of a blend between Aryan and pre-Aryan forms that prevailed in the North; these eight forms are mentioned in the *Tolkāppiyam* and other works, and much ingenuity is spent in accommodating them to Tamil forms. The Tamils had a relatively simple conception of marriage; they recognized the natural coming together of man and woman, and the natural differences in the manifestations of love, possibly due ultimately to differences in the physical conditions of the different parts of the country. These they designated as the five *tiṇais*. They had also names for unilateral love, *kaikkiḷai* and improper love, *perundiṇai*. Into this framework an attempt was made to squeeze the eight Aryan forms with results by no means happy. Such difficulties of synthesis apart, the most tangible result of the meeting of the Tamil and the Aryan was the tremendous richness and fecundity that was imparted to the Tamil idiom thereby and the rise of a beautiful literature which combined classic grace with vernacular energy and strength. This literature of the Śangam, the earliest stratum of Tamil literature now available, is also in many ways the best.

The land was fertile and there was plenty of grain, meat and fish; the Chera country was noted for its buffaloes, jack-fruit, pepper and turmeric. In the Chola country, watered by the Kaveri, it was said that the space in which an elephant could lie down produced enough to feed seven, and a *vēli* of land yielded a round thousand *kalams* of paddy. The little principality of Pāri abounded in forest produce like ‘ bamboo-rice ’, jack-fruit, *valli*-root and honey. Many rural activities like the cultivation of *rāgi* and sugar-cane, the making of sugar from the cane, and the harvesting and drying of grain are described in the Śangam poems in a vivid and realistic manner.

The people were organized for the most part in occupational groups living apart from one another but in fairly close proximity within each village or town, and their life was regulated by a pervasive sense of social solidarity. Differences in status and economic conditions were accepted by all as part of the established order, and there is little evidence of any tendency to protest or revolt against them. The poets describe with equally intimate touches the unlettered Maḻavar who thrive on robbery in the northern frontier of the Tamil land, the hunters (*eyinar*) with their huts full of bows and shields, the homes of shepherds where quantities of curds and ghee are produced for sale, and those of learned Brahmins versed in the Vedas and performing their daily ritual duties including the entertainment of guests. Apparently Brahmins ate meat and drank toddy without incurring reproach. One poem in the *Puṟanāṉūṟu* affirms that there are only four castes (*kuḍi*), viz., *tuḍiyan*, *pāṇan*, *paṟaiyan* and *kaḍamban*, and only one god worthy of being worshipped with paddy strewn before him, namely the hero-stone recalling the fall of a brave warrior in battle. These castes and this worship were of very great antiquity, perhaps survivals from pre-Aryan times. The practice of erecting hero-stones and of offering regular worship to them continued throughout the Śangam age and many centuries after. Foreigners (Yavanas) were numerous in the ports on the sea-coast like Toṇḍi, Muśiri and Puhār (Kāvēri-paṭṭinam) which they visited for trade. Although unable to speak Tamil they were employed as palace-guards in Madura and on police duty in the streets. Curiously wrought lamps and wine in bottles figure prominently among the articles of trade brought to India by the Yavanas.

Hereditary monarchy was the prevailing form of government. Disputed successions and civil wars were not unknown, as we have seen, and sometimes caused grave misery to the people. The king was in all essential respects an autocrat whose autocracy, however, was tempered by the maxims of the wise and the occasional intercession of a minister, a poet or a friend. The sphere of the state's activity was, however, limited, and in a society where respect for custom was deep-rooted, even the most perverse of autocrats could not have done much harm; indeed it must be said that the general impression left on the mind by the literature of the age is one of contentment on the part of the people who were proud of their kings and loyal to them. As the people took the king for their model, it was his duty to set up a high moral standard by his personal conduct; in many poems he was exhorted to keep a strict mastery over his passions in order to rule successfully. He was to be liberal in his patronage of religion, arts and letters. He was to show paternal care for his subjects and to be impartial as among different sections of them. He held a daily durbar (*nāḷavai*) at which he heard and set right all complaints. The onerous character of the royal task is emphasized by a poet who compares a king to a strong bull which drags a cart laden with salt from the plains to the uplands; another affirms that the king, much more than rice or water, is the life of the people. To Brahmins was assigned an important role in the state; they were the foremost among those (*śuṟṟam*) on whose assistance the king relied in his daily work; and the highest praise of a monarch was to say that he did nothing which pained the Brahmins. Agriculture was the mainstay of polity and the basis of war; and a good king was believed to be able to command the course of the seasons. The ideal of the ' conquering king ' (*vijigīshu*) was accepted and acted on. Victory against seven kings meant a superior status, which the victor marked by wearing a garland made out of the crowns of the seven vanquished rulers. The most powerful kings were expected to undertake a *digvijaya*, which was a conquering expedition in a clockwise direction over the whole of India. The idea of a *chakravarti*, 'wheel-king', whose *digvijaya* was led by the march of a mysterious wheel of gold and gems through the air is mentioned in one of the poems in the *Puṟanānūṟu*. Another poem in the same collection mentions the companions of a king who committed suicide when the king died—an early anticipation of what later became a widespread institution under such names as Companions of Honour (Abu Zayd), *vēḷaikkārar*, *garuḍas*, *sahavāsis*, *āpattudavigaḷ* and so on.

The *sabhā* or *manṟam* of the king in the capital was the highest court of justice. The sons of Malaiyamān were tried and sentenced, and later released by the intercession of Kōvūr Kiḻār, in the *manṟam* of Uṟaiyūr; and Pottiyār, after the death of his friend Kōpperunjōḻan, could not bear the sight of the same *manṟam* bereft of him. The elders are said and were doubtless expected to have laid aside their personal quarrels when they attended the *sabhā* to help in the adjudication of disputes. We may infer that the assembly was used by the king for purposes of general consultation as well. The *Kuṟaḷ*, clearly a post-Śangam work, definitely regards the *sabhā* as a general assembly dealing with all affairs. Even less specialized, and more entangled in the social and religious complex of village life, was the *manṟam*. Each village had its common place of meeting, generally under the shade of a big tree, where men, women and children met for all the common activities of the village, including sports and pastimes. There may also have been a political side to these rural gatherings, the germ out of which grew the highly organized system of village government which functioned so admirably in later Chola times.

Land and trade were the chief sources of the royal revenue. The *mā* and *vēli* as measures of land were already known; but the king's share of the produce of agriculture is nowhere precisely stated. Foreign trade was important and customs revenue occupied a high place on the receipts side of the budget; the *Paṭṭinappālai* gives a vivid account of the activity of customs officials in Puhār (Kāvēri-paṭṭinam). Internal transit duties on merchandise moving from place to place were another source of revenue, and the roads were guarded night and day by soldiers to prevent smuggling. Moderation in taxation, however, was impressed on the rulers by many wise sayings of the poets. If their word may be trusted, booty captured in war was no inconsiderable part of royal resources. The Cholas are said to have had a strongly guarded treasury at Kumbakonam in the Śangam age.

The streets of the capital cities were patrolled at nights by watchmen bearing torches, and the prison formed part of the system of administration.

Each ruler maintained an army of well-equipped professional soldiers who no doubt found frequent employment in those bellicose times. Captains of the army were distinguished by the title of *ēnādi* conferred at a formal ceremony of investiture where the king presented the chosen commander with a ring and other insignia of high military rank. The army comprised the traditional four arms—chariots (drawn by oxen), elephants, cavalry and infantry. Swords, bows and arrows, armour made of tiger-skins, javelins, spears and shields (including a protective cover for the forearm) are among the weapons of offence and defence specifically mentioned. The drum and the conch were employed on the field for signalling and the former to summon soldiers to arms. Each ruler and chieftain certainly had a war-drum among his insignia. Not only was it carefully guarded, but it was bathed periodically and worshipped with loud *mantras*. The occasions for war were numerous, but we need not suppose that the refusal of one king to give his daughter in marriage to another was as frequent a cause as the poets assert. A campaign might be started by the capture of the enemy's cattle, or a Brahmin messenger might be sent with a formal declaration before hostilities started. The military camp was often an elaborate affair, with streets and roads and a separate section for the king guarded by armed women; in this camp the hours of day and night were announced by watchers of water-clocks; the gnomon was employed to indicate midday and a drum beaten early every morning. Camp fires kept off the cold when necessary, and there were towers at important points from which a regular watch was maintained against surprises from the enemy. Death in battle was welcome to the soldier and even to his mother, for it was held to lead him straight to heaven. To the warrior, a peaceful death in bed was looked upon as a disgrace, and in the families of ruling chieftains the body of a man who died otherwise than in war was cut with the sword, and laid on *darbha* grass, and *mantras* were chanted to secure him a place in the warriors' heaven (*vīrasvarga*). Soldiers who fell in war were commemorated by hero-stones which bore inscriptions detailing their names and achievements; these stones were often worshipped as godlings. Wounded soldiers were carefully attended to, their wounds being cleaned and stitched where necessary.

Kings often took the field in person and delighted to rejoice with the common soldiers in their successes; on the other hand, if a king was killed or even seriously wounded in the midst of the fight, his army gave up the struggle and accepted defeat. The vanity of the victor often inflicted deep personal humiliations on his vanquished foe, the memory of which rankled and brought on further strife. The crowns of defeated kings furnished the gold for the anklets of the victor, while a woman's anklet and a garment of leaves were forced on the defeated party who was compelled to wear them; his guardian tree was destroyed and its trunk converted into a war-drum for the victor. The conquered country was at times ruthlessly laid waste, even cornfields not being spared.

The *Kaḷavaḻi* is one of the most detailed descriptions we possess of a battle-field in the Tamil country, and the poem supplies in a casual way much interesting information on military affairs. The soldiers, infantry and cavalry alike, wore leather sandals for the protection of their feet. The nobles and princes rode on elephants, and the commanders drove in pennoned chariots. The poet says that women whose husbands were killed bewailed their loss on the field of Kaḻumalam; unless this is mere rhetoric, we must suppose that women, at least of the higher orders, sometimes accompanied their husbands to the field.

Besides being the head of the government and leader in war, the king also held the first rank in society. He patronized poetry and the arts, and kept open house. War and women were, in fact, the universal preoccupations of the leisured classes, besides wine and song and the dance. The king and his *ēnādis* with their retinues must have formed a gay, boisterous crew at the top of society with a boundless capacity for enjoying the pleasures of life.

No occasion was lost for holding a feast and the poets are most eloquent in their praise of the sumptuous fare to which they were so often asked. One poet declares to his patron: 'I came to see you that we might eat succulent chops of meat, cooled after boiling and soft like the carded cotton of the spinning-woman, and drink large pots of toddy together.' Another speaks of wine poured into golden goblets by smiling women decked with jewels in the court of Karikāla. The flesh of animals cooked whole, such as pork from a pig which had been kept away from its female mate for many days and fattened for the occasion, *āppam* (pudding) soaked in milk, the flesh of tortoises and particular kinds of fish are mentioned as delicacies served at such feasts. Among drinks particular mention is made of foreign liquor in green bottles, of *munnīr* ('triple water')—a mixture of milk from unripe coconut, palm fruit juice and the juice of sugar-cane, and of toddy well matured by being buried underground for a long time in bamboo barrels.

The habit of eating betel-leaves with lime and areca-nut perhaps came into use only after the Śangam age. Women are said to have given up eating greens and bathing in cold water when their husbands fell in battle. The lot of widows was a hard one; they had to cut off their hair, discard all ornaments, and only eat the plainest food. No wonder, perhaps, that some wives preferred to die with their husbands and earn fame as *satīs*. The tonsure of widows, it may be noted by the way, like the tying of the *tāli* at the marriage ceremony, was obviously a pre-Aryan Tamil custom taken over and perpetuated into later times.

Easily the most cultured amusements open to the upper classes in those days were poetry, music (particularly singing) and dancing, which often went together. The poets were men and women drawn from all classes of society; they composed verses to suit the immediate occasion, and were often rewarded generously for their exertions, as when Karikāla is said to have given the author of *Paṭṭinappālai* 1,600,000 gold pieces. Their poems, especially the shorter ones, are full of colour and true to life. They abound in fine phrases giving compact and eloquent expression to the physical and spiritual experiences of the poet. Nor do they lack width of range: besides short lyrics, odes and religious hymns were known. The metres employed were simple and flexible, the more elaborate Sanskrit forms not having come into vogue.

Some of the poets were the resident companions and advisers of kings and chieftains, while others moved from one court to another in search of patronage. The lasting friendships between Kapilar and Pāri, between Piśir Āndaiyār and Kōpperunjōḷan, and between Auvaiyār and Adigaimān Anji are among the best known instances of life-long attachment between poet and patron. Ungenerous princes who delayed their gifts or were niggardly sometimes provoked the poets into pillorying their stinginess in song. One poet refused to accept a present sent to him by a prince who had not granted him the usual interview. Golden lotuses and lilies, land, chariots, horses, and cash are enumerated among the presents usually given on such occasions. Besides general and probably exaggerated statements, such as Karikāla's more than princely gift already mentioned, the gift of an elephant is mentioned in one instance, though it is not clear what use the poet could have for the animal.

The courts were also enlivened by roving bands of musicians followed by women who danced to the accompaniment of their music, the *pāṇar* and *viṟaliyar* who moved about the country in companies carrying with them all sorts of quaint instruments. They seem to have been the representatives of primitive tribal groups who preserved the folk-songs and dances of an earlier age. Their numbers and their dire poverty form a recurring theme of poems, and from all accounts they lived from hand to mouth and seldom knew where their next meal was to be had. Here is a humorous account of their experiences after meeting a generous patron: 'The Chola king showered on us great quantities of wealth in (the form of) fine and costly jewels not suited to our condition; on seeing this, some among the large group of my kinsfolk, used (only) to abject poverty, put on their ears ornaments meant for the fingers; some wore on their fingers things meant for the ear; others put on their necks jewels meant for the waist; others again adorned their waists with ornaments properly worn on the neck; in this wise, like the great group of red-faced monkeys which shone in the fine jewels (of Sītā) that they discovered on the ground, on the day when the mighty *rākshasa* carried off Sītā, the wife of Rāma of the swift chariot, we became the cause of endless laughter.' Literary convention evolved a class of poem, the *ārruppaḍai* ('setting one on the path'), in which a poet, *pāṇan* (or *viṟali*) told of the gifts he had received from a patron and exhorted his friends to visit him.

The arts of music and dancing were highly developed and popular. Musical instruments of various types are described and included many kinds of *yāḻ* (a stringed instrument like the lute) and varieties of drums. Karikāla is called 'the master of the seven notes of music'. The flute is quaintly described as the 'pipe with dark holes made by red fire'. Conventions had grown up regarding the proper time and place for each tune. *Viṟalis* sometimes danced at night by torchlight and particular dance-poses of the hands are mentioned by name as in the *Nāṭyaśāstra* of Bharata. Mixed dances in which men and women took part were also known. In this sphere a conscious and systematic attempt was made to bring together and synthesize the indigenous pre-Aryan modes (*dēśi*) with those that came from the North (*mārga*), the result of which is reflected fully in the *Śilappadi-kāram*, a work of the succeeding age. This subject, however, is too complicated and technical to be pursued further here.

Among other sports and pastimes, the hunting of dogs and hares, wrestling and boxing matches among warriors are mentioned. Old men engaged in dice-play, and women and girls played with balls and molucca-beans on the terraces of houses. Mixed bathing and picnic parties, children playing in the *manṟam* and their toy bows and arrows also find casual mention in the poems.

Boys and girls bathed together in tanks and rivers. The dancing-girl was often a serious rival to the wife, and the whole plot of the celebrated story of Kōvalan and Kaṇṇagi turns on this rivalry. Like Vātsyāyana's *Kāmasūtra*, the *Maṇimēkalai*, a work of the period after the Śangam, indicates that hetaerae underwent a regular course of instruction extending over a number of years and comprising court dances, popular dances, singing, playing on the lute and flute, cookery, perfumery, painting, flower-work and many other fine arts.

The richer classes dwelt in houses of brick and mortar; the walls often bore paintings of divine figures and pictures of animal life. Royal palaces were surrounded by gardens tastefully laid out. Houses and palaces were constructed according to rules laid down in the *śāstra*, care being taken to start at an auspicious hour carefully determined beforehand. The *Neḍunalvāḍai*, one of the 'Ten Idylls', contains a detailed description of the women's apartments in the palace of Neḍunjeḻiyan, their walls and pillars and the artistic lamps manufactured by the Yavanas; this is followed by an account of the equipment of the bedroom in the palace, its ivory bedsteads and superior cushions. High life even in those early days was thus no stranger to refined luxuries. The wife was highly honoured and was held to be the light of the family. The common folk dwelt in humbler structures in the towns and villages, while outcastes and forest tribes lived in huts of sorts which are also described in the poems. The making of rope charpoys by *pulaiyans* and the use of animal skins as mats for lying on deserve to be noted. The *Paṭṭinappālai* gives a vivid account of the life of the fisherfolk of Puhār, the *paradavar*, including some of their holiday amusements.

Valuable hints on popular beliefs and customs are scattered among the poems. There was much faith in omens and astrology; one song mentions the portents which preceded the death of 'Śēy of the elephant eye'. A woman with dishevelled hair was a bad omen. There were fortune-tellers who plied a busy trade. Children were provided with amulets for warding off evil; and rites were practised which were supposed to avert the mischief of demons (*pēy*), to bring about rain, and produce other desired results. The banyan tree was considered to be the abode of gods, while eclipses were held to be the result of snakes eating up the sun and the moon. Crows were believed to announce the arrival of guests, and particularly the return of the absent husband to his lonely wife, and were fed regularly in front of royal palaces, as well, perhaps, as in every household. Mass feeding of the poor was also known.

Trade, both inland and foreign, was well organized and briskly carried on throughout the period; Tamil poems, classical authors and archaeological finds in South India all speak with one voice on this subject. The great port-cities were the emporia of foreign trade. Big ships, we are told, entered the port of Puhār without slacking sail, and poured out on the beach precious merchandise brought from overseas. The extensive bazaar of that great city was full of tall mansions of many apartments each with doorways, wide verandahs and corridors. The family life of the rich merchants was carried on in the upper floors while the lower ones were set apart for business. Besides the flags waving on the masts of ships in harbour, various other kinds of flags advertised the different kinds of merchandise as well as the fashionable grog-shops. Śāliyūr in the Pāndya country and Bandar in Chera are counted among the most important ports in the poems. Horses were imported by sea into the Pāndyan kingdom, and elsewhere. The repairing of merchant ships after their voyages is mentioned, as also lighthouses. People from different countries gathered in the ports, and life in them was truly cosmopolitan. The Yavanas sailed their large ships to Muśiri (Cranganore) bearing gold, and returned laden with pepper and 'the rare products of the sea and mountain' which the Chera king gave. So far the evidence of the poems.

The author of the *Periplus* (*c.* A.D. 75) gives the most valuable information about this trade between India and the Roman Empire. He mentions the ports of Naura (Cannanore), Tyndis —the Toṇḍi of the poems, identified with Ponnāni—and Muziris (Muśiri, Cranganore), and Nelcynda very near Kōṭṭayam, as of leading importance on the west coast. Muziris abounded in ships sent there with cargoes from Arabia and by the Greeks. Nelcynda was part of the Pāndyan kingdom. Bacare (Porakad) was another port on the same coast. On the nature of the trade, the words of the author are worth citing: 'They send large ships to these market towns on account of the great quantity and bulk of pepper and malabathrum (to be had there). There are imported here, in the first place, a great quantity of coins; topaz, thin clothing, not much; figured linens, antimony, coral, crude glass, copper, tin, lead; wine, not much, but as much as at Barygaza; realgar and orpiment, and wheat enough for the sailors, for this is not dealt in by the merchants there. There is exported pepper, which is produced in quantity in only one region near these markets, a district called Cottonara. Besides this there are exported large quantities of fine pearls, ivory, silk cloth, spikenard from the Ganges, malabathrum from the places in the interior, transparent stones of all kinds (principally beryls of the Coimbatore district for which there was a constant demand in Rome), diamonds and sapphires, and tortoise-shell; that from Chryse Island and that taken among the islands along the coast of Damirica.' This trade increased in volume after Hippalus, an Egyptian pilot, showed the possibility of large ships sailing with the monsoon straight across the ocean instead of small vessels hugging the coast and exposing themselves to many risks. Other ports of South India mentioned by the author in order are: Balita (Varkalai), a village by the shore with a fine harbour; Comari, a fine harbour and a sacred place of pilgrimage; Colchi (Koṟkai) where were the pearl fisheries of the Pāndyan kingdom worked by condemned criminals; Camara (Kāvēri-paṭṭinam), Poduca (Pondicherry, Arikamedu) and Sopatma (Markāṇam). There were three types of craft used on the east coast: ships of the country coasting along the shore; other large vessels made of single logs bound together, called *sangara*, and those which made the voyage to Chryse and to the Ganges which were called *Colandia* and were very large. He mentions Argaru (Uṟaiyūr) as the place to which were sent all the pearls gathered on the coast and from which were exported muslins called Argaritic. About the ports on the east coast he adds: 'There are imported into these places everything made in Damirica, and the greatest part of what is brought at any time from Egypt comes here.' He notes further that a great quantity of muslins was made in the region of Masalia (Andhra country), and that ivory was a special product of the country further north, Dosarene (i.e., Daśārṇa, Orissa).

The large quantities of gold and silver coins struck by all the Roman emperors down to Nero (A.D. 54-68) found in the interior of the Tamil land testify to the extent of the trade, the presence of Roman settlers in the Tamil country, and the periods of the rise, zenith and decay of this active commerce. Its beginnings may be traced to the reign of Augustus if not to an earlier time, as a phenomenally large number bearing his stamp (and that of Tiberius) have been found. In that reign, despite ' embassies ' from the Pāndya ruler, this commerce was by no means extensive or economically important. Soon, however, it assumed new and unexpected proportions and ceased to be a mere trade in luxuries. After the death of Nero, the traffic was not so much confined to the Tamil land as before but spread more evenly along the Indian coasts, and was conducted by barter rather than with money—the emperors subsequent to Nero not being so well represented in the coin finds. Towards the end of the second century A.D. the direct trade between the Egyptian Greeks of the Roman empire and India declined, the traffic passing into the hands of the Arabians and, still more, the Auxumites of East Africa. A new era commenced with the rise of Constantinople in the fourth century A.D. Roman coins reappeared in South India, and embassies were received by Constantine from the people of the Maldives and Ceylon among others. Ceylon was becoming important in the trade of the Indian ocean at this time. But the activities of the Byzantine period bear no comparison with those of the earlier age which had drained the Roman empire of much of its treasure and evoked protests from the financiers of the empire as well as its moralists. The trade of the early Roman empire had wide ramifications and was bound up with much exploration and colonization on the part of Graeco-Romans and Indians. Says Schoff: ' The numerous migrations from India into Indo-China, both before and after the Christian era, give ample ground for the belief that the ports of South India and Ceylon were in truth, as the *Periplus* states, the centre of an active trade with the Far East, employing larger ships, and in greater number, than those coming from Egypt.' We shall see that when, after a long eclipse, the power of the Chola kings revived in the tenth and eleventh centuries, the seafaring instincts of the people had not deserted them and that, in the favourable conditions then obtaining, they attempted tasks more venturesome than anything they had achieved in the earlier age.

Internal trade was also brisk; caravans of merchants with carts and pack-animals carried their merchandise from place to place and from fair to fair. Salt was an important commodity of trade and salt-merchants moved with their families in carts provided with spare axles against contingencies. Barter played a large part in all transactions; honey and roots, for example, might be exchanged for fish-oil and toddy, and sugar-cane and *aval* (rice-flakes) for venison and arrack, while in Muśiri fish was sold for paddy. Agriculture was the mainstay of the national economy, and most of its operations were carried on by women of the lowest class (*kaḍaiśiyar*) whose status appears to have differed little from that of the slave. The bulk of the land was owned by *veḷḷālar*, the agriculturists *par excellence*, who commanded a high social rank. The richer among them did not plough the land themselves, but employed labourers to do it. Besides owning land, they held official posts in the civil and military administration, and the titles *vēḷ* and *araśu* in the Chola country and *kāvidi* in the Pāndya were applied to them. They not only enjoyed the *jus connubii* with royal families, but shared with the king the duties of war and the pleasures of the chase and of the table. The poorer *veḷḷālar* did not shun manual labour, but worked on their own small farms, as do the peasantry everywhere. Spinning and weaving of cotton, and perhaps also of silk, had attained a high degree of perfection. Spinning was then, as always, the part-time occupation of women. The weaving of complex patterns on cloth and silk is often mentioned in literature and, according to the *Periplus*, Uṟaiyūr was a great centre of the cotton trade. The poems mention cotton cloth as thin as the slough of the snake or a cloud of steam, so finely woven that the eye could not follow the course of the thread. Scissors and needles were known and employed in cutting hair and in dress-making; a kind of hair pomade (*tagaram*) is mentioned also.

In the sphere of religion and ethics the influence of Northern ideas is most marked. The practice of walking some distance to escort a departing guest was observed by Karikāla who went on foot for a distance of 'seven steps' (*saptapadi*) before requesting him to mount a chariot drawn by four milk-white steeds. The slaughter of a cow, the destruction of a foetus, and the killing of a Brahmin were accounted heinous offences; though ingratitude, according to the established code, was held to be even worse.

No single method was adopted for the disposal of the dead; both cremation and inhumation with or without urns are freely mentioned. A widow offered a rice-ball to her dead husband on a bed of grass (*darbha*) and the *pulaiyan* had a part to play in this funeral ritual. *Satī* was fairly common though by no means universal. The heroism and devotion of the *satī* were doubtless applauded by public opinion, but the practice was certainly not encouraged, much less enforced. The perfect wife was held to be one who, at the death of her husband, entered the burning pyre with as little concern as if she were entering cool water for a bath.

That Vedic religion had struck root in the South must have become clear from the references to the costly sacrifices performed by the monarchs of the age. Brahmins devoted to their studies and religious duties held a high position in society, and a song of Āvūr Mūlam Kiḻār portrays in much detail the life of Viṇṇandāyan, a Brahmin of the Kaundinya-gōtra who lived in Pūnjāṟṟūr in the Chola country. The followers of the Veda had often to engage in disputations with rival sectaries, and many are the references to such disputations proclaimed by the flying of flags and carried on with much gesticulation of the hands. The rival sects are not named, but they were doubtless Jainism and Buddhism which became more prominent in the succeeding age. From all accounts Hinduism was the dominant creed in this age. The worship of Subramanya (Murugan) and the legendary achievements of that deity are often alluded to. Other members of the pantheon were Śiva, Balarāma, Vishnu, Krishna, Ardhanārīśvara, and Anantaśāyi. The details of Vishnu worship with *tulasi* (basil) and bell are set forth in the *Padiṟṟuppattu*, and the custom is mentioned of people starving in the temple to invoke the grace of the god. Women went with their children to offer worship in the temples in the evenings. Asceticism was honoured and *tridaṇḍi* (triple staff) ascetics are particularly mentioned. The worship of Murugan was of ancient origin and embodied some indigenous features like the *vēlanāḍal*, an ecstatic dance in his honour. Indra also came in for special worship on the occasion of his annual festival held in Puhār. The epic poems of the post-Śangam period show that music and dancing were intertwined with religious rites from early times, the worship of Koṟṟavai by the hunters, of Krishna by the shepherdesses and of Murugan by the *kuṟavas* being the most striking instances of this. A temple of Sarasvatī is mentioned in the *Maṇimēkalai* which also alludes to the *kāpālikas*, an austere class of Śaiva ascetics. Belief in reincarnation, the effects of *karma* in successive births and the power of fate was the common basis of all religion in India, and this was generally accepted in the Tamil country also. The joyous faith in good living that generally animates the poems of the Śangam age gradually gives place to the pessimistic outlook on life that is, in the last resort, traceable to the emphasis laid by Buddhism on the sorrows of life and its doctrine that the only way of escape was the repression of the will to live. This note of sadness, already noticeable in some poems towards the close of the Śangam age, becomes more pronounced in the setting of the *Maṇimēkalai* which contains a round denunciation of the fools who, not meditating upon the ruthlessness of death, spend their time in the blind enjoyment of carnal pleasures.

A long historical night ensues after the close of the Śangam age. We know little of the period of more than three centuries that followed. When the curtain rises again towards the close of the sixth century A.D., we find that a mysterious and ubiquitous enemy of civilization, the evil rulers called Kalabhras (Kaḻappāḷar), have come and upset the established political order which was restored only by their defeat at the hands of the Pāndyas and Pallavas as well as the Chālukyas of Bādāmi. Of the Kalabhras we have as yet no definite knowledge; from some Buddhist books we hear of a certain Accutavikkanta of the Kalabhrakula during whose reign Buddhist monasteries and authors enjoyed much patronage in the Chola country. Late literary tradition in Tamil avers that he kept in confinement the three Tamil kings —the Chera, Chola and Pāndya. Some songs about him are quoted by Amitasāgara, a Jaina grammarian of Tamil of the tenth century A.D. Possibly Accuta was himself a Buddhist, and the political revolution which the Kalabhras effected was provoked by religious antagonism. At any rate the Kalabhras are roundly denounced as evil kings (*kali-araśar*) who uprooted many *adhi-rājas* and abrogated *brahmadeya* rights; there was no love lost between these interlopers and the people of the lands they overran. The Cholas disappeared from the Tamil land almost completely in this debacle, though a branch of them can be traced towards the close of the period in Rayalaseema—the Telugu-Chodas, whose kingdom is mentioned by Yuan Chwang in the seventh century A.D.

The upset of the existing order due to the Kalabhras must have affected the Chera country as well, though there is little evidence on this country in this period apart from the late legends of the *Keralotpatti* and *Keralamāhātmyam*. According to these, the rulers of the land had to be imported from neighbouring countries, and they assumed the title of Perumāl. Possibly the Vaishnava saint Kulaśekhara Āḻvār was one of these Perumāls; in his poems he claims sovereignty over Chera, Chola and Pāndya, besides the Kongu country and Kolli mountain. His age cannot be determined with any certainty, though a date as early as the sixth century has been suggested for him, on the ground that at no later period could his claim to rule over Pāndya and Chola be plausible. It seems more likely, however, that this claim was merely rhetorical, and that he belonged to a much later time, say the ninth century A.D.

This dark period marked by the ascendancy of Buddhism, and probably also of Jainism, was characterized also by great literary activity in Tamil. Most of the works grouped under the head '*The Eighteen Minor Works*' were written during this period as also the *Śilappadikāram*, *Maṇimēkalai* and other works. Many of the authors were the votaries of the 'heretical' sects.

BIBLIOGRAPHY

K. Gopalachari: *The Early History of the Andhra Country* (Madras, 1941)
B. L. Rice: *Mysore and Coorg from Inscriptions* (London, 1909)
Śanga Ilakkiyam (in Tamil) (Madras, 1940)
K. A. N. Sastri: *Foreign Notices of South India* (Madras, 1939)
K. A. N. Sastri: *The Colas*, Vol. I (Madras, 1936)
R. E. M. Wheeler, A. Ghosh and Krishna Deva: 'Arikamedu: an Indo-Roman Trading-station on the East Coast of India' (*Ancient India*, No. 2, July 1946)

CHAPTER VIII

CONFLICT OF THREE EMPIRES

General outline—Chālukyas: Pulakeśin I, Kīrtivarman I, Mangaleśa, Pulakeśin II and his conquests—Pallavas: Simhavishnu, Mahendravarman I—Chālukya-Pallava wars—Narasimhavarman I Pallava, Mahāmalla—death of Pulakeśin II followed by confusion—Mahāmalla's achievements—Mahendravarman II and Parameśvaravarman—Pāndyas: Kaḍungōn, Māṟavarman Avaniśūḷāmaṇi, Śēndan, Arikēsari Māṟavarman—Chālukya Vikramāditya II—Arab inroads checked—Pallava wars renewed—Narasimhavarman II Rājasimha, Parameśvaravarman II, Nandivarman II—Pāndya Kōccaḍaiyan; Māṟavarman Rājasimha I and his wars against Nandivarman II—Vikramāditya II invades Kānchī—Kīrtivarman II defeated by Pāndya Rājasimha I—fall of Chālukya power and rise of Rāshtrakūta Dantidurga—Nandivarman II fails in his attempt to check Pāndyan power—Varaguṇa I, Śrīmāṟa Śrīvallabha—Dantivarman—Rāshtrakūta Krishna I, Govinda II, Dhruva, Govinda III—Nandivarman III and his wars—Nripatunga—end of Pāndya Śrīmāṟa's reign—Rāshtrakūta Amoghavarsha I—Chera history—Gangas of Kalinga.

Polity—general features—village community: *sabhā*, *nagaram*—larger administrative units—provinces and officials—justice—king—succession—insignia—queens—checks on royalty.

For a period of 300 years from the middle of the sixth century A.D., the history of South India is virtually the story of mutual conflict among three powers each seeking constantly to extend its empire at the expense of its neighbours. The three powers were the Chālukyas of Bādāmi, the Pallavas of Kānchī and the Pāndyas of Madura. All of them rose into prominence in the sixth century; but the Chālukyas quit the stage about a century earlier than the two other powers, their place on the political map being more or less exactly filled from the middle of the eighth century by their successors, the Rāshtrakūtas of Mānyakheta (Malkhed). Besides the main house of Bādāmi, the Chālukyas established themselves in two other branches, more or less independent of the main line: the Chālukyas of Lāta, and the Eastern Chālukyas of Vengi. Together with the Gangas of Mysore, the Eastern Chālukyas took sides in the conflicts of the three kingdoms, sometimes with decisive results. The Cholas of the Tamil country had practically disappeared except that a line of Telugu rulers bearing their name and claiming a traditional connexion with their capital at Uṛaiyūr ruled in the area now known as Rayalaseema.

Political conflict was, however, no obstacle to cultural growth. A vast and many-sided Hindu revival checked the spread of Jainism and Buddhism, created a great volume of soul-stirring devotional literature and advanced philosophic speculation. Under the stimulus of this religious impulse, remarkable advances were registered in architecture, sculpture, painting and music. All these influences overflowed into the numerous Hindu colonies across the sea.

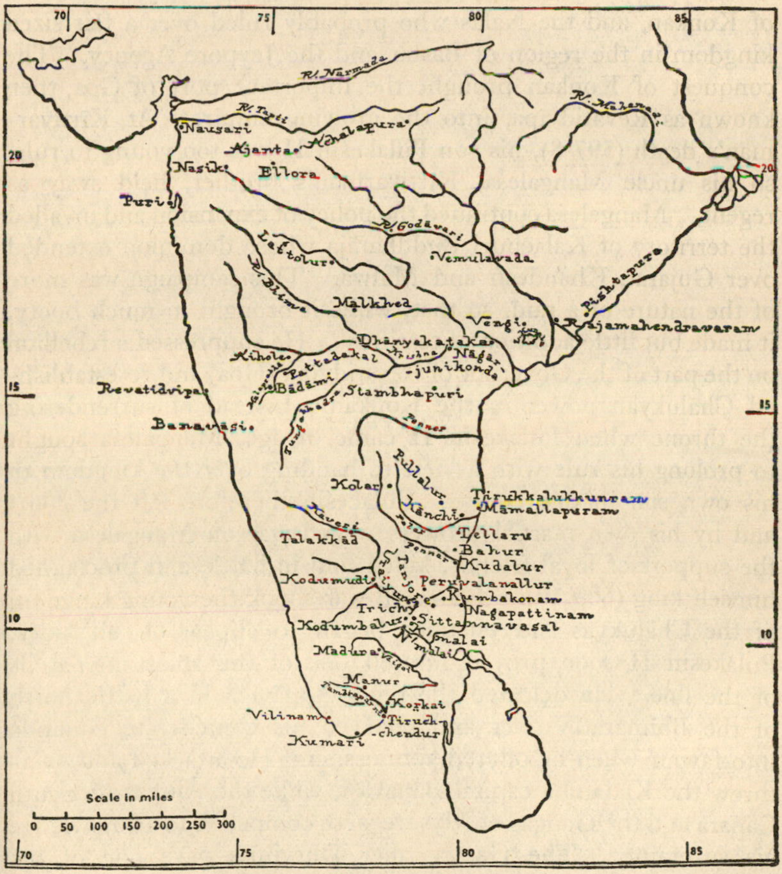

SOUTH INDIA : A.D. 500-850

The founder of the Chālukya line was Pulakeśin I. The name probably means 'the great lion'. He fortified the hill near Bādāmi into a strong fortress in 543-4, and declared his independence by performing a horse sacrifice. The new fortress stood on a defensible eminence within three miles of the Malaprabhā river. Among the hills to the east is Mahākūta; five miles farther in the same direction and on the river is Pattadakal, and another eight miles down the river is Aihōle—all witnessing to the age of Chālukyan ascendancy by their temples and inscriptions. Pulakeśin's son Kīrtivarman I (566-7) expanded the kingdom by wars against the Kadambas of Banavāsi, the Mauryas of Konkan, and the Nalas who probably ruled over a fair-sized kingdom in the region of Bastar and the Jeypore Agency. The conquest of Konkan brought the important port of Goa, then known as Revatidvīpa, into the growing empire. At Kīrtivarman's death (597-8), his son Pulakeśin II was too young to rule, so his uncle Mangaleśa, Kīrtivarman's brother, held sway as regent. Mangaleśa continued the policy of expansion and invaded the territory of Kalachuri Buddharāja whose dominion extended over Gujarat, Khandesh and Malwa. This campaign was more of the nature of a raid, so that, while it brought in much booty, it made but little addition of territory. He suppressed a rebellion on the part of the Governor of Revatidvīpa (Goa) and re-established Chālukyan power in the Konkan. Instead of surrendering the throne when Pulakeśin II came of age, Mangaleśa sought to prolong his rule with a view to handing over the kingdom to his own son in due course. Pulakeśin therefore left the court and by his own martial prowess waged war on Mangaleśa with the support of loyal friends, killed him in battle and proclaimed himself king (609-10). This civil war shook the young kingdom of the Chālukyas and enemies began to appear on all sides. Pulakeśin II soon proved himself one of the ablest monarchs of the line. He defeated the rebel Āppāyika in a battle north of the Bhīmarathi river and received his confederate Govinda into favour when he offered submission. He attacked and overthrew the Kadamba capital Banavāsi, while the Ālupas of South Canara and the Gangas of Mysore were compelled to acknowledge his suzerainty. The Ganga ruler Durvinīta gave one of his daughters in marriage to Pulakeśin, and she became the mother of Vikramāditya I. The Mauryas of northern Konkan were once more reduced to submission by a successful attack on their capital Purī (on the island of Elephanta), the Lakshmī of the western ocean. The fame of Pulakeśin's arms and fear of the growing power of Śrī Harsha in Northern India induced the Lātas, Mālavas and Gurjaras to offer their submission one after another to Pulakeśin. The northern frontier of the Chālukyan empire was thus extended at one bound to the river Mahī. When Harsha sought to invade the Deccan, Pulakeśin met and heavily defeated him on the banks of the Narmada, capturing many elephants—the only check in Harsha's otherwise victorious career. All these achievements were in the first three or four years of Pulakeśin's reign.

Pulakeśin then made his younger brother Vishnuvardhana *yuvarāja* and, leaving him in charge of the capital, he started on an extensive campaign of conquest in the eastern Deccan. Southern Kosala and Kalinga made their submission first. Pishtapura was then attacked and reduced. In a hard-fought battle on the shores of the Kunāla (Colair) lake, the power of the Vishnukundins was broken and subdued. Then came the turn of the Pallavas whose rise we must now trace before proceeding further.

The political confusion that reigned in the Tamil country after the incursion of the Kalabhras was ended in the last quarter of the sixth century by the activities of two monarchs, the Pallava Simhavishnu and the Pāndya Kaḍungōn with their capitals at Kānchī and Madura respectively. Simhavishnu was the son of Simhavarman one of whose copper-plate grants dated in the sixth year of his reign has turned up recently; it records a grant to a Jaina institution (a contemporary Ganga copper-plate records another gift to the Jainas made by Simhavishnu's mother)—and without giving any historical details of the reigning king, it details the achievements of his son who must have been *yuvarāja*. So we may consider Simhavishnu the virtual founder of the Pallava power in this period. The new inscription states that he overthrew another Simhavishnu, perhaps a Telugu Choda ruler, and the Bhrājishnu-vamśa (literally 'shining family', perhaps meaning Oḷiyar). Further, Simhavishnu not only suppressed the Kalabhras but conquered the whole country up to the Kaveri and even came into conflict with the Pāndyas and the ruler of Ceylon. He was a worshipper of Vishnu and had the title

Avanisimha (lion of the earth). His portrait and that of his son Mahendravarman I are found sculptured in relief in the Varāha cave at Māmallapuram (Mahābalipuram). He may be taken to have ruled between 560 and 580. He was followed by Mahendravarman I, a many-sided genius, great alike in war and in peace. He had many titles such as Mattavilāsa, Vicitra-citta and Guṇabhara. He was a great builder, a poet and a musician. He professed Jainism for a time but discarded it in favour of Śaivism, possibly under the influence of Appar. At the beginning of his reign (580-630), as in that of his father, Pallava rule extended in the north up to and perhaps a little beyond the river Krishna and bordered on the kingdom of the Kandaras and Vishnukundins.

After their overthrow, Pulakeśin II sought to measure his strength against Mahendravarman I whose growing power rivalled his own. His forces penetrated far into the Pallava territory and were not stopped until they reached Pullalūr, only fifteen miles north of the Pallava capital. There a pitched battle was fought, and although Mahendravarman was able to save his capital he lost the northern provinces to his enemy. This was the beginning of the long-drawn-out conflict between the Chālukyas and the Pallavas.

After his return (*c*. 621) Pulakeśin sent Vishnuvardhana to rule over the Andhra country as viceroy and complete the process of conquest, which he did by about 631. Then, with his brother's approval, he founded a dynasty of rulers who held sway in the Telugu country for over five centuries thereafter.

Pulakeśin sent an embassy to the Persian court of Khusru II in 625-6 and perhaps this courtesy was returned.

Pulakeśin's ambition prompted him to undertake another expedition against the Pallavas in the hope of achieving more decisive results. Mahendravarman had quitted the stage and his son Narasimhavarman I Mahāmalla (630-68) had begun his rule. Pulakeśin began his campaign by an attack on the Bānas who were ruling in Rayalaseema as feudatories of the Pallavas. After overrunning their kingdom he invaded the Pallava territory proper and once more threatened the capital. But Narasimhavarman defeated the Chālukyas in several battles including one at Manimangala about 20 miles to the east of Kānchipuram. In these battles Narasimha was ably assisted by a Ceylonese prince, Mānavarma, whom he afterwards helped to gain the throne of

Ceylon. Pulakeśin's expedition was thus a failure and was soon followed by terrible retribution. Narasimhavarman, encouraged by his successes, invaded the Chālukya country in force and, rapidly advancing to the capital, Bādāmi, made himself master of the city and its fortress. Pulakeśin II must have fallen fighting, and following upon his death his kingdom was threatened with disruption. Narasimha's occupation of the Chālukya capital is attested to by his title Vātāpikonda and by an inscription engraved on a rock behind the temple of Mallikārjunadeva in Bādāmi and dated in the thirteenth year of his reign.

This was indeed a crisis in the history of the Chālukyan kingdom. The feudatories of the empire declared their independence and even two of Pulakeśin's sons who were ruling as viceroys sought to follow the same course. Another son, however, Vikramāditya—aided by his maternal grandfather, the Ganga Durvinīta—set himself the task of repelling the Pallava invasion and restoring the unity of his father's empire. He compelled Narasimhavarman to retire from Bādāmi and defeated his brothers and those other feudatories who wanted to divide the empire among themselves. He then proclaimed himself king of the restored kingdom in 654-5 and rewarded his younger brother, Jayasimhavarman, who had stood by him all along, with the viceroyalty of Lāta or southern Gujarat.

The Pallava monarch must have returned to his capital soon after 642. Thereafter he sent two naval expeditions to Ceylon to aid Mānavarma. Though the second expedition was successful and Mānavarma put the rival king to death and captured Anurādhapura, he was later once more driven into exile and he sought refuge in the Pallava court—probably after the death of Narasimhavarman.

Narasimhavarman is said to have vanquished the Cholas, Cheras and Kalabhras as well as the Pāndyas, but no details of these battles are known. There can be no doubt, however, that under him the Pallava power attained a strength and prestige which it had not known since its revival under Simhavishnu (560-580). He was a great builder, and Māmallapuram, the chief port of the kingdom, was greatly embellished in his day. Yuan Chwang travelled in his kingdom as well as in that of Pulakeśin II a little before his expedition against Bādāmi and has left us an interesting account of what he saw. Narasimhavarman died about 668, and was succeeded by his son Mahendravarman II, who in his short reign came into conflict with Vikramāditya I. Mahendravarman was followed in his turn by his son, Parameśvaravarman I, in whose reign Chālukya Vikramāditya renewed his conflict, having secured the alliance of the contemporary Pāndya ruler Arikēsari Parānkuśa Māṟavarman I (670-700).

A word must now be said about the rise of the Pāndya kingdom. It started on its career about the same time as the Pallava or a little later, but we know little of the history of its first two monarchs, Kaḍungōn (590-620) and his son Māṟavarman Avaniśūḷāmaṇi (620-45). There is no doubt, however, that they put an end to Kalabhra rule in their part of the country and revived the Pāndya power. The third, Śēndan or Jayantavarman, imposed his rule on the Chera country and took to himself the title Vānavan. An inscription in Tamil and Vaṭṭeḻuttu discovered in 1959 records his excavation of a rock-cut cave temple at Malaiyaḍikurichi (Tirunelveli district). His son Arikēsari Māṟavarman (670-700) was a great soldier who fought many battles for the extension of Pāndya power, some of them against his Pallava contemporary. It is very probable that he entered into an alliance with the Pallavas' enemy on the other side, namely Chālukya Vikramāditya I.

That ruler, after rescuing his country from the invasion of Narasimhavarman I and consolidating his power, turned to the task of avenging the fate of his father. Hostilities began even in the reign of Mahendravarman II, who sustained defeat and perhaps death somewhere in the Mysore (Ganga) country; and early in the reign of Parameśvaravarman, Vikramāditya advanced to the neighbourhood of Kānchipuram, and Parameśvaravarman had to seek refuge in flight. Vikramāditya pursued him to the banks of the Kaveri and encamped at Uṟaiyūr where he probably effected a junction with his ally, the Pāndya king. From his exile Parameśvaravarman gathered a large army and offered battle at Viḷande to Bhūvikrama, the Ganga ally of Vikramāditya. The battle went against him and he lost to his enemy a valued crown jewel, the necklace which contained the gem 'Ugrodaya'. Nothing daunted, he managed to send a counter-expedition into the Chālukya kingdom in order to divert the attention of his enemy. He then met the invading forces in battle at Peruvaḷanallūr, two miles north-west of Uṟaiyūr, and inflicted a decisive defeat on them. The expeditionary force returned with much booty after encounters with Vinayāditya and Vijayāditya, the son and grandson of Vikramāditya who had to leave the Pallava territory and retire to his own kingdom.

There was a lull in the conflict between the Chālukyas and Pallavas during the generally peaceful and prosperous reign of Vikramāditya's son, Vinayāditya (681-96). Vinayāditya led an expedition into Northern India, in which his son Vijayāditya greatly distinguished himself, but that is all. Vijayāditya's was the longest reign (696-733) of the Bādāmi period and perhaps also the most prosperous and peaceful. It was marked by great activity in temple-building. He was followed by his son Vikramāditya II (733-44) in the first years of whose reign the Arabs who had established themselves in Sind and conquered the neighbouring lands made a push into the Deccan, but were stopped effectively by Pulakeśin, a son of that Jayasimhavarman who had stood by his brother, Vikramāditya I. Vikramāditya II so appreciated the service of Pulakeśin that he conferred on him the title, among others, of Avanijanāśraya, meaning 'refuge of the people of the earth'. The Rāshtrakūta Dantivarman, another feudatory of the Chālukya emperor, also co-operated in the war against the Arabs and earned the appreciation of his suzerain.

The chief interest of the reign of Vikramāditya II lies in his wars with the Pallavas. He is said to have overrun Kānchī three times—which brings us back to the Pallavas.

After his victory against Vikramāditya I, Parameśvaravarman I continued to rule in Kānchī until his death which occurred about 700, and was succeeded by his son Narasimhavarman II Rājasimha (700-728). His reign, like that of his Chālukya contemporary, was marked by peace and prosperity and by the construction of large and beautiful temples like the Shore Temple at Māmallapuram and the Kailāsanātha at Kānchipuram. It was also marked by literary activity, the great rhetorician Dandin probably spending many years at his court. Rājasimha sent embassies to China and maritime trade flourished greatly in his time. His son Mahendravarman III who took part in the construction of the Kailāsanātha temple of Kānchī predeceased his father, and may well have been the Pallava *yuvarāja* mentioned in a West Ganga inscription of A.D. 713 as having two sons Jaya Pallavādhirāja and Vriddipallavādhirāja. Rājasimha was followed by his son Parameśvaravarman

II (728-31), who perhaps built the Śiva temple at Tiruvadi which bears an inscription of the third year of his reign but has been repaired many times over.

Towards the end of his short reign Parameśvaravarman's capital was attacked by the Chālukya crown prince Vikramāditya II assisted by the Ganga prince Eṟeyappa, son of Śrīpurusha. The Pallava ruler had to purchase peace at a heavy price. His attempt at retaliation against Śrīpurusha ended in disaster; he was killed in battle at Viḷande by the Ganga ruler, who seized the royal Pallava umbrella together with the title Permānaḍi.

The death of Parameśvaravarman is said to have led to a crisis in the kingdom. There was no one to succeed him in the direct line and the officials of the capital acting with the *ghaṭikā* (college of learned Brahmins) and the people chose a prince from a collateral branch, Nandivarman II, the son of Hiraṇyavarman. This is the account given in the labels beneath the sculptured panels in the Vaikuṇṭhaperumāl temple which narrate the history of the Pallavas from their legendary origin to the accession of Nandivarman. They base the choice of Nandivarman on the fact of his being of pure descent both on his father's and mother's side. There were apparently other princes, perhaps the two sons of Mahendravarman III noticed above, ready to contest Nandivarman's accession. One of them apparently lost his life opposing Nandivarman's entry into Kānchī, while another, Chitramāya, as seen from other inscriptions, gained some support not only within the kingdom, but of the Pāndya ruler as well. We have also Ko Vijaya Skandaśishya Vikramavarman, whose grant issued in his fourteenth regnal year is known as the Rāyakota plates and who certainly seems to belong to this period. It is tempting to identify him with Chitramāya and to trace in his title Vikramavarman evidence of the support he got from Vikramāditya II. Surely the Vaikuṇṭhaperumāl label inscriptions are a partisan account of the revolution which brought about Nandivarman II's accession, and much of it still awaits satisfactory elucidation. Further, we learn that Nandivarman had to take a long strenuous journey through dense forests and mountains and possibly cross the sea before reaching Kānchipuram, but we get no clue to the identity of the place where the prince was living with his father Hiranyavarman and from which he started on his journey to Kānchipuram.

In the Pāndya kingdom, Arikēsari Parānkuśa was succeeded by his son Kōccaḍaiyan, also called Raṇadhīra (*c.* 700-30). This monarch waged aggressive wars against his neighbours and extended the Pāndya power into the Kongu country. He also suppressed a revolt of the mountain chieftain Āy who occupied the hilly country between Tirunelvēli and Travancore. His reign ended about 730, and his son Māṟavarman Rājasimha I succeeded him. Early in his reign Rājasimha formed an alliance with Chālukya Vikramāditya II, espoused the cause of Chitramāya, and after inflicting a number of defeats on Nandivarman Pallavamalla besieged him in a place called Nandigrāma, i.e., Nandipuram, near Kumbakonam. The able Pallava general Udayacandra, who encountered the Pāndya forces in many battles, raised the siege of Nandigrāma, beheaded Chitramāya, and thus made the Pallava throne secure for his monarch. He also dealt with other enemies of Pallavamalla like the Śabara king Udayana and the Nishāda chieftain Prithivīvyāghra who were probably acting in collusion with the Chālukya, Vikramāditya II. The invasion of Vikramāditya (*c.* 735), in which his Ganga feudatory Śrīpurusha also co-operated, was indeed the greatest danger that threatened the kingdom of Pallavamalla in the early years of his long reign. But Vikramāditya behaved on the whole very considerately; though he defeated Nandivarman and occupied his capital for a time, he did no damage to the city, pleased the people by his liberal gifts and returned to the Kailāsanātha and all other temples the heaps of gold that belonged to them. After recording these transactions in a Kannada inscription engraved on a pillar in Kailāsanātha and thus wiping out the disgrace that had befallen the Chālukyas by the occupation of Bādāmi by Narasimhavarman I, Vikramāditya withdrew to his own country leaving the Pallava ruler to continue his war with the Pāndya before resuming charge of his kingdom. We have no means now of determining the exact relative chronology of the events in these early wars of Pallavamalla with his enemies on the north and south. Towards the end of his reign Vikramāditya sent out another expedition against the Pallava under his son Kīrtivarman, who carried out a successful raid and returned with many elephants and much gold and jewellery captured from the enemy.

Vikramāditya's reign was also marked by the construction of new temples, an activity which was continued by his son

Kīrtivarman II who succeeded him in 744-5. Kīrtivarman II and his Ganga feudatory Śrīpurusha came into conflict with the Pāndya ruler Māṟavarman Rājasimha I who was extending the Pāndya power over the Kongu country and beyond. Rājasimha crossed the Kaveri and subjugated Maḻakongam on the borderland between the Tiruchirāpalli and Tanjore districts, defeated the Chālukya ruler and his feudatory in a big battle at Veṇbai and made peace with them, accepting the hand of a Ganga princess for his son (*c.* 750).

Kīrtivarman II was the last ruler of the Chālukya line of Bādāmi. His power was steadily undermined by the activity of the Rāshtrakūta prince Dantidurga who was in occupation of Ellora in 742. But the main scene of Dantidurga's early activities lay on the banks of the Mahī, Narmada and Mahanadi. He subdued the Gurjaras of Malwa, the rulers of Kosala and Kalinga and the Telugu-Chodas of the Śrīśailam country. Above all, he went down to Kānchī and, after a demonstration of force, struck up an alliance with Nandivarman Pallavamalla to whom he gave his daughter Rēvā in marriage. Having thus deprived Kīrtivarman of his outlying provinces and strengthened his political position, Dantidurga delivered the final assault on Kīrtivarman some time in 752 or 753 and proclaimed himself the sovereign power in Deccan. Kīrtivarman continued to rule in an obscure way for two or three years more but, as the later inscriptions say, 'In his reign the *rājyaśrī* of the Chālukyas disappeared from the face of the earth'.

To return to the reign of Nandivarman II: he led an expedition against the Ganga kingdom, defeated Śrīpurusha and forced him to surrender much wealth and restore the necklace which contained the precious gem called 'Ugrodaya'. Some territory was also taken from the Ganga and handed over to Jayanandivarman, the Bāna feudatory of Nandivarman. This was perhaps about 760. Nandivarman also came into conflict with Jaṭila Parāntaka Neḍunjaḍaiyan, *alias* Varaguṇamahārāja I (765-815), the son and successor of Pāndya Rājasimha I. The Pallava forces sustained a defeat at Peṇṇāgaḍam on the south bank of the Kaveri river (*c.* 767).

Pallavamalla sought to restrain the growing power of the Pāndya king by organizing a confederacy against him. He entered into an alliance with the rulers of Kongu and Kerala as well as the Adigaimān of Tagaḍūr (Dharmapuri). But the Pāndya king was equal to the occasion, won victories in several battles, put the Adigaimān to flight, and captured the king of western Kongu, with many elephants, and sent him into confinement at Madura, annexing the whole of the Kongu country to the Pāndya empire. In the course of war, he penetrated far into the Pallava country and fixed his camp at Iḍavai in the heart of Tanjore District. The coalition against him thus failed utterly, and Nandivarman did not succeed in his attempts to check the Pāndya.

Varaguṇa I had still other successes to his credit. He led an expedition into Vēṇāḍ, South Travancore, attacked the strongly fortified port of Vilinam and brought the country under his rule. He also waged successful war against the Āy chieftain of the intervening mountainous country who had perhaps been friendly to the ruler of Vēṇāḍ. As a result of these wars, Pāndya sway extended well beyond Tiruchirāpalli into the Tanjore, Salem and Coimbatore districts, and all that lay south was under him. The expansion continued under his son and successor Śrīmāṟa Śrīvallabha (815-62) who invaded Ceylon in the reign of Sena I (831-51), ravaged the northern province and sacked the capital. Eventually Sena made terms with the conqueror and the Pāndya forces quitted the island. Śrīmāṟa had next to deal with a formidable combination formed against him again under the leadership of the Pallavas. We must now turn for a while to Pallava history.

After the failure of his plans against Varaguṇa, Nandivarman Pallavamalla continued to rule till about 796. Pallavamalla was a worshipper of Vishnu and a great patron of learning. He renovated old temples and built several new ones. Among the latter was the Vaikuṇṭhaperumāl temple at Kānchipuram which contains inscribed panels of sculpture portraying the events leading up to the accession of Pallavamalla to the throne. The great Vaishnava saint Tirumangai Āḻvār was his contemporary.

Nandivarman was succeeded by his son Dantivarman (*c.* 796-847). The northern expansion of the Pāndya power under Varaguṇa I and Śrīmāṟa deprived Dantivarman of a considerable part of his territory in the south; and in addition, he had to face the hostility of the rising power of the Rāshtrakūtas. It is now necessary to trace the history of that power.

Dantidurga died childless and was succeeded about 756 by his uncle Krishna I. He completed the overthrow of the Chālukya power and expanded the new kingdom in all directions. He conquered southern Konkan and established the Śilāra family there as a feudatory power. He invaded the Ganga territory, defeated Śrīpurusha (768) and compelled him to acknowledge his suzerainty. Against the Eastern Chālukya kingdom of Vengi he dispatched an expedition under the crown prince Govinda II to whom Vijayāditya I (752-73), ruler of Vengi, made his submission without a fight (769-70). Krishna who excavated the celebrated Kailāsa temple at Ellora, was succeeded by Govinda II some time between 772 and 775. In 777-8, Govinda co-operated with Nandivarman Pallavamalla in assisting Śivamāra II the son of Śrīpurusha to gain the Ganga throne against the opposition of his brother, Duggamāra Eṟeyappa. Govinda was an easygoing monarch and his ambitious brother Dhruva planned to seize the throne for himself. Govinda sought the aid of the Pallava and the Ganga, and the rulers of Vengi and Malwa; but Dhruva defeated them all and thus became king. How exactly Govinda ended his life is not known. Dhruva's accession took place about 780 and his first task was to punish Govinda's allies. He caught and imprisoned Śivamāra II, and levied a tribute of elephants from Pallavamalla (783-4). He crossed the Vindhyas and drove the Gurjara king of Malwa, Vatsarāja by name, into the desert. He proceeded against Vengi, and Vishnuvardhana IV had to purchase peace by parting with some territory besides offering the hand of his daughter Śīlamahādevi to Dhruva. Dhruva followed up his success in Malwa by a raid into the Ganges-Jumna doab where he met and defeated Dharmapāla of Bengal. Towards the close of his reign, Dhruva abdicated and made Govinda III, the ablest of his sons, emperor. This led to trouble soon after Dhruva's death in 793-4, when Govinda III had to face the hostility of his disinherited brothers, particularly that of Kambha, the eldest. To gain support, Govinda released Śivamāra II from prison, but contrary to expectations that monarch threw in his lot with Kambha. Single-handed, Govinda defeated the confederacy of twelve rulers but used his victory with moderation, even reinstating Kambha as viceroy over Gangavādi; while Indra, a younger brother of Govinda who had stood by him, was rewarded with the viceroyalty of Lāta. Śivamāra II, however, was again put in prison. After putting down opposition at home Govinda III carried his arms into Northern India.

He inflicted a decisive defeat on the Gurjara ruler of Malwa. Nāgabhaṭa II, and on his ally Chandragupta, of unknown identity. Malwa was annexed for a time to Lāta. Govinda proceeded farther north and received the submission of Chakrāyudha of Kanauj and his protector Dharmapāla. On his return (802) he fixed his camp at Śrībhavana on the banks of the Narmada where a son was born to him, the future Amoghavarsha I. From Śrībhavana, he dashed across the Deccan into the Pallava country (803-4). He defeated Dantivarman, entered his capital Kānchī and there received the submission offered by an embassy from Ceylon before he retired to the banks of the Tungabhadra and fixed his camp at Rameśvara-*tīrtha*. The rulers of Vengi, Vishnuvardhana IV, and his successor Vijayāditya II (808), felt the impact of Govinda's power. Vijayāditya was a great fighter who earned for himself the title Narendramrigarāja (Lion among Kings). Govinda III created trouble for him by supporting his half-brother Bhīma Saluki's rival claims to the throne of Vengi. One of the greatest monarchs of the line, Govinda's achievements go far to justify the claim of his court-poets that after his birth the Rāshtrakūtas became as unassailable as the Yādavas after the birth of Śrī Krishna.

To return to affairs farther south; during his fairly long reign, the Pallava Dantivarman found himself unable to resist the aggression of the Pāndyas from the south or even hold his own against the Rāshtrakūtas in the north. For a good part of his nominal reign, between the twenty-first and forty-ninth regnal years, no inscriptions of Dantivarman are known, and from a Pāndyan copper-plate charter recently discovered it seems possible that Tondaimandalam passed under the rule of the Telugu-Chola ruler Śrīkaṇṭha of the Pottappi family. Śrīkaṇṭha was apparently collaborating with the Pāndyas against the Pallavas, and his daughter Aggalanimmati was the queen of Śrīmāṟa Śrīvallabha who gave birth to his second son Parāntaka Vīranārāyaṇa.

Dantivarman was followed by his son Nandivarman III (846-69), a much abler monarch than his father. In the last years of his father's reign, he organized a strong confederacy against his aggressive Pāndya contemporary Śrīmāṟa Śrīvallabha, and his father-in-law Śrīkaṇṭha and inflicted a severe defeat on them at Tellaru in the Wandiwash taluk of the North Arcot district. His allies were the Gangas, the Tamil Cholas, and even the

Rāshtrakūtas. The location of the field of battle shows the extent to which foreign aggression had developed, and this doubtless made it easy for Nandivarman to find support. The victory of Tellaru was a turning point. It gave Nandi the permanent title 'Teḷḷāṟeṟinda' and was followed up by further successes as a result of which the Pāndya forces were rolled back into their home country, and the Pallava army made a dash as far as the banks of the Vaigai, in the heart of the Pāndya kingdom.

Later, however, Śrīmāṟa recovered his strength and about 859 was able to defeat Nandivarman and his confederates in a battle near Kumbakonam.

Nandivarman III was undoubtedly too great a monarch to suffer by this defeat. Not only did he restore the Pallava power to its former glory, but he was also a liberal patron of literature and the arts in general. He is also said to have maintained a powerful fleet: a Tamil inscription at Takua-pa in Siam, on the opposite coast of the Bay, attests to his overseas connexions by mentioning a Vishnu temple and a tank called Avanināraṇam after one of his titles. Nandivarman was succeeded by his son Nripatunga who had became *yuvarāja* about 860, and whose mother was the Rāshtrakūta princess Śankhā. Nandivarman had two other sons, Aparājita and Kampavarman, by other queens. Soon after his accession, the young Nripatunga avenged the defeat of his father at Kumbakonam by a decisive victory against the Pāndyas in a battle on the banks of the river Ariśil, a branch of the Kaveri which enters the sea at Kāraikkāl.

Śrīmāṟa's defeat at Ariśil was, however, not an isolated event. His aggressive campaigns which had earned for him the title *Paracakrakolāhala* (Confounder of the Circle of his Enemies) naturally roused the hostility of his neighbours. Sena II (851-85) of Ceylon, nephew and successor of Sena I, had allied himself with the Pallavas and a Pāndya prince who sought his aid: this prince was probably Śrīmāṟa's son whose claim to the throne had been overlooked when his stepbrother Vīranārāyaṇa was made *yuvarāja* (*c.* 860). Sena sent an expedition into the Madura kingdom at about the same time as the battle of Ariśil and the invasion was a complete success. The capital was sacked, Śrīmāṟa died of his wounds, and his son Varaguṇavarman II was enthroned in his place by the Sinhalese commander-in-chief (862). Varaguṇa II had to acknowledge the overlordship of Nripatunga.

In the Rāshtrakūta kingdom Govinda III was succeeded (814) by his young son Amoghavarsha, also called Nripatunga. The early years of the boy-king's reign were full of trouble. There was a widespread rebellion of the officials supported by the Eastern Chālukya Vijayāditya II and the Ganga Rācamalla I. Amoghavarsha, however, found a loyal ally and strong protector in his cousin Karka of Lāta; the rebellion was suppressed and Amoghavarsha was secure on his throne before 821. At no time during his long reign of 66 years can peace be said to have prevailed all over his extensive dominions. With the Eastern Chālukyas war broke out again about 850 when Guṇaga Vijayāditya III, the grandson of Vijayāditya II and one of the ablest monarchs of his line, made a strenuous effort to free the Vengi kingdom from the Rāshtrakūtas. Amoghavarsha won a decisive victory in the sanguinary battle of Vīngāvalli near Stambhapuri (Kambham) in the Kurnool district, whereafter Guṇaga Vijayāditya submitted and remained loyal for the rest of Amoghavarsha's reign. The Ganga Eṟaya, known as also Nītimārga and Raṇavikrama (837-70), son of Rācamalla I, revolted soon after and was joined by other feudatories. Amoghavarsha's general Bankeśa dealt with them successfully; but before he could complete his task Amoghavarsha recalled him to the capital where other disturbances had arisen, in which the crown prince Krishna himself was involved, as well as the ruler of Lāta, Dhruva I, son of that Karka who had so ably protected Amoghavarsha earlier. Bankeśa killed Dhruva I in battle and continued the war with his son Akālavarsha and his grandson Dhruva II. Dhruva II was, however, threatened in his rear by the Gurjara ruler Mihira Bhoja, and some of his own kinsmen had turned hostile to him at home. He thus thought it wise to compose his quarrel with Amoghavarsha in 860, and was thereby enabled to thwart the designs of the Gurjara and his hostile kinsmen, so that we find him secure on his throne again in 867.

After the recall of Bankeśa, the war against the rebels in the Ganga kingdom was entrusted to Guṇaga Vijayāditya who led an expedition into the Nolamba kingdom as its ruler Nolambādhirāja I, also called Mangi, had joined the rebellion. Mangi was slain in battle and the road to Gangavādi opened up. Then the Ganga army was beaten in its turn and Nītimārga obliged to make peace.

By temperament Amoghavarsha was a religious man who loved literature more than fighting. He is said to have retired from his court more than once to spend time in the company of Jaina monks. It is doubtful, however, whether he formally renounced Hinduism, though a small Jaina catechism entitled *Praśnottara-ratna-mālikā* is attributed to him. He was himself an author and a liberal patron of authors. He is also celebrated as the maker of the city of Mānyakheta, the city built to excel that of Indra. His palace was full of fine workmanship and included an extensive apartment for the royal princesses and a tank. Amoghavarsha was succeeded by Krishna II (880).

The history of the Chera country during this period is still obscure. Apparently the land continued under the Perumāls, though several rulers of different dynasties claim to have overrun Kerala, generally a vague assertion not supported by tangible evidence. We have seen that Pallava Narasimhavarman I claimed victory over the Cheras as also the Pāndya Śēndan. Nandivarman II Pallavamalla allied himself with the ruler of Kerala against his Pāndyan contemporary, Varaguṇa I. Other Pallava rulers like Simhavishnu and Nandivarman III also claim suzerainty over Kerala. Cultural contact between the Chera country and the Pallava court is rather well attested. The *Mattavilāsa* of Mahendravarman became one of the favourite theatricals of the Chākkiyār, the hereditary play-actors of Malabar. In his *Avantisundarī Kathāsāra* Dandin reveals a vivid knowledge of Kerala and refers to several learned brahmins of Kerala who visited Kānchī while he was in the Pallava Court. Among the Pāndyas, besides Śēndan, almost every other ruler claims success against the Chera, as do also Pulakeśin II, Vikramāditya I, Vikramāditya II and Kīrtivarman II among the Bādāmi Chālukyas, and Dantidurga, Govinda III and Krishna III among the Rāshtrakūtas.

One of the latest Perumāls of the period was the celebrated Cheramān Perumāl, end of the eighth and early ninth century, whose history is much overlaid by legend. We may doubt the authenticity of the story of his conversion to Islām and his pilgrimage to Mecca. He must have been a devoutly religious man as the Jains, Christians, and Śaivites, besides Muslims, claim him as one of their fold. His relation to Sundaramūrti, according to Śaiva legend, will be noticed later. He may have renounced the world, and effected a partition of his realm among his relatives or vassals before doing so. He seems to have vanished somehow about A.D. 825, the epoch of the Kollam era. But whether that era commemorates Cheramān's partition of Kerala or Śankarāchārya's imposition of his religious prescriptions on that country, or the establishment of the Jewish merchant community in Kollam (Quilon)—other possibilities have also been suggested—cannot be determined yet. There are epigraphical references which connect the era both with the appearance and the destruction of Kollam.

In concluding the political history of the period we may note that Kalinga was throughout under the rule of the line of Eastern Gangas, who in spite of their name have no apparent connexion in this period with the Gangas of Mysore. They dated their inscriptions in an era of their own, beginning with the equivalent of A.D. 498. Their external contacts were few, though sometimes the politics of the Telugu country to the south under the Vishnukundins and their successors, the Eastern Chālukyas, occasionally forced itself on their attention. They made their submission to Pulakeśin II (*c*. 620) when he invaded the eastern Deccan and later perhaps also to the Rāshtrakūta Dantidurga (*c*. 750). But to judge from their grants they generally led a peaceful existence without disturbing their neighbours or being troubled by them.

In proceeding to sketch the polity of the period, emphasis should be laid, at the outset, on certain fundamental characteristics in the Indian attitude to political organization in ancient times. First, they looked to the state for very little. The ruler was expected to uphold the existing social order and protect it from internal trouble and foreign invasion, and receive as his wage the taxes paid by the people, particularly a sixth part of the produce of the land. The social order itself had its roots elsewhere—in revelation (*śruti*), tradition (*smriti*), and the practice of the *élite* (*ācāra*). The ruler had ordinarily little control over the numerous social, economic and religious concerns of the people, except by way of dispensing justice when disputes were brought before him or his courts. The details of the daily life of the people were looked after by numberless autonomous groups and associations bound by ties of locality, caste, occupation, or religious persuasion. These groups generally followed custom and ancient practice though they were by no means unwilling to try new methods should occasion demand it. Each group had its own constitution, generally well-understood by its members, and flexible enough for meeting new situations. There was usually a general assembly which met rarely, except perhaps once a year on some definite festive or ceremonial occasion, and an executive body in charge of the daily routine. The executive was often chosen by lot from among persons possessing certain prescribed qualifications. Decision by majority of votes was not unknown, but usually the aim was to reach unanimous and integrated decisions by reconciling the different interests and points of view. Guilds of merchants like the Nānādeśis, the Maṇigrāmam and the Five Hundred of Ayyavole, associations of craftsmen, artisans and manufacturers like the braziers, oil-mongers and weavers, and of students, ascetics, temple servants, priests, and so on, besides the territorial assemblies of the village and higher divisions—all functioned more or less independently of the government of the ruler.

Secondly, the duty of protecting society was cast by theory on a special class, the Kshatriyas, and by a natural and easy transition anyone who felt equal to the task of undertaking the rule of a particular area and did not hesitate to do so was more or less readily accepted as the ruler. Each successful adventurer became a king and gained respectability by maintaining a liberal court, patronizing learning and the arts, and causing *praśastis* (praises) to be composed in honour of himself and his family. Moreover, aggrandizement was the recognized duty of the ruler; he had to be a *vijigīshu* (one who wishes to conquer) and the general acceptance of this ideal led to frequent wars and skirmishes resulting in changes in the relative precedence of the different powers involved. Lastly, and as a consequence of these two factors, political changes did not have in India such profound effects on the structure of society and civilization as elsewhere, although the establishment and the continued prosperity of an empire often, indeed, meant an era of high endeavour and achievement in literature and the arts.

The organization which made for the continuity of life and tradition, held society together, and carried it safe through the storms and turmoils of political revolution was the autonomous, self-sufficient village. It was the primary cell of the body politic, and the vitality of its institutions is well-attested by hundreds of inscriptions from all parts of the country. Usually, it comprised a number of families, each occupying a house of its own in the residential quarter of the village, owning its own share of the arable land, and enjoying privileges like the right to graze cattle and gather firewood in the waste land and forest lying round about and held in common by the villagers as a body. A Pallava grant mentions some land in a village as the property of the king, which goes directly against the view sometimes expressed that all land belonged to the king in the ancient Indian State. A careful record of the boundaries of a village and of the individual estates in it was maintained. The villagers met periodically to consider matters of common concern and for the settlement of disputes and the administration of justice. Everywhere rural administration grew from timid and tentative improvisations to the more elaborate and complicated machinery of committees and officials that we find described in the Chola inscriptions of the tenth and eleventh centuries, and in this evolution the Tamil country appears to have been more progressive than the rest of South India. The village had a headman, variously called *mutuḍa*, *kiḻān*, *grāmabhōjaka* and so on, who was its leader and mediator with the royal government. How he was appointed and whether the office was hereditary cannot be determined. The village elders are also particularly mentioned besides the headmen and the assembly.

From the eighth and ninth centuries A.D. three types of village assemblies are traceable in Tamil inscriptions, namely the *ūr*, the *sabhā*, and the *nagaram*. The *ūr* was the common type which included all classes of people who held the land in the village. The *sabhā* was an exclusively Brahmin assembly of villages given as gifts to Brahmins where all the land belonged to them. The *nagaram* was quite another type pertaining to localities where traders and merchants were in a dominant position. In many instances the different types existed side by side in the same locality. Whenever necessary, there was mutual consultation among these different assemblies and other local associations, and the general rule was to consult all the interests concerned in a matter before a decision was taken on it. The village assembly regulated irrigation rights, administered charitable endowments, maintained tanks and roads and managed the affairs of temples, either directly or by means of executive officers and committees working under it. It also made rules for regulating its own procedure.

In the Deccan we come across many references to the *mahājanas* of villages who were in charge of the local administration under the leadership of *gāmuṇḍas* (headmen). The royal officials stood in closer relation to the working of the village assemblies here than in the more autonomous townships of the Tamil country.

Unless specially exempted, the villages were liable to visits from royal officers for digging for salt, the manufacture of sugar and the arrest of culprits. They also had to supply draught bulls to help the progress of touring officers, besides other amenities such as accommodation, beds, boiled rice, milk, curds, grass, fuel, and green vegetables, besides free labour on specified public works. In addition to the land tax and these occasional demands from officials, the people were subjected to a variety of imposts, direct and indirect. Houses and professions were taxed, market dues and tolls on merchandise moved from place to place were collected, besides judicial dues and fines. Arab writers who knew western India well thought that the people of India were heavily taxed, so that their monarchs might have their treasuries full. To complete the picture, we must note that besides these compulsory levies, central and local, a number of voluntary imposts for particular purposes such as the maintenance of a tank, temple, feeding house, college or hospital were undertaken by particular corporations, mostly of merchants.

Above the *grāma* was the administrative division called *āhara*, *rāshṭra*, *nāḍu*, *kōṭṭam*, or *vishaya* at different times and places. *Rāshṭra* and *vishaya* often figure as two categories, one larger than the other. In the Tamil country the larger division was often called *vaḷanāḍu* or *manḍalam*. The size of these units often depended on accidents of history, e.g. Bānarāja-vishaya of the Bādāmi period. In this division also there was an assembly of elders and a chief executive official known as *deśabhōjaka*, *nāṭṭukkōn* and so on.

Provincial offices were often held by princes of the royal family. This was an advantage when there was unity in the family but when differences arose it easily led to civil war and disruption, as for instance in the Chālukya empire of Bādāmi during the interval between the death of Pulakeśin II and the accession of Vikramāditya I. There were groups of officers charged with the maintenance of the peace and securing the safety of life and property who went by different names in different kingdoms. Local policing was to some extent done by village officials. There were also bailiffs (*śāsana sancārin*) who went about the country enforcing the execution of the orders of government and the decrees of law-courts, and they were aided in the discharge of their duties by a constabulary (*bhaṭas*). We hear also of a superintendent of the treasury (*kośādhyaksha*) and officers engaged in the survey and assessment of cultivated lands (*nilakkaḷattār* and *adhikāri*). Lastly there were the *vāyil kēṭpār*, i.e., hearers of oral orders issued by the king, also called *rahasyādhikrita*. They were the secretaries who attended on the king, listened to his orders, and subsequently wrote them out in proper form and had them communicated to the officials concerned for proper action. Such orders were called *rājaśrāvitam* under the Chālukyas and the Rāshtrakūtas. Besides village courts and caste and guild *panchāyats* for the settlement of disputes, there were law-courts called *adhikaraṇas* or *dharmāsanas* maintained by the central government for the administration of justice. They were presided over by state officials assisted by advisers learned in the law (*dharmāsanabhaṭṭas*). A scene in the farce *Mattavilāsa* by king Mahendravarman suggests that the courts were not altogether free from corruption. In the absence of other evidence ordeals (*divya*) were resorted to for proof.

There is no clear proof of the existence of a regularly constituted council of ministers although the *mantrimaṇḍala* (group of ministers) took part in the events preceding the coronation of Nandivarman II Pallavamalla.

The king was the head of the state, the fountain of honour, judge, and leader of the armed forces. The early kings in this period called themselves *dharmamahārājādhirājas*, in token of their active promotion of Vedic *dharma* as against Buddhism and Jainism which had made much headway in the country in the earlier period, but there were Jaina monarchs also, particularly among the Gangas. The kings specially favoured the particular religious creed they professed but never sought to impose it on all their subjects; rather they patronized as a matter of policy all the other creeds. After a political revolution, social and economic stability was ensured by express proclamations that all pre-existing rights of property and the charitable foundations would be respected by the new rulers.

Succession to the throne was usually hereditary in the eldest male line. Princes were educated according to the best standards of the time in literature, law, philosophy and the martial arts, and trained in administrative positions suited to their capacities and tastes. The attempt of Mangaleśa to shut Pulakeśin II, for whom he acted as regent, permanently out of his rights met with a deserved failure as public opinion supported Pulakeśin. The success of Vikramāditya in checking the disruption of the Chālukya empire after the death of Pulakeśin II has also been noticed above, and Vikramāditya was not the eldest son of Pulakeśin. The choice of Nandivarman II as king from a collateral branch when succession failed in the main line may also be recalled. Pāndya Śrīmāṟa's preference for his younger son led to a disastrous foreign invasion and the temporary submission of the Pāndya to the Pallava power. The history of the Rāshtrakūtas and of the Eastern Chālukyas was marred by a number of disputed successions and civil wars. Among the latter this was accentuated by the interference of the Rāshtrakūtas. The choice of Govinda III for succession by Dhruva led inevitably to a civil war started by his eldest son Kambha whose claims had been passed over, but the event justified the choice of Govinda for rule.

Each royal family had its own banner (*dhvaja*) and seal (*lāñchana*) mentioned prominently in their inscriptions. The royal palace was maintained in great state, and elephants and horses captured in war were exhibited at the palace gate. Queens occupied a position of equal importance with the king. Śīlabhaṭṭārikā, Dhruva's wife, bore the imperial titles *Parameśvarī* and *Paramabhaṭṭārikā*, made grants of land at her own will, and issued her own orders to the executive officers or government. Rangapatākā, the wife of Pallava Rājasimha, interested herself in the construction of the Kailāsanātha temple.

Though the king was in theory an autocrat, there were several modifying factors in practice. All the members of the royal family shared in the administration as far as possible and had opportunities of influencing the king's policy. Then there were the high officials of the state, some of whose offices were hereditary and who commanded the respect of the monarch by their descent, ability, and character. The presence of numerous feudatory monarchs and the domination of social life by the numerous corporate organizations spoken of above went far to mitigate the bad consequences of the rule of incapable or misguided sovereigns.

BIBLIOGRAPHY

A. S. ALTEKAR: *The Rāṣṭrakūṭas and their Times* (Poona, 1934)

H. W. CODRINGTON: *A Short History of Ceylon* (London, 1929)

J. F. FLEET: *Dynasties of the Kanarese Districts* (*Bombay Gazetteer*, Vol. I, Pt. II, Bombay, 1896)

R. GOPALAN: *Pallavas of Kānchī* (Madras, 1928)

Indian Archaeology Annual Review (Arch. Survey of India)

G. JOUVEAU-DUBREUIL: *The Pallavas* (Pondicherry, 1917)

C. MINAKSHI: *Administration and Social Life under the Pallavas* (Madras, 1938)

B. L. RICE: *Mysore and Coorg from Inscriptions* (London, 1909)

K. A. N. SASTRI: *Pandyan Kingdom* (London, 1929)

CHĀLUKYAS OF BĀDĀMI

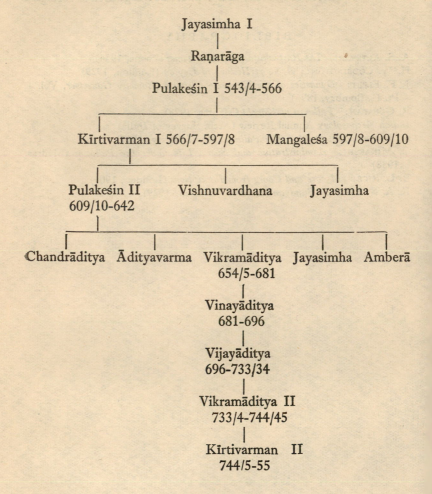

- Jayasimha I
  - Raṇarāga
    - Pulakeśin I 543/4-566
      - Kīrtivarman I 566/7-597/8
        - Pulakeśin II 609/10-642
          - Chandrāditya
          - Ādityavarma
          - Vikramāditya 654/5-681
            - Vinayāditya 681-696
              - Vijayāditya 696-733/34
                - Vikramāditya II 733/4-744/45
                  - Kīrtivarman II 744/5-55
          - Jayasimha
          - Amberā
        - Vishnuvardhana
        - Jayasimha
      - Mangaleśa 597/8-609/10

PALLAVAS

1. Simhavarman (A.D. 550-60)
    - 2. Simhavishnu (A.D. 560-80)
        - 3. Mahendravarman I (A.D. 580-630)
            - 4. Narasimhavarman I (630-668)
                - 5. Mahendravarman II (668-670)
                    - 6. Parameśvaravarman I (670-700)
                        - 7. Narasimhavarman II (700-728)
                            - Mahendravarman III (Yuva 720-28)
                            - 8. Parameśvaravarman II (728-731)
    - Bhīmavarman
        - Buddhavarman
            - Ādityavarman
                - Govindavarman
                    - Hiraṇyavarman
                        - 9. Nandivarman II (731-796)
                            - 10. Dantivarman (796-847)
                                - 11. Nandivarman III (846-869)
                                    - 12. Nripatungavarman (859-899)
                                    - 13. Aparājita (885-903)
                                    - 14. Kampavarman (870-912?)

PĀNDYAS A.D. 590-920

1. Kaḍungōn (590-620)
   |
2. Māṟavarman Avaniśūḷāmaṇi (620-645)
   |
3. Śēndan (654-670)
   |
4. Arikesari Māṟavarman (670-700)
   |
5. Kōccaḍaiyan (700-730)
   |
6. Māṟavarman Rājasimha I (730-765)
   |
7. Jaṭila Parāntaka Neḍunjaḍaiyan (756-815)
   |
8. Śrīmāṟa Śrīvallabha (815-862)

9. Varaguṇavarman II (862-885)

10. Parāntaka Vīranārāyana (860-905)
    |
11. Māṟavarman Rājasimha II (905-920)

CHAPTER IX

THE BALANCE OF TWO EMPIRES

General outline—Vijayālaya, Chola Āditya I—battle of Śripuṟambiyam—overthrow of Pallava Aparājita—Parāntaka I and his conquests—Rāshtrakūta Krishna II—battle of Vallāla—Indra III, Govinda IV, Amoghavarsha III, and Krishna III—Invasion of Chola country—battle of Takkōlam—results—Vengi and Malwa—Khottiga, Karka II, rise of Chālukya Taila II—Chola affairs after Parāntaka I—Rājarāja I and his work—Taila II and Paramāras—Satyāśraya—Vengi affairs—Chālukya-Chola war—and of Rājarāja's reign—Rājendra I—Vikramāditya V, Jayasimha II—his interest in Vengi affairs and wars with Rājendra—Chola expedition against Śrī Vijaya—end of Rājendra's reign—Someśvara I—his policy in Vengi and wars with Cholas Rājādhirāja I, Rājendra II, and Vīrarājendra—end of Someśvara I—Someśvara II—ambitious policy of Vikramāditya VI as *Yuvarāja*—death of Vīrarājendra—Adhirājendra, revolution, accession of Kulottunga I, and of Vikramāditya—end of Chola power in Ceylon—revolt in Pāndya and Kerala suppressed—embassy to China—Vengi—Vikramāditya suppresses the Hoysala revolt—and takes Vengi—estimate of Kulottunga I—Vikrama Chola—Someśvara III—Rājarāja II, Kulottunga II, Rājadhirāja II—civil war in Pāndya country, and Chola and Sinhalese intercession—Kulottunga III—his Pāndya campaigns—rise of Hoysala Vishnuvardhana under Jagadekamalla II and Taila III—Kākatīyas—Kalacuri Bijjala—Someśvara IV—Yādavas and Hoysalas put an end to Chālukya power—wars of Kulottunga III in the Telugu country.

Polity—monarchy—royal household—officials—administrative divisions—taxes—rural autonomy—justice—police—condition of the people.

THE emergence of the Chola power from obscurity, its rise to an imperial position and its conflicts—first with the Rāshtrakūtas from beyond the Tungabhadra and later with their successors, the Chālukyas of Kalyāni—form the dominant features of the history of the next 350 years (850-1200). The whole country south of the Tungabhadra was united and held as one state for a period of two centuries and more. The power of the new empire was proclaimed to the eastern world by the celebrated expedition to the Ganges which Rājendra I undertook and by the overthrow after an unprecedented naval war of the maritime empire of Śrī Vijaya, as well as by the repeated 'embassies' to China. In their wars with their enemies across the Tungabhadra, the Cholas were generally aided by the Eastern Chālukyas, a feudatory dynasty which drew closer and closer to the Cholas by marriage alliances until at last, in 1070, one ruler occupied both the Chola and the Vengi thrones.

The result of this union was an intensification of the hostility of the Western Chālukyas. Towards the close of the twelfth century, the two major powers had become thoroughly exhausted by their conflicts and were on their decline. Smaller powers standing in a subordinate relation to them were beginning to show new vigour and getting ready to take advantage of the weakening of their suzerains and proclaim their independence—the Pāndyas in the extreme south, the Hoysalas in Mysore, and the Yādavas and the Kākatīyas in the northern Deccan.

The Cholas built up a remarkably efficient administrative system which combined vigorous central control with a very large measure of local autonomy. The great temples of Tanjore and Gangai-kondaśōḻapuram as also those of Dārāśuram and Tribhuvani, not to speak of numerous smaller temples elsewhere, attest to this day the grandeur and the excellence of Chola architecture and sculpture. Other fine arts like painting, music, and dancing were liberally patronized. Literature flourished much more than ever before.

The capture of Tanjore by Vijayālaya, some time about 850, and his founding of a temple there to the goddess Nishumbhasūdinī (Durgā) were the first steps in the rise of the Chola power. He was perhaps a Pallava feudatory at the time, and he must have wrested Tanjore from the Muttarayar who had transferred their allegiance from the Pallava to the Pāndya. The success of Vijayālaya may have been obtained quietly when the Pallavas and Pāndyas were preoccupied with their own affairs from the battle of Tellāṟu to the enthronement of Varaguṇavarman II with Ceylonese aid. But after Varaguṇa became a subordinate ally of the Pallava power, that power naturally grew jealous of the newly growing influence of Vijayālaya and called upon Varaguṇa for aid in suppressing Vijayālaya. So Varaguṇa led an expedition into the Chola country. The invasion began well enough; Iḍavai on the north bank of the Kaveri in the Tanjore district was reached, and a camp was set up further north at Araśur on the banks of the Peṇṇar. It seems likely that Varaguṇa spent some years in the north aiding his protector and patron Nripatunga.

Meanwhile Nandivarman III died (869), and differences arose between Nripatunga and his step-brother Aparājita, probably owing to the latter's ambition to rule the kingdom in his own right. Both sides looked for allies. Nripatunga continued to have Varaguṇa on his side; Aparājita won over the Ganga Prithvīpati I and most probably also Āditya I (acc. A.D. 871), the son and successor of Vijayālaya Chola. The rival armies met at Śrīpuṟambiyam near Kumbakonam about A.D. 885 where the decisive battle was fought in which Prithvīpati I lost his life but only after securing victory for his ally Aparājita. This was the virtual end of Nripatunga's reign and the beginning of Aparājita's. There are no inscriptions of Nripatunga for the next fifteen years, from his twenty-sixth to the forty-first year, a period which practically coincides with Aparājita's rule.

But the real gain from this fratricidal fight went to the Chola Āditya I. Varaguṇavarman seems to have lost his zest in life after his defeat, and turned a saint, with the illustrious Māṇikka-vāśagar to keep him company; his brother Vīranārāyana became the uncontested ruler of the Pāndya country. Āditya I was not only allowed to keep what his father had taken from the Mutta-rayar, but some new territory was added to it by his grateful Pallava overlord Aparājita. Āditya I, however, did not rest content with a subordinate position. He planned and carried out the overthrow of the effete power of his suzerain. He invaded Tondaimandalam, and in a battle that ensued he pounced upon Aparājita when he was mounted on an elephant and slew him. That was the end of Pallava rule in Tondainād, and the whole of the Pallava kingdom now became Chola territory which henceforth bordered on that of the Rāshtrakūtas (903). Nripatunga died about 899, and his brother Kampavarman led an obscure life as a chieftain in North Arcot district in the Western part of Pallava territory till about the same time or a little later.

The Ganga Prithvīpati II, grandson of Prithvīpati I, soon afterwards acknowledged the suzerainty of Āditya. Āditya next conquered the Kongu country also, perhaps from the Pāndya ruler Parāntaka Vīranārāyana (860-905), the younger brother of Varaguṇavarman. Āditya was on friendly terms with the contemporary Chera ruler Sthāṇuravi, whose daughter was married to his son Parāntaka. He is said to have built tall stone temples of Śiva on both banks of the Kaveri from the Sahyādri to the sea. He died at Tondaimānād near Kālahasti, and a temple was erected over his remains by his pious son Parāntaka, who succeeded him on the throne in 907 and ruled for forty-eight years. The best part of his reign was marked by increasing success and prosperity, although it ended in disaster and gloom brought about by the hostility of the Rāshtrakūtas which began to pursue him almost from the beginning. Soon after his accession, as early as 910, he invaded the Pāndyan country and assumed the title Maduraikonda (' Capturer of Madura '). The Pāndyan ruler at the time, Mār̤avarman Rājasimha II (905-20), the son of Parāntaka Vīranārāyana, appealed for help to Kassapa V, ruler of Ceylon, who sent an army to his aid. In due course, however, Parāntaka defeated the combined armies at the battle of Veḷḷūr. Rājasimha had to flee to Ceylon and the Chola conquest of the Pāndya country was completed soon after. After staying in Ceylon for some years, Rājasimha left his crown and all his wealth behind, and betook himself to Kerala, the home of his mother. Some years later, in the reign of Udaya IV of Ceylon (940-53), Parāntaka made an unsuccessful attempt to capture the insignia of the Pāndyan king. His failure was remembered and made up for several years later by his powerful descendant Rājendra I.

While the Pāndyan conquest was in progress, Parāntaka had to encounter an invasion from the Rāshtrakūta Krishna II who had succeeded Amoghavarsha in 880. With the aid of his Lāta feudatory and kinsman, Krishna II successfully resisted an invasion by the Gurjara ruler Bhoja I and soon after abolished the viceroyalty of Lāta, extending his own direct rule into that country. His attempt to subjugate the powerful Vengi ruler Guṇaga Vijayāditya III ended in disaster. He had to seek refuge in the court of his father-in-law, the Chedi king Kakkala, whither the Eastern Chālukya general Pandaranga pursued him. The war ended when Krishna submitted to Vijayāditya, in return for which his capital and kingdom were restored to him. He renewed the conflict, however, after the death of Guṇaga Vijayāditya III, in 892, and invaded Vengi before the new ruler Chālukya Bhīma I, a nephew of Vijayāditya, could celebrate his coronation. Chālukya Bhīma was defeated and taken prisoner, but soon regained his freedom, cleared the country of the Rāshtrakūta forces and duly crowned himself king. Some years later Krishna made another unsuccessful attempt to reduce Vengi, but was beaten in two battles at Niravadyapura and Peruvangūru.

One of Krishna's daughters married the Chola monarch Āditya I and bore him a son called Kannaradeva. When Parāntaka became king, at the death of Āditya I, and prince Kannara was kept from the throne, Krishna espoused the cause of his grandson and invaded the Chola territory with the assistance of the Bānas and Vaidumbas. Parāntaka was assisted by the Ganga ruler Prithvīpati II, and a decisive battle was fought at Vallāla, modern Tiruvallam in the North Arcot district, which ended in disaster for Krishna and his allies. The Bānas lost their territory, which was handed over to Prithvīpati II, and the Vaidumbas also suffered for the support they had offered. The Rāshtrakūta war took place before 916.

From about 940 Parāntaka began to experience increasing difficulty in defending his empire. His loyal feudatory, Prithvīpati II, was no more; and as Būtuga II, the ruling Ganga monarch, had married a Rāshtrakūta princess (the sister of Krishna III) the alliance between Gangas and Rāshtrakūtas became closer. Those Bānas and Vaidumbas whom the Chola had uprooted were also by the side of the Rāshtrakūta ruler. To meet the expected trouble from the north-west frontier of his kingdom, Parāntaka stationed his eldest son Rājāditya there with a large army including an elephant corps and some cavalry, and sent another son, Arikulakesari, to assist him.

We must now turn once more to Rāshtrakūta history. Krishna II was succeeded by his grandson Indra III about 915. Even as *yuvarāja*, Indra had checked an invasion from the North by the Paramāra ruler Upendra of Malwa. Upendra sought to take advantage of the preoccupation of Krishna II in the Chola war and invaded the Rāshtrakūta kingdom. Indra defeated him, and compelled him to acknowledge Rāshtrakūta suzerainty. After his accession, Indra waged successful war against the Pratīhāra ruler, Mahīpāla I of Kanauj (913-43). Mahīpāla lost his kingdom for a while though he recovered it later, with the aid of the Chandela ruler, Harshadeva. Towards Vengi, Indra followed the usual policy of setting up opposition to the ruling king Amma I who, however, held his own and ruled the kingdom for seven years till 926. But his death was followed by a period of confused succession disputes which gave Indra III occasion to bring the bulk of the Vengi country under the occupation of his officers and nobles for a period of seven years. Indra was succeeded by his son Amoghavarsha II in 927. After a reign of only three years, he fell a victim to the foul play of his ambitious younger brother

Govinda IV, a dissolute and incompetent ruler, who had Vīramādēvi, a daughter of Chola Parāntaka for his queen. In his turn Govinda was removed from the throne by his feudatories who bestowed the kingdom on Baddega Amoghavarsha III, a half-brother of Indra III. Govinda seems to have sought refuge in the country of his father-in-law, the Chola kingdom. Amoghavarsha III was a gentle and peaceful monarch, but not so his young and energetic son Krishna III, whom he made *yuvarāja*. By waging war against Rācamalla, Krishna enabled his brother-in-law, Būtuga II, to attain the Ganga throne. He became king at the death of his father in 939. Within a few years thereafter he naturally thought of paying off old scores against the Chola power and punishing it for sheltering Govinda IV, and was urged to the task by the insistence of the Bānas and Vaidumbas and perhaps also of Būtuga II. With Būtuga he invaded the Chola kingdom and won a decisive victory (949) in a battle at Takkōlam, six miles to the south-east of Arkonam, in which Būtuga killed Rājāditya with a well-aimed arrow when he was on elephant-back. Even this decisive battle did not mean the collapse of all resistance to Krishna's advance, however, and he still had some years of hard fighting before he could establish himself in the South. Eventually he succeeded in occupying a large part of the northern half of the Chola empire and established his own men in the rule of that country. He assumed the title ' Conqueror of Kacci (Kānchī) and Tanjai (Tanjore) ', and thus caused the Chola empire a rude shock at the close of Parāntaka's reign. Indeed, it almost ceased to exist as its vassals in the south took advantage of its disasters in the north and proclaimed their independence.

Like most of his predecessors Krishna III fomented trouble in Vengi by setting up against Amma II, his elder half-brother, Dānārnava and two princes of a collateral branch, Bādapa and Tāḷa II. With many interruptions Amma continued to hold on to his kingdom until 970 when he was slain in a battle by Dānārnava.

Towards the close of his reign, about 963, Krishna invaded Northern India and compelled the Paramāra ruler, Harsha Sīyaka of Malwa, once more to acknowledge Rāshtrakūta suzerainty. In this expedition Krishna was ably assisted by the Ganga Mārasimha, son of Būtuga II. An able soldier and generous friend, Krishna would appear to have lacked statesmanship, for his policy stored up trouble for his successors. He unduly encouraged the Gangas and irritated the Paramāras without being able to subjugate them. He was reckless in awarding fiefs (*aṇuga jīvita*) to his lieutenants as when he gave the province of Tardavādi in the heart of the empire to Āhavamalla Tailaparasa of the Satyāśraya family, some time before 965.

Krishna III was succeeded by his half-brother Khottiga early in 967. In his reign, the Paramāra Harsha Sīyaka invaded the Rāshtrakūta kingdom after defeating its forces on the banks of the Narmada and sacked the capital Mānyakheta (Malkhed) in 972-3. Once more Mārasimha II assisted his overlord in regaining the capital after the Paramāra forces withdrew. Khottiga died soon after the Paramāra raid, and was followed by his nephew Karka II (973). He was dethroned within a few months by the Chālukya, Taila II, who had been biding his time ever since he got Tardavādi for his fief from Krishna III. Later tradition hailed Taila as an incarnation of the Lord Śrī Krishna who fought 108 battles against the race of Ratta demons and captured 88 fortresses from them. Taila's success was the beginning of the Chālukyan empire of Kalyāni. Mārasimha II made a futile attempt to revive Rāshtrakūta power by setting up Indra IV, the issue of a son of Krishna III by a sister of Mārasimha himself. Mārasimha killed himself by starvation (*sallekhana*) in 975. His feudatory Pāncāladeva who claimed sovereignty over the whole country south of the Krishna river was also killed by Taila in battle. Indra IV also performed *sallekhana* in 982.

In the Chola kingdom, the thirty years (955-85) that followed the close of Parāntaka's reign formed a period of weakness and confusion. His immediate successor was his son Gandarāditya, who with his queen Śembiyan-mahādevi claims a bigger place in the domain of religion than of politics. At his death in 957, the Chola kingdom had shrunk to the size of a small principality, and Krishna III still continued in occupation of Tondaimandalam. Gandarāditya's brother Arinjaya had a short reign (956-7) and was succeeded by his son Sundara Chola Parāntaka II (957-73). His young son Āditya II was made *yuvarāja* almost at the beginning of the reign. Sundara Chola turned his attention to the south, where Vīra Pāndya claimed independence after defeating a Chola king, probably Gandarāditya. As usual, the Pāndya had Mahinda IV, ruler of Ceylon, as his ally. In the war that followed, Sundara Chola defeated Vīra Pāndya in two battles; Āditya II killed Vīra Pāndya on the second occasion. Sundara Chola's forces also invaded Ceylon (959). These wars in the south did not result in the re-establishment of the Chola power there, but better success seems to have attended Sundara's attempts in the north. He is said to have died in 973 in his golden palace at Kānchī while still engaged in directing campaigns in the north. His last years were clouded by a tragedy. Uttama Chola, son of Gandarāditya, conspired to murder the *yuvarāja* Āditya II (969), and then compelled the aggrieved father to recognize him as heir-apparent in preference to his own younger son Arumoḻi (afterwards Rājarāja I). Uttama Chola accordingly became king at Sundara's death (973). By then the bulk of Tondaimandalam had been recovered from the Rāshtrakūtas for the Chola empire. The Rāshtrakūtas had given place to Taila II Chālukya who claims a victory against Uttama Chola about 980.

The real greatness of the Chola empire dates, however, from the accession of Arumoḻivarman, who crowned himself as Rājarāja in the middle of 985. The thirty years of his rule constitute the formative period of Chola imperialism. A relatively small state at his accession, hardly recovering from the effects of the Rāshtrakūta invasion, the Chola kingdom grew under him into an extensive and well-knit empire efficiently organized and administered, rich in resources, and possessed of a powerful standing army and navy, well tried and equal to the greatest enterprises.

Rājarāja began his conquests by attacking the confederation between the rulers of the Pāndya and Kerala kingdoms and of Ceylon. In two campaigns he destroyed the Pāndyas and conquered the haughty Kerala kings by attacking Kāndaḷūr and Vilinam. In a third campaign, a naval expedition, he overran the northern part of Ceylon, forcing Mahinda V to take refuge in the hill country in the south-east of the island. Anurādhapura was destroyed, and Polonnaruva became the capital of a Chola province. Elsewhere Gangapādi, Nolambapādi, and Tadigaipādi, all parts of modern Mysore, were conquered and annexed, which intensified the conflict with the new power of the Chālukyas under Taila II. The first battle fought in 992 went against the Cholas. Rājarāja's chief enemy, however, was Satyāśraya, the son and successor of Taila II. Before recounting their trial of strength we must now turn for a while to Chālukyan history.

After the overthrow of the Rāshtrakūta power, Taila II, who ruled from Mānyakheta, spent several years consolidating his sway in the western Deccan over the whole area between the Narmada and the Tungabhadra. When Paramāra Munja of Malwa invaded his kingdom from the north, he defeated him and put him to death after some years of confinement during which he developed a liaison with Mrinālavati, the sister of Taila II, and was subjected to many humiliations. In all his wars Taila was assisted by his elder son Satyāśraya who became king after his death in 997. Satyāśraya continued the aggressive policy of his father, his chief enemy being the rising Chola power under Rājarāja who was establishing a strong hold on the eastern Deccan by active intervention in the affairs of the Vengi kingdom.

In Vengi, Dānārnava had a short and troubled rule for three years, at the end of which he was slain in battle (973) by the Telugu Choḍa chief, Jaṭā-Choda Bhīma, probably a grandson of Chālukya Bhīma II. Dānārnava's sons sought refuge in exile while Jaṭā-Choḍa Bhīma ruled the Vengi kingdom for twenty-seven years (973-1000), the period described as an interregnum in later Eastern Chālukya inscriptions. Bhīma imposed his suzerainty on the Eastern Gangas of Kalinga and the Vaidumbas. He finally invaded Tondaimandalam and started a war against Rājarāja I because he had received Dānārnava's exiled sons, given his daughter Kundavai in marriage to the younger, and promised to restore the elder (Śaktivarman I) to his ancestral throne. Jaṭā-Choḍa Bhīma was defeated and taken prisoner, so that the way became clear for Śaktivarman to start his rule in the Vengi kingdom, though only as a subordinate of the great Chola monarch who had helped him.

Unable to brook this extension of Chola power into the eastern Deccan, Satyāśraya invaded Vengi in 1006, his general Bāyalanambi reducing the forts of Dhānyakataka (Dharanikota) and Yanamadala to ashes, and established himself in Chebrolu in the Guntur district. Acting on the principle that attack is the best form of defence, Rājarāja ordered his son Rājendra to invade Western Chālukya at the head of a strong army (1007). Rājendra marched up to Donūr in the Bijapur district and, in the words of a Chālukya inscription, ' plundered the entire country, slaughtering women, children and Brahmins'. He also captured Banavāsi and a good part of the Raichur doab, and sacked Mānyakheta. At the same time another section of the army operating from Vengi advanced on Kollipākkai (Kulpak), 45 miles north-west of Hyderabad, and captured its fortress. Satyāśraya was thus compelled to withdraw his forces from Vengi and only with difficulty succeeded in freeing his country of the Chola army, which retired behind the Tungabhadra with much booty.

Towards the close of his reign Rājarāja conquered and annexed the Maldives. He formally installed Rājendra as *yuvarāja* in 1012. The magnificent Śiva temple Rājarājeśvara at Tanjore, completed in 1010, fittingly commemorates the glory of his reign which came to an end with his death in 1014. Rājarāja encouraged Śrī Māra Vijayottungavarman, the Śailendra ruler of Śrī Vijaya (Palembang) and Kaṭāha (Kedah) across the Bay, to build a Buddhist *vihāra* at Negapatam. The *vihāra* was called Cūdāmani *vihāra* after the father of the ruler of Śrī Vijaya.

Rājendra I was a worthy son of his father, and raised the Chola empire to the position of being the most extensive and most respected Hindu state of his time. Early in his reign (1018) he installed his son Rājādhirāja I as *yuvarāja*. He invaded Ceylon and completed the conquest of the island begun by his father. Mahinda V was taken prisoner and transported to the Chola country where he died twelve years later. Thereafter his son Kassapa became the centre of Sinhalese resistance against the Tamil power, and after a war of six months in which a great number of Tamils were killed by the Sinhalese forces, he made himself king of the southern half of the island, Rohana, and ruled as Vikramabāhu I for twelve years from 1029.

Rājendra made a triumphal march at the head of his army through the Pāndya and Kerala countries, and appointed one of his sons as viceroy over both with the title Chola-Pāndya, Madura being the headquarters of the new viceroyalty. About 1020-1, Rājendra had to turn his attention once more towards the Western Chālukya.

Satyāśraya was succeeded in 1008 by his nephew Vikramāditya V who after a short and uneventful reign was followed by his brother Jayasimha II in 1015. Jayasimha had to fight on many fronts. The Paramāra Bhoja of Malwa, wanting to avenge the fate of Munja, invaded the Chālukya kingdom from the north and for some years occupied Lāta and portions of Konkan. After hard fighting Jayasimha succeeded with the aid of his loyal feudatories in recovering the territory occupied by Bhoja. But it was the Chola Rājendra who was his most formidable enemy. Soon after his accession, Jayasimha tried to retrieve the losses sustained in the wars of Satyāśraya and for a time circumstances seemed to favour him, Rājendra being busy with the conquest of Ceylon and the settlement of Pāndya and Kerala. In Vengi, Vimalāditya, who had succeeded his brother Śaktivarman I in 1011, either retired from the throne or died in 1018. Jayasimha II supported the claims of Vijayāditya VII to succeed him against those of Rājarāja, another of Vimalāditya's sons by his Chola queen Kundavai. In the pursuit of this plan Jayasimha crossed the Tungabhadra and occupied Bellary and possibly even a part of Gangavādi. In Vengi, Vijayāditya captured Vijayavāḍa (Bezwada) and made it impossible for his rival Rājarāja to celebrate his coronation. But then Rājendra soon turned his attention actively against Jayasimha and put two forces simultaneously in the field, one marching into the Raichur doab and the other into Vengi for the relief of Rājarāja. In the west Jayasimha was defeated in a battle at Maski, but this led to no further aggression on the part of Rājendra, the Tungabhadra being recognized tacitly as the boundary between the two kingdoms. In Vengi the Chola forces defeated Vijayāditya in several battles, took possession of the country on behalf of Rājarāja and proceeded farther north into Kalinga, probably because the Eastern Ganga ruler of that country, Madhukāmārnava (1019-38), had sided with Jayasimha. After punishing him the army went still farther north for a grand military display in the form of an expedition to the valley of the Ganges. But with the departure of the Chola army to the north, trouble broke out in the rear and threatened its communications. To meet the situation Rājendra I marched towards the north and encamped on the banks of the Godāvari. He tried to secure the line of return for his army which had advanced to the Ganges, and celebrated the coronation of his nephew Rājarāja with due pomp on 16 August 1022. The victorious army from the north joined him soon after, and he returned to the new capital that was rising in the wilds of the Tiruchirāpalli district—Gangaikondaśōḻapuram.

Very soon after, Rājendra sent a large naval expedition against the kingdom of Śrī Vijaya. Śrī Vijaya was the powerful maritime state which ruled the Malayan peninsula, Sumatra, Java and the neighbouring islands, and controlled the sea routes from India to China. The relations between Śrī Vijaya and the Chola empire had been quite friendly in the time of Rājarāja and in the early years of Rājendra's reign when Rājendra's friendship was sought also by the ruler of Kambuja. The Chola monarchs sent embassies, partly diplomatic and partly commercial, to China which reached that country in 1016, 1033, and 1077. Rājendra's war against Śrī Vijaya (1025) occurred between the dates of the first and second embassies to China. Whether it was rendered necessary by an attempt on Śrī Vijaya's part to obstruct the Chola intercourse with China or was simply the result of Rājendra's desire to win glory by extending his *digvijaya* to the countries across the sea, we cannot say. Whatever the reason, the expedition was a complete success. Kaḍāram (Kaṭāha) and the capital Śrī Vijaya itself were sacked and king Sangrāma Vijayottungavarman, Māra Vijayottungavarman's successor, was taken captive. The campaign apparently ended with the restoration of the kingdom to its ruler subject to his acknowledging Chola suzerainty. A fragmentary Tamil inscription from Sumatra bearing the date 1088 shows that active intercourse between the Chola kingdom and Śrī Vijaya was maintained continuously for several generations.

Rebellions in the Pāndya and Kerala kingdoms called for strong action in the course of a fairly extensive campaign conducted by the *yuvarāja* Rājādhirāja, and several princes of the two rebel royal families were either put to death or forced to seek refuge in flight. There was trouble in Ceylon also, where Vikramabāhu kept up the war against the Tamils, and forced Rājādhirāja to lead an expedition against him in 1041. After Vikramabāhu's death, which occurred about that time, anarchy supervened outside the Chola province, and Sinhalese adventurers, dispossessed Indian princes from the Pāndyan country and a certain Jagatīpāla from distant Kanauj asserted authority over portions of the island. They all had this in common however, that they led risings against the Chola power and suffered for it.

In the closing years of Rājendra's reign war broke out once more with the Western Chālukyas and the affairs of Vengi were, as usual, involved in it. In the Chālukyan kingdom Jayasimha II was succeeded by his son, Someśvara I Āhavamalla (1042). He removed the capital from Mānyakheta to Kalyāni, adorning it with many new buildings and generally adding to the amenities of the new capital. He continued the war begun by his father against the Bhoja of Malwa, and received his submission after a raid on his capital Dhārā. He extended his power across Vidarbha and part of modern Madhya Pradesh, into Kosala and Kalinga, and imposed his sovereignty on the Nāgavamśi ruler Dhārāvarsha of Cakrakūta. It deserves to be noted that the Kākatīya chieftain Prola I and his son Beta assisted Someśvara in his wars, and received from him as fief the Anumakonda Vishaya. In another direction Someśvara attacked Vengi and thus challenged the Chola power. In Vengi Rājarāja had no peace after his coronation in 1022. His half-brother Vijayāditya renewed his struggle for the throne, perhaps with the aid of Chālukya Jayasimha II, drove Rājarāja out of Vengi, and made himself king (1031) with the title Vishnuvardhana Vijayāditya VII; but by 1035 Rājarāja had regained his kingdom. Vijayāditya sought refuge in the Western Chālukya court where he was received with open arms and entertained royally. Someśvara's invasion of Vengi was undertaken ostensibly in furtherance of the claims of Vijayāditya and news of it quickly reached Rājendra I. The king was too old to take the field himself, his son Rājādhirāja was engaged in the south, so a trusted Brahmin general, assisted by three able lieutenants, was ordered to go to Rājarāja's relief. The Chola army engaged the enemy in a sanguinary but indecisive battle at Kalidindi. Meanwhile Rājendra I died and was succeeded by Rājādhirāja I (1044). He was eager to restore Chola power in Vengi, and himself led an expedition into the Telugu country soon after he ascended the throne. He defeated the Western Chālukya forces in a battle at Dannaḍa (Dhānyakataka) on the Krishna and compelled Vikramāditya, Someśvara's son, and Vijayāditya, Rājarāja's rival, to retreat in disorder. He then entered Western Chālukyan territory and set fire to the important fort of Kollipākkai (Kulpak). These successes enabled Rājarāja to breathe freely for a time. They were followed by campaigns on the western front where the Chola forces captured several generals and feudatories of the Chālukyas, demolished the Chālukya palace in the city of Kampili, and inflicted a defeat on the enemy in a pitched battle at Pūndūr on the banks of the Krishna. Crossing that river, the victorious camp of the Chola was fixed at Yetagiri (Yadgir), where a pillar of victory with the tiger emblem on it was planted. After more fighting, the Chālukya capital Kalyāni was itself sacked, and Rājādhirāja performed the *vīrābhisheka* (coronation of victor) in the enemy capital and assumed the title 'Vijayarājendra'. A fine image of a *dvārapālaka* which used to be at the entrance to the Dārāśuram temple (Tanjore district) and has since been removed to the Tanjore Art Gallery, bears the Tamil inscription: 'the *dvārapālaka* brought by *Uḍaiyār* Śrī Vijayarājendradeva after burning Kalyānapuram'.

Before 1050, Someśvara succeeded in driving the Chola forces out of his territory. He also re-established his influence in Vengi and compelled Rājarāja to acknowledge his suzerainty in the place of that of the Cholas. Lastly, he sent a counter-expedition into Chola territory which returned after making a dash against Kānchī. These successes were only spurs to further effort on the part of Rājādhirāja, although, for reasons not now clear, he did not make any attempt to recover Vengi or Kalinga where Someśvara had established himself. Rājādhirāja, assisted by his younger brother and *yuvarāja* Rājendra II, led another expedition against Someśvara (1053-4) and a battle was fought at Koppam (Kopbal), a place of great natural strength on the river Krishna. It was hotly contested and Rājādhirāja fell mortally wounded. Rājendra who had held himself in reserve then pressed forward and turned the defeat into victory. He put several Chālukyan generals to death and forced their army to retreat in disorder leaving many elephants, horses, camels, and much booty to fall into the hands of the Cholas along with several women, including some of the queens. Rājendra II crowned himself king on the battlefield and advanced to Kollāpura where he planted a pillar of victory (*jayastambha*) before he returned to his capital, Gangaikondaśōḻapuram.

Anxious to wipe out the disgrace of Koppam, Someśvara soon renewed the war. The death of Rājarāja in Vengi (1061) enabled him to put Śaktivarman II, the son of Vijayāditya VII, on the throne and send a strong force to his assistance under Chāmundarāja. He also sent his sons Vikramāditya and Jayasimha into Gangavādi to invade that part of the Chola territory. Rājendra II met the challenge on both fronts aided by his son Rājamahendra and his brother Vīrarājendra. In Vengi Chāmundarāja was defeated and killed, Śaktivarman II also meeting his end in the same engagement. The Chālukya invaders of Gangavādi were driven back in disorder and heavily defeated in a battle at Kūḍal-

Śangamam, that is, Kūḍali at the junction of the Tunga and Bhadra in the Mysore country. Someśvara's attempt to reverse the verdict of Koppam thus ended in failure (1061-2). Soon after occurred the deaths of the Chola *yuvarāja* Rājamahendra and his father Rājendra II, and Vīrarājendra became king (1063).

The death of Rājendra II necessarily meant a lull in Vīrarājendra's campaigns against the Chālukya. But Someśvara I knew that the attack would be renewed and prepared to meet it on both fronts. In the east he counted on help from his vassals, the Nāgavamśi ruler Dhārāvarsha and the Eastern Ganga Vajrahasta III. He also stationed in the neighbourhood of Bezwada a strong army under Jananātha of Dhārā, a Paramāra prince in his service. In the west, he sent Vijayāditya to carry the war into the enemy country. Vīrarājendra soon returned to the charge as expected. The Chālukya forces suffered small defeats in Vengi, but at first the Cholas did not have any decided success. In the west, Someśvara's forces were defeated with heavy loss on the banks of a river, perhaps Tungabhadra, in 1066. But he soon reorganized his forces and sent a message to Vīrarājendra challenging him to another contest, fixing Kūḍal-Śangamam as its venue. The Chola monarch gladly accepted the challenge and took the field. But Someśvara did not turn up though his forces had assembled at the appointed spot. After awaiting Someśvara's appearance in vain for a month, Vīrarājendra attacked the Chālukya army, inflicted a crushing defeat on it, and set up a pillar of victory on the banks of the Tungabhadra. He then proceeded with his forces to Vengi whither Vijayāditya had also gone earlier to organize the defence on the opposite side. A great battle ensued near Bezwada which ended in defeat for the Chālukya. Vīrarājendra crossed the Krishna and marched into Kalinga, where much fighting followed, and in the neighbouring Nāgavamśi principality of Cakrakūta. There, besides Vijayāditya, and Rājarāja, the son of Vajrahasta III, Vikramāditya also took part on the Chālukyan side, and prince Rājendra, the future Kulottunga I, on that of the Cholas. Meanwhile, unable to endure the illness which had prevented his keeping his martial engagement with Vīrarājendra, Someśvara I met his end and performed *paramayoga* by drowning himself in the Tungabhadra river at Kuruvatti on 29 March 1068. Thus departed one of the greatest rulers of the Chālukya line. He succeeded in keeping Vengi under his control practically throughout his reign and reducing to temporary subjection two major powers of Northern India, the Paramāras and Pratīhāras. In spite of many reverses he maintained the wearisome struggle with the Cholas with undiminished vigour to the end of his life. He was greater as diplomat than as warrior, else he could not have succeeded in making his influence felt by so many states and for so long, and that with a military record none too bright. He had great faith in himself and succeeded in imparting it to his many able generals, including his famous son Vikramāditya. He was not unmindful of the arts of peace; the noble city of Kalyāni was his creation.

Someśvara I was succeeded by his eldest son of the same name, but the ambition of his younger brother Vikramāditya began to assert itself almost from the beginning. Hardly had Someśvara II come to the throne than Vīrarājendra led a vigorous attack against him, laid siege to Gutti and attacked Kampili. Vikramāditya turned the troubles of his brother into his opportunity. He seduced his feudatories from loyalty to their lawful monarch, and with their aid entered into negotiations with Vīrarājendra. The result was a total revolution in the diplomatic relations among the states and a virtual partition of the Chālukyan kingdom. Vijayāditya made his submission to Vīrarājendra and consented to rule the Vengi kingdom as his feudatory. Two of Vīrarājendra's daughters were given in marriage, one to Vikramāditya himself and the other to the Kalinga Ganga prince Rājarāja; and within the Chālukyan kingdom Vikramāditya VI was installed as *yuvarāja* with almost independent rule over the southern half of the empire. Thus it looked as if the eternal feud between the Cholas and the Chālukyas had at last come to an end.

But the death of Vīrarājendra in 1069 altered the situation. Before explaining this, however, we must mention some events of the reign of Vīrarājendra. Some time before 1067 he sent an expedition against Ceylon, where the Sinhalese king Vijayabāhu I was making a strong effort to put an end to the Chola power on the island. Vijayabāhu was defeated and his queen taken captive, he himself being forced to seek shelter at Vātagiri (Wakirigala in Kegalla district). We shall see that better success attended Vijayabāhu within the next few years. Vīrarājendra also sent another naval expedition for the conquest of Kaḍāram on behalf of a prince who had come in search of his aid and protection (1068).

After the death of Vīrarājendra, Vikramāditya found his Chola alliance no longer an asset but a liability. He had to divide his attention between the pursuit of his differences with his brother at home and the protection and maintenance of his young brother-in-law Adhirājendra on the Chola throne against the designs of the Eastern Chālukya prince Rājendra II (Kulottunga I). The intermarriages between the Eastern Chālukya and Chola families and the position of Rājendra Kulottunga in both may be seen from the following table:

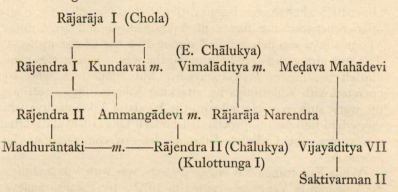

Rājarāja I (Chola)
Rājendra I — Kundavai *m.* (E. Chālukya) Vimalāditya *m.* Meḍava Mahādevi
Rājendra II — Ammangādevi *m.* Rājarāja Narendra — Vijayāditya VII
Madhurāntaki——*m.*——Rājendra II (Chālukya) (Kulottunga I) — Śaktivarman II

The bestowal of the Vengi kingdom on Vijayāditya VII by Vīrarājendra had kept Rājendra (Kulottunga) out of the throne that was rightfully his, and that able prince naturally took advantage of the death of Vīrarājendra to press his claims both to Vengi and to the Chola throne. Vikramāditya proceeded to Kānchī, nipped a rebellion in the bud, installed Adhirājendra formally on the throne at Gangaikondaśōḷapuram and returned after a month to the banks of the Tungabhadra. Soon after, he heard that the Chola king had lost his life in a popular rising and that Rājendra, the ruler of Vengi, had captured the vacant Chola throne. It is thus clear that Rājendra made excellent use of the short interval after the death of Vīrarājendra to expel Vijayāditya from Vengi and capture the Chola throne as well.

Vikramāditya thus found himself placed between two enemies, his brother Someśvara at home and Kulottunga I in the Chola and Vengi countries. It was the task of Vikramāditya during the next six years to extricate himself from this dangerous situation. He continued to undermine the position of his brother Someśvara by inducing the feudatories of the empire to desert his cause.

Among them were, besides his younger brother Jayasimha, and Vijayāditya, who were already on his side, the Kadamba ruler Jayakeśi of Konkan, Vinayāditya and his son Ereyanga of the Hoysala family just coming into prominence, the Pāndya ruler of Uccangi and even the distant Yādava ruler Seuna II of Devagiri. Someśvara had a difficult time, but he did his best with the support of a few loyal lieutenants to maintain himself at the head of the state and entered into an alliance with Kulottunga I. The preparations on both sides, military and diplomatic, were completed by about 1075 when the war began with a clash at Nangili in the Kolar district between the forces of Vikramāditya and Kulottunga. Vikramāditya was defeated and pursued by the Cholas up to the Tungabhadra with heavy fighting all the way. Kulottunga made himself the master of Gangavādi. But Someśvara who co-operated with Kulottunga by attacking Vikramāditya's rear was the worst sufferer. He fell into the hands of Vikramāditya who threw him into prison, proclaimed himself king (1076) and started a new era—the Chālukya-Vikrama era—to commemorate his accession.

While Kulottunga was engaged in the war with Vikramāditya, the kingdom of Vengi was raided in 1072-3 by Yaśahkarnadeva, the Haihaya ruler of Tripuri. This, however, was an episode with no permanent results, military or political, although in another direction Kulottunga sustained a permanent loss of territory. In Ceylon Vijayabāhu resumed his efforts to rid the island of its Tamil rulers and succeeded. From the extreme south of the island he put three armies in the field all of which advanced simultaneously. Polonnaruva fell, and Anurādhapura surrendered in about 1070. Vijayabāhu's coronation as monarch of Lankā, which was delayed by a rebellion, took place in 1072-3. Kulottunga had to reconcile himself to the loss, and Vikramāditya hailed Vijayabāhu as his natural ally and sent him a friendly embassy with rich presents.

Kulottunga could not afford to neglect the revolt of the Pāndya and Kerala countries on the mainland. He led a strong expedition to the south, and after some hard-fought battles at Semponmāri, Kōṭṭāṟu, Vilinam, and Śālai he subjected the whole country once more and compelled the numerous Pāndya and Kerala princes who had opposed him to acknowledge his supremacy. He established a number of military colonies along the important routes of communication in both countries, but the old administrative arrangements of Rājarāja I and Rājendra were not revived and the local rulers were left in charge of internal affairs. About 1084-5 Vijayabāhu of Ceylon declared war on the Cholas when he heard that the envoys he had sent to Vikramāditya VI had been mutilated. While he was preparing the expedition, the *vēḷaikkāra* mercenaries, 'unwilling to fight their Tamil kinsmen, mutinied, and burnt the royal palace. The king fled to Wakirigala, but returning crushed the insurrection, the ringleaders being burnt at the funeral pyre of the royal generals whom they had murdered. The *vēḷaikkāra* forces learnt the lesson, and at the end of the reign set up the fine Tamil stone inscription, still extant at Polonnaruva, in which is recorded their agreement to protect the Tooth Relic temple.'[1] Kulottunga apparently made his peace with Vijayabāhu for one of his daughters, Śuttamalli, married Virapperumāl, a Sinhalese prince.

A Chola embassy of seventy-two merchants reached China in 1077 and received '81,800 strings of copper cash, that is, about as many dollars in return for the articles of tribute comprising glassware, camphor, brocades, rhinoceros horns, ivory, incense, rose water, putchuck, asafoetida, borax, cloves, etc.' There was active trade with Śrī Vijaya during this period, so much so that in 1090 its king sent an embassy to Kulottunga I to consult about the regulation of the affairs of the two *vihāras* his ancestors had erected at Negapatam.

After the death of Vijayāditya VII (1076) Kulottunga sent his sons to rule as viceroys in Vengi: Rājarāja Mummudi Chola (1076-8), Vīra Choda (1078-84), Rājarāja Chodaganga (1084-9), Vīra Choda again (1089-92), and lastly, Vikrama Chola (1092-1118). About 1097 the chieftain of Kolanu entered into a league with Anantavarman Choda Ganga of Kalinga and rebelled against the viceroy. Among those who assisted Vikrama Chola was Parāntaka Pāndya from the extreme south. Kolanu was sacked, and southern Kalinga invaded. The rebel chieftain made his submission, and Anantavarman himself had to follow suit. Some years later, about 1110, Anantavarman Choda Ganga withheld tribute and brought about a second Chola invasion of Kalinga. This was led by the famous general of Kulottunga, Karuṇākara Tondaimān. The invading army spread destruction throughout Kalinga and

[1] Codrington, p. 57.

defeated Anantavarman, who had to seek safety in flight. The victorious Chola army returned with vast booty but the campaign was devoid of any permanent results, though it formed the subject of a celebrated poem, *Kalingattupparaṇi* of Jayangondār.

Up to 1115 the extent of the Chola empire remained undiminished under Kulottunga, except for the loss of Ceylon, and included the entire country south of the Krishna and Tungabhadra extending at least up to the Godāvari on the east coast. The emperor maintained diplomatic relations with distant kingdoms like Kanauj in Northern India, Kambhoja (Cambodia) in Indo-China, and with Kyanzittha (1084-1112), the ruler of Pagan. But towards the end of his reign troubles arose in the Mysore and Vengi countries owing to the renewal of the hostility of Chālukya Vikramāditya to whom we must now turn our attention.

After the accession of Vikramāditya, he as well as his great antagonist Kulottunga recognized their limitations, and suspended active hostilities against each other. Vikramāditya's reign was, in general, peaceful and his court was adorned by learned poets and authors like Bilhana and Vijñāneśvara. About 1083, however, his younger brother Jayasimha rebelled but was defeated in a hard-fought battle and taken prisoner. Jayasimha had appealed to Kulottunga for help but in vain.

More serious danger threatened Vikramāditya from the Hoysalas. Hoysala Vinayāditya and his son Eṟeyanga, as we have seen, served Vikramāditya in the war against Kulottunga. After Vinayāditya, Eṟeyanga ruled for less than two years and was succeeded by Ballāla I (1100-10). These rulers professed allegiance to Chālukya rule but steadily built up their power and extended their territory. The results of this policy declared themselves in the reign of Ballāla's younger brother, Biṭṭiga, better known as Vishnuvardhana. He was a great soldier and an ambitious monarch. He attacked the Chola province of Gangavādi and after defeating Adigaimān, the Chola governor of Talakād, annexed the province (1116). He then turned against Vikramāditya himself and at first attained much success. He won over to his side the Pāndya ruler of Uccangi and Kadamba Jayakeśi II of Goa and advanced to the Krishna in the north. But Vikramāditya dealt firmly with the situation with the assistance of loyal feudatories, particularly Sinda Ācugi II of Yelburga. Vishnuvardhana was expelled from the Chālukyan territory he had attempted to occupy, Goa was sacked and burnt, and the Pāndya was pursued and pressed with great vigour. The Hoysala had to seek safety in the mountain fortresses of his home-country, and thither he was pursued in strength by the imperial forces. There were many battles and the campaign was a long one, but in the end (1122-3) Vishnuvardhana made his submission and returned to his allegiance.

While still engaged in suppressing the Hoysalas, Vikramāditya renewed his designs against Kulottunga; possibly the success of the Hoysalas against that monarch in Gangavādi encouraged him to do so. We cannot say whether he had anything to do with the revolt of the Kolanu chieftain and the contumacy of Anantavarman Choda Ganga which led to two wars during the viceroyalty of Vikrama Chola. But he did interfere in Vengi from about 1115 and much more actively after 1118 when, at the instance of Kulottunga, Vikrama Chola left Vengi for the Chola country as *yuvarāja*. In 1118 Anantapāla, Vikramāditya's famous general, is described as ruler of Vengi, other Chālukyan commanders are found established in other parts of the Telugu country, and the Chola power practically disappears for a number of years thereafter.

Thus Kulottunga sustained another curtailment of his empire which by the end of his reign was practically confined to the Tamil country and a relatively small area of the adjoining Telugu districts. All the same, Kulottunga must take rank among the great Chola monarchs. His long reign was, for the best part, characterized by unparalleled success and prosperity. He avoided unnecessary wars, and the permanent results of his policy appeared under his successors. Until the end of Kulottunga III's reign (1216), for about a century, the empire, though not so extensive as in the eleventh century, held well together, and there was on the whole less of the chronic warfare of the period before the accession of Kulottunga I. The wisdom of Kulottunga's statesmanship lay in adjusting his aims to his resources and in preferring the well-being of his subjects to the satisfaction of his personal vanity. Tradition and epigraphy alike give him the title '*Śungam tavirtta*' (He who abolished the tolls), but there is no account of the nature and scope of this reform.

Vikrama Chola dates his rule from 1118 though his father Kulottunga I continued to live four years longer. The seventeen years of his reign were on the whole a period of peace. He made extensive additions to the temple at Chidambaram to which the Chola monarchs were particularly attached—at least from the days of Parāntaka I—and to the shrine of Ranganātha at Śrīrangam. The death of Chālukya Vikramāditya VI (1126) and the accession of his son, the mild Someśvara III, enabled Vikrama Chola to re-establish Chola power in Vengi. It was a gradual process which began about 1127 and reached its completion in a battle on the banks of the Godāvari about 1133 at which Someśvara was present. Fighting on the Chola side, Velananti Choda Gonka II routed the army of the Western Chālukyas and their Eastern Ganga ally Anantavarman Choda Ganga, taking captive some prominent generals and capturing much booty in gold, horses, and camels. In Gangavādi Vikrama Chola's attempt to restore Chola power was not so successful, though he did recover parts of the Kolar district.

He was followed on the throne by his son Kulottunga II who was formally installed in 1133. He had a peaceful reign till 1150 and associated his son Rājarāja II with the actual conduct of the administration from 1146. Kulottunga II continued the renovation and extension of the temple at Chidambaram begun by his father and in the course of this work he removed the image of Govindarāja from the courtyard of the Natarāja shrine and cast it into the sea. Rāmānuja is said to have recovered it and enshrined it at Tirupati. It was restored to its original place long after by Rāmarāya of Vijayanagar.

Rājarāja II ruled generally in peace till about 1173. Having no son, he chose Rājādhirāja II, the grandson of Vikrama Chola by a daughter, for the succession and appointed him *yuvarāja* in 1166. Rājarāja II's empire extended over the whole of the Telugu country up to Dākshārāma (Drākshārāma) and over large sections of Kongunād and the eastern part of Gangavādi. The hold of the central administration over the outlying parts of the empire was becoming less firm; and even at the centre, the administrative system was beginning to betray signs of weakness. Everywhere feudatory chieftains were becoming more and more assertive.

Soon after the installation of Rājādhirāja II, a fierce succession dispute in the Pāndya country led to the intervention of the Chola and Sinhalese rulers on opposite sides which brought no good to either. Out of the ashes of this civil war arose the Pāndya power which in its renewed strength soon swallowed both the Chola and Ceylonese kingdoms. After the conquest of the Pāndya country by Kulottunga I, the princes of the local royal family were allowed to rule as they liked, subject to the vague suzerainty of the Cholas. Parāntaka Pāndya, as we have seen, took part in the first Kalinga war of Vikrama Chola. But hardly any Chola inscriptions are found in the Pāndya country after the reign of Kulottunga I. About 1166, Parākrama Pāndya of Madura and Kulaśekhara quarrelled about the succession, and Kulaśekhara invested the city of Madura. Parākrama appealed to Parākramabāhu I (1153-86) of Ceylon, but before aid could reach him from Ceylon, Kulaśekhara took Madura and killed Parākrama, his queen and some of his children. In spite of this, Parākramabāhu sent word to his general Lankāpura that he should continue the war until the kingdom of Madura was taken and bestowed on a prince of the house of Parākrama Pāndya. Kulaśekhara put up a brave resistance: the war was so protracted that Lankāpura had to get reinforcements from Ceylon. Kulaśekhara then appealed to the Chola monarch, and a large force was sent to his aid under the command of Pallavarāya. Nevertheless the war went at first against Kulaśekhara who was defeated in a number of battles in the Ramnad district, and the Ceylonese commander installed Vīra Pāndya, a son of Parākrama Pāndya, on the throne. Soon, however, the Chola army under Pallavarāya began to make itself felt and the Sinhalese troops were beaten. The heads of their commanders, including that of Lankāpura, were nailed to the gates of the city in literal fulfilment of the orders of the Chola monarch. Kulaśekhara re-entered Madura, and the conversion of the Pāndya country into a province of Ceylon was thus averted.

Hearing that Parākramabāhu was preparing another attack on the mainland, Pallavarāya espoused the cause of Śrīvallabha, a nephew of Parākramabāhu and a rival claimant to the throne of Ceylon. An expedition was sent with Śrīvallabha at its head and many places in Ceylon were captured and destroyed. Seeing that his attempt to support the line of Parākrama Pāndya had brought on him nothing but disaster, Parākramabāhu now recognized Kulaśekhara as the rightful king, and entered into an alliance with him against the Cholas. Kulaśekhara's treachery was discovered by the capture of Parākramabāhu's letters and presents. The Chola policy at once changed. After further fighting, some of which took place in Chola territory proper, Pallavarāya set up Vīra Pāndya on the throne of Madura and drove Kulaśekhara into exile. Thus Parākramabāhu's designs were frustrated and his candidates steadily kept out of the throne of Madura. All these events may be placed between 1169 and 1177 but that date by no means fixes the end of the struggle.

The growing independence of the central power on the part of feudatories noticed in the reign of Rājarāja II became more pronounced under Rājādhirāja. The Śāmbuvarāya, Kāḍavarāya, Malaiyamān chieftains and the Telugu-Chodas of Nellore were making wars and alliances among themselves in the northern half of the Chola kingdom without any reference to the ruling monarch.

Rājādhirāja II's successor was Kulottunga III whose exact relationship to the main line is not clear. He began his reign in July 1178, though Rājādhirāja lived up to 1182. By his personal ability, Kulottunga delayed the disruption of the Chola empire for about a generation, and his reign marks the last great epoch in the history of Chola architecture and art as he himself is the last of the great Chola monarchs.

Pāndya affairs first claimed his attention. The tireless Parākramabāhu renewed his efforts against the Cholas and even persuaded Vīra Pāndya to make common cause with him, and the ruler of Vēṇāḍ also probably joined the combination. A certain Vikrama Pāndya, perhaps some relation of Kulaśekhara, who must have died in the interval, sought Kulottunga's help against Vīra Pāndya. There followed an invasion of the Pāndya kingdom as a result of which the Pāndya and Sinhalese forces were defeated in battle, Vīra Pāndya being driven into exile, and Vikrama Pāndya installed on the throne of Madura. This campaign must have come to an end before 1182. From his exile, with the aid of his allies, Vīra Pāndya made another effort to retrieve his fortune, but the attempt was crushed on the battlefield of Nettūr. Thence he fled to Ceylon. But there was no further fighting as both the ruler of Vēṇāḍ and Vīra Pāndya made up their minds to submit to Kulottunga, and offered obeisance to him in his open durbar at Madura. On the same occasion, according to (probably exaggerated) Chola inscriptions, Kulottunga 'placed his foot on the crown of the king of Ceylon'. This second campaign occurred sometime before A.D. 1189. Vīra Pāndya was treated better than he had a right to expect. His life was spared and he was allowed some land and other wealth suited to his new station.

After the second Pāndya war, Kulottunga undertook a campaign in Kongu to check the growth of Hoysala power in that quarter. He re-established Chola suzerainty over the Adigaimāns of Tagaḍūr, defeated a Chera ruler in battle and performed a *vijayābhisheka* in Karuvūr (1193). His relations with the Hoysala Ballāla II seem to have become friendly afterwards, for Ballāla married a Chola princess.

Some time later Jaṭāvarman Kulaśekhara, who came to the Pāndyan throne after Vikrama Pāndya in 1190, provoked Kulottunga by his insubordination. About 1205 Kulottunga led a third expedition into the Pāndya country, sacked the capital and demolished the coronation hall of the Pāndyas—conduct which may be taken to prove Kulottunga's consciousness of the increasing weakness of his own position. As the war ended with the restoration of Kulaśekhara, the success of Kulottunga was by no means complete and the seed was sown for a war of revenge.

Kulottunga waged other wars in the north before the Pāndya war of reprisal overwhelmed him towards the close of his reign and the situation was saved to some extent by the intervention of the Hoysalas. These events can only be understood in the light of occurrences outside the Chola empire.

To begin with the Western Chālukyas of Kalyāni, Someśvara III was a peaceful monarch and in his reign Hoysala Vishnuvardhana not only threw off his allegiance to the Chālukyan power, but sought to extend his dominions at their expense, particularly in the regions of Nolambavādi, Banavāsi and Hangal. Vishnuvardhana continued his aggression in the reigns of the two sons of Someśvara III, Jagadekamalla II (1138-51) and his younger brother Taila III (1150-6). By 1149 Vishnuvardhana stationed himself at Bankāpura in Dharwar and left his son Narasimha in charge of his capital Dōrasamudra. The Chālukya empire was beginning to dissolve, although its trappings continued intact and even the Hoysalas occasionally paid nominal allegiance to the emperor, not to speak of the Kalacuris who had held a fief in Tardavādi, in the heart of the empire, from the time of Someśvara III. So also the Kākatīyas, who had received the district of Sabbi 1000 from Vikramāditya VI, and were making other additions to their original fief of Anumakonda; and the Yādavas of Devagiri who had been generally loyal to the Chālukyas from the days of Taila II. Taila III was a feeble and incompetent ruler, and the Kalacuri chieftain Bijjala of Tardavādi won his confidence and arrogated to himself more and more power in quick stages. By 1157 Bijjala assumed imperial titles and a new era may be said to have started; but almost to the end of his reign Taila continued to retain his nominal suzerainty which even powerful monarchs like Hoysala Narasimha I acknowledged, though fitfully. Taila waged war against the Kākatīya Prola II and attacked the city of Anumakonda, but Prola captured him and only released him out of loyalty and mercy. The hostilities, however, outlasted the reign of Prola, and Taila is said to have died of ' dysentery caused by his fear of Rudra ', the son of Prola (1163).

The Kalacuri revolution now ran its course and Bijjala set up rule in the Chālukya capital. He attacked Hoysala Narasimha I and took Banavāsi. He was still ruling in 1168 although a certain Jagadekamalla III was also ruling with full imperial titles at the same time. According to some doubtful legends Bijjala lost his life on account of the hostility of the newly risen sect of Lingāyats whom he persecuted. Three of his sons ruled in quick succession up to 1183, but none of them had the ability to turn Bijjala's usurpation to good account, though they continued to war against the Hoysalas under Ballāla II (1173-1220), son of Narasimha I, and met with some initial successes. In 1183 Someśvara IV, the son of Taila III, became ruler after sweeping away the last remnants of Kalacuri power and thus putting an end to the confusion they had caused. This he was enabled to do by general Brahma or Barmideva who deserted the Kalacuris and went over to the service of Someśvara.

The Yādava feudatory of Someśvara IV, Bhillama (1187-91), was the first to realize the utter weakness of Someśvara's position and take advantage of it. He invaded the Chālukya kingdom and seized its northern districts before 1189. But the Yādavas, like the Kalacuris, experienced difficulty in gaining recognition as an imperial power from those who had stood to the Chālukyas in the same relation as themselves. The Rattas, Śilāhāras, and Kadambas never gave them their allegiance, and the Hoysalas were stimulated to a fresh effort by the example of the Yādavas. Bhillama spent some years in the south organizing his new conquests. His pressure compelled Someśvara and his general Brahma to shift their headquarters to Banavāsi. Kalyāni passed into the hands of the Yādavas. Meanwhile Ballāla II struck a blow on his own account and defeated Someśvara and Brahma in a series of battles, the last of which occurred in 1190. That was the end of the Chālukya power. Someśvara continued to live in obscurity for less than a decade. There naturally ensued a contest between Ballāla II and Bhillama for possession of the empire. Several battles were fought and in the final engagement near Soratūr and Lakkundi near Gadag, Bhillama was defeated (1191), and Ballāla advanced the northern frontier of his empire to the Malaprabha and the Krishna rivers, while the Yādavas retained most of the territory that lay further north. Bhillama founded the city of Devagiri and made it his capital. The Kākatīyas also gained some territory as a result of the final dissolution of Chālukyan hegemony.

Ballāla II was not left in undisturbed possession of his northern conquests. Bhillama was succeeded by his son Jaitugi who declared war against Kākatīya Rudra, killed him and took his nephew Ganapati captive (1196). Rudra was followed by his younger brother Mahādeva on the Kākatīya throne. Mahādeva's short reign was marked by a rebellion and perhaps also by another war with the Yādavas. After Mahādeva's death (1199), Jaitugi released his son Ganapati from prison and set him on the throne. Jaitugi's son and successor Singhana resumed the war against the Hoysala ten years after his accession (1210) and was assisted by the Kadambas of Konkan and other feudatories who had been resisting Ballāla already for some years. As a result of Singhana's campaigns, Ballāla lost almost all the territory he had gained by his wars against Someśvara IV and Bhillama (1216).

In Vengi, from about the end of the reign of Rājarāja II, the Chodas of Velanādu declared their independence. They were followed by the Nellore branch of the Telugu-Chodas which began with Bēta, a feudatory of Vikrama Chola. There is no evidence of the rule of Rājādhirāja II in Nellore or the Northern Circars. But there was a recovery under Kulottunga III whose sway was acknowledged by the Telugu-Choda rulers, Nallasiddha and his brother Tammu Siddha, from 1187 to the end of Kulottunga's reign. There was, however, an interlude during which Nallasiddha occupied Kānchī in 1192-3 and was driven out of the city by Kulottunga III in 1196. The Telugu-Chodas made another and a more successful bid for independence towards the close of

Kulottunga's reign when he was hard pressed by a Pāndya invasion of the Chola country, as we shall see in the following chapter. Kulottunga waged war once again in the north in 1208 when he claims to have subdued Vengi and entered the Kākatīya capital, Wārangal, perhaps an exaggeration because the Kākatīya kingdom was ruled at the time by the powerful monarch Ganapati.

There is little steady light on the history of the Chera country in this period. There are inscriptions of the several kings of the ninth century of whom Sthāṇuravi, the contemporary of Āditya I noticed above, was the most important. He ruled in the last quarter of the ninth century, and the Syrian Christian Kottayam copper plates are associated with him. These grants record the settlement of workmen on the church called Tariśāpalli erected at Kollam by one Iso Tapir. Sthāṇuravi was perhaps succeeded by Vijayarāgadeva, described as manager of the temple or palace (*kōyil adigārigaḷ*) in the Kottayam plates, and as Kerala rāja in the Tiruvoṟṟiyur epigraph. Among the kings that followed, Bhāskara Ravivarman (*c.* A.D. 1047-1106) deserves mention. Śrīvallabhan Kodai and Govardhana Martāndavarman of Vēṇāḍ were his contemporaries. A copper-plate grant now in the possession of the Jews of Cochin was issued by Bhāskara Ravivarman: it records a royal gift to Isuppu Irappan (Joseph Rabban) of the rights of the Anjuvaṇṇam together with the 72 proprietory rights, such as the collection of tolls and other revenue as also the perpetual right to use a palanquin, for him and his successors. The inscriptions of Bhāskara Ravivarman have been found spread over a relatively large area from Changanasseri in the south to Tirunelli temple in Wynāḍ taluq in the north. Under Rājarāja I and his successors, the Chola rule extended over the bulk of Chera country. The country revolted during the troubles preceding the accession of Kulottunga I whose reconquest of and establishment of military colonies in south Chera country have been noticed above. In the twelfth century there are inscriptions of the rulers of Vēṇāḍ, identified with Cheranādu on the one hand, and Kūpakadeśa on the other; one of these rulers was conquered by Parāntaka Pāndya, a feudatory of Vikrama Chola.

In this age as in the last the form of government was hereditary monarchy. But there was little in common between the simple, personal rule of the earlier time and the Byzantine royalty of this age with its numerous palaces, officials, and ceremonials, and its majestic display of the concentrated resources of extensive empires. The coronation was an important and impressive ceremony and the occasion of great liberality. The Chālukyas held the ceremony usually at Pattadakal (literally 'the coronation-stone'), the Cholas at different places—Tanjore, Gangaikondaśōḻapuram, Chidambaram and sometimes Kānchipuram. Succession disputes were not unknown, but generally the rule of succession in the eldest male line was respected, and the choice of the *yuvarāja* during the lifetime of the reigning monarch diminished the chances of dispute. The murder of Chola Āditya II by his uncle Uttama Chola was an extreme and unusual assertion of political ambition, viewed with more leniency than it deserved by the ruling king Parāntaka II and his son Rājarāja I. Vikramāditya VI, whose ability was equal to his ambition, trumped up charges of misrule against his elder brother before waging war on him and deposing him. Chola Rājarāja I initiated the system of prefacing the stone inscriptions of the reign with an account in set terms of its chief events kept up to date by additions from time to time. The relations between the emperor and his feudatories varied with time and circumstance. The administration of the Chola empire was stricter and more centralized than that of the Chālukyas, who employed a staff of highly trained diplomats (*sandhivigrahis*) to serve as liaison officers between the emperor and the feudatories in the various parts of the empire. Princes of the royal family were often employed as viceroys over important sections of the empire.

The royal household comprised numerous servants of varied descriptions including bodyguards of sorts. The coronation hall and kitchen establishments comprised mostly women. The palace servants of the Cholas were organized into *vēḷams* and settled in separate quarters in the capitals. Chau Ju-kua, a Chinese author of the early thirteenth century, observed of the Chola kingdom: 'At state banquets both the prince and four court ministers salaam at the foot of the throne. Then the whole company present break into music, song and dancing. He (the prince) does not drink wine but he eats meat, and, as is the native custom, dresses in cotton clothing and eats flour cakes. For his table and escorts he employs fully a myriad dancing girls, 3,000 of whom are in attendance daily in rotation.' The Chālukya palace had a *manevergaḍe* (chamberlain) and a *bhāṇasavergaḍe* (steward) besides other officials. The princes of the royal family and the nobles all maintained similar establishments suited to their own tastes and means.

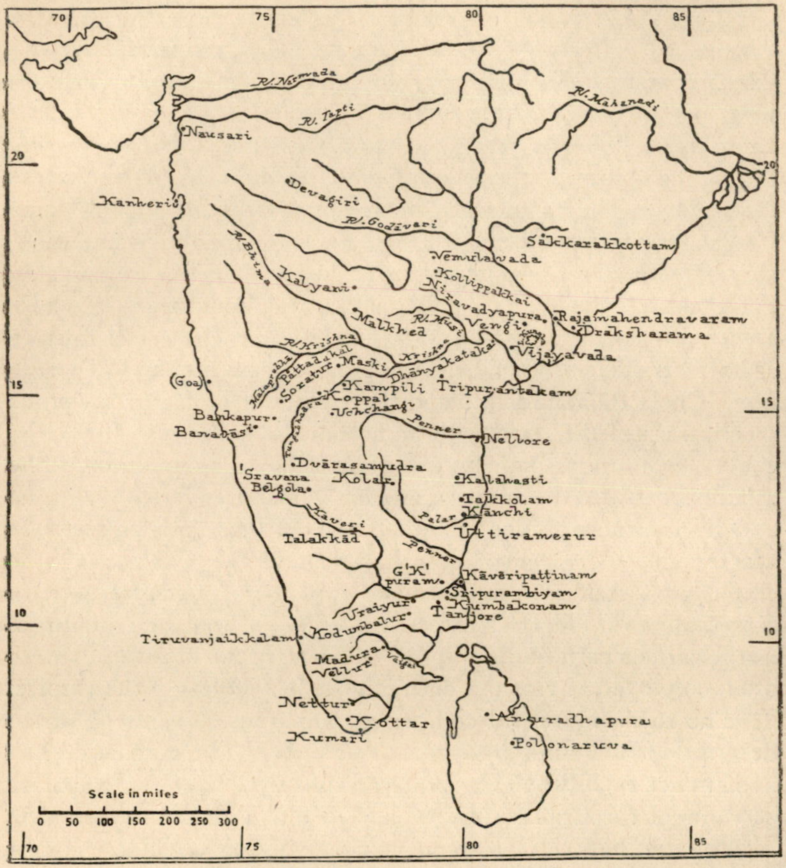

SOUTH INDIA: A.D. 850-1200

The monarch disposed of business by means of oral orders, but an elaborate procedure was observed both before securing them and in putting them into execution. The Chola monarch had an *uḍankūṭṭam*, immediate attendants, a group of ministers representing all the chief departments of administration to advise him on the disposal of business, besides a chancery (*ōlai*). There were corresponding officials in the Chālukya court.

The Chola administrative machinery was an elaborate and

complicated bureaucracy comprising officials of various grades. The officials tended to form a separate class in society, organized in two ranks, an upper *perundanam* and a lower *śiṟudanam*. Offices tended to become hereditary and there was no clear distinction

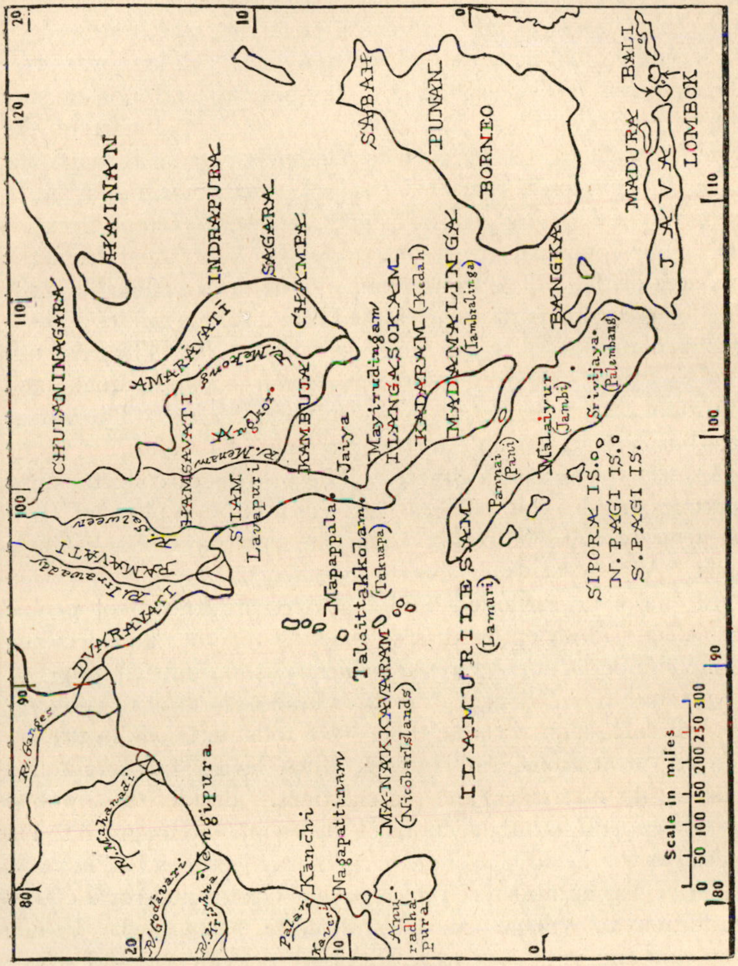

GREATER INDIA

between civil and military employment. We know little of the methods of recruitment or the principles that governed promotion. The officials were often remunerated by assignments of land (*jīvitas*) suited to their station. Titles of honour and shares in booty taken in war formed other rewards of public service.

For purposes of administration the empire was divided into convenient areas with lower subdivisions in the Chola empire, the divisions in descending order being *vaḷanāḍu* or *maṇḍalam*, *nāḍu*, and *kūṟṟam*. Large townships formed a separate *kūṟṟam* by themselves, being known as *taniyūr* or *tankūṟṟam*. Land revenue being the mainstay of public finance, great care was bestowed on the recording of land rights and revenue dues. All land was carefully surveyed and classified into tax-bearing and non-taxable lands. In every village and town, the residential part of the village (*ūr nattam*), temples, tanks, channels passing through the village, the *paṟaccēri* (pariahs' hamlet), *kammāṇaccēri* (artisans' quarters), the burning ground (*śuḍugāḍu*) were exempt from all taxes. The total extent of such areas was subtracted from the gross area of the village to ascertain the net area of taxable land. In its turn, taxable land was classified into different grades according to its natural fertility and the crops raised on it. The existence of immunities and exemptions in favour of individuals and institutions was also carefully noted in the accounts. The village as a whole was responsible for the payment of the entire revenue due from it to the king's officers. The process of collection was sometimes harsh, and villages had reason to complain of their treatment by royal officers even in the best days of the Chola empire. When central control weakened, local oppression became more unrestrained, and instances are known of people from villages in an entire district meeting together and deciding upon common action to resist arbitrary and unusual imposts. The revenue was collected in cash or kind according to convenience. Besides land revenue there were tolls on goods in transit, taxes on professions and houses, dues levied on ceremonial occasions like marriages, and judicial fines. Besides these public dues of a general nature, sections of the people often agreed to tax themselves voluntarily for some particular object they had in view.

Justice was administered by regularly constituted royal courts in addition to village courts and caste *panchāyats*. Usage, documents and witnesses were admitted as evidence, and where no human evidence was forthcoming, trial by ordeal was resorted to; sometimes titles to property were proved by the self-immolation of people who were ready to prove the title with their lives. Treason (*rājadrōham*) was dealt with by the king himself and involved confiscation of property besides death as punishment.

Fines and imprisonment were the common punishment for ordinary crimes, and Chau Ju-kua notes: 'When any one of the people is guilty of an offence one of the court ministers punishes him; if the offence is light the culprit is tied to a wooden frame and given fifty, seventy, or up to an hundred blows with a stick. Heinous crimes are punished with decapitation or by being trampled to death by an elephant.'

The most striking feature of the Chola period was the unusual vigour and efficiency that characterized the functioning of the autonomous rural institutions. A highly developed committee system (*vāriyams*) for the administration of local affairs was evolved and the *sabhā* of Uttiramērūr which revised its constitutional arrangements twice at short intervals in the reign of Parāntaka I is only the leading example of a number of similar attempts going on everywhere to evolve improved methods of administration in the light of experience. Besides the staff of village officials engaged in the routine affairs of village administration, there were special arrangements by which a local chieftain or a powerful official undertook to protect life and property in a particular area in return for a separate police tax (*pāḍikāval kūli*) paid to him and the need and importance of this system increased with the weakening of the central government.

This sketch of administration in its details has had particular reference to the Chola empire, but the conditions elsewhere in South India were generally similar though the administrative terms differed in the different kingdoms.

Speaking generally, the medieval polity has the appearance of being designed specially for the benefit and comfort of the upper classes of society and would seem to have neglected the common man. But the excesses to which the system was liable corrected themselves more or less automatically by the social uses to which wealth was put. The rich generally sought distinction by competing in the service of the gods and of the poor. To build a temple, endow a *maṭha* and to attach a school or a hospital to either, to reclaim land and to promote irrigation, such were the most common roads to social eminence and public recognition. The king, the nobles and the temples drew largely in various ways upon the products of the industry of the common people. But much of this wealth was returned to them in ways that advanced their common good. It was a wonderful social harmony based not on equality of classes or individuals but on a readiness to give and take, a mutual goodwill that had its roots deep down at the foundations of communal life.

BIBLIOGRAPHY

H. W. Codrington: *A Short History of Ceylon* (London, 1929)

J. D. M. Derrett: *The Hoysalas* (Oxford University Press, 1957)

J. F. Fleet: *Dynasties of the Kanarese Districts* (*Bombay Gazetteer*, Vol. I, Pt. ii, 1896)

F. Hirth and W. W. Rockhill: *Chau Ju-kua* (St. Petersburg, 1912)

H. C. Ray: *Dynastic History of Northern India*, 2 Vols. (Calcutta, 1931, 1936)

K. A. N. Sastri: *Colas*, Vols. I and II (Madras, 1935, 1937), Second edition 1955.

N. Venkataramanayya: *The Eastern Chālukyas of Vengi* (Madras, 1950)

CHĀLUKYAS OF KALYĀNI

1. Taila II *m.* Bonthādevi A.D. 973-97

2. Satyāśraya Iṟivabeḍanga A.D. 997-1008 — Daśvarman *m.* Bhāgyavatī

Mahādevi *m.* Iṟivanolambādirāja

3. Vikramāditya V 1008-15 — 4. Ayyana 1015 ? — Akkādevī — 5. Jayasimha II 1015-42

6. Someśvara I 1042-68 — Āvalladevi *m.* Seuna Bhillama III

7. Someśvara II 1068-76 — 8. Vikramāditya VI 1076-1126 — Jayasimha III

Jayakarna — 9. Someśvara III 1126-38

10. Perma Jagadekamalla II 1138-55 — 11. Tailapa III 1149/50-63 — 12. Jagadekamalla III 1163-83

13. Someśvara IV 1184-1200

EASTERN CHĀLUKYAS

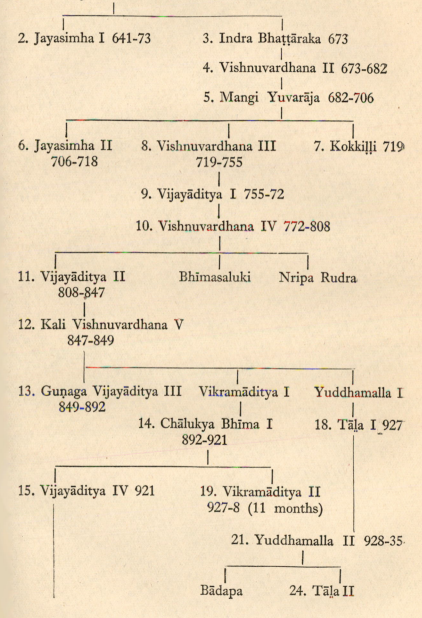

1. Kubajavishnuvardhana A.D. 624-641
   - 2. Jayasimha I 641-73
   - 3. Indra Bhaṭṭāraka 673
     - 4. Vishnuvardhana II 673-682
       - 5. Mangi Yuvarāja 682-706
         - 6. Jayasimha II 706-718
         - 8. Vishnuvardhana III 719-755
           - 9. Vijayāditya I 755-72
             - 10. Vishnuvardhana IV 772-808
               - 11. Vijayāditya II 808-847
                 - 12. Kali Vishnuvardhana V 847-849
                   - 13. Guṇaga Vijayāditya III 849-892
                   - Vikramāditya I
                     - 14. Chālukya Bhīma I 892-921
                       - 15. Vijayāditya IV 921
                       - 19. Vikramāditya II 927-8 (11 months)
                   - Yuddhamalla I
                     - 18. Tāḷa I 927
                       - 21. Yuddhamalla II 928-35
                         - Bādapa
                         - 24. Tāḷa II
               - Bhīmasaluki
               - Nripa Rudra
         - 7. Kokkiḷḷi 719

EASTERN CHĀLUKYAS (*continued*)

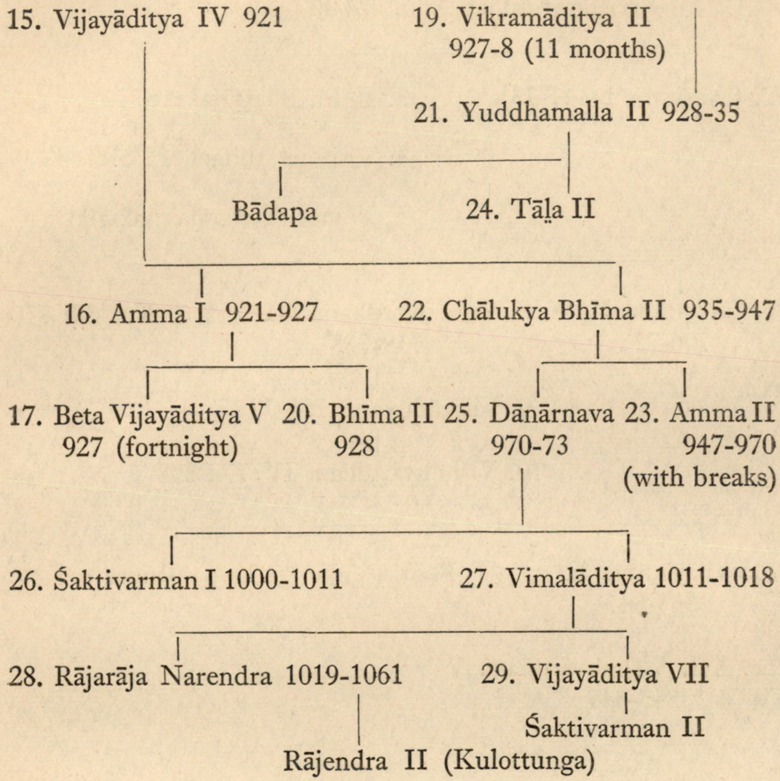
15. Vijayāditya IV 921
19. Vikramāditya II
927-8 (11 months)
21. Yuddhamalla II 928-35
Bādapa
24. Tāḷa II
16. Amma I 921-927
22. Chālukya Bhīma II 935-947
17. Beta Vijayāditya V
927 (fortnight)
20. Bhīma II
928
25. Dānārnava
970-73
23. Amma II
947-970
(with breaks)
26. Śaktivarman I 1000-1011
27. Vimalāditya 1011-1018
28. Rājarāja Narendra 1019-1061
29. Vijayāditya VII
Śaktivarman II
Rājendra II (Kulottunga)

CHOLAS

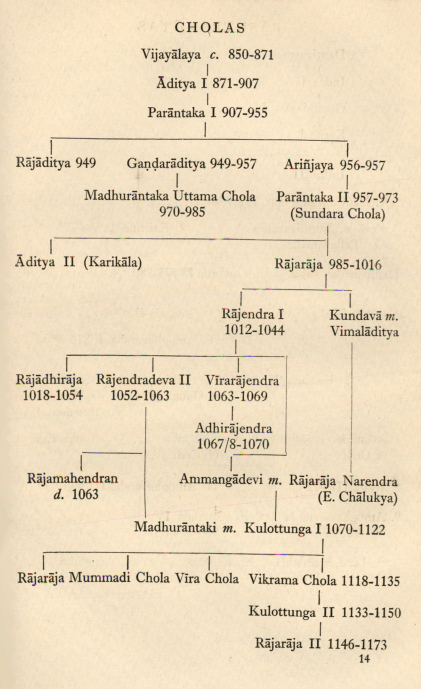

- Vijayālaya *c.* 850-871
  - Āditya I 871-907
    - Parāntaka I 907-955
      - Rājāditya 949
      - Gaṇḍarāditya 949-957
        - Madhurāntaka Uttama Chola 970-985
      - Ariñjaya 956-957
        - Parāntaka II 957-973 (Sundara Chola)
          - Āditya II (Karikāla)
          - Rājarāja 985-1016
            - Rājendra I 1012-1044
              - Rājādhirāja 1018-1054
              - Rājendradeva II 1052-1063
                - Rājamahendran *d.* 1063
                - Madhurāntaki *m.* Kulottunga I 1070-1122
              - Vīrarājendra 1063-1069
                - Adhirājendra 1067/8-1070
              - Ammangādevi *m.* Rājarāja Narendra (E. Chālukya)
            - Kundavā *m.* Vimalāditya
              - Rājarāja Narendra (E. Chālukya)

- Ammangādevi *m.* Rājarāja Narendra (E. Chālukya)
  - Madhurāntaki *m.* Kulottunga I 1070-1122
    - Rājarāja
    - Mummadi Chola
    - Vīra Chola
    - Vikrama Chola 1118-1135
      - Kulottunga II 1133-1150
        - Rājarāja II 1146-1173

RĀSHTRAKŪTAS

```
Dantivarman
    |
Indra I
    |
Govindarāja I
    |
Karka I
    |
    |_____
    |                                |
Indra II                            |
    |                                |
1. Dantidurga c. A.D. 752-756       |
    |                                |
Revā m. Nandivarman        2. Krishna I 756-775
    Pallavamalla                     |
    |                      _____|_____
    |                     |                     |
Dantivarman Pallava   3. Govinda II 775-780  4. Dhruva 780-92
    |                     |                          |
 ___|_____|_____        ___|_____
|          |            |                 |      |            |
Kambha  Karka  Suvarnavarsha  5. Govinda III 792-814  Indrarāja
                              |
                        6. Amoghavarsha I 814-880
                              |
        _____|_____
       |                      |                          |
7. Krishna II 880-915      Abbalabbe                  Śankhā
       |                 m. Ganga Būtuga I         m. Pallava
       |                                          Nandivarman III
       |                                                 |
Lakshmī m. Jagattunga m. Govindāmbā        Nripatunga Pallava
   of Cedi |              |        of Cedi
          _|_____|_____
         |                                           |
8. Indra III 915-27              11. Amoghavarsha III 935-939
    ___|_____                              |
   |                   |                             |
9. Amoghavarsha II   10. Govinda IV                  |
   927-930             930-934/35                     |
                      ___|_____|_____
                     |                  |                          |
                12. Krishna III   13. Khottiga              Nirupama
                    939-966           967-97                    |
                     |                                   14. Karka 972-973
                    son
                     |
                15. Indra IV
```

CHAPTER X

THE AGE OF THE FOUR KINGDOMS

General outline—Pāndya revival under Māṟavarman Sundara—Chola Rājarāja III aided by Hoysalas against Pāndya and Kādava Kōpperunjinga—Chola recovery under Rājendra III shortlived—Jaṭāvarman Sundara Pāndya and his wars—Māṟavarman Kulaśekhara and Hoysalas—Pāndya conquest of Ceylon—end of Kulaśekhara's reign—Hoysala Rāmanātha, Narasimha III and Ballāla III—Kerala—Yādava Singhaṇa, Krishna, Mahādeva and Rāmachandra—Kākatīya Ganapati, Rudrāmbā and Pratāparudra II—Gangas of Kalinga.

Marco Polo on Ma'bar, Kāyal, horse-trade, pearl-fishing, and social conditions—on Ceylon and west coast.

THE Chālukya empire disappeared at the end of the twelfth century and the Chola tottered at the beginning of the thirteenth. For a century thereafter, the history of South India is the history of the four kingdoms that rose on the ruins of the vanished empires and filled the annals of the century with their mutual antagonisms. The kingdoms were the Pāndya and the Hoysala in the south, and the Kākatīya and Yādava in the north. Minor powers like the Telugu-Chodas of Nellore played their part as auxiliaries to the chief powers. The period was marked by no striking developments in polity or society although industry, trade and the arts continued to flourish with their normal vigour. Marco Polo who visited many parts of the country in 1292-3 gives a vivid account of prevailing conditions. The Muslim invasions of the Deccan which began towards the end of the century upset all the four kingdoms and caused a period of confusion terminated by the rise and expansion of the Bāhmanī and Vijayanagar kingdoms in the second quarter of the fourteenth century.

Jaṭāvarman Kulaśekhara, the Pāndya ruler whom Kulottunga III humiliated in a signal manner in 1205, was followed on the throne, more than ten years later, by his younger brother, Māṟavarman Sundara Pāndya (1216). Sundara wanted to avenge the wrongs he had shared with his brother and invaded the Chola territory soon after his accession. Kulottunga's age and the swiftness of the attack rendered Chola resistance feeble. After sacking Uṟaiyūr and Tanjore, Sundara Pāndya drove his suzerain into exile along with his *yuvarāja*, Rājarāja III. Sundara performed a *vīrābhisheka* in the coronation hall of the Cholas at Āyirattali, Tanjore district, and marched up to Chidambaram where he worshipped at the famous shrine of Naṭarāja. On his way back he fixed his camp at Pon Amarāvati (Pudukkōṭṭai).

SOUTH INDIA: A.D. 1200-1325

Meanwhile Kulottunga had appealed for aid to Hoysala Ballāla II who promptly sent an army under his son Narasimha to Śrīrangam. Sundara Pāndya therefore had to make peace and restore the Chola kingdom to Kulottunga and Rājarāja after they made formal submission at Pon Amarāvati and acknowledged him as suzerain. This was the beginning of the second empire of the Pāndyas though it was not yet quite the end of that of the Cholas.

Kulottunga III died soon after (1218) and Rājarāja III proved to be an incompetent ruler under whom confusion increased and the dissolution of the Chola kingdom was hastened. In some unknown way a company of Oḍḍa (Oriya) soldiers penetrated to the heart of the Chola country (*c.* 1223) and created disturbances in Śrīrangam until they were dislodged by Sundara Pāndya (1225). In the north, Hoysala forces were present in Kānchī, perhaps pursuing hostilities with the Telugu-Chodas of Nellore and their suzerains, the Kākatīyas. The Kādava chieftain Kōpperunjinga became more and more powerful and entered into an alliance with Sundara Pāndya against the Cholas and their Hoysala protector. Little realizing the increasing difficulty of his position, Rājarāja III defied Sundara Pāndya by withholding the annual tribute due to him and starting hostilities. Sundara Pāndya repelled the feeble Chola invasion and took the offensive. Rājarāja was defeated with much loss of wealth and his chief queen was taken prisoner. Sundara Pāndya performed a *vijayābhisheka* at Muḍikondaśōḻa-puram (Āyirattali). Rājarāja made an attempt to join his allies, the Hoysala forces of Narasimha II in the north, but he was intercepted and, after a battle at Teḻḻāṟu, was taken prisoner by the Kādava Kōpperunjinga and confined in the fortress at Śēnda-mangalam.

Hearing of the disasters that had befallen the Chola monarch, Narasimha II promptly moved to his aid. He attacked and over-powered the ruler of the Magara kingdom (Salem and South Arcot), an ally of the Kādava, and marched towards Śrīrangam. From there he sent an army under his generals Appanna and Goppayya with instructions to carry destruction into the country of Kōpperunjinga and to reinstall the Chola emperor. The generals carried out their instructions to the letter. They captured many important places held by Kōpperunjinga and, after a battle at Perambalūr, advanced by way of Toḻudūr to Chidam-baram, punishing on the way some officers of Rājarāja and Parāk-ramabāhu, a prince of Ceylon, who had joined the enemy. After worshipping the god of Chidambaram, they devastated the country south of the river Gaḍilam and east of Śēndamangalam. Finally they made preparations to invest that fortress when Kōpperunjinga sent word to Narasimha that he was ready to restore the Chola emperor to liberty and his throne, and Narasimha transmitted the offer to his commanders. They then received the Chola emperor with honour and accompanied him back to his country (1231).

Meanwhile Narasimha himself had met Sundara Pāndya in battle at Mahendramangalam on the Kaveri and defeated him. Sundara Pāndya had to acquiesce in the restoration of Rājarāja. The war with the Kādava went on for some more years, but peace was finally made among the Hoysalas, Pāndyas, and Cholas and sealed by dynastic marriages. Someśvara (1233-4), the son and successor of Narasimha II, is called uncle (*māmaḍi*) by the successors of both Sundara Pāndya and Rājarāja III.

Rājarāja continued to rule until 1256, the extent of his empire outside the Pāndya country nominally being the same as at the beginning of his reign in spite of reverses. But instances of treason, disorder, and alliances for mutual defence among local chieftains and of defiance of express orders issued by the king were becoming more and more numerous, while Hoysala influence over the whole area of the Chola kingdom and even in the Pāndya country increased steadily from about 1220 to 1245, a period which may be well described as that of Hoysala hegemony in the south. This was due to Someśvara leaving the administration of his home territory in the hands of his ministers and devoting all his time to the consolidation of the Hoysala position in the Tamil country.

Rājendra III, who was installed as *yuvarāja* in 1246, was a much abler prince than Rājarāja III. He made a strenuous effort to revive Chola power and would have succeeded even better than he did but for Someśvara's interference. Rājendra attacked the Pāndyas and defeated two Pāndyan princes, one of whom was Māṟavarman Sundara Pāndya II (*acc.* 1238). Someśvara now took the side of the Pāndyas to prevent the complete restoration of Chola authority, defeated Rājendra in battle and then made peace with him. In the north Rājendra commanded the alliance of Choḍa Tikka of Nellore, also called Gandagopāla, who had been attacked by Someśvara in 1240. Tikka by his wars checked the power of the Śāmbuvarāyas and Kādavarāyas and thereby strengthened that of Rājendra. He even fought against Someśvara though he took Kānchī for himself as a reward for his services and had another allegiance, namely that to Kākatīya Ganapati of Wārangal, also an enemy of the Hoysalas.

The alliance between Rājendra and Someśvara became closer after the accession to the Pāndya throne of the celebrated Jaṭāvarman Sundara Pāndya in 1251, one of the most famous warriors and conquerors of South India under whom Pāndyan power attained its greatest splendour. In the first years of his reign Sundara Pāndya fought many wars and rapidly extended his sway to Nellore and beyond, and to Ceylon, confining the Hoysalas to the Mysore plateau. Kānchipuram became a secondary Pāndya capital, while Ceylon and Kerala were firmly held and administered for a time. In his wars, Sundara commanded the active co-operation of other princes of the royal family, Jaṭāvarman Vīra Pāndya (1253) being most prominent among them.

Sundara Pāndya proceeded with a small force against the Chera king Vīraravi Udaya Mārtāndavarman, and destroyed him and his forces after ravaging the Malainādu. He compelled the warlike Chola Rājendra to acknowledge his suzerainty and pay him tribute. He invaded Ceylon and exacted a vast quantity of pearls and many elephants from its ruler. He then attacked the Hoysalas in the region of the Kaveri and captured the fortress of Kannanūr Koppam. Several Hoysala generals were killed, including the brave Singana, while numerous elephants and horses were captured together with a large amount of treasure and a number of women. Sundara only stopped fighting when Someśvara withdrew into the plateau; but shortly afterwards Someśvara renewed the war in which he was to meet his death at Sundara Pāndya's hands (1262). Sundara then attacked the rich city fortress of Śendamangalam and fought several engagements 'which struck terror into the heart of the Kādava' (Kōpperunjinga). Having thus become master of his territory, forces and treasure, Sundara restored him to the rulership of his land and left for Chidambaram where he worshipped Naṭarāja before proceeding to Śrīrangam. 'Here he wore the garland of victory, performed many *tulābhāras*, which pleased the eyes and hearts of all spectators and evoked blessings from learned poets'; and in that temple which he roofed with gold he sat upon a splendid throne with his queen, wearing a golden crown and 'emulating the morning sun rising on the top of the mountain'.

Sundara Pāndya's conquests included the Magadai (Bāna) and Kongu countries which must have been taken during the wars against the Hoysalas and Kōpperunjinga. Finally, he led an expedition further north in which he killed Gandagopāla in battle and occupied Kānchī. He also came into conflict with Kākatīya Ganapati and his other feudatories, defeated a Telugu army at Muḍugūr (Nellore district) and drove a Bāna chief into exile. At the end of the campaign he performed a *vīrābhisheka* at Nellore.

Between 1262 and 1264, on an appeal for help from a minister of Ceylon, Jaṭāvarman Vīra Pāndya invaded the island, defeated and killed one Ceylonese prince and received the submission of another as also that of a son of Chandrabhānu of the Malay peninsula who ruled over a principality in the north of Ceylon. Both the Pāndya invasions of the island fell in the reign of Parākramabāhu II who appears never to have gained mastery over the northern half of the island but left its fate to be settled by local adventurers and foreign invaders.

The vast treasure that fell into the hands of Sundara as a result of his wars was used to beautify and enrich impartially the great shrines of Śiva and Vishnu at Chidambaram and Śrīrangam.

Sometime before his death, Hoysala Someśvara, being pressed by enemies from both north and south, had effected a virtual division of his kingdom, assigning the northern half to his elder son Narasimha III and the southern Tamil area to his younger son Rāmanātha. After his father's death, Rāmanātha recovered Kannanūr and held his own against Sundara Pāndya who died in 1268 and was succeeded by Māṟavarman Kulaśekhara I, also a great ruler.

During this period the rule of the Pāndya kingdom was shared among several princes of the royal family, one of them enjoying primacy over the rest. Such an arrangement seems to have been of long standing in that country; even Kulottunga I is said to have subjugated five Pāndya princes together. Kulaśekhara pressed the war against Hoysala Rāmanātha, who had allied himself closely with Chola Rājendra III, and defeated both in 1279. That is the last we hear of Rājendra III and the Cholas. Kulaśekhara became unquestioned master both of the Chola country and of those Tamil districts of the Hoysala empire over which Rāmanātha had ruled. He also fought in Kerala (Travancore) where, perhaps, he suppressed a local rising. Sometime later he took advantage of a famine in Ceylon to send his minister Āryachakravarti to invade the island where he 'laid waste the country on every side', entered the fortress of Śubhagiri (Yāpahu), and carried away to the Pāndya country 'the venerable Tooth Relic and all the solid wealth that was there'. This was at the close of the reign of Bhuvanaikabāhu I, and there followed a period of some twenty years during which the island formed part of the Pāndya empire. The next ruler of Ceylon, Parākramabāhu III (1303), adopted peaceful methods with Kulaśekhara, went on a personal embassy to the Pāndya court, and persuaded Kulaśekhara to surrender the Tooth Relic. Ceylon regained her independence only during the civil war and the Muslim invasion that followed Kulaśekhara's death (1308-9). His last years were embittered by quarrels between his sons. He wanted his younger son by a favourite mistress, Vīra Pāndya, to succeed him. The result was that the elder son, Sundara Pāndya, started a war after the death of his father, for which, according to some writers, Sundara was himself responsible. The war went in favour of Vīra Pāndya, and Sundara had to invoke the aid of the Muslim invader Malik Kafur (1310).

After the loss of his Tamil territory Hoysala Rāmanātha started a civil war against his brother Narasimha III who was hard pressed by other enemies like the Yādavas of Devagiri and the Kākatīyas. Rāmanātha succeeded in capturing some territory for himself in the Bangalore, Kolar, and Tumkur districts, and ruled it with Kundāni as his capital. Narasimha III died in 1292 and was succeeded by Ballāla III. His accession was not disputed by Rāmanātha who, however, kept up a hostile attitude till his death three years later, as did his son Viśvanātha also for a few years until he too disappeared from the scene. Ballāla then once more ruled over a united Hoysala kingdom before 1300. He took advantage of the civil war in the Pāndya country that followed the death of Kulaśekhara, and went out to the aid of one or other of the parties in the hope of regaining the territory lost by Rāmanātha. But his plans were thwarted by the sudden appearance of Malik Kafur in his rear.

In the thirteenth century in Kerala, some kings of Vēṇāḍ known chiefly from their donative records claim to belong to the Yadukula, thus tracing their descent from the Āy kings of the eighth century who in turn connected themselves with Āy Aṇḍiran of Śangam literature. In the last quarter of the century Ravivarman Kulaśekhara who calls himself Chera emperor shot into a short-lived eminence by raiding extensive territories including the Pāndya country and right up to Kānchipuram and Poonamallee; he was an accomplished ruler and liberal patron of letters. Kollam (Quilon) was his capital. His exploits will be referred to again in the next chapter. Not far removed from him in time was Vīrarāghava Chakravarti, author of the Kottayam plates conferring the title of Maṇigrāmam and certain other honours on Iravikoṟṟan; the grant is attested among others by the authorities of Vēṇāḍ, Odanāḍ, Ernāḍ and Valluvanāḍ, important divisions of the Kerala country.

After this period, the history of Kerala remains as fragmentary and obscure as ever, and becomes mixed up with the rivalries of the Portuguese and the Indian powers and those among the Dutch, English and French themselves later. It does not lie within the scope of this book to study these developments which link up medieval with modern times in India, and in the following chapter the history of Kerala particularly the wars between Calicut and Cochin and the activities of the European Companies together with their consequences will be left on one side.

To turn now to the northern states, the Yādava Jaitugi was succeeded by his son Singhana (1200-47) under whom the Yādava empire attained its greatest extent. He invaded Gujarat twice in 1231-2 and 1237-8, while in the south he waged war first against Hoysala Ballāla II and deprived him of considerable territory to the south of the Krishna and Malaprabha. He still kept up the pressure against the Hoysalas in the reign of Narasimha II, who had to abandon the Sagar taluq and the Bellary district. Narasimha's successor Someśvara, however, succeeded in retrieving the position sufficiently for him to be able to encamp near Pandarpūr in 1236 and to endow the Vitthala temple of that place by the grant of a village. Singhana's general Vīcana, the governor of the southern province, not only drove him back but carried his arms into Hoysala country up to the banks of the Kaveri (1239). Indeed, so disastrous were Someśvara's sallies against the Yādavas that by the end of his reign he had lost even more territory to them than his predecessors had. Singhana's empire, on the other hand, was extended and established by Vīcana all over what had been the central, western, and south-western regions of the Western Chālukya empire. Singhana also waged rather indecisive wars against Kākatīya Ganapati and the ruler of Malwa.

Singhana's chief astrologer was Changadeva, the grandson of the famous astronomer Bhāskarācārya, and son of Lakshmīdhara, the chief pundit of Jaitugi I. He founded a college at Patna for the study of his grandfather's *Siddhāntaśiromaṇi* and other works.

The Yādava throne descended to Singhana's grandson Krishna (1247-60)—his son Jaitugi II having died in his father's lifetime. Although he lost some territory in the south-western Andhradesh to Kākatīya Ganapati, he may be said in general to have passed on undiminished the extensive empire he had inherited. His reign is chiefly remarkable for its literary activity: his minister and general Jalhana compiled an anthology of Sanskrit verse, and Amalānanda's *Vedāntakalpataru* also dates from this time. Krishna himself seems to have been a religious man who performed many sacrifices.

Krishna was succeeded by his brother Mahādeva (1260-71). He fought a successful war against Kākatīya Rudrāmbā, capturing her elephants and some of her insignia but sparing her life as she was a woman. He invaded northern Konkan, defeated its Śilāra ruler Someśvara in a naval battle and annexed his territory to the Yādava empire. The celebrated Hemādri was minister (*śrikaraṇādhipa*) under him and his successors. A voluminous writer himself, Hemādri encouraged many other writers by his patronage, and built so many temples that a style of architecture came to be associated with his name.

Krishna's son Rāmachandra succeeded to the throne in 1271 after a short war with Āmana, the son of Mahādeva, who tried to usurp his place. Rāmachandra also waged other wars, by no means decisive in their results, against the ruler of Malwa and the Kākatīya Pratāparudra II, Rudrāmbā's successor. About 1276-7, his famous general Sāluva Tikkama invaded the Hoysala territory of Narasimha III and laid siege to the capital Dōrasamudra. He returned with much booty from a victorious campaign, but left Narasimha in full possession of his territory. Narasimha's brother Rāmanātha was also attacked but with no decisive results. Hostilities against the Hoysalas continued into the reign of Ballāla III, who attempted to extend the kingdom northward, but the advance of Muslim power in the Deccan during the last decade of this century considerably curbed Rāmachandra's activity. The great Maratha saint Jñāneśvara flourished during his reign and completed his great Marathi exposition of the *Gītā* on the banks of the Godāvari in 1291.

Turning to the Kākatīyas, perhaps the ruler with most claim to greatness was that Ganapati whom Jaitugi had released from prison and set on the throne. In his long reign of over sixty years (1199-1262) he earned the reputation of being a good administrator. In the Andhra country, the power of the Velanānti Chodas had disappeared after 1186, and its distracted political condition was an invitation to a ruler like Ganapati to enter and exploit its fertile lands, its iron and diamond mines and its ports. This conquest he completed between 1209 and 1214 and made the Telugu-Chodas of Nellore acknowledge his suzerainty. Their wars with Kulottunga III, after their capture of Kānchī, involved him, as we have seen, in hostilities with that monarch also. He also fought against Ananga Bhīma III (1211-38) of Kalinga, who was hard pressed by his Muslim enemies from the north and by the Chedi rulers of Tummana, and in another indecisive war about 1231 with the Yādava Singhana. More decisive was his defeat (1239) of the Kāyasthas in Cuddapah and Kurnool, represented by Gangaya Sāhini and his nephews Tripurāntaka and Ambadeva. Soon after this, Ganapati proclaimed his daughter Rudrāmbā heir-apparent, even calling her by the masculine name Rudradeva Mahārāja, and associated her actively in the administration. He also issued a charter of security to foreign merchants trading in Mōtupalli. Jaṭāvarman Sundara Pāndya's aggressive wars, that brought him into conflict with the Telugu-Chodas and their suzerain Ganapati, have been narrated already. When Sundara Pāndya withdrew, Ganapati, at the instance of the poet Tikkana, assisted Manuma Siddhi, the son of Choda Tikka, against his domestic enemies and seated him firmly on the Nellore throne. Even that turbulent Kādava chieftain Kōpperunjinga acknowledged Ganapati's overlordship.

Ganapati's daughter Rudrāmbā was his successor. The early years of her reign were marked by troubles created by Kōpperunjinga and other rebellious feudatories, but these were firmly suppressed by the loyal Kāyastha chieftain Ambadeva. Yādava Mahādeva invaded Rudrāmbā's kingdom with results already noted. The hostility of the Yādavas continued after Mahādeva's reign, and the young prince Pratāparudradeva, grandson of Rudrāmbā, won his spurs as a warrior in these conflicts. He was made *yuvarāja* about 1280, and when, eight years later, Ambadeva rebelled and got support from the Hoysalas and Yādavas, the *yuvarāja* succeeded in suppressing the revolt by about 1291.

Pratāparudra II succeeded his grandmother in 1295 and ruled till 1326. Early in his reign one of his generals led an expedition into Kuntala, capturing the forts of Ādavāni (Adoni) and Raichur, among others, after driving out the Yādava garrisons, and brought the territory under Kākatīya rule. Pratāparudra reformed the administrative system by dividing the kingdom into 77 nāyakships, confining recruitment thereto to the Padmanāyaka community and thoroughly overhauling the staff of *nāyakas*. Some of the great *nāyakas*, like Kāpaya Nāyaka, who later played a great part in resisting the Muslims, were the products of this system which, incidentally, was later adopted and elaborated by the rulers of Vijayanagar.

Throughout the thirteenth century, and later, the Gangas continued to rule the kingdom of Kalinga. In the reign of Rājarāja III (1198-1211), grandson of Anantavarman Choda Ganga, occurred the first Muslim invasion of Orissa. The army sent by Ikhtiyār-ud-din Muhammad-i-Bhaktyar Khilji (1205) againt Jajnagar was successfully repulsed. Similar results attended another effort against Orissa by the Bengal Muslims between 1211 and 1224 in the reign of Rājarāja's successor Aniyanka Bhīma III. Aniyanka Bhīma also fought against Kākatīya Ganapati, and his troops went as far afield as Kānchipuram and possibly even Śrīrangam. His son Narasimha I (1238-64) took the offensive against the Muslim rulers of Bengal and fought three campaigns against them, though they were not uniformly successful. Bhānudeva II (1306-28) was definitely defeated by the Tughlak invasion under Ulugh Khan and had to surrender a number of elephants to the victor. In his turn, Bhānudeva III (1352-78) had to face Firoz Tughlak to whom he had to submit as a condition of peace. The last great Ganga ruler was Narasimha IV (1378-1414), in whose time the Muslim ruler of Malwa tried to invade Orissa but without gaining any advantage. This long-lived dynasty ended with Bhānudeva IV (1414-32) who died childless, leaving the throne to be occupied by his commander-in-chief Kapileśvara Gajapati.

We may stop for a while for an account of the impressions gathered by Marco Polo, that 'prince of medieval travellers', who spent several months in South India and used them very well. The name by which the country was known to foreigners was Ma'bar, a word which in Arabic signifies 'passage' or ferry, and was applied to the part of the Indian coast most frequented by travellers and merchants from Arabia and the Persian Gulf. Ma'bar 'extends in length from Kulam (Quilon) to Nilawar (Nellore)', says a contemporary Muslim chronicler. Writing on Kāyal, the chief emporium of the Pāndya kingdom, Marco Polo says that the king to whom the city belongs 'possesses vast treasures and wears upon his person a great store of rich jewels. He maintains great state and administers his kingdom with great equity and extends great favour to merchants and foreigners so that they are very glad to visit his city.' 'It is at this city that all the ships touch, that come from the west as from Hormos and from Kis and from Aden, and all Arabia, laden with horses and with other things for sale. And this brings a great concourse of people from the country round about, and so there is great business done in this city of Cail.' Marco Polo notes that a great part of the wealth of the country was wasted in purchasing horses, a statement fully confirmed by the observations of contemporary Muslim chroniclers who say that the unfavourable climate of South India and the ignorance of Indian horse-keepers necessitated large annual imports of fresh animals. From the earliest times, the Pāndya country has been famous for its pearls, and Marco Polo gives a substantially correct account of the fisheries, adding that the king derived great revenue from them. 'Moreover nobody is permitted to take out of the kingdom a pearl weighing more than half a *saggio* unless he manages to do it secretly.' Marco Polo describes at some length the institution of the King's Trusty Lieges, the band of bodyguards sworn to defend the king with their lives. Amazed at the scantiness of the dress worn by the common people, Marco Polo exaggerates their nakedness and denies the existence of tailors in the country, though tailors are mentioned in inscriptions long preceding Marco Polo's visit. He mentions the custom of *satī* and refers to the practice of allowing a condemned criminal who was sentenced to death to sacrifice himself to some god or other of his choice. He says quaintly: 'And let me tell you the people of this country have a custom of rubbing their houses all over with cowdung. Moreover all of them, great and small, king and barons included, do sit upon the ground only. . . . It is their practice that everyone, male and female, do wash the body twice every day; and those who do not wash are looked on much as we look on the Patarins. You must know that in eating, they use the right hand only . . . . So also they drink only from drinking vessels, and every man hath his own; nor will anyone drink from another's vessel. And when they drink they do not put the vessel to the lips but hold it aloft and let the drink spout into the mouth. . . . They are very strict in executing justice upon criminals and as strict in abstaining from wine. Indeed they have made a rule that wine-drinkers and seafaring men are never to be accepted as sureties.' He mentions the custom by which a creditor drew a circle round his defaulting debtor and 'the latter must not pass out of this circle until he shall have satisfied the claim, or given security for its discharge.' He mentions the presence of experts in the arts of physiognomy, astrology and sorcery, and the readiness of people to consult them. He refers to temples as 'certain abbeys in which are gods and goddesses to whom many young girls are consecrated' (*devadāsis*). He notices the widespread use of betel leaves with camphor and other aromatic spices mixed with quicklime. He notes that 'the nobles and great folks slept on beds made of very light cane work, hanging from the ceiling by cords for fear of tarantulas and other vermin: while the common folk slept on the streets'.

He mentions the richness of Ceylon in precious stones and narrates the legends he heard about Adam's Peak. He records the embassy sent to Ceylon in 1284 by Kublai Khan to get from there some of the hair and teeth of Adam. He sets down in detail the legends narrated to him of St Thomas the Apostle, and the manner of his death in the neighbourhood of Mylapore. He knew that the Andhra country was ruled by a queen (Rudrāmbā), a lady of much discretion, and he describes the different methods by which diamonds were gathered from the mines in her kingdom. He adds: 'In this kingdom also are made the best and most delicate buckrams and those of the highest price; in short, they look like tissue of spider's web! There is no king nor queen in the world but might be glad to wear them. The people have also the largest sheep in the world, and great abundance of all the necessaries of life.'

He notices the presence of Jews and Christians in the kingdom of Quilon and says that the king was tributary to no one. Pepper and indigo were abundant in the country which was visited regularly by merchants from China, Arabia, and the Levant. 'Corn they have none but rice. So also their wine they made from (palm-) sugar; capital drink it is, and very speedily it makes a man drunk. All other necessaries of a man's life they have in great plenty and cheapness.'

In the kingdom of Eli (Mount D'Ely), pepper and ginger and other spices in quantities were to be had, but any merchant ship touching its ports by stress of weather was seized and had its cargo plundered. Piracy was rampant throughout the Malabar coast. 'The ships that come from the East bring copper in ballast. They also bring hither clothes of silk and gold and sandals; also gold and silver, cloves and spikenard, and other fine spices for which there is a demand here and exchange them for products of these countries.'

BIBLIOGRAPHY

R. G. BHANDARKAR: *Early History of the Dekhan* (*Bombay Gazetteer*, I, ii, 1894)

H. W. CODRINGTON: *Short History of Ceylon* (London, 1929)

J. D. M. DERRETT: *The Hoysalas* (Oxford University Press, 1957)

J. F. FLEET: *Dynasties of the Kanarese Districts* (*Bombay Gazetteer*, I, ii, 1896)

K. A. N. SASTRI: *Colas*, Vol. II (Madras, 1936)

—: *Foreign Notices of South India* (Madras, 1939)

—: *The Pāndyan Kingdom* (London, 1929)

HOYSALAS (1022-1342)

1. Nripakāma 1022-1047

2. Vinayāditya 1047-1098

3. Eṟeyanga 1063-1100

4. Ballāla I 1100-1110

5. Vishnuvardhana 1110-1152

Udayāditya

6. Narasimha I 1152-1173

7. Ballāla II 1173-1220

8. Narasimha II 1220-1238

9. Someśvara 1233-1267

10. Narasimha III 1254-1292

Rāmanātha 1254-1295

11. Ballāla III 1291-1342

Viśvanātha 1295-1300

12. Ballāla IV

KĀKATĪYAS

1. Beta I 1000-1030
   |
2. Prola I 1030-1075
   |
3. Tribhuvanamalla Beta II 1075-1110
   |
4. Prola II 1110-1158
   |
   - 5. Pratāparudra I 1158-1196
   - 6. Mahādeva 1196-1199
     - 7. Ganapati 1199-1262
       - 8. Rudrāmbā 1262-1296
         |
         Mummaḍāmbā *m.* Mahādeva
         |
         9. Pratāparudra II 1295-1326
       - Ganapāmbā
     - Mailāmbā

CHAPTER XI

THE BĀHMANĪS AND THE RISE OF VIJAYANAGAR

First Khilji invasion of the Deccan and subjugation of Devagiri—subsequent invasions—Malik Kafur—invasion of Hoysala and Pāndya countries—Hindu reaction—kingdom of Kampili—Pāndya civil war and Tughlak invasion—end of the Yādava and Kākatīya kingdoms—rebellion of Baha-ud-Din Garshasp and its results—fall of Kampili—movement for liberation—Kāpaya Nāyaka and Ballāla III—Harihara and Bukka—Vidyāranya—foundation of Vijayanagar—Sultanate of Madura and Ballāla III—expansion of Vijayanagar till 1346.

Foundation of the Bāhmanī kingdom—Ala-ud-din I Bahman Shah—Muhammad I—Mujahid—Daud—Muhammad II—Ghiyas-ud-din—Shams-ud-din—Firuz—Ala-ud-din II Ahmad—Humayun—Nizam Shah—Muhammad III—Mahmud—end of the Bāhmanī kingdom—nominal rule of the four sons of Mahmud.

THE sultanate of Delhi was established towards the close of the twelfth century, and for a hundred years thereafter its attention was confined to Northern India. The idea of subjugating the Deccan and the land beyond began with the Khiljis, although the first Muslim attack on a Deccani kingdom was a quasi-private enterprise planned in secret and carried out with suddenness. The story is that Garshasp Malik, the future Ala-ud-din, nephew and son-in-law of Sultan Jalal-ud-din, resented the supercilious conduct of his wife towards him and wanted to punish her. Before he could do so, however, he had first to gather strength and resources enough to be able to oppose the sultan and his sons. First he obtained the sultan's permission to lead an expedition against Malwa, but in fact went much farther south and advanced rapidly against the Yādava kingdom of Devagiri (February 1296) at a time when its army was engaged on a distant expedition. The reigning king, Rāmadeva, was overwhelmed by the swiftness of the onslaught, and sued for peace at the end of a week's siege of his capital. He surrendered much treasure and many elephants and horses, and even gave one of his daughters in marriage to the conqueror. When Singana, his son, heard of the threat to the capital, he hastened back with his army and wanted to resume hostilities. By the time he arrived, however, peace had been concluded, Rāmadeva was in the hands of the enemy, and Singana himself also had to make his submission, at least for the time.

Rāmadeva's kingdom was restored and he and Ala-ud-din exchanged vows of lifelong friendship. The treasure he took from Devagiri played no small part in paving Ala-ud-din's way to the throne which he seized soon after by murdering Jalal-ud-din.

As sultan, Ala-ud-din pursued a policy of plunder and loot in the South in preference to the extension of his territories. In 1303-4 he sent an expedition against Wārangal by way of Bengal. It was led by Malik Fakhr-ud-din Juna (later Muhammad bin Tughlak) and ended in failure; the Telugu army met the invader before he could reach Wārangal, inflicted severe losses on him, and compelled him to retreat. This disaster so lowered the prestige of the sultanate in the Deccan, that Singana of Devagiri withheld the tribute his father had agreed to pay and gave shelter to the refugee king of Gujarat and his daughter who had fled their country to escape falling into the hands of the sultan's forces. Either out of loyalty to Ala-ud-din or pursuit of a deeper policy Rāmadeva denounced his son, and asked Ala-ud-din to take steps to restore his authority before it was too late. An army was sent immediately (1307) under the sultan's favourite slave Malik Kafur; Singana was defeated near Devagiri and fled. Malik Kafur plundered the city, took possession of the kingdom in the name of his master and carried off Rāmadeva and his family as prisoners to Delhi. But the sultan treated Rāmadeva with great kindness; he kept him by his side for six months before sending him back, loaded with money and presents, to rule over a kingdom extended by the addition of portions of Gujarat. The sultan's generosity was rewarded, for Rāmadeva remained loyal to him for the rest of his life and gave valuable aid to his forces in their operations in the South.

Later in 1309 Malik Kafur was sent against Wārangal to wipe out the disgrace of the last defeat sustained by the imperial armies at that place. He first proceeded to Devagiri where Rāmadeva was all attention to his requirements. Thence he crossed the Yādava territories and entered the Telugu country, reaching the neighbourhood of Wārangal by rapid marches early in 1310. The siege of the double-walled city lasted a month; the outer fortress was taken by storm, and the consequent overcrowding in the inner fort made it imperative for Pratāparudra to open negotiations with the invader. The sultan's price for raising the siege was the surrender of a vast amount of treasure, many elephants and horses, and an annual tribute. Malik Kafur returned to Delhi with the booty in June 1310 where he was received with honours by his master.

Early next year, Malik Kafur again set out on another expedition to the South, this time against the kingdoms of Dōrasamudra and Ma'bar, i.e., the Hoysala and Pāndya kingdoms in the far South. Devagiri again became the base of operations, where Rāmadeva was glad to offer help, for the Hoysala ruler, Ballāla III, was no friend of his, having at one time seized some of his territory. Kafur's army waited to attack the Hoysalas until Ballāla was away on an expedition in the Pāndya country. That land was disturbed by quarrels among Kulaśekhara's sons, and Ballāla hoped to turn the situation to his advantage and to regain territory that Kulaśekhara had seized some time before. Kafur's advance was therefore practically unchecked and he spread destruction and panic throughout his journey to the Hoysala capital. Ballāla returned in haste, but saw that resistance was hopeless, and overruled his nobles and officers who wanted to fight. He consented to become a tributary (*zimmi*) to the sultan and to surrender his wealth, elephants and horses.

Kafur spent less than a fortnight in Dōrasamudra, and then started towards Ma'bar. Ballāla accompanied him and guided the army along the difficult mountain routes that led from the tableland to the plains. Though divided among themselves, the Pāndya princes were at one in resisting the invader, harassing him incessantly, but avoiding pitched battles and taking care not to shut themselves in fortresses that might easily be reduced. Malik Kafur first marched against Bīr Dhūl, the capital of Vīra Pāndya in the neighbourhood of Uṟaiyūr. The king escaped before the city fell into the enemy's hands, and Kafur's further operations were hampered by rains. He braved the weather, however, and pursued Vīra Pāndya who was reported to have fled to Kandūr (not identified). On the way he seized a convoy of treasure from the backs of a hundred and twenty elephants, but even when he reached Kandūr, and took it, there was no sign of Vīra Pāndya. He therefore marched to Kānchipuram (or Marhatpuri to the Muslim historians) where he plundered and desecrated the temples before returning to Bīr Dhūl. Thence he planned a sudden descent upon Madura, the Pāndya's main capital, where Sundara Pāndya was king; but Sundara was forewarned and abandoned the city, taking his family and treasure into the country. At this stage Vikrama Pāndya, Sundara's uncle, came out of retirement to lead the Pāndyas against the Muslims and inflicted a decisive defeat on them. Malik Kafur was 'obliged to retreat and bring back his army'; but he managed to keep the vast booty he had taken from Vīra Pāndya and convey it safely to Delhi. He reached the imperial capital in October 1311 and later presented Ballāla III's son to the sultan, speaking highly of the help the invaders had received from his father. The Hindu prince was treated with kindness and then sent back to his father whose kingdom was also returned to him. The Ma'bar expedition was thus only a military raid, and not a very successful one at that; it had no permanent results, though indeed South India was drained of a vast amount of treasure: 'six hundred and twelve elephants, ninety-six thousand *mans* of gold, several boxes of jewels and pearls, and twenty thousand horses', according to Barni.

About a year later, in 1312, Rāmadeva died and his son Singana came to the throne of Devagiri. His hostility to the sultanate was well known, and Malik Kafur was sent out with an army once again, this time to seize and annex the Yādava kingdom to the empire of Delhi. This was easily accomplished, without any fighting, as Singana fled. Kafur behaved with moderation to convince the people that they had nothing to fear from their new rulers. He regulated administrative affairs with commendable wisdom, though in one respect he was inexorable; he insisted on pulling down temples and erecting mosques in their place. A great mosque was built at Devagiri itself and named after the sultan in accordance with his wishes. Nevertheless, considerable areas of the Yādava kingdom did not submit to the new rule, and the kingdom of Kampili proclaimed its independence under Singeya Nāyaka and his more famous son Kampiladeva. This new kingdom included the present Bellary, Raichur and Dharwar districts, and three important forts—Kampili itself, Kummata and Hosadurg (Anegondi?)—all on the Tungabhadra. Malik Kafur led one indecisive expedition against Kampili; and before he could make another attempt he was recalled to Delhi where he died in the political revolution that intervened between the death of Ala-ud-din (1316) and the accession of Kutb-ud-din Mubarak Shah.

The same revolution led to the voluntary withdrawal of the Muslim government from Devagiri because Kafur recalled the lieutenant he had left behind. Harapāla Deva, Rāmadeva's son-in-law, was thus able to re-establish the Yādava power for a time, but soon after his accession, Mubarak Khilji again marched south in 1318, with an army led by his favourite slave Khusrau Khan, resolved to retake Devagiri. The reduction of Harapāla involved some hard fighting in mountainous country; he was wounded in the final encounter, taken prisoner and put to death—flayed alive, according to Barni. The sultan's return to Delhi was delayed by rains, so during his enforced stay in Devagiri he reorganized the administration. Malik Yak Lakhy was made governor of Devagiri; subordinate officers and collectors of revenue were stationed at different places, and garrisons posted at strategic points. An attempt to force a garrison on the Hoysala capital Dōrasumudra failed. When the sultan returned to Delhi (August 1318) he left Khusrau Khan behind to deal with Pratāparudra II of Wārangal who had not sent his annual tribute after the death of Ala-ud-din. Khusrau therefore marched in, collected all the arrears due and easily restored the sultan's supremacy.

Shortly afterwards, however, Khusrau had to march south again to suppress the rebellious governor of Devagiri and then to bring the country of Ma'bar under Muslim rule. Malik Yak Lakhy had set up independent rule under the title Shams-ud-din and began to mint coins in his own name; but his easygoing and profligate nature made him thoroughly unpopular, so that the nobles of his court joined together to capture him and hand him over to Khusrau when he advanced towards Devagiri. The unfortunate rebel was sent, bound hand and foot, to Delhi, while Khusrau proceeded further southward.

The civil war between Vīra Pāndya and Sundara Pāndya continued after Malik Kafur's return (1311). Sundara fared so badly in the struggle that at first he sought Muslim aid which was given only in very small measure and availed him little. The ruler of south Travancore, Ravivarman Kulaśekhara, who professed allegiance to Sundara till about 1312, took advantage of the confusion to invade the Pāndya country and marched as far north as Kānchipuram. Vīra Pāndya seems to have joined him, and Sundara Pāndya appealed to the Kākatīya ruler Pratāparudra II for aid. A large army was sent in his support in 1317, under the leadership of Muppidi Nāyaka, the governor of Nellore, who defeated Ravivarman Kulaśekhara and Vīra Pāndya, compelled the former to withdraw into his own kingdom, and installed Sundara Pāndya on the throne at Vīradhavalapattanam (Bīr Dhūl). Then came Khusrau's invasion. The Pāndya followed his usual policy of evading battle by evacuating his capital, taking his family and all his wealth with him. A rich Muslim merchant who stayed behind hoping his religion would protect him was robbed and insulted by Khusrau, and finally committed suicide. Nevertheless, Khusrau's expedition was not a success. Rains hampered his movements; and, what is more, he himself seems to have contemplated rebellion. When this was discovered and disapproved of by his followers, he had to submit to being carried back in fetters to Delhi.

The political revolution in Delhi which ended Khilji rule and ushered in that of the Tughlaks gave Pratāparudra II the opportunity of declaring himself free once again. His example spread and caused disaffection even in that part of Mahārāshtra which was under a governor of the sultanate. Ghiyas-ud-din Tughlak resolved, therefore, to do away with the Hindu kingdoms of the South one after another until the sway of Islam extended to Cape Comorin. He began in 1321 by sending against the kingdom of Wārangal an expedition led by his son and heir, Ulugh Khan. The army marched as usual by way of Devagiri laying waste the country and investing fortresses as soon as it entered Telengana. Pratāparudra retreated and shut himself and his forces up in the well stocked and strongly fortified capital city. The siege that followed lasted six months, at the end of which dissensions arose in the camp of the invaders, his lieutenants turned against Ulugh Khan and entered into negotiations with Pratāparudra. The Hindu monarch agreed to let them go back in peace, and when they did so, he fell upon the rump of the army under Ulugh Khan and compelled it also to retreat. Nor was it left in peace until Ulugh Khan entered into negotiations with the rebel section of his army and succeeded in interposing it between himself and the Wārangal forces, so that his further retreat to Devagiri might be unhampered. On his way, however, he came by another section of the army which, under the command of Majir Abu Rija, was engaged in the vain attempt to reduce the fortress of Kotgir. Majir was cordial to Ulugh Khan and offered to help him in dealing with his rebel lieutenants; he sent instructions round that zamindars and heads of districts were to attack the rebels, seize them and send their chiefs to the court of the king. He then accompanied Ulugh Khan back to Devagiri. His way of dealing with the rebels proved effective; some of them fell fighting, others fled and hid themselves, and others were caught and sent to Delhi to be executed under the orders of the sultan.

Elated by his success against the invader, Pratāparudra dispersed the troops and provisions he had gathered in his capital, and acted as if he had secured perpetual immunity from further attack. To Ghiyas-ud-din, on the other hand, the failure of his son in Telengana was but a spur to a further and stronger effort to reduce that country. He sent large reinforcements to Devagiri, and Ulugh Khan soon led a second expedition against the Kākatīya kingdom. Bidar on its western frontier and several other forts including Bodhan were captured by the invading troops, and Wārangal itself invested. Ill-prepared as Pratāparudra was, he held out for five months after which famine compelled him to sue for peace. He delivered himself and his family into the hands of Ulugh Khan (1323) who sent him under a strong escort to Delhi, but he seems to have put an end to his own life on the way. Ulugh Khan plundered and devastated Wārangal, and subjugated the rest of the country by fighting where resistance was offered, but generally by accepting the submission of the Hindu chieftains in the different localities.

Ulugh Khan also sent an army into Ma'bar. The country was conquered and, for a time, brought under the sway of Delhi, whither the Pāndya king, Parākramadeva, was taken as a prisoner. Ma'bar, in fact, was still counted as a province of the Delhi empire when sultan Muhammad bin Tughlak made Devagiri its capital in 1326. Ulugh Khan led yet another expedition against Jajnagar in the Ganga kingdom of Orissa. Here his aim was not so much to conquer that kingdom as to secure the frontier of Wārangal on that side.

Thus at the accession of Muhammad bin Tughlak considerable portions of the Deccan and South India acknowledged the sovereignty of the Delhi sultanate. Devagiri and Wārangal were under the effective control of imperial officers, and a viceroy was set over distant Ma'bar charged with the duty of consolidating the new conquests and firmly establishing and extending imperial authority. Prominent among the Hindu states that still continued to enjoy their independence were Kampili and Dōrasamudra.

The famous king of Kampili, himself called Kampiladeva, rose to prominence in the first years of the fourteenth century when he rendered valuable service to his suzerain Rāmadeva of Devagiri in the wars against Hoysala Ballāla III. He was a consistent opponent of the growing power of Islam in the South, but was much hampered by his feuds with the neighbouring states of Dōrasamudra and Wārangal. All the same, he built up a kingdom of considerable size which included parts of the present-day Anantapur, Chitaldrug and Shimoga districts besides Raichur, Dharwar and Bellary; the Krishna river separated it from the Maratha province of the Delhi empire. He treated with contempt a demand for tribute from the officers of the Tughlak sultanate, and entered into friendly negotiations with Baha-ud-din Garshasp, a cousin of Muhammad bin Tughlak and governor of Sagar, in the neighbourhood of Gulbarga, who had some grievance against his cousin, laid claim to the Delhi throne, and set up the standard of revolt. Thereupon the sultan ordered Malik Zada, governor of Gujarat, and Majir Abu Rija, governor of Devagiri, to deal with the rebel. A battle on the banks of the Godāvari ended disastrously for Garshasp who fled to Sagar pursued by the victorious imperial army. He soon left Sagar with his women and children and took refuge with Kampiladeva. Meanwhile the sultan had taken the field in person and come down to Devagiri where he got news of the defeat of Garshasp and of his flight to Kampili. The task of reducing the defiant Hindu ruler who harboured the defeated rebel engaged his attention at once, but it proved more troublesome than he had anticipated, and two expeditions failed to take the strong fortress of Kummata. The third attempt led by Malik Zada ended in success; Kummata was overthrown, and Kampiladeva was forced to shut himself up in Hosadurg (Anegondi?), which was invested on all sides by the sultan's troops. Lack of provisions made it impossible for the besieged to hold out longer than a month; but meanwhile, Kampiladeva succeeded in sending Garshasp and his family to the court of Dōrasamudra, commending them to the care of Ballāla III. Kampiladeva met his end with courage and determination. He announced to his women that he had made up his mind to die fighting, and advised them to burn themselves in advance to escape falling into the hands of the enemy. They did so cheerfully, and their example was followed by the wives and daughters of the ministers and nobles of the kingdom. Thereupon Kampiladeva and his followers sallied out of the fort, fell upon the enemy and wrought havoc in their ranks before they fell in the fight. Kampiladeva's head was stuffed and sent to the sultan to announce the victory, and a garrison was posted at Hosadurg to hold the country round about (1327).

Malik Zada then began to plan an invasion of the Hoysala kingdom in pursuit of Baha-ud-din. Ballāla III had no mind to risk his kingdom and fortune by sheltering a rebel Muslim sent to him by Kampila, with whom he had never been friendly. He therefore seized Baha-ud-din when he presented himself and sent him to Malik Zada, at the same time acknowledging the supremacy of the sultan of Delhi. This pleased Malik Zada who withdrew his forces and returned to Devagiri.

For some time after the fall of Kampili, Muhammad bin Tughlak remained in Devagiri, making arrangements to complete the transfer of the imperial capital to that place. Also, after a siege of eight months, he captured the strong fortress at Kandhyāna (Sinhagad) near Poona, and forced its Hindu chieftain, Nāga Nāyaka, ruler of the Kolis, into subjection. Nāga Nāyaka was treated with honour when he made his submission and the fort passed into the hands of the sultan who returned north very shortly afterwards.

With pardonable exaggeration, Muslim historians include the whole of the Deccan and South India in the empire of Delhi in this period (1324-35). They divide it into the five provinces of Devagiri, Tiling, Kampili, Dōrasamudra and Ma'bar; some adding Jajnagar (Orissa) as a sixth, although there is less justification for this. Each of these provinces had a governor (*naib*) set over it who was assisted by a military coadjutor in charge of the provincial army, and a *kotwal* who policed the capital of the province. Except in Devagiri, however, the power of the sultan was nowhere firmly established. Dōrasamudra, for example, owed nothing more than nominal allegiance, and the bulk of the people—especially in the rural areas—was not reconciled to the new rule. The system of *iqtas* (military fiefs) by which the land was parcelled out among Muslim chieftains who had to maintain a quota of troops and pay a stipulated amount to the treasury did not make for peace or smooth administration. No wonder that this loose fabric crumbled quickly at the first touch of revolt which came naturally not long after.

The movement for the liberation of the Deccan from the Muslims may be said to have begun immediately after the sultan left for Northern India in 1329. The people had never willingly accepted Muslim rule. At this time, moreover, they and their leaders were under the influence of a strong revival of Śaivism and in no mood to submit passively to the profanation and destruction of their temples and to the corruption and overthrow of their long-established usages. In its single-minded devotion to Śiva, its fanatical intolerance of the followers of any other creed, whom it stigmatized as *bhāvis* (infidels), and in its ideal of perfect equality among the *bhaktas*, the new Śaivism was a worthy rival of Islam, and the impetus it gave to politics had not a little to do with the failure of Tughlak rule to take root in many parts of the Deccan. The abrogation of religious and charitable endowments, and the extortions to which the farmers and artisans were subjected by the sultan and his provincial governors, added the stimulus of material interest and strengthened the movement for liberation. Prominent among its leaders were Prolaya Nāyaka and his cousin Kāpaya Nāyaka, the Kanhaya Nāyaka of Muslim historians. Tradition affirms that no fewer than seventy-five lesser Nāyakas heartily assisted them in their enterprise, the celebrated Prolaya Vema, founder of the Reddi kingdom of Addanki and Kondavīdu, among them. By 1331, or a little later, the entire coastal region from the Mahanadi to the Gundlakamma in Nellore district had been freed from the Muslims, and Hindu chieftains had entered upon the task of restoring and reconstructing the civic life of the people on its old lines. At the same time, Somadeva, who claimed descent from the ancient line of the Chālukyas and became the progenitor of the later Aravīdu kings of Vijayanagar, led the Hindus of the western Telugu country in revolt against their Muslim overlord Malik Muhammad, governor of Kampili. With the centre of his power in the neighbourhood of Kurnool, he seized the forts of Anegondi, Raichur and Mudgal. As the Hoysala Ballāla III also threw off his allegiance to the sultan and invaded the province of Kampili, Malik Muhammad was helpless. He told the sultan (as Nuniz records) that 'the land was risen against him', 'everyone was lord of what he pleased, and no one was on his side'; the people came to 'besiege him in the fortress, allowing no provisions to go in to him, nor paying him the taxes that had been forced on them'. On the advice of his councillors that order could only be restored by someone connected with the late Rāja of Kampili, the sultan sent Harihara and his brother Bukka to govern the province of Kampili after taking oaths and pledges of loyalty from them.

Harihara and Bukka belonged to a family of five brothers, all sons of Sangama. They were at first in the service of Pratāparudra II, but after the Muslim conquest of his kingdom in 1323 they went over to Kampili. When Kampili also fell in 1327, they became prisoners and were carried off to Delhi where, because they embraced Islam, they stood well with the sultan. Now, once again, they were sent to the province of Kampili to take over its administration from Malik Muhammad and to deal with the revolt of the Hindu subjects. What really happened after their arrival in the South does not emerge clearly from the conflicting versions of Muslim historians and Hindu tradition. Both are agreed, however, that the two trusted lieutenants of the sultanate very soon gave up Islam and the cause of Delhi, and proceeded to set up an independent Hindu state which soon grew into the powerful empire of Vijayanagar. They started by doing the work of the sultan, their former connexion with Anegondi making their task easy, though their Muslim faith set some people against them. They followed a policy of conciliation which pacified the people, and only used force where it was absolutely necessary.

Gutti and its neighbourhood appear to have acknowledged Harihara earlier than the rest of the country, but a war undertaken against Ballāla III was not very successful at first. Then, Hindu tradition avers, the brothers met the sage Vidyāranya and, fired by his teaching, returned to the Hindu fold and accepted the mission of upholding the Hindu cause against Islam. A second expedition against Ballāla had better results, and left Harihara free to pursue his schemes of conquest and consolidation.

Meanwhile important political changes elsewhere proclaimed the approaching doom of the Tughlak empire in the South. Jalal-ud-din Hasan Shah, the governor of Ma'bar, asserted his independence after doing away with the loyal lieutenants of the sultan, and began to issue gold and silver coins in his own name from Madura (1333-4). Sultan Muhammad bin Tughlak got news of the revolt and marched to Wārangal, where the outbreak of an epidemic decimated his army and the sultan himself caught the infection. He therefore had to retrace his steps, having achieved nothing, and thus destroyed what remained of the prestige of the Delhi sultanate in the South. A false rumour that the sultan had died of the plague added to the confusion, and the rebels, both Hindu and Muslim, felt greatly heartened.

Prolaya Nāyaka was dead, but his work was continued by his cousin Kāpaya. He saw that the considerable number of *amirs* and their slaves, the Muslim merchants and the numbers of Hindu converts to Islam scattered all over the country, might throw effective obstacles in the way of his attempts to restore Hindu rule and Hindu *dharma* in the Deccan. He set about his work with caution and entered into an understanding with Ballāla III of Dōrasamudra, who was the most powerful Hindu ruler in the South at that time. Ballāla strengthened the northern marches of his kingdom and prepared to meet any attacks from Devagiri. He also sent aid to Kāpaya Nāyaka in his struggle against the Muslims in Telengana where a defeat was inflicted on Malik Maqbul, the governor of Wārangal, who fled to Devagiri, and thence to Delhi, leaving Telengana free from Muslim rule (1336). Soon after, Kāpaya and Ballāla together entered the northern districts of Ma'bar, the area known as Tondaimandalam. They ousted the Muslim garrisons from the forts of that country and entrusted the task of its administration to a scion of the line of Śāmbuvarāyas, the native rulers of the region at the time. Other Hindu kingdoms came up elsewhere. The Koppula chiefs of Pithāpuram made themselves masters of the coastal region from the Godāvari to Kalinga; the Reddis of Kondavīdu formed a principality which extended from Śrīśailam to the Bay of Bengal; and the Velamas raised a small state round Rājakonda in the hilly tract of the Nalgonda district of Andhrapradesh. The power of the Tughlak sultans was thus completely broken all over the Deccan except in the Maratha provinces. In Ma'bar half the territory had been recovered for Hindu rule, and although the rest was held by a Muslim ruler, he was a rebel against the sultan.

We may well believe that this general anti-Islamic movement did much to disturb the loyalty of Harihara and Bukka to the sultan and to kindle in their minds a longing to serve their country and their ancestral religion in the old way. Their meeting with Vidyāranya (' Forest of Learning ') thus probably furnished them with the best and perhaps the only means of following the promptings of their hearts; it needed a spiritual leader of his eminence to receive them back from Islam into Hinduism and to render the act generally acceptable to Hindu society. Thus it happened that the trusted Muslim agents of the sultan of Delhi, who were sent to restore his power in the Deccan, turned out to be the founders of one of the greatest Hindu states of history which later distinguished itself pre-eminently in the defence of ancient Hindu culture against the onslaughts of Islam. After establishing their sway over Kampili at first for the sultan, and conquering more territory in the same manner, the two Sangama brothers returned to the Hindu fold, proclaimed their independence, and founded a new city opposite to Anegondi on the south bank of the Tungabhadra to which they gave the significant names Vijayanagara ('City of Victory') and Vidyānagara ('City of Learning'), the second name commemorating the role of Vidyāranya in these momentous events. Here, in the presence of God Virūpāksha, Harihara I celebrated his coronation in proper Hindu style on 18 April 1336. He undertook the rule of the kingdom as the agent of the deity to whom all the land south of the Krishna river was supposed to belong, and his successors kept up the practice he started of authenticating all their acts of state by the sign manual of Śri Virūpāksha.

Ballāla's part in the establishment of Śāmbuvarāya power in the northern districts of Ma'bar involved him in continuous hostilities with the newly-established sultanate of Madura and this led very soon to the absorption of the Hoysala kingdom in the rising state of Vijayanagar. At Madura, Jalal-ud-din Hasan Shah fell by assassination (1340) after a rule of five years, and was succeeded by one of his *amirs*, Ala-ud-din Udauji, a warlike prince who planned an expedition against Ballāla. The Hoysala monarch stationed himself at Tiruvannamalai in 1340; Udauji's invasion came in 1341; but in the hour of victory an arrow shot by an unknown hand struck him and he died at once. Ballāla converted defeat into victory, and for a time it looked like the end of the small Muslim state of Madura. The late sultan's son-in-law was put on the throne by the nobles, but being found unsatisfactory he was murdered. The next ruler was Ghiyas-ud-din Damghani, a blood-thirsty monster not, however, devoid of ability. At the time of his accession, Ballāla was investing the strong fortress of Kannanūr-Koppam, after a decisive victory against the Muslim forces in the open field. The siege lasted for six months at the end of which Ballāla acted with unaccountable folly and brought on his own doom. When the besieged forces opened negotiation, he consented to allow them to get into touch with the sultan at Madura to settle the terms of surrender; this naturally led to Ghiyas-ud-din's marching quickly to the relief of the beleaguered garrison with some 4,000 troopers, all he could gather in the straits to which he found himself reduced. Ballāla was taken completely by surprise when his camp was attacked by the Madura army. Nasir-ud-din, the sultan's nephew and afterwards his successor, overtook an old man and was about to kill him when one of his slaves identified him as the Hindu sovereign; he was then made prisoner and taken before the sultan. Treating him at first with apparent consideration, Ghiyas-ud-din persuaded him to part with all his riches, horses and elephants; and then had him killed and flayed. 'His skin was stuffed with straw and hung upon the wall of Madura, where,' says Ibn Batuta, 'I saw it in the same position' (1342).

Ballāla III was succeeded by his son Virūpāksha Ballāla IV who held his coronation in August 1343; but this is all we know of him, for his kingdom was overrun and annexed by the newly risen kingdom of Vijayanagar. Bukka had seized Penugonda while Ballāla III was still alive, and his tragic end enabled Bukka to complete the work of conquest. He was firmly established in the vicinity of Hosapattana and Harihar in the middle of 1344, and 'the circle of earth belonging to the Hoysala family' had become 'an ornament to his arm'. The conquest of Tulu-nāḍ on the west coast followed soon after; that country had been conquered by Ballāla III and made part of his kingdom, but had regained its independence at the end of his reign. In 1345, or perhaps even earlier, it acknowledged the supremacy of Harihara whose brothers, in the decade that followed the foundation of Vijayanagar, were engaged in expanding their power over other territory and in bringing the smaller kingdoms under their suzerainty. As early as 1340, Bādami had become part of the new empire.

If the new danger from Islam was to be effectively combated, it was necessary that the power of the various Hindu states should be consolidated by welding them into one strong state, and that they should be prevented from continuing in their normal condition of mutual hostility. Harihara had gone a long way towards securing this so that, in 1346, the entire family of five brothers and their chief relatives and lieutenants could meet at Śringeri, the seat of the Hindu pontiff, to celebrate the conquest of dominions extending from sea to sea by holding a great festival (*vijayotsava*) in the presence of the most eminent spiritual leader of the Hindu community.

But the very next year (1347) witnessed the birth of the Muslim sultanate of the Deccan which made the danger from Islam to the Hindu culture of the South much more immediate and constant. Harihara and his brothers had not entered upon their work a day too soon. In the rest of this chapter we shall trace the rise and history of the Bāhmanī sultanate, reserving the further history of Vijayanagar for the next.

The Bāhmanī kingdom arose out of one of the many revolts that broke up the Tughlak empire towards the close of the reign of Muhammad bin Tughlak. The numerous foreign officials of the revenue department in the province of Daulatabad fell under the suspicion of the sultan because they had failed to collect the enormous revenue which they were required to make up; these '*amirs* of the hundred' or 'centurions' were sent under escort by the governor of Daulatabad to Broach in accordance with the sultan's orders. But news of the sultan's merciless killing of the centurions of the neighbouring province of Malwa reached them, and they were by no means inclined to submit tamely to such treatment. They therefore revolted at the end of the first day's march, returned to Daulatabad, imprisoned its weak governor, and proclaimed one among themselves, Ismail Mukh, the Afghan, king of the Deccan under the title Nasir-ud-din Shah. An imperial army led by Muhammad himself soon made its appearance on the scene from Broach, defeated the rebels and shut them up in the citadel of Daulatabad. Some of them, including Ismail Mukh's brothers, contrived to make their escape to Gulbarga under the leadership of Hasan Gangu *alias* Zafar Khan. After about three months, Hasan gathered a considerable army, including some contingents from Kāpaya Nāyaka of Wārangal, and marched to Bidar. Meanwhile, Muhammad was called away by a rebellion in Gujarat, and Hasan easily defeated and dispersed an imperial army after slaying its commander. As he approached Daulatabad, the royal troops gave up the siege and retired to Malwa. The aged and ease-loving Nasir-ud-din Ismail Shah, the new king of the Deccan, now readily abdicated his troublesome charge in favour of Hasan who proclaimed himself ruler of the Deccan on 3 August 1347 under the name Sultan Abu'l Muzaffar Ala-ud-din Bāhman Shah. He is said to have traced his descent from a half-mythical hero of Persia, Bāhman, the son of Isfandiyar. Ferishta, however, records that he called himself Gangu Bāhmanī, in honour of the Brahmin Gangu whose slave he had formerly been.

Sultan Ala-ud-din Bāhman Shah reigned for eleven years till his death in February 1358. He spent most of his time waging war or conducting negotiations calculated to extend the territory under his sway. He had to encounter much opposition at first from nobles who were or professed to be loyal to their Tughlak suzerain. By a judicious mixture of force and clemency, Ala-ud-din changed the situation in a few years. Even Kāpaya Nāyaka of Wārangal had to surrender the fort of Kaulas and promise him tribute. As early as 1349 he attacked the territory of Vijayanagar and captured Karaichur. Five years later, as a result of an understanding with the new sultan of Madura who was a relative of his, Ala-ud-din attacked Vijayanagar a second time. While Muslim accounts claim for him the conquest of all territory up to the Tungabhadra, Hindu sources say that Harihara I inflicted a defeat on the sultan. However that may be, Ala-ud-din had become master of an extensive kingdom when he died. It extended up to the sea on the west and included the ports of Goa and Dabhol, the eastern limit was marked by Bhongir, while the Penganga and Krishna rivers bounded the kingdom on the north and the south. He gained recognition from the caliph, and his coin legend, ' A second Alexander ', shows that he had further designs of conquest. He made Gulbarga his capital, and began adorning it with fine buildings. He organized the administration of the kingdom by dividing it into four provinces (*tarafs*) each under a governor; three were named after their chief cities—Gulbarga, Daulatabad, and Bidar—and the fourth was Berar.

Ala-ud-din was followed on the throne by his eldest son, Muhammad I (1358-77), a diligent and methodical administrator whose institutions long survived him and influenced the polity of later kingdoms. He established a council of eight ministers including the Peshwa, and greatly decentralized the provincial administration—a step that made for efficiency and sound government so long as the king was strong and undertook frequent tours of the realm, but led ultimately to its dismemberment. He reorganized the bodyguard into four reliefs (*naubats*), each doing duty by turns for four days at a time. He took strong measures for the suppression of highway robbery, and no fewer than 20,000 brigands lost their lives before the sultan was satisfied that the safety of the roads had been secured. The great mosque of Gulbarga was completed in 1367. It is perhaps the only mosque in India which has no open courtyard and has been described as 'a noble building impressive in its massive solidity'. He secured recognition from the puppet caliph of Egypt as a result of his mother's journey to Mecca (1361).

Muhammad waged wars with Telengana and Vijayanagar and had to suppress a revolt in Daulatabad. The neighbouring Hindu rulers sent hostile messages to Muhammad—Kāpaya Nāyaka demanded the restoration of Kaulas, and Bukka the cession of the Raichur doab, both conquered from them by his predecessor, and threatened to join Delhi in taking measures against him. Muhammad merely detained their messengers for eighteen months, during which time he completed his preparations. He then sent back haughty answers calling upon his 'vassals' to explain their failure to make the customary offerings at his accession, and to make it good by sending him all their elephants laden with gold, jewels and other treasure. Kāpaya Nāyaka's reply was to send an army under his son Vināyak Deo (or Nāgdev according to some accounts) against Kaulas, aided by a body of 20,000 horse sent by Bukka. Vināyak Deo, however, was beaten back by Bahadur Khan who advanced to Wārangal and collected 100,000 gold *huns* and 26 elephants before he left Telengana. This resulted in permanent estrangement between the two kingdoms and continued hostilities. For example, in 1362 a caravan of horse-dealers reported that horses meant for Gulbarga had been forcibly purchased by Vināyak Deo, whereupon Muhammad captured and executed the Hindu prince and caused the devastation of much of the Telengana country, though not without serious losses to himself.

Nor was Muhammad without other troubles, for during his excursion into Telengana, his cousin Bahram Khan Mazandarani, governor of Daulatabad, revolted. He made common cause with Kāpaya Nāyaka and sent a futile message to Delhi seeking the aid of Firuz Tughlak. Muhammad sent an army against Daulatabad, while he himself took the field once more against Telengana. Wārangal and Golconda were besieged; Kāpaya Nāyaka had to flee to the jungles and was only able to purchase peace by the promise of fealty and the cession of the town of Golconda, much gold and many elephants. He also yielded a throne studded with turquoises meant originally for Muhammad bin Tughlak. On 21 March 1365, Muhammad sat on the throne at Gulbarga, and celebrated the occasion with great *éclat*. He ordered, according to Ferishta, that the singers and dancers who entertained him on this occasion should be paid by a draft on the treasury of Vijayanagar, and despite his ministers' remonstrances he insisted on the literal execution of this rash order. When his messenger took the draft to Vijayanagar, Bukka (Ferishta calls him Krishnarāya) had him paraded on an ass in his city, and then crossed the Tungabhadra and seized Mudgal. Muhammad was furious and incontinently marched against Bukka though only with a moderate force. Bukka withdrew with his cavalry to Adoni, leaving the infantry to face the enemy and defend the country. Muhammad plundered and killed the defenceless inhabitants in the villages before he retired into Mudgal for the rains. The rest of his army then joined him; he marched in the direction of Adoni and, early in 1367, a battle was fought at Kauthal, south of the Tungabhadra. The Muslims gained the victory, thanks to their guns and their cavalry, the Hindu artillery not coming into play till it was too late, and their commander Mallinātha being mortally wounded. Ferishta is very definite that guns were used by both sides on this occasion and that the gunners were generally Europeans and Ottoman Turks. After his defeat, Bukka eluded Muhammad's pursuit for three months, and finally shut himself up in his capital. Not having the strength to besiege the vast city, Muhammad feigned sickness and retreated. Bukka ventured to attack him, but he had to retire into the city again after losing many men and some treasure. Muhammad then took to the promiscuous slaughter of all the inhabitants of the country and proclaimed his intention of not stopping until his draft was honoured by the ruler of Vijayanagar; the war was then ended by Bukka consenting to this. Four hundred thousand Hindus, ten thousand Brahmin priests among them, lost their lives in the massacre. So shocked were both sides by the dimensions of the slaughter that an agreement was made to spare non-combatants in future wars. Though violated on occasions, this agreement did do something to mitigate the horrors of the perpetual contest between the two states.

Ferishta's account of Muhammad's wars with Vijayanagar cannot be accepted at face value. He retails as a cause of the first war an improbable story of a large issue of gold coins by Muhammad which were melted down by the Hindu bankers of his kingdom at the instance of the Hindu rulers of neighbouring kingdoms. In his account of the second war he calls the Vijayanagar ruler Krishnarāya and mentions his general Bhojmal of whom history knows nothing. Again, according to Ferishta himself, the Krishna river was recognized as the boundary between the two kingdoms by the terms of the treaty which ended the war: this virtually conceded the claim of Vijayanagar to the territory between the Krishna and Tungabhadra, which would not have been the case if Muhammad had been so uniformly successful in the war as Ferishta would have us believe.

After the end of the war with Vijayanagar, Muhammad easily suppressed the revolt in Daulatabad; Bahram Khan fled and was pursued to the frontiers of Gujarat.

Muhammad gets a good character from Ferishta to whom cruelty to infidels was, if anything, a commendation. The author of the *Burhan-i-Ma'asir* says that he died as a result of an 'irreligious manner of living', meaning perhaps indulgence in drink. The internal affairs of the kingdom during the reign were managed by Saif-ud-din Ghori, who had served the first sultan well and continued in service till the accession of the sixth sultan when he died at an age of more than 100.

Muhammad was succeeded by his eldest son Mujahid, who provoked a quarrel with Vijayanagar by demanding territory and then invaded that kingdom. Bukka adopted the plan of wearing out his enemy by avoiding battle and finally retired into his capital. Although its outer defences were carried by the enemy, they soon afterwards sustained a decisive defeat. A futile siege of Adoni for nine months was followed by peace. Mujahid rebuked his uncle, Daud Khan, for the inefficiency of his operations against the city of Vijayanagar. Daud Khan retaliated by conspiring to procure Mujahid's murder on 15 April 1378 and made himself king. Within a month, however, Mujahid's sister contrived to have Daud murdered, and Muhammad II, son of the youngest son of Ala-ud-din I, was proclaimed king.

Muhammad II was a man of peace, devoted to religion and poetry. He sent large presents to Hafiz of Persia together with an invitation to visit him, but the poet was frightened by a storm in the Persian Gulf and would not continue his journey to India. A less amiable side of his character, however, is to be seen during the years of famine between 1387 and 1395, when the relief measures he organized were confined to his Muslim subjects. Muhammad II died of a fever in April 1397 and was succeeded by his elder son—Ghiyas-ud-din, a strong-willed and indiscreet youth of seventeen. Within two months (June 1397) he was dethroned and blinded by an angry Turkish slave, Tughalchin, who raised to the throne Shams-ud-din Daud, Ghiyas-ud-din's younger half-brother, and made himself regent. Firuz and his brother Ahmad, sons-in-law of Muhammad II and grandsons of Ala-ud-din I, wanted to redeem the royal line from domination by a slave, and, after an initial failure, succeeded in overpowering Tughalchin and his master in the palace in November 1397. Firuz became king under the title Taj-ud-din Firuz Shah.

Firuz had a vigorous body and a keen mind. Ferishta considered him the greatest of the Bāhmanī kings, and the author of the *Burhan-i-Ma'asir* speaks of him as a ' good, just, and generous king who supported himself by copying the Quran, and the ladies of whose harem used to support themselves by embroidering garments and selling them '. But these are exaggerated estimates, and there is no doubt that Firuz drank hard and his character degenerated as his reign advanced; he ruined his vigorous body by excessive indulgence in the company of women. He built a new city, Firuzabad, on the Bhima where he set up a harem of 800 women of various nationalities; he was reputed to be a master of many languages and able to converse with each of his mistresses in her own tongue. Firuz made his brother Ahmad chief minister, and regulated the administration efficiently, not hesitating to employ Brahmins in important posts.

In 1398, Harihara II invaded the Raichur doab, and there was at the same time a rebellion of the Kolis on the north bank of the Krishna led by a Hindu chief. The Koli rebellion was crushed, but the armies of Berar and Daulatabad that came to aid Firuz against Harihara II had to go back to deal with the Gond rāja of

Kherla who had invaded Berar. Firuz only had 12,000 horse with him as he advanced on the Krishna, while Harihara was encamped on the southern bank with a vast but ill-organized array. Firuz saw the difficulty of crossing the river for the attack in the face of the enemy, and Quazi Siraj-ud-din suggested a stratagem and offered to carry it out himself; he disguised himself and a number of his friends as a company of strolling performers and went into the enemy camp. In a few days they made a reputation for themselves and gained permission to perform before the son of Harihara when in the course of a dance with naked swords they suddenly fell upon the prince and killed him on the spot. Such confusion arose in the Hindu camp that Firuz was able to cross the river unopposed and Harihara fled to Vijayanagar, carrying with him the corpse of his ill-fated son. Firuz pursued him and took large numbers of prisoners, including 10,000 Brahmins, but released the captives on payment of a big ransom, and the war came to an end. Firuz now separated the Raichur doab from the home province of Gulbarga, and appointed Fulad Khan as its first military governor.

Soon after, Firuz led a successful expedition against Narsingh of Kherla who had to surrender 40 elephants, much money and a daughter into the hands of Firuz as the price of peace. In 1401 Firuz sent a mission with presents to Timur, and Timur issued a decree bestowing the Deccan, Malwa and Gujarat on Firuz. The rulers of Malwa and Gujarat were alarmed and entered into negotiations with Harihara II who now began to withhold tribute and defy Firuz successfully; fearing an attack from the north, Firuz let Harihara alone. Harihara died in 1404, and two years later his son Devarāya I started a war, according to Ferishta, on account of a pretty girl, the daughter of a goldsmith of Mudgal, who had caught his fancy. Devarāya's attempt to seize her by force miscarried, and he laid waste some villages in the neighbourhood of Mudgal. This act of aggression provoked Firuz who invaded Vijayanagar and attacked the city; being wounded himself, he had to withdraw to a fortified camp some distance away, from where he sent his lieutenants to ravage and conquer the country to the south of the city up to Adoni. Devarāya had to make peace on the sultan's terms which included the gift of a daughter in marriage, the surrender of Bankapur as her dowry, besides pearls, 50 elephants, 2,000 boys and girls skilled in song and dance, and a large cash indemnity. The marriage was celebrated with due pomp, but as the king did not accompany Firuz far enough out of the city when he left it, they parted in anger. Firuz secured for his son Hasan Khan the girl whose charms had brought on the war. The story of the goldsmith's daughter is, however, unknown to other writers.

In 1412, the Gond governor of Mahur rebelled against Firuz who marched into Gondwana but had to return without suppressing the revolt. About this time Firuz began to suspect his brother Ahmad of plotting against him, as the saint Jamal-ud-din Husaini prophesied his accession to the throne. Two slaves became the sultan's favourites and received the titles Ain-ul-Mulk and Nizam-ul-Mulk. In 1417, an expedition against Telengana was successful in killing Kāṭayavema Reddi of Rajahmundry in battle and enforcing subordination in that country. But in 1420 the attack on Pangal, which had been taken by Vijayanagar, ended in disaster; the siege of the fortress lasted for two years at the end of which disease began to decimate the ranks of the Bāhmanī forces. The success of Vijayanagar was complete on this occasion, and Firuz had to retreat leaving the southern and eastern districts of his kingdom in the occupation of the enemy. Firuz was completely shaken by this defeat and was henceforth a broken man; he spent the rest of his life in works of piety, according to his light, and left the affairs of state more and more to the two favourite slaves.

Ahmad's position was endangered by their ascendancy, and he fled from the capital with some adherents, including a rich merchant from Basra by name Khalaf Hasan. On his advice, Ahmad assumed the royal title in his camp near Kalyāni, defeated troops sent against him, and pursued them to the capital. Firuz was too ill to do anything, and his army deserted him in favour of Ahmad, who accepted his brother's abdication and took charge of his two sons Hasan Khan and Mubarak Khan (September 1422). Firuz died within a few days, it was said, strangled or poisoned under Ahmad's orders.

Ahmad Shah (1422-35) richly endowed the saint who had prophesied his accession and had advised him on several occasions when he was in difficulty; he also rewarded his other friends, like the merchant of Basra, with offices and rank. He ordained that each provincial governor was to rank as a commander of 2,000;

but this did not mean that the troops under him were restricted to this number.

Ahmad proceeded against Vijayarāya of Vijayanagar to avenge the disasters of the last reign; a battle on the banks of the Tunga-bhadra was followed by the most ruthless devastations of Vijaya-nagar country. Indiscriminate slaughter and enslavement of the civil population, destruction of temples and the slaughter of cows were the special features of this campaign.

In March 1423, while out hunting, Ahmad pursued an antelope until he was separated from his bodyguard. At this disadvantage, he was spotted by a body of Hindu cavalry, but was saved by the timely arrival of a detachment of his own troops under a faithful officer Abdul Qadir. The latter was rewarded with the title of Khan Jahan and the governorship of Berar, and his brother, Abdul Latif, became Khan A'zam and governor of Bidar. Foreign mounted archers played a great part in the rescue and were hence-forth a strong corps in the Bāhmanī army. The war against Vijayanagar was only concluded when Vijayarāya agreed to pay the 'arrears of tribute', a vast amount; his son Devarāya accom-panied the sultan on his way back as far as the Krishna. The sultan carried away many prisoners with him, among them two able Brahmin youths who became Muslims, one of them later becoming the first independent sultan of Berar, and the other the father of that Ahmad who founded the Nizam Shahi line of Ahmadnagar.

In both 1423 and 1424 the rains failed and there was famine. Ahmad prayed for rain publicly on the top of a hill outside the capital and when his prayer was apparently answered, he was hailed a saint (*wali*). This, however, did not prevent him, at the end of 1424, from invading Telengana, where he captured Wārangal, and slew its king. The governor of Bidar was left to reduce the rest of the country and extend the kingdom to the sea. This was the end of that Hindu kingdom.

In 1425 Ahmad proceeded against Mahur, whose rebellious rāja was enticed by a promise of pardon and then slain along with 6,000 of his followers. Ahmad next led a raid into Gondwana and spent a year in Ellichpur, rebuilding the forts of Gawilgarh and Narnala on his northern frontier, as a preparation for the conquest of Gujarat and Malwa which had been granted by Timur to his brother. To the same end, he entered into a close alliance with

Khandesh, a small state over which both Gujarat and Malwa had claims of suzerainty. In his turn, Hushang Shah of Malwa had, by 1422, compelled Narsingh of Kherla, a vassal of the Bāhmanī sultan, to swear fealty to Malwa. In 1428 he invaded Kherla to collect tribute, and on Narsingh's appeal for aid, Ahmad marched to Ellichpur. Hushang pressed on with the siege of Kherla, but Ahmad was assailed by doubts about the morality of attacking a brother Muslim in defence of an infidel, and gave up the cause of Narsingh and retired to his own country. Hushang attributed Ahmad's retreat to cowardice, and pursued him with a considerable force, whereupon Ahmad defeated him decisively on the banks of the Tapti; 200 elephants and all the baggage in Hushang's camp along with the ladies of his harem fell into the hands of the victor. Narsingh issued from Kherla and pursued Hushang's beaten troops into Malwa, while Ahmad advanced to Kherla. There he was well entertained by Narsingh. He sent the women back to Hushang under a strong escort.

On his return from this campaign, Ahmad stayed in Bidar for some time, where he was so struck by its situation and climate that he decided to build a new city near its ancient fortress and called it Ahmadabad-Bidar. This became the new capital where he settled in 1429. About the same time his eldest son, Ala-ud-din Ahmad, married the daughter of Nasir Khan of Khandesh. In 1430, Ahmad ordered a wanton attack on Gujarat, then under Ahmad I; the Deccan army was twice defeated, and an attempt on Mahim on the island of Bombay also resulted in great losses. But Ahmad Bāhmanī obstinately persisted in his effort so that there was much fighting in 1431 on the southern frontier of Gujarat, although the Deccan troops gained no advantage. In 1432, Ahmad put his sister's son Sher Khan to death, suspecting him of designs upon the throne. Sher Khan had been among those who had advised Ahmad earlier in his life to end his brother's feeble rule and make himself king.

The Gujarat war exhausted Ahmad, and Hushang of Malwa, who knew this, captured Kherla and killed Narsingh. Ahmad marched north to avenge this insult, but Nasir Khan intervened and made peace between them on terms by no means favourable to Ahmad. Kherla was acknowledged to be a fief of Malwa, while the rest of Berar remained a province of the Deccan. Ahmad then punished some of the petty chieftains of Telengana and restored order (1434-5) in the province ruled by one of his sons. He died in 1435 aged about sixty-four. Unlike his brother Firuz, whose learning had imparted a touch of scepticism to his outlook on life, Ahmad was a superstitious Muslim, with a tinge of fanaticism, apt to show too much reverence to any long-haired 'saint'. But he was not altogether incapable of enjoying wit and learning, and at his instance the poet Āzarī or Isfarāyīn in Khurasan composed the *Bāhman-nāmā*, a versified history of the dynasty, now lost. From such quotations as have survived, we know it to have been a rather poor imitation of the *Shāh-nāmā*. Āzarī retired to his native place before Ahmad's death, but continued writing his history up to his death in 1462; it was added to regularly by other hands till the end of the dynasty.

The regular employment of foreigners—Turks, Arabs, Moguls and Persians—in the civil and military offices of the state gave rise to rivalry between them and the local Muslims, the Deccanis, who were backed by African negroes as well as by the offspring of African fathers and Indian mothers. The 'foreigners' alleged that the disasters of the Gujarat war were due to the cowardice of the Deccanis, and the quarrels between the rival factions often led to pitched battles and bloody massacres. The 'foreigners' were generally Shiahs while the Deccanis were Sunnis, and this added acerbity to their disputes which had no small share in weakening the Bāhmanī sultanate and its succession states.

Ahmad the Saint was succeeded by his eldest son Ala-ud-din II (1436-58). He surrounded himself with foreigners and the jealousy and intrigues of the Deccanis were the source of much trouble during his reign. He sent his brother Muhammad to recover 'arrears of tribute' from Devarāya II of Vijayanagar, which he did. This success turned Muhammad's head, and he demanded equal power with the sultan or one half of the kingdom for himself. The result was a war in which he was beaten, but he was pardoned and made governor of the Raichur doab and remained loyal to his brother ever after.

Parts of Konkan were conquered in 1437, and the rāja of Sangameśvar gave his daughter in marriage to the sultan, who preferred her to his first wife, the daughter of Nasir Khan of Khandesh. To avenge this slight, Nasir Khan invaded Berar, induced many officials of the province to take his side, and confined its governor, Khan Jahan, to the fortress of Narnala. At this juncture, the

Deccani party recommended caution to the sultan, while the Malik-ut-Tujjar Khalaf Hasan Basri, the governor of Daulatabad and leader of the foreigners, declared his readiness to take the field if he was given foreign troops and no Deccanis. He had his way and won a splendid success as a result of which the supremacy of the foreign party seemed assured; they took the place of honour on the right side of the throne, while the Deccanis were relegated to the left.

Meanwhile Devarāya II had reorganized his army and made it an efficient striking force of all arms. In 1443, he invaded the Raichur doab, captured Mudgal, besieged Raichur and Bankapur, and laid waste the country up to Bijapur and Sagar. On the approach of Ala-ud-din, he withdrew to Mudgal, and Malik-ut-Tujjar was able to raise the sieges of Raichur and Bankapur. Three battles between the two armies followed in as many months. In the first, the Hindus won the day, while the Muslims won the second; in the third, Devarāya's elder son was killed and his troops driven headlong back to Mudgal. Two important Muslim officers of the Bāhmanī army were captured and imprisoned; but when the sultan sent word that the lives of 200,000 Hindus would be the price of these officers, Devarāya agreed to make peace and to pay 'tribute' regularly in future.

Ala-ud-din's character degenerated with age and he began to indulge in gross sensual pleasures to the neglect of public business. The Deccanis took advantage of this to compass the destruction of the foreigners' party. In 1446-7, an expedition against the Konkan was organized, with Malik-ut-Tujjar Khalaf Hasan appointed to the command. The intrigues of the Deccanis with two Hindu princes, one of them the rāja of Sangameśvar, brought about the defeat of the army and the slaughter of large numbers of the foreigners including Malik-ut-Tujjar himself. The survivors gathered in the fort of Chākan to the north of Poona, but the Deccanis followed up their game by bringing false accusations of treason against them and persuading the sultan to agree to their assassination. They then contrived to murder all the officers at a banquet, and to slaughter 1,200 Sayyids and 1,000 other foreigners besides numerous children, appropriating to themselves the wives, daughters and goods of their victims. The few who escaped, Quasim Beg and two other officers among them, managed to convey to the sultan a true account of what had happened.

Ala-ud-din was overcome by remorse, executed the leaders of the Deccani party, and reduced their families to penury. Quasim Beg became governor of Daulatabad, and his two companions were promoted to high rank. The foreign party regained its ascendancy, and in 1451 the king got a letter from the poet Āzarī of Isfarāyīn urging him to abandon the use of wine and dismiss all Deccani officials. He did both and began to take more interest in state affairs.

During 1453 the sultan was confined to his palace for a time by an injury to his leg, and rumours of his death began to spread. Sikandar, governor of Telengana, rebelled and invited Mahmud I of Malwa to invade Berar and joined him there in 1456. When Ala-ud-din took the field in person, Mahmud, who had been led to believe that he was dead, retired to Malwa. Sikandar and his father were defeated and captured after a siege by Mahmud Gawan, a foreigner who was just rising to power, but the sultan pardoned them.

Ala-ud-din died in 1458. While he drank wine himself, he sternly discouraged its use among his subjects. He built a free hospital at Bidar and displayed his piety by sitting through long sermons, and by building mosques with the material acquired from the Hindu temples he destroyed. Before he died he designated his eldest son Humayun as his successor.

Humayun (1458-61) had an evil reputation for cruelty and the savage deeds that marked his reign earned for him the title of *zalim* or ‘ tyrant ’. At the start of his reign, some officers made attempts to enthrone Humayun’s brother, Hasan Khan, and paid for it by death, imprisonment or flight; Hasan Khan himself was both blinded and imprisoned. Humayun favoured the foreigners and made Mahmud Gawan lieutenant of the kingdom (*malik naib*) and governor of Bijapur. The Deccanis, however, were not altogether excluded from office. There were two rebellions: one in Telengana led by Sikandar Khan and his father Jalal Khan, and another in the capital when the king and his minister were absent in Telengana. Both were suppressed with a maniacal ferocity unexampled even in the bloodstained annals of Bāhmanī rule. Neither the able minister Mahmud Gawan nor the talented queen Makhdumah Jahan (who distinguished herself greatly during the minority of her sons after her husband’s death) seems to have been able to restrain the excesses of the sultan. His subjects heaved a sigh of relief when Humayun died in September 1461, 'assassinated during a fit of intoxication by his own servants, who were tired out by his inhuman cruelties'.

Humayun's son, Nizam Shah, was only a lad of eight at his accession, so his mother managed the affairs of state with the help of Malik Shah Turk, surnamed Khvaja Jahan, and Mahmud Gawan. Underrating the efficiency of the new regime, the Hindu ruler of Telengana and Orissa invaded the kingdom as did Mahmud I of Malwa also. The former was met and turned back twenty miles from the capital, Bidar; but the invasion of Mahmud I was a more serious danger. The Bāhmanī forces sustained a defeat near Kandhar, the capital had to stand a siege, and the queen-mother retired to Firuzabad with her young son. Relief came when Mahmud Begarha, the ruler of Gujarat, responded to Mahmud Gawan's appeal for help. The Gujarat and Bāhmanī forces joined and together threatened the rear of the Malwa army which was thus compelled to retreat. Another raid from Malwa in the following year did not advance beyond Daulatabad thanks once again to the timely intervention of the ruler of Gujarat.

The young sultan died suddenly on 30 July 1463, and was succeeded by his brother Muhammad III, then only nine years of age. The regency council carried on the government during the king's minority, as in the previous reign, but Khvaja Jahan's ambition disturbed the harmony. The queen-mother suspected his designs when she found that Mahmud Gawan was, in effect, banished from the capital and kept constantly employed on the frontier. She arranged for her son to order the execution of Khvaja Jahan as a traitor. She then recalled Mahmud Gawan, who had bestowed great care on the education of the king, to the capital where he became chief officer with the title Amir-ul-Umara. The queen-mother retired when her son was fifteen, and retained his affection and respect throughout her life.

A campaign against Kherla, then in the possession of Mahmud I of Malwa, was undertaken in 1467; but nothing was gained by this, peace was made, and Kherla continued to be a fief of Malwa as in the reign of Ahmad the Saint. Mahmud Gawan, who still retained the government of Bijapur, undertook an expedition against the Hindu rājas of the Konkan, a country that was never completely subjugated by the Bāhmanī sultans. In particular, Mahmud Gawan wanted to prevent the rājas of Khelna (Viśālgarh) and Sangameśvar from using their fleets off the west coast to harass Muslim merchants and pilgrims. By patience and the calculated employment of force and corruption he gained several successes, and finally captured Goa, then the best port of the Vijayanagar empire. This last victory was important not only as an achievement against the permanent enemy of the Bāhmanī kingdom, but as giving to that kingdom a virtual command over the west coast trade, besides guaranteeing the safety of Muslim pilgrims to Mecca. Mahmud Gawan returned to the capital in 1472 after an absence of over three years and was received with high honours.

Before Mahmud Gawan's return, news of a war of succession in Orissa, following the death of Kapileśvara Gajapati, reached Muhammad III in the form of an appeal for aid from Kapileṣvara's son Hambar (Hamvīra) against an usurper named Mangal, by whom Purushottama Gajapati, another of Kapileśvara's sons, seems to be meant. Malik Hasan, one of the two Brahmin youths brought from Vijayanagar by Ahmad the Saint, was sent against the usurper whom he was successful in defeating and thus secured the throne for Hambar. Hambar was to repay Malik Hasan later on when he helped him to reduce the Reddis of Rajahmundry and Kondavīdu. Malik Hasan's achievements received due recognition when he returned to the capital, but Purushottama soon displaced Hambar and won the throne of Orissa for himself, Hambar consenting to rule in Kimedi as a subordinate vassal.

The Bāhmanī kingdom now for the first time extended from sea to sea, and honours were fairly divided between the foreigners and Deccanis. Of the four provinces, two—Gulbarga with Bijapur, and Daulatabad—were held by Mahmud Gawan and Yusuf Adil Khan, both foreigners, and two others—Telengana and Berar—by Malik Hasan and Fathullah Imad-ul-Mulk, the other Brahmin youth from Vijayanagar. Fathullah was friendly with the foreigners, but not so Malik Hasan; Mahmud Gawan was relatively free from party spirit. The leader of the foreigners was Yusuf, and round him gathered many foreigners who enabled him to complete the conquest of northern Konkan. This earned for him higher honours than Hasan's who thus became more hostile than ever to the foreigners.

At the end of 1472 the rājas of Belgaum and Bankapur were urged by Virūpāksha of Vijayanagar to recover Goa for the Hindu empire. Muhammad III and Mahmud Gawan marched against

Bankapur, whose ruler Birkana withstood a siege for some time and then surrendered; his territory was annexed and added to the charge of Mahmud Gawan. Soon after, the queen-mother, whose advice had been sought almost every day by her son even after her retirement, died in camp, and her body was sent to Bidar for burial, while Muhammad III halted at Bijapur as the guest of Gawan. She had been a steady supporter of Mahmud Gawan who felt her loss even more keenly than her son did.

About 1476 the people of Kondavīdu rose against their oppressive Muslim governor, put him to death and delivered the town to Hamir, an Oriya nobleman. The person so described by the Muslim historians was doubtless Dakshina Kapileśvara Kumāra Hamvīra Mahāpātra, a son of Hambar (Hamvīra) who had contested the throne of Orissa with Purushottama. Hamir sent word that the time had come for Purushottama to recover his lost territory, so he invaded Telengana and besieged Malik Hasan in Rajahmundry. Muhammad, however, marched across the country and relieved him, the Orissan king retired to his country whither Muhammad followed him in 1478, when he had to make peace at the cost of many elephants and other rich presents to the sultan. Hamir, who had shut himself up in Kondavīdu, eventually surrendered and was spared his life. Muhammad destroyed the great temple at Kondavīdu, built a mosque on its site, and earned for himself the title of *ghazī* by killing with his own hand the Brahmin priests of the temple.

Muhammad now spent over three years in Telengana, completing its subjugation. The province, which had grown administratively unwieldy because of the addition of so much newly-conquered territory, was divided into two, east and west, with capitals at Rajahmundry and Wārangal. This was part of a general scheme of administrative reform planned by Mahmud Gawan; but Malik Hasan, who had hoped to become governor of undivided Telengana, resented the new scheme and resolved on the destruction of its author.

Muhammad also planned an expedition against the eastern Carnatic ruled over by Sāluva Narasimha, viceroy of Vijayanagar, who had helped Purushottama in the recent war. Malik Hasan offered to go with him, leaving his son Ahmad as his deputy in Rajahmundry. Ahmad, the better soldier, was then holding a fief in the Mahur district in Berar, evidently because it was felt necessary to keep father and son separated. He was now summoned from Mahur and installed in Rajahmundry. The invasion began, and Kondapalli became the headquarters of the Bāhmanī army. Here Muhammad left his son Mahmud with Mahmud Gawan, while he personally led a daring raid against Kānchipuram, plundered its rich temples, and slew a number of priests. The Muslim chronicler of this episode wildly exaggerates its results and writes that the Bāhmanī troops 'levelled the city and its temples to the ground and overthrew all the symbols of infidelity'. On his way back to Kondapalli, Muhammad lost much of his booty to Narasimha's troops, but succeeded in capturing Masulipatam.

At Kondapalli, Mahmud Gawan completed his scheme of administrative reform. Each of the four overgrown *tarafs* was divided into two under separate governors. At the same time, the power of the *tarafdars* (governors) was much curtailed, because 'several places in each of the eight divisions were reserved especially to meet the king's private expenses, and district collectors were appointed from the court to manage them'. Again, the new order was that only one fort in each province was left in the governor's hands, 'the remainder being entrusted to officers and troops distinctly appointed by the king and paid from headquarters'. This was calculated to make rebellion difficult if not impossible. Thirdly, the allowances for the maintenance of troops were increased, but stricter supervision and control was introduced and *pro rata* reductions made for missing numbers. Mahmud Gawan also improved the administration of land revenue by organizing a proper survey and proper assessment. These reforms made him very unpopular with the Deccanis who held five out of the eight governorships.

The hostile party carried to the sultan many tales against Mahmud Gawan, and as proof of their allegations, they contrived to get his seal affixed to a blank sheet of paper on which they wrote a letter purporting to be from Mahmud Gawan to the king of Orissa telling him that the people of the Deccan were weary of Muhammad's tyranny and perpetual drunkenness and urging him to invade the country. They placed the letter in the sultan's hands pretending that they had intercepted the messenger who was carrying it. Mahmud Gawan was sent for at once; disregarding the remonstrances of friends who sought to dissuade him from obeying this unusual call and advised him to flee to Gujarat, the minister presented himself before the king. Muhammad Shah sternly asked him what punishment was proper for one whose treason against his sovereign was proved. 'Death' was the unhesitating answer. The sultan showed him the forged letter; the minister admitted that the seal was indeed his, but protested that he had not written the letter. The sultan paid no attention but 'ordered his Abyssinian slave Jowhur to put the minister to death on the spot', and so it was done (5 April 1481). Thus died the only counsellor of the Bāhmanīs who combined loyalty with an ability which entitled him to the rank of a statesman, and who served his masters with unswerving devotion for thirty-five years. In private life, Mahmud Gawan was simple, generous, charitable, learned and blameless, and he might have healed the feud between the 'foreigners' and 'Deccanis' but for the implacable rancour of Malik Hasan.

Mahmud Gawan's camp was plundered by the troops and the mob, and his followers fled, together with the other 'foreigners', to Yusuf Adil Khan who was in the field. When questioned, Gawan's treasurer told the king that his master had distributed all his earnings in charity and had left no hoard; he further accused the sultan of having shed innocent blood and challenged him to prove the guilt of Mahmud Gawan or at least get at the messenger who was supposed to have carried the letter to the king of Orissa. Too late the sultan discovered the truth and sent the body of Gawan for burial with honour at Bidar. But the king was now feared and distrusted by all the foreigners and the respectable section of the Deccanis, who declined to have anything more to do with him, refused to attend court or camp and saluted him from a distance when they did so at all.

The king was thus thrown into the hands of the betrayers of his late minister and had to make it up with them, instead of punishing them as he had intended. Malik Hasan became lieutenant of the kingdom and his son Ahmad governor of Daulatabad in the place of Yusuf, who took the fiefs formerly held by Mahmud Gawan—Belgaum and Bijapur. Muhammad went to Belgaum hoping to conciliate Yusuf Adil Khan. When he heard that Narasimha of Vijayanagar was preparing to attack Goa, he wanted to go there, but his nobles would not accompany him. He therefore sent Yusuf Adil Khan to its relief, and himself returned to Firuzabad where he drowned his humiliation in drink. He formally nominated his young son Mahmud as his successor and died at Bidar on 22 March 1482, crying out that Mahmud Gawan was slaying him. He was only twenty-nine at the time.

Ferishta says that, next to Firuz Shah, he was the most learned prince that ever filled the Bāhmanī throne. He was a high-spirited, energetic monarch and a good soldier; and he had a number of competent ministers, Mahmud Gawan being the best among them. But drink was his arch-enemy which ruined his reputation by betraying him into rash acts and brought him to a premature end. He was in fact the last king of the line worth the name; five more followed him on the throne, but they were little more than puppets in the hands of unscrupulous ministers.

Muhammad III's son Mahmud was enthroned, at the age of twelve, by Malik Hasan, at a mean ceremony from which the nobility deliberately stayed away. Yusuf Adil Khan came back from Goa to Bidar to pay his respects to the new monarch, but suspicion and intrigue and the open fights between the Deccanis and his followers induced him to retire to Bijapur, leaving Malik Hasan supreme in the capital. An attempt by the boy-sultan to gain his freedom by having Malik Hasan assassinated failed, and he was more closely guarded ever after. It became well known that the king was a helpless prisoner, and the governors of provinces began to defy the orders of Malik Hasan, the *malik naib*. In 1486, for instance, the governor of Telengana rebelled and there were also revolts in Goa and Chākan supported by Yusuf Adil Shah. It was not long before the king openly expressed his disgust with Malik Hasan who thereupon left for Bidar with the intention of capturing the treasury and winning the army over to his side. He was caught, however, and, under the king's orders, strangled by Dilpasand Khan, the governor of the city. But his removal came too late; the king returned to Bidar and plunged into idleness and debauchery, neglecting public affairs. A conspiracy of the Deccanis to dethrone him in November 1487 was foiled by the intercession of the foreign troops, and the Deccanis and Africans suffered a terrible reprisal in the form of a general massacre which lasted three days.

In 1490, at the suggestion of Malik Ahmad Nizam-ul-Mulk, the late Malik Hasan's son, Yusuf Adil Khan of Bijapur and Fathullah Imad-ul-Mulk of Berar joined him in assuming the royal title and announced themselves free from the suzerainty of

Bidar. Their example was followed later by Qutb-ul-Mulk of Golconda (1512) and Barid-ul-Mulk of Bidar itself. Such was the origin of the five kingdoms of the Nizam Shahis of Ahmadnagar, Adil Shahis of Bijapur, Imad Shahis of Berar, Qutb Shahis of Golconda, and Barid Shahis of Bidar. Ahmad's motive was almost certainly disloyalty to the sultan who had ordered the murder of his father; but the others set up their independence because they could no longer tolerate a king who allowed himself to be swayed by whichever ambitious minister held his favour at the moment. That post was then held by Quasim Barid who soon reduced Sultan Mahmud to greater impotence than ever, and some are inclined to date the rise of the Barid Shahis from 1490.

Quasim Barid sought to bring the provincial governors under control, and proceeded against Bijapur after inciting Narasa Nāyaka, the regent of Vijayanagar, to attack it by invading the Raichur doab. He also expected Ahmad Shah to aid him, but was disappointed, and Yusuf gained a success against him. In 1493, Mahmud Begarha of Gujarat complained to the king of the Deccan against the piratical acts of his vassal Bahadur Gilani of Goa. In his attempts to reduce him, Quasim had the help of Yusuf, Ahmad and Fathullah, all of whom were interested in saving the Deccan from a Gujarati invasion. Bahadur was killed and his lands were bestowed on Ain-ul-Mulk Kanani, specially chosen by Quasim as likely to hold his own against Yusuf Adil.

There is no need to pursue in detail the intrigues, rebellions and faction fights that marked the remaining years of Mahmud's nominal rule. In 1504, Quasim Barid died and his place was taken by Amir Ali Barid who, in the midst of many vicissitudes, managed to retain control of the king and foil his efforts to secure his freedom. Mahmud died in December 1518, and was followed on the throne by his four sons: Ahmad (1518-21); Ala-ud-din (1521) who was deposed, imprisoned, and put to death for his attempt to get free of the control of Ali Barid; Wali Ullah (1521-4) who met the same fate after a nominal rule of three years; and Kalimullah. The last ruler sent a messenger to Babur promising to surrender the provinces of Daulatabad and Berar to him if he would rid the king of the Deccan of his jailor and restore to him the rest of his kingdom. No answer came; but

Amir Ali Barid got scent of the mission, and Kalimullah fled to Bijapur in 1527. He was received coldly there, and so went to Ahmadnagar where he died soon afterwards. His body was sent to Bidar for burial.

Such was the end of Bāhmanī rule, by no means an attractive chapter in the history of the country. Among the eighteen sultans of the line, there were few who were not drunkards and debauchees surrounded by informers and self-seekers. Faction and party strife dominated court-life and sometimes led to terrible blunders like the murder of Mahmud Gawan. Some of the kings were bigots, and none of them had any genuine sympathy for their subjects who were Hindus. Something was done to promote irrigation and agriculture, and though this was largely to increase the revenue to the crown, still it did good to the people as well. The Russian merchant Athanasius Nikitin who lived in Bidar for some time (1470-4) records: 'The land is overstocked with people; but those in the country are very miserable, whilst the nobles are extremely opulent and delight in luxury. They are wont to be carried on their silver beds, preceded by some twenty chargers caparisoned in gold, and followed by 300 men on horseback, and by 500 on foot, and by horn men, ten torchbearers and ten musicians.' The army and its leaders often sucked the country dry, and the people were helpless against them. The wars with the neighbouring Hindu states, particularly Vijayanagar, were marked by sickening horrors, and there were occasions when several hundreds were made 'converts'. Numbers of foreigners —Persians, Turks, Arabs and Moguls—came in search of trade or office, settled in the country and formed unions with the women of the land. All the same, the bulk of the population continued Hindu, and the number of Muslims in the former 'Hyderabad state' never exceeded fifteen per cent.

The Bāhmanī sultans erected a number of well-designed fortresses, and the cities of Gulbarga and Bidar owe their chief monuments to them and their ministers. The architecture of these buildings will be discussed in chapter XVI on 'Art'.

The history of the five separate kingdoms that arose out of the Bāhmanī kingdom need not be pursued in detail, and will only be touched on in the next chapter in so far as it concerns their relations with Vijayanagar. Golconda and Bijapur were the most important among them, and had a longer history than the rest. Muhammad Kasim, better known by his surname Ferishta, wrote his celebrated history to the command of Ibrahim II of Bijapur (1580-1626).

BIBLIOGRAPHY

J. BRIGGS: *History of the Rise of the Muhammadan Power in India* (Ferishta), Vol. II, pp. 283-559 (Calcutta, 1909)

SIR WOLSELEY HAIG: *The Kingdom of the Deccan*, 1347-1436 (*Cambridge History of India*, Vol. III)

J. S. KING: *The History of the Bāhmanī Dynasty* (London, 1900)

H. K. SHERWANI: *Mahmud Gawan* (Allahabad, 1942)

M. SOMASEKHARA SARMA: *A Forgotten Chapter of Andhra History* (Madras, 1945)

N. VENKATARAMANAYYA: *The Early Muslim Expansion in South India* (Madras 1942)

BĀHMANĪ KINGS OF THE DECCAN

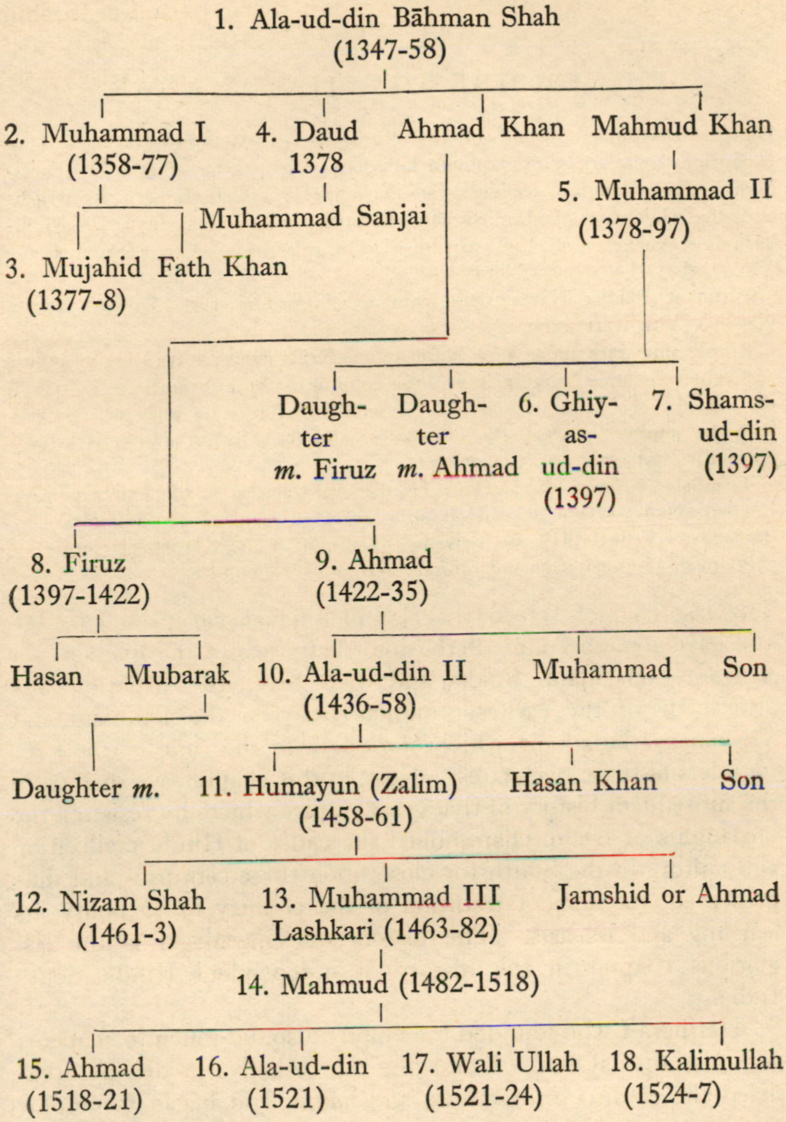

CHAPTER XII

THE EMPIRE OF VIJAYANAGAR

Harihara I—Bukka I—end of the Sultanate of Madura—Harihara II—expansion—relations with Bāhmanī kingdom—Virūpāksha—Bukka II—Devarāya I—Rāmachandra —Vijayarāya—Devarāya II—relations with the Reddis and the Gajapatis—Abdur Razzak—Bāhmanī wars—Vijayarāya II—Mallikārjuna—weakness of the empire—Oḍḍa expansion—loyal feudatories—Virūpāksha II—Sāluva Narasimha.

Wars of Sāluva Narasimha—Immaḍi Narasimha and Tuluva Narasa Nāyaka—Vīra Narasimha.

Revolts and wars under Vīra Narasimha—Krishnadeva Rāya—his greatness and achievements—Achyuta Rāya—the coming of the Portuguese—the rise of the Nāyaks of Madura—Venkata I—Sadāśiva—Rāmarāja and his relations with the southern powers, the Portuguese and the Muslim states—Rakshasi-Tangadi—destruction of Vijayanagar.

Tirumala—Śrīranga I—Venkata II—Revival—arrival of the Dutch and the English—civil war and confusion after death of Venkata II—Śrīranga II—Rāmadeva—Venkata III and Śrīranga III—end of the Karnataka empire.

Political, administrative and military system of the empire.

THE last chapter traced the rise of Vijayanagar prior to 1346 and gave some account of the joint activities of the five sons of Sangama—Harihara, Bukka and their brothers. Mention was also made of the earliest conflicts between the Bāhmanī and Vijayanagar kingdoms which started from the time of the very founders of those two states. Now, in this chapter, we shall trace the subsequent history of that great empire which, by resisting the onslaughts of Islam, championed the cause of Hindu civilization and culture in the South for close upon three centuries and thus preserved the ancient tradition of the country in its polity, its learning and its arts. The history of Vijayanagar is the last glorious chapter in the history of independent Hindu South India.

Harihara I who founded the empire also did much to shape its administrative system. Following the Kākatīya model, he organized the country into *sthalas* and *nāḍus*, and began to employ numbers of Brahmins as *karṇams* (in preference to goldsmiths and *velamas* who had held the positions before). He also reclaimed to the plough large areas of land in the Ceded Districts. His reign must have come to an end shortly after 1357 as that is the last date occurring in the known inscriptions of his reign. Before he died he had already nominated Bukka, the ablest of his brothers, to succeed him; indeed this 'prop of the throne' became joint ruler as early as 1346, with Gutti as his capital.

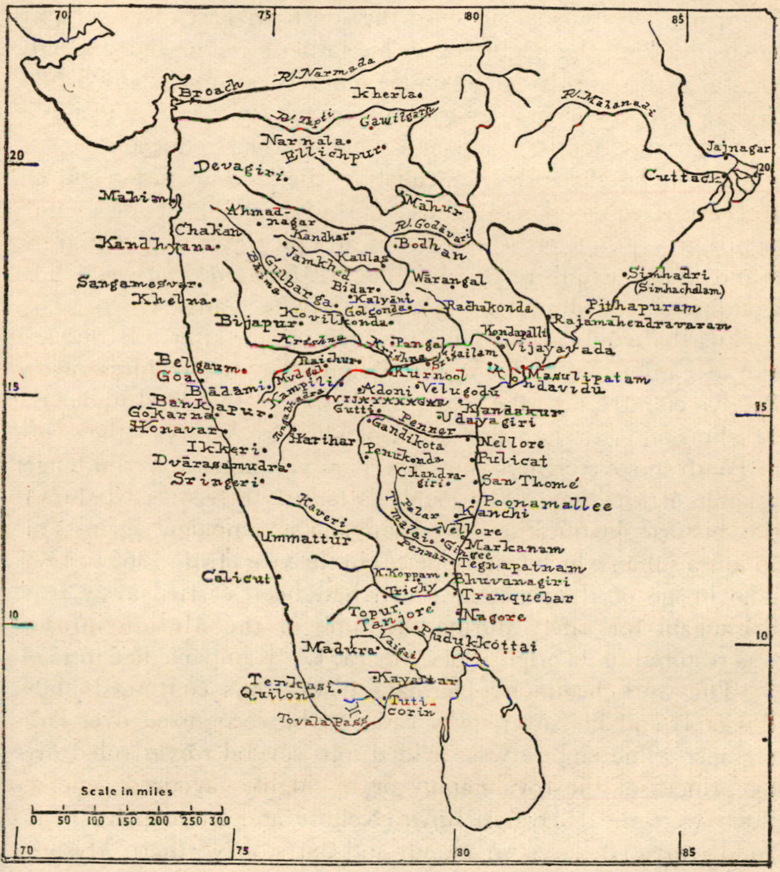

SOUTH INDIA IN VIJAYANAGAR TIMES

Bukka I's reign as sole sovereign lasted for exactly twenty years to 1377. In the field of foreign affairs his most notable act was to send an embassy to China, as is recorded under the year 1374 in the annals of the Ming dynasty. At home, there were frequent, and mainly disastrous, wars against the Bāhmanī sultans, Muhammad I and Mujahid, as recorded in the last chapter. The accession of Muhammad II to the throne of Gulbarga in 1378 brought a welcome lull in the perpetual hostilities, for the new sultan was essentially a man of peace.

In importance, however, the most notable event of Bukka's reign was the overthrow of the Madura sultanate by his son, Kumāra Kampana. Kampana had ruled the southern part of the empire as viceroy from the beginning of his father's reign, and was ably assisted in this work by such famous generals as Gopana and Sāluva Mangu. Kampana first made his power felt by the Śāmbuvarāyas of North and South Arcot, and when he had reduced them to subjection he succeeded in enlisting their co-operation in his enterprise against the Muslims of Madura. The details of this campaign are not forthcoming, but an epic version of it is to be found in the exquisite Sanskrit poem *Madhurā Vijayam* (' The Conquest of Madura ') by Kampana's wife Gangā Devī. This tells us that while sojourning at Kānchipuram after his conquest of the Śāmbuvarāya, Kampana dreamt that the goddess of the Pāndya country described the pitiful state of that land under the Muslims and gave him a sword dispatched by Agastya—the sword of Pāndyan sovereignty which the Pāndyan kings were no longer capable of wielding. The Pāndya's failure to recover Madura is the historic justification for Kampana's campaign against the Madura sultan which history places in the years from 1365 to 1370. The image of Ranganātha, which had been carried away from Śrīrangam for safety during the time of the Muslim inroads, was restored to its original place in 1371. Kampana died in 1374.

The work begun by Harihara I was thus continued under Bukka I, and his sovereignty came to be recognized over large regions. The empire was divided into several *rājyas* ruled over by princes of the royal family or by highly favoured generals. Such were the Udayagiri *rājya* (Nellore and Cuddapah), Penugonda *rājya* (Bellary, Anantapur and parts of Northern Mysore), Mulvāyi *rājya* (parts of Mysore, Salem and South Arcot districts), Araga or Maleha *rājya* (Banavāsi, Chandragutti and Goa) and the Tulu *rājya* also called Barakūr-Mangalūru *rājya*, besides the Rājagambhīra *rājya* and others in the south.

Bukka I was followed on the throne by his son Harihara II who ruled for twenty-seven years (1377-1404) and consolidated the supremacy of Vijayanagar all over southern India. The celebrated Sāyaṇa-ācārya, the brother of Mādhava, was his chief minister.

Harihara replaced his cousins by his own sons as governors of provinces and sought thus to forestall the tendencies to disruption due to the ambitions of his more distant relatives. Thus Devarāya was made the governor of Udayagiri.

In Telengana an important change had followed the invasion of Anapota, the Velama chieftain of Rājakonda, which had resulted in the defeat and death of Kāpaya Nāyaka sometime about 1369. Anapota was friendly to the Bāhmanīs, and this alliance spelt danger to Kondavīdu and Vijayanagar. Prince Bukka II, son of Harihara II, led two expeditions into Wārangal territory before the end of 1390, but failed to achieve any decisive results. Seven years later, Pangal was taken. This should have been an important gain, since it gave Bukka a forward base for future operations in Telengana; but it seems to have been lost soon after.

Extensions of territory were achieved in other directions as well. In the north-west, the ports of Goa, Chaul and Dabhol were taken from the Muslims, as also Kharepatan; and the Krishna became the northern frontier of Vijayanagar for a time. The Reddis of Kondavīdu were deprived of their possessions in Kurnool, Nellore and even parts of Guntur (1382-5); and the power of the empire in the southern country was strengthened by an expedition led by prince Virūpāksha which even reached Ceylon and laid it under tribute. These successes, particularly those in the north, were doubtless due, at least in part, to the peaceful character of Muhammad II Bāhmanī and the confusion caused after his death by the mischievous activity of the ambitious Turkish slave Tughalchin.

In 1398-9 another fierce war raged between the Vijayanagar and Bāhmanī kingdoms in which Firuz pursued the army of Harihara II from the banks of the Krishna to the capital. He inflicted great slaughter on the Hindu population, and only agreed to an armistice after collecting a heavy ransom for the numerous prisoners he had taken. The treaty which both sides then signed contained such vague declarations as that the boundaries of the two kingdoms were to be the same as before the war, and that each party was to refrain from molesting the subjects of the other. Widespread famine over a great part of the Deccan added to the sufferings of the people during this period. The tribute which Harihara promised to pay annually was withheld two years later when the Sultans of Malwa and Gujarat became his allies.

When Harihara II died in August 1404 the succession was violently disputed between his surviving sons. At first Virūpāksha succeeded in securing the throne, but was soon ousted by Bukka II who ruled for two years (1405-6). Finally, Devarāya I became king and celebrated his coronation on 5 November 1406.

According to the Portuguese chronicler Nuniz, Bukka II and Devarāya greatly extended the city of Vijayanagar, raising fresh walls and towers, and building further lines of fortification. But, says Sewell, their 'great work was the construction of a huge dam in the Tungabhadra river, and the formation of an aqueduct fifteen miles long from the river into the city. If this be the same channel that to the present day supplies the fields which occupy so much of the site of the old city, it is a most extraordinary work. For several miles this channel is cut out of the solid rock at the base of the hills, and is one of the most remarkable irrigation works to be seen in India.'

Early in his reign Devarāya was at war with Firuz Shah Bāhmanī—as a result, according to Ferishta, of the Hindu monarch's infatuation for a beautiful girl who lived in Mudgal; but another account attributes it to Firuz's determination to wage a *jihad* (holy war) against the Hindu monarch. The war went badly for Firuz at first but ended in a peace humiliating to the Hindu monarch who had to surrender the strategic fort of Bankapur, which commanded an important route from Vijayanagar to the Arabian Sea, and to give one of his daughters in marriage to the sultan.

The Reddis of Kondavīdu, who were possibly in league with Firuz, took their chance to attack Udayagiri and captured territory belonging to that province from which they were not expelled until 1413.

Anadeva, a Telugu-Choda chief of the region between the Krishna and Godāvari, was another ally of Firuz. To counteract his influence, Devarāya entered into an alliance with his brother-in-law Kātayavema, the Reddi chief of Rājamahendravarman (Rajahmundry). Fighting began in 1415 and at first went against Anadeva until Firuz came to his rescue and Kātayavema was killed. Devarāya's forces were also beaten so that Firuz was able to maintain his suzerainty in Telengana. Devarāya retaliated by capturing Pangal, thus threatening Firuz's line of communication; the town was then subjected to a siege lasting two years. The defection of the Velamas of Rājakonda, who joined Devarāya, weakened the Bāhmanī forces, so that when plague further reduced their strength, Devarāya won an overwhelming victory (1419). The Reddi kingdom of Rajahmundry recovered under Allāḍa, Kātayavema's general, who upheld the cause of his master's son Kumāragiri. Kondavīdu, however, was partitioned between Devarāya and the Velamas of Rājakonda (1420) and suffered extinction. In all these battles and wars, Devarāya was notably assisted by his son Vīra Vijaya Rāya and his minister Lakshmīdhara who is said to have saved the king from a plot to murder him. When Devarāya died in 1422, his son Rāmachandra occupied the throne for a few months, and was then followed by his brother Vīra Vijaya Rāya. Towards the close of Devarāya's reign the Italian Nicolo Conti visited Vijayanagar and his description of the city has survived to this day.

The duration of Vīra Vijaya Rāya's reign has been variously estimated; tentatively it may be said to have lasted for about five years (1422-6). Nuniz says he 'did nothing worth recording'. His son, who in due course succeeded him as Devarāya II, was associated with him in the administration almost from the beginning. The traditional enmity with the Bāhmanīs continued, so it was not long before Ahmad Shah began a war against Vijaya and inflicted a defeat on his forces and great slaughter and destruction on the civil population of the country. The armies met on the banks of the Tungabhadra; Vijaya's camp was surprised in the early morning and the king hurriedly made his escape to a sugarcane plantation. He was found by the Muslim soldiers; but they mistook him for a common labourer and, when they came to know of the sultan's victory, they left him and hastened to join their friends. Ahmad Shah then overran the open country, and 'laying aside all humanity, whenever the number of the slain amounted to twenty thousand, he halted three days, and made a festival in celebration of the bloody work. He broke down the idol temples, and destroyed the colleges of Brahmins'. Before peace could be had, Vijaya had to pay a vast sum as arrears of tribute, and to acquiesce in the conqueror's carrying many of his subjects, including several learned Brahmins, into captivity.

Vijaya Rāya was succeeded by his son Devarāya II in about 1426. Devarāya's title *gajabeṭekāra* ('Hunter of Elephants') has been explained in two ways—as a metaphor referring to his victories over enemy kings who were strong as elephants, and more literally as indicating the monarch's addiction to the sport of hunting elephants. By about 1428 Devarāya effected the conquest and annexation of the Kondavīdu country which had been in a weak and disorganized state after the death in 1420 of the intrepid Peda Komati Vema. He followed this up by invading the Gajapati kingdom of Orissa, possibly because the conquest of Kondavīdu brought Devarāya into conflict with Gajapati's subordinates; but before hostilities could proceed, Allāḍa Reddi of Rajahmundry intervened and brought about peace between the combatants. Allāḍa died shortly after this and was succeeded by his sons Allaya Vema and Vīrabhadra who followed their father's general policy of aggrandizement at the expense of Kalinga. The accession of Kapileśvara, an energetic ruler in Kalinga, in 1435, naturally resulted in a Gajapati invasion of the kingdom of Rajahmundry. The rulers of Rajahmundry sought help from the Vijayanagar ruler connected with them by ties of political and dynastic alliance. Devarāya II responded, and his troops drove the Kalinga army back and secured a temporary respite for the kingdom of Rajahmundry until it was swallowed up by Kapileśvara after Devarāya II's death.

Devarāya also carried his arms into Kerala, subjugating the ruler of Quilon and other chieftains. The Zamorin of Calicut, however, seems to have continued to retain his independence. Abdur Razzak, the Persian ambassador who visited South India in this reign, states that although the Zamorin was not under Devarāya's authority, he lived in great fear of him, and when he received a letter from the Vijayanagar monarch that the Persian ambassador should be sent to his court without delay he instantly carried out the order. The same writer bears testimony to the supremacy of Devarāya over the whole of South India, saying that his dominions extended from Ceylon to Gulbarga and from Bengal (Orissa) to Malabar. Nuniz asserts that Devarāya also exacted tribute from the rulers of Quilon, Ceylon, Pulicat, Pegu and Tenasserim and elsewhere.

With the Bāhmanī kingdom, however, Devarāya's relations continued to be hostile. Soon after his accession in 1436, sultan Ala-ud-din II sent his brother Muhammad against Vijayanagar to recover ' the arrears of tribute ', and Devarāya had to pay a large amount. The Vijayanagar armies were so consistently defeated in their contests with Bāhmanī forces that Devarāya held a council of his nobility to explore the causes of Muslim successes and devise means of counteracting them. As a result, Mussalmans were thenceforth eligible for service in his army and allowed the free exercise of their religion; a Koran was placed before his throne that they 'might perform the ceremony of obeisance in his presence, without sinning against their laws'. Further, the Hindu soldiers received better training, particularly in archery. After this reorganization the army became a more efficient striking force.

Abdur Razzak relates that while he was staying at Calicut in 1443, a brother of Devarāya II attempted to murder the king at a banquet. The plot was a failure, however, because the king excused himself on the score of health, though many nobles fell into the trap and lost their lives. Ala-ud-din Bāhmanī II evidently knew of the conspiracy, and tried to take advantage of the confusion by demanding from Devarāya the payment of 'seven lakhs of *varāhas* (pagodas)'. Devarāya returned a defiant answer which he soon followed up by an invasion of the Raichur doab. The campaign began very well; Mudgal was taken, Raichur and Bankapur were besieged and the country up to Bijapur laid waste. But the Bāhmanī forces soon rallied and compelled Devarāya to fall back on Mudgal. In the last of three engagements that followed, Devarāya's elder son was killed, and his troops were driven back into the fortress of Mudgal. Two important Bāhmanī generals, however, were taken prisoners until the sultan threatened a wholesale massacre of the Hindu population if they were not released; and Devarāya did not feel strong enough to refuse the Sultan's terms.

Devarāya was a great builder and a patron of poets. Himself a scholar and author, he is reputed to have presided with conspicuous success over many literary disputations. In one such, the Telugu poet Śrīnātha was held to surpass the poet-laureate who belonged to the celebrated Ḍiṇḍima family, and is said to have been bathed in a shower of golden *tankas*.

Devarāya's long, and generally prosperous, reign came to an end with his death in May 1446. He was succeeded by a Vijaya Rāya II and then, very shortly after, by his own son Mallikārjuna who was crowned some time before May 1447.

Mallikārjuna was weak and incompetent so that, from his accession, there began a period of dissension, decline and confusion until the strength of the empire was restored, over forty years later, by the martial ability and statesmanship of Sāluva Narasimha. The interval is marked by much agitation, discontent, and opposition to the members of the old royal family, several of whom met with violent deaths. At the start of his reign, the Velamas made a new home for themselves in Velugodu (Kurnool district) when their capital Rājakonda was seized by the Bāhmanīs and the neighbouring princelings then disturbed the peace and weakened the realm—a situation of which both Ala-ud-din II and Kapileśvara Gajapati took advantage. They laid siege to Vijayanagar; but, true to its name, that city defied all their efforts to capture it and the invading armies had to retire without accomplishing much.

Kapileśvara, however, kept up the war, capturing Rajahmundry and Kondavīdu before 1454, being aided in his enterprise by the Kshatriya and Velama chieftains of Telengana. His conquests extended up to Śrīśailam and included a large part of the Kurnool district. He sent his son Hambar against Mahmud Gawan, whom he defeated, to capture Wārangal in Telengana, and later, on Humayun's death in 1461, Bidar. He then conquered Udayagiri in Nellore, and Kānchipuram and Trichinopoly in the southern provinces of the empire of Vijayanagar (1463).

The Oḍḍa empire reached its greatest extent at this time, its influence being felt from the Ganges to the Kaveri. But unlike the Telugu districts, which became part of the empire of Orissa for some years, the southern lands did not pass out of the control of Vijayanagar, and the Oriya invasion of the South was only a sudden raid followed by speedy withdrawal. The sovereignty of Vijayanagar was upheld by its powerful nobles ruling in almost complete independence of the emperor Mallikārjuna; such were Sāluva Gopa Timma, also known as Tirumalaideva Mahārāja who held Trichinopoly, Tanjore and Pudukkōṭṭai, and Sāluva Narasimha, equally prominent in the centre and in the eastern parts of the empire. The latter was assisted by Īśvara, an able soldier of Tuluva extraction. Mallikārjuna died some time between June and October 1465.

He left behind an infant son, Rājaśekhara, but the throne was occupied by his cousin Virūpāksha II. Virūpāksha was the son of Pratāpadevarāya, a younger brother of Devarāya II, and had been ruler of Penugonda for several years before he assumed the imperial crown. Nuniz records that ' he was given over to vice, caring for nothing but women, and to fuddle himself with drink.' It is not surprising, therefore, that large tracts of land were lost to the Muslims including Goa, Chaul and Dabhol. The authority of the central government continued to decline, and total disruption was, once again, only prevented by the initiative of powerful provincial governors. Most prominent among these was Sāluva Narasimha, ruler of Chandragiri *rājya*, whose inscriptions begin as early as 1456. His dominions must have suffered during the Oḍḍa invasion of 1463, and he now began a war against the Gajapati and captured Udayagiri after a siege (1470). He suppressed a rebellion in the Tamil districts and, taking advantage of the civil war in Orissa that followed Kapileśvara's death, he expelled the Oriyas from the eastern districts of the empire and made himself master of all the territory up to the Godāvari. Kondavīdu and Masulipatam fell into his hands before 1477. It seems probable that Narasimha helped Purushottama Gajapati to regain the throne of Orissa from which he had been expelled by Hambar with the aid of the Bāhmanī sultan Muhammad III. Narasimha and Purushottama had to face the hostility of that sultan, and the war that followed, in 1478-81, has been described in the last chapter. The Tuluva general Īśvara particularly distinguished himself by recapturing much of the booty which the sultan had gathered by his daring raid on Kānchipuram.

Virūpāksha II continued to rule till the middle of 1485 when he was murdered by his eldest son. The parricide, however, declined the throne and had his younger brother, Padearao (Praudhadevarāya), crowned king. The first act of the new king, however, was to procure the assassination of the brother to whom he owed the throne, and then to plunge into debauchery and neglect the affairs of state. Sāluva Narasimha saw that the only way to save the kingdom was to put an end to the old dynasty and to assume the royal title himself. He therefore commanded his general Narasa Nāyaka to proceed against Vijayanagar and capture the city. 'Nuniz gives us a graphic account of the last scenes; how Narasimha's captain arrived at the city gates and found them undefended; how he penetrated the palace and found no one to oppose him; how he even went as far as the harem "slaying some of the women"; and how at last the craven king fled.' Thereupon Narasimha was 'raised to be king' (1486) and the kingdom came to be called after him. There can be no doubt that by this act of ' usurpation ' Narasimha and his supporters saved the empire from disruption. All the same, there was much opposition to Narasimha's elevation and he had to spend time and energy in fighting and subduing recalcitrant chieftains like the Sambetas of Peranipādu (Cuddapah district), the *pālayagars* of Ummattur near Mysore, and others. He certainly overcame his internal troubles but they greatly weakened his capacity to resist his foreign enemies. For instance, when Purushottama Gajapati took advantage of the weakness of the Bāhmanī kingdom after the death of Muhammad III and conquered all the eastern coastal country south of Orissa up to the Gundlakamma river in the Nellore district by about 1489 and even advanced to Udayagiri and laid siege to it; Narasimha's attempt to raise the siege proved disastrous. Defeated in battle and taken prisoner, he only secured his release by agreeing to surrender the fort and the surrounding country.

The loss of the western ports in the reign of Virūpāksha II had dislocated the horse trade of the Arabs on which the Vijayanagar army depended for its cavalry. Narasimha, however, revived the trade by conquering the Tulu country and manning the ports of Honavar, Bhaṭṭakkula (Bhatkal), Bākanūr and Mangalore. ' He caused horses to be brought from Ormuz and Aden into his kingdom, and thereby gave profit to the merchants, paying them for the horses just as they had asked ' (Nuniz). He also took steps to strengthen the efficiency and the martial spirit of his troops.

He did not long survive his defeat at Udayagiri, however, and died in 1491. He left behind two young sons whom he commended to the care of his loyal general Narasa Nāyaka, the son of Tuluva Īśvara. Narasa at first made the elder prince Timmabhūpa king, but Tymmarasa, a rival of Narasa Nāyaka, had him murdered. The crown then descended to the younger prince, Immaḍi Narasimha (1491); but Narasa Nāyaka retained all real power in his hands as regent, and even assumed the royal style along with his Sāluva titles. Friction thus naturally arose between him and the king which was increased when Immaḍi Narasimha refused to punish Tymmarasa, the murderer of his elder brother, as Narasa Nāyaka wanted, but received him into favour. The breach between them reached such a pass that Narasa Nāyaka marched with his troops from Penugonda to lay siege to Vijayanagar (1492), and, as the price of peace with the regent, Immaḍi Narasimha had to abandon Tymmarasa who was punished with death. The king was now removed to Penugonda where he was kept under close surveillance. It was indeed a second usurpation, which necessarily led to a crop of fresh internal troubles which hampered Narasa Nāyaka throughout the twelve or thirteen years he was the virtual ruler of the kingdom.

At his death, Sāluva Narasimha had besought Narasa Nāyaka to capture the forts of Raichur and Udayagiri, which had rebelled against him but 'which he could not subdue because time failed him'. In 1492-3 Quasim Barid, the Bāhmanī minister, offered Narasa Nāyaka the forts of Raichur and Mudgal in return for an attack on Yusuf Adil Khan of Bijapur, now an independent monarch. Narasa accepted the terms and sent into the Raichur doab an army which 'having crossed the river Tungabhadra, laid waste the country as far as Mudgal and Raichur' (Ferishta). Adil Khan was in no position to resist the invader immediately as he had also to contend with other enemies whom Quasim Barid had set up against him at the same time. As soon as he had succeeded in repelling them, and found himself free to attempt the recovery of Raichur, Narasa Nāyaka had to defend his recent conquests. Yusuf Adil Khan met with little success, however; he was defeated and forced to seek refuge in the fortress of Manvi, north of the Tungabhadra in the neighbourhood of Adoni. He then pretended submission and invited Narasa to a peace conference where the Bijapur ruler treacherously attacked him and his followers and put seventy persons of rank to death. The Hindu army fled and gave Adil Khan the victory; but the doab continued to remain part of the Vijayanagar empire till 1502 when, as the result of a *jihad* undertaken by the Bāhmanī nobles at the instance of Mahmud, it passed into the hands of Yusuf Adil Shah along with the fortresses of Raichur and Mudgal.

In the south there had been no effective assertion of the authority of the empire after the raid of Kapileśvara Gajapati in 1463-4. Sāluva Narasimha had been too busy nearer home, and it is doubtful if his authority was acknowledged south of the Kaveri. About 1496, or perhaps a little earlier, Narasa Nāyaka marched south, controlled the tyrannical oppression of officials like Kōnētirāja, Governor of Trichinopoly and Tanjore, against whom the Vaishnavas of Śrīrangam had many complaints, and subjugated the whole land up to Cape Comorin, compelling the local Chola and Chera rulers, and Mānabhūsha of Madura, to acknowledge the suzerainty of Vijayanagar. He also attacked Śrīrangapattana (Seringapatam) after throwing a bridge across the Kaveri, and its Heuṇa chieftain Nanjarāja had to submit. Further conquests on the west coast and a march to Gokarna (1497) closed this extensive and successful campaign.

Narasa Nāyaka again came into conflict with the Gajapati king towards the close of his rule. Purushottama died in 1496 after a reign of thirty years and was succeeded by his son Pratāparudra. He attacked Vijayanagar territory with a view to conquering the south (*c.* 1499). Narasa was quite equal to holding his own and the campaign ended without any marked gains to either side, and the boundary of the Gajapati kingdom continued to be to the south of the Krishna river.

When Narasa Nāyaka died in 1503, he could truthfully claim to have continued the work of his master Sāluva Narasimha and to have imparted fresh strength to the empire. He had established its authority effectively over the whole of its extensive dominions and had reorganized the army. Indeed he may be said to have laid the foundations on which his talented son, Krishnadeva Rāya, built the glorious age that followed.

Immediately after his death, however, his place as regent was taken by his eldest son Immaḍi Narasa Nāyaka, better known as Vīra Narasimha. The lawful sovereign, Immaḍi Narasimha, continued to be kept under tutelage, though he must in fact have been old enough to look after affairs. He was finally assassinated early in 1505, and was shortly afterwards succeeded by Vīra Narasimha, who thus inaugurated the third, or the Tuluva dynasty of the Vijayanagar kingdom. Nuniz notes that after Narasa's death 'the whole land revolted under its captains', and the murder of the king and the following usurpation could not have made the position of Vīra Narasimha any the easier. His six-year reign was almost wholly spent in fighting and success did not always attend him. Yusuf Adil Khan again sought to extend his dominion beyond the Tungabhadra which he crossed to lay siege to Kurnool. Rāmarāja of the Aravīḍu family and his son Timma stood by Vīra Narasimha, forced Adil Khan to retire and, by pursuing the retreating army, inflicted a defeat upon it. They expelled the treacherous captain of Adoni, which they occupied and later received, along with the fortress of Kurnool, as fiefs from their grateful emperor.

Meantime, the Heuṇa chiefs of Ummattur and Śrīrangapattana had set up the standard of revolt, and Vīra Narasimha left his half-brother Krishnarāya in charge of the capital while he marched to the south to lay siege to Ummattur. Failing to take the place after three months, he raised the siege and proceeded to attack Śrīrangapattana but with no better results. Some minor successes, however, attended him in the Tulu country. He also entered into friendly relations with the Portuguese who were just establishing themselves on the west coast, and sent an embassy to Almeida at Cannanore with a view to the better training of his armed forces and the procuring of horses for his cavalry. When Almeida wanted to build a fortress at Bhatkal, however, he sent him no answer. He tried to make his people more warlike by encouraging his nobles to settle their disputes by duelling, and he rewarded skill in swordsmanship by presenting the winners with beautiful girls.

Vīra Narasimha also tried to recover Goa. The Italian traveller Varthema recorded that the Muslim governor of that place was at war with the king of Vijayanagar (1506); but the result of the campaign is not known. He was concerting measures to renew his attack on Ummattur when he died in 1509. Munificent gifts to all the important shrines of South India, such as Rāmeśvaram, Śrīrangam, Kumbakonam, Chidambaram, Śrīśailam, Kānchipuram, Kālahasti, Mahānandi and Gokarna, are recorded in his name in the inscriptions of his time. Nuniz records that, while on his death-bed, he sent for his minister Sāluva Timma and ordered him to put out the eyes of Krishnadeva Rāya in order to secure the throne for his eight-year-old son, and that the minister satisfied the dying king by producing before him the eyes of a she-goat. There is, however, no evidence that the relations between the two half-brothers were anything but friendly, and indigenous tradition avers that Vīra Narasimha himself chose Krishnadeva Rāya for the succession.

The earliest inscription of Krishnadeva is dated 26 July 1509. His coronation was celebrated about a fortnight later on the birthday of Śrī Krishna, to convey the suggestion that the king was an incarnation of the Lord. The reign of Krishnadeva Rāya was 'the period of Vijayanagar's greatest success, when its armies were everywhere victorious, and the city was most prosperous'. Krishnadeva was between twenty and twenty-five years of age at his accession. Paes, who saw him about ten years later, said: ‘ The king is of medium height and of fair complexion and good figure, rather fat than thin; he has on his face signs of smallpox. He is the most feared and perfect king that could possibly be, cheerful of disposition and very merry; he is one that seeks to honour foreigners, and receives them kindly, asking about all their affairs whatever their condition may be. He is a great ruler and a man of much justice, but subject to sudden fits of rage.’ Krishnadeva kept up his bodily strength by hard physical exercise, he was a fine rider and his noble presence made a pleasant impression on all who came into contact with him. He often led his armies in person and exhibited great steadfastness and courage in the face of danger. He had great care for the welfare of the rank and file of the forces, and visited the wounded after each engagement and arranged for their proper care. He was loved and respected by all and was, says Paes, ‘ gallant and perfect in all things ’.

At the time of Krishnadeva’s succession, however, the condition of the empire was by no means reassuring. The rebel chieftain of Ummattur was contesting the lordship of the best part of the Mysore country; the Gajapatis of Orissa were in occupation of the north-eastern districts and Pratāparudra was openly hostile and aggressive; and though the Bāhmanī kingdom had virtually split up into five separate states, still the Muslim pressure from the north, especially from Bijapur, continued unabated in its strength. There was also the newly-risen power of the Portuguese to contend with—a power which was rapidly establishing control over the routes and the maritime trade of the west coast and seeking profitable political contacts with ‘ the country powers ’. Nevertheless, within ten short years Krishnadeva succeeded in firmly establishing the authority of Vijayanagar all over the country; there was no thought of revolt and no great discontent anywhere within his vast realm, and the Portuguese became his friends.

His first task was to repulse the Bāhmanī forces which invaded his territory in pursuit of the policy of annual *jihad* resolved upon by Mahmud in 1501. As usual, prominent Bāhmanī nobles assembled in Bidar and started with the Sultan Mahmud on their annual raid into the Rāya’s kingdom (1509); but they soon discovered that they were no longer free to plunder and ravage. The progress of the Muslim armies was checked at the unidentified town of Diwani where they were decisively defeated in the battle that followed. The sultan himself was thrown off his horse and sustained serious injuries from which he recovered only slowly, whereupon his nobles ' folded up the carpet of contention and war ', and returned to Bidar. Krishnadeva pursued the retiring armies, particularly that of Yusuf Adil Khan, who turned round to oppose him near Kovilkonda and lost his life in the battle that followed. The citadel of Kovilkonda became Krishnadeva's before he returned to his capital.

At the start of this war, the Portuguese governor, Albuquerque, sent an agent to offer aid to Krishnadeva in return for Vijayanagar support against the Zamorin of Calicut; he also promised to supply Arab and Persian horses only to Vijayanagar, and not to send any to Bijapur. Eager as Krishnadeva was to secure a monopoly in the horse trade, he did not immediately accept the offer. The second Portuguese embassy to Krishnadeva renewed Almeida's request to erect a fort at Bhatkal and gained its object. This was after Albuquerque had attacked and captured Goa at the end of 1510—the result of many months' fighting during which the town changed hands several times between the Portuguese and Bijapur troops.

After this preliminary canter against his foes, Krishnadeva spent some time in his capital reorganizing his army and converting the motley feudal levies into an effective fighting force. He then invaded the Raichur doab and took the Raichur fort, finding his opportunity in the differences that had arisen between Bijapur and the Bāhmanī sultan. Yusuf Adil Khan had been succeeded by his young son Ismail Adil Shah as nominal ruler in Bijapur, but Kamal Khan was all-powerful and had his own designs on the throne; Kamal Khan also knew that Krishnadeva was friendly with the Portuguese, and so the opposition from Bijapur to Krishna's invasion on this occasion was very feeble. Kamal Khan was assassinated in May 1511 by a hireling employed by Ismail's mother, which led to fresh troubles for Bijapur from Persian and Khurasani nobles who were the friends of the murdered regent. Krishnadeva, however, was entirely free to pursue his designs, so that after the capture of Raichur he marched on Gulbarga, defeated Amir Barid, the minister and gaoler of Mahmud and took the city. From there he marched on Bidar, captured it after a short siege, released Mahmud and assumed the title ' establisher of the Yavana (Muslim) kingdom '.

At the same time, Krishnadeva was also fighting his other enemies: the rebellious chieftain of Ummattur and the Gajapati ruler of Orissa. The war against Gangarāya of Ummattur who had been in revolt since the last years of Vīra Narasimha's reign was undertaken soon after the repulse of the Bāhmanī invasion, and may be said to have lasted from August 1510 to the end of 1512. It began with an attack on Penugonda, which had passed into the hands of the rebel; the capture of this strong fortress was followed by attacks on Ummattur and Śivanasamudram (the headquarters of Gangarāya). The latter took over a year to reduce; Gangarāya fled and was drowned in the Kaveri, and his seat was razed to the ground. The conquered territory became a new province with Śrīrangapattana as its capital; Sāluva Govindarāya was appointed its first governor, while the local administration was entrusted to three local chieftains, the famous Kempe Gauda of Bangalūru (Bangalore) being one of them.

A third front was opened against the Orissa ruler, who had been in occupation of the coastal districts in the east from the days of Sāluva Narasimha, soon after the king's accession. It was only pressed with vigour, however, after the close of the campaign against Gangarāya. An army was then sent to lay siege to Udayagiri in 1513, and soon Krishnadeva himself joined it and conducted the operation. The fort was taken after the siege had lasted for a year and a half during which Krishnadeva had many new paths cut up the rocky hills to enable his troops to reach the walls of the inaccessible citadel.

On his way back to his own capital Krishna and his queens Tirumala Devi and Chinna Devi visited Tirupati and gave thanks to Venkateśvara (July 1514). His religious orthodoxy was also shown by the capture from Udayagiri and re-erection in Vijayanagar of a fine image of Bālakrishna. The sage Vyāsarāya composed songs celebrating the occasion.

Pratāparudra's attempt to raise the siege of Udayagiri resulted in defeat and the pursuit of the retiring forces up to Kondavīdu. To the Vijayanagar army it was a triumphal march all the way, the smaller forts either submitting or being easily captured. Then began the siege of Kondavīdu, first by Sāluva Timmarasa and later by the king. Being the chief city of the Gajapati dominions south of the Krishna river, it was strongly guarded and many chiefs of the kingdom were stationed in it. Only after many months, when many of its inmates had died of starvation, were the walls scaled and the garrison overcome. Many Oriya nobles, including a son and the wife of the Gajapati ruler, were taken captive, and the prisoners sent by road to Vijayanagar.

Krishnadeva Rāya entrusted the administration of the district of Kondavīdu to Sāluva Timma before he and his queens proceeded to Amaravati to offer worship to Amareśvara. From there he went back to the capital after visiting Śrīśailam to make magnificent gifts to Mallikārjuna.

Soon he was on the march once more to join his army in the field, but he found time to visit the shrine of Narasimha at Ahobalam on his way to Vijayavāḍa, which was taken and made the advanced base for further operations. A few miles to the north-west was Kondapalli, a strong and well-defended fort with lofty walls. Krishnadeva laid siege to it; an army sent for its relief by Pratāparudra was met on the banks of the Krishna and thoroughly defeated. The siege was then pressed for two months longer until the fortress surrendered. The seizure of many other forts in Telengana, and the occupation of large parts of the Nalgonda and Wārangal districts then under the suzerainty of the Gajapati, speedily followed.

This campaign effectively completed the conquest of Telengana. Krishnadeva next turned his attention to the country of Kalinga proper where Rājamahendravaram (Rajahmundry) was one of the first cities to be taken. A few feeble attempts were made to stop its progress, but the Vijayanagar army continued its triumphal march, devastating the territory of the Gajapati all along the road, up to Potnūr-Simhādri. There Krishnadeva set up a pillar of victory and then returned to his capital by way of Rajahmundry (1516). His invading and victorious army pressed on, however, and marched further into Kalinga until its capital, Cuttack, was reached. Reduced to extremity, Pratāparudra sued for peace and offered the emperor the hand of his daughter, which was accepted. Krishnadeva, indeed, was magnanimous and returned all the territory north of the Krishna.

While Krishnadeva was busy with his Orissa campaign (which may be called one of the most brilliant military episodes in the history of sixteenth-century India) Ismail Adil Khan recaptured Raichur. Krishnadeva's campaign for its recovery (1520) is described by Nuniz. Determined to try conclusions once for all with the Adil Shah, Krishnadeva marched against him with an army consisting ' of about a million of men, if the camp-followers be included ' and over five hundred elephants; he pitched his camp to the east of Raichur and began a regular siege of the fortress. Ismail came to its relief with strong contingents of cavalry and advanced to within nine miles of Raichur where he entrenched himself, leaving the Krishna river about five miles behind. The decisive battle was joined on the morning of 19 May 1520. It opened with a frontal attack by the Vijayanagar troops which drove the Muslims back to their trenches; but then the artillery of the Muslims came into play and wrought much havoc among the close ranks of the Hindus who fell back and were charged by the enemy. Krishnadeva, who was in command of the second line, then mounted his horse and ordered a forward movement of the remaining divisions. Their impetuous onslaught overcame and scattered the ranks of the Muslim forces who were relentlessly pursued right up to the river, and the threatened defeat was converted into brilliant victory. The Shah's camp was seized and he himself barely escaped with his life on an elephant. ' The spoil was great and the result decisive.' The sultan of Bijapur thenceforth cherished a wholesome dread of Krishnadeva Rāya and did not venture to renew the contest during his lifetime. Krishnadeva returned to Raichur and shortly afterwards recaptured it. Its fall was in large measure due to the assistance rendered by some Portuguese soldiers with Christovao de Figueiredo at their head; with their arquebuses they ' picked off the defenders from the walls ' and enabled the besiegers ' to approach the lines of fortification and pull down the stones of which they were formed'. The Portuguese commander was specially honoured by the king in the next *Mahānavami* festival in the capital.

This resounding success against the Adil Shah had important political results. Krishnadeva personally became haughty and made provocative demands on his defeated foe; he kept his ambassador waiting at Vijayanagar for over a month and then sent word that if the Adil Shah would come and kiss his foot in obeisance, his lands and fortresses would be restored to him. The Muslim sultans saw the danger to their position in the rising military strength of Vijayanagar and in its capacity to interfere in their affairs, which led, by and by, to more concerted action on their part against Vijayanagar. Lastly, the Portuguese on the coast gained by the result of the battle of Raichur: 'Goa rose and fell simultaneously with the rise and fall of the third Vijayanagar dynasty; and necessarily so, considering that its entire trade depended on Hindu support.'

The machinations of one Asad Khan Lari, a wily courtier of Ismail Shah, who had been sent to Vijayanagar to conclude a treaty, led Krishnadeva into yet another campaign against Bijapur in 1523. According to Asad Khan's undertaking, the Adil Khan or his mother would meet Krishnadeva at a certain point on the northern frontier of the kingdom. As he did not find them, however, he marched on Gulbarga by way of teaching them a lesson, and razed its fortress to the ground. He also captured the fortress cities of Firuzabad and Sagar, and led his army up to Bijapur 'which for a time he occupied and left sadly injured'. At Gulbarga he liberated the sons of Mahmud Bāhmanī, made the eldest of them sultan, and brought the others with him to Vijayanagar and treated them with much consideration. But this attempt to resuscitate Bāhmanī sovereignty under Hindu patronage lacked all possibility of success and perhaps only served to irritate the more the sultans of the five succession states.

Nuniz narrates that Krishnadeva in his own lifetime made his six year old son king and himself took up the post of minister. This must have been about 1524 when we have the inscriptions of prince Tirumalai Rāya, who was obviously made *yuvarāja* at the time. Nuniz also states that during the festivities of the coronation which lasted eight months, Tirumalai Rāya took ill and died, poisoned by the son of Sāluva Timma whose position as chief minister had been lowered by the elevation of the prince. When Krishnadeva Rāya came to know of it, he sent for the minister, accused him in open court of the dastardly crime, and cast him and his whole family into prison. In this, certain Portuguese at his court helped him; and when one of Timma's sons escaped, he was caught and blinded with the remaining prisoners.

The Adil Shah now advanced again to try to retrieve his broken fortunes, but when Krishnadeva Rāya took the field against him, he retreated in haste. The king was preparing for an attack on Belgaum, then in the Adil Shah's possession, when he took seriously ill and died soon after (1529). He nominated his half-brother, Achyuta Rāya, to be his successor.

Pre-eminent as a warrior, Krishnadeva Rāya was equally great as statesman, administrator, and patron of the arts. The grandeur of his court excited the warm admiration of many foreign visitors and their description of the great wealth of Vijayanagar, its festivals, its military strength and its heroic king make eloquent reading. All South India was under Krishnadeva Rāya's sway, and many quasi-independent chiefs—like those of Bankapur, Gersoppa, Bhatkal, and so on—were his vassals. The empire, although under his direct rule, was itself divided into a number of governorships under generals, each of whom enjoyed practical independence so long as he maintained a certain quota of horse, foot and elephants in constant readiness for action and paid his annual contribution to the central treasury. For such a system to work efficiently, the monarch had to command the universal respect of his subjects and exhibit great energy, tact and vigilance in the performance of his public duties. Krishnadeva proved himself more than equal to this task, and there was no confusion or disorder anywhere in the realm during his reign. He was a scholar and poet and the Telugu poem *Āmuktamālyada* passes under his name; it contains an exposition, by the way, of the principles of political administration practised by the monarch. The illustrious Telugu poet Allasāni Peddana graced his court as Poet Laureate, and many of the foremost scholars of the time were attracted by the discriminating liberality of the emperor. 'King Krishna Rāya was in no way less famous for his religious zeal and catholicity. He respected all sects of the Hindu religion alike, though his personal leanings were in favour of Vaishnavism. Krishna Rāya's kindness to the fallen enemy, his acts of mercy and charity towards the residents of captured cities, his great military prowess which endeared him alike to his feudatory chiefs and to his subjects, the royal reception and kindness that he invariably bestowed upon foreign embassies, his imposing personal appearance, his genial outlook and polite conversation which distinguished a pure and dignified life, his love for literature and for religion, and his solicitude for the welfare of his people, and, above all, the almost fabulous wealth that he conferred as endowments on temples and Brahmins, mark him out indeed as the greatest of the South Indian monarchs.'

Krishnadeva Rāya was a great builder and added much to the beauty and amenities of the capital. At the beginning of his reign he built a new *gōpura* (tower) and repaired another in the temple of Virūpāksha. In 1513, as already mentioned, he erected the shrine of Krishnasvāmi to house worthily the image of Bālakrishna he had brought from Udayagiri. With the aid of a Portuguese engineer, whose services he borrowed from the Governor-General of Goa, he improved the irrigation of the dry lands round about Vijayanagar. He added a beautiful suburb to the capital on its southern approaches, and called it Nāgalāpūr in honour of his mother Nāgalā Devī; the new city's water supply came from the new tank which was under construction at the time Paes visited the city. The temple of Viṭṭhalasvāmi on the river bank was also embellished by Krishna Rāya; it marks the extreme limit in the ' florid magnificence ' to which the Vijayanagar style advanced. Work on it continued for many years afterwards, and was perhaps only stopped when the Mussalmans destroyed the city in 1565. The enormous statue of Narasimha, hewn out of a single boulder of granite, that lay near the south-western angle of the Krishnasvāmi temple was one of the latest monuments of the reign (1528). Though much mutilated, it is still a striking object amongst the ruins of the city.

Nuniz, who spent some time in Achyuta Rāya's court, affirms that the new king gave himself over to vice and tyranny, that he lacked honesty and courage, and that the people and captains of the kingdom were much discontented with his evil life and inclinations. Achyuta does not, in fact, appear to have been such a bad monarch. He was specially chosen by Krishnadeva for the succession in preference to his infant son who was only eighteen months old. Yet it cannot be denied that his position was difficult at the time of his accession (1529). The infant son of Krishna Rāya was proclaimed king by Rāma Rāya; but Rāma's attempt to seize power in the name of the infant was foiled by Sāluva Vīra Narasimha who kept the throne vacant for Achyuta till he could come up from Chandragiri where he had been confined by Krishnadeva Rāya, along with other princes of the family, in order to secure the peace of the realm. On his way to Vijayanagar, Achyuta Rāya held two coronations, one at Tirupati and the other at Kālahasti, in an attempt to forestall Rāma Rāya's efforts to enthrone another king.

Krishnadeva's death was the signal for all the enemies of Vijayanagar to renew their attacks on that kingdom. Ismail Adil

Khan once again invaded the Raichur doab and seized Raichur and Mudgal, before Achyuta could do anything to prevent it. (This is almost the only occurrence of the entire reign noticed by Nuniz.) The Gajapati ruler, however, who led an invasion at the same time was defeated and turned back; so also the sultan of Golconda, Quli Qutb Shah, whose attempt to seize Kondavīdu was likewise foiled.

When he finally reached Vijayanagar, Achyuta came to terms with Rāma Rāya and agreed to share the power with him. This greatly displeased Sāluva Vīra Narasimha who retired from the court and set up the standard of revolt in the south with the aid of the chieftains of Ummattur and the Tiruvaḍi *rājya* in south Travancore. Achyuta Rāya marched against them, with an army commanded by his brother-in-law Salakarāju Tirumala. The campaign was one victorious progress up to the banks of the Tambraparni where a pillar of victory was set up. The Pāndya ruler who had suffered at the hands of the rebels was restored to his kingdom and his daughter accepted as the emperor's bride. Sāluva Vīra Narasimha and his allies were not only defeated in battle but captured and brought as prisoners to the king's camp at Śrīrangam. Achyuta returned to his capital via Ummattur to receive the submission of local chieftains on the way.

When Krishnadeva Rāya's infant son died soon afterwards, Rāma Rāya's position was considerably weakened. It brought about a change in Achyuta Rāya's attitude; he advanced his own powers still further by invading that much disputed territory, the Raichur doab, and subduing the Bijapur country as far north as the Krishna. This was possible because Ismail Adil Khan's death, in 1534, left the Bijapur throne to his unpopular son Mallu Adil Khan. The nobility rose against him at the instance of the notorious Asad Khan Lari, and Achyuta was not slow to take advantage of the situation, with Mallu consenting to make peace on Achyuta's terms.

The history of the subsequent years is obscure. A rebellion in Gutti seems to have been suppressed in 1536-7, after which he paid a visit to Tirupati with his officers. Rāma Rāya was strengthening his position by removing old servants and appointing his own relatives and friends in their place. He also took into his service 3,000 Muslim soldiers whom Ibrahim Adil Khan, the new sultan of Bijapur, had dismissed from his service on his accession in 1535. He then made bold to seize Achyuta when he returned to the capital, kept him imprisoned and proclaimed himself king; but the opposition of the nobles forced him to abandon the scheme, enthrone Sadāśiva, a nephew of Achyuta, and carry on the government in his name. This went on until rebellions in the south forced Rāma Rāya to leave the capital, when he put Achyuta into the charge of a trusted servant. The campaign in the south was no unalloyed success, and lasted longer than Rāma Rāya had expected. Meanwhile, the trusted servant in charge of Achyuta set him free and assumed the office of chief minister. He was soon done away with by Salakarāju Tirumala, however, who took the direction of affairs into his hands. These occurrences made it expedient for Rāma Rāya to patch up his quarrels with the rebels in the south and return to the capital.

Troubles come not singly and Ibrahim Adil Khan chose this moment to march against Vijayanagar and lay siege to it. He entered Nāgalāpūr and 'razed it to the ground' perhaps by way of reprisal for the treatment of Bijapur by Krishnadeva Rāya. Both Achyuta and Rāma Rāya were afraid of Ibrahim joining forces with the other party, while the machinations of the wily Asad Khan brought about an invasion of Bijapur by the sultan of Ahmadnagar. Ibrahim opened negotiations with both the Hindu princes and settled their quarrel before he retired to his own territory. It was agreed that Achyuta would be king, but Rāma Rāya was to be free to rule his estate without interference. Ibrahim was richly rewarded with large sums of money for his service, and the terms of the compact were observed by both parties till the death of Achyuta in 1542.

The whole of Achyuta Rāya's reign was spent in a struggle against adverse conditions created by internal revolts, foreign aggression and the intrigues and ambitions of Rāma Rāya. Trade everywhere was hampered and pilgrim traffic suffered from the activities of bandits who infested, if they did not control, the highways. Achyuta put up a brave fight against his many difficulties and does not merit the harsh judgement passed on him by Nuniz and others who have accepted a low estimate of his character. His life forms the subject of an ornate poem in Sanskrit, the *Achyutarāyābhyudaya*, by the court-poet Rājanātha Ḍiṇḍima, written during the lifetime of the monarch: even after making all possible allowances for the intemperate eulogies which the poem contains, we can still sense that Achyuta had uncommon and praiseworthy characteristics.

Meanwhile, both during the reign of Achyuta Rāya and in the period that followed, the Portuguese had been busily establishing their empire on the coasts of South India, building forts wherever the protection of their trade demanded them. Wars with the Zamorin of Calicut and the feudatories of the empire were frequent, though they still kept up the appearance of friendly relations with the emperor himself. They acted throughout as if they had 'a divine right to the pillage, robbery, and massacre of the natives of India. Not to mince matters, their whole record is one of a series of atrocities.' They delighted particularly in plundering all rich temples within their reach, even Tirupati not escaping their predatory attentions (1545).

Viśvanātha Nāyaka, son of Nāgama Nāyaka, was regarded by his descendants in later times as the founder of the celebrated Nāyak dynasty of Madura. He must have followed Achyuta in his southern campaign and fought in the wars against Sāluva Vīra Narasimha, Tiruvaḍi and others, until he was finally appointed representative of the emperor in the Pāndya country. He was governor of the Madura country from 1533 to the end of Achyuta's reign (1542) when he gave place to another officer. There is nothing to show that he established the separate Nāyak kingdom of Madura; that came later and may have been the work of his son Krishnappa.

Achyuta Rāya was succeeded by his son Venkata I, but as he was not yet of age, his maternal uncle Salakarāju Tirumala became regent despite the opposition of the nobles. The queen-mother, Varadādevi, suspected her brother's motives and sought the assistance of the Adil Khan; but Tirumala bought off the sultan when he was already on his way to Vijayanagar. As a counter-move Rāma Rāya now liberated Sadāśiva from prison at Gutti, proclaimed him emperor, and in his turn appealed to Bijapur for aid. Nothing loth, the Adil Khan invaded Vijayanagar, but Tirumala, who had been proclaimed king by the bewildered citizens of the capital, inflicted such a defeat on the Shah that he had to turn back. Tirumala's next step to clear his path of all rivals was to cause Venkata I and all the members of the royal family to be assassinated. Thereafter the tyranny became so intolerable that the nobles once again invited the Bijapur sultan to come to their rescue. He came, but his overweening pride aroused hatred all round, and he went back in fear of his own safety. Rāma Rāya moved at last to seize the kingdom in the name of Sadāśiva; he captured Penugonda, defeated Tirumala in a series of battles, put him to the sword in a final engagement on the banks of the Tungabhadra and then proceeded to Vijayanagar to perform the coronation of Sadāśiva (1543).

For the first seven or eight years after his coronation Sadāśiva was the only king; but the real power was always in Rāma Rāya's hands and in due course Rāma Rāya assumed the royal titles. Sadāśiva was kept under close guard, although Rāma Rāya and his brothers Tirumala and Venkatādri 'went on one day every year and prostrated themselves before their lawful sovereign in token of his rights over them'.

Ferishta says that Rāma Rāya destroyed many of the ancient nobility and raised his own family to the highest rank, a point which is confirmed by the evidence of other writers and of the inscriptions. Rāma Rāya also began to admit large numbers of Muslims into the army, a practice that had, indeed, been started in a small way by Devarāya II. No important offices at that time had been entrusted to them, but Rāma Rāya departed from this prudent policy employing Muslims in places which gave them an intimate knowledge of the internal affairs of the state. Further, he made it a point to avail himself of every opportunity of interfering in the relations between the Muslim states of Deccan and playing them off one against another, hoping thus to keep them weak and to increase his own power. The Muslim rulers, needless to say, saw clearly what was happening and closed their ranks; and Rāma Rāya paid heavily for his miscalculations. His policy opened the direct road to the disaster of Rakshasi-Tangadi (Talikota).

Soon after Sadāśiva's coronation, Rāma Rāya was once again called away to the south. His opponents, who could not bear to see him established at the head of the state, sought to defy his authority and created confusion in the land to the south of Chandragiri, which was under their control. In the extreme south, the rulers of the Travancore country were once more in revolt, actually driving out the chieftain of Kayattār, the Pāndya feudatory of the empire. The Roman Catholic missionaries, headed by St Francis Xavier, were not only converting to their faith large numbers on the pearl-fishery coast of the Gulf of Mannar, but induced the fishermen to transfer their allegiance to the king of Portugal on the grounds that they could thereby escape from the rapacity of the Muslim traders and the oppression of the Hindu governors from which they had been suffering for many years. The Franciscan friars and Jesuits were busy demolishing temples and building churches in the coastal cities, and the Portuguese governor of Goa was reported to be organizing a plundering raid against the rich temples of Kānchipuram. The presence of many petty local rulers, their mutual jealousies and negotiations with the Portuguese further complicated a tangled situation.

At this juncture Rāma Rāya ordered his cousin China Timma to lead a large army south and evolve order out of this chaos. Chandragiri was first wrested from the rebels; then the Chola country was entered and the fort of Bhuvanagiri stormed. Marching thence along the coast and crossing the Kaveri, the expedition reached the port of Nagore where a temple of Ranganātha which had suffered ruin at the hands of the Catholics was restored; and the local chiefs of Tanjore and the Pudukkōṭṭai territory were reduced to subjection and arrears of tribute taken from them. Farther south still, the displaced Pāndya was restored to his kingdom and the pride of Bettumperumal, the chief of Kayattār and Tuticorin, crushed. The forces of the 'Five Tiruvaḍis' of Travancore were met at Tovaḷa Pass, beaten and dispersed; the rest of Travancore was invaded and its defeated ruler ('Iniquitibirim') was received into favour and set to rule over much of the territory that had earlier been his. China Timma worshipped at the shrine of Padmanābha at Trivandrum, set up a pillar of victory at Cape Comorin and then returned to the capital leaving his brother Vitthala, who had rendered yeoman service throughout the campaign, in charge of the conquered territory.

With the Portuguese, Rāma Rāya's relations were by no means always friendly, and the advent of Martin Alfonso de Sousa as governor of Goa in 1542 brought about a change for the worse. He attacked and plundered the port of Bhatkal soon after he came to Goa, and his activities on the Coromandel Coast have been noticed above. With his successor, Joao de Castro, Rāma Rāya concluded a treaty in 1547 by which he secured the monopoly of the horse trade. There followed some years of friendship and peace until, in 1558, Rāma Rāya made a sudden attack on San

Thomé. He had received complaints of the destruction of temples by Roman Catholic monks and, being persuaded that the inhabitants were possessed of vast riches, he thought he could both defend his religion and refill his treasury at one stroke. He demanded a tribute of 100,000 pagodas, half to be paid immediately and the rest a year later, for which five hostages were taken from among the chief citizens. At about the same time, to prevent help reaching San Thomé, Goa also was attacked by Vitthalarāya, Rāma Rāya's cousin, aided by the Ikkeri chieftain Sankanna Nāyaka. In spite of these setbacks, the Portuguese continued their depredations along the Malabar coast in the succeeding years.

We must now turn to the details of Rāma Rāya's relations with the Muslim states and to the train of events that led to the decisive battle of Rakshasi-Tangadi (Talikota) to which passing reference has already been made. In 1542-3, Bijapur and Ahmadnagar made up their differences and agreed that the former was to have a free hand against Vijayanagar, and the latter against Bidar. Ibrahim Adil Shah then invaded Vijayanagar, but gained nothing as his forces were turned back by the generalship of the Keladi chief Sadāśiva Nāyaka. In 1548 Rāma Rāya aided Burhan Nizam Shah in the capture of the fort of Kalyāni from Bidar, and the fort remained in Burhan's possession till his death in 1553. His son, Husain Nizam Shah, entered into an alliance with Ibrahim Qutb Shah of Golconda, renewed the war with Bijapur and laid siege to Gulbarga in 1557. Ibrahim Adil Shah called on Rāma Rāya for help and he promptly responded by marching in person at the head of his army. Anxious to avoid bloodshed, Rāma Rāya brought about a meeting of all the parties at the junction of the Bhima and Krishna rivers which resulted in a treaty of mutual alliance and protection by which, if any one of the contending parties became the victim of an unjust attack, the others were to join him against the aggressor—a plan of collective security as it would now be called.

Ibrahim Adil Shah died soon after this meeting of the four kings and was succeeded by his young son Ali Adil Shah. An unusual step was taken by Ali to cement his friendly relations with Vijayanagar, says Ferishta. Rāma Rāya lost a son about this time, and Ali went to Vijayanagar to offer his condolence in person. He was received with the greatest respect, and Rāma Rāya's wife adopted the sultan as her son. When, however, Ali took his leave after a stay of three days, Rāma Rāya failed to attend him out of the city, and Ali 'treasured up the affront in his mind'. Rāma Rāya, perhaps, on his part felt that the fortunes of Bijapur must have sunk rather low that its sultan should so far humble himself to secure his friendship.

The first of the high contracting parties to disregard the Four Kings' Peace was Husain Nizam Shah who invaded Bijapur in 1560. Ali fled to Vijayanagar and implored the assistance of Rāma Rāya, who responded to the appeal and also called upon Ibrahim Qutb Shah of Golconda to fulfil his part according to the treaty. He did so with reluctance, but at the approach of the combined forces, the Nizam Shah retreated into his dominions and made over the defence of Kalyāni to one of his Hindu officers, Bhopal Raj. The allied army left behind a division of its forces to invest Kalyāni and pressed on to Ahmadnagar. The Nizam Shah was beaten in a battle at Jamkhed, and the fleeing sultan pursued up to Daulatabad. He then realized the futility of further resistance and made peace by surrendering Kalyāni to Ali Adil Shah, who thus had good reason to be grateful to Rāma Rāya. After this, Rāma Rāya invaded Bidar and inflicted a defeat on the Barid Shah, who had thenceforth to take part in Rāma Rāya's wars against his enemies.

As Rāma Rāya's career began with a short period of service in the Qutb Shahi court of Golconda, he had a first-hand knowledge of the internal conditions of that kingdom, and had friends among the nobles of that court. With Ibrahim Qutb Shah his relations were at first friendly as he had received him with favour when he fled to Vijayanagar from his brother's wrath and helped him to gain the throne when that brother died (1550). But gradually their conflicting interests drove them apart, and Ibrahim cooperated in the war against Ahmadnagar only in a half-hearted manner. Later, he openly allied himself with Ahmadnagar, went against Bijapur and laid siege to Kalyāni. Rāma Rāya went to the relief of the fortress and ordered at the same time an invasion of the southern districts of the Golconda kingdom led by his brother Venkatādri. Thereupon the allied sultans retreated from Kalyāni; Rāma Rāya pursued the Nizam Shah while the Bijapur troops chased the Qutb Shah. Ahmadnagar was besieged a second time by Vijayanagar forces, but now without success as the flooding of the adjacent river compelled the invading army to retire with losses. Ibrahim Qutb Shah was defeated in battle, and reached his capital with difficulty, where he found everything in disorder owing to Venkatādri's invasion. Soon Rāma Rāya also returned from Ahmadnagar and marched towards Golconda. Ibrahim sought to divert him by attacking Kondavīdu, but met with no success, being once more beaten in the field. His country was thus devastated and the principal forts captured by the enemy. In the end he had to purchase peace by surrendering the forts of Kovilkonda, Ganpura and Pangal (*c.* 1563). The war widened the breach between Golconda and Vijayanagar, and Ibrahim became more than ever determined to destroy the Hindu power which had become a source of repeated humiliation to its Muslim neighbours in the north, even their ambassadors not being received properly.

The Muslim rulers saw clearly that their disunion gave the advantage to Rāma Rāya. Ibrahim Qutb Shah and Husain Nizam Shah, who had suffered most, perhaps took the lead in the formation of the confederacy against Vijayanagar. Ferishta avers that the excesses committed by the Hindu forces against the Muslim population and sacred places in their invasions of Ahmadnagar and Golconda had no small share in rousing feeling against Rāma Rāya. Accordingly embassies passed to and fro among the sultans, their differences were made up, and steps taken to form a general league of the faithful against the Hindu monarch. Dynastic marriages cemented the political alliance between Ahmadnagar and Bijapur—Ali Adil Shah marrying Chand Bibi, the daughter of Husain Nizam Shah, and Husain's eldest son marrying one of Ali's sisters at the same time. Soon after the marriages, preparations began for the holy war. Hindu sources generally speak of all the five sultans as the opponents of Rāma Rāya, though Muslim historians leave the sultan of Berar out of account. Ali Adil Shah clearly played a double game throughout, professing friendship with both the parties. The Muslim armies met on the plains of Bijapur and began their march to the south towards the end of 1564.

Rāma Rāya knew that the decisive trial of strength was to begin soon, and, on *Vijayadaśami* day (15 September 1564), he informed the nobles of the impending war and ordered them to gather together all their available strength without delay. Though little reliance can be placed on the large figures given by several writers, there is no doubt that very large numbers of troops were engaged on both sides. The Muslims reached Talikota, a small fortress-town in the neighbourhood of the Krishna river, on 26 December 1564. Rāma Rāya faced the situation with the utmost confidence. He first sent his brother Tirumala with a considerable force of all arms to guard the Krishna and prevent the enemy from crossing it. Then he sent up his other brother, Venkatādri, and finally himself came up with the rest of the forces of the empire. The Hindu camp was on the south side of the Krishna, while the Muslims occupied both banks. Several partisan accounts have been written of the antecedents of the decisive engagement and of that engagement itself, but it is by no means easy to reconstruct the exact course of events. The actual field of battle was on the south bank of the Krishna; but as the two villages of Rakshasi and Tangadi, ten miles apart on its north bank, lie much nearer the field than Talikota, some historians refer to the battle as Rakshasi-Tangadi rather than Talikota.

The rival armies were opposing each other for over a month, during which there were preliminary trials of strength. In one of these the Nizam Shah and the Qutb Shah sustained a severe defeat, and felt the need to resort to a stratagem. They gave out that they intended to make peace with the powerful Rāya and even started negotiations; at the same time they secured the firm adherence of Ali Adil Shah to their cause by remonstrating with him, and possibly also entered into communication with the Muslim officers in Rāma Rāya's army. When everything was ready, the main body of the Muslim army crossed the river by means of a feint which drew off the Hindu forces guarding the ford, and proceeded to attack the Hindu camp. Rāma Rāya, though surprised, was able to organize the defence. In the decisive engagement that followed —the day was Tuesday, 23 January 1565, according to Sewell and Ferishta—Rāma Rāya and his two brothers all took part. In spite of his age Rāma Rāya insisted on directing operations from a litter. He held command of the centre and was opposed by Husain Nizam Shah; his left, under his brother Tirumala, was opposed by the Bijapur forces under Ali; and his right, under Venkatādri, opposed the sultans of Ahmadabad-Bidar and Golconda. At first the Hindus fought with success and nearly won the battle; but the issue was decided by the desertion of two Muslim commanders of Rāma Rāya's army, each in charge of seventy to eighty thousand men. Says Caesar Frederick: 'And when the armies were joined, the battle lasted but a while, not the space of four hours, because the two traitorous captains in the chiefest of the fight, with their companies turned their faces against their king, and made such disorder in his army, that astonied they set themselves to flight.'

Rāma Rāya fell prisoner into the hands of the Nizam Shah who immediately decapitated him and had his head raised on a spear for the Hindu troops to see. Above a hundred thousand were slain in the pursuit that followed. There was great confusion and no attempt was made to take up a fresh position or organize the defence of the capital. The road to the great city lay open; first to enter it were the dejected soldiers and princes from the field bringing the bad news; but Tirumala made good his escape with all the treasures of the emperor loaded on to one thousand five hundred and fifty elephants. He left the city and its inhabitants to their fate, taking with him only the captive emperor Sadāśiva and the women of the royal family.

The victorious army was preceded by hordes of robbers and jungle-folk who fell upon the helpless people and looted their houses and shops. 'With fire and sword, with crowbars and axes, they carried on day after day their work of destruction. Never perhaps in the history of the world has such havoc been wrought, and wrought suddenly, on so splendid a city, teeming with a wealthy and industrious population in the full plenitude of prosperity one day, and on the next seized, pillaged, and reduced to ruins, amid scenes of savage massacre and horrors beggaring description.' Vijayanagar never recovered from the blow, and the attempt made by Tirumala shortly afterwards to revive the city appears to have met with only indifferent success.

He took up his abode in Penugonda and began rebuilding an army by all possible means; in his dire need, he is said to have taken several horses from Portuguese merchants and refused to pay for them. He gave up Vijayanagar partly because opinion in that city favoured the claims of Rāma Rāya's son Peda Tirumala, *alias* Timma, for the regency. Six years of anarchy and confusion intervened before Tirumala actually became king. Rāma Rāya's evil policy of breaking up the trained civil service for the sake of promoting relatives now added to the troubles of the realm in the crisis; there were rebellions everywhere; crime increased and the tyranny of *pālayagars* and dacoits also grew apace. The effective independence of the Nāyaks of Madura, Tanjore and Gingee may be traced to this period.

Even from so great a disaster as this defeat, Peda Tirumala seems to have been able to learn nothing; he invoked the aid of Ali Adil Shah against his uncle. The sultan first marched to Vijayanagar, and thence sent an army to lay siege to Penugonda; but the fort held its own under its able general Savaram Chennapa Nāyaka, and Tirumala in his turn appealed to the Nizam Shah who invaded Bijapur and brought about the retreat of the Adil Shah from Vijayanagar (1567). Soon Tirumala was called upon to join the Nizam Shah and Qutb Shah against Bijapur and did so; but the Adil Shah made peace with his Muslim neighbours, and fell upon Tirumala and invaded his territory with all his strength in 1568, laid siege to Adoni and dispatched a force against Penugonda to prevent any relief going to Adoni. Penugonda again put up a successful resistance, but Adoni fell.

Yet Tirumala seems somehow to have held the bulk of the empire together; he tacitly approved the new status of the Nāyaks of the south and made them his friends. The Voḍeyars of Mysore and the Nāyaks of Vellore and Keladi still owed allegiance as before. He set up each of his three sons as viceroy over a linguistic area for general control and supervision: Śrīranga, the eldest, over the Telugu area with Penugonda as his capital; Rāma, his second son, over the Kannada country, to rule from Śrīrangapattana; and Venkatapati, the youngest, to rule over the Tamil country from Chandragiri. He assumed the title 'Reviver of the Decadent Karnātaka Empire' and had himself crowned emperor in 1570. But he was already an old man, and seems to have retired after a short rule, and been succeeded by Śrīranga in 1572. Tirumala's work restored the empire, though in a truncated form, and prolonged its life for about a century.

The fate of Sadāśiva is uncertain. Caesar Frederick heard in 1567 that he was assassinated by one of Tirumala's sons, but this may only have been scandal spread against the new ruling house of Aravīḍu by its enemies. It seems as probable that Sadāśiva, being a docile prince whom no one would have troubled to kill, may have languished in prison until he died in natural death. His name occurs in inscriptions till 1576.

Śrīranga I began to rule in 1572 though his father continued to live in retirement for some six years longer. He carried on the work of restoration, but there were many obstacles in his way. In addition, two of his Muslim neighbours continued their invasions, resulting in loss of territory. In 1576, Ali Adil Shah sent out an army from Adoni to lay siege to Penugonda. Śrīranga entrusted the defence of his capital to his able general Chennapa and went off to Chandragiri with the treasures. Penugonda stood a three months' siege, which gave Śrīranga time to appeal successfully for help to Golconda and he himself took steps to send relief to Chennapa. He bought over one of the Adil Shah's Hindu lieutenants and thus enabled Chennapa to inflict a defeat on the sultan on 21 December 1576, after which he retired into his own territory. But within three years, Ibrahim Qutb Shah forgot his recent alliance with Śrīranga and invaded his territory: quite likely he was in league with some of the discontented nobles of Vijayanagar and chose his opportunity for aggrandizement. The rich temple of Narasimha at Ahobalam was plundered in 1579 by Murhari Rao, a Maratha Brahmin in the service of Golconda, and much territory was captured and ravaged although it was later recovered.

The Golconda ruler returned to the charge and invaded the Kondavīdu territory. There were struggles round the forts of Vinukonda, Kondavīdu and Udayagiri, and though inscriptions say that Śrīranga took these forts, the truth seems to be that Ibrahim gained considerable success and took much territory from Vijayanagar on this occasion which the Hindu empire never recovered. Śrīranga's failure was due to the virtual division of the empire which limited the resources at his command, since his brothers gave him little aid. The dissensions among the nobles, which led to many petty fights and wars and intrigues with the enemy, weakened the defence still further. When Śrīranga died without issue in 1585, his younger brother Venkata succeeded him, superseding the two sons of his elder brother Rāma who had been viceroy of Śrīrangapattana under Tirumala. These two boys were young at a time when strong rule was needed. The nobles, therefore, headed by Jaggadevarāya, chose Venkata to rule, and he fulfilled their expectations in an ample measure. He celebrated his coronation in 1585-6 and his reign of twenty-eight years was marked by a revival of strength and prosperity

It was during the reign of Venkata that the Dutch and the English began to establish themselves on the east coast. In 1605 the Dutch opened negotiations with Golconda and established factories in Nizampatam and Masulipatam. They soon felt the need for ' a footing in the Hindu territory further south in order to obtain the patterned goods demanded so largely in the spice-markets '. In 1608, therefore, they got permission from the Nāyak of Gingee to open a factory at Tegnapatam (Fort St David), and two years later Venkata allowed them to have a factory at Pulicat with exclusive privileges of trade. Pulicat was open to attack from the Portuguese at San Thomé, and when the Queen of Venkata delayed building a fortress for its protection, the Dutch completed the fortress at their own cost—a step which stood them in good stead in the period of civil war and confusion that followed the death of Venkata. The English made a futile attempt to land at Pulicat in 1611, but succeeded soon after in opening trade at Nizampatam and Masulipatam. Their negotiations with Vellore had led to no result at the time of Venkata's death; they were admitted to trade in Pulicat in 1621 by a treaty with the Dutch, but the English factory moved soon after, first to Armagon a short distance to the north, and ultimately to Madras (1639-40). The Danes settled at Tranquebar in 1620.

Although Venkata II had several wives he had no son. His love for one of them made him wink at a fraud she practised on him of borrowing a baby from one of her maids and calling him her own. Hoping to stop the mischief from going further, Venkata nominated Śrīranga to the succession. But the presence of the putative ' son ' was a complication, and Śrīranga was no paragon of strength or wisdom. He alienated the sympathies of the nobles by making injudicious appointments and avaricious demands for lands, money and jewels. The nobles fell into two camps; the son's party headed by Gobbūri Jagga Rāya, the brother of Venkata's favourite queen; and Śrīranga supported by Velugōti Yāchama Nāyaka. With the co-operation of Timma Nāyaka and Makarāja, two of his lieutenants, Jagga Rāya seized and threw Śrīranga and all the members of his family into prison, crowned the putative ' son ' as emperor, and persuaded some of the nobles to do him homage. Yāchama defied Jagga Rāya and gathered forces to rescue the lawful emperor; he also had prince Rāma, Śrīranga's second son, smuggled out of the prison by a washerman. An attempt to rescue Śrīranga by means of an underground tunnel, however, was discovered and led to stricter incarceration. Yāchama made yet another effort to rescue the emperor and his family. He took advantage of Jagga Rāya's absence to arrange with a captain of Vellore fort, one Ite Obalesa, to slay the guards. On hearing that they were dead, Yāchama was supposed to come and take possession of the fort. Unfortunately the news reached Jagga first, and he returned before Yāchama had time to strike. Śrīranga and his whole family were killed within four months of his accession, as the only certain way of preventing all future intrigues for their rescue and restoration.

The massacre of the royal family sent a thrill of horror through the kingdom, and Jagga Rāya and his partisans came to be deeply hated. Sympathy grew for Rāmadeva, the sole survivor of the family. He owed his survival to the forethought of Yāchama, who now proclaimed him emperor, and there ensued a long-drawn out civil war in which the whole empire took part. Yāchama defeated Jagga Rāya in battle and forced him to flee to the jungles for refuge. The Gobbūri estates in the south-west of the Nellore district were captured. But, nothing daunted, Jagga became active again, and secured the support of Muttu Vīrappa Nāyaka of Madura and Krishnappa Nāyaka of Gingee. Yāchama on his side paid a visit to Tanjore and secured the adherence of Raghunātha Nāyaka to Rāma's cause. Jagga Rāya and his allies gathered their forces in the neighbourhood of Trichinopoly; Yāchama led his army from Vellore in that direction and was joined by Raghunātha's forces on the way. The decisive engagement took place at Topur, a village near the Grand Anicut. Jagga Rāya fell in the battle with many of his lieutenants, his army broke up and fled, and Yāchama's victory was complete (1616). The putative son of Venkata, the cause of all the trouble, was captured, and Krishnappa Nāyaka lost all his forts except Gingee; his subsequent attempt to recover them only resulted in another defeat followed by captivity. The war was kept on by Etirāja, Jagga Rāya's younger brother, and by differences among the Nāyaks. The death of the putative son in 1619, followed by reconciliation between Rāmadeva and Etirāja, whose daughter he married, put an end to the war and brought about the recognition of Rāma in Karnātaka, though the Madura Nāyak went his own way. Etirāja now stood by his son-in-law, as did Raghunātha Nāyaka who helped to restore the imperial authority over contumacious vassals. The reconciliation of Rāma with Etirāja estranged Yāchama, however, who had longed to confiscate all the Gobbūri lands, including Pulicat and its surroundings, which belonged to Etirāja himself. After much local fighting Rāmadeva's authority came to count for something in the remnants of the empire by about 1629, and the Nāyak of Gingee gave up his hostile attitude and became a friendly vassal. Even Yāchama's partisans were subdued and Pulicat and its environs firmly secured for Etirāja and the empire. Thus the struggle of a decade and a half ended in a tolerable measure of success for Rāma.

But the civil war had given Bijapur its opportunity. The sultan at last realized his ambitions of capturing the western Telugu country. In 1619-20 he sent Abdul Wahab Khan against Kurnool where Gōpālarāja offered stout resistance in which he was aided by Golconda; Abdul Wahab Khan was defeated and forced to make peace. But this was only a truce, for in 1624 he came back and attacked Kurnool once more. Gōpālarāja was now aided by his friends in the neighbourhood; but the Bijapur forces won the battle that followed, and Gōpālarāja abandoned the fort and fled. Rāma was too preoccupied to intervene. His death in 1630 at an early age of twenty-eight set the seal on the Muslim conquest of Kurnool which passed to Bijapur for good.

With no son or brother, Rāma had nominated his cousin, Peda Venkata, a grandson of the great Rāma Rāya, to succeed to the throne; but Timma Rāja, a paternal uncle of Rāma, thought he had a better claim, and seized the government, compelling Venkata III to remain at his native place Anegondi. Gingee, Tanjore and Madura declared for Venkata, and Timma got no support and was generally looked upon as a usurper. He was nevertheless able to make trouble, and civil strife continued till his death in 1635. In the early stages he gained some successes, but prince Śrīranga, son of Chenna Venkata, the younger brother of Venkata III, took the field on behalf of his uncle. With help from the Dutch at Pulicat, he beat Timma and compelled him to accept Venkata's claim to the throne. He was, however, allowed to retain some of the places he had captured; but when he again stirred up trouble, the Nāyak of Gingee defeated and slew him in 1635. Peace was thus restored. Venkata went and lived in Vellore, entrusting the defence of Penugonda (once again threatened by the sultan of Bijapur) to Kondi Nāyaka who managed to keep it secure till the dissolution of the empire some fifteen years later.

Thinking he was too friendly with the Nāyak of Gingee, the rulers of Tanjore and Madura plotted to seize Venkata. They failed and war began in 1637 but was soon ended by a patched-up peace. For reasons that are not clear, Śrīranga, once so loyal to his uncle, turned against him and actually engineered two invasions from Bijapur in 1638 and 1641. On the first occasion the sultan's forces invested Bangalore, and Venkata had to buy peace at the cost of a large indemnity early in 1639. Later in the year, with the help of troops sent by the southern Nāyaks, he gained a moderate success which put a temporary check on Muslim inroads. The invasion of 1641 was led by Randhula Khan who was joined by Śrīranga; they marched upon Vellore after capturing some forts on the way, and pitched their camp within twelve miles of the capital. Once more aid from the Nāyaks saved Vellore for a while.

Watching the course of events in the Carnatic, the sultan of Golconda sent an army from the east along the coast in April 1642 to capture as much territory as possible from the Hindu empire, which was now in the last stages of dissolution. Velugōti Timma, lord of Armagon in the extreme south of Nellore, and Dāmerla Venkata, ruler of Madras and Poonamallee, offered resistance, but it was not effective. Venkata III himself retired to the jungles near Nārāyanavanam in the Chittoor district where he died in a helpless condition on 10 October 1641.

Venkata III had no children and was succeeded by his treacherous nephew Śrīranga III. When he learnt that Venkata lay dying on the hills, Śrīranga deserted the Bijapur general and put himself forward as the defender of his ancestral kingdom and made himself king on the 29 October 1642. But he was by no means equal to undoing as king the mischief he had started as rebel; and many of the nobles—like Dāmerla Venkata and Krishnappa Nāyaka of Gingee—were against him. For a time, however, jealousy among the Muslim states appeared to give Śrīranga a chance, and the aid of Bijapur in January 1644 enabled him to check the advance of Golconda beyond Udayagiri for a time. He now felt strong enough to demand and collect large sums of money from the southern Nāyaks, part of which he paid over to Bijapur as the price of its help. Madura and Gingee soon rose again in rebellion, and another Golconda invasion reached Pulicat without opposition and was only repulsed by the Dutch commandant of the fort. To stop the Nāyak of Gingee from joining the Golconda army, Śrīranga made peace with him; he even gained a success against Golconda and pursued the invading army up to Kandukur in the north of the Nellore district. When Bijapur and Golconda reached an understanding, Śrīranga was unable to face their combined forces, and had to retire. The Golconda general, Mir Jumla, was preparing to advance by way of Kurnool, when the sultan of Golconda suddenly countermanded the war and compensated Bijapur, perhaps as the result of an understanding with Śrīranga. The danger of invasion ceased for a while until the southern Nāyaks with Tirumala Nāyaka of Madura at their head rebelled and appealed to Bijapur which sent Mustafa Khan against Vellore. Śrīranga, who had gone south to meet the Nāyak forces, had to hurry back to the defence of his capital. Golconda also struck at the same time in the direction of Vinukonda and Udayagiri. Utterly overwhelmed and helpless, Śrīranga made a last appeal to Hindu nationalism and exhorted his subjects to rally to the protection of the state, temples, Brahmins and religion. The ears of the Nāyaks were deaf to such appeals, and the great Mogul had asked Bijapur and Golconda to attack and partition the Carnatic between themselves. Defeated in battle by his own feudatory Nāyaks in December 1645, Śrīranga fell back on Vellore; pressure from Bijapur diminished for a time as the commanders went to Bijapur to settle disputes that had arisen among themselves; but Golconda was active and Mir Jumla came and occupied parts of Nellore and Cuddapah. Mustafa Khan of Bijapur came back and prepared to attack Vellore. Then the Nāyaks realized too late the danger that was threatening them all together. Even so Tirumala Nāyaka of Madura stood aloof. All other resources being spent, the jewels of the women of Vellore and the treasures of the Tirupati temple were used to maintain the defending forces. A slight success against Mustafa Khan won outside Vellore was not followed up by Śrīranga owing to dissensions among his allies who abandoned him and retired inside the fortress. Another big battle followed at Virinchipuram (4 April 1646) in which Śrīranga was again defeated despite aid from Mysore, Madura and Tanjore. Mustafa then besieged Vellore. Meanwhile Mir Jumla took all the territory in the east coast up to Pulicat; but the Dutch still refused to recognize Golconda for a while. Śrīranga finally had to abandon all resistance and seek refuge in Tanjore. Madura and Mysore were unable to ward off the Muslim conquest of the Carnatic which was completed by 1652. When Tanjore, like Gingee a little before, submitted to Bijapur in 1649, Śrīranga repaired to Mysore where he kept his court at Bellūr with the aid of the Keladi chiefs, dreaming of the reconquest of Vellore until death came to him as a relief some time about 1672.

The fall of the Carnatic was not the fall of the Hindu cause, however, for even as Bijapur was ravaging it and driving Śrīranga into exile, Śivāji commenced his eventful career, and Śrīranga did not come to his end till a little before Śivāji crowned himself Chatrapati (1674). Madura and Mysore continued as independent Hindu states well on into the eighteenth century.

Thus, nevertheless, ended the Karnātaka-Vijayanagar empire more than three centuries after its foundation. During that long period it had maintained a constant struggle against its Muslim neighbours on the north, destroyed the sultanate of Madura, and kept Southern India free from the inroads of Islam. True, we find Hindus in the service of Muslim rulers and Muslim troops engaged by the Hindu emperors of Vijayanagar. Diplomatic, and even dynastic alliances, also occurred often enough between these two continuously contending parties; but they do not alter the basic nature of the historic role of Vijayanagar, which was to preserve South India as the last refuge of the traditional culture and institutions of the country. The great commentary on the Vedas composed by a syndicate of scholars with Sāyaṇa at their head, and the impressive additions made to the structure of almost all important temples in the country by the rulers of Vijayanagar, form the most typical monuments of the work of the great Hindu empire. The Portuguese and Jesuits sought to Christianize the population, and to that extent they incurred the displeasure of the emperors and their feudatories, and their efforts in this direction were not allowed to proceed very far.

It now remains to say something on the political, administrative and military system of the empire before concluding the chapter. The empire was in theory a hereditary monarchy; but the times were hard, and the hostility of the Muslim states on the one side and the intransigence of feudatories on the other made it imperative that the king should be possessed of high attainments in diplomacy and war. No wonder that weak kings were either imprisoned or dethroned by able and ambitious ministers, and that there was a change of the ruling dynasty on three occasions as the result of usurpations in which the nobles of the court played their own parts and took sides with rival claimants. On the whole, however, political factions in Vijayanagar did not develop the rancour that marked the politics of the Bāhmanī court and of its successors; with rare exceptions, the leaders of the Hindu empire showed a readiness to recognize facts, and to prefer compromise, whenever possible, to open rebellion.

The king was advised by a council of ministers whom he often consulted; but he was not bound to accept their advice, and was free to follow his own bent or the counsel of individual favourites. Even the most powerful minister held his office at the pleasure of the king, and was liable to be degraded and summarily punished, as Sāluva Timma was punished by Kṛishnadeva Rāya when he was suspected of having procured the murder of the heir apparent.

It was customary for the emperor to have a plurality of wives and to maintain innumerable maids of honour to wait on them as well as on himself. They had well-appointed, separate apartments, and the maintenance of the harem was no small item in the expenditure of the palace. The royal princes were often employed in administrative offices suited to their capacity. A strong monarch like Krishnadeva Rāya imposed restrictions on the movements of those who might have any pretensions to the throne and kept them under surveillance.

The work of the central government was apportioned among a number of departments, and there was a well-organized secretariat with its office near the palace. There were two treasuries, a smaller one for current remittances and withdrawals, and a larger reserve to which every king made it a point to add something and of which Paes says, it 'is kept locked and sealed in such a way that it cannot be seen by anyone' and is 'not opened except when the kings have great need'.

Crown lands, annual tributes from feudatories and provincial governors paid at the time of the *Mahānavami* festival, port and customs dues from the commerce passing through the numerous ports of the empire, formed the chief sources of revenue which was collected both in cash and in kind. The land was carefully surveyed and assessed according to its quality, the rates differing between wet and dry lands and in accordance with the crops and the yield. The proportion of produce claimed as revenue varied from the traditional sixth to as much as half the gross yield. The state often handed over to temples and learned Brahmins the privilege of enjoying its share of the land revenue in accordance with prescribed terms. Taxes on professions and houses, fees for licences of various kinds, transit and market dues and judicial fines were other sources from which the state got its money. Most of these taxes were farmed out to the highest bidder both in areas directly administered from the centre and in the provinces, and the impression produced is that of high and even oppressive taxation.

The chief items of expenditure were the upkeep of the palace, the upkeep of the army, and charitable endowments. Krishnadeva Rāya laid down the theory that income should be divided into four equal parts: one quarter went to maintain the palace establishment and to charity, two went to the army, and the remaining quarter was deposited in the Reserve Treasury. Doubtless this was only the ideal, and practice depended entirely on current exigencies.

Vijayanagar was perhaps the nearest approach to a war-state ever made by a Hindu kingdom; and its political organization was dominated by its military needs. The emperor maintained a large standing army consisting of an elephant corps, cavalry and infantry in this force, 'the soldiers receive their pay', noted Abdur Razzak, 'every four months, and no payment is ever made by a draft upon the revenues of any province'. In addition, military fiefs studded the whole length and breadth of the empire, each under a *nāyak* or military leader authorized to collect revenue and to administer a specified area provided he maintained an agreed number of elephants, horses, and troops ever ready to join the imperial forces in war. Nuniz counted more than two hundred such *nāyaks*. There were regular military schools where men were trained in archery, swordsmanship, and so on, and prepared for enlistment in the army; the artillery, however, seems generally to have been manned by foreigners. A military camp was a moving city, 'arranged in streets with many open spaces'. The number of non-combatant camp-followers was too large not to impede the troops, but this was a common feature of the times. Fortresses played a large part in the defence organization, and the arts of siege were well known and extensively practised. There must have been a navy of some sort for the Rāyas had the command of several ports and of parts of Ceylon; but we have no definite information on its strength or organization.

The details of the organization of provincial government depended on the historical antecedents of each locality. In the extreme south and on the west coast, the older rulers of the land were allowed to carry on in a subordinate capacity, paying tribute and submitting to the general supervision of a high official of the empire, usually a prince of the blood-royal; such were the Pāndyas, the Tiruvaḍis, and the chiefs of Gersoppa, Karkal and other places. In the Tamil districts the ancient Chola territorial divisions, together with the deeply-rooted system of autonomous village assemblies, were allowed to continue and no attempt was made to impose arrangements perfected by the Rāyas elsewhere in the Telugu and Kannada areas. The autonomy of villages, however, suffered considerable abridgement in this period as their officials came to be linked up more and more closely with the central government and its representatives. The names of divisions and offices differed with the locality; but everywhere the provincial governor appointed from the centre was more the military commander of a strategic fort than an ordinary civil servant of the crown. The boundaries of provinces, or *rājyas*, were changed from time to time to suit immediate administrative needs; and some territories, especially in the northern sections of the empire which constantly passed to and fro between Vijayanagar and its Muslim enemies, must have experienced many changes in their rule. These governors and *nāyaks* were allowed to rule their fiefs by deputy and therefore appointed and maintained their agents in the capital when they were not present in person. A regular system of espionage performed the duties of the modern intelligence service and kept the emperor informed of the doings of his subordinates all over the empire as well as of the designs and movements of neighbouring rulers. Captains of fortresses at the frontiers were generally very trustworthy men who were specially exempted from attendance at the capital.

The police system was fairly efficient, the rule being that when a theft occurred the property was recovered or made good by the police-officers. Wherever trouble was expected from jungle tribes, *pālayagars* were posted with a considerable body of retainers maintained from *jāgirs*—land assignments—set apart for the purpose. In towns the streets were patrolled regularly at nights, and the police arrangements of the capital were particularly efficient and received the commendation of foreign observers like Abdur Razzak.

Justice was administered by a hierarchy of courts, the emperor's *sabhā* being the highest appellate authority. Some of these courts appear to have been peripatetic, being held wherever the officers concerned were encamped. The *smriti* of Yājnavalkya and Mādhava's great commentary on Parāśara's code commanded special authority in the decision of doubtful legal points. Minor offences and violation of caste and trade rules were dealt with in the first instance by village courts and caste and guild organizations, and perhaps seldom found their way to the courts of the crown. When human evidence failed trial by ordeal was not unknown. By modern standards punishments were harsh and even barbarous, including as they did, in extreme cases, mutilation, impalement, and being thrown to the elephants.

The emperors of Vijayanagar addressed themselves deliberately to the task of preserving the Hindu social and political order from being destroyed by Islam, and in this task they were eminently successful in spite of repeated reverses in the field of battle. That today South Indian society presents a striking contrast in many respects to society in North India, that South India is still adorned by a large number of great temples that enshrine the artistic achievements of successive generations of Hindu master-builders, and that the Hindu-Muslim ' problem ' was virtually unknown in the South furnish some measure of the success that attended the efforts of Vijayanagar and its rulers.

BIBLIOGRAPHY

T. V. MAHALINGAM: *Administration and Social life under Vijayanagar* (Madras, 1940)

—: *South Indian Polity* (Madras, 1955)

—: ' Tirumalaideva Maharaya ' (*Proceedings, Ninth All-India Oriental Conference* 1937, pp. 827-32, Trivandrum, 1940)

K. A. N. SASTRI and N. VENKATARAMANAYYA: *Further Sources of Vijayanagar History* (Madras, 1947)

R. SATYANATHA AIYAR: *History of the Nāyaks of Madura* (Madras, 1924)

R. Sewell: *A Forgotten Empire* (London, 1924)
N. Venkataramanayya: *Studies in the History of the Third Dynasty of Vijayanagar* (Madras, 1935)
V. Vriddhagirisan: *The Nāyaks of Tanjore* (Annamalainagar, 1942)

I. SANGAMA DYNASTY

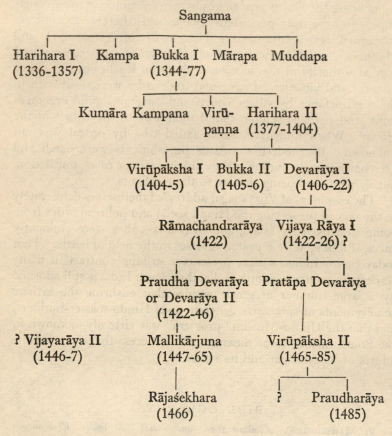

- Sangama
  - Harihara I (1336-1357)
  - Kampa
  - Bukka I (1344-77)
    - Kumāra Kampana
    - Virūpaṇṇa
    - Harihara II (1377-1404)
      - Virūpāksha I (1404-5)
      - Bukka II (1405-6)
      - Devarāya I (1406-22)
        - Rāmachandrarāya (1422)
        - Vijaya Rāya I (1422-26) ?
          - Praudha Devarāya or Devarāya II (1422-46)
            - Mallikārjuna (1447-65)
              - Rājaśekhara (1466)
          - Pratāpa Devarāya
            - Virūpāksha II (1465-85)
              - ?
              - Praudharāya (1485)
  - Mārapa
  - Muddapa

? Vijayarāya II (1446-7)

II. SĀLUVA DYNASTY

- Guṇḍa
  - Sāluva Narasimha (1486-91)
    - Tirumala or Timma
    - Dammarāya or Immadi Narasimha
  - Timma

III. TULUVA DYNASTY

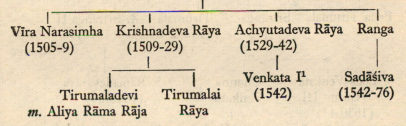

- Īśvara Nāyaka
  - Narasa Nāyaka
    - Vīra Narasimha (1505-9)
    - Krishnadeva Rāya (1509-29)
      - Tirumaladevi *m.* Aliya Rāma Rāja
      - Tirumalai Rāya
    - Achyutadeva Rāya (1529-42)
      - Venkata I[1] (1542)
    - Ranga
      - Sadāśiva (1542-76)

[1] Assassinated by his maternal uncle Salākaraju Tirumala whose tyrannical rule for a few months intervened between the reigns of Venkata I and Sadāśiva.

IV. ARAVĪḌU DYNASTY

- Aravīṭi Bukka
  - Rāmarāja
    - Śrīranga
      - (Aliya) Rāma Rāja (*m.* Tirumaladevi, d. of Krishnadeva Rāya) (1542-65)
        - Peda Tirumala
        - Śrīranga
          - 6. Peda Venkata or Venkata III (1630-41)
          - Chenna Venkata
            - 7. Śrīranga III (adopted by Gōpālarāja of Kandanavolu) (1642-9) Lived till 1672
      - 1. Tirumala (1570-2)
        - 2. Śrīranga I (1572-85)
        - Rāma
          - Tirumala (Timma Rāja)
          - 4. Śrīranga II (1614)
            - 5. Rāmadevarāya (1618-30)
        - 3. Venkata II (1586-1614)
      - Venkatādri
        - Śrīranga
          - Gōpālarāja of Kandanavolu

CHAPTER XIII

SOCIAL AND ECONOMIC CONDITIONS

Plan of remaining chapters—territorial divisions—people—court life—king—army and navy—war and camp—Brahmins—caste—food and dress—education—learning—the temple—sports and pastimes—town and village life—agriculture and irrigation—industries—transport—merchant guilds and articles of trade—maritime trade: under Bāhmanī and Vijayanagar—on the east coast in the sixteenth and seventeenth centuries—currency, weights and measures.

IN this and the succeeding chapters we shall try to sketch the social and economic conditions that prevailed in South India from the sixth to the seventeenth centuries A.D., and to trace in outline the principal movements of culture in the spheres of literature, religion and art. The ground is vast and the material abundant; only a summary treatment of selected topics will be possible within the limits of this book.

The country was divided into certain well-marked territorial divisions, e.g., Kuntala, Andhra, Tondainād, Chola, Pāndya and Chera, and the people of each division tended to develop and cherish separate traditions and habits of their own. These local patriotisms did not by any means prove an obstacle to the formation of larger political units, as happened under the Chālukyas of Bādāmi and Kalyāni, the Rāshtrakūtas, the Cholas and Vijayanagar; and they played a great part in mitigating the evils which resulted from the break-up of the larger units.

There is no means of forming a reliable estimate of the population at any time during this long period we are now reviewing; even the Cholas, although they kept a minute record of property in land, never thought of taking a census of the population. In the ports on the seaboard, and in the capitals of kingdoms, particularly in Vijayanagar, there were undoubtedly considerable numbers of foreigners, including Arabs, Jews, Persians, Chinese, people from Malaya and the eastern archipelago; and later, the Portuguese and other European nations. The presence of Parsis is noticed by Friar Jordanus at the beginning of the fourteenth century. Necessarily and obviously, however, the bulk of the population was always and everywhere Hindus organized in castes. There was some connexion between caste and occupation, but this was by no means unalterable, and the pressure of new factors and situations was always bringing about changes, in spite of protests from conservatives and even occasional attempts on the part of the political power to stop them.

Then, as now, the service of the state in its civil departments, as well as the army and the navy (where one was maintained), furnished openings for all classes of the population; and many are the instances of Brahmin generals who distinguished themselves in war. Krishnadeva Rāya had a high opinion of their loyalty and considered that they should be put in charge of important forts in all strategic places. Forest and hill tribes furnished a favourite recruiting-ground for the army, especially in time of war. The roads were often infested by robbers, and any sharp local quarrel or the turbulence of a chieftain might lead to a village being attacked or its cattle being taken away; in such circumstances the people generally had to defend themselves, and numerous inscriptions attest the bravery of many village heroes, especially near forests and mountains.

Conquests sometimes led to the large-scale migration of people from one part of the country to another, and to new adjustments in economic and social relations. The most recent instance of this, and one whose effects are still clearly traceable, was the coming into the Tamil country of numbers of Telugus and Kannadigas with the extension of the empire of Vijayanagar and, perhaps, of the Hoysala power earlier. They must have come in as officers and soldiers upholding the authority of the rulers and their migration was doubtless encouraged by grants of land and other concessions at the expense of the people of the conquered territory. Royal patronage of learning, the arts, and religion were other causes of similar movements.

The king and his court led an extravagant and luxurious life in striking contrast to the modest living standard of the rest of the population. The pomp and ceremony of the court became more and more dazzling in the course of centuries and may be said to have reached its culmination under the Rāyas of Vijayanagar. The palace always had a large establishment attached to it; in theory there were seventy-two departments (*niyōgas*) in a palace as in a temple. On the establishment there were large numbers of women, specially chosen for their youth and beauty. Some were imported from abroad while others were captured in war and enslaved. Many, needless to say, were courtesans, skilled in the arts of music and dancing, while others were the concubines of princes, nobles and courtiers. A mistress of the Chālukya king Vijayāditya of Bādāmi, Vināpōṭigaḷ by name (notice the honorific plural), performed the *hiraṇyagarbha* at Mahākūta and presented to the deity a pedestal (*pīṭha*), set with rubies, with a silver umbrella over it. The Rāshtrakūta Amoghavarsha regularly employed courtesans as his emissaries and his feudatories had to receive batches of them from the emperor and entertain them in their courts.

Princesses of the royal family generally received a good education in literature and the fine arts; some were quite equal, on occasions, to the tasks of administration and war. The Chālukyan princess Akkādevi, elder sister of Jayasimha II, carried on the administration of a province and personally and actively engaged in fights and sieges. Hoysala Ballāla I's queens were highly accomplished in music and dancing, and Sovaladevi, the queen of Kalacuri Sovideva (1174) used to display her accomplishments in these arts in large assemblies attended by nobles, scholars and artists from different countries. The Portuguese chronicler Paes (1520-2) and other foreign writers often described the number and costly establishments of the Vijayanagar queens as well as the large numbers of women attendants, the lavishness of their clothing and jewellery, and the sundry light duties allotted to them in the daily routine of the palace. We learn, for instance, that in the provincial court of Raghunātha Nāyaka of Tanjore there were many learned women poets who were capable of expounding works written in various languages. The role of women in high society was varied, important, and, generally speaking, pleasant. *Satī* was not unknown, especially among the upper classes, but by no means common.

The king made his appearance in open durbar at least once a day, when all high officials and nobles had to be in attendance, and nothing was omitted that could increase the splendour of the display. It was then that he generally transacted public business, heard complaints, received ambassadors from foreign countries and tribute from subordinate rulers. Such scenes have been repeatedly described by travellers from abroad, and the following account by Nicolas Pimenta (1599) of the interview he had with the Naick (*nāyak*) of Gingee at Chidambaram may be considered more or less typical. 'The Naickus of Gingi was come hither, in whose dominion it standeth. He commanded that we should be brought to his Presence. Before us two hundred Brachmanes went in a ranke to sprinkle the house with Holy water, and to prevent Sorcerie against the King, which they use to do every day that the King first entreth into any house. We found him lying on a silken carpet leaning on two Cushions, in a long silken Garment, a great Chaine hanging from his necke, distinguished with many Pearles and Gemmes, all over his breast, his long hair tyed with a knot on the Crowne, adorned with Pearles; some Princes and Brachmanes attended him. He entertained us kindly, and marvelled much that we chewed not the leaves of Betele which were offered to us, and dismissed us with gifts of precious clothes wrought with Gold, desiring a Priest of us for his new Citie which he was building.' In 1443, the king of Vijayanagar interviewed the Persian ambassador Abdur Razzak twice a week when he stayed in the city, and on one occasion he said to the ambassador through his interpreter: 'Your monarchs invite an ambassador, and receive him to their table; as you and we may not eat together, this purse full of gold is the feast we give to an ambassador.' The sultans of the Bāhmanī kingdom and their nobles were, if anything, even more luxurious and extravagant in their mode of life, as the Russian merchant Athanasius Nikitin testifies. About Bijapur, Varthema (1505) wrote: 'The king lives in great pride and pomp. A great number of his servants wear on the insteps of their shoes rubies and diamonds, and other jewels; so you may imagine how many are worn on the fingers of the hand and in the ears. . . . They are all Mahommedans . . . The ladies go with their faces quite covered, according to the custom of Damascus.'

In war the king sometimes took the field in person, but more often sent his trusted generals. The traditional fourfold division of the army is often spoken of, particularly in literary works, but there is no tangible evidence of the chariot playing any part in battle. Elephants retained their importance to a very late date, and Yuan Chwang observed that in Mahārāshtra they were made drunk before an engagement. Cavalry was so important that kings often competed with one another in the terms they offered to Arab merchants in the busy trade in horses. Firearms came into use in the wars between the Bāhmanī and Vijayanagar kingdoms, although the gunners were usually foreigners. Forts played a prominent part in the defence system from very early times, but the art of besieging and reducing them was also well understood. Details of the recruitment, training and equipment of armies are lacking till we come to the period of Vijayanagar. It is clear, however, that they included men from all strata of society, and that their numbers were increased by the addition of fresh recruits and feudal levies when a war was on. A select body of troops often served as a king's chosen bodyguard who shared a meal with the king at the time of his accession and were thereafter always bound to defend him with their lives. They were called by various names—*Sahavāsis* under the Chālukyas, *Vēḷaikkārar* under the Cholas, *Garuḍas* under the Hoysalas, and *Āpattudavigaḷ* under the Pāndyas. The institution seems to have fallen into desuetude in later times. Though total war was altogether unknown, war was not always confined in its effects to the fighting forces. Although instances of clemency, such as Narasimhavarman I sparing Bādāmi, and Vikramāditya II the citizens of Kānchī, are indeed known, the wars between the Cholas and the Chālukyas of Kalyāni, and those between Bāhmanī and Vijayanagar, were undoubtedly marked by much wanton destruction and cruelty. Nuniz describes an expeditionary force of the Vijayanagar army in the following terms: 'All were equally well armed, each after his own fashion, the archers and musqueteers with their quilted tunics, and the shieldmen with their swords and poignards in their girdles; the shields are so large that there is no need for armour to protect the body, which is completely covered; the horses in full clothing, and the men with doublets, and weapons in their hands, and on their heads headpieces after the manner of their doublets, quilted with cotton. The war elephants go with their howdahs from which four men fight on each side of them, and the elephants are completely clothed, and on their tusks they have knives fastened, much ground and sharpened, with which they do great harm. Several cannon were also taken.' On the camp, the same writer observed: 'All the camp was divided into regular streets. Each captain's division has its market where you found all kinds of meat, such as sheep, goats, pigs, fowls, hares, partridges and other birds, and this in great abundance; so much, so that it would seem as if you were in the city of Bisnaga.' There were gymnasia in the capital and other important centres where the troops were systematically trained in military exercises in peace-time. Commanders who were defeated were given women's clothes to wear, as Yuan Chwang observed, and as has been confirmed by Chola inscriptions of the eleventh century.

Not much information is forthcoming about the navy, though we hear of naval operations, great and small. The conquest of Rēvatidvīpa and Purī on the West Coast by the Chālukyas of Bādāmi, and that of Ceylon and the Maldives by the Pallavas, Pāndyas and Cholas as well as by Vijayanagar, above all the great naval expedition of Rājendra Chola against the maritime empire of Śrī Vijaya could not have been executed without an efficient naval organization. Furthermore the maritime trade of the country, which was always considerable, must have required protection from the depredations of pirates and hostile powers. The opinions of Chola mariners expressed in treatises on navigation were quoted with approval by their Arab successors in the fifteenth and sixteenth centuries. There is no doubt that the kingdoms of South India had a fairly continuous maritime tradition which served their immediate purposes; but it failed them altogether against the more adventurous nations of Europe.

In civil life the Brahmins occupied a highly respected position. With the exception of the few who entered the state service in the army and elsewhere, they generally devoted themselves to religious and literary pursuits and stood outside the race for wealth and power. They lived on voluntary gifts from all classes of people from the king downwards. Hundreds of inscriptions proclaim the continued solicitude of kings, nobles and merchants for the maintenance and encouragement of a class of men who devoted themselves exclusively to learning and teaching, who were capable of detached thinking on all problems of social welfare, and whose presence in every town and village was calculated to provide not only patterns of ethical and religious conduct for the rest of the population, but active helpers and disinterested arbitrators in the numerous concerns of their daily life. 'The intellectual superiority of the Brahmans as a caste', says Sir Charles Eliot, 'was sufficiently real to ensure its acceptance and in politics they had the good sense to rule by serving, to be ministers and not kings. In theory and to a considerable extent in practice, the Brahmans and their gods are not an *imperium in imperio* but in *imperium super imperium*.' It cannot be denied that the Brahmin did not always live up to the ideals of his vocation, and that some movements, like that of the Lingāyats, raised a protest against the position accorded to the Brahmin in society; but as a rule he proved true to his trust, and the rest of the community willingly acknowledged the justice of it in every way.

In fact the institution of caste with all its social and economic implications was accepted almost universally, and the upholding of the social order organized on its basis was held to be the primary duty of the ruler. This accounts at once for the prevalence of much social exclusiveness in matters of food and marriage among different sections of the people, and for the readiness with which they came together and co-operated on matters of common concern like the management of a temple and its adjuncts, the regulation of land and irrigation rights in the village, and the administration of local affairs generally. The emphasis was throughout on the performance of duties attaching to one's station rather than on the rights of the individual or group. The general atmosphere was one of social harmony and contentment with the existing order; differences and disputes there were—there has been no society without them—but they were seldom acrimonious. Even the quarrels between 'right-hand' and 'left-hand' castes, a distinction which has an early start and whose origin is a mystery, did not attain the violence that characterized them in subsequent times. Both in towns and villages, the castes tended to live in separate quarters of their own and follow their own peculiar customs and habits. The outcastes who tilled the land and did menial work (under conditions little different from slavery) lived in hamlets at a distance from the village proper.

Some curious instances of mixed castes and their trades occur in the inscriptions. Towards the close of the reign of Kulottunga I, for instance, the *bhaṭṭas* of a village consulted the codes and laid down the professions to be followed by the *anuloma* caste of Rathakāras as architecture, coach and chariot-building, the erection of *gōpuras* with icons on them, the manufacture of sacrificial instruments and so on—a decision in conformity with the nearly contemporary manual of law, the *Mitāksharā* of Vigñānesvara. Sometimes the privileges of particular castes became, for specific reasons, the subject of royal regulation. For instance, the stonemasons (*kanmāḷar*) of South Kongu and some other areas were granted the following privileges by a Chola monarch: the blowing of two conches, the beating of drums and so on at domestic occurrences, good or bad, the use of sandals when they went out of their homes; and the plastering of the walls of their residences with lime plaster. A barber Kondōja pleased Sadāśiva and Rāma Rāya so much that he was able to secure exemption for his entire community from taxes and dues like forced labour, land-rent, *Mahānavami* torches and so on; and a number of inscriptions recording this fact contain engravings of razors, strops, mirrors, scissors and others of the barbers' tools of trade.

Food and dress varied with the time, place and the class of people concerned. Much authentic and detailed information on these subjects can be gathered from epigraphs, literature, and the observations of foreign travellers which become more copious and detailed after the foundation of Vijayanagar. Here, for instance, is Varthema's account of what he saw in Vijayanagar early in the sixteenth century: 'Their dress is this: the men of condition wear a short shirt and on their head a cloth of gold and silk in the Moorish fashion, but nothing on the feet. The common people go quite naked, with the exception of a piece of cloth about their middle. The king wears a cap of gold brocade two spans long, and when he goes to war he wears a quilted dress of cotton, and over it he puts another garment full of golden piastres, and having all around it jewels of various kinds. His horse is worth more than some of our cities, on account of the ornaments which it wears. When he rides for his pleasure he is always accompanied by three or four kings, and many other lords, and five or six thousand horse. Wherefore he may be considered to be a very powerful lord.'

Some sections of the population—Brahmins, Jains, and Śaivas—were strict vegetarians. There was generally a good supply of the prime necessaries of life, and scarcity and famine are only rarely heard of.

Of the system of education, we get more positive information on higher studies in Sanskrit than on popular education; while the former formed the subject of liberal endowments recorded in inscriptions of considerable length, we have to make inferences about the latter from the mention of the village teacher and his share in the arable land of the village and also occasional direct endowments, as for the teaching of Tamil, Marathi, and Prakrit in the schools in Kuntala. What we should now call technical or vocational training was a private affair; the father brought up his children in his calling, and learning went side by side with doing. The erection of a temple or palace must have been the occasion as much for the discovery of fresh talent as for the application of known abilities; and, judging from the monuments that have survived, we may well conclude that at no time was there a dearth of artisans who were also great artists. The beauty and accuracy which mark the engraving of most inscriptions on stone and copper attest the high degree of the literacy and skill of the engravers, while the literary quality of many of the inscriptions, as well as the volume of literature produced in all languages, shows that the cultivation of the popular speech of each locality and its employment in administration and education was by no means neglected. All we lack is clear knowledge of the processes by which these results were achieved, especially during the earlier period when the *maṭhas* had not come up in such large numbers as they did later to foster vernacular learning and culture. The 'three Rs' were taught in village schools which met under the shade of a tree or in the verandahs of temples, and the village teacher (*vātti* or *akkariga*) was among the regular village officials who held assignments of land from the village on the condition that they fulfilled specified duties. The Italian traveller Pietro Della Valle (1623) has left a vivid account of the village schools and the methods of instruction they followed, including the process of learning by rote and the use of fine sand strewn on the floor for writing, methods which survived in full force till the other day and have perhaps not quite gone out yet in remote villages. Ibn Batuta (1333-45) records: 'I saw in Hanaur thirteen schools for the instruction of girls, and twenty-three for boys, a thing I have not seen anywhere else.' Robert de Nobili, in a letter of 1610, says that in Madura there were 10,000 students who went to the Professor in Theology and Philosophy. When the Christian missionaries came, they began to start schools which, besides hospitals, formed the main channels for the propagation of their gospel. They had schools at Madura, San Thomé and Chandragiri.

'Adult education' was provided throughout the country by endowments in temples for the recitation and exposition of the epics and Purāṇas. An intelligent and popular expositor seldom confined himself to the words of his text, but at once instructed and amused his audience by ranging over a variety of topics including shrewd comments on current affairs. This form of popular instruction is not unknown even at the present day. The singing of devotional hymns in temples by choirs regularly maintained for that purpose and the training of young men for the same purpose in schools generally attached to *maṭhas* is another side of education that deserves notice. Besides *maṭhas*, Jain *pallis* and Buddhist *vihāras* played a part in educating the people wherever they existed, and they had large libraries of books in all branches of learning which were being copied from time to time.

Sanskrit learning tended to be the monopoly of Brahmins, though there were exceptions, and it was particularly encouraged by means of large special endowments. Sometimes only four, and sometimes as many as fourteen or eighteen subjects of study were enumerated. The four subjects were: philosophy (*ānvīkshikī*), Veda (*trayī*), economics (*vārttā*), and politics (*daṇḍanīti*) —a group which was particularly suited to kings and which in fact first occurs in Kauṭilya's *Arthaśāstra.* The fourteen *vidyās* were: the four *Vedas;* six *angas* (auxiliaries)—phonetics, prosody, grammar, etymology (of difficult words), astronomy and ritual; *purāṇa*; logic (*tarka*); exegesis (*mīmāmsā*); and law (*dharmaśāstra*). To these were added *āyurveda* (medicine), *dhanurveda* (archery), *gāndharvaveda* (Music) and *arthaśāstra* (politics) to make up the tale of eighteen. Brahmins learned in many of these sciences served as *Rājagurus* (teachers of kings) and spread themselves all over the land edifying the lives of the inhabitants of every town and village. Gifts of land and houses were frequently offered as inducements to Brahmins to come and settle where they were wanted. In several places they were organized into corporate colleges called *brahmapurīs* and *ghaṭikās*, like the *brahmapurī* at Belgaum or the *ghaṭikā* at Kānchī. A Vaishnava *maṭha* and its scholars are mentioned in an inscription of Nripatunga's reign from Kāveripākkam. Another record of the same monarch proves the flourishing condition of a college at Bāhūr, near Pondicherry, where the fourteen *vidyās* were pursued. At Salatgi was another eminent college to which pupils came from different *Janapadas* (countries) and whose *vidyārthisangha* was richly endowed in 945 by Nārāyana, the minister of Krishna III, with the revenues of houses, land, and levies on marriages and other ceremonies. We also hear (1058) of a *ghaṭikā* at Nāgai with ample provision for

200 Veda students, 50 students of the *śāstras*, three teachers of the Vedas, and three teachers of the *śāstras*—one each for Bhāṭṭa, Prābhākara-mīmāmsā and Nyāya—besides a librarian who brings up the strength to 257 in all. At Eṇṇāyiram in South Arcot the Chola Rājendra I endowed a large college of (1) 270 junior students of whom 40 studied the elements of grammar according to the *Rūpāvatāra*, 10 studied the *sūtras* of Bodhāyana, and the rest learnt the Vedas by rote; (2) 70 senior students, 10 studying *vedānta*, 25 *vyākaraṇa*, and the rest Prābhākara-mīmāmsā; and (3) a teaching staff of 14. In another college, in the same neighbourhood at Tribhuvani, there were 260 students and 12 teachers. Full details have been preserved of the food and residence of the pupils of a smaller institution at Tirumukkūdal in Chingleput district in an inscription of the reign of Vīrarājendra (1067) which also gives equally interesting details about the stock of medicines maintained in a good-sized hospital in the same place. A medical school at Tiruvāḍuturai where the *Ashṭāngahridaya* and *Caraka Samhitā* were taught, and a school for the study of Pāṇini's grammar at Tiruvoṟṟiyūr, may also be noted. The study of Law and Astronomy found special encouragement from the Yādavas of Devagiri. Education and learning continued to receive generous support from the Rāyas of Vijayanagar and their numerous feudatories. The Bāhmanī kingdom and its successors naturally devoted more attention to Muslim education and Islamic studies, in such large and well-equipped colleges as the one at Bidar, established by the celebrated minister Mahmud Gawan.

The apparent geographical isolation of Kerala did not mean any cultural aloofness. Kerala appears in many ways in the literature of the rest of India. In Kerala itself the Nambūdiri Brahmins allowed only the eldest son to contract a permanent marriage and rear a family; the younger sons freed from family cares devoted themselves generally to study and teaching, and helped in the promotion of literacy among the masses. Sanskrit learning was patronized by the chiefs as can be seen from a grant of the Āy king Karunandaḍakkan, middle of the ninth century, endowing a college and hostel for the maintenance of ninety-five vedic students who were admitted after an entrance test in *Vyākaraṇa* (grammar), *Mīmāmsā* (exegetics), *Paurohitya* (priest-craft) and *Trairājyavyavahāra* (Law and usage of the three countries, perhaps Pāndya, Chola and Kerala). The college was to function in a Vishnu temple at Pārthivaśekharapuram in South Travancore, and indeed, the many temples of the land as well as the *maṭhas* and *sattras* tended each in its way to become a centre of learning of the *gurukula* type.

The temple was not merely a place of worship; it filled a large place in the cultural and economic life of the people. Its construction and maintenance offered employment to numbers of architects and craftsmen who vied with one another in bold planning and skilful execution. The making of icons in stone and metal gave scope to the talents of the best sculptors of the country; some of the larger bronzes cast in the Chola period take their place among the wonders of the world for the mass of metal manipulated as well as for the grace of form attained in the result. The daily routine, especially of the larger temples, gave constant employment to numbers of priests, choristers, musicians, dancing-girls, florists, cooks and many other classes of servants. The periodical festivals were occasions marked by fairs, contests of learning, wrestling-matches and every other form of popular entertainment. Schools and hospitals were often located in the temple precincts, and it also served often as the town hall where people assembled to consider local affairs or to hear the exposition of sacred literature. The large endowments in land and cash bestowed on each temple by successive generations of pious donors tended to make it at once a generous landlord and a banker whose aid was always available to those that needed it. The practice of decorating images, particularly those used during processions, with numerous jewels set with precious stones encouraged the jeweller's art to a considerable extent. There can be no better record of the details of the economy of a large temple than is provided by the numerous inscriptions of the Great Temple of Tanjore. There the gifts of Rājarāja came largely from booty captured in successful warfare and included well over 41,500 *kaḻañjus* of gold, or, taking a *kaḻañju* to be about 70 grains, well over 500 lb. troy weight. The value of jewels was 10,200 *kāśus*, equal to half as many *kaḻañjus* in gold. Of silver he gave 50,650 *kaḻañjus* or over 600 lb. troy weight. He set apart lands in villages throughout his dominions, including Ceylon, with an annual income of 116,000 *kalams* of paddy, equal at the then prevailing prices to 58,000 *kāśus*, besides a cash income of 1,100 *kāśus*. For the service of the temple, 400 *devadāsis* were impressed from those attached to other temples in the empire, each one receiving a *pangu* (share) consisting of a house and one *vēli* of land yielding a net revenue of 100 *kalams* of paddy a year. About 180 further such shares were set apart to maintain 212 male dancing-masters, musicians, drummers, tailors, goldsmiths, accountants, and so on. These men-servants included three people to sing the *Āriyam* and four others the *Tamil*, which apparently are the two systems of music called *ahamārgam* and *dēśi* elsewhere. A choir of 50, on a daily wage of three *kurunis* of paddy, recited the *Tiruppadiyam* to the accompaniment of musical instruments. This choir had the additional privilege of filling vacancies by co-option if any of their number died or emigrated without leaving behind a suitable relative to take his place. Rājarāja's elder sister Kundavai was another generous contributor to temple funds. On one occasion she presented gold weighing nearly 10,000 *kaḻañjus* and utensils valued at 18,000 *kāśus*. Others, too—queens, high officials and regiments of soldiers—made gifts which have been recorded with equal care and precision on the walls and pillars of the temple. Cash endowments, which amounted to several thousands of *kāśus*, were loaned to numerous village assemblies at rates of interest fixed in kind or money, and generally about 12 per cent per annum. Camphor, cardamom-seeds, champak-buds and khus-khus roots were among the products provided for by means of cash endowments.

The inscriptions contain accurate and detailed descriptions of numerous icons, some of which were cast in the form of complex groups of figures illustrating favourite themes from legends. They also contain an equally minute and complete account of the ornaments and jewels of the temple, and record periodical inquests into the management of temple affairs by officers of state, and sometimes even by the king himself—clear proof that the business side of the temple administration was properly controlled. All systems of public administration were not as efficient as the Chola system, and all temples were not so well off as that of Tanjore. As a matter of course, however, every temple held more or less the same position in relation to its neighbourhood that the Great Temple held in the Chola capital; the difference was only one of degree. And it is no exaggeration to say that the temple gathered round itself all that was best in the arts of civilized existence and regulated them with the humaneness born of the spirit of *dharma*.

As an agency of social well-being the medieval Indian temple has few parallels.

Of the sports and pastimes of the different classes of people, the inscriptions do not give us many authentic accounts of a detailed nature. The Rāshtrakūta Govinda III took part in a boar-hunt on the banks of the Tungabhadra when he was camping there after his conquest of Kānchī in 804, and the Ganga Būtuga II's hound 'Kāli' died after fighting a boar. (A memorial was erected over its remains at Ātakūr and a *gorava* appointed to offer regular worship to it.) A ball game on horseback, much like polo, is said to have been the favourite game of the Rāshtrakūta prince Indra IV. Paes states that, every morning before daylight, Krishnadeva Rāya drank gingelly-oil and exercised himself with earthenware weights and a sword till he had sweated out all the oil. He then wrestled with one of his wrestlers and after that went riding before his morning bath. There were arenas inside the royal palace in Vijayanagar where, for the amusement of the monarch and his court, fights between animals and wrestling matches took place, the latter sometimes among women. Gambling, racing, cock and ram fights were the pastimes of common people, besides the festivals and fairs of which there was no lack. Then there were peripatetic entertainers like the snake-charmer and troupes of acrobatic performers whose visits furnished much genuine amusement at very little cost. Picnics and folk-dances offered other means of diversion. The following account of what Pietro Della Valle saw in the streets of Ikkeri of an evening (in 1623-4) is of great interest from several points of view:

'We saw going along the streets several companies of young girls, well clothed, after their manner, with some of the above-mentioned wrought and figured silk from the girdle downwards; and from thence upwards either naked, or else very pure linen, either of one colour, or striped and wrought with several, besides a scarf of the same work cast over the shoulder. Their heads were decked with yellow and white flowers formed into a high and large Diadem, with some sticking out like sun-beams, and others twisted together and hanging down in several fashions which made a pretty sight. All of them carry'd in each hand a little round painted stick, about a span long, or a little more which they struck together after a musical measure, to the sound of Drums and other instruments, and one of the skilfullest of the company sang one verse of a song, at the end of which they all reply'd seven or eight times in the number of their meter with the word *Colé*, *Colé*, *Colé*, which signifies I know not what, but, I believe, 'tis a word of joy . . . I imagined it was for some extraordinary Festival.'

Another citation, from the same observer, relating to Calicut, is well worth making for its vivid portraiture of conditions many of which were obviously not confined to that city: 'We went to see the Bazār which is near the shore; the Houses or rather Cottages are built of Earth and thatched with Palm-leaves, being very low; the streets also are very narrow, but sufficiently long; the Market was full of all sorts of Provisions and other things necessary to the livelihood of that people, conformably to their custom; for, as for clothing they need little, both men and women going quite naked, saving that they have a piece either of Cotton, or silk, hanging down from the girdle to the knees and covering their shame; the better sort are either wont to wear it all blew, or white striped with Azure, or Azure and some other colour; a dark blew being most esteemed amongst them. Moreover both Men and Women wear their hair long and ty'd about their head; the women with a lock hanging on one side under the ear becomingly enough as almost all Indian women do; the dressing of whose head is, in my opinion, the gallantest that I have seen in any other nation. The Men have a lock hanging down from the crown of the head, sometimes a little inclined on one side; some of them use a small coloured head-band, but the Women use none at all. Both sexes have their Arms adorned with bracelets, their ears with pendants, and their necks with jewels; the Men commonly go with their Swords and Bucklers, or other Arms, in their hands, as I said of those of Balagate.'

The vast majority of the population lived in villages and agriculture was their main occupation. Great prestige attached to ownership of land, and everyone, whatever his occupation, aimed at having a small plot he could call his own. The village was thus primarily a settlement of peasants, and its assembly an association of landlords. A periodical redistribution of the arable land of a village among its inhabitants prevailed in many parts of the country till comparatively recent times. Besides the landowners, great and small, there was a fairly large class of landless labourers, an agrarian proletariat, who assisted in the operations and shared the proceeds of agriculture; some of them were in a condition of serfdom, and all of them had less to do with the management of local affairs than the landowners. The artisans of the village had shares from the common land of the village, which were of the nature of retainers or inducements to them to stay in the village, ready to take up work as it came to them, the wage of each engagement forming the subject of separate negotiation between the parties. There was also a staff of menial servants from the outcastes who were likewise rewarded by shares in the common land. Day labour was usually paid for in grain, and even the small peasant was ready to hire himself out in his spare time. Tenancy cultivation was quite common, especially on lands belonging to temples and other corporate institutions, the terms of the tenancy being fixed either by the terms of the original endowment or by separate negotiation in each case. Very often such tenants had rights which made them more or less part-owners of the land they cultivated. The distinction between garden land, including flower-gardens and orchards, in the neighbourhood of capital cities, land under wet cultivation and that under dry cultivation, and forest land, was carefully maintained for taxation and other purposes, wet lands being further divided into several grades according to their natural fertility. Besides cultivating food grains and pulses on both wet and dry land, intensive flower and vegetable growing and the raising of commercial crops like cotton and sugar-cane were also widely practised. Black land and red land are particularly mentioned in Chālukya records besides the usual wet land, garden land and waste land. Betel and areca-nuts, ginger and turmeric, fresh fruits and flowers, were the chief items of garden produce. Abdur Razzak noticed the number of rose merchants in Vijayanagar and added that roses seemed as necessary as food to the people of that city. The importance of irrigation was well understood from early times; dams were erected across streams and channels taken off from them wherever possible. Large tanks were made to serve areas where there were no natural streams, and the proper maintenance of these tanks was regularly provided for. The extension of agriculture was encouraged at all times by granting special facilities and tax concessions for specified periods to people who reclaimed land and brought it under cultivation for the first time. The prosperity of the cultivator depended to some extent on the seasons, but to a large measure on the conditions of his tenure and on the tax-collecting agency. Tenant conditions were probably easier on lands set apart for religious and charitable uses and of which temples, *maṭhas* and Brahmins were the landlords. But where rights were assigned to high officials and nobles, or where, as often happened, the collection of the land tax was farmed, both the rate of tax and the manner of collecting it might have pressed hard on the cultivator. Even in the heyday of liberal and efficient administration—under the imperial Cholas—there were complaints of the tax-gatherer's oppressive methods; and after the weakening of Vijayanagar, under the Nāyaks, the ryots were generally compelled to purchase the state's share of the grain at prices arbitrarily fixed by the tax-gatherer. Closely allied to agriculture was cattle-raising and dairy farming, and land was set apart for pasture; this industry must have been widespread at all times, but in the inscriptions we hear more of the cattle belonging to temples and eating-houses, of the cowherds in charge of them, and of the obligations they owed to the temple or other owner. Ghee was not only an important item of food among the upper classes, but was used in considerable quantities for burning in lamps in the larger temples.

In most of the common industries the rule was production for the local market; but the movements of individual merchants from one part of the country to another, and the highly developed organization of mercantile corporations in different parts of it, provide adequate evidence of a brisk internal trade in certain sorts of goods. Spinning and weaving formed a major industry which occupied considerable numbers, and guilds of weavers were generally in a flourishing condition and took an active part in many local concerns. The export of the finer varieties of cloth from various parts of the country is proved by records during the entire period covered by this survey. Wārangal specialized in the manufacture of carpets which were much sought after, and other places had other specialities. The metal industries and the jeweller's art had reached a high state of perfection. Household utensils of metal were apparently confined to the rich, earthenware being in more common use to judge from the frequency with which it is mentioned in connexion with cooking and eating in *śālas* (or charitable feeding-halls). Iron was used for making arms, and some places like Palnad attained celebrity for the excellence of their output. The manufacture and sale of salt was generally the concern of government which derived a considerable revenue from it. This industry was naturally concentrated at important centres on the sea-coast, as was pearl-fishing in the Gulf of Mannar —an important industry which attracted the notice of foreign visitors (including Marco Polo) who have often described it.

Almost all the arts and crafts were organized in castes and guilds of their own, and work was clearly done on a corporate basis, for we hear little about individual artists, not even the names of the architects, sculptors and painters who added so much beauty to life in the country. One of the very few and notable exceptions to this rule is Śrī Guṇḍan Anivāritachāri, the builder of the Lokeśvara temple (now called Virūpāksha) at Pattadakal, who procured many privileges for his class from the contemporary Chālukya ruler of Bādāmi besides winning for himself the title Tenkanadiśeyasūtradhāri, 'the architect of the South'. It was he who designed the sculptures of scenes from the *Rāmāyana* which adorn the walls of this temple. Śrī Guṇḍan is said to have been an expert in planning cities, constructing palaces, vehicles, thrones and bedsteads. Several Hoysala sculptors 'signed' their creations, the most famous names among them being Malitamma, Baicoja, Caudaya, Nanjaya, and Bāma.

It is not possible to give a detailed account of the conditions of internal transport. There was as little scope then as now for the use of natural waterways for the carriage of merchandise in the interior, and there is no evidence that canals were made for any purpose other than irrigating agricultural lands. Roads are mentioned in inscriptions from all parts of the country, and to maintain them, great and small, in good repair was part of the duty of local authorities, the villagers being generally expected to give their labour free. The breadth of a main road was about twenty-four feet; but there were also tracks, only slightly better than foot-paths, which were apparently impassable for wheeled traffic. There was regular coastal shipping. Up-country, merchandise was carried in carts, on the heads or shoulders of men (*kāvaḍis*), and on the backs of animals. The roads were not always safe and brigandage increased in unsettled times. Soon after the battle of Rakshasi-Tangadi, Caesar Frederick was detained in Vijayanagar for seven months ' until the ways were clear of thieves, which at that time ranged up and down'.

Merchants were generally organized in powerful guilds and corporations which often transcended political divisions and were therefore not much affected by the wars and revolutions going on about them. The most celebrated guilds from fairly early times were the Maṇigrāmam and the Nānādeśis or Aiññūṟṟuvar. The records of the Kākatīyas speak of merchants of the home country (*svadeśabēhārulu*), merchants of another country (*paradeśabēhārulu*), and merchants from different countries (*nānādeśis*). The first were the local merchants organized in local guilds—*nagarams*. The second were like the first except that they came from another country—perhaps combining pleasure with business while on a visit to their neighbours, or possibly acquiring religious merit by attending *yātras* and festivals in famous shrines. The last were the powerful guilds already mentioned which included merchants from all countries, with established branches in all of them, and perhaps playing a prominent part in the foreign trade of the country as a whole. The name Maṇigrāmam is generally explained as a corruption of Vaṇik-grāmam, 'an association of merchants', and this may well be correct. They are mentioned in many early South Indian inscriptions and in a Tamil inscription at Takua-pa (Siam) of the reign of Nandivarman III, Pallava. The fact that this merchant guild had established itself on the opposite coast of the Bay of Bengal with sufficient permanence for it to be put in charge of a Vishnu temple and a tank gives a clue to a yet little-known chapter in the annals of our ancient politics and commerce.

The Aiññūṟṟuvar, often styled the Five Hundred Svāmis of Ayyavolepura (Aihole), were the most celebrated of the medieval South Indian merchant guilds. Like the great kings of the age, they had a *praśasti* of their own which recounted their traditions and achievements. They were the protectors of the *Vīra-Baṇañju-dharma*, i.e., the law of the noble merchants, *Baṇañju* being obviously derived from Sanskrit *Vaṇija*, merchant. This *dharma* was embodied in 500 *vīra-śāsanas*, edicts of heroes. They had the picture of a bull on their flag and were noted 'throughout the world' for their daring and enterprise. They claimed descent from the lines of Vāsudeva, Khandaḷi and Mūlabhadra, and were followers of the creeds of Vishnu, Maheśvara and Jina. Among the countries they visited were Chera, Chola, Pāndya, Maleya, Magadha, Kausala, Saurāshtra, Dhānushtra, Kurumba, Kāmbhoja, Gaulla, Lāta, Barvvara, Parasa (Persia), and Nepāla. They traversed land-routes and water-routes, penetrating all the countries of the six continents. They traded in elephants, bloodstock, sapphires, moonstones, pearls, rubies, diamonds, lapis lazuli, onyx, topaz, carbuncles, emeralds and other precious articles; cardamoms, cloves, bdellium, sandal, camphor, musk, saffron, *malegaja* and other spices and perfumes. They either sold them wholesale or hawked them about on their shoulders; they paid the *śunka* regularly and filled the royal treasury with gold and jewels, and replenished the kings' armoury; they bestowed gifts on pandits and sages 'versed in the four *samayas* and six *darśanas*'. There were among them the sixteen *seṭṭis* of the eight *nāḍs*, who used asses and buffaloes as carriers, and many classes of merchants and soldiers, viz., *gavẹ̄ṟas*, *gātrigas*, *seṭṭis*, *seṭṭiguttas*, *ankakāṟas*, *bīras*, *bīravaṇijas*, *gaṇḍigas*, *gāvuṇḍas* and *gāvuṇḍasvāmis*. A fragmentary Tamil inscription from Sumatra (1088) and a temple of Vishnu which they erected at Pagan and which was still flourishing in the thirteenth century attest the truth of their claim to trade with foreign countries beyond the seas. In the Chola country they had their own settlements called *vīra-paṭṭanas* where, with the sanction of the local powers and the central government, they enjoyed special privileges in matters of trade. Historians have generally tended to ignore the effect of trade on the outlook of the people of those comparatively remote times. There is no doubt, for instance, that the continuous meeting and intermingling of people of diverse social backgrounds tended to create a liberal and cosmopolitan, as opposed to an insular, attitude to life.

The maritime trade of South India in the early centuries of the Christian era has been briefly described in Chapter VII. In the Chinese annals of the fifth, sixth and seventh centuries, all the products of Ceylon and India are classed, with those of Arabia and Africa, as products of Persia. The direct sea-route between India and China, however, is known to have come into common use by the fifth century; Fa Hien travelled from Ceylon in a merchantman which carried no fewer than two hundred Indian and Ceylonese merchants; and I-tsing mentions the names of thirty-seven of his contemporaries who took this route to India at different times. There were Brahmin temples and merchants in Canton in A.D. 750.

By the ninth century A.D. the countries of southern Asia had developed an extensive maritime commerce which brought great prosperity. The T'ang empire in China, Śrī Vijaya under the powerful line of the Śailendras, and the Abbasid Khalifat at Baghdad were the chief states outside India that flourished on this trade. Owing to political troubles China became unsafe for foreigners in the latter part of the ninth century, but Chinese ships regularly called at the ports of the Malay Peninsula and Sumatra to buy foreign goods. This was the beginning of Chinese navigation of the high seas. From the twelfth to the fifteenth century, Chinese sea-going junks were frequent visitors to the west coast of India. Siraf, on the eastern coast of the Persian Gulf, was the chief emporium in the west and the rich merchants of that city feasted the numerous merchants from China, Java, Malaya, and India who visited their city—every Indian insisting on having a separate plate exclusively reserved for him!

At the end of the tenth century, the political situation in China became normal again, and the Sung government of the day showed great interest in foreign trade. It became a government monopoly and strenuous efforts were made to increase it. Eager to take advantage of the new conditions, the Cholas sent 'embassies' to China. One such trade delegation left towards the end of Rājarāja's reign and reached China in 1015 after spending over three years on the way. Another, sent by Rājendra I, reached the celestial court in 1033, and a third went in 1077. The chief articles of merchandise in this long-distance trade were necessarily goods that carried great value for small bulk. For instance, the chief imports of Siraf were aloes, amber, camphor, precious stones, bamboo, ivory, ebony, paper, sandalwood, Indian perfumes, drugs and condiments. The import of horses to India from Arabia was important at all times, and grew to great proportions after the rise of the Bāhmanī and Vijayanagar kingdoms in the fourteenth century. The Portuguese, as we have seen, sought to acquire a monopoly in this trade when they gained command of the routes in the Indian waters. Imports into China were of two distinct categories of goods: manufactured textile fabrics mostly of cotton, spices and drugs; and, by far the more valuable intrinsically, jewels and semi-precious substances like ivory, rhinoceros horn, ebony, amber, coral, various aromatic products and perfumes. This trade was at first welcomed in China; but in the twelfth century, the drain of currency and precious metals resulting from this expansion of the trade in luxuries caused serious concern to the Chinese government. They therefore prohibited the export of precious metals and coined money, and put restrictions on the trade with ‘ Ma’bar ’ and ‘ Kulam ’—that is the Coromandel coast and Quilon. All the same, the trade continued with more or less regularity to the end of the thirteenth century. The testimony of the Jewish traveller Benjamin of Tudela (1170) on conditions of trade in Quilon under Chola rule is worth citing: ‘ This nation is very trustworthy in matters of trade, and whenever foreign merchants enter their port, three secretaries of the king immediately repair on board their vessels, write down their names and report them to him. The king thereupon grants them security for their property, which they may even leave in the open fields without any guard. One of the king’s officers sits in the market, and receives goods that may have been found anywhere, and which he returns to those applicants who can minutely describe them. This custom is observed in the whole empire of this king.’

The Kākatīya monarch Ganapati gave an impetus to the foreign trade of the Andhra country in the middle of the thirteenth century by his charter of security (*abhayaśāsana*). Under this charter the cargo of shipwrecked merchants would no longer be seized, as had been the custom till then; moreover, the duty on all exports and imports would not exceed 1/30 of their value. This edict was renewed a century later by Annapota Reddi (1378), and corresponded to the general practice that prevailed in all the enlightened and progressive ports of South India, though Colombo still retained the older practice in the fourteenth century. In the last quarter of the thirteenth century, the restless ambition and insatiable curiosity of Kublai Khan, added to the unsettled political conditions of the Pāndya kingdom, resulted in a very active exchange of embassies, more political than commercial, between the Chinese court and the South Indian powers. Again in the fifteenth century, under the third Ming emperor (1403-25), large fleets of Chinese junks, led by the famous general Cheng Ho, made no fewer than seven voyages across the Indian ocean and visited many South Indian ports, particularly those on the west coast.

Our information on conditions of industry, trade and travel becomes more copious and precise after the foundation of the Vijayanagar and Bāhmanī kingdoms, thanks to the many interested foreigners who visited these famous kingdoms and left records of what they saw. And the establishment of the Portuguese power followed by the advent of the trading companies of other European nations, whose factors gained intimate knowledge of the industries of the country, also resulted in the collection and recording of much valuable information on the economic conditions of South India in the sixteenth and seventeenth centuries. Much of this material still awaits critical study, and here we must rest content with a brief reference to some outstanding observations. Abdur Razzak (1443) described the kingdom of Vijayanagar as a place extremely large and thickly peopled, and its king as 'possessing greatness and sovereignty to the highest degree, whose dominion extends from the frontier of Serendib (Ceylon) to the extremities of the country of Kalbergah'. The country was for the most part well cultivated and very fertile. It contained about 300 ports and its army included 1,000 elephants and eleven lakhs of troops.

Calicut, where Razzak landed on his arrival, was a secure harbour for ships from Africa and Arabia; considerable numbers of Muslims were permanent residents there and had built two mosques. Security and justice were firmly established. 'Officers of the custom house look after the merchandise, and levy duty of 1/40 on sales, no charge being made on unsold articles.' There was a flourishing pepper trade with Mecca, and straying vessels were not plundered in this port as elsewhere. More than seventy years later, Duarte Barbosa found that the trade of Calicut was very large, and on that account natives of divers lands—Arabs, Persians, Guzerates, Khorassanians and Daquanis—settled there. The Moors had a governor of their own who ruled and punished them without interference from the king, except that he was obliged to account for certain matters to the king. Shipbuilding particularly flourished; keeled ships of 1,000 to 1,200 *bahares* burden were built, without decks and without any nails, the whole hull being sewn with thread. Here they loaded goods from every place, and every monsoon ten or fifteen ships sailed for the Red Sea, Aden and Mecca, whence the goods went through intermediaries up to Venice. The principal exports were pepper, ginger, cinnamon, cardamom, myrobalan, tamarind, canafistula, precious stones of every kind, seed-pearls, musk, ambergris, rhubarb, aloes, cotton cloth and porcelain. The chief imports into Calicut, which were loaded at Juda, were copper, quicksilver, vermilion, coral, saffron, coloured velvets, rose-water, knives, coloured camlets, gold and silver. As early as 1510, the Portuguese had a fort and settlement at Cochin where they repaired their ships and built new ones ' in as great perfection as on the Lisbon strand '. The Italian Varthema (1505) noted that an immense quantity of cotton was produced near Cambay so that every year forty or fifty vessels were laden with cotton and silk to be carried to different countries. Carnelians and diamonds also came to Cambay from mountains at six and nine days' journey from there. At Cannanore—another fine, large city—the king of Portugal had a strong castle; and there horses from Persia disembarked. On every one, customs duty of 25 ducats had to be paid before they could proceed on the fifteen-day journey to Vijayanagar. Another shipbuilding centre, owing to the excellent timber in the neighbourhood, was Dharmapatnam, 12 miles from Cannanore. Barbosa (1515) noted that wheat, rice, millet and gingelly, besides fine muslins and calicoes produced in the Bāhmanī kingdom, were exported from Chaul. A few miles inland from Chaul was a big market where ' they bring their goods laden on great droves of trained oxen with pack-saddles, like those of Castille; a driver drives 20 or 30 oxen before him '. Of Malabar, Barbosa makes the very true remark: ' albeit the country is but small, yet it is so fulfilled of people, that it may well be called one town from Mount Dely to Coulam ' (Quilon). Caesar Frederick (1567) found much silk imported into Cochin from China, and sugar from Bengal. According to Ralph Fitch (1583-91) ' all merchandise carried to Goa in a ship wherein were horses paid no custom in; the horses paid custom, and the goods paid nothing '. If there were no horses, the goods paid 8 per cent. ' The Moores cannot pass except they have a passport from the Portugals.' In Chaul there was great traffic in all sorts of spices and drugs, silk and cloth of silk, sandals, elephants' teeth and much ' China work '. Fitch calls the palm tree ' the profitablest tree in the world ' and notices the existence in Cambay of hospitals to keep lame dogs and cats, and for birds. ' They will give meat to the ants.'

The accounts of one English and two Dutch factors, who spent some years in Masulipatam and its neighbourhood, give an unusually vivid picture of the state of industry and trade on the east coast, particularly in the Golconda region. The country was mainly agricultural; in the lowlands the staple crops were rice, millets and pulses, while, on a smaller scale, the dye crops, indigo and chay-root, were produced for the weaving industry. Tobacco, then recently introduced, was grown largely for export. Cotton was not grown extensively, but was brought from the interior. The chief minerals were iron and steel of high quality, manufactured some distance inland, and exported from Masulipatam. Diamond-mining on an important scale had developed at Kollūr. Among industries cotton-weaving stood by itself. It was practised all over the area, both for local consumption and for export in large quantities. The weavers worked in their own houses, but as they depended on advances of capital from buyers they had to produce the quality and quantity of goods prescribed by their customers. There were two main classes of cotton goods—plain goods like calico and muslin, brown, bleached or dyed; and patterned goods of the type now called 'prints' made of either calico or muslin, with coloured patterns produced by the indigenous processes. This work was carried out mainly on the coasts and carefully adapted to the needs of markets in Java and the Far East, each with its own peculiar tastes and requirements. The export trade for plain goods was localized on the Golconda coast, while Pulicat specialized in the patterned variety.

The main exports of Golconda were thus cotton goods, iron and steel. Indigo was transported to the west coast and thence to Persia; cotton yarn went to Burma, and other minor items contributed to what was for the time large export trade. The volume of imports was smaller; spices, dye-woods, metals other than iron, camphor, porcelain, silk and other goods, mainly luxuries, were brought for sale on the coast, and the excess of exports was paid for in gold and silver. There was also a large coasting trade, northward to Bengal and southward to Ceylon.

Caesar Frederick noted the existence of regular trade from San Thomé to Pegu.

There was at all times a great multiplicity of currencies, weights and measures—each locality having its own system. At important trade centres money-changers assisted trade by settling fair exchange-rates. In liquid and grain measures, and particularly in the measurement of land, mention is often made in the inscriptions of the major dynasties of a 'royal measure'; this doubtless implies some effort at standardization. The Rāshtrakūta inscriptions, for instance, mention the *dramma* besides the *suvarṇa* and the *gadyāna*. The first recalls the Indo-Bactrian *drachma*, a silver coin of 65 grains. In Tamil inscriptions of even the eleventh and twelfth centuries occurs the name *tiramam* as that of a coin, perhaps of silver, which was a fifth or sixth of the standard gold coin—the *kāśu* of the Cholas. But golden *drammas* are mentioned in the Rāshtrakūta records and their value cannot be determined. In general two systems of weights are traceable in the ancient coins of South India. The gold *gadyāna* of the Deccan averages 58 grains, the heaviest reaching 60.1 grains; this was the old *gadyāna* (*kaccānam*) or *kaḻañju* (Tamil). But in the Chola period the more usual standard was a heavier *kaḻañju* of twenty *mañjāḍis* equal in theory to 72 grains but sometimes going up to 80. A coin of this standard was called *pon* or *māḍai*, and the *kāśu* was exactly half of this. But the records contain the names of many varieties of *māḍai* and *kāśu*, and it does not appear that standardization ever attained any tangible measure of success. And in many small day-to-day transactions coins seldom played a part, as barter was the rule, or grain served as currency. Coinage was never the monopoly of a single central power, though this condition was very nearly realized for some time under Vijayanagar. Abdur Razzak mentions the royal mint, and adds: ' In this country they have three kinds of money, made of gold, mixed with alloy: one called *varāha* weighs about one *mithkal*, equivalent to two dinars, *kopeki*; the second, which is called *pertab*, is half of the first; the third, called *fanom*, is equivalent in value to the tenth part of the last mentioned coin. Of these different coins, the *fanom* is the most useful. They cast in pure silver a coin which is the sixth of the *fanom*, which they call *tar*. This latter is also a very useful coin in currency. A copper coin worth the third of a *tar* is called *djitel*. According to the practice adopted in this empire, all the provinces, at a fixed period, bring their gold to the mint.' About sixty years later, Varthema records other relations among the smaller currency units, saying that sixteen *tars* went to the *fanom*, and sixteen *cas* to the *tar*, though he counts twenty *fanoms* to the pagoda (*pardao*, *varāha*) all right. Duarte Barbosa pays a high compliment to the integrity of the currency system and says: ' Coins of this place are perfectly genuine, not one of them has been ever found false, nor is now so found.' But the multiplicity of currencies persisted and caused inconvenience, and Caesar Frederick grumbles that a new governor's country meant new coins, 'so that the money we took this day would not serve the next'.

BIBLIOGRAPHY

T. V. Mahalingam: *Administration and Social Life under Vijayanagar* (Madras, 1940)

—: *Economic Life in the Vijayanagar Empire* (Madras, 1951)

C. Minakshi: *Administration and Social Life under the Pallavas* (Madras, 1938)

W. H. Moreland: *Relations of Golconda in the Early XVII Century* (Hakluyt Society, London, 1931)

S. Purchas: *His Pilgrimages*, Vol. X (Glasgow, 1912)

K. A. N. Sastri: *The Pandyan Kingdom* (London, 1929)

—: *Foreign Notices of South India* (Madras, 1939)

—: *The Colas*—2 vols. (Madras, 1935, 1937, second edition 1955)

Sir R. C. Temple (ed.): *The Itinerary of Ludovico di Varthema of Bologna, 1502- 1508* (London, 1928)

N. Venkataramanayya: *Studies in the history of the Third Dynasty of Vijayanagara* (Madras, 1935)

CHAPTER XIV

LITERATURE

1. *Sanskrit*: Sūtras—exegesis—*Bhāgavata*—commentaries on the epics—belles-lettres and rhetoric—philosophical literature: Nyāya; Pūrvamīmāmsā; Advaita; Viśishtādvaita, Vaishnava and Śaiva; Dvaita—Dharmaśāstra—lexicography—grammar—role of Kerala—music and dance.

2. *Tamil*: Late Śangam literature—second period (500-850): didactic works; devotional literature, Śaiva, Vaishnava; general literature—third period (850-1200): general literature; devotional literature, Śaiva, Vaishnava, Jaina; grammar; lexicography; beginnings of Śaiva-siddhānta—fourth period (1200-1650): Śaiva-siddhānta; devotional and religious literature, Purāṇas, Vaishnava *rahasyas*, secular literature, anthology; grammar, commentaries, lexicography, religious lore, the ballad.

3. *Kannada*: Before Pampa—'The three Gems'—Chāvundarāya—Durgasimha and his contemporaries—Nāgachandra—Karnapārya—other Jaina writers—Vīra-śaiva literature—Vaishnava literature: Dāsas—Bhaṭṭākalanka and other writers of early seventeenth century—stories.

4. *Telugu*: Beginnings of the language and literature—Nannaya and his contemporaries—Vīra-śaiva writers—Tikkana and other translators of the Epics—contemporaries of Tikkana—mathematical literature, translations—age of Śrīnātha—the age of Krishnadeva Rāya—literature of late sixteenth and early seventeenth centuries.

5. *Malayālam*: Beginnings—*Uṇṇunīli Sandēśam*—folk songs—*Rāmacaritam* and *Rāma Kathāppāṭṭu*—Chākkiyār Kūttu and Campūs—Niraṇam poets—Cheruśśēri Nambūdiri—local songs and ballads—Eḻuttaccan—Kathakaḷi.

SANSKRIT was the language of higher culture throughout South India, and a considerable volume of literature in its various branches arose from the activity of poets and scholars through the centuries. We shall trace the history of this activity in outline before proceeding to a study of the literatures in the languages of the people, viz., Tamil, Kannada, Telugu and Malayālam, to name them in the probable order in which they developed their literary idioms. All these literatures owed a great deal to Sanskrit, the magic wand whose touch alone raised each of the Dravidian languages from the level of a patois to that of a literary idiom, and the influence they exercised on one another was also not inconsiderable; but their interaction cannot be adequately considered in the brief sketch that follows.

The beginnings of Marathi literature fall indeed within the period dealt with in this book, but they will not be traced here, because Marathi is more properly regarded as a North Indian vernacular. The bulk of the Marathi literature falling in our period was primarily devotional in nature and is represented by such authors as Jñāneśvara (1290), Nāmdev (1425), Eknāth (1608) and Tukārām (1608-49), names greater in the field of religion than in that of literature.

SANSKRIT

The Vedic religion of sacrifice had spread all over the country by the beginning of the Christian era, if not earlier, and Vedic literature and exegesis therefore naturally claim our first attention in the domain of Sanskrit. Āpastamba, the author of a complete set of *śrauta*, *grihya* and *dharma sūtras* that has luckily been preserved in its entirety, must have flourished somewhere about 300 B.C. in the Godāvari valley. His language seems to be of an age preceding that of Pāṇini, and the followers of his school abound in the land south of the Narmada. The school of Satyāshāḍha Hiraṇyakeśins, whose *Dharmasūtra* shows clear traces of Āpastamba's influence, came into prominence in the Sahya region (Malabar and S. Kanara?) between the first century B.C. and the first century A.D. A third school which can also be definitely assigned to South India is that of the Vaikhānasas whose *Grihya sūtra* shows many influences of the idiom of the Dravidian languages. The manuals of these two schools also are complete.

The foundation of the Chola and Vijayanagar empires was marked by notable efforts to elucidate the Vedas. In the reign of Chola Parāntaka I, Venkata Mādhava, who lived in a village on the banks of the Kaveri, wrote the *Rigarthadīpikā*. Under the patronage of the early Vijayanagar sovereigns, notably Bukka I, a large syndicate of scholars, headed by Sāyaṇa, undertook and completed the stupendous task of commenting upon the Samhitas of all the four Vedas and many of the Brāhmaṇas and Āraṇyakas.

Coming long after the age of the texts they annotated, these scholars obviously did not always succeed in interpreting them correctly or convincingly; but the most critical of modern scholars cannot deny the debt they owe to the commentaries which recorded the traditional interpretations current in the Vedic schools of the tenth and fourteenth centuries in South India. Bharatasvāmin's commentary on the *Sāmaveda* written under Hoysala Rāmanātha also deserves notice among the pre-Sāyaṇa Vedic commentaries. In the interval between Venkata Mādhava and Sāyaṇa came also another great commentator, Shaḍguruśishya, 'the pupil of six teachers', whose personal name has not been handed down to us. He commented on the *Aitareya Brāhmaṇa* and *Āraṇyaka* and Kātyāyana's *Sarvānukramaṇī*, probably about the middle of the thirteenth century.

Besides Vedic texts proper, ancillary works like the Prātiśākhyas (manuals of phonetics) and the Kalpa sūtras (ritual) were also annotated. Shaḍguruśishya himself wrote a commentary on *Āśvalāyana Śrauta sūtra*, and the *Āpastamba Śrauta* was annotated twice over by Tālavrintanivāsin and by Caundapācārya (fourteenth century); the latter was also the author of *Prayogaratnamālā*, an independent treatise on ritual practices. The *Bodhāyana Śrauta* also had two commentaries, one by Bhavasvāmin (ninth or tenth century), and the other by the famous Sāyaṇa who was himself a follower of the Sūtra. Haradatta is another well-known annotator of the same school whose commentaries *Anāvilā* on the *Āśvalāyana Grihya sūtra*, *Anākulā* on *Āpastamba Grihya sūtra*, and *Ujjvalā* on the *Dharma sūtra* are rightly celebrated. He also wrote the *Mitāksharā* on *Gautama-dharmasūtra*, and a commentary on *Bodhāyana Śrauta sūtra* of which only an insignificant fragment has been traced so far.

Devarāja's *Nighaṇṭu Vyākhyā*, written at Śrīrangam in the fifteenth century, marks an important stage in the history of Vedic scholarship as it is a very learned exposition of Yāska's celebrated treatise on Vedic lexicology.

Among the Purāṇas, the *Bhāgavata* was composed somewhere in South India about the beginning of the tenth century. It summed up the tenets and outlook of the neo-*bhakti* cult which had been developing from the fourth or fifth century in the course of the conflict between Hinduism and the non-Vedic creeds of Jainism and Buddhism. The *Bhāgavata* combines a simple surging emotional *bhakti* to Krishna with the Advaita philosophy of Śankara in a manner that has been considered possible only in the Tamil country in that period. The *Vishṇu Purāṇa*, perhaps the shortest and the best work of its class, was commented on by Vishnu Chitta in the twelfth century from the standpoint of Viśishtādvaita. We must also notice the more famous commentaries on the

Rāmāyaṇa and *Mahābhārata* for the place they hold in literary criticism as well as in religious thought. Ātreya Varadarāja, otherwise known as Uḍāli, composed his *Vivekatilaka* on the *Rāmāyaṇa* in the twelfth century; he came later than Rāmānuja and is cited in the *Īḍu*, the great thirteenth-century commentary on *Tiruvāymoḻi*. The much better-known *Bhūshaṇa*, also the work of a Vaishnava author, was produced by Govindarāja, a native of Kānchipuram and contemporary of Krishnadeva Rāya and Rāma Rāya of Vijayanagar. He is said to have got his inspiration to write the work during one of his visits to the famous shrine at Tirupati. Mādhava Yogi was the author of *Kataka*, an important commentary on the *Rāmāyaṇa*; the author put forward many interesting points of textual criticism and held Rāma to be an avatar of Brahmā as the Lord of Gāyatrī. Again, the *Vālmīki-hridaya* of Ahobala was based on the comments on select verses from the *Rāmāyaṇa* scattered throughout the *Īḍu*. Īśvara Dīkshita of the Kaundinya *gōtra* wrote two commentaries on the epic, a *laghu* and a *brihad vivaraṇa* in 1517; the work was done at Hemakūṭa in Vijayanagar under the patronage of Krishnadeva Rāya. Altogether about a score of commentaries on the *Rāmāyaṇa* were produced in South India. On the *Mahābhārata*, the *Lakshābharaṇa* of Vādirāja, written some time during the sixteenth century, is the best known of the extant commentaries from South India; the author has sought in his own way to determine the authentic text of the 100,000 verses of the great epic. About the same time or a little earlier came the *Vyākhyāratnāvali* of Ānandapūrna Vidyāsāgara who wrote from Gokarna on the west coast and was a contemporary of the Kadamba Kāmadeva, father-in-law of Harihara II of Vijayanagar. A third commentary by Sarvajña Nārāyana, only fragments of which survive, is perhaps the oldest work of its class so far known from the South.

In belles-lettres, the first work that claims attention is *Sattasaī*, an anthology in Mahārāshtri Prākrit passing under the name of the Sātavāhana ruler Hāla and comprising about seven hundred verses. Each verse is a vignette characterized by an unusual degree of realism, and the collection as a whole depicts ' simple loves set among simple scenes, . . . the work of poets who wished really to express the feelings as well as describe the externals of the people of the land, the cowherds and cowherdesses, the girl who tends the garden or grinds corn at the mill, the hunter, the handworker '.

On linguistic grounds the work is assigned by critics to the period A.D. 200-450; but it may possibly be a revised version of an earlier work. Another notable work of the age of the Sātavāhanas was the *Brihatkathā* of Guṇāḍhya, reputed to have been composed in the Paiśācī dialect but no longer available except through a number of later Sanskrit recensions; many legends are told about the composition and fate of the book, and its widespread influence on later literature in many languages is universally admitted. The tales of the *Brihatkathā* had for their hero Naravāhanadatta, a son of Udayana, and borrowed motifs from the *Rāmāyaṇa* and from Buddhist sources. The work seems to have survived till about the eighth or ninth century and is highly praised by such famous authors as Bāna and Dandin.

Sundara Pāndya's *Nītidvishashṭikā* must be older than the sixth century; the author's identity remains a mystery, but the work has great merit and its verses deserve a high place in the literature of *nīti* (policy). Kumāradāsa's long poem in twenty cantos, *Jānakīharaṇa*, handles the familiar story of Rāma; the author was clearly an admirer of Kālidāsa and his work contains many echoes of that great poet. Tradition, late and not very reliable, identifies Kumāradāsa with a king of Ceylon who ruled in the sixth century. This poem has had a curious history; till recently it was only known from a Sinhalese paraphrase and a restoration of a part of it in Sanskrit by a certain Rājasundara, but the original was recovered recently in Malabar. Much better known and of greater literary merit is Bhāravi's *Kirātārjunīyam* which describes, in eighteen cantos, the conflict between Śiva and Arjuna ending in the latter's attainment of the valuable weapon Pāśupata *astra*. The poem is remarkable for its vigour and its imagery. In an inscription dated 634 the poet is mentioned as having attained great fame already. Tradition connects him with Vishnuvardhana, the founder of the line of Eastern Chālukyas, and with Simhavishnu of Kānchī; it also affirms that the Ganga king Durvinīta annotated the fifteenth canto of the poem; but all this is very doubtful.

In passing it may be observed that the inscription just mentioned comes from Aihole and records the achievements of Pulakeśin II in a short poem of no mean literary quality; its author, Ravikīrti, affirms that, by his composition, he deemed himself the peer of Bhāravi and Kālidāsa! A somewhat earlier inscription from

Mahākūta is composed in ornate prose which could stand comparison with Bāna. In fact a complete history of Sanskrit literature must devote attention to inscriptions as much as to books. This is, in fact, equally true for all languages; but it is a subject that cannot be pursued here. Vijayabhaṭṭārikā, the wife of king Chandradityā who was a son of Pulakeśin II, has been plausibly identified with the poetess Vijayānkā or Vijjikā, who describes herself as a dark Sarasvatī (the Goddess of Learning, usually depicted as white), and whom the great critic Rājaśekhara placed next only to Kālidāsa for style. The few verses of this poetess which have been preserved in the anthologies go far to justify this high estimate.

The ' curious-minded ' Pallava ruler of Kānchī, Mahendravarman I, found time to compose two delectable farces (*prahasanas*), *Mattavilāsa* and *Bhagavadajjuka*, which succeed in turning the laugh against the *Kāpālikas* and Buddhist *Bhikshus*, and afford a pleasing contrast to the growing intensity of sectarian feeling in his day. The authorship of *Bhagavadajjuka* is, however, doubtful, and the work has been attributed to Bodhāyana. The relatively dry subject of prosody was expounded in *Chandoviciti-Janāśraya*, perhaps by or under Mādhavavarman II of the Vishnukundin line (whose title was Janāśraya). If tradition preserved in the *Avantisundarīkathā* is true, the illustrious Dandin was the great-grandson of Dāmodara, a friend of Bhāravi, and adorned the Pallava court of Narasimhavarman I (630-68). The *kathā* just mentioned is itself a long prose work which has only been preserved in part; the kernel of the extant *Daśakumāracarita* is most likely a part of this work, its beginning and end being by other hands. The superb manual of rhetoric *Kāvyādarśa*, by which Dandin is best known, marks an epoch in the history of literary criticism as it made the Vaidarbhī style the touchstone of good poetry. It also formed the basis of *Daṇḍiyalangāram* in Tamil.

Though most of Bhavabhūti's work was done in Northern India, still, as he was born in Berar and is said to have had his education under Kumārila, it may not be wrong to include the great dramatist's name in this survey. Two of his dramas—the *Mahāvīracarita* and *Uttara-rāma-carita*—are based on parts of the Rāma saga, while the third—*Mālatīmādhava*—is a work of the poet's imagination. He flourished at the end of the seventh century and the beginning of the eighth.

Kulaśekhara, one of the later *āḻvārs*, and a ruler of Kerala, probably in the ninth century, produced a splendid devotional lyric in the *Mukunda-mālā* which has retained a wide popularity to this day. Kulaśekhara is believed to have been the patron of Vāsudeva, author of the four Yamaka Kāvyas, *Yudhishṭhira Vijaya*, *Tripuradahana*, *Śaurikathā* and *Nalodaya*. Though Yamaka (sound jingle) often leads to queer expressions and forced constructions, Vāsudeva must be deemed to have succeeded in a remarkable measure in escaping the defects of the method. The *Yudhishṭhira Vijaya* was commented on by Rājānaka Ratnākara of Kashmir. Vāsudeva also wrote the *Vāsudeva Vijaya*, a Kāvya in five cantos on the model of the *Bhaṭṭikāvya*, illustrating the rules of Sanskrit grammar laid down by Pāṇini. The *Āścarya-cūḍāmaṇi* of Śaktibhadra claims to be the first full-blown drama (*nāṭaka*) to be produced in the southern country; its theme is the perennial Rāma story, and some of the author's innovations are real improvements. The poetry and prose are alike of high quality, and the work has always been very popular among the actors of Malabar. Another play by the same author, *Unmādavāsavadattā*, is no longer extant. He is reputed to have been a pupil of Śankara and may be assigned to the early ninth century.

Trivikrama Bhaṭṭa, contemporary with Rāshtrakūta Indra III (915), was the author of *Nalacampū* or *Damayantī-kathā*, the earliest extant Campū in Sanskrit. The story is that the work was composed with the aid of Sarasvatī to meet the challenge of a rival at a time when his father, a court-poet, was absent. It is said to have been left unfinished because the father returned and rendered the son's effort otiose. Both verse and prose are no more than mediocre. The *Madālasācampū* is also attributed to Trivikrama. The earliest extant Campū from Kerala is the *Amogharāghava* by Divākara (A.D. 1299)—on the Bālakāṇḍa story of the *Rāmāyaṇa*; this type became much more common later both in Sanskrit and Malayālam.

A second Kulaśekhara from Kerala (935-55) wrote two dramas —*Tapatīsamvaraṇa* and *Subhadrādhanañjaya*—which dramatized minor incidents from the *Mahābhārata* in a very stage-worthy form. Kulaśekhara was also the author of a prose work *Āścarya-manjarī* cited in a Bengali commentary (A.D. 1159) on the *Amarakośa*. In his time according to tradition there was a reform in the mode of staging Sanskrit dramas by the Chākkiyārs; they are professional actors, who appear to have been a survival in Kerala of the older institution of *sūtas* who recited the Purāṇas to popular audiences. The repertoire of the Chākkiyārs included the *Mattavilāsa*, *Bhagavadajjuka* and *Kalyāṇasaugandhika*, among others. The last mentioned work is a play by Nīlakantha, a Vyāyoga depicting a tussle between Hanumān and Bhīma ending in a compromise on their recognizing their common parentage. Bilvamangala-svāmi, also called Krishna-līlā-śuka, or Līlā-śuka for short, was another protégé of the king; his *Krishṇa-karṇāmrita* is a devotional poem of unsurpassed beauty in three *āśvāsas*. He composed other works of an erudite nature; but by this poem he lives in the hearts of Sanskritists.

The great Jaina writer Somadevasūri (950) flourished in the court of Arikesari II of Vemulavāda (Andhra Pradesh), a subordinate of Rāshtrakūta Krishna III, where the illustrious Kannada poet Pampa also lived. Somadeva was the author of *Yaśastilaka campū*, *Nītivākyāmrita*, and other works. The tale of the Campū is by no means dull, but the main objective of the author is the propagation of Jaina tenets and ethics. The *Nītivākyāmrita* reviews the subject-matter of Arthaśāstra from the standpoint of Jaina morals. The author's style is at once learned, pithy and clear. Another contemporary of Krishna III was Halāyudha, author of *Kavirahasya*, a pedantic work which seeks to illustrate the formation of the present tense of Sanskrit roots and at the same time to eulogize the Rāshtrakūta king. Vādirāja, a pupil of Somadevasūri—a Jain, like his guru—wrote *Yaśodharacaritra* in which he mentions the *Pārśvanāthacaritra* as an earlier work of his; but it is not extant.

The prose romance *Udayasundarī Kathā* of Soḍḍhala, a Kāyastha of Lāta, was written about A.D. 1000 under the patronage of Mummunirāja of Thana; the author took Bāna's *Harshacarita* as his model, but falls far short of it. From Kerala we get in this period the quasi-historical *Mūshakavamśa* of Atula, a chronicle of the Mūshaka or Rāmaghata kings in fifteen cantos, and the exquisite unfinished poem *Krishṇavilāsa* by Sukumāra whose date and nativity are, however, not beyond dispute. The *Vikramānkadevacarita* of Bilhaṇa, the Kashmirian Vidyāpati of Vikramāditya VI, is a Mahākāvya in eighteen cantos, which recounts in epic style the life and deeds of the Chālukyan emperor. The author gives his own life-history in the last canto and says that he composed the poem out of gratitude for the great honour shown to him late in his life by the ruler of Karnāta. Not all its statements on the relations of Vikramāditya with his elder brother Someśvara can be accepted as true, but the verse is easy and flowing though the descriptions are disproportionately long. Bilhaṇa wrote other works from which citations have survived in anthologies; but there is no proof that the *Pañcāśikā*, a moving though somewhat outspoken portrayal of the pleasures of illicit love, can properly be attributed to him. Purporting to be the work of Chālukya Someś-vara III, but most likely a composition of one or more of his court-poets, is the *Mānasollāsa* or *Abhilashitārtha cintāmaṇi* (1129-30), intended for the benefit of all classes in the state. It consists of five books of twenty chapters each. Its range is cyclopaedic, and obviously it lays under contribution many older technical treatises on medicine, magic, veterinary science, the valuing of precious stones and pearls, fortifications, painting and music, games and amusements and on the many other subjects it treats of. No great merit is evident in the choice of topics or their sequence, though the work is valuable as a record of the state of knowledge on many topics at that time. An astrologer and poet who flourished under Someśvara III was Vidyāmādhava whose *Pārvatī-Rukmiṇīya* is a *tour de force*, each verse yielding two meanings, one narrating the marriage of Śiva and Pārvatī and the other that of Krishna and Rukminī. Another and better effort in the same deplorable line was the *Rāghava-Pāṇḍavīya* of Kavirāja Mādhava Bhaṭṭa setting forth the story of the *Rāmāyaṇa* and the *Mahābhārata*. The poet lived in the court of Kadamba Kāmadeva (1182-97) and also wrote the *Pārijātaharaṇa*, a poem in ten cantos on a well-known episode from the Krishna cycle of legends.

A family of hereditary poets held the position of *vidyācakravarti* (poet-laureate) in the Hoysala court but their names have not been preserved. One of them, who seems to have obtained recognition also from the Pāndyas and other rulers of the South, wrote the quasi-historical *Gadyakarṇāmrita*, an eloquent prose work dealing with the war between Hoysala Narasimha II and the Pāndyas in the first quarter of the thirteenth century. Another composed a poem of high quality, the *Rukmiṇīkalyāṇa*, and wrote commentaries on the *Alankārasarvasva* and the *Kāvyaprakāśa*—two celebrated works on poetics; this was in the reign of Ballāla III (1291-1342).

To the thirteenth century also belonged Śāradātanaya, born of a scholarly family in the Chingleput district, and author of the well-known *Bhāvaprakāśa*, an important work on literary criticism, which cites many writers and works otherwise unknown; he also wrote the *Śāradīya*, a treatise on music. Another celebrity of the same age and neighbourhood was the great Vaishnava teacher Venkatanātha or Vedānta Dēśika (*b.* 1268) who, though better known for his works on religion and philosophy, achieved distinction in the domain of general literature as well. His Mahākāvya on Krishna's life, called *Yādavābhyudaya*, was commented on by the great Appaya Dīkshita; the *Hamsa-sandeśa*, an imitation of Kālidāsa's *Meghasandeśa*, the devotional poem *Pādukāsahasra*, and the drama *Samkalpasūryodaya* (a Viśishtādvaitic counterblast to the Advaitic drama *Prabodhacandrodaya* of Krishna-miśra), deserve particular mention among his other general works.

Kerala was prolific in Sandeśa-Kāvyas which have been found there in scores. The *Śukasandeśa* of Lakshmīdāsa (A.D. 1100) is the earliest and perhaps the best. The *Kokilasandeśa* of Uddaṇḍa Kavi (fifteenth century), and the *Mayūrasandeśa* of Udaya, the commentator of *Locanā* (same century), and the *Bhringa Sandeśa* of Vāsudeva (sixteenth century) also deserve mention. Apart from their lyrical merit, these poems have a historical and topographical interest as they refer to contemporary personalities and events and contain detailed descriptions of the routes of the respective messengers. King Ravivarman Kulaśekhara of Travancore found time for literary pursuits in the midst of his stormy career; he wrote the *Pradyumnābhyudaya*, a drama in five acts on the marriage of Pradyumna and Prabhāvatī, and was the patron of Samudrabandha, the author of a learned commentary on the *Alankāra-sarvasva* of Ruyyaka of Kashmir.

Similar in spirit and manner are two works on dramaturgy, both composed about 1300 and both including a play calculated to glorify the author's patron and illustrate the rules of the drama: these are the *Ekāvali* of Vidyādhara, written under Narasimha II of Orissa, and *Pratāparudra-Yaśobhūshaṇa* of Vidyānātha whose patron was Pratāparudra II, the Kākatīya ruler of Wārangal. The last-named ruler was himself the author of a *nīti* work, extracts from which appear in the anthology *Sūktiratnākara* of Sūrya and on which the Telugu *Baddana-nīti* is based. Vidyānātha is often identified with Agastya, the reputed author of seventy

Kāvyas in all, among which are *Bālabhārata*, a poetic summary of the great epic in twenty cantos commented on by Sāluva Timma, the minister of Krishnadeva Rāya; the *Krishṇa-carita*, a prose summary of the *Bhāgavata*; and *Nalakīrtikaumudī* which narrates the familiar story of Nala and Damayantī. Viśvanātha, the author of *Sāhityadarpaṇa*, a comprehensive work covering the entire field of poetics, flourished (*c*. 1350) in the court of one Narasimha, probably the third king of that name to rule over Orissa.

The achievements of Kumāra Kampana, the second son of Bukka I of Vijayanagar, are celebrated in a beautiful poem by his wife Gangādevī—*Maḍhurāvijayam* ('Conquest of Madura'). One of Vidyāraṇya's pupils was Vāmana Bhaṭṭa Bāna, patronized by the Reddi king Pedda Komati Vēma of Kondavīdu (1398-1415), whom he celebrated in a prose romance of considerable length, the *Vemabhūpāla-carita*. The author's aim was to rival Bāna as a prose writer, and he achieved a notable measure of success in his endeavour. His other works were *Nalābhyudaya*, *Raghunātha-carita-kāvya*, and two plays, *Pārvatī-pariṇaya* and *Kanakalekhā Kalyāṇa*. The Reddi ruler Pedda Komati himself passes as the author of commentaries on *Amaruśataka*, a centum of erotic verses, and *Saptaśatī-sāra*—a selection of 100 verses from Hāla's Prākrit anthology; two independent works on poetics and music, *Sāhitya-cintāmaṇi* and *Sangīta-cintāmaṇi* are also attributed to him. Like him, his predecessor Kumāragiri was also author and patron; he wrote a work on *nāṭya* (dance) called *Vasantarājīya*, after one of his titles. His brother-in-law (and minister) Kātayavema wrote well-known commentaries on the plays of Kālidāsa.

Passing over several minor works of poetry, drama and criticism of the early Vijayanagar period, we may notice the *Rasārṇavasu-dhākara*, a masterly treatise on *rasa* and the rules of dramaturgy. This work is said to be by Simhabhūpāla of Rājakonda (*c*. 1350), but possibly owes much to his court-poet Viśveśvara, who wrote *Camatkāracandrikā*—also a good manual of rhetoric. The family of Ḍiṇḍimas in the village of Mullandram in North Arcot district produced many authors of distinction. Rājanātha's *Sālvābhyu-daya*, a quasi-historical poem on the wars of his patron Sāluva Narasimha (latter half of the fifteenth century), the *Bhāgavata-campū* and *Acyutarāyābhyudaya* of a later Rājanātha, who lived [illegible] the sixteenth century in the reign of Achyuta Rāya, deserve [illegible]lar mentio[illegible] This last poem is a useful guide to the events of Achyuta Rāya's reign. Krishnadeva Rāya was scholar and poet as well as soldier and statesman, and wrote with great power in both Sanskrit and Telugu; his drama *Jāmbavatīkalyāṇa* is marked by a fairly high order of poetic and dramatic skill. Tirumalāmbā's *Varadāmbikāpariṇaya* is another historical Campū of the period to commemorate the marriage of king Achyuta Rāya with Varadāmbikā.

The next great name is that of Appaya Dīkshita (1520-92), author of over a hundred works in many branches of Sanskrit learning, who was patronized by the Nāyak chieftains of Vellore, particularly by Chinna Bomma. His commentary on the *Yādavābhyudaya* has been mentioned already. Other contributions which he made to poetry and poetics include *Citramīmāmsā* and *Lakshaṇāvalī* on literary criticism and the appreciation of poetry; the *Kuvalayānanda* which, though in form an amplification of Jayadeva's *Candrāloka*, almost attains the level of an independent treatise on figures of speech; *Vrittivārttika*, a treatise on the significance of words in their poetic use; *Varadarājastava*, and many other devotional poems. The family of Appaya Dīkshita produced a considerable number of talented authors, all of whom cannot be mentioned here. Nīlakantha Dīkshita, Appaya's great-nephew, was a greater poet than his uncle and wrote several works which attained a degree of literary force and charm which had been unknown for several centuries; the *Nīlakaṇṭha-Vijaya-campū* (1637), *Gangāvataraṇa*, *Nalacaritanāṭaka* and the *Śivalīlārṇava*, all exhibit the superior talent of the author, who is reputed to have been minister to Tirumalai Nāyaka of Madura.

At the Nāyak court of Tanjore, at about the same period, flourished Govinda Dīkshita, held in high esteem by Śevvappa Nāyaka, the founder of the line, and his descendants. His *Sāhitya Sudhā* treats of the history of the two later rulers Achyutappa and Raghunātha; he also composed the *Sangītasudhānidhi*. Two of Govinda's sons also gained distinction as writers; one, Yajñanārayana, wrote two works on the life of Raghunātha Nāyaka—a poem *Sāhityaratnākara*, and a drama in five acts, *Raghunātha Vilāsa*; the other, Venkatamakhi, was a versatile writer on all Śāstras, but his Kāvya *Sāhityasāmrājya* is not available. Raghunātha Nāyaka himself composed several works like *Pārijātaharaṇa*, *Vālmīkicarita*, *Gajendra-moksha*, *Nalacarita*, and *Acyutendrābhyudaya*, the last being obviously a biography of his father. He also wrote on music.

The *Raghunāthābhyudaya* of Rāmabhadrāmbā also has the life of the Nāyaka for its theme and gives clear proof of the intense devotion that the ruler evoked in the talented poetess.

Yet another family of Dīkshitas rose to literary fame under the Nāyaks of Gingee. Ratnakheṭa Śrīnivāsa Dīkshita of Satyamangalam is reputed to have written eighteen plays and sixty poetical works—most of which have been lost, however; his allegorical drama *Bhāvanāpurushottama* was composed at the instance of Sūrappa Nāyaka, and the *Bhaishmīpariṇaya-campū* is a small work on the marriage of Rukminī and Krishna. Śrīnivāsa had three sons, the best known being Rājachūdāmani Dīkshita who migrated to Tanjore and became the pupil of Venkatamakhi. While still in his teens he is said to have written *Kamalinī Kalahamsa*; another drama, *Ānanda-rāghava*, a poem *Rukmiṇī Kalyāṇa* and a biography of Śankarācārya called *Śankarābhyudaya* were among his other works. He also wrote on Mīmāmsā and other subjects which will be mentioned further on.

Turning next to philosophical literature, Vātsyāyana (*c*. 350-400), the author of the commentary on the *Nyāya-sūtras* of Gautama, is ascribed by tradition to South India. But the first writer on Nyāya definitely known to belong to South India is Varadarāja, the author of *Tārkikarakshā* and of a commentary (*Bodhinī*) on *Kusumāñjali* of Udayana; he lived most probably in the middle of the twelfth century. Aparārka's commentary on the *Nyāyasāra* of Bhāsarvajña can be assigned to about the same date. The author was the Silāhāra ruler of Konkan, better known for his commentary on *Yājñavalkya-smriti*. Two commentaries were written on *Tarkabhāshā*, one by the famous Mallinātha (thirteenth century) and the other by Chennubhaṭṭa (fourteenth century). The most popular manual of logic, *Tarkasangraha* (*c*. 1625), and the gloss *Dīpikā* on it were the work of Annambhaṭṭa, a native of the Chittoor district who also wrote commentaries on other classics on this subject.

The popularity of Pūrva-Mīmāmsā studies in the South is indicated by a number of inscriptions recording endowments—particularly in favour of the school of Prabhākara, who was the pupil as well as the rival of the great Kumārila, the founder of these studies in this part of the country. Kumārila is generally regarded as an Andhra by birth and an elder contemporary of Śankarācārya (eighth century); his main works are *Ślokavārttika*, *Tantravārttika*, and *Tuptīkā* which together form a complete commentary on the classic *Bhāshya* of Śabarasvāmin on the *Mīmāmsā sūtras* of Jaimini. Prabhākara (a native of North Travancore according to tradition) also wrote two commentaries on Śabara's *Bhāshya*, a short *Laghvī* or *Vivaraṇa*, no longer extant, and a more extensive *Brihatī* or *Nibandhana* which has survived in part and gives unmistakable evidence of the author's originality and dialectical skill. Mandana Miśra, another elder contemporary of Śankara, discussed two fundamental topics of Mīmāmsā in his *Vidhiviveka* and *Bhāvanāviveka*. The *Bhāshyadīpa* of Kshīrasāgaramiśra (eleventh century) is another commentary on Śabara written from the standpoint of Prabhākara; the same writer also composed a tract called *Arthavādādivicāra*. Varadarāja expounded in the *Nayaviveka-dīpikā* the tenets of the same school in the twelfth century. The volume of Mīmāmsā literature that developed in South India is very great and cannot be reviewed here in its entirety. Only the names of the most important authors and their works can be noted. They are: Someśvara's *Nyāyasudhā* (*c.* 1200), an elaborate commentary on Kumārila's *Tantravārttika*; another commentary on the same work—the *Nyāyapārāyaṇa* (mid-thirteenth century) of Gangādhara-miśra; the *Mīmāmsāpādukā* and *Seśvaramīmāmsā* of Vedānta Dēśika, who sought to synthesize the views of the two rival schools; the *Nyāyamālā* and its *vistara* by Sāyaṇa's brother Mādhava (fourteenth century), an abstract in verse and an explanation in prose on the subject-matter of each section of Śabara's *Bhāshya*; a number of tracts on Mīmāmsā by Appaya Dīkshita such as *Vidhirasāyana*, *Upakramaparākrama* and *Vādanakshatra-mālā* besides his *Mayūkhāvalī* a commentary on the *Śāstradīpikā*, a classic exposition of the Kumārila school by Pārthasārathi Miśra.

In the domain of Vedānta, all the three major schools had their origin in the South. The first and greatest name here is that of Śankara, the founder of Advaita Vedānta as we know it. Few authentic details of his life are known, though he is believed to have been born at Kāladi (North Travancore) in 788 and to have died in 820 at the age of 32. His principal works are the great Bhāshyas on the *Brahma-sūtras*, the principal Upanishads, and the *Bhagavadgītā*, besides certain independent treatises like the *Upadeśa-sāhasrī*. Many other works, particularly Stotras (devotional poems), pass as his but there is no reason to think that Śankara wrote them. The literary force and philosophic depth of

Śankara's works entitle him to a very high place among the master minds of the world. His pupil Sureśvara, who may perhaps be identified with Viśvarūpa, wrote the commentary *Bālakrīḍā* on *Yājñavalkyasmriti.* He also succinctly re-stated his master's fundamental principles in his *Naishkarmyasiddhi,* and wrote monumental *vārttikas* (elucidations) on Śankara's Bhāshyas on the *Taittirīya* and the *Brihadāraṇyaka* Upanishads. Śankara had other pupils who became authors; but their provenance is unknown. Mention may be made, however, of Padmapāda's *Pañcapādikā,* a commentary on Śankara's Bhāshya on the *Brahmasūtras*; the work is now only available for the first four Sūtras. Padmapāda was a Brahmin from Kerala. Mandana Miśra, whom we have already mentioned as a contemporary of Śankara, held different views on Advaita which he expressed in *Brahmasiddhi.* Sarvajñātman was the next great Advaita author; he flourished in Travancore at the end of the tenth century. His authoritative *Samkshepa-śārīraka,* with its fine literary flavour, is his chief work, but he also wrote *Pañcaprakriyā* and *Pramāṇa-lakshaṇa.* This last work, on epistemology, is accepted by Mīmāmsakas as well as Vedāntins. Jñānaghana's *Tattavaśuddhi* is another treatise of about the same time; its author finds mention in the Śringeri list of pontiffs. Jñānottama, who commented on Sureśvara's *Naishkarmyasiddhi,* is the author of two independent works—*Nyāyasudhā* and *Jñānasiddhi*—and his more celebrated pupil, Chitsukha of Simhāchalam (*c.* 1200), deserves notice next. Chitsukha's *Bhāshya-bhāva-prakāśikā* is a highly esteemed commentary on Śankara's Bhāshya on the *Brahmasūtras*; among his other works the best known is an independent treatise on Advaita, *Tattvapradīpikā.* He had pupils like Sukhaprakāśa who also became writers of repute. Amalānanda, a pupil of Sukhaprakāśa, lived near Nasik on the banks of the Godāvari in the reigns of the Yādava kings Krishna and Mahādeva (1246-71); his *Vedānta-kalpataru* is an extensive commentary on Vāchaspati Miśra's *Bhāmatī,* itself a commentary on Śankara's *Brahmasūtra-bhāshya*; and the *Śāstradarpaṇa* is a more concise statement of the doctrines of the Bhāmatī school. Śankarānanda (*c.* 1250) wrote the *Ātmapurāṇa* which brings together the gist of the Upanishads in a standard work in *anusṭup* verse; he also wrote commentaries on the principal Upanishads and on the *Brahmasūtra-bhāshya* of Śankara. The *Sarvamatasangraha* of Rāghavānanda Muni of Kerala is an epitome of several systems of Hindu philosophy, and a forerunner of the better-known *Sarva-darśana-sangraha* of Mādhava Ācārya. Rāghavānanda's commentaries on *Paramārtha-sāra*, on *Mukundamālā*, and on the *Bhāgavata Purāṇa* called *Krishṇapadī* exhibit his high learning in several branches of literature. This task of commenting on ancient classics and refining and restating doctrines went on steadily from generation to generation, and we can only note the most prominent works in this later derivative literature. Such were: the *Vivaraṇa-prameya-sangraha*, and *Jivanmuktiviveka* of Vidyāraṇya and the *Pañcadaśī* ascribed to his teacher Bharatītīrtha, but held by some to be in fact the work of the pupil; the *Sarvadarśana-sangraha* of Sāyaṇa-Mādhava which establishes the superiority of Advaita by reviewing many of the rival systems of philosophy; Ānanda-pūrna's (*c.* 1410) commentaries on the *Khaṇḍana-khaṇḍa-khādya*, *Brahmasiddhi*, and *Vivaraṇa* as well as his *Nyāyacandrikā*; Appaya Dīkshita's sub-commentary *Vedānta-kalpataru-parimala* and his *Siddhāntaleśa sangraha*, a compendium of the various schools of advaitic thought, and *Madhvatantra-mukhamardana*, a polemic against the dualism of Madhva; and lastly, the *Vedāntaparibhāshā* of Dharmarājādhvarin, the best known among the manuals of Advaita.

The literature of Viśishtādvaita (qualified monism) philosophy may be said to start with the *Yogarahasya* and the *Nyāyatattva* by Nāthamuni, or Ranganātha-muni (824-924), the first of the great *ācāryas* of Vaishnavism who followed the *āḻvārs*. Then came the somewhat more systematic exposition of Yāmunācārya (*b.* 917), the grandson of Nāthamuni, in his works *Siddhitraya*, *Gītārthasangraha* and *Āgamaprāmāṇya*. He also wrote other works like *Stotraratna*, a devotional poem. The true founder of the system in its entirety was of course Śrī Rāmānuja (*b.* 1018) whose *Śrībhāshya* on the *Brahma-sūtras* is its great classic. He also annotated the *Bhagavadgītā* from his point of view, and wrote the *Vedārthasangraha* to demonstrate that the Upanishads support his system rather than that of Śankara. His *Vedāntasāra* and *Vedānta Dīpa* are simple commentaries on the *Brahma-sūtras*. Parāśara Bhaṭṭa, who succeeded Rāmānuja in the pontificate at Śrīrangam in 1137, wrote the *Tattvaratnākara*, no longer in existence, and a commentary on *Vishṇusahasranāma*. The *Nītimālā* of Nārāyaṇārya, composed some time before 1200, and the *Prameya-*

mālā and *Tattvasāra* of Naḍādūr Ammāl (*b*. 1155) are important re-statements of the system, while the latter's *Prapannapārijāta* develops the doctrine of *prapatti* (surrender) with great elaboration. Sudarśana Bhaṭṭa, a pupil of Naḍādūr Ammāl, wrote the celebrated commentary known as *Śrutaprakāśikā* on Rāmānuja's *Śrībhāshya*. Tradition avers that he was born in A.D. 1175 and that he fled from Śrīrangam, burying his commentary in the sands of the Kaveri, when the place was sacked by the Muslim invader; both these statements, however, cannot be true. The commentary is a voluminous and erudite work and has been itself much commented on since. Sudarśana also wrote *Śrutapradīpikā*, and commentaries on Rāmānuja's *Vedārthasangraha* and the *Bhāgavata*, the last work bearing the name *Śukapakshīya*. Another pupil of Naḍādūr Ammāl was the famous Piḷḷai Lokācārya, author of *Vacanabhūshaṇa*, *Ācārya Hridaya*, and *Tattvaviveka*, besides many works in Tamil, and founder of the Tengalai (southern branch) *sampradāya*. A third pupil of Naḍādūr Ammāl was Ātreya Rāmānuja (*b*. 1220), author of *Nyāyakuliśa* which seeks to establish doctrines of general Vedānta, and emphasizes the differences between Advaita and Viśishtādvaita only in some of its chapters. His other works have not survived. A nephew (sister's son) and pupil of Ātreya Rāmānuja was the famous Vedānta Dēśika (1268-1369) who wrote commentaries on Rāmānuja's *Śrībhāshya* (*Tattvaṭīkā*) and *Gitā-bhāshya* (*Tātparyacandrikā*) besides independent treatises on Viśishtādvaita like *Nyāyasiddhāñjana*, *Sarvārthasiddhi* and *Tattvamuktākalāpa*. His *Śatadūshaṇī* is a polemic against Advaita. In spite of his decided preference for Tamil, the famous Tengalai saint Maṇavāḷamahāmuni (*b*. 1370) wrote some philosophical works in Sanskrit such as *Tattvatraya*, *Rahasyatraya*, *Śrivacanabhūshaṇa*, *Jñānasāra* and *Prameyasāra*. Vaishnavism waxed strong under the patronage of Vijayanagar rulers, but though many authors wrote, there was little real advance in philosophic thought.

Viśishtādvaita was the philosophy also of Śaivism. The earliest Śaiva writer in Sanskrit is perhaps Haradattācārya (*d*. 1116) whose *Śruti-sūkti-mālā* (also called *Caturvedatātparya-sangraha*) delineates the salient features of Śaiva thought, while his *Harihara-tāratamya* is a sectarian polemic. He was followed by Śrīkantha whose *Brahma-mīmāmsā-bhāshya* expounds the Sūtras of Bādarāyana from the Śaiva viewpoint. Śrīkantha may well be identical with the *ācārya* who, according to Aghoraśivācārya, came down from Gauda to worship Naṭarāja at Chidambaram and whom Vikrama Chola adopted as his *guru*. There are notable verbal coincidences between Srīkantha's Bhāshya and the *Śrībhāshya* of Rāmānuja. Śrīkantha's system is called Śivādvaita to distinguish it from the Śaiva-siddhānta system developed in the Tamil books. Attempts have been made to treat both the systems as one, but they cannot be regarded as successful. Aghoraśivācārya's (*c*. 1158) commentaries on *Tattvaprakāśikā* of Bhojadeva and on the highly philosophic *Mrigendrāgama* are important in the history of Śaiva philosophy. Umāpatiśivācārya's (*c*. 1290-1320) Bhāshya on the *Paushkara Samhitā* is a powerful plea that Śiva is the one deity for everyone to worship. Ñānaśivācārya of the *maṭha* at Sūrya-nārkōyil in the Tanjore district, and preceptor of Śevvappa Nāyaka of Tanjore, commented on the *Śivajñānabodha*, not the Tamil work of Meykaṇḍār, but a section of the *Raurava Āgama*, from the more usual Śaiva-siddhānta standpoint; the commentary is notable for its many valuable citations from works no longer extant. His other works were *Śāiva Paribhāshā*, a manual in five sections on the categories of Śaivism, and the *Śivāgrapaddhati* and *Kriyādīpikā* on the rituals of worship and renunciation. Śrīkantha's work was carried further by Nīlakantha (*c*. 1400) whose *Kriyāsāra* is a metrical compendium of Śrīkantha's Bhāshya which attempts to discover common ground between his system and that of the Vīra-śaivas; and by Appaya Dīkshita's striking contributions to Śaiva philosophy, particularly in his monumental commentary on Śrīkantha called the *Sivārkamaṇidīpikā*.

The philosophy of Dvaita (dualism) was elaborated by Madhva, also called Ānanda Tīrtha (1198-1275), in his Bhāshya on the *Brahma-sūtras* and in the *Anuvyākhyā*, a further commentary supporting the conclusions of the Bhāshya; he also commented on the Upanishads and the *Bhagavadgītā*, and wrote an epitome of the *Mahābhārata* entitled *Bhāratatātparyanirṇaya*, besides a commentary on some hymns of the Rigveda called *Rigveda-vyākhyā*. He wrote also a number of polemical works rebutting the doctrines of rival schools. He relied for support more on the Purāṇas than on Vedic texts or logical proofs. Jayatīrtha (*d*. 1388), a pupil of Madhva's pupil Akshobhyatīrtha and contemporary of Vidyāraṇya, was the greatest elucidator of the works of Madhvācārya, and earned for himself the title *Ṭīkācārya*. He also wrote two polemics, the *Nyāya-sudhā* on the *Brahmasūtra-bhāshya* of Madhva, and *Vādāvali*. The next great name in the history of Dvaita is that of Vyāsarāya (1447-1539) who was highly honoured by the great Krishnadeva Rāya of Vijayanagar. His *Bhedojjīvana* and *Tātparya-candrikā* are summary re-statements of the doctrines of his school; *Nyāyāmrita* was directed against Advaita, and *Tarka-tāṇḍava* against the conclusions of the logicians (*Naiyāyikas*). Vādirāja, a pupil of Vyāsarāya, wrote the *Yuktimallikā*, a critique of the doctrines of Śankara. Vijayīndra (1576), another pupil of Vyāsarāya, was held in great esteem by Śevvappa Nāyaka of Tanjore. He wrote commentaries on the works of Vyāsarāya besides the *Upasamhāravijaya*, and *Madhva-tantra-mukha-bhūshaṇa*, refutations of Appaya Dīkshita's works of the opposite names, and *Paratattvaprakāśa*, an answer to the same writer's *Śiva-tattva-viveka*. He spent his last days at Kumbakonam writing other works.

In legal literature (Dharmaśāstra), the earliest work that calls for notice after the Sūtras mentioned above is the *Bālakrīḍā*, Viśvarūpa's commentary on *Yājñavalkya-smriti*. The author, who was also called Sureśvara, was a pupil of Śankara. Another writer of fairly early date was Bhāruci who commented on the *Vishṇu Dharmasūtras* and *Manusmriti*; the first work is lost and the second was only recently recovered in a fragmentary form. Perhaps the greatest name in this sphere is that of Vijñāneśvara who adorned the court of Chālukya Vikramāditya VI; his *Mitāksharā*, a commentary on Yājñavalkya, is an important treatise on law based on many earlier writings and it has found acceptance in the whole of South India and large parts of the North. The work was commented on more than once by subsequent writers; Colebrooke, who translated into English the section on inheritance, gave it currency in British Indian courts. Another work ascribed to Vijñāneśvara is the *Āśauca-daśaka* or *Daśaślokī*, ten terse verses treating of pollution consequent on death. A pupil of this great author, Nārāyana by name, compiled an independent digest on civil law called *Vyavahāraśiromaṇi* which has survived only in part. The Śilāhāra ruler of Konkan, Aparārka or Aparāditya I, already mentioned as a writer on Nyāya, wrote an extensive commentary on Yājñavalkya early in the twelfth century; even more than the *Mitāksharā*, it is more an independent digest than a commentary hugging its text. Varadarāja's *Vyavahāranirṇaya*, for which various dates are assigned like A.D. 1297 and A.D. 1500, is valuable for its interpretation of juristic rules in the light of Mīmāmsā principles, and deserves particular notice among the legal digests of South India, as also the more extensive *Smriticandrikā* of Devana Bhaṭṭa often cited by Hemādri. To the latter half of the thirteenth century may be assigned the famous Haradatta whose commentaries on the Dharmasūtras of Āpastamba and Gautama are models of their kind; he is cited by Viśveśvara (1375), author of the *Subodhinī* on the *Mitāksharā*. Hemādri, minister of the Yādava king Mahādeva (1260-71) and his successor, was the author of a cyclopaedic digest called *Caturvargacintāmaṇi* comprising five large sections on Vrata, Dāna, Tīrtha, Moksha and Pariśesha. Two more sections on Prāyaścitta (expiation) and Vyavahāra (civil law) are supposed to have been compiled by him though they are not now extant. The published portion covers over 6,000 pages and forms perhaps the most extensive digest on the subjects it treats of. Part of the glory that was Vijayanagar was the work of Mādhava, the brother of Sāyaṇa, whose commentary on *Parāśarasmriti*, the *Parāśara Mādhavīya*, is a most erudite work which includes an independent treatise on Vyavahāra which was neglected in the text of Parāśara. And Sāyaṇa himself wrote a number of lesser manuals called *Sudhānidhis* treating of Prāyaścitta (expiation), Yajñatantra (Vedic ritual), Purushārtha (the aims of human endeavour) and so on. The two brothers wrote in the first half of the fourteenth century. Dalapati's extensive work in twelve sections, *Nrisimhaprasāda*, deals with all phases of religious and civil law; Dalapati (1490-1533) was a highly placed Hindu officer in the Nizam Shahi court of Ahmadnagar. Pratāparudra Gajapati of Orissa composed the *Sarasvatī-vilāsa* with the avowed intention of reconciling the apparent discrepancies between the views of Vijñāneśvara, Aparārka, Bhāruci and other authors who preceded him. Only the Vyavahāra section of this work has been found. The royal authorship of the work has, however, been doubted as it is counted among the writings of the polyhistor Lolla Lakshmīdhara. The *Smritiratnākara* of Hārīta Venkatācārya (Tōḻappar) (1450-1500), a native of the Chingleput district which was so prolific of Vaishnava scholars, is accepted to this day as an authoritative exposition of religious law by the Vaishnavas of the South. Vaidyanātha Dīkshita's *Smritimuktāphala*, written probably early in the seventeenth century, holds a similar position among the Smārtas. In the sixteenth and seventeenth centuries under the Nāyak rulers of South India many other works were written in the field of Dharmaśāstra as in other branches of literature.

In lexicography, the *Vaijayantī* of Yādavaprakāśa, the teacher of Rāmānuja, has commanded great authority in the eyes of later authors; it is a work in two sections—one on synonyms and the other on homonyms. Dhanañjaya, a Digambara Jaina writer (1150) of Karnātaka, compiled the *Nāmamālā*, a lexicon of synonyms in about two hundred verses. Jātaveda Dīkshita (1250), also from Karnātaka, annotated the *Amarakośa* in his *Brihadvritti*. Lastly, Vāmana Bhaṭṭa Bāna, whose writings in prose and drama have been noted already, produced two lexicons of merit—*Śabdaratnākara* and *Śabdacandrikā*.

In grammar, Śarvavarman, a reputed contemporary of Guṇāḍhya in the Sātavāhana court, wrote the *Kātantra sūtras*, a simplified system of grammar, for the benefit of his patron and thus began the Kātantra school which flourished subsequently more in Bengal than anywhere else. Another system that arose in the South was that of Śākaṭāyana, of the reign of the Rāshtrakūta Amoghavarsha I (A.D. 817-77); he wrote the *Śabdānuśāsana* in four chapters as also a commentary on it called *Amoghavritti* after his patron, besides the ancillary treatises needed to complete his new system. The earliest South Indian writer on the system of Pāṇini was Haradatta (ninth century) whose commentary *Padamañjarī* on the *Kāśikā* of Vāmana and Jayāditya is a work of outstanding merit and authority. In the thirteenth century a certain Krishnalīlāśuka wrote a commentary called *Purushakāra* on the *Daiva* of Deva, a terse metrical treatise in 200 verses on roots of similar form. The commentary described itself as a *vārttika* and deservedly enjoys a high place among grammatical works. The *Mādhavīya-dhātuvritti* of Mādhava, the great commentator on the Vedas, is a commentary on the *Dhātupāṭha* (list of roots) of Pāṇini which, by the way, suggests the derivation of quite a large number of words whose origin is not given in any other work. The *Siddhānta Kaumudī* of Bhaṭṭoji Dīkshita, a younger contemporary of Appaya Dīkshita, is today the most popular manual of Sanskrit grammar.

In some ways Kerala occupied from the beginning a special position as regards Sanskrit learning and institutions for its promotion, and this became more apparent from the fifteenth century when the Zamorins of Calicut began to stand out as the most powerful rulers of Kerala. An early ruler of the line instituted an annual convocation of scholars and poets for public debates, the most meritorious among them being awarded the title of Bhaṭṭa and money-presents; the whole occasion was known as Bhaṭṭadānam. This went on for about a century and a half and attracted to Calicut scholars from distant countries. Mānavikrama, the Zamorin who ruled in the middle of the fifteenth century, was a distinguished scholar himself and a patron of letters; emulating the legendary Vikramāditya of Ujjain who had 'nine gems' (poets) adorning his court, Mānavikrama gathered eighteen literary gems about himself, and an inspired Malayālam poet Punam, recognized as a half-poet; the names of only a few of these eighteen-and-a-half (Padienettarakkavigaḷ) have survived. In this constellation, the Bhaṭṭatiris of Payyūr who specialized in Mīmāmsā literature stood out prominently; they were great writers in the field of belles-lettres also. There were three Parameśvaras among them; the earliest of them wrote two commentaries on the *Nyāya-kaṇikā* (Mīmāmsā) of Vāchaspati Miśra. He wrote also the *Haricharita*, an artificial composition of 263 stanzas each beginning with one of the *chandra-vākyas* of Vararuchi in order. His grandson Parameśvara II was known as Mīmāmsā-chakravarti. He composed scholarly commentaries on Maṇḍana Miśra's *Sphoṭa-siddhi* (on the sphoṭa doctrine) and *Vibhrama-viveka* (on the five Khyāti-vādas); on Vāchaspati Miśra's *Tattvabindu* (on the source of verbal cognition); and on Chidānanda's *Nīti-tattvā-virbhāva* (Mīmāmsā). In the commentary on the *Sphoṭa-siddhi* he claims to come of a family whose members were the sole authority on the interpretation of the works of Maṇḍana. He has a brother Vāsudeva II, a poet who, after the manner of his earlier namesake of the ninth century A.D. wrote three Yamaka (alliterative) Kāvyas, viz. *Devīcharita*, *Satyatapahkathā* and *Achyutalīlā*. The third Parameśvara was grandson of the second, and author of *Mīmāmsā-sūtrārtha-sangraha*, a commentary on Jaimini's sūtras on the lines of Śabarasvāmin, besides other works.

Uddaṇḍa (A.D. 1430) from Lāṭapura on the Pālār river in Chingleput district held a prominent place in the court of Mānavikrama. He wrote the drama *Mallikāmāruta* modelled on Bhavabhūti's *Mālatīmādhava*. It is not possible to mention all the poets and works of this prolific period; but mention must be made of Chennas Nambūtiri's *Tantrasamuccaya*, an authoritative treatise on temple architecture, iconography, rituals and related matters.

Very soon after the literary group of Mānavikrama flourished Melpattūr Nārāyaṇa Bhaṭṭatiri (1560-1666), a star of the first magnitude in the literary firmament. He was a polymath who adorned everything he touched. His celebrated *Nārāyaṇīya* sings the glory of the divinity of Guruvāyūr in 1,000 stanzas and forms the best devotional poem in Sanskrit, regarded in Kerala as of equal sanctity with the *Bhāgavata Purāṇa*. His *Prakriyā Sarvasva* is a work on grammar which enjoys as much popularity in Kerala as the *Siddhānta Kaumudī* does outside that area. He maintained that great poets were not bound by the strict rules of grammar and that grammar should follow their usage, and upheld the position in his polemical work *Apāṇinīya-prāmāṇya-sādhana*; in this respect he followed his teacher Achyuta Pisharoti who departed from Pāṇini and simplified grammar in his *Praveśaka*, a primer of the subject. Among other works, Nārāyaṇa wrote the Māna section of *Mānameyodaya*, a primer of Bhāṭṭamīmāmsā, which was completed when the Meya section was written by another Nārāyaṇa, a protégé of Mānaveda of Calicut. Nārāyaṇa Bhaṭṭatiri composed several Campūs for recitation by Chākkiyār. His *Niranu-nāsika-prabandha* is a literary *tour de force* containing no nasal letters as it describes the complaint of Śūrpaṇakhā to Rāvaṇa after her nose had been cut off. Bhaṭṭatiri lived to be well over a hundred years old and his fame elicited the admiration of Yajñanārāyaṇa, the chief minister of Raghunātha Nāyaka of Tanjore (1650).

There were families in Kerala which specialized for generations in particular subjects, like the Thaikkāṭṭu *illam* in architecture. *Vāstuvidyā*, *Manushyālaya chandrikā* and *Śilparatna* are well known contributions on the subject from Kerala. In Āyurveda (medicine) the eight great families, hereditary custodians of the science and practice of medicine, are well known. To the departments of astronomy and astrology again Kerala made very striking contributions. The Kaṭapayādi system of numerals was the invention of a Vararuchi of Kerala, author of the *Chandra Vākyas* used for calculating the position of the moon on any day of the year. Bhāskara I expounded the astronomical system of Āryabhaṭa in his *Mahābhāskarīya* some five centuries before the better-known Bhāskarāchārya, author of *Siddhāntaśiromaṇi*; the work is still widely current in Kerala. Govindasvāmi wrote an extensive Bhāshya on it, and his pupil Śankaranārāyaṇa wrote in A.D. 869 a commentary on *Laghubhāskarīya*, another work of Bhāskara I. Śankaranārāyaṇa's patron, Ravivarma of Mahodayapuram, was a great astronomer and set up an observatory and is also said to have inaugurated the Kollam era. Haridatta, another and an earlier authority in astronomy, wrote his *Grahachāranibandhana* about A.D. 700. This work has been regarded as the basic text of the Parahita system of computation employed for many centuries in Kerala. *Veṇvāroha*, a small treatise on the calculation of the correct position of the moon, was written by Mādhavan Nambūtiri of Sangamagrāma about A.D. 1400. But the most notable figure in astronomy was a Parameśvara who from his direct personal observation of the movements of the sun and the moon invented the system of *driggaṇita* in 1431, a correction of the Parahita system. He was a prolific writer on astronomy and astrology. His *Bhaṭadīpikā*, a commentary on the *Āryabhaṭīya* and *Goladīpikā* in two versions are the most notable among them. The next great authority in the field was Nīlakantha Somayājin (1442-1545), a pupil of Dāmodara, son of Parameśvara; of his many works, the most notable is a Bhāshya on *Āryabhaṭīya*. Then we may note Achyuta Pisharoti (1550-1621), the teacher of the celebrated Nārāyaṇa Bhaṭṭatiri; he wrote *Karaṇottama*, a manual on astronomical calculations, and *Uparāgakriyākrama*, on eclipses, besides other works including a Malayālam commentary on *Veṇvāroha*. Astrology was also studied and written on extensively, but these works cannot be noticed here in any detail.

There were notable grammarians also in Kerala. The *Vāraruchasangraha* is a concise treatise in twenty-five verses (*kārikas*) on the major topics of Vyākaraṇa; the commentator on the work, Nārāyaṇa Nambūri of Agnihotri *illam* near Cochin, says that the author Vararuchi was almost the equal of Pāṇini. Nārāyaṇa has also written an extensive commentary on the *Bhāshya pradīpa* of Kaiyaṭa. We owe to another Nambūri of Kāśi *illam* the voluminous *Vrittiratnam*, a metrical commentary in verse on the *Kāśikāvritti*; the same author wrote a *Laghu vritti* in 2,720 verses, and the *Bālamitram*, an elucidation of Mādhava's *Dhātuvritti*. Among other works may be noted the *Subhadrāharaṇa*, a Kāvya in twenty cantos, by another Nārāyaṇa Nambūri which illustrates the rules of Pāṇini mostly by *anushṭup* verses and excels in lucidity the similar works of Bhaṭṭi and Bhauma.

Kerala specialized also in temple worship and rituals and contributed to the literature on the subject; *Prayogamañjari* of Ravi in twenty-one chapters, and the *Paddhati* of Īśāna Śivaguru, an encyclopaedic work in 18,000 verses, are among the best specimens in this line.

This sketch may be concluded with a brief notice of the more important Sanskrit treatises on music and dance. The musical inscription of Kuḍumiyāmalai (Pudukkōṭṭai), which consists of exercises to be practised on stringed instruments, has been without good reason assigned to Pallava Mahendravarman I; we read at the end of the inscription that it was the work of a Śaiva monarch who was the pupil of Rudrācārya, evidently a famous music master of the seventh or eighth century. Chālukya Jagadekamalla (1138-50) of Kalyāni wrote the *Sangītacūḍāmaṇi*, a work in five chapters. In the reign of the Yādava Singhana (1210-47) of Devagiri Śārngadeva wrote a work of outstanding merit, *Sangītaratnākara.* The book in its seven chapters covers the whole range of music and dance. Jayasenāpati, a general of Kākatīya Ganapati, composed the *Nrittaratnāvalī* (1254), in eight chapters on Dancing. Harapāla-deva, an unidentified Chālukya prince, was the author of *Sangīta-sudhākara* on dance and music. The fine arts received great encouragement from the rulers of Vijayanagar and their feudatories, and the theory and practice of music and dancing made notable advances. The great Vidyāraṇya wrote the *Sangītasāra.* Kallinātha, a writer on music, flourished under Mallikārjuna, and his grandson Rāma Amātya who wrote the *Svara-melakalānidhi* was patronized by Rāma Rāya. The *Sangīta-sūryodaya* was the work of Lakshmīnārāyaṇa, the court-musician of Krishnadeva Rāya. The *Sangīta-sudhā*, composed by Govinda Dīkshita in the name of Raghunātha Nāyaka, and the *Caturdaṇḍiprakāśikā* of Venkateśvara Makhi, the son of Govinda Dīkshita, are works of outstanding merit produced in the Nāyak Court of Tanjore.

From very early times South India held an important place in the evolution of Indian music. Even the early writer Bharata mentions a melody-mode known as Āndhrī-jāti and details of other early southern modes are recorded by later writers like Matanga and Śārngadeva. The large place of choric singing in the religious revival of the seventh and eighth centuries is well-known. The great musician and composer Gopāla Nāyaka was invited to Northern India by Ala-ud-din Khilji at the instance of Amir Khusru. Kallinātha cites a composition of Gopāla Nāyaka called Rāga Kadamba, and Venkatamakhi states that he claimed to be the promulgator of Caturdaṇḍi, that is, a fourfold delineation of Rāga forms in Gīta, Prabandha, Ṭhāya, and Ālāpa. The Vaishnava saint Purandara Dāsa was the author of numerous compositions which had a great influence in shaping the tradition of Karnatic music. The four generations of Tallapākkam composers who produced many *kīrtanas* on Lord Venkateśa of Tirupati and a short treatise on the nature and features of *kīrtana* called *Samkīrtana Lakshaṇa* and the celebrated composer Kshetrajña of Maruvāpuri (Guntur district) are famous musicians who flourished towards the close of our period.

TAMIL

Some account has been given in Chapter VII of the literature of the Śangam Age, the oldest body of works now known in the Tamil language. That literature was the result of the meeting and fusion of two originally separate cultures, the Tamil and the Aryan. Its beginnings are no longer traceable, and the schematic anthologies that have been handed down doubtless represent a relatively late phase in that epochal literary movement, and to this phase we have suggested the period A.D. 100-300. A close study of the grammar and vocabulary of the different works as also of their ideas enables the trained reader to discern the outlines of a progressive development and to arrive at tentative conclusions on their relative chronology. The *Tolkāppiyam*, for instance, is best placed towards the close of the age indicated above, and at least two of the anthologies, the *Kalittogai* and *Paripāḍal*, may well be taken to at least a century later. The theme of all the 130 poems of the *Kalittogai* is love as manifested in the five *tiṇais* (types of landscape), and the treatment of the subject is much more sophisticated in these poems than in the *Ahanānūṟu*. This sophistication is found also in the *Paripāḍal* and both works mention new names of ornaments like *vāhu-valaiyam* (armlets), and *mekalai* (girdles) unknown to the earlier poems. A certain Nallanduvanār was the author of the verses in one section (*neydal*) of the *Kalittogai* by one account, and the compiler of the entire anthology according to another. The *Paripāḍal* takes its name from the type of verse employed in the poems in the collection; the original collection included seventy songs on different deities, and of these only twenty-four entire songs and a few fragments of some others have survived; Tirumāl (Vishnu), Muruga, and the river Vaigai form the themes of all these poems and fragments. This is the first instance of a work set to music and belonging to the class of *iśait-tamiḻ*, 'musical Tamil'. The songs show much familiarity with Upanishadic and Purāṇic lore, and are replete with advanced philosophic concepts belonging to different schools of thought. The story of Prahlāda in all its details is mentioned, as also the story of Indra's misconduct with Ahalyā, the wife of the sage Gautama; the six mothers of Muruga and the dances of Vishnu with the shepherdesses are other myths indicating a relatively late age for the collection.

The next great epoch in the annals of Tamil literature extends over a period of three and a half centuries (500-850). In this age the inflow of northern Sanskritic influences became even more marked than before; numerous words and concepts in the domain of ethics, religion and philosophy were freely borrowed and incorporated in Tamil; the Sanskrit codes and law books were accepted as the basis of a considerable volume of didactic literature which forms a striking feature of the time; sometimes whole works in Sanskrit or allied dialects were translated or adapted into Tamil. There was a preponderance of Jaina writers to start with as Jainism and Buddhism were then waxing strong. But the rising tide of Hindu reaction soon produced a great volume of popular devotional literature, which was set to music and ravished the hearts of the common folk. Notable developments occurred in belles-lettres, grammar and lexicography, but here the Jains and Buddhists continued to hold the palm. Almost all writing was in verse, and there was little prose worth mentioning.

Most of the important didactical works composed in the period have been grouped together under the title 'The eighteen *kīḻkkaṇakku*' from about the thirteenth century, because of their being composed in various short metres, generally types of the *veṇbā*. Certainly the best known of them all, and possibly also among the earliest, is the *Kuṟaḷ* of Tiruvaḷḷuvar, a comprehensive manual of ethics, polity and love. It contains 1,330 distichs divided into 133 sections of ten distichs each—the first 38 on ethics (*aṟam*), the following 70 on political and economic topics (*poruḷ*) and the rest on love (*kāmam*). The author was most probably a learned Jaina divine and his close acquaintance with the works of Manu, Kauṭilya and Vātsyāyana is unmistakable. We have little authentic information of his life, and the great merits and continued influence of his work have naturally led to the growth of many popular legends around his name. If, as is often affirmed, he and some other writers of this age belonged to a Śangam, it must have been a later institution than the one which flourished in the early centuries of the Christian era: 450-550 may be suggested as the best data for the *Kuṟaḷ*. To the same period must be assigned the *Kaḷavaḻi* of Poygaiyār, already noticed, and the *Mudumoḻikkāñji*, a short work of 100 stanzas on mutability by Kūḍalūrkiḻār of Madura.

The age of the remaining works in the collection may be given, tentatively and within broad limits, as follows: between 550 and 650—*Kārnāṟpadu*, *Innā-nāṟpadu*, *Aindiṇai-aimbadu*, *Nālaḍi*, *Nānmaṇikkaḍigai*, and *Paḻamoḻi*; between 650 and 750—*Tirikaḍukam*, *Aindiṇai-yeḻubadu*, *Tiṇai-mālai-aimbadu*, *Kainnilai*, *Ēlādi*, *Tiṇai-mālai-nūṟṟaimbadu*, *Śiṟupañcamūlam*, *Iniya-nāṟpadu* and *Āśārakkōvai*. The figures *nāṟpadu* (40), *aimbadu* (50), and so on, with which some of these names end, indicate the number of stanzas in the work. The *Kār-nāṟpadu* is a love poem in which a love-lorn lady is supposed to describe the dreadful approach of the rainy season in the absence of her lover; the four other poems whose titles contain the word *tiṇai*, as well as *Kainnilai*, are also on the theme of love and belong to the class of *aham* works. *Innā-nāṟpadu* and *Iniya-nāṟpadu* are catalogues of painful and unpleasant, and pleasurable and joyous, things and deeds respectively. *Nālaḍi* is a Jaina anthology (400 verses) put together by Padumanār and arranged in forty chapters on the lines of the *Kuṟaḷ*; the names of the poets whose songs are collected are unknown, but the reference to Muttaraiyar in two of the stanzas gives the clue to the date of the collection. *Nānmaṇikkaḍigai* (100 stanzas) by a Vaishnava poet, Viḷambi Nāganār, contains four sententious statements in each stanza; it is a work of high literary merit and ranks next only to the *Kuṟaḷ*. The *Paḻamoḻi* is a Jaina work of 400 *veṇbās*, each citing a proverb and mentioning some incident or story to illustrate it. *Tirikaḍukam* ('three pungents'), *Ēlādi* (cardamom and others) and *Śiṟupañcamūlam* ('the five minor roots') take their names from well-known medicinal preparations; just as the medicines cure the illnesses of the body and restore health, the morals inculcated in these works cure the diseases of mind and spirit and set the reader on the road to virtue and happiness. The author of *Tirikaḍukam* was a worshipper of Vishnu; the other two works were by Jains. The *Āśārakkōvai* is a veritable Tamil *smriti* by a Śaiva author based avowedly on Sanskrit originals. It is among the latest, if not the last, works of this type in this period.

The widespread Hindu religious revival for which many Śaiva *nāyanārs* and Vaishnava *āḻvārs* worked together furnished a powerful stimulus to the growth of a popular devotional literature. It was of great importance alike for its volume and for its influence on the life of the people. Groups of devotees headed by some prominent religious leader moved from place to place and shrine to shrine singing the hymns they composed in the course of these pilgrimages. The result was the use of simple diction and catchy tunes. In this golden age of Tamil Hinduism there must have come into existence a much larger volume of literature than has been preserved in the canonical editions of hymns made in the tenth century by Nambi Āṇḍār Nambi for the Śaiva group, and Nāthamuni for the Vaishnava. For instance, a hymn of Ñānasambandar, which is unknown to the canonical collection, is found engraved on stone in the temple of Tiruviḍaivāyil in the Tanjore district.

Perhaps the earliest author in the group whose works have entered the Śaiva canon is Kāraikkāl Ammai, 'the woman of Kāraikkāl'. Tradition makes her the contemporary of Pūdam, one of the early *āḻvārs*, and both may be assigned to about 550. The Ammai sang the praises of the deity of Tiruvālangādu where she witnessed the dance of Śiva. The two other poems she wrote which mark the beginning of Prabandha literature in Tamil—a *genre* which counted in course of time no fewer than ninety-six types—are *Tiru-iraṭṭai-maṇi-mālai* with twenty pairs of stanzas each including a *kalitturai* verse and a *veṇbā* and the *Adbhutat-tiruvandādi* of 100 *veṇbā* verses. Next comes Aiyaḍigaḷ Kāḍavarkōn who is reputed to have handed over the rule of his principality to his son and devoted himself to a religious life. His *Kshetrattiru-veṇbā* is an *andādi* (a poem in which the last word or syllable of one verse recurs at the beginning of the next) and contains a list of twenty-one Śaiva shrines including Ujjain (Mākāḷam) which were held in esteem in his day. The 307 *padigams* (hymns) of Appar constitute books 4-6 of the Śaiva canon. They contain many notable anticipations of the Śaiva-siddhānta philosophical system; the intensity of devotion that characterizes them is excelled only in the *Tiruvāśagam* of Māṇikka-vāśagar. Ñānasambandar, the most celebrated Śaiva hymnist, heads the canon, and 384 hymns sung by him constitute its first three sections. It is said that he began singing hymns of his own composition at the age of three, and that he met Appar and Śiṟuttoṇḍar in person, but the story of his meeting with the Vaishnava saint Tirumangai seems to be no more than a beautiful legend. Sambandar's hymns are marked by an exceptionally high literary quality, but towards the end of each one the Buddhists and Jains come in for round denunciation—evidence of the most active part he took in the campaign against the heretical faiths.

The *Tirumandiram* of Tirumūlar is a manual of Śaiva mysticism in 3,000 verses. It constitutes the tenth book in the canon, though it does not appear to be mentioned by name by any author before Śēkkiḻār. The life of Tirumūlar is wrapped in a fantastic legend: a *siddha* from Kailāsa, the abode of Śiva, migrated to the South to meet his friend Agastya; near Tiruvāḍuturai he entered the dead body of a shepherd out of pity for the herd which had just lost him; he led the herd back home in the evening, and then abandoned the shepherd's family; then as a penance he sat under a tree for 3,000 years composing the work at the rate of one verse per year. In spite of its almost unredeemed obscurity, it is held in great veneration by Tamil Śaivas.

Sundaramūrtti, the last of the three hymnists of *Dēvāram*, contributed the 100 hymns which make the seventh book of the canon. His devotion to God was that of an intimate friend and he was known as the 'Friend of God' (*tambirān tōḻan*). Legend credits him with having sent the deity as a messenger to his first love when she was cross with him for his temporary unfaithfulness. His *Tiruttoṇḍattogai* sung at Tiruvālūr in the presence of *Aḍiyārs* (devotees) is the classic list of Śaiva saints, individual and collective, of whom sixty-two are named, including the author's father and mother; by adding Sundaramūrtti himself we get the celebrated sixty-three *nāyanārs*, the story of whose lives was told briefly by Nambi Āṇḍār Nambi in the tenth century and, with epic elaboration, by Śēkkiḻār in the twelfth. One of Sundara's friends, Cheramān Perumāl, was the author of other devotional works of high literary quality: *Tiruvālūr-mummaṇik-kōvai*, a schematic poem of ten groups of three stanzas each in a different metre—an *ahaval* followed by a *veṇbā* and a *kalitturai*; *Ponvaṇṇattandādi* in a hundred verses; and the *Tirukkailāya-ñāna-ulā* reputed to be the first poem in this *genre* and to have been promulgated at Kailāsa after the *nāyanār* reached the sacred mountain in the company of Sundaramūrtti.

Last but by no means least of the Śaiva saints of this period who earned themselves an abiding place in the literature and hearts of the Tamils was Māṇikka-vāśagar whose *Tiruvāśagam* forms the eighth book of the canon, to which some would add his *Tirukkōvai* also. The transparent sincerity of the passionate outpourings of the saint in the *Tiruvāśagam* makes a deep impression on the reader's mind, and the fifty-one hymns, in spite of their many strange mythical allusions, strike him as a true record of a vivid religious experience which traces the progress of a soul from the bondage of passion and ignorance to the liberty of light and love. The supreme power of divine grace to liberate the soul is the main theme. Some would trace Christian influences in the trend of the saint's thought and feeling; the parallel with some aspects of Christian experience is clear enough, but of any direct borrowing there is no proof; and on the whole the differences are more important than the resemblances. The *Tirukkōvai* is among the earliest of the full-fledged *kōvais* which treat of love in a schematic poem of 400 stanzas, each depicting a particular situation. Māṇikka-vāśagar's poem has a double meaning throughout, the main theme being the love of the soul for God. Some are inclined to doubt the authorship of the poem, which is, however, marked by a devotional intensity not unworthy of the author of the *Tiruvāśagam*, though its diction is less popular. The *Kārikkōvai* of Kāri-nāyanār and the *Muttaraiyar-kōvai* mentioned in the commentary to the *Yāpparungalam* (tenth century) may be earlier than *Tirukkōvai*, but they are no longer extant; and the *Pāndikkōvai*, also perhaps an earlier poem, is available only in numerous citations.

Side by side with the Śaiva *nāyanārs*, the Vaishnava *āḻvārs* also laboured along the same lines for the revival of Hinduism, and their devotional songs constitute in their final redaction the 'Four

Thousand Sacred Hymns'—*Nālāyira Divyaprabandham.* The three earliest *āḻvārs* were Poygai, Pūdam, and Pēy, and later literary tradition avers that Pūdam was the contemporary of Karaikkāl Ammai. These saints are each represented by one *andādi* of one hundred *veṇbās*, remarkable for their non-sectarian outlook and for the purity and gentleness of their devotion. Then came Tirumaḻiśai, a contemporary of Mahendravarman I, in whose works, the *Nānmugantiruvandādi* and *Tiruccandaviruttam*, a somewhat more controversial tone can be traced than in the writings of the first three *āḻvārs.* He is reputed to have tried both Jainism and Buddhism before turning Vaishnava *yogi*, and this explains the state of religion in his day and the tone of his poems. Tirumangai (eighth century) was a much more voluminous writer and a keen controversialist. His poems constitute about a third of the entire collection in volume, and ensure him a high place both as poet and devotee. In its literary quality and in sentiment his work has many resemblances with that of Sambandar. He has many flings at Jains and Buddhists, and some even against Śaivas. Periyāḻvār and his daughter Āṇḍāḷ contribute nearly 650 verses to the collection between them. The daughter claimed that the Lord of Śrīrangam was her lover, and her poems are suffused by her passionate longing for companionship with the Lord; she is reputed to have been accepted as his bride, and her poems, with her father's, are placed first in the canon. The cycle of Krishna stories is most effectively used to rouse the devotion of the hearer, and to a Hindu the repeated allusions to the tales in different settings constitute not the least attractive feature of her work. The hymn of Āṇḍāḷ which starts with the words *vāraṇam-āyiram* ('one thousand elephants'), telling of her dream-marriage with Vishnu, is sung at all Vaishnava Brahmin marriages to this day. Tiruppāṇ and Toṇḍar-aḍip-poḍi may be placed next; the former has only one hymn while the latter has two, *Tirumālai* and *Tiruppaḷḷiyeḻucci*, to his credit. The last-named presupposes the existence of the order of worship in temples as the offering of royal honour, *rājopacāra*, to the deity; it is a song meant to rouse the god from his sleep at break of day. Tirumangai, Toṇḍar-aḍip-poḍi and Kulaśekhara are said to have been contemporaries, but we may well doubt this. Kulaśekhara calls himself king of Kongar, Kūḍal and Kōḻi in his poems. He was the author of a notable devotional poem in Sanskrit, *Mukundamālā*, besides the 105 Tamil verses forming the

Perumāḷ Tirumoḻi in the Tamil canon of the Vaishnavas. The Veḷḷāla saint Nammāḻvār, also called Śaṭhakōpa, and his Brahmin pupil Madhurakavi were the latest of the *āḻvārs*. Nammāḻvār's work is held in the highest respect as it is believed to embody the deepest philosophical truths taught by the Upanishads. The 1,101 stanzas comprising the *Tiruvāymoḻi* hold the place of honour and have been most elaborately commented on by later expositors of the Viśishtādvaita system of philosophy. The *Tiruvāśiriyam*, *Tiruviruttam* and *Tiruvandādi* are other works comprising together less than 200 stanzas. They relate to the deities of some thirty shrines, of which all but six are found in the Pāndya and Chera countries. Nammāḻvār was a *yogi*, and his *Tiruvāymōḻi* is replete with a convincing narration of his mystical experiences. Like the other *āḻvārs*, he delights in the contemplation of the avatārs of Vishnu and their achievements, and his handling of themes from the lives of Rāma and Krishna has found expression in some very charming child poetry. Not only as philosopher and mystic, but even as a pure literary artist, Nammāḻvār takes a very high rank. Nāthamuni, the first of the *ācāryas* of the next epoch, is said to have been his pupil and received from him the entire canon of 4,000 hymns. The other pupil, Madhurakavi, himself an *āḻvār*, wrote only one hymn in praise of his *guru*. It it quite probable that the last two *āḻvārs* lived for many years after 850, the limit of our second period.

In the field of general literature, the three most outstanding works are by Jaina and Buddhist authors. The *Śilappadikāram* is an unsurpassed gem, though its authorship and date are not free from besetting doubts. The work is in some ways unique in the whole range of Tamil literature, and the vivid portraiture of its scenes and its skilful metrical effects are practically unknown to any other work. Its theme is an old popular saga, the story of a merchant prince, Kōvalan, who neglects his wife Kaṇṇagi and loses his fortune through love of the celebrated hetaera Mādhavi of Puhār. A quarrel between the lovers sends Kōvalan back to his wedded wife, and they both migrate from Puhār to Madura to start a new life with the money to be raised by the sale of Kaṇṇagi's jewels—particularly her precious anklet (*śilambu*) which gives the name to the poem. As the result of the machinations of the royal goldsmith, Kōvalan is suspected of being the thief who stole the queen's anklet from the palace and is cut down by the king's officers in the streets of Madura. When Kaṇṇagi hears the news, she rushes to the palace with the second anklet as proof of Kōvalan's innocence. The king realizes his injustice and dies of a broken heart. Kaṇṇagi wreaks her vengeance on Madura by consigning the city to flames, and moves into the Chera country where she is received into heaven with her husband. Śenguṭṭuvan enshrines her as the Goddess of Chastity. Despite it supernatural elements, the bulk of the story is a moving human tale powerfully told, its scenes laid in all three kingdoms of the Tamil land. The author is called Iḷango Aḍigaḷ (' Prince ascetic ') and is reputed to be the brother of the Chera monarch Śenguṭṭuvan; but of such a brother the Śangam poems have no knowledge. The mystery deepens when we learn further that Iḷango was a contemporary of Śāttanār, a grain-merchant of Madura, the author of *Maṇimēkalai*. This is a Buddhist poem, which tells the life-story, mainly of religious interest, of Maṇimēkalai, the daughter of Mādhavi by Kōvalan. The prologues to the two poems say that each was read out to the author of the other. And there is actually among the Śangam poets a Śīttalaic-Cāttanār, who contributes ten poems to four of the eight anthologies, though there is no trace of any leaning to Buddhism on his part. In its present form the *Maṇimēkalai* contains a long exposition of fallacies in logic which is obviously based on the *Nyāyapraveśa* of Dinnāg, a work of the fifth century A.D. And the literary form of the two epics is so different from anything known in the real age of Śangam literature that it would not be wrong to postulate an interval of several centuries between that age and that of the *Śilappadikāram* and *Maṇimēkalai*.

The *Perungadai* (Sanskrit, *Brihat-kathā*) of Kongu-Vēḷir is another great poem by a Jaina author, of which only parts are available. It tells of the adventures of Naravānadatta, the son of the celebrated Udayana of Kauśāmbī and is apparently based on a Sanskrit original which was a rendering of Guṇāḍhya's famous poem in the Paiśācī dialect. The Western Ganga king Durvinīta is said to have composed a Sanskrit version of that work at the end of the sixth century. As a narrative poem the *Perungadai* has exceptional merits and is deservedly popular. *Vaḷaiyāpati* and *Kuṇḍalakēsi* are the names of two other Kāvyas, respectively Jaina and Buddhist, in Tamil which have been lost but were once counted among the five great Kāvyas. The commentary on the

Yāpparungalam, a Jaina grammar of the next period, cites many works on grammar by Jaina authors which must have been composed at this time; so also the commentary on the *Vīraśōḻiyam*, a Buddhist grammatical work of the eleventh century, cites verses from many Buddhist Kāvyas of this period no longer accessible to us.

The commentary on the *Iṟaiyanār Ahapporuḷ* traditionally ascribed to Nakkīrar must have been composed late in this period. It is worthy of note as the earliest of the great prose commentaries which occupy so conspicuous a place in the development of Tamil prose. The style of the commentaries is by no means easy or popular, and is often marred by the authors' desire to show off their learning and by their straining after alliteration; the earliest commentary exhibits in full all the demerits of this class of writing.

The *Muttoḷḷāyiram* must have been a work of 900 *veṇbās*, made up of 300 verses in praise of each of the three monarchs of the Tamil country. It is now known only from about 100 verses which are often very good poetry, cited by different writers, but its authorship cannot be traced. The *Tagaḍūr-Yāttirai* is another lost work of the age, which is likewise only known from stray citations. Its theme was the war between the Chera monarch and Adigaimān of Tagaḍūr which took place relatively late in the Śangam Age.

Finally, mention must be made of two works of the time of Pallava Nandivarman III. The anonymous *Nandikkalambakam*, that has come down with many interpolations, is a quasi-historical poem of about eighty stanzas dealing, in various metres, with events of the reign of the last great Pallava monarch. The *Bhāratam* of Perundēvanār of which only a small part has survived raises questions which cannot now be satisfactorily answered. The extant portions include the whole of the Udyoga and Bhīshma *parvas*, and part of the Droṇa *parva*,—to the battle on the thirteenth day. The work consists of *veṇbās* interspersed with connecting prose passages, and thus attains the form of a Campū. But it has been doubted if the poetry and prose are from the same pen, and the problem is complicated by the fact that the *Bhāratam* was rendered into Tamil by a Perundēvanār in the Śangam Age. The present work, poetry and prose taken together, is a straightforward and simple narrative of the main story not devoid of eloquence and charm. It may well be that the entire work was written by a single author in the ninth century, his poetry conforming to a long established tradition regarding its diction, while his prose was modelled on the style of the learned commentaries, the only prose then known.

The age of the imperial Cholas (850-1200) was the golden age of Tamil culture, and it was naturally marked by the widespread practice and patronage of literature. The Prabandha form became dominant and the systematic treatment of Śaiva-siddhānta in philosophical treatises began. Great Śiva temples were built anew and celebrated in hymns on the model of those of the previous period by new authors (among whom was a prince), and the hagiology of Śaivism was standardized in a great Purāṇa by Śēkkiḻār. A quantum of Vaishnava devotional literature and commentaries on the canon also came into existence. Jaina and Buddhist authors continued to flourish though not in such numbers as in the earlier age. Many works mentioned in the numerous inscriptions of the period have been lost beyond recovery.

In general literature, the *Jīvakacintāmaṇi* of the Jaina ascetic and poet Tiruttakkadēvar was composed early in the tenth century. It follows late ninth-century Sanskrit originals and tells the life story of Jīvaka, an ideal hero, equally distinguished in the arts of war and peace, the perfect saint no less than the charming lover. After a stormy youth marked by many adventures Jīvaka finds himself, in the prime of life, the monarch of a splendid kingdom. For some years thereafter he leads a life of pleasure in the company of his eight queens; in fact the poem has another name, *Maṇa-nūl*, 'The Book of Marriages', on account of each of Jīvaka's early adventures culminating in a happy marriage. Jīvaka is shaken from his complacency by an incident, trivial in itself, but full of deep significance to him. He sees in a moment's flash the hollowness of human life and the wisdom of seeking release from its bonds. He installs his son on the throne and seeks the peace of the forest, and attains salvation in the end. In its present form the work contains 3,154 stanzas, of which it is thought that only 2,700 were composed by the original author, two contributed by his *guru*, with whose permission he wrote the poem, and the rest by a later writer. The annotator has marked out the *guru's* two verses, but there is no means of identifying the work of the third writer. The art of Tiruttakkadēvar is marked by all the qualities of great poetry and even, as is well known, furnished the model for the genius of Kamban. The poem is said to have been the author's answer to a challenge that while Jaina writers were admittedly distinguished in the field of religious literature, they could make no contribution to the literature of love. Tiruttakkadēvar was allowed to take up the challenge and write this long erotic poem after he had satisfied his *guru* that he had the literary capacity for the task and that he would not lose his spiritual balance by writing it. He is thought to have been a Chola prince by birth. Another Jaina writer of the time was Tōlāmoḻi ('a man of unsurpassed eloquence') whose *Śūḷāmaṇi* handles a Jaina purāṇic theme in very mellifluous verse and is counted among the five minor Kāvyas of Tamil literature.

Kallāḍanār, the author of *Kallāḍam*, must be distinguished from his namesake of the Śangam Age. He can perhaps be identified with the author who figures in the eleventh book of the Śaiva canon. Kallāḍam is a place-name and possibly the writer was born there. He is said to have chosen one hundred verses from the *Tirukkōvai* as the basis of his work which deals with the sixty-four sacred sports of Śiva. The style of the work is very stilted as a result of the author's attempt to revive the poetic forms and diction of the Śangam Age. The whole poem of 100 pieces, each purporting to depict a particular mood of love (*ahatturai*) is a curious instance of extreme pedantry. The *Kalingattupparaṇi* of the poet-laureate of the Chola court, Jayangondār, dates from the end of the reign of Kulottunga I and is the earliest and best of the Paraṇis now accessible. It is a splendid little masterpiece which keeps clear the line between history and fictitious convention; its choice diction and the sustained harmony between the metres employed and the incidents portrayed are unique. The Paraṇi is the war poem *par excellence* and depicts not only the pomp and circumstance of war, but all the gruesome details of the field. The Kalinga war of Kulottunga, the theme of this poem, was celebrated in several other works, none of which could survive in the face of Jayangondār's poem. Another poet-laureate of the Chola court was Kūttan or Oṭṭakkūttan who graced the reigns of three successors of Kulottunga (viz. Vikrama Chola, Kulottunga II and Rājarāja II) and sang eloquent Ulās of each of them. Born of a poor Śengundar (weaver) family in Malari, a village in the Chola country, Kūttan sought service under Śankaran, the chieftain of Puduvai and father of Śaḍaiyan, the patron of the more celebrated Kamban. Kūttan had other patrons like Gāngēya, whom he praised in a *Nālāyirakkōvai*, and a certain Soman of Tribhuvani. When his fame rose he was invited to the imperial court and entertained there as Kaviccakravarti ('Emperor of Poets') by the three successive monarchs named. Besides the three Ulās, he composed a Paraṇi, no longer extant, on the Kalinga war of Vikrama Chola, and a *piḷḷaittamiḻ* (a poem describing the hero's childhood) on Kulottunga II. The last is easily the best of the poet's compositions on account of its copious diction, the rich melody and fine imagery of its verse. The same poet's *Takkayāgapparaṇi*, obviously an imitation of *Kalingattupparaṇi*, in its metres and style, handles the legendary theme of Daksha's sacrifice with considerable force and power, but must take a rank well below its model. Other poems attributed to him are *Sarasvatiyandādi* in praise of the Goddess of Learning by whose grace he became a poet, reputed to be his first composition, and *Arumbaittoḷḷāyiram*, besides *Īṭṭiyeḻupadu* and *Eḻuppeḻupadu*, poems of no merit about the composition of which popular imagination has trumped up wild legends which reflect no credit on their inventors or the poet. The village of Kūttanūr on the banks of the Ariśil river (Tanjore district) keeps the poet's memory alive, and has a Sarasvatī temple with a record of the twelfth century mentioning the installation of the image of the goddess by Kavipperumāl alias Ōvāda-Kūttar, the grandson of Oṭṭakkūttan.

A greater poet than Kūttan was Kamban, the celebrated author of the Tamil *Rāmāyaṇam* or *Rāmāvatāram*, who flourished in the reign of Kulottunga III. This poem is the greatest epic in Tamil literature, and though the author states that he follows in the wake of Vālmīki, still his work is no translation or even adaptation of the Sanskrit original. Like the other great poets who have enriched the literatures of the different languages of India by their works on the Rāma saga, Kamban imports into his narration the colour of his own time and place. Thus his description of Kosala is an idealized account of the features of the Chola country, and he compares the brightness of moonlight to the fame of his patron, Śaḍaiyan of Veṇṇai-nallūr. Rāma himself was as much master of the Tamil idiom as of Sanskrit. Sometimes Kamban yields to the somewhat rigid canons of Tamil poetics as when he enters on an elaborate analysis of the emotions of Rāma and Sītā after a chance meeting which takes place immediately after Rāma's entry into Mithilā. Elsewhere, as in the description of Sītā's behaviour on receiving Rāma's ring from Hanumān, Kamban elaborates a brief hint thrown out by Vālmīki who says that she rejoiced as if she had rejoined her husband. He compresses Vālmīki's account at other points, as in Daśaratha's *aśvamedha*. Few authentic details of the poet's life are forthcoming. He is believed to have belonged to the *Uvaccar* caste, priests in the temples of Kāli and similar deities and stray verses attributed to him seek to bring him into some relation with all the great monarchs of South India including the Pāndya and Kākatīya rulers. Kamban's poem carried the story of Rāma up to his return to Ayodhyā and his coronation as king; the *Uttarakāṇḍam* being the work of another hand. The *Rāmāvatāram* soon attained great popularity which it has retained to this day. Two mediocre poems, *Ēreḻupadu* and *Śaṭakōparandādi*, are attributed to Kamban; the former is in praise of agriculture, and the praise of Śaṭakōpa (Nammāḻvār) is said to have been composed to please the god of Śrīrangam whose approval was sought by the poet for the *Rāmāyaṇa* and who ordered him to praise his beloved devotee in a centum of verses. One of the best known works of secular literature belonging to the late Chola period is the *Kulōttungankōvai*, on Kumāra Kulottunga, afterwards Kulottunga III. Little is known of the author, and the poem has no conspicuous merit except that it has a great Chola monarch for its hero and contains passing allusions to some of his achievements in war.

The impulse to produce devotional religious literature which was so active in the last period (500-850) continued with some force far into this (850-1200), and the extant arrangement of the Śaiva canon into eleven books was the work of Nambi Āṇḍār Nambi who lived at the close of the tenth and the beginning of the eleventh century. His part in the collection and editing of the canon became the subject of Umāpatiśivācārya's poem *Tirumuṟai-kaṇḍa-purāṇam* (fourteenth century). Nambi's own works include six Prabandhas on Ñānasambandar and one on Appar, besides *Tiruttoṇḍar-tiruvandādi* which gives brief accounts of the lives of the sixty-three saints and is based on Sundaramūrtti's *Tiruttoṇḍattogai*. All these and the poems he wrote in praise of Vināyaka and Chidambaram, find a place in the eleventh book of the canon. The same book includes five compositions of

Paṭṭinattu-piḷḷaiyār in which this senior contemporary of Nambi celebrates the Śaiva shrines of Chidambaram, Kaḻumalam (Shiyali), Tiruviḍaimarudūr, Kānchipuram and Oṟṟiyūr. Earlier than Nambi but not far removed from him were the authors represented in the ninth book of the canon, *Tiruviśaippā*. There are nine of them including Gandarāditya, the son of Parāntaka I, and a Karuvūr Dēvan who has hymns on the three famous Chola temples newly erected in his day—the Ādityēśvara at Kaḷandai, the Rājarājēśvara at Tanjore and the Gangaikonda-śōḻēśvara at Gangaikonda-śōḻapuram.

The *Tiruttoṇḍar-purāṇam* or *Periya Purāṇam* of Śēkkiḻār composed in the reign of Kulottunga II (1133-50) is a landmark in the history of Tamil Śaivism. Umāpati-śivācārya has celebrated the event in a short Purāṇa called *Śēkkiḻār-nāyanār-purāṇam*. A Veḷḷāla by caste, Śēkkiḻār was born at Kunṟattūr very near Madras, and having entered the service of the Chola monarch, he rose to a high position and earned the title Uttamaśōḻa Pallavarāyan. He built a Śiva temple closely modelled on that at Tirunāgēśvaram (near Kumbakonam), a shrine to which he was greatly devoted. The story goes that the king's study of *Jīvaka-cintāmaṇi* offended Śēkkiḻār's deeply religious nature and that he exhorted the king to abandon the pursuit of impious erotic literature and turn instead to the lives of the Śaiva saints celebrated by Sundaramūrtti and Nambi Āṇḍār Nambi. The king thereupon commanded Śēkkiḻār to expound these lives, and being greatly attracted by the theme, he wanted Śēkkiḻār to write them out *in extenso* in a great poem and gave him much wealth to enable him to do so. Śēkkiḻār then went over to Chidambaram, and with his mind filled with divine grace—there was a voice commanding him to begin his work with the words *Ulagelām*—he began to compose the Purāṇa in the beautiful thousand-pillared *maṇḍapa* within the precincts of the temple. On its completion, the Chola monarch himself came to Chidambaram and, in accordance with another divine command, he listened attentively to Śēkkiḻār's exposition of the work from day to day for a whole year. It was hailed universally as a veritable fifth Veda in Tamil and immediately took its place as the twelfth and last book in the Śaiva canon. It has influenced profoundly the lives of all the Śaivas of the Tamil country and of those in Andhra and Karnātaka through translations and adaptations. It is one of the masterpieces of Tamil literature, and worthily commemorates the great age of the Imperial Cholas and their sustained devotion to Śaivism.

Vaishnava religious literature during this period was mostly composed in Sanskrit. It is possible that the last two *āḻvārs* lived far into this period, but the *ācāryas* who succeeded them, Nāthamuni, the redactor of the 4,000 hymns, his grandson Āḷavandār or Yāmunācārya and the great Rāmānuja himself wrote almost all their works in Sanskrit, a rather strange transformation for a movement which began with a more popular appeal than Śaivism. Even the commentators on the early Tamil hymns like Piḷḷān, the author of the shortest extant commentary on *Tiruvāymoḻi*, Nañjīyar, Nambiḷḷai, Periyavāccān and Vaḍakkuttiruvīdippiḷḷai, all authors of more elaborate commentaries, developed a quaint style, *maṇipravāḷa* (*lit.* crystal and coral), loaded with Sanskrit words not easily understood outside the narrow learned circle. The centum of verses in praise of Rāmānuja, the *Rāmānuja-nūṟṟandādi*, by his disciple Tiruvarangattu Amudanār, is a conspicuous exception; it is a poem in simple devotional style held in great esteem to this day and often repeated as a daily prayer; the central idea of the poem is that there is no way to salvation without the grace of the *guru*.

Jīvasambodanai of Devendra-munivar is a Jaina work expounding in detail twelve modes of meditation in the form of an address to the soul. The work is replete with mythical stories and anecdotes, and its metres resemble those employed in contemporary Tamil inscriptions.

In the field of Tamil grammar, the *Yāpparungalam* and *Yāpparungalakkārigai*, two authoritative works on prosody, were composed by Amitasāgara, a Jaina ascetic of the close of the tenth century. Both the works have lucid commentaries, that on the *Kārigai* being by a certain Guṇasāgara, also a Jaina ascetic and most probably a pupil of Amitasāgara. The *Yāpparungalam* is unique in its range and offers an exhaustive treatment of the metres in Tamil, and the *Kārigai* (Skt. *Kārikā*) is its abridgement. Amitasāgara quotes the *Śūḷāmaṇi* and is himself quoted by Buddhamitra, the Buddhist author of *Vīraśōḻiyam*. Both Amitasāgara and Buddhamitra were patronized by the contemporary Chola monarchs and granted liberal assignments of territory. The latter mentions king Vīrarājendra as a great Tamil scholar. His work written in *kalitturai* metre attempts a synthesis between the Tamil and Sanskrit systems of grammar, and comprises all the five sections of a complete treatise—*sandhi* (*eluttu*), *śol*, *porul*, *yāppu* and *alankāra* (*aṇi*). The work is full of interest for a student of the history of grammatical theory in Tamil; it has a commentary by Perundēvanār, a pupil of the author. The *Daṇḍiyalangāram* treats mainly of figures of speech and, as its name implies, it is modelled on the famous *Kāvyādarśa* of Dandin. It is composed in sūtra (aphoristic) style and, like its model, it treats of the nature of poetry and Kāvya, and of figures of speech under two generic heads—*arthālankāra* (*poruḷaṇi*) and *śabdālankāra* (*śollaṇi*). Each sūtra is followed by an explanation and illustration, all believed to be by the author, and some of the illustrative stanzas are in praise of Anapāya Chola (Kulottunga II). The name of the author and the details of his life are lost. The *Nēminādam* of Guṇavīrapandita is a short treatise of less than 100 verses in the *veṇbā* metre treating of the orthographs and parts of speech (*eḻuttu* and *śol*) of the Tamil language. The author, a Jain of the time of Kulottunga III, named his work after Neminātha, the *tīrthankara* of South Mylapore. Another work of the same writer on prosody was *Vaccaṇandi-mālai* ('the Garland of Vaccaṇandi'), named after the author's *guru*; it is also known as *Veṇbāppāṭṭiyal*. The *Nannūl* ('The Good Book') was the work of Pavaṇandi, another Jaina grammarian patronized by a Ganga feudatory of Kulottunga III. It treats only of *eḻuttu* and *śol*, and it is not known whether the author stopped there or the rest of the work has been lost. By its simplicity and terseness, it has practically displaced all other books as the beginner's handbook of Tamil grammar. The *Puṟapporuḷ-veṇbāmālai* of Aiyanāridanār, yet another Jaina writer, defines the conventions governing the *tuṟais* (situations) of *puṟam* and illustrates each *tuṟai* by a *veṇbā*; in some respects it differs from the *Tolkāppiyam*, and is said to be based on an early work called *Pannirupaḍalam*.

In lexicography the concise *nigaṇḍu* (lexicon) called *Pingalam* after its author belongs to this period. Its topical divisions are different from those of *Divākaram*, the earliest extant lexicon, composed by Divākara under the patronage of a Śēndan of Ambar sometime in the eighth century A.D. Little is known of the author of *Pingalam;* he is mentioned in the *Nannūl* and seems to have been a Śaiva.

The philosophical literature of Śaiva-siddhānta had its beginnings late in this period in two works, *Tiruvundiyār* by Tiruviyalūr-uyyavanda-dēvar and *Tirukkaḷirruppaḍiyar* by Tirukkaḍavūr-uyyavanda-dēvar; the latter is said to have been the pupil of the former and these two works composed in 1148 and 1178 are the only ones among the fourteen works comprising the Siddhānta-sāstra that precede *Śiva-Ñāna-Bōdam* of Meykaṇḍār, the celebrated manual of Śaivism.

The fourth and last great period of Tamil literature that will engage our attention extended from 1200 to 1650 and was marked by a large output of philosophical works, commentaries, Purāṇas and Prabandhas. Much of this literature is derivative and second-rate, and one gets the impression that the age of creative achievement has given place to imitation and criticism. A somewhat arid scholasticism found much encouragement in the numerous *maṭhas* that began to play a prominent part in the educational system of the country. The numerous authors of the period belonged mostly to the Śaiva or Vaishnava sects, though some Jaina writers continued to write also. Though the emperors of Vijayanagar and most of their feudatories even as far south as Madura were Telugus with a decided preference for Sanskrit and Telugu, there is no reason to think that there was any setback in Tamil literary work, and the Pāndyas, confined to the extreme south from the fifteenth century, bestowed particular attention on the cultivation of Tamil.

Early in this period, in the first half of the thirteenth century, came Meykaṇḍār who formulated the tenets of Śaiva-siddhānta in his *Śiva-Ñāna-Bōdam*, a short treatise of a dozen Sūtras, perhaps translated from a Sanskrit original. The author has added *vārttikas* which explain and illustrate the argument of each of the Sūtras. The scheme of the work is simple: the first three Sūtras affirm the existence of the three entities—God (*pati*), Bondage (*pāśa*), and Soul (*paśu*); the three next define and explain their nature and interrelation; the next triad deals with the means of release; and the last with its nature. 'The Veda,' it has been said, 'is the cow; its milk is the true *āgama*; the Tamil sung by the four in *Dēvāram* and *Tiruvāśagam* is the ghee extracted from it; and the virtue of the Tamil work of Meykaṇḍār of the celebrated (city of) Veṇṇai is the fine taste of the ghee.' After the *Bōdam*, the next work of importance on Śaiva doctrine is the *Śiva-Ñāna-Śittiyār* of Aruṇandi, reputed to have been first the *guru* of Meykaṇḍārs' father and then the disciple of Meykaṇḍār himself. Written altogether in verse, this work is a statement of the true doctrine (*supakkam*) in *viruttam* verses, following the order of the Sūtras in the *Bōdam*; this statement is preceded by a critical discussion of rival systems (*para-pakkam*) of which no fewer than fourteen, including four schools of Buddhism and two of Jainism, are passed under review. This is the great classic of Tamil Śaiva doctrine; often commented on, it has been the most widely read manual on the subject. The *Irupāv-irupahdu* by the same writer owes its name to the alternate use of two metres in its twenty verses in the from of a dialogue between teacher and pupil. The name of the author's *guru*, Meykaṇḍār, occurs in each of these twenty verses. The *Uṇmai-viḷakkam* ('Explanation of the Truth') of Manavāśa-gangaḍandār of Tiruvadi (South Arcot) is the simplest of the manuals on the doctrine, true to the essence of the Āgamas. Umāpatiśivācārya (end of the thirteenth and early fourteenth century) was the author of the remaining eight works which complete the tale of the fourteen Śaiva-siddhānta-śāstras.[1] One of them, *Sankaṟpanirākaraṇam*, is dated 1313. Like the *para-pakkam* of the *Śittiyār*, it is a critique of other creeds; but, unlike the earlier work, it is much exercised with the minute differences within the fold of Śaivism. Both these works were commented on in the sixteenth century by Ñānaprakāśar of Tiruvoṟṟiyūr who also composed a Purāṇa on his birthplace (*c.* 1580).

At the end of the fourteenth and beginning of the fifteenth century came Svarūpānanda Dēśikar and his pupil Tattuvarāyar, authors of two celebrated anthologies bearing on the philosophy of Advaita. The *Śivaprakāśap-perundiraṭṭu* comprising 2,824 verses is the work of the teacher; that of the pupil, called *Kuṟun-diraṭṭu*, (short anthology), includes almost exactly half as many verses as the bigger work. The two anthologies together conserve much of the religious and philosophical literature of the silver age of Śaivism in the Tamil country that would otherwise have been lost. Tattuvarāyar was an ascetic, like his *guru*, and author of many devotional poems and songs, some of which were remarkable for the simplicity of their diction and their wide appeal to the common man; the songs in particular were of the nature of ditties and created many new models that were extensively

[1] Some Mss. include *Tugaḷaṟubōdam* of Śiṟṟambalanāḍigaḷ of Shiyali (fourteenth century) in the place of *Uṇmaineṟiviḷakkam* ascribed to Umāpati.

followed by subsequent composers. Among the poems may be named *Pāḍuturai*, *Ñānavinōdan Kalambakam*, *Mōhavadaip-paraṇi* and *Aññavadaipparaṇi*. Even wider in its appeal was the *Tiruppugaḻ* of Aruṇagirinātha, over 1,360 songs in various metres handled with the utmost skill and characterized by a unique lilt. The diction is highly Sanskritized and the imagery vivid; the author's wide knowledge of the sacred lore of Hinduism is evident in every song. His mention of Praudhadeva Rāya places him in the fifteenth century. His life has become the subject of many legends, but the references in the songs show that for a time he led the life of a libertine which he afterwards regretted. He accepted Muruga or Kārttikeya as the supreme deity, and in philosophy he followed the Śaiva-siddhānta system. He seems to have visited all the shrines of Muruga and been particularly attached to Paḻani which figures largely in the *Tiruppugaḻ*. A number of shorter devotional poems, all in praise of Muruga, are also attributed to him. A certain Śivaprakāśar of Madura (1489) wrote valuable commentaries on *Irupāv-irupahdu* of Aruṇandi and *Śivaprakāśam* of Umāpati. Haridāsa was a Vaishnava poet who adorned the court of the celebrated Krishnadeva Rāya of Vijayanagar, and wrote the *Irusamaya-viḷakkam*, an exposition of the two systems, viz. Śaivism and Vaishnavism, with a bias towards the latter. The *Śivadarumōttaram* (1553) of Maṟaiñānasambandar, who lived in a *maṭha* in Chidambaram, contains over 1,200 verses in twelve sections based on the Āgamas and dealing with cosmology, with the temple and its constitution, and with theology. The same author wrote also the *Śaiva-samaya-neṟi* ('the path of the Śaiva creed'), 727 small stanzas (*kuṟal veṇbās*) on the daily religious observances of Śaivas. About the same time (1564) Śivāgrayogi *alias* Śivakkoḻundu Dēśikar composed an authoritative commentary on the whole of the *Śittiyār*, besides other works on ritualism, asceticism and other religious subjects. Another famous writer who flourished at the same time was Kamalai Ñānaprakāśar, the author of many manuals of Śaiva worship, besides the Purāṇa on Tirumaḻuvāḍi, and a *kōvai* on Tiruvaṇṇāmalai. Māśilāmaṇi Sambandar's Purāṇa on Uttara-kōśamangai is very important for the life-story of Māṇikka-vāśagar. Niramba Aḻagiya Dēśikar wrote *Sētu-purāṇam* which is popular among scholars as it uses all the rare words listed in the lexicons and is considered helpful in enriching the vocabulary of aspiring writers. He wrote also Purāṇas on Tirupparangiri and Tiruvaiyāṟu, and a commentary on the *Śittiyār*, differing in some ways from his elder contemporary Śivāgrayogi. He had many pupils who composed several minor Purāṇas and religious works including the well-known *Tiruvālūr-purāṇam* (1592). Turaśai Ambalavāṇa-Dēśikar (*c.* 1605) was the author of many religious works like the *Śittānta-śikāmaṇi*, *Niṭṭai-viḷakkam* and *Sanmārgaśittiyār* besides the *Pūppiḷḷai-aṭṭavaṇai*, an easy prose exposition of Śaiva philosophy said to have been composed for the edification of a loyal attendant.

A certain Tuṟaiyūr Śivaprakāśa-svāmi was a contemporary of Lingama Nāyaka of Vellore (early seventeenth century). He is said to have embraced Vīra-śaivism to win the Nāyaka's favour and induce him to restore worship in the shrine of Naṭarāja at Chidambaram, interrupted by the intolerance of the Vaishnava officials of Vijayanagar. Among his works *Advaita-veṇbā* expounds the Śaiva philosophy in 218 verses based on the Āgamas, particularly the Vātula, while others like *Gaṇa-bhāshita-ratnamālai* and *Śatakatrayam* deal with the theology and philosophy of Vīra-śaivism. Of more than ordinary interest is the work of Mādai Tiruvengaḍanāthar, an officer of the Nāyak of Madura at Kayattār in the Tinnevelly district about 1633. He undertook the exposition of Advaita Vedānta in a long Tamil poem and sought to excel Krishna Miśra who expounded the same system in the allegorical Sanskrit drama *Prabodha-Candrodaya*. The Tamil work also bears the name of its model and has an alternative name *Meyññānaviḷakkam* (exposition of true knowledge), with 48 cantos comprising 2,019 verses. Being a high official, Tiruvengaḍa patronized many poets. One of the latest works of Śaiva philosophy was *Ñānābharaṇa-viḷakkam*, a commentary on *Śiva-Ñāna-Śittiyār* by Veḷḷiyambala Tambirān (*c.* 1650), a disciple of the famous Kumaraguruparar. It is an extensive Bhāshya replete with citations from Āgamas of which the author also translated some into Tamil.

The philosophical and religious literature of Vaishnavism during this period as in the last comprises mostly Sanskrit works. There was very little writing in Tamil other than commentaries and subcommentaries on the canonical hymns and a class of esoteric theological works called Rahasyas (secrets), of which it is not easy to gather an authentic account. The commentaries adopted the *maṇipravāla* style. Piḷḷai Lōkācārya, author of eighteen Rahasya works, and his pupil and younger brother Aḻagiya Maṇavāḷaperumāḷ Nāyanār, author of more Rahasyas and commentaries on parts of the canon, came very early in the period and belonged to the first decades of the thirteenth century. Vedānta Dēśika, an eminent divine and prolific writer in Sanskrit, was also the author of a number of Tamil works like *Mummaṇik-kōvai*, *Navaratnamālai*, *Arthapañcakam* and *Aḍaikkalappattu*. His son and pupil Nayinār Ācāriyār wrote a poem in praise of his father and *guru* in twenty verses known as *Piḷḷaiyandādi*, and other works of theology and polemics; both father and son were keen controversialists and travelled incessantly to hold religious disputations. Tiruvāymoḻi Piḷḷai (1307) wrote commentaries on the hymns of Periyāḻvār and on *Śri-vacanabhūshaṇa*, one of Piḷḷai Lōkācārya's eighteen Rahasyas; Maṇavāḷa Mahāmuni (1370), pupil of Tiruvāymoḻi Piḷḷai, wrote commentaries on many canonical works and on the *Rāmānuja-nūṟṟandādi*; he is held in the highest esteem by one section of the Vaishnavas, the Tengalais (southern branch).

A considerable part of the religious and philosophical literature of the age took the form of Purāṇas, some of which have been named already. Other prominent works in the same class may now be noticed. The *Kōyiṟpurāṇam* of Umāpati-śivācārya is among the earliest of the Sthalapurāṇas and narrates the legends of the celebrated Śaiva shrine in Chidambaram; it follows the Kāvya style and ranks fairly high as literature. There is also a *Cidambara-purāṇam* (1508) by Purāṇa Tirumalaināthan, who also wrote the *Cokkanāthar-ulā* in praise of the deity of Madura. More popular in its diction and content is the *Ariccandira-purā-ṇam* (1524) of Nallūr Vīrakavirāyar which sets forth the trials which Hariścandra had to endure on account of his devotion to truth. The work comprises twelve sections and 1,225 easy-flowing verses; the poet is said to have been a goldsmith of Nallūr in Ramnad district. We may next mention three large works on the sixty-four sacred sports of Śiva at Madura. The *Sundara-pāṇḍiyam* of Anadāri was composed at the request of Tiruvirun-dān, a general of Vīrappa Nāyaka (1572-95) of Madura; the poem is a translation and bears the name of its Sanskrit original; only a fragment of over 2,000 verses has survived. Two other poems, both called *Tiruviḷaiyāḍal*, also handle the same theme with many variations; the shorter one was by Perumbaṟṟappuliyūr-nambi who has been assigned on rather slender grounds to the thirteenth century, but might have lived much later; the larger version (purporting to give the names of the Pāndya kings in whose reigns each of the sports took place) was by Parañjōti of Vēdāraṇyam, perhaps written at the beginning of the seventeenth century. The *Kandapurāṇam* of Kacciyappa Śivācārya (1625) closely follows Kamban's poetry as a model and is based on a section of the Sanskrit *Skandapurāṇa*. The last section of this book was completed by a pupil of the author, Ñānavarōdaya Paṇḍāram. The work comprises over 13,000 verses including 2,600 at the end by the pupil. Among minor Sthalapurāṇas composed towards the close of our period may be mentioned: *Vriddhācalapurāṇam* of Ñānak-kūttar, a pupil of Tuṟaiyūr Śivaprakāśa; *Tiruvāñjiya-purāṇam* of Kaḷandaikkumaran (1616); the Purāṇas on Kumbakonam, Vedāraṇyam and Tirukkānappēr by Aghōra Munivar, who had for his pupil the celebrated grammarian Vaidyanātha Dēśikar; and the *Paḷanit-tala-purāṇam* (1628) of Bālasubramanya Kavirāyar, a native of Paḷani. There are two versions of the *Bhāgavatam* in Tamil, by Śevvaiccūḍuvār of Vēmbaṟṟūr in the Madura district and by Varadarāja Aiyangar of Nellinagar (1543); the former is the earlier and better work.

In secular literature, the *Tañjai-vāṇan-kōvai* of Poyyāmoḻi of Vañji comes first. The Vāṇan of Tañjai, the hero of the poem, is described as 'the eye of the Pāndya who conquered the *malai-nāḍu*.' This must be a reference to Māṟavarman Kulaśekhara I (1260-1308) especially as the *kōvai* illustrates systematically the rules of the *Nambi Ahapporuḷ*, a work on grammar composed and published by Nāṟkavirājanambi under Kulaśekhara. Tañjai, the residence of the Bāna hero of the *kōvai*, is modern Tañjākkūr near Madura. The *Naḷaveṇbā* of Pugaḻēndi is an easy and moving narration of the tragic story of Nala and Damayanti; nothing authentic is known of the author except that he was patronized by a chieftain named Chandran Suvarkki, ruler of Muḷḷūr in Maḷḷuva-nāḍ; he certainly came after Kamban and the popular stories that connect him with Oṭṭakkūttan and Auvaiyār deserve no credence. The *Bhāratam* of Villiputtūrar (*c.* 1400) is a poem of great merit which tells the entire story of the Great Bhārata War in 4,350 well-turned verses. The narrative style of the author and his rich diction marked by a profuse admixture of Sanskrit words and expressions make the poem very attractive reading. The author was patronized by a certain Varapati Āṭkoṇḍān of the Kongar family. Contemporary with Villiputtūrar were the two brothers, one lame and the other blind, known as Iraṭṭaippulavar (twin poets), authors of *Ēkāmra-nādar-ulā* and two *kalambakams*; in the Ulā which celebrates the Śaiva shrine of Kānchī they refer to Mallināthan Rājanārāyana Śambuvarāyan (1350), the last of the Śengēṇi chieftains of North Arcot and Chingleput districts.

An Ulā on another famous Śaiva shrine, that of Tiruvānaikkā on the island of Śrīrangam, was the work of Kālamegham, the accredited author of many witty verses besides; he was supported by Sāluva Tirumalairāja, the son of Goppaya, and ruler of the Chola country under Vijayanagar in the middle of the fifteenth century. Śaiva Ellappa Nāvalar, a *veḷḷāla* poet of the Tanjore district, flourished in the sixteenth century (*c.* 1542-80), and wrote an excellent *kōvai* on Tiruvārūr (496 verses), besides *Aruṇaiandādi* and *Aruṇācalapurāṇam*, both on the shrine of Tiruvaṇṇāmalai, and *Tiruviriñjaipurāṇam*; he also wrote a commentary on the Tamil *Soundaryalahari*, a translation by Vīrai Kavirājapanditar.

About the same time the Pāndyan king Ativīrarāma of Tenkāśi (*c.* 1564) achieved literary distinction by his *Naiḍadam* with its twelve *paḍalams* and 1,172 verses written in high style and full of conceits not always pleasing to a modern reader, but held in high esteem by pandits; it contains many echoes of phrases and sentiments from older classics like the *Jīvakacintāmaṇi* and the *Rāmāyaṇam* of Kamban. Easier in their style are the same royal poet's translations from Sanskrit originals—the *Kāśikaṇḍam* and *Kūrmapurāṇam*; and the small book on morals known as *Veṟṟivēṟkai* or *Naṟundogai* is simple enough to be followed by children, for whom it is meant. A contemporary of this royal author was Śērai Kavirājapiḷḷai who wrote *Tirukkāḷatti-nādar-kaṭṭaḷaikkalitturai-mālai* on the deity of Kālahasti at the request of the king; other works of Kavirājapiḷḷai were *Tirukkāḷatti-nādar-ulā*, *Tiruvaṇṇāmalaiyār-vaṇṇam*, *Śēyūr-Murugan-ulā* and *Rattinagiri-ulā*. All the poems are marked by elegant diction and deep religious feeling. Varatungarāma Pāndya, a cousin of Ativīrarāma, was also a litterateur with varied interests; his three *andādis* on the Śiva shrine at Karuvai, i.e. Karivalam-vandanallur in Tinnevelly district, take high rank as pure literature; one of them employs ten metres and is called *Padiṟṟuppattandādi*; and the others are known from their metres as *Veṇbāvandādi* and *Kalitturai-andādi*. His *Piramōttirakaṇḍam* is a theological poem in twelve *adhyāyas* of 1,310 verses on religious subjects. He also translated into Tamil the work on erotics known as *Kokkoha* after the name of the composer of the Sanskrit original. In the first half of the seventeenth century, Kandasāmi Pulavar (1621) of Tiruppūvaṇam wrote an Ulā on the local Śaiva shrine and a Purāṇa on Tiruvāppanūr. More famous was Andakakkavi Vīrarāghava Mudaliyār, pupil of Kacciyappaśiva who wrote the *Kandapurāṇam* and was the author of a Purāṇa and an Ulā on Tirukkaḻukkunṟam, an Ulā on Tiruvārūr and other works of the same type; he also wrote some poems no longer extant in praise of patrons and rulers, such as a *piḷḷaittamiḻ* on Vittinar Ammaiyappan of Śēyūr, a *vaṇṇam* on Pararājasinghan of Ceylon and an Ulā on the ruler of Kayattār, i.e. Mādai Tiruvengaḍanāthar mentioned above as the author of *Prabōdacandrōdayam*.

Other famous authors of the period of Tirumalai Nāyaka were Kumaragurupara and Tuṟaimangalam Śivaprakāśar. The former was born at Śrīvaikuṇṭham, had his initiation at the hands of Māśilāmaṇi Dēśika—the fourth in succession to the headship of the *maṭha* at Dharmapuram—and spent a good part of his life in Northern India conducting disputations with rival sectarians including Muslims. He is said to have performed miracles, met the Mughal emperor and received from him a gift of land in Benares for the erection of a temple and a *maṭha*. Born a mute, he gained the power of speech in his sixth year by the grace of the deity of Tiruccendūr and celebrated him in his first poem *Kandar-kali-veṇbā*. His other literary productions included *Kayilaikkalambakam* on the deity (Śiva) of his birthplace which was also called Kailāsam; a *piḷḷaittamiḻ*, and *iraṭṭaimaṇi-mālai* on the goddess Mīnākshī of Madura; *Maduraikkalambakam*, a work of 102 stanzas celebrating Chokkalinga (Śiva), the deity of Madura, and his sports; *Tiruvārūr-nānmaṇi-mālai*, forty verses in four metres on Tyāgarāja (Śiva) of Tiruvārūr; a *piḷḷaittamiḻ* on Muttukumarasvāmi (Muruga) of Vaidīśvarankōvil; *Kāśikkalambakam* and other devotional works. His *Sakalakalā-valli-mālai*, in praise of Sarasvatī, the goddess of learning, in ten verses, is said to have been composed during his residence at Benares for gaining proficiency in Hindustani to meet and converse with the emperor of Delhi. He also wrote *Cidambaracceyyuṭkōvai*, a work on Tamil prosody, which defines and illustrates the different metres; and the *Nītineṟiviḷakkam*, comprising 102 *veṉbās* on ethical conduct, written at the request of Tirumalai Nāyaka who asked for an abstract of the contents of the *Kuṟaḷ* for his guidance.

Śivaprakāśar is associated with Tuṟaimangalam as he accepted the friendship and patronage of Aṇṇāmalai Reddi of that place. Born in Kānchipuram, Śivaprakāśar had his education under Veḷḷiyambalavāṇa Tambirān of Tinnevelly; he spent some time with Aṇṇāmalai Reddi both on his way to Tinnevelly and back; patron and protégé were alike Vīra-śaivas by persuasion, but the poet at any rate was no fanatic, as among his thirty works there are many that show his deep knowledge of and regard for the philosophy of Śaiva-siddhānta and for the four Samayācāryas of Tamil Śaivism and their works. He is said to have met a Christian missionary for a disputation, (this could not have been Father Beschi as is often stated), and to have composed a polemic refuting the Christian creed—*Ēśumada-nirākaraṇam*, no longer extant. Besides devotional poems on the deities of Tiruccendūr, Tiruvengai (near Tuṟaimangalam), Tiruvaṇṇāmalai and other places, he wrote the *Prabhulinga-līlai*, a translation from a Kannada original on the sports of Allamadēva, an incarnation of Śiva honoured of the Vīra-śaivas; it is a long poem in 25 sections containing 1,157 stanzas. It bears the date 1652. Other notable works of the author are: *Siddhāntaśikhāmaṇi*, a Vīra-śaiva manual, translated from Sanskrit; *Vedānta-cūḍāmaṇi*, a translation of a Kannada version of a portion of *Vivekacūḍāmaṇi* of Śankarācārya; *Tarukkaparipāḍai*, a translation of the Sanskrit manual *Tarkaparibhāshā*; and *Nanneṟi*, a short work on ethics in forty *veṇbās*. Śivaprakāśar remained a bachelor to his death at the early age of thirty-two.

To the first half of the fifteenth century has been assigned an important anthology, *Puṟattiraṭṭu*, which followed the *Kuṟal* in the selection and arrangement of topics and sections, and brought together perhaps 2,000 verses and more from all works in the language to the date of the anthology; no work later than Kamban's seems to have found a place in it. Its last part, on Love, has not been recovered except in an abstract of 65 poems. Many poems no longer accessible were known to the anonymous compiler of the anthology.

Among works of grammar composed in this period, after *Nambi Ahapporuḷ*, already mentioned, we have the *Cidambarappāṭṭiyal* by

Parañjōti, the son of Tirumalai-nāthan (1508) of the *Cidambara-purāṇam*; the *pāṭṭiyal* explains the conventions governing the composition of different types of Prabandhas. Another work on the same subject was the *Navanītappāṭṭiyal* of Navanīta-naṭan which has evoked a very valuable commentary. Next may be placed a fragmentary and anonymous work based on the *Kaḷaviyal* or *Ahapporuḷ* of Iṟaiyanār, and named *Kaḷaviyaṟ-kārigai* for that reason by the editor of this precious fragment, Mr S. Vaiyapuri; the work, more particularly its commentary, is valuable for its numerous citations from many otherwise unknown authors and works. *Māṟan-Alankāram* by Kurugai Perumāl Kavirāyar (*c.* 1575) is a work on rhetoric which cites many earlier writers and incidentally celebrates Māṟan, i.e. Nammāḻvār. The author wrote also the *Tirukkurugā-mānmiyam*, a *sthalapurāṇam* on Āḻvār-Tirunagari, the birthplace of Nammāḻvār. The *Ilakkaṇaviḷak-kam* of Vaidyanātha Dēśikar of Tiruvārūr belongs to the first half of the seventeenth century and is rightly celebrated as *Kuṭṭit-Tolkāppiyam*, as it is like the *Tolkāppiyam*, a complete exposition of the entire range of Tamil grammar. It is said to have grown out of the lessons given by the author to the children of Mādai Tiruvengaḍanāthar, already noticed as ruler of Kayattār under Tirumalai Nāyaka. Dēśikar also composed devotional works like *Pāśavadaip-paraṇi* and the extensive *Nallūrp-purāṇam* of over 1,000 verses.

The period 1200-1650 was also the age of many celebrated commentators whose work is important enough to find a place even in a short sketch of Tamil literary history. The dates of many of them cannot be ascertained accurately though there is good reason to assign all of them to this period. The commentaries of Mayilaināthar on *Nannūl* and of Perundēvanār on *Vīra-śōḻiyam*, both works of grammar, were among the earliest. Then came the gloss of Aḍiyārkkunallār on *Śilappadikāram*, a very learned and eloquent commentary remarkable for its extensive and instructive citations from numerous old works now lost. Śēnāvaraiyar on the *śol* section of *Tolkāppiyam* and Parimēlaḻagar on *Kuṟaḷ* may be placed next. The latter's comment on *Kuṟaḷ*, now recognized as the best, is said to have been preceded by nine other commentaries; however that may be, Parimēlaḻagar is at once learned, concise and clear; he often traces the ideas of the *Kuṟaḷ* to their sources in Sanskrit or helps one to do so.

He is said to have been a native of Madura, and is therefore probably different from the homonymous annotator of *Paripāḍal* who belonged to Kānchī and was a Vaishnava by faith. Pērāśiriyar and Naccinārkkiniyar were other great commentators. The former elucidated *Tolkāppiyam* and 380 out of the 400 poems in the *Kuṟundogai*, a Śangam anthology. The latter completed the gloss on *Kuṟundogai*, and also annotated the *Tolkāppiyam*, *Pattuppāṭṭu*, *Kalittogai* and *Jīvakacintāmaṇi*. The anonymous commentaries on the Śangam anthologies of *Puṟa-nānūṟu*, *Padiṟṟuppattu* and *Ainguṟunūṟu* must also have been written some time in this period. So also the commentary on *Puṟapporuḷveṇbāmālai* by Chāmuṇḍi-dēvanāyakan. Tirumēnik-kavirāyar, born in Tentiruppērai in Tinnevelly district, was a contemporary of Tirumalai Nāyaka; he wrote a commentary on *Māṟan-Alankāram*, and a prose abstract of the *Kuṟaḷ* known as *Tirukkuṟaḷ-nuṇ-poruḷmālai*; a similar work based on *Tolkāppiyam* attributed to him is not now available. The importance of the commentaries is twofold; they are almost the only considerable prose works in Tamil; and they mention many authors, works and historical and social facts that we have no other means of knowing.

In lexicography, the most popular lexicon *Nigaṇḍu-cūḍāmaṇi* was composed by a Jaina author by name Mandalapurusha, most probably in the reign of Krishna Rāya whose name figures prominently in the lexicon, but he may be either a Rāshtrakūta ruler or the better known Rāya of Vijayanagar. The work follows the scheme of *Divākaram*, but is written in verse instead of in the form of Sūtras. Then came the *Agarādi-nigaṇḍu* (1594) of Chidambara Rēvaṇa Siddar, a Vīra-śaiva, the first to attempt an alphabetical arrangement of the words treated; the first word (*agarādi*) in the name of the work meaning 'alphabetic order' has since come to mean a dictionary. The *Kayādaram* (*c.* 1550) of a Brahmin author, Kayādarar by name, cited in *Māṟan-Alankā-ram*, and the *Uriccolnigaṇḍu*, a short lexicon by a certain Śaiva author named Gāngēyan (early seventeenth century), are also worth noting.

Tamiḻākara-munivan of Tinnevelly set forth portions of religious law from Sanskrit in two Tamil works called *Prāyaccitta-samuccayam* (1633) and *Āśaucadīpikai*; their names show that they dealt respectively with penances for sin and pollution due to death. He also wrote other works like *Nītisāram* and *Nellaiti-ruppaṇi-mālai*. Much more interesting is the anonymous ballad *Rāmappayyan-ammānai*, giving an account of the wars of a general of Tirumalai Nāyaka, which belongs to a class of works of which few specimens have survived.

KANNADA

Among South Indian languages, after Tamil, Kannada possesses the oldest literature. Its beginnings are not clearly traceable, but a considerable volume of prose and poetry must have come into existence before the date of Nripatunga's *Kavirājamārga* (850), the earliest extant work on rhetoric in Kannada. In that work the Kannada country is said to have extended from the Kaveri to the Godāvari, and thus included much territory in the north where now Marathi is the spoken language. The district round about Puḷigere was held to be the well of pure Kannada undefiled. Durvinīta, mentioned in the same book as one of the best writers of Kannada prose, might well have been the Ganga monarch of the sixth century. Another early writer was the celebrated Śrīvardhadeva, also called Tumubulūrācārya from the place of his birth; his *Cūḍāmaṇi*, a commentary on the *Tattvārtha-mahāśāstra*, in 96,000 verses, was known to the great Kannada grammarian Bhaṭṭākaḷanka (1604) who calls it the greatest work in the language. Another writer of this early period (*c*. 650) was Śyāmakundācārya. Both these *ācāryas*, like most early Kannada writers, were Jains.

The *Kavirājamārga* is based in part on Dandin's *Kāvyādarśa*, and must have been inspired if not actually composed by the Rāshtrakūta emperor Nripatunga Amoghavarsha I, its ostensible author. But the first extant work of real literature is the *Vaḍḍārādhane* of Śivakōṭi (*c*, A.D. 900), a prose work on the lives of the older Jaina saints, written mostly in the oldest Kannada style called *pūrvahaḷa-kannaḍa*. Then we have Pampa, who came of a family from Vengi and flourished in the court of a feudatory of Rāshtrakūta Krishna III, Arikesari II of Vemulavāḍa. Pampa is said to have composed two great poems at the relatively early age of thirty-nine (941). His *Ādipurāṇa* narrates the life-story of the first Jaina Tīrthankara; the other work, *Vikramārjuna Vijaya*, contains the author's own version of the Mahābhārata story, and is called *Pampa-Bhārata* on that account; the poet makes Arjuna the hero of the poem and identifies him with his patron Arikesari and introduces into the narrative many interesting details of contemporary history. Critics have unanimously hailed Pampa as the most eminent among Kannada poets. Pampa's junior contemporary was Ponna whose principal work is the *Śāntipurāṇa*, the legendary history of the sixteenth Tīrthankara. He wrote also the *Bhuvanai-karāmābhyudaya* now known only from citations in later works, and the *Jīnāksharamāle*, 'an acrostic poem in praise of the Jinas'. His family also had its origin in Vengi. He got the title Ubhayakavicakravarti, 'supreme poet in two languages' (Sanskrit and Kannada) from Krishna III.

Ranna, who, with Pampa and Ponna, completes 'the Three Gems' who usher in Kannada literature in full panoply, adorned the court of the Chālukya king Taila II and his successor. Born in 949 of a family of bangle-sellers in Muduvoḷal, Ranna rose to the rank of Kavicakravarti (poet-laureate) in the Chālukya court and enjoyed the honours of the golden rod, *chauri*, elephant and umbrella. His *Ajitapurāṇa* (993) is a Campū in twelve *āśvāsas* on the life of the second Tīrthankara. The poem was written at the request of Attimabbe, the pious wife of general Nāgavarma, who survived her husband for some years and promoted the cause of Jainism in many ways. The *Sāhasabhīmavijaya* or *Gadāyuddha* (982) is also a Campū of ten *āśvāsas* which reviews the story of the *Mahābhārata* with particular reference to the last fight with clubs (*gadā*) between Bhīma and Duryodhana, as well as the wars and achievements of Iṟivabeḍanga Satyāśraya on whom the poet confers the title Sāhasa-bhīma ('daring Bhīma'). Two other works of Ranna—*Paraśurāma-carita* and *Cakreśvara-carita* are no longer extant; and a lexicon *Ranna Kanda* in which the verses generally end with *kaviratna* may well be his production also.

Chāvundarāya, one of Ranna's early patrons, was a feudatory of Ganga Rācamalla IV who conferred on him the title Rāya for his having set up the colossus of Gommaṭēśvara at Śravana Belgola. He composed in 978 the *Cāvuṇḍarāya-purāṇa* or *Trishashṭilakshaṇamahāpurāṇa*, one of the earliest extant prose works in Kannada, treating of the legends of twenty-four Tīrthankaras, twelve Cakravartis, nine Balabhadras, nine Nārāyanas and nine Pratinārāyanas, sixty-three in all. Nāgavarma I was another protégé of Chāvundarāya, and, like him, a pupil of Ajitasena. He came of a Brahmin family which like Pampa's came from the

Vengi country. His *Chandombudhi*, 'ocean of prosody', addressed by the author to his wife, is the earliest work on the subject in Kannada. The *Karnāṭaka-Kādambari* is a Campū based on Bāna's prose romance in Sanskrit; its sweet and flowing style is valued highly by critics.

The next writer of note was Durgasimha, a Brahmin Śaiva minister under Jayasimha II Jagadekamalla; his *Pañcatantra* is a Campū professedly based on Guṇāḍhya's *Brihatkathā*; it is a learned work perhaps too full of sound jingles (*prāsa*) to suit modern taste. Durgasimha mentions many of his predecessors and contemporaries. Among the latter was Chandrarāja, a Brahmin polyhistor of the Vājigotra, whose *Madanatilaka*, a Campū in eighteen *adhikaraṇas*, is a work on erotics in the form of a dialogue between his patron and his wife; the author claims that he has used the most modern language of his time (*posa-kannaḍa*). Another Brahmin Advaita Śaiva protégé of Jayasimha was Chāvuṇḍarāya, author of *Lokopakāra* (A.D. 1025), a guide to daily life, a cyclopaedic miscellany in good verse on various subjects such as astronomy and astrology, sculpture, construction of buildings, omens, divination of water, medicinal herbs and their uses, scents, cookery and toxicology. Śrīdharācārya, a Jaina Brahmin, showed his capacity for scientific writing (*śāstrakavitva*) in his *Jātaka-tilaka* (1049), the earliest work on astrology in Kannada, and his capacity in belles lettres (*kāvya kavitva*) in his *Candraprabhacarite*, no longer extant. The Advaiti Nāgavarmācārya, patronized by Ganga Udayāditya (1070), a feudatory of Someśvara II at Banavase, was the author of *Candracūḍāmaṇiśataka*, a centum of easy verses in *mattebha* metre on the ethics of renunciation.

The next great writer was Nāgachandra (*c.* 1105), a Jain and a man of means who built the Mallinātha Jinālaya dedicated to the nineteenth Tīrthankara at Bijapur and also wrote the *Mallināthapurāṇa*, a Campū. But Nāgachandra is best known for his *Rāmacandra-caritapurāṇa* which gives the Jaina version of the Rāma legend in a Campū of sixteen sections, the story proper beginning only with the third. The poem was a necessary complement to the *Bhārata* of Pampa, and earned for its author the title Abhinava (new) Pampa. The story differs in many ways from Vālmīki's; Rāma gets the *Jinadīkshā*, becomes a Jaina ascetic and attains *Nirvāṇa* at the end. To the first quarter of the twelfth century belong also a Jaina polemic *Samayaparīkshe* of Brahmaśiva which seeks to establish the superiority of Jainism over all other creeds, and the *Gōvaidya* of Kīrttivarma, a work on veterinary science, half-medicine and half-magic. Round about 1145, Karṇapārya wrote the life of the twenty-second Tīrthankara in his *Nēmināthapurāṇa*, a Campū in fourteen *āśvāsas* in which the story of Krishna and the *Mahābhārata* are also cleverly worked in. To the same time belongs Nāgavarma II, the author of *Kāvyāvalōkana*, an important work on the grammar and rhetoric of Kannada in five sections; it takes the form of Sūtras in verse illustrated by examples from literature. Another work of Nāgavarma on grammar is the *Karnāṭakabhāshābhūshaṇa*; here the Sūtras and a short explanation are both in Sanskrit, while the illustrations come from Kannada literature. The *Vāstukōśa*, a third work of Nāgavarma II, is a relatively short lexicon of 800 *granthas*, giving Kannada equivalents of Sanskrit terms. Nāgavarma was *Kaṭakopādhyāya* (camp-teacher) under Jagadekamalla II whom he survived for many years, becoming the teacher of the poet Janna (*c.* 1209). *Udayādityālankāra* (*c.* 1150) is a short work on the art of poetry based on Dandin's *Kāvyādarśa* by a Chola prince whose name it bears. A work on medicine, Pūjyapāda's *Kalyāṇakāraka*, was translated from Sanskrit into Kannada at this time by a Jaina author Jagaddala Sōmanātha; 'the treatment it prescribes is entirely vegetarian and non-alcoholic.' Rājāditya (1190), a Jain of Pūvinabāge, showed great skill in reducing to easy verse the mathematical subjects he dealt with in several *gaṇita* works like *Vyavahāra-gaṇita*, *Kshetragaṇita* and *Līlāvatī*.

Most of the writers so far mentioned were Jains, and it may be well to continue and complete the account of Jaina authors before turning to those of the two other classes, Vīra-śaivas and Vaishnavas, who began to influence Kannada literature from the twelfth and fifteenth centuries respectively.

Jaina writers continued to flourish under the later Hoysalas, and the lives of the Tīrthankaras formed the theme of many Purāṇas in the form of Campūs. Nemichandra, court-poet under Vīra Ballāla, wrote the *Līlāvatī*, a plain romance with Banavase as its scene of action, where a prince and princess dream of each other, meet after delays, and are wedded to live happily for ever. Nemichandra undertook to write the *Nemināthapurāṇa*, at the instance of Ballāla's minister, but died before completing it, and the work came to be known as *Ardha Nemi*, 'unfinished (life of) Nemi'. Janna was not only a poet but a minister and a builder of temples; he wrote the *Yaśodharacarite* (1209), the story of a king who was about to sacrifice two boys to Māriamma, but on hearing their story gave up the idea, released them and abandoned the practice of sacrificing live victims. The *Anantanāthapurāṇa* (1230) on the life of the fourteenth Tīrthankara was also his work; his style is noted for its dignity and grace. Bandhuvarma, a *vaiśya*, wrote the *Harivamśābhyudaya* and *Jīva Sambodhana*. The latter is a work on morals and renunciation in the form of an address to the soul. A new form of composition, *sāngatya*, meant to be sung to the accompaniment of a musical instrument, was introduced by Śiśumāyaṇa (*c*. 1232) who wrote two works in this style—*Añjanācarita* and *Tripura-dahana*; the latter is an allegorical poem on the destruction of the triple fortress of Birth, Decay and Death. Āṇḍayya's *Madana Vijaya* (Triumph of Cupid), composed about 1235, is remarkable for its total avoidance of assimilated Sanskrit words (*tatsamas*), limiting itself to indigenous (*dēśya*) and naturalized Sanskrit (*tadbhava*) words; the experiment was not continued by later authors. The story of the poem is that Śiva imprisoned the moon, and Cupid, in his anger, assailed Śiva with his arrows and was cursed by him to be separated from his bride; he contrived, however, to free himself of the curse and rejoin his bride. The work is known by other names—*Kāvana Gella* ('Victory of Kāma'), *Kabbigara Kāva* ('Poets' Defender'), and *Śobagina Suggi* ('Harvest of Beauty'). A brother-in-law of Janna was Mallikārjuna (*c*. 1245), an ascetic who compiled an anthology *Sūkti-sudhārṇava*, which arranges extracts from many works under eighteen topical headings, of which only fifteen have yet been found. Keśirāja (*c*. 1260) the son of Mallikārjuna, was the author of *Śabdamaṇidarpaṇa* ('Mirror of Word-jewels'), the standard grammar of Kannada. The rules are set forth in *kanda* metre and followed by a prose commentary by the author himself; like other works of its class it refers to the usage of writers of repute and is of high scientific and historical value to the student of the language. Kumudendu (*c*. 1275) wrote a *Rāmāyaṇa* according to Jaina tradition in *shaṭpadi* metre; the work was largely influenced by the *Pampa Rāmāyaṇa* already noticed. Other works of note produced under the Hoysalas were: *Raṭṭa-Mālā* or *Raṭṭasūtra* (*c*. 1300) of Raṭṭa-kavi, treating of 'natural phenomena such as rain, earthquakes, lightning, planets and omens'; *Puṇyāsrava* (*c.* 1331) of Nāgarāja, a Campū containing fifty-two tales of Purāṇic heroes said to be translated from Sanskrit for the guidance of house-holders; and a work on toxicology, *Khagēndra-maṇi-darpaṇa* (*c.* 1360), by Mangarāja I.

In the Age of Vijayanagar (1336-1650) the Jains were being steadily pushed out by the rising influence of Śaivas of different schools and Vaishnavas; yet they continued to write in Kannada on the lives of Tīrthankaras and other holy persons. Madhura (1385), patronized by ministers of Harihara II and Devarāya I, wrote *Dharmanāthapurāṇa* on the fifteenth Tīrthankara and a short poem in praise of Gommaṭēśvara of Śravana Belgola; his style resembled that of the earlier Jaina poets. There was also Vritta Vilāsa, author of *Dharmaparīkshe*, a Kannada version of a Sanskrit original of the same name by Amitagati, and *Śāstrasāra*, both works of quasi-religious import. The life of Jīvandhararāja was a favourite subject and was handled three times over in *shaṭpadi* metre by Bhāskara of Penugonda (1424), Bommarasa of Teṟkaṇāmbi (*c.* 1485) and Koṭeśvara of Tuluvadeśa (*c.* 1500). Bāhubali of Śringeri (*c.* 1560) narrated the story of Nāga-Kumāra who despised riches and took to a religious life.

Jainism flourished in the Tuluva country more than anywhere else in this period, when two colossal Jaina statues were erected—one at Kārkala in 1431 and the other at Yēnūr in 1603. Accordingly we have four authors from that country. First was Abhinava Vādi Vidyānanda of Gersoppa, an able champion of Jainism in public debates at Vijayanagar and many provincial capitals; in 1533 he compiled the *Kāvyasāra*, an anthology with forty-five different heads, similar to, but much more useful than, Mallikārjuna's *Sūkti-sudhārṇava*, as he gives the names of many of the poets of the period 900-1430. Sālva (*c.* 1550), court-poet of a petty prince of Konkan, produced a Jaina version of the *Bhārata*, in *shaṭpadi* in sixteen *parvas*; this was perhaps meant to be a rival to the *Krishṇa Rāya Bhārata* which had completed the Vaishnava version about 1510. Ratnākara-varni, a Kshatriya of Mudabidire, wrote a number of works; his *Trilōkasāra* (1557) is an account of Jaina cosmogony; the *Aparājita-śataka* treats of philosophy, morals and renunciation; the *Bharatēśvara-carita* gives the story of the legendary emperor Bharata, the son of the first Tīrthankara who turned Jaina ascetic. Many songs by this author are still current among Jains and are known as *Annagaḷapada*, 'songs of the brothers'. Nemanna's *Jñāna-bhāskara-carite* (1559) exalts meditation and study as means of emancipation above rites and austerities.

Lastly may be mentioned a poet of uncertain date assigned by some to *c.* 1400, Āyata-varma whose *Ratna-karaṇḍaka*, a Campū translated from Sanskrit, treats of 'the beliefs and duties of the Jains under the heads of the three Jaina "jewels"—right belief, right knowledge, and right conduct'.

After the Jains, the Vīra-śaivas did most for the development of Kannada language and literature; they wrote many religious works in Kannada and showed a decided preference for the prose medium. Basava and his contemporaries (twelfth century) brought into existence the Vacana literature in simple prose easily understood by the common folk and well calculated to popularize the new creed. There were over two hundred writers, many women among them, with Mahādēviyakka at their head. E. P. Rice characterizes their work thus: 'In form the Vacanas are brief disconnected paragraphs, each ending with one or another of the numerous local names under which Śiva is worshipped. In style they are epigrammatical, parallelistic and allusive. They dwell on the vanity of riches, the valuelessness of mere rites or book-learning, the uncertainty of life, and the spiritual privileges of the Śivabhakta. They call upon men to give up the desire for worldly wealth and ease, to live lives of sobriety and detachment from the world, and to turn to Śiva for refuge. They are seldom controversial, but almost entirely hortatory, devotional and expository. They are still recited by Lingāyat *ācāryas* for the instruction of their followers.' Some of the Vacanas have a section called *Kālajñāna*, a messianic forecast of the future, speaking of the arrival of an ideal king, Vīra Vasanta Rāya, who would rebuild Kalyāni and restore the Lingāyat religion to its full glory. The Vacanas often bear the *mudras* (marks in set phrases) of their authors.

Besides Basava himself, to whom six works of this type are attributed, and his nephew Chenna Basava, special mention must be made of two groups of highly honoured teachers and writers. First the 'three *paṇḍitas*'—Mañcanna known as Śivalenka (bodyguard of Śiva), Śrīpati Pandita, and Mallikārjuna Panditārādhya; and the 'five *ācāryas*'—Rēvaṇa Siddha or Rēṇukācārya of

Kollipāka, Maruḷa Siddha of Kollāpura, Panditārādhya just mentioned as one of the three *paṇḍitas*, Ekōrāmi Tande, and Viśvēśvarācārya. They were either contemporaries of Basava or lived a little before or after him.

This period forms a definite transition marked by some notable changes in Kannada language and literature. The letter *ḻa* tends to disappear giving place to *ḷa*, and *pa* in particular positions changes into *ha*. The Campū form of composition goes out of use, and new metres distinctive of Kannada like *shaṭpadi* and *tripadi*, verses with six and three lines respectively, and *ragaḷes*, lyrical poems with refrains, come into vogue.

We may now notice the chief Lingāyat writers other than the authors of Vacanas. The first is Harīśvara, who came of a family of Karanikas (accountants) of Halebid and was a contemporary of Hoysala Narasimha I (1152-73). He spent several years at Hampi, and among his works is *Pampāśataka*, a centum of verses in praise of Virūpāksha of Hampi. His *Girijā-kalyāṇa* is still in the old style of Jaina works, a Campū of ten sections on the marriage of Śiva and Pārvatī. His *Śiva-gaṇada-ragaḷegaḷu* has all the characteristics of the new school which starts with him; it treats of the lives of the sixty-three saints of early Śaivism, of Basava and other devotees. A nephew and disciple of Harīśvara was Rāghavānka, a native of Hampi, who was the first to use *shaṭpadi* metre. His *Hariścandra-kāvya*, though very good as poetry, contains several *dēśya* words and occasionally violates the strict rules of grammar. The *Sōmanātha-carite* giving the life of Somayya of Puḷigere, and the *Siddharāma-purāṇa* on the life of Siddharāma of Sonnalige are works of Lingāyat hagiology. The *Harihara-mahatva* is in praise of Harīśvara of Hampi. Other works attributed to him are *Vīreśvara-carita* and *Śarabha-caritra*. Kereya Padmarasa held office under Narasimha I and got his title by constructing the Belūr tank. He was called from his retirement to meet an itinerant Telugu Brahmin preacher of Vaishnavism who as the result of the contest had to accept the Śaiva creed. Padmarasa wrote the *Dīkshā-bodhe*, a work of *ragaḷes* in dialogue form in which a *guru* instructs his disciple in the faith, citing Sanskrit verses in support of the true doctrine. Padmarasa became the hero of a *Padmarājapurāṇa* written by one of his descendants (*c*. 1385). Though Rāghavānka and Padmarasa were contemporaries of Basava, neither of them makes any reference to him. Pālkuriki Sōmanātha born at Pālkuriki in the Godāvari district, was the author of several works on Vīra-śaivism in Telugu and Kannada. Legend credits him with victory in many contests with other sectarians, particularly Vaishnavas, and final *mukti* at Kailāsa. His life became the subject of a Purāṇa by Tōṇṭadārya (*c.* 1560). He was a great admirer of Basava and his Telugu *Basava-purāṇa* was used by Bhīmakavi (1369) when he wrote a Kannada work of the same name. Sōmanātha's chief works in Kannada are *Śīlasampādane*, *Sahasragaṇanāma*, and *Pañcaratna*, besides several *ragaḷes* and Vacanas. *Sōmēśvara-śataka*, a popular work on moral subjects, was perhaps the work of a contemporary and namesake of Sōmanātha from Puḷigere. Two works of romance belonging to this period are the *Kusumāvaḷi* of Deva-kavi (*c.* 1200) which resembles *Līlāvatī* of Nemichandra in its story, and *Śringārasāra* of Sōmarāja (1222), also called *Udbhaṭakāvya* as it has Udbhaṭa, a ruler of Gersoppa, for its hero.

The Lingāyat literature of the Vijayanagar period (1336-1650) falls under two heads—stories of reformers and devotees, and expositions of doctrine. The *Basava-purāṇa* of Bhīmakavi, an Ārādhya-Brahmin, completed in 1369, is an important and a very popular work on hagiology. Written in *shaṭpadi* metre, it treats of Basava as an incarnation of Nandi, specially sent to re-establish Vīra-śaiva faith on earth, and dwells at great length on the miracles performed by Basava in his life-time. Another account of Basava's life written about 1500 is *Mala-Basava-rāja-carita* of Singirāja, also known as *Singirājapurāṇa*, recounting the eighty-eight miracles of Basava and giving particulars of his opponents at Bijjala's court. Prabhulinga, also called Allama-prabhu, an associate of Basava, is the hero of *Prabhulinga-līle* of Chāmarasa, an Ārādhya-Brahmin poet of the court of (Praudha) Devarāya II (1422-46). Prabhulinga is here regarded as an incarnation of Ganapati, and Pārvatī is said to have taken the form of a princess of Banavase to test the strength of his detachment from the world. The work is said to have been read out to Devarāya who caused it to be translated into Telugu and Tamil. Chāmarasa held disputations with Vaishnavas in the king's presence and was a rival of Kumāra Vyāsa, the author of the Kannada *Bhārata*. Over a century later came Virūpāksha Pandita (1584), author of *Cenna-Basava-purāṇa*. The hero, Cenna Basava, is regarded as an incarnation of Śiva for the instruction of Siddharāma of Sonnalige in the entire Śaiva lore including stories of saints. The popular Purāṇa identifies the messianic Vīra Vasanta Rāya with the contemporary ruler Venkaṭapati Rāya of Vijayanagar, who, in some of his inscriptions styles himself 'Lord of Kalyānapura', though with little justification. There are also lives of many *ācāryas* and *purātanas* (elders). Panditārādhya and Rēvaṇa Siddha were the most popular among the *ācāryas*, and became heroes of many works.

In the literature of the doctrine, several works were produced under Devarāya II who had two zealous Lingāyat ministers. One was Lakkaṇṇa who wrote the *Śiva-tattva-cintāmaṇi*, a treatise on the tenets and rites of the sect. The other, Jakkanārya, not only wrote a work entitled *Nūrondusthala* (hundred and one topics), but liberally patronized other scholars like Kumārabanka-nātha and Mahālinga-deva. An eminent *guru* of the time was Guru Basava, author of seven works, *Sapta-kāvya*, six in *shaṭpadi* metre expounding aspects of the doctrine in the form of dialogues between teacher and pupil, and the *Avadhūtagīte*—'Songs in Praise of Detachment'. There were also one hundred and one teaching *jangamas* of whom several wrote Vacanas and works on the doctrine. Acute rivalry between Lingāyats and Vaishnavas led to 'organized processions through the town in honour of the books of their respective faiths'. Out of this rivalry also arose the *Prauḍharāya-carita* of Adriśya (*c.* 1595), stories of Śaiva saints narrated by Jakkanārya to Devarāya II to divert his mind from the Brahminical version of the *Bhārata*.

A famous teacher of the time of Virūpāksha (1465-85) was Tōṇṭada Siddheśvara or Siddalinga-yati, who practised Śiva-yoga for a long time in a garden and came to be known on that account as *tōṇṭada*, of the garden. A *maṭha* and a temple mark the place of his burial at Yediyūr, near Kunigal. He wrote a prose work of 700 Vacanas called *Shaṭsthala-Jñānāmrita*, and had many disciples who wrote similar works. Virakta Tōṇṭadārya (*c.* 1560) composed the *Siddheśvara-purāṇa* on the life of his teacher. Nijaguṇa-śiva-yogi, at first a petty ruler of the territory round Śambhulinga hill near Yelandur and afterwards Śiva-yogi, was a prolific writer who employed *tripadi*, *sāngatya*, *ragaḷe* and prose in his works. Notable among them are a commentary on the Sanskrit work *Śiva-yoga-pradīpika* meant for those who cannot read Sanskrit and desire emancipation, and

Viveka-cintāmaṇi, a cyclopaedia of 'Sanskrit terms and Vīra-śaiva lore'. Mallanārya of Gubbi lived in the reign of Krishnadeva Rāya (1509-29) and wrote both in Kannada and Sanskrit. His chief works in Kannada were: *Bhāva-cintāratna* (1513), said to be based on a Tamil work of Ñānasambandar; *Satyendra-chola-kathe*, the story of a Chola king to illustrate the power of the sacred *mantra* of five letters of the Śaivas; and *Vīraśaivāmrita* (1530), describing twenty-five sports of Śiva and giving the lives of the saints, old and new. Virūparāja (1519), author of a *sāngatya* work on the life of king Cheramānka, a *purātana*, and his son Vīrabhadra-rāja who wrote five *Śatakas* on Vīra-śaiva doctrine and morals were other writers of the period. Towards the close of it came Sarvajñamūrti whose *Sarvajñapadagaḷu* is in *tripadi* metre: about a thousand of these *padas* are current and treat of religion, morals and society, in much the same manner as the sayings of Vemana in Telugu or Nāmdev and Tukārām in Marathi. Like them he exalted sincerity in life above externals such as the worship of idols, pilgrimages and rituals.

The earliest writer of note on Vaishnava topics in Kannada was Rudra-bhaṭṭa, a *Smārta* Brahmin of the time of Vīra Ballāla (1173-1220). His *Jagannātha-vijaya* is a Campū on the life of Krishna up to his fight with Bānāsura and based on the *Vishṇu-purāṇa*. In 1281 Narahari-tīrtha, third in succession from Madhva, composed songs in praise of Vishnu. But the Vaishnava movement began to exert a strong influence on Kannada literature only from the time of Krishnadeva Rāya. And this new Vaishnava literature in the form of translations of Sanskrit classics also marks the transition from medieval to modern Kannada. The first ten *parvas* (sections) of the *Mahābhārata* had been translated by Nāraṇappa, a Brahmin author, who had the title Kumāra Vyāsa and was a rival of Chāmarasa in the reign of Devarāya II; his work, dedicated to the deity at Gadag, came to be known as *Gadugina Bhārata*. The remaining *parvas* were translated in 1510 by Timmaṇṇa who named his work after his patron *Krishṇa-rāya Bhārata*. Then followed the *Torave Rāmāyaṇa*, so called because it was produced in Torave in Sholapur district. This is the first brahminical version of the story in Kannada and the author was Narahari who calls himself Kumāra Vālmīki; his date is not quite settled. Mention must also be made of the *Jaimini Bhārata* of Lakshmīśa composed some time in the seventeenth century. A free rendering in *shaṭpadi* metre of a Sanskrit original ascribed to the legendary sage Jaimini, the work is 'esteemed alike by learned and unlearned, and universally studied'. The subject is the wanderings of the horse appointed for Yudhishthira's horse-sacrifice, and thus corresponds to a portion of the Aśvamedhaparva of the *Mahābhārata*, though there is no correspondence in details. The *Bhāgavata* found its translator in Cāṭu Viṭṭhalanātha who flourished under Krishnadeva Rāya and his successor Achyuta. He also wrote a fuller rendering of portions of the *Mahābhārata* which had been greatly abridged by Kumāra Vyāsa—the Pauloma and Āstika *parvas*. This was a great period not only for Kannada, but for other languages as well—Sanskrit, Telugu and Tamil. And not only Vaishnavas, but Lingāyats and Jains, were patronized by Krishnadeva Rāya and Achyuta.

Popular songs in *ragaḷe* metre by *dāsas* (mendicant singers) was another form of Vaishnava literature in Kannada in this period. These singers got their inspiration from Madhvācārya and Vyāsarāya, and the visit of Chaitanya to the South in 1510 did much to stimulate the growth of this popular type of song. Purandara Dāsa was 'the earliest, most prolific and most famous' of these singers; he visited Vijayanagar in the reign of Achyuta Rāya and died at Pandarpur in 1564; all his songs bear the imprint Purandara Viṭṭhala. Kanakadāsa of Kāginele in the Dharwar district was a contemporary of Purandara, who, like him, owed his adoption of a religious life to Vyāsarāya, head of the Madhva *maṭha* at Sosile, himself a composer of lyrics in praise of Krishna. Besides songs in praise of Vishnu, Kanakadāsa wrote *Mōhana Taranginī* ('River of Delight') narrating stories of Krishna in *sāngatya*, and two works in *shaṭpadi*—*Nala-carita* and *Hari-bhakti-sāra*, the latter being a popular book of morals for children. A little poem of Kanakadāsa called *Rāma-dhānya-caritre* exalts *rāgi*, the grain which above all other grains forms the staple food of a great part of Karnātaka. Kanakadāsa came of the caste of hunters (*bēḍa*) according to some accounts, and of shepherds (*kuruba*) according to others. There were many other *dāsas* besides.

This sketch of Kannada literature may close with the notice of some important works of the early seventeenth century. Most notable among them is the *Karnāṭaka Śabdānuśāsana* (1604) of Bhaṭṭākaḷanka Deva, the most comprehensive grammar of Kannada in 592 Sanskrit Sūtras with a gloss (*vritti*) and commentary (*vyākhyā*) in the same language. Its references to previous authorities and citations from leading Kannada writers are of value to the student of the history of the language. The author was a Jain and was reputed to be learned in six languages. The reconsecration of the Gommaṭa statue at Śravana Beḷgola in 1612 was described by poet Pañcabāna of that town in his *Bhujabali-caritra* (1614). The Kārkala image was rededicated in 1646 and its history and that of Gommaṭa form the subject of *Kārkaḷa-Gommaṭēśvara-caritra* of Chandrama of the Tuluva country. *Bijjala-rāja-caritra*, giving the Jaina version of Basava's life at Kalyāna, and *Jina-munitanaya* on Jaina morals are other works of the period.

Mention may also be made of collections of short stories the dates of which are not settled, but which came into existence about the sixteenth century—*Battīsa-puttali-kathe*, *Bētāla-pañca-vimśati-kathe* in the three forms of Campū, *tripadi* and prose, *Śuka-saptati*, and so on. *Tenāli-Rāmakrishṇa-kathe* is a collection of funny anecdotes of the famous court jester of the court of Krishnadeva Rāya.

TELUGU

In ancient times the Telugu country was often called Trilinga, the country which contained or was bounded by the three *lingas* of Kālahasti, Srīśailam and Dākshārāma, and Telinga-Telugu as the name of the country and language may well be traced to this word. It is also suggested that Tel(n)ugu comes from *tene*, 'honey' or *tennu*, 'way'. The beginnings of the language can be traced from stone inscriptions of the fifth and sixth century A.D., and its basic elements have unmistakable affinities with Tamil and Kannada. But, from the beginning, the literary idiom depended very largely upon Sanskrit and the *Janāśrayachandas*, an early work on prosody, fragments of which have recently come to light, though it includes some metres peculiar to Telugu and unknown to Sanskrit, is itself written in Sanskrit throughout; the author was most probably the Vishnukundin monarch Mādhavavarman II (580-620), who had the title Janāśraya. The inscriptions of the dynasty are in Sanskrit with an admixture of Prākrit and Telugu words.

In the beginning Telugu had much in common with Kannada and this affinity persisted to a relatively late stage in the development of the two languages. Pampa and Ponna, two of the greatest Kannada poets, came from the Telugu country, and the great Telugu poet Śrīnātha styles himself a poet in Karnāta-bhāshā. Early Telugu prose and verse can now be traced only in inscriptions like those of the Telugu-Chodas and the Eastern Chālukyas; a well-developed verse in *sīsa* metre adorns the grant of General Pānduranga (845-6). Beyond doubt there must have existed much unwritten literature of a popular character which enlivened the daily life of the common folk; such *dēśi* compositions may have included *lālipāṭalu* (songs of the cradle), *mēlukolupulu* (songs of the dawn), *mangala hāratulu* (songs of festivity), *kīrtanalu* (devotional songs) and *ūḍupu pāṭalu* (songs of the harvest).

Higher literature strongly influenced by Sanskrit was said to be in the *mārga* style. Of this class no work earlier than the eleventh century has survived. The beginnings and early history of this type of writing can no longer be traced. Some are inclined to doubt the existence of a separate *mārga* style altogether.

Telugu literature as we know it begins with Nannaya's translation of the *Mahābhārata* undertaken in the reign of Rājarāja Narendra (1019-61). Nannaya undertook the great work at the king's instance and had for his assistant a certain Nārāyana Bhaṭṭa, also a talented poet, who was rewarded richly by the monarch. Rājarāja's reign was a troubled time, and it is not known if the political troubles hampered the work of Nannaya. He was able to complete the translation of only two *parvas* (Ādi and Sabhā) and of a part of the third (Vana). The translation was not literal, and the poet allowed himself free scope for the exercise of his powers of imaginative creation; he set the model for later translators. Nannaya's vocabulary is dominated by Sanskrit, but he is never obscure; and the majesty of his diction induced Yeṟṟāpragaḍa, another translator of the *Mahābhārata*, to compare it to a noble elephant (*bhadragaja*). Nannaya was perhaps also author of *Āndhra-śabda-cintāmaṇi*, the first Telugu grammar which systematized the language by standardizing words and their usage and earned for the author the title *Vāganuśāsana*, law-giver of the language.

An eminent younger contemporary of Nannaya was Vēmulavāḍa Bhīma Kavi, associated by tradition with the Eastern Ganga emperor Anantavarman Chodaganga (1078-1148). He was the author of *Kavijanāśraya*, a Telugu grammar, and *Bhīmeśvara Purāṇa* relating legends of the shrine of Bhīmeśvara at Dākshārāma. He seems to have written also *Rāghava-Pāṇḍavīya*, giving the story of both the *Rāmāyaṇa* and *Mahābhārata* together, the whole book being a sustained *double entendre;* it is no longer extant. There is much uncertainty about the life and works of Bhīma Kavi who has become a centre of many myths and miracles.

From the twelfth century Vīra-śaivism became an important factor in the religious life of the Telugus and a sectarian outlook became more and more common. The poets of the period were generally supporters and propagandists of this faith. Famous among them was Mallikārjuna Pandita, *guru* of Nanne Choda; his *Śiva-tattva-sāram* is an exposition of Vīra-śaivism in about five hundred verses. Nanne Choda, a Telugu-Choda prince, son of Chodaballi of Pākanādu, was the author of *Kumārasambhava*, a Mahākāvya which has recently come to light; it is based on the Sanskrit works on the same theme by Kālidāsa and Udbhaṭa, and draws also upon the Śaiva literature known to the author. Nanne Choda employed Kannada and Tamil words in his poetry, and he had a partiality for Kannada metres. The author's style has not commanded universal praise. Atharvaṇa, the grammarian, considered Nanne Choda as a poet who courted death by using inauspicious metres. Pālkuriki Sōmanātha was a contemporary of Kākatīya Pratāparudra II (1291-1330). Sōmanātha was a staunch Lingāyat and a prolific writer in Sanskrit, Kannada and Telugu. He was an active pamphleteer and disputant in the cause of Vīra-śaivism. His major works in Telugu are *Paṇḍitārādhya Carita*, *Dvipada Basava Purāṇa* and *Anubhava Sāra*. The first was used by Śrīnātha when he wrote a work of the same name. Another *Basava Purāṇa* in Telugu verse was that of Piḍuparti Sōmanātha (1510). Pālkuriki Sōmanātha's *Vrishādhipa Śatakam*, a centum of verses addressed to Basava, became very popular.

The translation of the *Mahābhārata* was resumed by Tikkana (1220-1300), perhaps the greatest Telugu poet. He was a *niyogi* Brahmin of the court of Manumasiddhi, chief of Nellore and subordinate of Kākatīya Ganapati. The poet's grandfather was a minister and poet, and his father and cousin were renowned warriors. Tikkana himself was a successful courtier and diplomat, and on one occasion he secured Ganapati's aid for Manumasiddhi in regaining his throne. He performed a sacrifice and earned the title Somayāji. He commenced his translation with the Virāṭa *parva*, evidently because he did not wish to start where Nannaya's work had been so unhappily interrupted. Tikkana's translation is complete for the rest of the *Bhārata*. Many legends have grown up about Tikkana's prodigious learning and to account for his unfailing inspiration. His prologue was marked by originality, and it gave currency to certain conventions which have generally been adopted by his successors. He condemned incompetent poets and lavished praise on the true ones; he introduced a dream in which his grandfather delivered to him a message from Hari-hara-nātha asking that Tikkana's work should be dedicated to him; lastly he put in a hymn of praise with every word ending in the possessive case (*shashṭhyantamulu*). The first and last features are found in Nanne Choda's *Kumārasambhava* also. Tikkana's compact diction and his marvellous capacity for vivid portraiture and characterization earned for him the title Kavi Brahma. Before undertaking the translation of the *Bhārata*, Tikkana composed *Nirvacanōttara Rāmāyaṇa*, an all-verse work on the story of Rāma after his coronation; for some reason or other he left the last canto of this work to be completed later by another hand.

The gap in the Vana *parva* between Nannaya's and Tikkana's works was filled by Yeṟṟāpragaḍa (1280-1350). He was a *niyogi* Brahmin from Gudlur in the Nellore district, and his father, Śrī Sūrya, was a poet in Sanskrit and Telugu, and a *yogi*. Yeṟṟā-pragaḍa himself was a great devotee of Śiva and bore the title Śambhu-dāsa. He was attached to the court of Prolaya Vema Reddi. For fear of the possible evil consequences of continuing the ill-fated translation of Nannaya, he made it appear that his work was that of Nannaya himself by dedicating it to Rājarāja Narendra, Nannaya's patron. He says also that Tikkana appeared to him in a dream and urged him to complete the *Bhārata*. 'His ability as a poet is manifest from the fact that he begins his work in the style of Nannaya and, imperceptibly, passes into that of Tikkana.' He was called Prabandha Parameśvara. He also translated the *Harivamśa*, the epilogue to the *Bhārata* which traces the occurrences after the war. His other works are: *Rāmāyaṇa* (not extant), and *Lakshmī Nrisimha Purāṇa* also known as *Ahobala Māhātmya*.

The three translators of the *Mahābhārata* have always been held in the highest esteem as the '*Kavitraya*'—the three poets of Telugu, and subsequent authors generally began their writings by making obeisance to them.

A contemporary of Yeṟṟāpragaḍa was Nachana Soma (1355-77) who wrote the *Uttara Harivamśa* as he was dissatisfied with Yeṟṟāpragaḍa's achievement and wanted to produce a work worthy of the theme, and competent critics have held that the poet achieved his object.

The *Rāmāyaṇa* was translated by two poets of the thirteenth and fourteenth centuries. Kona Buddharāja, a feudatory of Kākatīya Pratāparudra II, produced the *Ranganātha Rāmāyaṇa* in *dvipada* metre, a work of great simplicity and sweetness and full of apt similes. Ranganātha's relation to the poem is by no means clear; either he was a court poet or possibly the *guru* of the king who dedicated the poem to him. Buddharāja's sons are said to have completed it by adding the *Uttara-Rāmāyaṇa.* The other translation is a Campū by Hullakki Bhāskara and his pupils dedicated to a Sāhinimāra, whose identity is not settled beyond dispute.

Among the contemporaries of Tikkana must be noticed Ketana, author of *Daśakumāracarita*, a translation of Dandin's work which got him the title 'Abhinava Dandi', of a grammar called *Āndhra-bhāshā-bhūshaṇa*, and of a translation of Vijñāneśvara's *Mitāksharā*; Mārana, a pupil of Tikkana, whose *Mārkaṇḍeya Purāṇa* became the basis of Peddana's *Manucaritra*; and Mañcana of Rajahmundry, author of *Kēyūrabāhucaritra.* Baddena, a Chola feudatory of Rudramadevi in the Shaṭsahasra country, wrote the *Nītiśāstra-muktāvali*, a treatise on politics in fifteen chapters, and probably also *Sumati Śataka*, a popular work of moral maxims.

Before proceeding to the next period, we must notice two works on mathematics, also translations from Sanskrit, which are the earliest scientific works in Telugu. Mallana (1060-70), a *niyogi* Brahmin *karṇam* of Pavalūr near Guntur, translated into verse a mathematical treatise of Mahāvīrācāryulu which contained chapters on mensuration, fractions and theory of numbers, among others. Eluganti Peddana translated the *Līlāvatī* of Bhāskara and called the work *Prakīrṇa Gaṇita*

The century and a half that followed 1350 may well be designated the age of Śrīnātha (1365-1440), held by some to be the greatest poet in the language. His great talents secured for him early in life the patronage of many chiefs and kings—the Reddis of Kondavīdu, the Velamas of Rājakonda, and Devarāya II of Vijayanagar. He moved on equal terms with them and their ministers, and enjoyed a full taste of the pleasures of life though in the end he died a poor man. His command of Sanskrit and Telugu was unrivalled, and he says that he wrote the *Marutrāṭ-caritra* as a boy and translated *Śālivāhana-sapta-śati* while yet in his teens; unfortunately neither has survived. His masterpiece was the translation of Śrī Harsha's *Naishadhakāvya* called *Śringāra Naishadha*, a majestic and stately poem in which all the great qualities of Śrīnātha's genius found full play. His other works were *Paṇḍitārādhya-carita*, *Śivarātrimāhātmya*, *Haravilāsa*, *Bhīmakhaṇḍa* and *Kāśikhaṇḍa*. Only the last four are available now and these show what a staunch Śaiva he was. Another work attributed to him is *Krīḍābhirāmam*, a drama which marked a new departure in Telugu and started the genre known as *vīthinā-ṭaka* in which one person narrates his experiences in the streets of Wārangal to another who is only a listener. *Śringāra-dīpika*, a work of poetics, purports to be the composition of Kumāragiri Reddi but is held by some to be the work of Śrīnātha. A heroic ballad of a very popular type, the earliest available work of its kind, *Palnāṭivīra-caritram*, which commemorates the achievements of the warriors of Palnad (Guntur district) in the thirteenth and fourteenth centuries, is also considered to be his work. Many Cāṭus or stray verses on miscellaneous subjects are reputed to be his and command great popularity to this day.

A striking contrast in almost every way to Śrīnātha was his brother-in-law and junior contemporary Bammera Potana (1400-75), a *niyogi* from Onṭimiṭṭa in Cuddapah district and translator of the *Bhāgavata Purāṇa*. Potana lived and died a poor man; he had no scholarly education, and his poetry, the result of inspiration born of an intense devotion, often overlooked the niceties of grammar. Potana is said to have met a *yogi* called Jītānanda whose grace converted him into a devotee with the gift of poesy. The *Bhāgavata* of Potana is more voluminous than the original, and its easy diction, vivid descriptions, and narrative power together with the intense spiritual experience conveyed by almost every verse have made the work much more popular than the translations of the *Rāmāyaṇa* and the *Mahābhārata*. The story goes that when Rao Singa wanted Potana to dedicate the poem to him, the Goddess of Learning appeared in a dream and begged Potana to guard her chastity by not casting her into the arms of Singhabhūpāla, and there is a notable verse purporting to be Potana's answer to the goddess. In any event, Potana did not publish his great work in his life-time but left it as a legacy to his son Mallana. Parts of the poem were found later to have suffered damage from insects, and the gaps had to be filled in by other hands. The sections of the poem on the release of the Gajendra (elephant lord) by Vishnu and the marriage of Rukminī carry an appeal even to the unlettered. Potana perhaps also wrote *Vīrabhadra Vijaya* in praise of Śiva, it is said, as an expiation for his having penned the words of abuse which the enemies of Śiva uttered against him on the occasion of Daksha's sacrifice.

The philosophical moralist Vemana, whose Śataka (centum) of verses has been well known to both young and old and has been translated into many other languages, most probably lived in the early fifteenth century.

Pillalmaṟṟi Pina Vīrabhadra Kavi is counted by tradition as a much younger contemporary of Śrīnātha than Potana. Vīrabhadra translated the *Jaimini Bhārata* which treats of the story of the Aśvamedha *parva* of the original *Bhārata*, and dedicated the work to Sāluva Narasimha. The poet is said to have claimed that Sarasvatī, the Goddess of Learning, was his queen and to have sustained the claim to the satisfaction of Narasimha's court. His *Śringāra Śākuntala*, a rendering of Kālidāsa's great drama, is his only other work now available, the rest of his writings being known only by their names. The subtle musical character of his verse has gained the appreciation of critics.

Of the other poets of this period, Nandi Mallaya and Ghaṇṭam Singaya (*c.* 1480) are important; they were joint authors of *Varāha Purāṇa* and *Prabodhacandrodaya*. The latter, in Prabandha form, is far more faithful to its Sanskrit original than either Śrīnātha's *Naishadha* or Pina Vīrabhadra's *Śākuntala*. The *Varāha Purāṇa*, also a translation from Sanskrit, is dedicated to Tuluva Narasānāyaka. Peram Rāju Jakkana (1450) was the author of *Vikramārka-carita* narrating the stories centring round the legendary monarch of Ujjain. Other notable names are: Duggupalli Duggaya (1480), author of *Naciketopākhyāna*, Dūbaguṇṭa

Nārāyaṇa (1470), author of *Pañcatantra,* Vennalakaṇṭi Sūranna (1460), author of *Vishṇupurāṇa* and Gaurana, author of *Hariścandropākhyāna.*

The reign of Krishnadeva Rāya was a glorious epoch in literature as in politics, war and art. The monarch was himself no mean scholar and poet, and the impetus he gave to Telugu literature lasted far beyond his time. Under his lead the practice of translating from Sanskrit originals was generally given up and independent Prabandhas which handled a purāṇic story or some invented theme after the manner of a Mahākāvya in Sanskrit came more into vogue. The earlier Prabandhas were marked by originality, variety, freedom and grace of matter and style; but in course of time in the hands of lesser poets the Prabandha tended to degenerate into stereotyped and monotonous forms which observed the formal rules of rhetoric, but fell far short of true literature.

Krishnadeva Rāya's *Āmuktamālyada* or *Vishṇucittīya,* one of the five great Kāvyas in Telugu, is among the first fruits of the new movement; it also marks the beginning of the influence of Vaishnavism on Telugu literature. It deals with the life of the *āḻvār* Vishnucitta (Periyāḻvār), his exposition of Vaishṇava philosophy and the love between his foster-daughter Godā and God Ranganātha. The style is involved and complex, the similes are sometimes far-fetched, but all the same the effect achieved is majestic and sublime. 'There is hardly a book in Telugu where there is such a continued flow of ideas, seeking an impetuous outlet in language which, though rich, is yet scarcely equal to the task of full and adequate expression. For insight into human nature, and for facility in depicting elusive moods by some striking phrase, Krishnadeva Rāya has no superior, and scarcely an equal.' He was the author of a number of Sanskrit works also.

Like the Nine Gems of Vikramāditya's court the *Ashṭadiggajas* (the Eight Elephants of the Quarters) of Krishnadeva Rāya's court are famous in legend. In either case, popular imagination has sought to glorify an intrinsically great name at the cost of historical truth. But there were doubtless many great poets who did adorn the court of Krishnadeva Rāya, and among them Allasāni Peddana, on whom the emperor conferred the title *Āndhrakavitāpitāmaha* (Grandfather of Telugu poetry), stands out foremost. He was the son of Chokkanāmātya and had his literary training under Śaṭhakopayati, a Vaishnava patriarch of the age. His chief work is the *Svārocisha-sambhava* or *Manucarita*. The story is taken from the *Mārkaṇḍeyapurāṇa*. An orthodox Brahmin by name Pravara refuses the love offered to him by the divine courtesan Varūthinī. A *gandharva* comes to know of this, assumes the guise of Pravara and lives with her. Their son was Svārocisha from whom the second Manu was born. As in Kālidāsa's *Kumāra-sambhava*, interest centres round the parents of the hero whose name the work bears, and Peddana's fame rests on his delineation of Pravara and Varūthinī. He borrowed from his predecessors like Śrīnātha some features in the development of the theme and in the use of Kannada words. *Manucarita* was dedicated to Krishnadeva Rāya who marked his appreciation of the poem by being a pole-bearer of Peddana's palanquin. Peddana survived his royal patron and bemoaned the years of desolation that followed. *Harikathā-sāra* attributed to him is no longer extant.

Nandi Timmana, the second great poet of Krishnadeva Rāya's court, was the author of *Pārijatāpaharaṇa*, which elaborates in beautiful verse a well-known episode in Śrī Krishna's life. The poem is said to have been composed to reconcile the emperor to one of his queens, who, he thought, had insulted him by sleeping with her legs stretched towards his portrait; Krishna's efforts to appease Satyabhāma, particularly the scene of his falling at her feet and being spurned by her with a kick, was calculated to hint to the emperor the extent of liberties permitted between lovers, and served its purpose. A pretty story, but most probably apocryphal.

Bhaṭṭumūrti, who came to be known later as Rāma Rāja Bhūshaṇa, had a long and distinguished literary career. His *Narasabhūpāliyam* is a work on rhetoric written in imitation of Vidyānātha's *Pratāparudrīya* and dedicated to Toragaṇṭi Narasarāju. His *Hariścandra-Nalopākhyānam* is a poem in which each verse has two meanings and tells the story of Nala as well as that of Hariścandra. But he is best known for his *Vasucaritra* which elaborates a simple story with great art. The theme is the marriage of prince Vasu with princess Girika, the daughter of the river Śuktimati and the mountain Kolāhala—a minor episode in the *Mahābhārata*. The musical cadence of his verse and the high imagination characteristic of his often over-elaborated descriptions have been highly esteemed by critics. The poem was written in the reign of Tirumala I, the brother of Rāma Rāya, and dedicated to him. It was translated into Sanskrit.

Dhūrjaṭi, a Śaiva poet from Kālahasti, evoked the admiration of Krishnadeva Rāya by his *Kālahasti Māhātmya* and a Śataka on the same shrine. His grandson, Kumāra Dhūrjaṭi, chronicled the conquests of the emperor in his *Krishṇadēvarāya-vijaya*. Mādayyagari Mallana was another court poet of the time whose *Rājaśekharacarita* is dedicated to Nadendla Appa, a nephew of Sāluva Timma and governor of Kondavīdu. The work is a typical Prabandha dealing with the wars and loves of Rājaśekhara, king of Avanti. Ayyalarāju Rāmabhadra, known as Pillala (of many children) Rāmabhadra, is believed to have gained the patronage of Krishnadeva Rāya by the good offices of Rāma Rāja Bhūshaṇa. He wrote the *Sakalakathāsāra-sangraha*, an abridgement of many purāṇic stories, at the instance of the emperor, and later the *Rāmābhyudayam*, on the story of Rāma, under the patronage of Gobbūri Narasarāju.

Pingali Sūranna, (Pingali is a village in the Krishna district), though counted among the *Ashṭadiggajas*, came later than the reign of Krishnadeva Rāya. His *Rāghava-Pāṇḍavīya*, as the name indicates, tells the story of the *Rāmāyaṇa* and *Mahābhārata* simultaneously. It commands a grace and simplicity hard to attain in this type of forced composition, and it is believed that Bhaṭṭumūrti (already mentioned) found his model in this work. Sūranna's *Kalāpūrṇodayam* is more a novel in poetry than a Prabandha, the only work of its type. The plot is a veritable comedy of errors and grips the attention of the reader. 'In the centre of the plot are Krishna and his seraglio, and in the background are Kāli worshippers with dark hints of human sacrifices, and Malayāli magicians with mystic garlands and strange spells. A noticeable feature of this work is that the writer altogether discards *śleshа*.' The *Prabhāvati Pradyumna* was esteemed by the author himself as the best of his works. It deals with a purāṇic theme in an original dramatic manner. The subject is the fall of the powerful Daitya king Vajranābha at the hands of Pradyumna, the son of Krishna, followed by the marriage of Prabhāvati, the daughter of the fallen Daitya, with Pradyumna. In this work Sūranna's 'characters are lifelike, their movements spontaneous, their conversations natural and the situations tense and vivid'.

In some ways the most interesting figure of the time was Tenāli Rāmakrishna who started his career under Krishnadeva Rāya but lived on to the reign of Venkata. Posterity remembers him more as a court jester who played many practical jokes on high-placed men, the monarch himself not excepted; but he was also a poet of talent, and his *Pānduranga Māhātmya*, counted among the five great Kāvyas in Telugu, is a work of high merit which narrates the story of a dissipated Brahmin's soul being successfully rescued from the servants of Yama by those of Vishnu, because he happened to die in Pandarpur. Rāmakrishna also wrote the *Udbhaṭācārya-carita* and dedicated it to an officer of Krishnadeva Rāya.

Though not counted among the 'great eight', Śankusāla Nrisimha Kavi was a distinguished poet of the time. Peddana, it is said, out of jealousy, obstructed his approach to the emperor, and the poor poet had to sell his poem, *Kavikarṇa Rasāyana*, in the market-place; one of its verses reached the emperor through his daughter Mohanāngi and, struck with its beauty, Krishnadeva Rāya sent for the poet, but he had left for Śrīrangam where he dedicated his work to the goddess of the shrine. It treats of the life of the mythical emperor Māndhātā, and in its prologue Nrisimha Kavi roundly denounces bad poets and kings.

Chintalapūdi Ellaya was the author of *Rādhā-mādhava-vilāsa* and *Vishṇumāyāvilāsa*; the first work was so much appreciated that the poet came to be known by its name. Molla, a poetess of the time, born of a low caste, was the author of the most popular version of the *Rāmāyaṇa*, in chaste and simple Telugu. Kamsāli Rudraya was the author of *Nirankuśōpākhyāna*, a fascinating story of a gifted gambler defeating the god Śiva, the stake being Rambhā, the divine dancer; Nirankuśa, the victor, lives with Rambhā though Indra tries to break up their companionship. Addanki Gangādhara (1570) wrote the *Tapatīsamvaraṇōpākhyāna* and Ponnaganti Telaganna the *Yayāticaritra*; they are both dedicated to Ibrahim Qutb Shah (1550-83), ruler of Golconda—called by the poets Ibha-rāmasauri in their dedication. Venkatanātha translated *Pañcatantra* into a Prabandha, instead of a collection of stories as in the original. Piḍuparti Sōmanātha's *Basava Purāṇa* is the only Śaiva work of the time; the author was a fanatical Vīra-śaiva and his intolerance of Vaishnavism which breaks out everywhere in his work is out of place in the tolerant age of Krishnadeva Rāya.

Sārangu Tammayya and Chadaluvāda Mallaya were authors of two *Vipranārāyaṇa-caritas*.

Among the scientific works of the time may be noted Manumañci Bhaṭṭa's *Hayalakshaṇa Śāstra* and *Līlāvatī-gaṇita* by Vallabhācārya. The first is an original work on horses and their training dedicated to Oba Kamparāya, a *daṇḍanāyaka* of Krishnadeva Rāya; it is now available only in parts. The second is a translation of *Līlāvatī-gaṇita* in verse form dedicated to an officer of Achyuta Rāya.

In the seventeenth century Vijayanagar lost its importance and its place was taken by the feudatory courts such as Gandikōta, Siddhavatam, Nellore, Gingee, Tanjore and Madura. Matli Ananta (1590-1610) of Siddhavatam (Cuddapah district) and his grandson were both poets and composed respectively the *Kākustha-vijayam* and the *Kumudvatī-kalyāṇam*. About the same time Tarigoppula Mallana wrote a Prabandha—*Candrabhānu caritra*—at the instance of Pemmasāni Timmānāyudu. Interesting in its own way, this Prabandha ranks far below the masterpieces of the age of Krishnadeva Rāya. Nellore was made famous by the work of Pushpagiri Timmana who rendered Bhartrihari's *Nītiśataka* into Telugu and described the exploits of Hanumān in a poem called *Samīrakumāravijayam*. He gathered round him a circle of talented friends including the celebrated Kankanti brothers—Pāparāja and Narasimha. Pāparāja's *Uttararāmāyaṇa* challenges comparison with the best works in Telugu; he also wrote a *yakshagāna Vishnumāyāvilāsa*. His less celebrated brother Narasimha was the author of a mechanical rendering into *dvipada* metre of the *Vishṇumāyāvilāsa Nāṭaka* of Rādhāmādhava Ellaya. The *Daśāvatāracarita* of Dharaṇidevula Rāmamantri is another notable poem of the period though the author's tendency to parade his learning makes his composition rather heavy. At Tanjore Raghunātha Nāyaka himself became the author of two delightful poems—the *Vālmīki-caritram* and *Rāmāyaṇam*. The former is the first important prose work in the language; the latter, though incomplete, shows Raghunātha's art at its best. Less talented than his father, Vijayarāghava, the son of Raghunātha, also composed poems and *yakshagānas* but his fame rests more securely on the poets patronized by him. Among them was the celebrated Chēmakūri Venkatakavi whose poems *Sārangadhara-caritram* and *Vijayavilāsa* handle respectively the themes of Chitrāngi's love for her step-son and Arjuna's pilgrimage to the sacred *tīrthas* and his marriages with the *nāga* princess Ulūcī and with Subhadrā, the sister of Śrī Krishna. The *Vijayavilāsa* is rightly counted as one of the great Kāvyas in Telugu. One of the queens of Vijayarāghava, Rangājamma, contributed to the development of the *yakshagāna* in her *Mannārudāsavilāsa* where she employs more characters than usual and frequently uses prose in conversations instead of song. Savaram Chinna Nārāyaṇarāju who lived in South Arcot and wrote an excellent Kāvya *Kuvalayāsvacaritra* was another poet notable for the grace of his manner and his wit. Lastly Kadirīpati, a cousin of Rāmarāja, the commander-in-chief of Śrīranga III, composed the *Śukasaptati*, a work of great literary excellence in which he perfected the art of story-telling.

MALAYĀLAM

Malayālam was the last of the South Indian languages to develop a separate existence and a literature of its own. In the Śangam age, the present Malayālam area was a land of Tamil speech though grammarians recognized that the dialect of the mountain country deviated from standard Tamil in many ways. The Śangam literature contains many words and expressions that survive in Malayālam today though they have gone out of use in Tamil. Attempts to derive Malayālam from Sanskrit or to postulate for it an origin independent alike of Sanskrit and Tamil are clearly misplaced, and there can be no doubt that it was a natural growth through centuries from the form of '*Koḍum-Tamiḻ*' that prevailed in Kerala at the beginning of the Christian era. The literary idiom of Malayālam, like that of Kannada and Telugu, borrowed freely from Sanskrit, and in order to express the Sanskrit sounds adequately, it had to discard the old Vaṭṭeḻuttu script and evolve a new script based on Tamil-grantha. This happened perhaps about the tenth century or a little later. The early inscriptions of the country used the *grantha* script for Sanskrit words in the midst of Tamil-Malayālam written in Vaṭṭeḻuttu.

The *Uṇṇunīli Sandeśam*, an anonymous poem of the fourteenth century, is the earliest extant literary work in the language. Its model was the *Meghasandeśa* of Kālidāsa, and it purports to be a message sent by a lover in Trivandrum to his lady love at Koḍungallūr and a detailed description of the route to be followed, the messenger in this case being a prince, Ādityavarma by name, and not a cloud or a bird as in other *sandeśa* poems. On his way the messenger is required to pay his respects to Ravivarman (Kulaśekhara), the great ruler of Quilon, and other contemporary rulers are also mentioned in the poem. The style of the work shows a large admixture of Sanskrit, and is in fact *maṇipravāḷam*, like most works of Malayālam literature. It is universally accepted as one of the most exquisite poems in the language. The *Chandrotsava* is another poem of the same period in Sanskrit metres, while the *Līlātilakam* (15th century) is a grammar of *maṇipravāḷam* style.

Prior to the date of the first *sandeśa* poem, there had come into existence popular ballads of various kinds, now known as Paḷaiya-pāṭṭus, old songs. Though in their present form they appear in a very modernized garb, competent critics hold that some of them at least must be of really early origin. There were many varieties of these folk songs such as *Brāhmaṇip-pāṭṭu* sung in marriages, *Bhadrakālip-pāṭṭu* and *Śāstāp-pāṭṭu* in praise of the respective deities, *Yātrakkaḷip-pāṭṭu* and *Tiruvādiraip-pāṭṭu* which take their names from the festive occasions when they were sung; they appear to have been generally accompanied by dance. Similar in character, but longer on account of the continuous themes they handled, were compositions like the *Payyanūr Paṭṭōla*, of which only the memory has survived. This early literature shows the least admixture of Sanskrit in its vocabulary. More systematic and much nearer true literature among these early poetic compositions were *Rāmacaritam*, a long metrical work on the story of the Yuddha-kāṇḍa of *Rāmāyaṇa*, believed to have been written by an ancient ruler of Travancore some time between the tenth and thirteenth centuries A.D.; and the somewhat later *Rāmakathāp-pāṭṭu* of a certain Ayyipiḷḷai Āśān. Both these works show signs of a strong Tamil influence in respect of words and metres. To this early period must also be assigned the anonymous *Bhāshākauṭilīya*, a Malayālam commentary on the *Arthaśāstra* of Kauṭilya; it follows the Sanskrit commentary *Jayamangalā*, and only six out of the fifteen *adhikaraṇas* are known.

From about the thirteenth century a strong impetus to literature came from the development of *Chākkiyār-kūttu*, a dance-recital of literary works which grew out of a simple and earlier form of the same art known as *Kūḍiy-āṭṭam* devoted to the exposition of dramas like *Nāgānandam* and *Āścarya-cūḍāmaṇi.* For enriching the repertoire of the Chākkiyār, many Campūs, works in mixed prose and verse, and Prabandhas came to be written under the inspiration of Sanskrit influences. Poetry follows Sanskrit metres and the prose passages are also really poetical in content and conception. Purāṇic stories and episodes form the themes of these compositions; but extraneous matter is often introduced and the Campūs abound in satirical references to contemporary usages and personalities. They were mostly written by Nambūdiri Brahmins, a class well known for their mordant wit and sarcasm, employed to good purpose in these works. Perhaps the most famous of them was Punam Nambūdiri of the fifteenth century to whom many Campūs are ascribed; the *Rāmāyaṇa-campū* is unquestionably his masterpiece. Second only to Punam was Maḷamangalam Nambūdiri, an inspired poet of the sixteenth century, who was gifted with a vivid imagination and an easy flow of language. His great work is the *Naishadha-campū* in which piquant situations like Nala leaving his kingdom and Damayanti lamenting over her separation from him are portrayed with great effect. These front-rank writers were followed by imitators of lesser calibre among whom Nārāyaṇan, the author of the *Bhārata-campū*, is the most notable.

Mention must be made of the Niraṇam poets, so called from their native village Niraṇam in central Travancore, who from the fifteenth century sought to develop an independent Malayālam style relatively free from the domination of Tamil and Sanskrit models. Most prominent among them was Rāma Paṇikkar, of the *Rāmāyaṇam*, popularly known as *Kaṇṇaśśa Rāmāyaṇam*, which narrates the whole of the Rāma story. He was also the author of *Bhārata Gāthā*, *Savitrī Māhātmyam*, *Brahmāṇḍapurāṇam*, and *Bhāgavatam.* His poems are marked by great narrative power and he has been called 'the Chaucer of Malayālam'. The translation of the *Gītā* by Mādhava Paṇikkar, the maternal grandfather of Rāma Paṇikkar, also deserves more than a passing mention. The Niraṇam poets also popularized a metre which takes its name after them, *Niraṇavrittam*, but even this is seen to have its prototype in Tamil.

Cheruśśeri Nambūdiri (early sixteenth century), author of the *Krishṇagāthā*, may be said to close the middle Malayālam period and herald the literature of modern Malayālam. The subject-matter of his great poem is the entrancing theme of the life of Śrī Krishna as narrated in the tenth *skandha* of the *Bhāgavata* and Cheruśśeri's *gāthā* is hailed by critics as a marvellous work of art which captivates the mind of the reader by the wealth of its imagery and the rich harmony of sense and sound.

For some time after Cheruśśeri, only local songs and ballads, like some of the *Vaḍakkan-pāṭṭukkaḷ*, the *Añju Tampurān-pāṭṭu* and *Eravikuṭṭipiḷḷa-pāṭṭu*, were produced. These continued the old tradition of popular songs on contemporary events which ushered Malayālam literature into being. The great luminary after Cheruśśeri was the renowned Tuñcat Rāmānujan Eḻuttaccan who gave shape to modern Malayālam. His chief works were: *Adhyātma Rāmāyanam Kiḷippāṭṭu*, *Bhāratam Kiḷippāṭṭu*, *Harināmakīrtanam*, *Cintāratnam*—a work on Advaita Vedānta, and perhaps also *Bhāgavatam Kiḷippāṭṭu* and *Dēvīmāhātmyam*. It will be seen that he covers practically the whole range of Hindu mythology giving his own versions of the two great epics and *Bhāgavatam*, and did not neglect religion and philosophy. The Kilippāṭṭu reached its perfection in his hands, and he is hailed as the genius who conferred literary dignity on the daily speech of the common man by adapting it to the highest purposes of literary art. Eḻuttaccan's date is not settled beyond dispute, but he may be placed late in the sixteenth or early in the seventeenth century.

A word must be said about Āṭṭakatha or Kathakaḷi. This variety of dance-drama was till a few years ago believed to be a development of recent origin, not older than two or three centuries at the most. Recent research has shown, however, that the first Āṭṭakathas were composed towards the close of the fifteenth century, and that the *Rāman-āṭṭam* of Koṭṭārakkara Tampurān, meant to be completed in eight performances, is the earliest of the extant Āṭṭakathas; though there is no direct evidence, the author may be taken to belong to the sixteenth century. Later contributions to this type of popular literature—about two hundred Kathas have so far been listed—lie outside the period covered by this book.

BIBLIOGRAPHY

Tamil

S. SOMASUNDARA DESIKAR: *Sixteenth-century Tamil Poets* (in Tamil: Madras, 1936)

—: *Seventeenth-century Tamil Poets* (in Tamil: Madras, 1936)

M. SRINIVASA AIYANGAR: *Tamil Studies* (Madras, 1914)

S. VAIYAPURI PILLAI: *History of Tamil Language and Literature* (Madras, 1956)

Kannada

R. NARASIMHACHARYA: *History of Kannada Literature* (Mysore, 1940)

—: *Karnataka Kavicarite* (3 vols. in Kannada: Bangalore, 1924, 1927 and 1929)

Telugu

T. ACHYUTA RAO: *A History of Andhra Literature in the Vijayanagar Empire* (2 parts in Telugu: Rajahmundry and Pithapuram, 1933 and 1940)

P. CHENCHIAH AND BHUJANGA RAO: *A History of Telugu Literature* ('Heritage of India Series', Calcutta, 1930)

P. T. RAJU: *Telugu Literature* (Bombay, 1944)

GURUJADA SRIRAMAIAH: *Kavipritamulu* (in Telugu: Madras, 1925)

K. VEERESALINGAM: *Kavula Carita* (3 vols. in Telugu: Rajahmundry, 1887, 1894 and 1911)

Malayālam

C. ACHYUTA MENON: *Eluttachan and his Age* (Madras, 1940)

P. GOVINDA PILLAI: *History of Malayalam Literature* (2 vols. in Malayalam: Trivandrum, 1889)

H. GUNDERT: *Malayalam Dictionary* (Mangalore, 1872)

P. KRISHNA NAIR: *Attakatha or Kathakali* (Madras, 1939)

R. NARAYANA PANIKKAR: *Kerala Bhasha Sahitya Caritram* (4 vols. in Malayalam: Trivandrum, 1927, 1929, 1941, 1944)

T. K. VELU PILLAY: *Travancore State Manual*, Vol. 1 (Trivandrum, 1940)

CHAPTER XV

RELIGION AND PHILOSOPHY

Introductory—early harmony among sects—reaction against Jainism and Buddhism—*bhakti* schools—*nāyanārs*—*āḻvārs*—Kumārila and Śankara—temples and *bhakti*—schools in the age of the Cholas—Rāmānuja—Nimbārka—Madhva—Vaishnava schism—saints of Mahārāshtra—Vallabhācārya—Pāśupata sects—temples of the Deccan—growth of Śaiva-siddhānta—Vīra-śaivism and the Ārādhyas—temples and festivals under Vijayanagar.

Buddhism, Jainism and Ājīvakas—Islam—Christianity.

In the sphere of religion, as generally in all matters of spiritual culture, South India began by being heavily indebted to the North; but in the course of centuries it more than amply repaid the debt and made signal contributions to the theory and practice of religion and to philosophic thought in its various aspects. Its saints and seers evolved a new type of *bhakti*, a fervid emotional surrender to God which found its supreme literary expression in the *Bhāgavata-purāṇa*, a *bhakti* very different from the calm, dignified devotion of the Bhāgavatas of the early centuries before and after Christ in Northern India. Again, from South India arose the two schools of Vedic exegesis—Mīmāmsā—that go by the names of Kumārilabhaṭṭa and Prabhākara. The founders of the three main systems of Vedānta—Śankara, Rāmānuja and Madhva—also hailed from the southern country. Yet another prominent philosophical system—the Śaiva-siddhānta—also found its exponents in the Tamil country. Lastly, the Vedas were commented on more than once in this part of the country, and the constant study of the ritual manuals of the different Vedic schools was kept up. The literature of these movements was reviewed in outline in the last chapter; here we shall seek to sketch the main stages in the history of these developments.

Till about the fifth century A.D., harmony and tolerance characterized the relations between the different religious sects. The worship of primitive godlings with offerings of blood and toddy went on side by side with the performance of elaborate Vedic sacrifices; the popular pantheon included many deities like Muruga, Śiva, Vishnu, Indra, Krishna, and others. Buddhists and Jains were found in considerable numbers in different parts of the country following their practices without let or hindrance. In the story of *Maṇimēkalai*, for instance, we find the heroine advised to study in Kānchī the philosophical systems of the Veda, Śiva, Vishnu, Ājīvika, Jaina and of the Sānkhya, Vaiśeshika and Lokāyata.

But soon a great change came—particularly in the Tamil country—and people began to entertain fears of the whole land going over to Jainism and Buddhism. At any rate, worshippers of Śiva and Vishnu felt the call to stem the rising tide of heresy. The growth, on the one hand, of an intense emotional *bhakti* to Śiva or Vishnu and, on the other, of an outspoken hatred of Buddhists and Jains, are the chief characteristics of the new epoch. Challenges to public debate, competition in the performance of miracles, tests of the truth of doctrines by means of ordeal, became the order of the day. Parties of devotees under the leadership of one gifted saint or another traversed the country many times over, singing, dancing and debating all their way. This great wave of religious enthusiasm attained its peak in the early seventh century and had not spent itself in the middle of the ninth.

Later tradition counted sixty-three *nāyanārs*, individual and collective, as the most prominent leaders of this revival on the side of the Śaivas. The individuals included a woman from Kāraikāl, and a pariah, Nandan from Ādanūr, besides a general of the Pallava forces, Siṛuttoṇḍar. But most prominent among them were the three great men whose hymns are collected together in the *Dēvāram*. First came Tirunāvukkaraśu, a Veḷḷāla from Tiruvāmūr and generally believed to be a contemporary of the Pallava ruler Mahendravarman I. Though born in an orthodox Śaiva family he was attracted to Jainism in his early years, and joined the Jaina monastery at Pātaliputra (Cuddalore) as a monk. His elder sister, who had watched his change of faith with untold regret, implored Śiva's help. Her prayer was answered; Dharmasena, for that was her brother's name in the monastery, became the victim of an incurable abdominal disorder. When all his fellow-Jains failed him, he was compelled to go and seek his sister's aid. She secured his cure by the grace of the God of Tiruvadigai. The news of his defection greatly upset the Jaina monks of Pātaliputra who trumped up many false charges against Dharmasena to poison the mind of the Pallava ruler of the country against him. He was subjected to many trials and tortures which, however, by the grace of Śiva he easily surmounted. Finally, the king himself was convinced of the superiority of Śaivism, and embraced it. Whatever elements of truth there may be in the life-story of Tirunāvukkaraśu or Appar which we have sketched above, a verse in the Trichinopoly inscription of Mahendravarman furnishes clear proof that the king did indeed turn to Śaivism from some other creed. It must, however, be admitted that the tradition regarding the persecution of Appar by Mahendravarman (whose name does not occur in the story narrated by Śēkkiḻār) is hard to reconcile with the spirit of the *Mattavilāsa*. The rest of Appar's long life of 81 years was spent in pilgrimages during which he met many contemporary *nāyanārs*, of whom Ñānasambandar was the most notable, indeed the greatest of them all.

Ñānasambandar was a Brahmin of the Kaundinya *gōtra* from Shiyāli in the Tanjore district. There are few Śaiva temples in the Tamil country today where worship is not offered to him. Legend avers that as a child of three he got the milk of divine knowledge from Pārvatī herself and narrated the incident to his father in song. The father at once realized the divinity of his child and carried him on his shoulders from one Śaiva shrine to another until he was relieved by the present from the gods of a pearl palanquin for his son's use. At that time the Pāndya country was almost completely overrun by Jainism, and the Pāndyan queen, a princess from the Chola country, and the minister Kulacciṟai, both of whom were Śaivas, sent Sambandar an urgent invitation to come and release the Pāndya and his country from the tightening grip of Jainism. Ñānasambandar betook himself to Madura, foiled all the conspiracies of the Jains against him, vanquished them in debate and converted the king and his subjects to Śaivism. The story goes that on this occasion 8,000 Jains were put to death by impalement, and a festival in the Madura temple is supposed to commemorate the gruesome event to this day. This, however, is little more than an unpleasant legend and cannot be treated as history. There is no reason to believe that, even in those days of intense religious strife, intolerance descended to such cruel barbarities. Nor are we asked to believe the story of his marriage. It is said that when, at the age of sixteen, he was married, the ceremony had hardly been completed when the newly wedded pair and all the wedding party were absorbed into the god-head. Sambandar had disputations with Buddhists also and visited many shrines and sang hundreds of hymns in his short life-time. He was the purest of all the saints, with no past to regret. He may be placed in the middle of the seventh century and his Pāndyan contemporary was either Māṟa-varman Avaniśūlāmaṇi or his grandson Arikesari Māṟavarman.

Some decades later came Sundaramūrtti of Nāvalūr. He was born of poor Brahmin parents but his beauty as a child was such that he attracted the attention of the local chieftain Narasinga Munaiyadaraiyan who, with the consent of the parents, brought him up. When his marriage with a girl of his own caste was about to take place it was stopped by the mysterious intervention of Śiva who claimed him as his slave. A little later Sundara fell in love with two women, one a dancing-girl of Tiruvālūr and the other a *śūdra* girl of Tiruvoṟṟiyūr. Their jealousies, it is said, could only be resolved by Śiva himself acting as a messenger to one of them. Like the other *nāyanārs*, Sundara is also credited with many miracles and the contemporary Chera ruler, Cheramān Perumāl, was his friend. They visited each other regularly and made their last journey to the abode of Śiva in Mount Kailāsa together, Sundara on a white elephant and Cheramān Perumāl on a horse. Sundara's devotion to Śiva was that of an intimate friend so that he was given the title *Tambirān-Tōḻan* ('Friend of God').

About a century after Sundara came the illustrious Māṇikka-vāśagar. Legend makes him the minister of a Pāndyan king; and on his account Śiva, the presiding deity of Madura, is said to have performed many miracles. His Pāndyan contemporary was most probably Varaguṇa II (862-85). Māṇikka-vāśagar is said to have debated with Buddhists from Ceylon at Chidambaram and to have utterly vanquished them. His hymns form the *Tiruvāśagam* ('The Sacred Word') and another work, *Tiruccir̤ram-balakkōvai*, is also ascribed to him.

The hymns of Sambandar, Appar and Sundara form a varied treasure-house of religious experience which tells of mystical raptures and ecstasies, of moments of light when there is a vision of God and the world is transfigured in the light of his love, and of periods of gloom when all is dark and the blind seeker is filled with a sense of fear. Somewhat different and more exuberant are the outpourings of Māṇikka-vāśagar whose confessions are more outspoken and whose devotion is more impassioned. Some of them were keen controversialists and had no soft word for Buddhists and Jains.

The Vaishnava wing of the movement is represented by twelve *āḻvārs* ('divers' into the qualities of God) for whom orthodox tradition gives an impossible chronology. Three of them—Poygai, Pūdam, Pēy, born respectively at Kānchī, Mallai and Mylapore—are believed to have come earliest. A beautiful legend tells how these three saints sheltered from the rain in a narrow room which could only just hold them standing, when Vishnu himself came seeking their company. The *bhakti* of these early saints is a gentle, simple devotion, altogether free from a sectarian outlook. This fact, and their employment of the *veṇbā* metre in their songs, points to a really early date for them—not later than the fifth or the sixth century A.D.

Then came Tirumaḻiśai, born in the village of that name in Chingleput district and most probably an elder contemporary of Pallava Mahendravarman I. The story goes that at birth he was a shapeless mass of flesh abandoned by his parents and brought up by a *śūdra*. He is said to have practised Jainism, Buddhism and Śaivism before settling down finally as a Vaishnava *yogi*. His poems show a more controversial tone than those of the first three *āḻvārs*, and this was quite natural to his age.

After him we might place Tirumangai, one of the most celebrated of the *āḻvārs*. He was the petty chieftain of Ālināḍu in the Tanjore district who, legend says, became a highwayman in order to carry off and marry the daughter of a Vaishnavite doctor of a higher caste, for whom he also changed his religion. He is said to have stolen a solid golden image of Buddha from a monastery in Negapatam to pay for renovating the temple of Śrīrangam. The clear reference to Vairamegha in his hymns places him in the middle of the eighth century, a date which discredits the story of his friendly meeting with Ñānasambandar at Shiyāli. None of the stories can be treated as history, though each in its own way furnishes a clue to what his followers believed in later times. His hymns, and they are many, are equally full of good poetry and attacks on Jainism and Buddhism. To Śaivism, on the whole, he evinced a more friendly attitude and there are many resemblances in literary form and religious sentiments between Ñānasambandar and Tirumangai.

A little later than Tirumangai, about the close of the eighth and the beginning of the ninth century, came a number of *āḻvārs*. Periyāḻvār, a Brahmin of Śrīvilliputtūr, won a religious disputation in the court of the Pāndya king Śrīmāṟa Śrīvallabha (815-62). The only woman among them, Āṇḍaḷ or Kōdai (Skt. Godā), was the real or adopted daughter of Periyāḻvār. In her intense devotion to Vishnu she dreamt of her marriage with that god, and described her experience in her hymns. This mystical union was the only one she knew, and in many ways the ardour of her devotion resembles that of Māṇikka-vāśagar, and her hymns are replete with allusions to Krishna stories. To about the same period belonged Tiruppāṉ, a minstrel of low caste, who was not permitted to enter the temple of Srīrangam and was thus the Vaishnava counterpart of Nandan; and Toṇḍar-aḍip-poḍi ('The dust of the feet of the devotees'), a Brahmin from Tanjore district whose real name was Vipranārāyaṇa and whose intolerance of Buddhism and Jainism was nearly as great as that of Tirumangai.

Kulaśekhara, the ruler of Kerala, proficient alike in Sanskrit and Tamil, was the next *āḻvār* who, among other shrines of Vishnu, sang of those at Chidambaram and at Tiruvāli—the latter, no doubt, a foundation of Tirumangai. Lastly came the celebrated Nammāḻvār and his pupil Madhurakavi. The former was born of a Veḷḷāla family of Āḻvārtirunagari (earlier called Kurugūr) in the Tinnevelly district. His personal name was Māṟan and he seems to have gained the name Śaṭhakopa on the occasion of his initiation. He renounced the world in his thirty-fifth year to practise *yoga*. His hymns, the largest in number after those of Tirumangai, are rightly regarded as embodying the deepest religious experience and philosophic thought of one of the greatest seers of the world.

Yuan Chwang, who visited South India in 642, when the Hindu revival was just gathering momentum, did not notice the new movement, although in speaking of Mahārāshtra he mentions the worshippers of Deva (Śiva) who covered themselves with ashes. He mentions with regret that his own creed—Buddhism—was on the decline, but remarks repeatedly that it had yielded to Digambara Jainism. The triumph of the revivalist movement was largely achieved in the two centuries that followed. Public disputations which led kings and rulers to transfer their allegiance from one creed to another did much to bring this about. More important, however, was the use of the popular speech by the *nāyanārs* and the *āḻvārs* in their soul-stirring compositions, and the fact that these were set to simple tunes which the masses loved to sing.

Another important, though less popular, aspect of the same revival is seen in the work of Kumārila and Śankara. They were Smārtas (traditionalists) who laboured in the cause not of any one sect in particular but of the ancient brahminical religion as it had been developed through the centuries. They held up as the religious ideal a youth occupied with ritual observances followed by an old age given up to philosophic contemplation. Kumārila frequently attacks Buddhists in his works, and tradition asserts that he did much to discredit them in the course of his many scholarly journeys. He elucidated the philosophy of ritualism (Mīmāmsā) in all its aspects, but Śankara was the greater thinker. Few details of his life are very well attested, but he is generally taken to be a Nambūdiri Brahmin from Kālaḍi on the banks of the Alwaye river in north Travancore, where he was born in 788. He lost his father early in life and turned ascetic, with Govinda *yogi*, a pupil of Gauḍapāda, as his *guru*. In a short life he travelled all over India propagating his new philosophy of a rigorously consistent monism and triumphing against all rivals who met him in debate. He reorganized the ascetic order of Hinduism on the model of the Buddhist order, and founded a number of *maṭhas* in different parts of India, the best known being those at Śringeri, Dvārakā, Badrīnāth, Puri and Kānchī. His philosophy, which traces all apparent multiplicity and difference to illusion (*māyā*), is indeed derived from the Upanishads, but clearly owes much in detail to Mahāyānist speculation; nevertheless, he regarded Buddhism as Hinduism's chief enemy. Some time after his death in 820, one of his pupils, Śivasoma, was spreading his doctrine in distant Kambuja across the seas. Not without justice, it has been said that Śankara 'would have a higher place among the famous names of the world had not his respect for tradition prevented him from asserting the originality which he undoubtedly possessed'.

The work of the poet-saints of the Pāndya-Pallava period was continued in the age of the Cholas by a succession of poets and teachers of second rank. The Tamil hymns of the last age came to be treated as equal to the Veda and were collected and arranged in canonical books. Gradually they were regularly employed in the daily worship in temples, and their authors came to be regularly worshipped as manifestations of divinity. In fact the rise of the temple to an important place in the religious and social life of the land was the direct result of the revivalist movement. The age of the Imperial Cholas saw the construction of stone temples, great and small, in almost every town and village in their extensive empire. The great temples of Tanjore and Gangaikondaśōḷa-puram were symbolic of the new age and, among many others, they were celebrated in hymns by contemporary poets.

The Śaiva canon, in which these hymns also found a place, was arranged in the first instance in the reign of Rājarāja I by Nambi Āṇḍār Nambi and continuously added to till about the middle of the twelfth century. The Vaishnava canon, on the other hand, received its definitive shape at the hands of Nāthamuni. In his works he expressed the clear need he felt for the support and guidance of a living God, and pointed the way to a philosophical justification of the path of love. His grandson Āḷavandār, also called Yāmunācārya in memory of his visit to the sacred spots of Krishna's youth, was the next great name in the succession of Vaishnava *ācāryas* of the period. In his early years he was a man of the world, but a follower of Nāthamuni called him to the higher life. He then turned ascetic and led the life of a religious teacher, gathering disciples round him and preaching, writing and conducting debates. In his writings, often cited by Rāmānuja, 'he sought to establish the real existence of the supreme soul, and the eternal independence of the individual soul'.

The greatest of the Vaishnava *ācāryas* was undoubtedly Rāmā-nuja. Born at Śrīperumbudūr, near Madras, in the first quarter of the eleventh century, he had his early philosophical training under Yādavaprakāśa of Kānchipuram who belonged to the school of Śankara. Yāmunācārya is said to have once met Rāmānuja at Kānchī but, unwilling to disturb the progress of the youth's studies, he uttered a prayer for the increase of Śrī Vaishnavas and went back to Śrīrangam. Rāmānuja then disagreed with the teachings of his *guru* and was strongly attracted by those of the Śrīrangam school. Yāmuna sent for him, but breathed his last before Rāmānuja could reach him. He succeeded Yāmuna as head of the *maṭha* at Śrīrangam, which gave him control over the temple and the school, and a position of authority in the sect. He soon proved his mettle as a teacher and organizer, and his influence grew day by day. In his lectures and writings he refuted the Māyāvāda of Śankara, demonstrated that the Upanishads did not teach a strict monism, and built up the philosophy of Viśishtādvaita which reconciled devotion to a personal God with the philosophy of the Vedānta by affirming that 'the soul, though of the same substance as God and emitted from him rather than created, can obtain bliss not in absorption but in existence near him'. He attempted to unify the sect by a reform of temple ritual wherever possible. Though he respected the rule that none but the twice-born may read the Veda, he was eager, like the *āḻvārs*, to spread the doctrine of *bhakti* among Sūdras and even among the outcastes. He arranged that in certain important temples the outcastes should have the privilege of entering the temple on one day in the year. He travelled throughout India to propagate his ideas, and these journeys may well account for the wide influence of the sect in Northern India.

The Cholas were ardent Śaivas and evidently did not view the growing influence of Rāmānuja with favour. We may not trust the legends of the persecution to which Rāmānuja and his followers were subjected in all their details, but the fact remains that he had to withdraw into Mysore about 1098 and could not return to Śrīrangam till 1122. During this time Rāmānuja won over the Hoysala king Vishnuvardhana from Jainism and established a well-organized *maṭha* at Melkote. After his return to Śrīrangam, Rāmānuja continued his work there till he died in 1137. He is worshipped as an avatar in all Vaishnava temples.

A younger contemporary of Rāmānuja was Nimbārka, a scholarly *Bhāgavata* Telugu Brahmin from Nimbāpura in Bellary district who spent most of his time in Brindāvan in Northern India. In religion he accepted the doctrine of surrender (*prapatti*) and translated it into a total devotion to Krishna and Rādhā. For him Rādhā is not merely the favourite mistress of Krishna but his eternal consort who lives with him for ever in Goloka, the highest heaven. Philosophically, he accepted the position that God, the soul, and the world were identical yet distinct, the position described as *bhedā-bheda*. Nimbārka thus became the founder of a new sect allied to, but distinct from, that of Rāmānuja. He expounded his views in a commentary on the

Vedāntasūtras and in another work called *Siddhāntaratna* or *Daśaślokī*.

The philosophic debate which, as against Śankara, laid increasing stress upon the reality of the world and the soul in distinction from Brahman ended in complete pluralism in the system of Madhva. Born shortly before 1200 in a Brahmin family at Kalyānapura in the Udipi taluk of South Kanara district, some forty miles west of Śringeri, he became a *sanyāsi* while he was still quite young and, like Rāmānuja, had his early training in the system of Śankara. But before his training was over, he broke away from that system and evolved his own based mainly on the *Bhāgavatapurāṇa*. Tradition credits him with a great capacity for physical endurance. A debate at Trivandrum with an *ācārya* of Śringeri ended in his discomfiture and he was robbed of his library and subjected to much annoyance and persecution. He toured Northern India where he had encounters with robbers, wild beasts and hostile chieftains in the course of his journeys. After resting for a while in Hardwar he retreated into the Himalayas for communion with Vyāsa and published his commentary on *Vedāntasūtras* on his return. Back at Udipi again, he built a temple to Krishna and spent his time preaching, converting, and defeating 'illusionists'. After a ministry of nearly eighty years, and at the age of ninety-six, he disappeared as he sat teaching and was seen no more. He claimed to be an incarnation of Vāyu, the Wind-god. He was a prolific writer who disdained fine-spun arguments and found support for his teachings mainly from the Purāṇas and other later literature. He taught that the Universe is ruled by God as two persons—Vishnu and Lakshmī—and that the souls in the world are eternally distinct from Him. He recognized different orders of souls and consigned some of them to eternal damnation, which has led some modern critics to hold that 'it is impossible not to see traces of Christian influence' in his teaching. The centre of his religion is *bhakti* to Krishna as taught in the *Bhāgavata*, Rādhā having no place in it; but all other avatārs are revered, Śiva is worshipped, and 'the five gods' (*Pañcāyatana*) are recognized.

The thirteenth and fourteenth centuries witnessed the rise of a schism among the followers of Rāmānuja due to a difference in their interpretation of *prapatti* (surrender). Some held that the devotee had to exert himself to win the grace of the Lord, while others thought that the Lord's grace by itself conferred salvation on the soul that had entered the path of surrender. The position of the first school, Vaḍagalai (northern branch), is commonly summed up in the phrase *Markaṭakiśoranyāya*, the rule that the young monkey clings to its mother with an effort, and that of the second school, the Tengalai, is called *Mārjāra-kiśoranyāya*, the rule of the kitten which is carried by its mother in her mouth. There are other differences between the two schools, one of them being a decided preference for Tamil as against Sanskrit on the part of the Tengalais. The southern school looks upon Piḷḷai Lōkācārya (b. 1213) as its founder. He was the author of eighteen esoteric treatises (*rahasyas*), and had to leave Śrīrangam with the sacred image during the period of the Muslim inroads. He found an influential expositor in Maṇavāḷa Mahāmuni (b. *circa* 1370), the next great teacher and writer in the southern school. The leader of the northern school was Vedānta Dēśika (b. 1268). He once hid himself under a mass of dead bodies in Śrīrangam on the occasion of a Muslim incursion and escaped to Mysore until the storm blew over. As we have seen, he was poet, philosopher, and man of affairs.

Another development of Vaishnavism based on the *Bhāgavata* was the rise from the close of the thirteenth century of a number of poet-saints whose popular songs stirred the life of Mahārāshtra as those of the *nāyanārs* and the *āḻvārs* had stirred the Tamil country centuries before. The earliest of them was Jñāneśvara, popularly called Dnyāndev Dnānōbā—a pupil according to some accounts of Vishnusvāmi, who was a dualist and founder of a sect of his own. Jñāneśvara was the author of an extensive work in Marāthī verse on the *Bhagavad-gītā*. His tone is Advaitic, though he also lays great stress on *yoga*; he was also the author of many *abhangs* or hymns. The movement begun by him continued through a succession of saints to Tukārām, the contemporary of Śivāji.

Vaishnavism continued to be one of the dominant forces influencing the life of the people. No striking developments took place in the rest of our period in doctrine or practice. Occasionally the cult, especially that of Rādhā, tended to degenerate into erotic excesses. This is particularly true of the followers of Vallabhācārya (1479-1531), a Telugu Brahmin contemporary of Chaitanya. He was born in Benares, wrote several works in

Sanskrit including a commentary on the *Vedāntasūtras* and became the founder of a system called Śuddhādvaita which exalted *bhakti* above knowledge. He is said to have vanquished Smārta scholars in public debate at the court of Krishnadeva Rāya. The *ācāryas* of the sect were known as Mahārājas and lived luxurious lives. The highest ambition of his followers was to become *gopis* and sport eternally with Krishna in his Heaven, an ideal which in practice degenerated into gross eroticism. Further, disputes between rival sects sometimes flared up with unusual violence. Nevertheless, Vaishnavism continued to be, in general, a noble and sweet influence on life. The Rāyas of Vijayanagar were great patrons of Vaishnavism; in 1556 Sadāśiva, at the request of Rāma Rāya, gave thirty-one villages to maintain the temple of Rāmānuja and the institutions attached to it at Śrīperumbudūr.

To return to the history of Śaivism; we must note that by the side of the pure school of *bhakti* represented by the three saints of *Dēvāram* and Māṇikka-vāśagar, there existed other types of worshippers of Śiva whose tenets and practices are gruesome and repellent to modern taste. Such were the Pāśupatas, Kāpālikas, Kālāmukhas, and others whose presence in considerable numbers in centres like Kānchī, Tiruvoṟṟiyūr, Melpāḍi and Koḍumbāḷūr is attested by inscriptions and literature from the seventh century onwards. Smearing the body with ashes from a burning ghat, eating food in a skull, and keeping a pot of wine, were some of the common practices of the Kālāmukhas; and some of these sects, if not all, were addicted to the worship of the female principle, which often degenerated into licentious orgies. The practice of the devotee offering his own head as a sacrifice to the goddess is shown in the sculpture and literature of the age of the Pallavas and Cholas.

In the Deccan, under the Chālukyas of Bādāmi and the Rāshtrakūtas of Mānyakheta, both Śaivism and Vaishnavism flourished, although Śaivism was, perhaps, the more favoured creed. Magnificent temples were built at Bādāmi, Pattadakal, Mahākūta, Ellora, and other places, *arcakas* (priests) were imported from the Śaiva *ācāryas* on the banks of the Ganges, and daily worship and periodical festivals in these temples were richly endowed. At the same time the performance of Vedic sacrifices was continued, *vratas* (religious vows) were observed and *dānas* (gifts) made. The worship of Kārtikeya attained such prominence in the Bellary region in the tenth century that two *tapovanas* were dedicated to him as the supreme deity, a development initiated by some teachers from Bengal. In the Andhra country also, where Buddhism had flourished in great strength in the early centuries of the Christian era, there came about a strong Hindu revival. Besides the more famous shrines of Kālahasti, Dākshārāma and Śrīśailam, the temples of Mahāsena (Kārtikeya) at Chebrolu, Humkāraśankari at Bidapura, and Mallēśvara at Bezwada became important centres of pilgrimage. *Maṭhas* grew up and were occupied by monks who fed the poor, tended the sick, consoled the dejected and set up schools for the education of youth, and in the process many Buddhist shrines and *vihāras* were turned to Hindu uses.

Hinduism has always been a house of many mansions, and the following description of the Arab geographer al-Idirīsī, who wrote at the beginning of the twelfth century basing himself on earlier writers, may well be taken to apply to the whole of the Deccan from the tenth to the twelfth centuries. 'Among the principal nations of India there are forty-two sects. Some recognize the existence of a Creator, but not of Prophets; while others deny the existence of both; some acknowledge the intercessory powers of graves and stones and others worship holy stones on which butter and oil is poured. Some pay adoration to fire and cast themselves into the flames. Others adore the sun and consider it the Creator and Director of the world. Some worship trees, others pay adoration to serpents which they keep in stables and feed as well as they can, believing this to be a meritorious work. Lastly there are some who give themselves no trouble about any kind of devotion, and deny everything.'

Two developments in Śaivism which occurred in the twelfth and thirteenth centuries in the Tamil country and in the Deccan deserve particular mention. The first is the development of the Tamil Śaiva-siddhānta philosophy based on the Āgamas. The Āgamas are first mentioned by Sundaramūrtti, and the *Tirumandiram* of Tirumūlar (ninth century) is the earliest work to reflect the theology of the Āgamas. Āgamic terminology is also found in the writing of Māṇikka-vāśagar, who frequently speaks of the Āgamas as revealed by Śiva and openly expresses his dislike of the Vedānta, by which he means the monism of Śankara. But the first definite formulation of the philosophy of the Tamil Śaiva-siddhānta was in the work of Meykaṇḍadēva, a pious Veḷḷāla who lived early in the thirteenth century on the banks of the Pennār river, south of Madras. He is reputed to have received instruction from Parañjōtimuni who was sent down from Kailāsa specially for that purpose. His *Śiva-Ñāna-Bōdam*, a translation into Tamil verse of twelve Sanskrit Sūtras from the *Raurava-āgama*, is looked upon as the fountainhead of the dogmatics of the system. The extensive philosophic literature that sprang from this work has already been reviewed. The progress of discussion led to the growth of different schools within the fold of the Śaiva-siddhānta. But in the main the system sought, like other philosophies of religion, to determine the relations of God, matter and the soul. It declared that matter and souls were, like God, eternal. The Absolute through its 'grace-form' is forever engaged in the rescue of souls from the bondage of matter and the three stains (*malas*) which defile their purity. 'As body and mind together form a unity so God is the soul whose body is the Universe of nature and of man. He is not identical with either; He is not their substance but he dwells in them and they in Him. Advaita is not Oneness, but inseparability. To realize this union is the high calling of the soul.' It is for the *guru* or the teacher to let in the light, but Śiva is the source of all enlightenment, sole embodiment of intelligence and grace, and hence the true object of all devout aspiration. The system transcends caste and ritual and calls for inner devotion. According to one writer, contentment, justice and wisdom are the flowers of worship.

The other development in Śaivism (also based on the twenty-eight Śaiva Āgamas) was the growth of Vīra-śaivism or the Lingāyat cult in Karnātaka and the Telugu country. Basava, the prime minister of Kalacuri Bijjala, king at Kalyāni (1156), is usually regarded as the founder of the sect. Lingāyat tradition avers that the sect is very old and was founded by five ascetics—Ekōrāma, Panditārādhya, Rēvaṇa, Maruḷa, and Viśvārādhya—who were held to have sprung from the five heads of Śiva. Basava, they say, was but the Reviver of the Faith; but we know for a fact that the five ascetics named were all contemporaries of Basava, some older, some younger. The early history of Vīra-śaivism is therefore still somewhat uncertain. Two features of the sect, however—the prominent place held by monasteries, and the more or less complete social and religious equality among the sectarians

—have been held to be due to the influence of Jainism and Islam. Lingāyats regard Śiva as supreme and must worship only Him; hence the name Vīra-śaivas, stalwart Śaivas. They must also worship each his own chosen *guru*. Each Lingayat, man or woman, carries a *linga* about his person, usually in a silver or wooden reliquary suspended from the neck. Reverence is paid by Lingāyats to the sixty-three *nāyanārs* of the Tamil country whom they recognize as Purātanas (elders) and to seven hundred and seventy later saints among whom are included Māṇikka-vāśagar, Basava, and his chief disciples. An account of Lingāyat literature has been given already.

The Ārādhya Śaivas of the Telugu country differed from the Lingāyats in some respects. They followed Mallikārjuna Panditārādhya, a contemporary of Basava, in refusing to accept the latter's rejection of the Veda and renunciation of caste. But the relations of Ārādhya Śaivism with Lingāyatism were friendly, and both joined together in the fourteenth century in resisting the inroads of Muslims and in preparing the way for the foundation of Vijayanagar.

Under the Rāyas of Vijayanagar all types of religion found encouragement, and most of the famous temples of South India were enlarged at this time, particularly by the addition of large *gōpuras* or entrance towers and corridors and *maṇḍapas*. A few temples were altogether rebuilt on a new integral plan, like that of Madura under Tirumalai Nāyaka (1623-59). The periodical festivals in most of these temples were also richly endowed, and brought together people from all classes of society including groups of peripatetic merchants and traders. The festivals of the capital city of Vijayanagar, in particular the Mahānavami (nine days' festival) in October, were occasions of great display which have been described by many foreign travellers who had occasion to witness them. Their accounts leave little doubt that there was widespread slaughter of buffaloes and sheep as sacrifices to the goddess, hook-swinging, and other bad practices of a similar character.

BUDDHISM, JAINISM, AND ĀJĪVIKAS

The early history of Buddhism in South India has been incidentally sketched in the opening chapters of this book. Its decline in Andhradeśa, where it had flourished in the early centuries A.D., was noticed by Yuan Chwang, and this decline proceeded further after his time. The renascent Hinduism of the period began the worship of the Buddha at Amarāvatī as an incarnation of Vishnu and seems likewise to have converted many other Buddhist centres into Hindu shrines. In the Tamil country, Buddhism declined rapidly as a result of the activities of the Hindu saints and reformers which we have noticed in this chapter, but it lingered on feebly in different parts of the country. Under the Cholas there were Buddhist settlements in Negapatam on the east coast and at Śrīmūlavāsam in the west; and Buddhism was considered sufficiently important for some scenes from Buddha's life to be represented in decorative panels in a balustrade of the great temple of Tanjore. The ancient Velgam Vehera on the banks of the Periyakulam tank near Trincomalee in Ceylon was remodelled and considerably extended, and renamed Rājarāja Perumbaḷḷi early in the eleventh century; a large life-size limestone image of the Buddha and an inscribed bronze lampstand are among the finds in the *vihāra* area—clear proof of the active interest of the great Chola monarch in the spiritual well-being of his subjects in Ceylon. An important work of Tamil grammar, the *Vīrasōḻiyam* composed in Vīrarājendra's time, has a Buddhist scholar for its author. One section of Kānchipuram bore the name of Buddhakānchī to a relatively late date, and a Buddhist monk from one of the monasteries there sang the praises of a Hindu ruler of eastern Java in the fourteenth century.

In the north-west of the Deccan also, new *vihāras* were coming up on behalf of Buddhism late in the ninth century. Thus, in 853, a monk from Bengal built a great monastery (*mahāvihāra*) in Krishnagiri (Kaṇheri) for the use of the *sangha* and endowed it with one hundred gold *drammas*. In the same neighbourhood a meditation hall was constructed for monks in 877 by a minister of the Śilāhāras of Konkan, and other endowments are recorded at the same time and place for the regular worship of the Buddha.

On the whole, however, Jainism had more influence than Buddhism on the life of the people, particularly in Karnātaka and in the Tamil country owing to the striking contributions made by Jaina authors to the literatures of Kannada and Tamil. Some account of them has already been given in the last chapter on literature. The Jaina temple built at Aihole by Ravikīrti in the reign of Pulakeśin II is said to have been the abode of all excellences, and Jaina temples and monasteries continued to be built everywhere in the extensive dominions ruled by the Chālukyas and the Rāshtrakūtas. Rāshtrakūta Amoghavarsha I, for instance, found solace by retiring to a Jaina monastery more than once in the course of his long reign. Many of the early Western Ganga monarchs were followers of Jainism, and it also found patronage under the Eastern Chālukyas. Amma II (mid-tenth century) built two Jinālayas and established *satras* (feeding houses) attached to them where *śramaṇas* (Jaina monks) of all the four castes were to be fed.

Jainism had much more in common with Hinduism than Buddhism, and many popular beliefs and practices were common to both the systems. Thus in 812 a Jaina temple was endowed for the removal of trouble caused to a Chālukya Vimalāditya by the planet Śanaiścara (Saturn). In many Jaina grants we find that the donees are required to use the proceeds of the endowment for their daily rites and observances in terms identical with those employed in Hindu donations; and influential guilds of merchants often included a strong Jaina wing in their membership. Soon after the establishment of Vijayanagar, Jains complained to king Bukkarāya of persecution by the Vaishnavas. The monarch interceded (1368) and decreed that both parties should practise their respective religions with equal freedom and without mutual interference. Though Jainism has been steadily losing ground it has not altogether disappeared from the country—particularly in parts of Gujarat.

Another sect outside the pale of Hinduism, which continued to count some adherents in South India though it had disappeared elsewhere, was that of the Ājīvikas. Founded by Gośāla Maskarīputra, a contemporary of the Buddha and Mahāvīra, this strictly deterministic school was influential in the Mauryan period in the North, and Aśoka and his successor Daśaratha presented fine rock-cut caves to it. They believed in an inexorable *Niyati* (Destiny) which man was unable to counteract. The South Indian Ājīvika monks practised severe asceticism, and probably influenced by Hinduism and Mahāyāna Buddhism, came to look upon Gośāla as 'an ineffable divinity'; they also developed the 'view that all change and movement were illusory, and that the world was in reality eternally and immovably at rest'. The inscriptions show that they were sometimes subjected to a special tax levied on them, at least by the Cholas.

ISLAM

The contact of South India with Islam is much older than that of the North. A Muslim fleet first sailed in Indian waters in 636, when a governor serving under Caliph Umar sent an army to Thāna; but Umar disapproved of this. Very soon afterwards, Muslim traders continuing the contacts of pre-Muslim days settled in numerous parts of the Malabar coast, married the women of the country, and the issue of such unions became the Māppiḷḷas (Moplahs). Such Muslim traders were encouraged by Hindu Rājas who used them to procure horses for their cavalry and to man their fleets. Al-Ishtakhrī, an Arab writer of the tenth century who knew India at first hand, says that there were Musalmans and Jumma Masjids in the cities of the Rāshtrakūta empire. A doubtful legend relates the conversion to Islam of the last of the Perumāl rulers of Kerala, Cheramān Perumāl. He is said to have made the pilgrimage to Mecca and to have sent directions from there to the rulers of his homeland to receive Muslims hospitably and to build mosques for them. Travellers like Masūdī (916) and Ibn Batūtā (fourteenth century) testify to the presence of Muslims and mosques all along the west coast. There were Muslim settlements on the east coast also, of which Kāyal-pattanam and Nagore were the most important. Islam, it is said, was preached actively near Trichinopoly early in the eleventh century by a Sayyid prince of Turkey, Nathad Vali, who became a missionary, came to India, and spent his last years converting many Hindus. His tomb is still pointed out in the city. According to Ibn Batūtā, the army of Hoysala Ballāla III included 20,000 Musalmans. The Muslim invasions from the North and their consequences, the rise of the Bāhmanī kingdom and its relations with Vijayanagar, have been dealt with elsewhere. By the beginning of the sixteenth century the Māppiḷḷas were estimated by Duarte Barbosa to have formed one-fifth of the population of Malabar, but the arrival of the Portuguese checked the growth of Muslim power and ruined the Arab trade.

It is very difficult to say how far Islam influenced Hindu religious thought and practice in the South. Some traits of the Hindu revival, such as the increasing emphasis on monotheism, on emotional worship, on self-surrender, on the need for devotion to a spiritual teacher, as well as the growing laxity in caste rules and indifference to ritual at least among some sects, have all been held to be in some way or other the result of Islamic influence. But these developments may well be explained from the internal history of Hinduism itself, and there is no direct evidence of the active influence of Islam on their growth. Perhaps, after all, it is not an accident that, as Eliot has observed, sects grew 'more definite in doctrine and organization, especially among Vishnuites, as Hindus became more familiar with Islam'. As we have shown, however, there were Musalmans in plenty who, in general, were left free both to worship and to proselytize.

CHRISTIANITY

A persistent but doubtful tradition ascribes the introduction of Christianity in South India to St Thomas, in the first century A.D. Cosmas, the Alexandrian merchant who travelled in South India in 522, found a church at Quilon and another in Ceylon, both Nestorian. Copper-plate grants to Malabar Christians, the earliest of which is dated 774, show that they had then gathered native converts, though they were not yet very numerous. The strength of the community was increased by a number of immigrations of Christians from western countries, from Baghdad, Nineveh, Jerusalem and other places.

There was a Christian community at St Thomas Mount, but no authentic evidence of its condition is forthcoming before Marco Polo (1293) who first reports the story of the martyrdom of St Thomas on the Mount, but the shrine on the Greater Mount was visited by Hindus and Muslims as well as by the Christians themselves. Thirty years after Marco Polo heard the story of St Thomas, Friar Odoric found some fifteen houses of Nestorians beside the church, but the church itself was filled with idols. A century later Conti reckoned a thousand Nestorians in the city; yet early in the sixteenth century Barbosa found the church in ruins, with a Muslim *fakir* charged to keep a lamp in it.

Christian travellers in the Middle Ages occasionally complain of the paucity of Christians in South India and of the persecution to which they were sometimes subjected, and Friar Jordanus (1321-30) wrote enthusiastically of the great scope that India offered for missionary activity in the cause of Christianity.

Active propagation of Christianity, however, began only after the arrival of the Portuguese and of St Francis Xavier (*c.* 1545). But these efforts did not make much headway except among the lower classes, and what is more, they led to the rise of acute schisms and quarrels between the new Catholic Christians and the other sects that had already established themselves in different parts of the country. The coming of other Christian nations like the Dutch only added to the confusion. We have already seen that the Portuguese policy of turning religious propaganda to political use roused the resentment of even the tolerant rulers of Vijayanagar and their feudatories.

It cannot be said that in the period covered by this book Christianity exerted any potent influence on the life of the people as a whole.

BIBLIOGRAPHY

Archaeological Reports of Ceylon, 1953, 1954

A. L. BASHAM: *The Wonder that was India* (London, 1954)

R. G. BHANDARKAR: *Vaishnavism, Śaivism and Minor Religious Systems* (Strassburg, 1913)

ESTLIN CARPENTER: *Theism in Medieval India* (London, 1921)

TARA CHAND: *Influence of Islam on Indian Culture* (Allahabad, 1936)

SIR CHARLES ELIOT: *Hindusim and Buddhism*, 3 vols. (London, 1921)

J. N. FARQUHAR: *An Outline of the Religious Literature of India* (London, 1920)

CHAPTER XVI

ART AND ARCHITECTURE

Caityas and *vihāras* of the north-western Deccan—Jaina caves of Orissa—Buddhist sanctuaries in the lower Godāvari and Krishna—rock-architecture of the western Deccan (fifth century)—paintings—temples at Aihole—rock-cut halls at Bādāmi—temples at Pattadakal—last phase of rock-architecture in the western Deccan.

Pallava rock-architecture—structural temples—early Chola temples—age of Rājarāja—Tiruvālīśvaram—the Great Temple of Tanjore—Gangaikondaśōḷapuram—Chola sculpture and bronzes—Pāndyan architecture—*gōpuras*—*maṇḍapas*—Jaina monuments.

Chālukya temples of the western Deccan—Hoysala architecture and sculpture.

Architecture of Orissa—Mukhalingam—Bhuvaneśvar—Puri—Konarak.

'Deccani' temples (eleventh and thirteenth centuries)—Hemadpanti style.

Age of Vijayanagar—pillared *maṇḍapas*—Viṭṭhala and Hazāra Rāma temples—secular buildings—Madura style.

Bāhmanī architecture, military and civil—its influence on Hindu architecture.

THIS brief sketch of the architecture and art of South India is more historical than aesthetic; aesthetic appreciation is a matter of individual taste, and the role of the art critic is different from that of the student of its history. Again, though the continuity in the evolution of art forms and the mutual influences of the different schools that flourished in different localities and ages will be taken account of in a general way, no attempt can be made here to study such questions in any detail. Our aim must be to give a general view of the salient features of the different schools and their productions in the light of the most recent studies on the subject.

The earliest monuments that call for notice are the *caityas* and *vihāras* of the north-western Deccan. These are often called 'caves' and 'cave-temples'; such names are misleading when applied to these wonderful excavations, many of which are large, well-planned temples and monasteries skilfully chiselled out of the solid rock with infinite forethought and patience. The term 'rock-architecture' has been suggested as more adequate by Percy Brown (to whose great work on Indian Architecture this account is much indebted).

Such work involved no great problems of constructional engineering, and is best regarded as a branch of sculpture, though 'on a grand and magnificent scale'. The *caitya* was primarily a temple or place of worship and was so called because in early Buddhism the object of worship was generally a *stūpa* (*caitya*); the *vihāra* was a monastery. In Hīnayāna Buddhism the Buddha was never represented in sculptured form, but his presence was indicated by a throne, a footstool, cushions and other symbols. The Buddha image came into use in later Mahāyāna Buddhism and then it was introduced into some of the early *caityas* as at Kanheri and Nasik. The Hīnayāna rock-cut monasteries and shrines are all situated in Bombay State within a radius of two hundred miles round Nasik. The *caitya* was generally 'a large vaulted hall having an apsidal end and divided longitudinally by two colonnades into a broad nave and two aisles. In the apse stood the *stūpa*, also carved out of the natural rock'. Circumambulation of the *stūpa* took place along the aisles and the apse, while the congregation assembled in the nave. The *vihāra* consisted of a 'central hall entered by a doorway' from a verandah in front and surrounded by square cells cut further into the rock, each serving as the abode of a monk. Architecturally the *caityas* are more notable than the *vihāras*. In both there was a close imitation of the wooden structures which were the originals of their designs; even in rock-cut buildings, much woodwork was put into both the facade and interior, so used were the early builders to wood before they started building in stone. But rock-architecture as it comes before us is fully matured, and the stages, if any, of its evolution are no longer traceable.

There are eight *caitya* halls of the second and first century B.C. and in their probable order of execution they are 'Bhāja, Kondane, Pitālkohra, Ajanta (No. 10), Bedsa, Ajanta (No. 9), Nasik and Karle', the first four belonging to the second century and the remainder to the first. Two *caitya* halls at Junnar are 'of the same type and date as that at Nasik'. The series may be said to close with the *caitya* at Kanheri (second century A.D.). In the earlier examples the pillars of the colonnades are copies of plain wooden posts, with an octagonal section and without capital or base, and they generally slope towards the interior; in later examples the inward slant disappears and the columns become more elaborate, with bases and capitals, and evolve into an 'order'.

The horseshoe archway above the entrance which dominates the façade also undergoes a corresponding evolution. Bedsa and Karle are the finest examples of this early series of *caityas*, and the façade as well as the column is marked by many innovations. At Bedsa the base of the column is vase-shaped and its capital is surmounted by a group of figures and animals 'each of which consists of a male and female figure lightly clad but with heavy ornaments seated astride kneeling animals, on the one side horses, and on the other elephants. These groups are exceptionally vivid and spirited examples of rock sculpture, evidently the work of a master craftsman in this medium.' The hall is 45½ feet long and 21 feet wide. Karle (Pl. I), the largest and best of the series, is 124 feet long, 46½ feet wide and 45 feet high. Here the façade consists of two stages, the lower wall pierced by three doorways and an upper gallery over which rises the enormous horseshoe window. The pillars of the colonnade have capitals more elaborate than at Bedsa, and they have the effect of a frieze and cornice. From them rise the wooden ribs attached to the domed stone of the roof. The spaces between the doorways in the lower stage of the façade are each decorated with sculptures of two human figures, very massive and grandly executed. 'The setting back of the entrance into the face of the rock forms an outer porch, the sides of which are sculptured in architectural façades of several storeys, the lowest supported by huge elephants, the second decorated with sculptured figures' like those of the lower stage of the façade. The entrance was preceded by a wooden antechamber or porch, and farther outside stands one of the two original monolithic *dhvajastambhas* with a capital of four lions which once supported a wheel. The arrangements carefully designed to deflect the glaring sunshine streaming through the horseshoe window of the façade have received high praise from Percy Brown who observes: 'There are few lighting effects more solemnly beautiful than the soft luminous atmosphere diffused in this manner through the sun-window at Karle'. The *caitya* at Kanheri is 'a decadent copy of that at Karle, but only about two-thirds its size'.

The *vihāras* are monastic houses excavated near the *caityas* in secluded places where the monks found freedom to pursue their religious observances without distraction. From a small beginning in course of time they developed a full complement of rooms: a dormitory, a common room, a refectory, and so on, besides cells for individual monks. Ajanta (No. 12) is 'a simple but typical example' of an early single-storeyed *vihāra*. Another *vihāra* of the same type is that to the left of the *caitya* at Kondane. At Nasik this type of *vihāra* is seen 'in its most decorative form . . . in a series of three examples', all of the first century A.D., viz. Nahapāna (No. 8), Gautamīputra and Śrīyajña, so-called from their inscriptions. 'All have columned porticos' but no pillars in their large central halls, from which open the individual cells generally containing stone beds.

Contemporary with these monasteries in the Western Ghats, another group—not Buddhist but Jaina—was excavated near Cuttack in Orissa. These rock-cut chambers are all located in two hills known as Khaṇḍagiri and Udayagiri, and were made within the century and a half preceding the Christian era. There are in all some thirty-five excavations but only half the number are at all important, only one of these being on Khaṇḍagiri. There was apparently no regular plan and they were cut in convenient places and connected by paths. The workmanship is clumsy and crude but that was perhaps at least in part due to the rough texture of the sandstone. Locally, these monasteries are known as *gumphas*, and each is distinguished by some prefix, like Hāthi (elephant). There are many unidentified sculptured scenes from Jaina legends in the more important *gumphas*. The style of the sculptures is at once original and vigorous. The Rāni and Gaṇeśa *gumphas* are both two-storeyed; and the courtyard of the Rāni, there is good reason to think, constituted an open-air theatre. In it are the remains of channels for the distribution of water throughout the structure. In the Gaṇeśa *gumpha* the entrance steps are flanked with figures of elephants, the first appearance of the sculptured-animal motif at the entrance to a rock-cut hall which was developed with such wonderful effect later at Ellora and Elephanta (where, however, the elephants are replaced by lions).

Remains of extensive Buddhist sanctuaries, rock-cut and structural, are found on many sites in the lower reaches of the Krishna and Godāvari rivers. Nearly all of them bear traces of an early foundation, for in this region Buddhist art found a refuge under the patronage of the Andhras and their successors and had a more or less continuous evolution from about 200 B.C. to A.D. 400. The monuments of this region form a precious link between the ancient schools of Barhut and Sānchī and medieval Hindu art.

Rock-cut architecture is found in two sites in Andhra state, one at Guṇṭupalli (Krishna district), the other on the Sankaram hills (Vizagapatam district). The small circular *caitya* of Guṇṭupalli (200 B.C.), 18 feet in diameter, and its ribbed domical roof are obvious imitations of a primitive hut, and the whole structure, perhaps, contains the clue to the beginnings of the more elaborate *caitya* hall. There are, besides, two *vihāras*, one large and the other small, ruins of a brick-built *caitya* hall, and several *stūpas* of various sizes, rock-cut and structural. There is no regular plan and the work is rather coarse. The remains on the Sankaram hills are perhaps later—about A.D. 350. A number of monolithic *stūpas* and rock-cut chambers scattered in an irregular way to suit the configuration of the hilltop and the foundations of an extensive structural monastery are the principal remains. Some of the monolithic *stūpas* here are the largest of their kind, one being 65 feet in diameter at the base. Here, as at Guṇṭupalli, the work is rather crude and unskilled.

The technical skill and artistic excellence of the Andhra craftsman are best seen in the structural monuments, particularly the *stūpas* distributed over an area of 75 miles all round Ellore. The most notable of them were at Goli, Jaggeyapeta, Bhaṭṭiprōlu, Ghaṇṭśāla, Amarāvatī and Nāgārjunikonda. As examples of Buddhist architecture and sculpture they had few equals at the beginning of the Christian era. Most of them had an exterior encasement of white marble, richly carved in low relief, and this gave them an imposing appearance. In the early examples, as at Bhaṭṭiprōlu, the *stūpa* was built solid, but later strength and economy of material were secured by means of cross-walls and 'other walls radiating towards the circumference like the spokes of a wheel'. The bricks themselves were of enormous size, 24″×18″×4″. At first, the *stūpa* was a low hemispherical mound, as at Sānchī, but in later examples the dome is raised by being set on a lofty plinth. The marble casing was never applied over the whole surface of the brick core, but only to its lower portion, the remainder being plastered and painted white. At the four cardinal points there were rectangular projections from the plinth which accommodated steps leading to the procession-path above the plinth. Above each of these projections stood five slender pillars which may have symbolized the five Dhyānibuddhas and were called *āryaka kambhas* ('worshipful columns'). 'As an ornamental attribution to the domical shape of the *stūpa*, this projection with its graceful pillars was an admirable device and gives an artistic distinction to the southern type.'

The largest of all these *stūpas*, that of Amarāvatī, had its beginning about 200 B.C., but was completely reconstructed between A.D. 150 and 200. The dome was 162 feet across at the base and the concentric railing outside enclosed the *pradakshiṇa* path 15 feet wide. The height of the dome must have been from 90 to 100 feet. Some 20 feet above the ground there was a higher processional path with the usual offsets and the *āryaka* pillars. There was a balustrade about 8 feet high round the terraced path and it was richly carved on the inner sides. All that remains now of this stupendous monument are the sculptural slabs and parts of the railing preserved in museums.

The sculptures of Amarāvatī, like those from several other *stūpas* in the neighbourhood, depict incidents in the life of the Buddha and scenes of worship, and contain many fine ornamental motifs. The figures of women and animals are in the Sānchī tradition and display a vigorous and supple realism, characteristic of all Indian sculpture, particularly of animals, from the days of Aśoka to the age of the Pallava sculptures at Māmallapuram. In the scenes depicting life in the women's quarters, there is an innocent delight in the nude and a refined sensuality with marked freshness. The Bodhisattvas and the Buddha are represented actually and not by mere symbols, and good reason has been shown to admit the presence of Roman influence in the art of Amarāvatī, which foreshadows that of Aihole and Māmallapuram. This side of Amarāvatī art leaves naturalism behind and develops an idealism of the highest order, 'a new canon of beauty and tranquillity', 'the aesthetic ideal of India'. 'The school of Amarāvatī,' says Grousset 'can show many a scene which is a veritable picture in stone, perfect in its composition, by some very great, though unknown, artist'. In the medallion (Madras Museum) depicting the taming of the elephant (Pl. II), for instance, the confusion caused by the mad beast contrasts remarkably with the calm after it is tamed by the power of Buddha's kindliness. In the various stories illustrated 'there are representations of walled cities, palace-buildings, *toraṇas* and *stūpas;* and more than one of the slabs portrays the *stūpa* of Amarāvatī itself as it must have appeared in the height of its glory'.

At Tēr in the Sholapur district and Chezārla in the Krishna district are found Buddhist *caitya* halls built in brick, perhaps in the fifth century A.D., and surviving to this day because they were appropriated to brahminical uses after the decline of Buddhism. We refer to the Trivikrama temple at Tēr and the Kapoteśvara temple at Chezārla. These two small buildings, each not more than 30 feet long, are now the only means of judging the external appearance of the Buddhist structural temples as the rock-cut *caityas* have no exteriors except their façades.

About the middle of the fifth century there was a revival of rock-architecture in the western Deccan under the stimulus of Mahāyāna Buddhism. The chief centres of this art were Ajanta, Ellora and Aurangabad, not to speak of some places of lesser importance in the same region. The *caitya* in its essential features remained the same as before except for the introduction of Buddha images, sometimes of colossal proportions. The *vihāra*, however, undergoes much alteration and the innermost range of cells which served originally as dormitories for monks now became sanctuaries containing images of the Buddha. And the *vihāra* thus became a place of worship as well as of residence.

The monastic retreats of Ajanta extend in a 'sickle-shaped curve along the face of the cliff for over a third of a mile, and overhanging the waters of a pretty stream, cascading through the ravine below'. Here are twenty-eight halls of various sizes and they have been numbered in order from west to east. Two *caityas* and three *vihāras* (Nos. 8, 9, 10, 12 and 13) had come into existence in the earlier Hīnayāna period under the Andhras (200 B.C.-A.D. 200); the others were added in the two centuries that followed A.D. 450. In these later examples the imitation of wooden construction is discarded, and a distinct advance made in the handling of the rock-medium. The walls and the ceilings of these halls were covered with a large number of mural frescoes which have survived in some of them almost intact.

The two *vihāras* (Nos. 16 and 17) made under the Vākāṭakas (about A.D. 500) are pillared halls (with the usual cells and shrines in the back walls) containing Buddhas seated in 'European fashion' (*pralamba pāda*). In the paintings of No. 16, there is a remarkable combination of figures with architectural motifs, while a striking narrative style marks the scenes of the life of the Buddha depicted in No. 17. No. 19 (Pl. III), with its highly embellished façade and

.te I KARLE: CHAITYA MAIN HALL

Plate II AMARAVATI : THE MIRACLE OF THE INFURIATED ELEPHA

Plate III

AJANTA: CAVE 19

Plate IVa AIHOLE: DURGA TEMPLE FROM THE S.W.

e V

ELLORA: KAILASA TEMPLE (GENERAL VIEW)

e IVb

HANTA: TRIMURTI

Plate VIa ELLORA: DUMARLE

ate VII MAMALLAPURAM: THE DESCENT OF THE GANGES

ate VIb

.ORA: KAILASA TEMPLE (DETAIL OF PLINTH)

Plate VIIIa MAMALLAPURAM : THE SHORE TEMPLE

ɩte IX TANJORE: GREAT TEMPLE (GENERAL VIEW)

ɩte: VIIIb
NCHIPURAM: VAIKUNTHAPERUMAL TEMPLE

Plate X DANCING SIVA, NATARAJA (TENTH CENTURY)

Plate XI LAKSHMI

Plate XII

HALEBID: HOYSALESVARA TEMPLE WALL DETAIL

e XIII SOMANATHAPUR: KESAVA TEMPLE WALL DETAILS

Plate XIV

BHUVANESVAR: LINGARAJA TEMPI

ate XV KONARAK: ROCK ELEPHANT

Plate XVI HAMPI: HIPPOGRYPH AND RIDER

Plate XIX

Plate XVII

MADURA: MINAKSHI TEMPLE

Plate X

Plate XX BIDAR: MADRASA OF MAHMUD GAWAN

its numerous Buddhas, marking a great development of Mahāyāna sculpture, may be dated about 550, thus forming a link between the earlier group and that of the seventh century. The pillars within this *caitya* are fluted columns richly ornamented. The capitals are of the pot and foliage variety. The chief painting here is the ' Return to Kapilavastu '. Nos. 1-5 and 21-6 were the last group to come into existence (*c.* 600-50). No. 1 contains the painting of the beautiful ' Bodhisattva with blue lotus ' and other famous frescoes including the ' Śibi-Jātaka ' and ' Banquet of Persians ', really a representation of the Buddhist god Pañcika. The painters of Ajanta ' had a complete command of posture. Their knowledge of the types and positions, gestures and beauties of hands is amazing. Many racial types are rendered; the features are often elaborately studied and of high-breeding, and one might call it stylistic-breeding. In some pictures considerable impetus of movement of different kinds is well suggested. Some of the schemes of colour composition are most remarkable and interesting and there is great variety.' A critic observes: ' It is impossible for anyone who has not seen them with their own eyes to realize how great and solid the paintings in the caves are; how wonderful in their simplicity and religious fervour.' But the simplicity was the result of a very conscious art-tradition of long standing and, as Grousset has said, ' every one of the chief subjects of the Ajanta frescoes is worthy of separate analysis '. The Ajanta style of painting is seen contemporaneously at Sigiriya in Ceylon and some centuries later in the paintings of a Jaina cave at Śittannavāśal (Pudukkōṭṭai), in the cave-temple at Tirumalaipuram (Tinnevelly district), and on the inner walls of the *garbhagriha* of the Great Temple at Tanjore.

The rock-architecture of Ellora was begun by the Buddhists from 450 to 650, with twelve rock-cut halls that fall into two sub-groups, one slightly later than the other and each comprising a prayer-hall with monasteries attached to it. The later group contains two monasteries which are the only examples in three storeys, rising to a height of nearly 50 feet with wide courtyards in front. The technique of rock-architecture reached its culmination in some of these *vihāras* in which ' lines are straighter, angles more correct, and surfaces more true than in any other examples '. At Aurangabad there are three groups of Buddhist excavations in a hill about 3 miles north of the city. One of them includes a *caitya* and four *vihāras*, another has four *vihāras*, and the third comprises three unimportant caves. They all belong to the sixth and seventh centuries. Some of the sculptures of deities and devotees, male and female, in these *vihāras* are remarkable for their massive proportions and bold relief and for their life-like presentation of the people of the period, their garments, head-dresses and ornaments.

A group of four pillared rock-cut halls at Bādāmi, three of them Hindu and one Jaina, are all of the same type, each comprising 'a pillared verandah, a columned hall, and a small square cella cut deep into the rock'. One of these (No. 3) is a Vaishnava cave exactly dated 578, and contains fine reliefs of Vishnu seated on Ananta and a Narasimha, both in the verandah. The workmanship in these caves is marked by a high degree of technical excellence. One noteworthy feature is the running frieze of *gaṇas* in various amusing postures carved in relief on each plinth. The front of these caves is otherwise unassuming but the interior is treated with great skill and care in every detail.

The beginnings of Hindu temple architecture in South India are best traced in the remains of the early brick temples of the Ikshvākus excavated at Nāgārjunakonda in 1959. Here the temple complexes are seen to comprise shrines with *ardha*—and *mahā-maṇḍapas* in one axial line, *prākāra*, *gōpura*, *dhvaja-stambha*, etc., at this early date. One of the temples has *parivārālayas*, subsidiary shrines, with square, octagonal and circular plans anticipating the later Nāgara, Drāviḍa and Vesara styles. The main shrines are generally apsidal, though square in one or two instances, an indication that temple forms were common to all creeds. The next stage is seen in the temple-complex at Aihole and its neighbourhood dating from about A.D. 600. Aihole is a town of temples and contains no fewer than seventy structures. The work started there was continued in the neighbouring towns of Bādāmi and Pattadakal. The temple at Aihole known as Ladh Khān, usually assigned to about 450 but really much later, say 620 or so, is a low flat-roofed building 50 feet square, with a small square cella and a porch set on the roof at a later date and forming an independent shrine of the Sun. Of the main temple three sides are completely enclosed by walls, two of which carry stone windows perforated in a variety of beautiful designs. On the fourth side, which forms the eastern front, there is an open porch on the pillars of which are figures, of the river-goddesses. The interior is a pillared hall containing 'two square groups of columns one within the other'. A large *nandi* fills the central bay, and the cella at the farther end is not a separate chamber leading off from the main hall, as one would expect, but built within it against the back wall. The entire disposition is totally inadequate for the purposes of a temple, and Percy Brown suggests that it was just a moot hall converted into a temple. In the pilasters at the exterior angles of the building may be traced the beginnings of the 'Dravidian order' with the tapering upper end of the column and its 'cushion capital with an expanded floral abacus supporting the bracket'. The construction of the roof is also peculiar as it consists of large flat slabs held together by long narrow stones covering the entire length of the joints and fitting into grooves cut in the slabs.

Very different from Ladh Khān is the Durgā temple (Pl. IVa), which was another experiment seeking to adapt the Buddhist *caitya* to a brahminical temple. This temple, perhaps of the eighth century, is an apsidal structure (60 feet by 36 feet) with a large portico 24 feet deep on its eastern front, making its entire length 84 feet. The temple stands on a high plinth with many mouldings. The top of its flat roof is 30 feet from the ground. A *śikhara* rises above the *garbhagriha* in the apse and there is a verandah roofed with sloping slabs carried on massive square columns with heavy brackets and this forms the *pradakshiṇa* path.

The *śikhara* or pyramidal tower over the sanctum is generally curvilinear in shape in Northern India, but in the far South it rises by square terraces of diminishing size. In the Deccan both styles were used. There was even a tendency, at times, to combine the features of the two styles. The *śikhara* of the Durgā temple, perhaps a later addition, is of the Northern variety.

Another temple very similar to the Durgā temple is the smaller and simpler Huccimalli-guḍi which contains one new feature, namely a vestibule or *antarāla* between the cella and the main hall. One of the fairly early temples to be built at Aihole was the Jaina temple of Meguti (634), which shows some progress in the erection of structural temples. It is unfinished and its shrine is detached from the back wall. Of nearly the same date is the small finely-proportioned and magnificently located Mālagitti Śivālaya at Bādāmi.

The next stage in the development of Chālukyan art is marked by the temples at Pattadakal, about ten miles from Bādāmi. There are ten temples here, four in the Northern style and six in the Southern. The Pāpanātha temple (*c.* 680) among the former, and Sangameśvar (*c.* 725) and Virūpāksha (*c.* 740) among the latter, are the most notable. The temple of Pāpanātha in its plan and elevation alike exhibits shortcomings due to uncertainty regarding the correct relation of the different parts of the temple structure to one another. The temple is 90 feet long and too low for its length, its tower in true Northern style is too small and stunted, and the *antarāla* too big—almost a supplementary hall. The outer walls carry a close and monotonous repetition of canopied niches representing a shrine. This temple was perhaps one of the first attempts to combine Northern and Southern features in one structure, and was not quite successful.

The vastly improved design and execution of the Virūpāksha temple, built by one of Vikramāditya II's queens, was most likely due to workmen brought from Kānchipuram, and to their direct imitation of the Kailāsanātha temple which had come into existence in the Pallava capital some decades earlier. 'There is a bold beauty,' says Brown, 'in the appearance of the Virūpāksha temple as a whole, which is best seen in the exterior. It is a comprehensive scheme as it consists not only of the central structure, but of a detached *nandi* pavilion in front, and it is contained within a walled enclosure entered by an appropriate gateway.' It measures 120 feet from the front of the porch to the back of the shrine, and the studied grouping of its parts produces a very pleasant total effect. The heaviness of the stonework is relieved by an increase in the amount and quality of the sculpture. The main shrine, distinct from the *maṇḍapa*, has a *pradakshiṇa* path. The pillared *maṇḍapa* has thick walls with perforated stone windows. The square *śikhara* rises in clearly defined storeys each of considerable elevation. The external wall surface is divided by pilasters into well spaced ornamental niches filled alternately with windows and sculptures. The sculptures include representations of Śiva, *nāgas* and *nāginis*, and scenes from the *Rāmāyaṇa*. To cite Brown once more: 'The sculpture flows into the architecture in a continuous yet disciplined stream. . . . The Virūpāksha temple is one of those rare buildings of the past in which the spirit still lingers of the men who conceived it and wrought it with their hands.' The neighbouring Sangameśvara temple, built some years earlier, is very much in the same style but has an open *maṇḍapa.*

Progress in the erection of structural temples did not mean the cessation of rock-architecture, which continued to flourish to the end of the ninth century. Its final manifestation occurred in three localities, namely: Ellora, already in the occupation of Buddhists for over 200 years; the islands of Elephanta and Salsette near Bombay; and the Pallava kingdom in the far South. At Ellora, the brahminical group (spread over half a mile along the west face of the hill) contains sixteen temples. They fall into three or four types. The simplest is still much under the influence of the Buddhist *vihāra* and is just a pillared portico with a cella beyond, like the Daśāvatār cave. The second type was similar to the first except for the passage round the cella, as in Rāvaṇa-kā-khai and Rāmeśvara. In the third type, the shrine stands in the centre of a cruciform hall having more than one entrance to it, as in the Dumarlena, the temple at Elephanta, and the Jogeśvara in Salsette. Lastly, the culmination of this architecture came in the monolithic temple of Kailāsa which stands in a class by itself and in which an entire structural temple in all its details is carved out of the living rock.

Of the first type, the Daśāvatār is the largest and best example. A rock-cut entrance leads to an open courtyard of irregular shape with a detached shrine in its centre, probably a *nandi-maṇḍapa.* Beyond this lies the façade of the temple, in two storeys defined by two rows of square pillars one above the other. Each floor consists of a large pillared hall, the pillars being generally ' simple square prisms with flat abacus capitals '. But the architecture was only meant to furnish the framework for the gigantic sculptures of Hindu mythology adorning the large sunk panels between pilasters at regular intervals on the surrounding walls. The sculptures on one side are mostly Vaishnava while those on the other are entirely Śaiva. One of the finest of these sculptures is that of the death of Hiraṇyakaśipu.

Both the Rāvaṇa-kā-khai and the Rāmeśvara of the second type are simple in their plan. On each side of the entrance to the monolithic cella in the Rāvaṇa-kā-khai are carved a number of figures, including two *dvārapālas*; and within is a broken image of Durgā. On the walls of the pillared hall are recesses between pilasters carrying bold sculptures in high relief, Śaiva subjects on the south and Vaishnava on the north. The Rāmeśvara contains a *lingam* in the cella guarded by giant *dvārapālas* and is remarkable for the wealth of carving which adorns it in all its parts. The handling of the female figures in particular shows ' a feeling for grace of pose and voluptuous beauty which is instinctive '.

The Dumarlena (Pl. VIa), the only example of the third type at Ellora, has three separate entrances, one at the front and one on each wing. It is much larger than the previous types in its area and in the scale of its parts, and the light entering the temple from three different directions makes the interior much more impressive than in the other types. The central feature of the *lena* is a massive shrine guarded by huge *dvārapālas* by the sides of each of its four doorways, reached by flights of steps. ' Leading up to this shrine and partly encircling it, is the main hall, a fine rectangular gallery 150 feet long and 50 feet wide divided into a nave and aisles by a colonnade of five pillars on each side, including the two forming the principal entrance.' Flanking the main hall are the transepts leading to the two lateral entrances, the width across the temple between the side-entrances being the same as its depth. Each of the three entrances is a wide pillared opening approached by a flight of steps guarded by sejant lions mounted on pedestals on either side. The pillars within the temple are of huge proportions, 15 feet high and 5 feet wide at the base, and carry ' cushion ' capitals.

The second example of this type, on the island of Elephanta, near Bombay, resembles the Dumarlena in many ways but is somewhat smaller (130 feet by 129 feet). But the Elephanta temple is better than all others of its kind in its sculptures, particularly those on the back wall. There are three large square recesses separated by pilasters each bearing a huge *dvārapāla*. The panel on the left contains a representation of Ardhanārī, the hermaphrodite form of Śiva, while the corresponding one on the right contains figures of Śiva and Pārvatī. In the central recess is the famous colossal three-headed bust (Pl. IVb) long called Trimūrti but in reality a representation of Maheśa. Of this magnificent sculpture Grousset remarks: ' The three countenances of the one being are here harmonized without a trace of effort. There are few material representations of the divine principle at once as powerful and as well balanced as this in the art of the whole world. Nay, more, here we have undoubtedly the grandest representation of the pantheist God ever made by the hand of man. In a magnificently poetic outburst Rodin has celebrated "this full, pouting mouth, rich in sensuous expressions, these lips like a lake of pleasure fringed by the noble, palpitating nostrils". Indeed never have the exuberant vigour of life, the tumult of universal joy expressing itself in ordered harmony, the pride of a power superior to any other, and the secret exaltation of the divinity immanent in all things found such serene expression.'

A third example of this style, the temple of Jogeśvarī (*c.* 800) in Salsette, is larger than the others, measuring 250 feet in a straight line, but has no other remarkable features about it.

The last type, a complete monolithic structural temple, is represented by the unique example of Kailāsa at Ellora (Pl. V), excavated under Rāshtrakūta Krishna I. In its general plan, it bears a certain resemblance to the Virūpāksha temple at Pattadakal though it is more than twice its size. The temple resolves itself into four parts—its main body, the entrance gateway, a *nandi* shrine in between, and cloisters round the courtyard. Supplementary chambers, probably of a slightly later date, have been cut on the sides of the courtyard, that in the north wall called the Lankeśvara being a large, pillared hall. The entrance to the temple is on the west, and its main body measures roughly 150 feet by 100 feet, with projections at intervals throughout the entire height of the structure. The lofty and substantial plinth 25 feet in height is marked by heavy mouldings, above and below, while the central face is taken up by a magnificent series of elephants and lions seeming to support the structure (Pl. VIb). We cannot do better than quote the description from Percy Brown:

'Standing high on this plinth,' says Brown, 'is the temple proper, approached by flights of steps leading to a pillared porch on its western side, and it is here that its designers rose to the greatest heights. There is no pronounced departure from the conventional combination of the *maṇḍapa* and the *vimāna*, but the manner in which various architectural elements, all definite and sharply outlined, such as cornices, pilasters, niches and porticos, have been assembled in an orderly and artistic manner to form a unified whole, is masterly. Then over all rises the stately tower in three tiers, with its prominently projecting gable-front, and surmounted by a shapely cupola, reaching up to a total height of 95 ft. But this is not all. Around the wide space of the platform at the base of the *vimāna* five subsidiary shrines have been fashioned out of the rock, each an elegant reproduction to a reduced scale of the main theme, to which they serve as a refrain. The interior consists of a pillared hall, from which a vestibule leads to the cella. This hall is a well-proportioned compartment measuring 70 feet by 62 feet having sixteen square piers in groups of four in each quarter, an arrangement which produces a cruciform central aisle with an effect of great dignity.'[1]

Noteworthy in the remaining parts of the scheme are the two *dhvajastambhas* 51 feet high, one on each side of the *nandi* shrine, in themselves striking works of art, which mark an important stage in the evolution of the Southern pillar style. Lastly the sculptural decoration of the entire temple fits its parts admirably and forms the crowning glory of the monument. The vigorous representation of Rāvaṇa's attempt to uproot mount Kailāsa specially deserves to be noted.

Also at Ellora are five Jaina excavations, all probably of the ninth century, but only three of them are notable. One is a copy of the Kailāsa, about a fourth of its size, and is known as Choṭā-Kailāsa. The other two—Indrasabhā and Jagannāthasabhā—are both two-storeyed. Indrasabhā is the larger and finer. The sculptures in its upper storey, as well as its frontage comprising three sides of a quadrangle elaborately carved into a façade with two storeys, are remarkable features.

Remains of frescoes can be found on the ceiling of the porch on the second storey of the temple known as Rangmahal (probably because of the coloured decoration which once covered all its interior). The paintings are of two periods, the earlier contemporary with the excavation and therefore of the eighth century, the second much later. The later layer overlaps and partly conceals the earlier and is decidedly inferior. The earlier painting is clearly related to the Ajanta school. Vishnu and Lakshmī borne through the clouds by *garuḍas* of the human type, a rider upon a horned lion and pairs of *gandharvas* floating amongst the clouds can be identified among the paintings, besides representations of lotus pools with elephants, fish, and so on. The quality of the painting is already much removed from the style of Ajanta with features connecting it with the medieval style of Gujarat.

[1] *Indian Architecture* (*Buddhist and Hindu*), p. 87.

In the far South, the Pallavas bridge the transition from rock-architecture to structural stone temples. Their architecture and sculpture constitute a most brilliant chapter in the history of South Indian art. Its first phase was entirely rock-cut and comprised two groups of monuments: one the pillared *maṇḍapas*, all of the reign of Mahendravarman I, who gloried in the construction of temples without the use of bricks, timber, metals or mortar; and the other, including similar but more elaborate *maṇḍapas* and monolithic temples known as *rathas*, all of the reign of Narasimha-varman I Mahāmalla and his immediate successors. The *maṇḍapas* of the Mahendra group are simple pillared halls with one or more cellas cut into the back wall. The main feature of the front façade is a row of pillars each 7 feet high, the shaft being square in section with a two-foot side above and below, and the corners chamfered in the middle third to give an octagonal section. A heavy bracket provides the capital. In the earliest examples (Maṇḍagappaṭṭu and Trichinopoly), there is no cornice above the pillars, but later a roll moulding was added as at Pallāvaram. In still later examples, e.g. Dalavanur, the roll cornice carries at intervals a new ornament known as the *kūḍu* which is really a much reduced version of the Buddhist *caitya* window.

But it is in the elaboration of the pillars that the beginnings of a distinctive Pallava ' order ' can be traced, and the figure of a lion is introduced and combined with the pillar in its lower portion and another in the capital. This order of pillar and capital was further refined and developed into a column of striking elegance in the productions falling in the second group called after Mahāmalla.

The rock-cut Anantaśayana temple at Undavalli (Guntur district) and other cave temples and monoliths in Bezwada, Mogalrajapuram etc., in the lower Krishna valley, must be deemed to be of Eastern Chālukya origin and definitely post-Mahendravarman in date. Likewise the Bhairavakonda cave temples near Udayagiri, excavated into a softer soapstone-like rock in a gorge in the hill separating the Nellore and Cuddapah districts, are different in style from Pallava and Chālukya, and must be assigned to a later date and to either the Eastern Chālukyas or Telugu Chodas of the region.

All the examples of the Mahāmalla group are found in the seaport town of Māmallapuram (Mahābalipuram) at the mouth of the Palar river, 32 miles south of Madras. A large granite hill 100 feet high, half a mile in length from north to south and a quarter of a mile wide, and a smaller granite outcrop further south, admirably served the purpose of the talented Pallava sculptors. Māmallapuram must have been a busy port with its royal residences, bazaars, warehouses and harbour. All the secular buildings of relatively perishable material have disappeared but the halls and sculptures quarried out of the natural rock with a religious intent have survived. There can be little doubt that Māmallapuram was one of the chief entrepôts of South India and that from it streamed forth strong cultural influences which shaped the art of Hindu colonies in Indonesia and Indo-China.

Clear traces survive of a carefully-designed system to supply the town with fresh water drawn from the Palar river and distributed to all parts of the port; and it is quite possible that the remarkable open-air sculpture 'The Descent of the Ganges' (Pl. VII), long known as 'Arjuna's Penance', was not unrelated to this system. This vast sculpture, in high relief, is nearly 30 yards long and 23 feet high, covering the sea-face of the cliff. There is a cascade in a natural fissure in the middle of the rock in which a band of *nāgas* and *nāgīs* sport and symbolize the sacred waters, and on both sides are sculptured figures of deities, human beings and animals of all kinds approaching or facing the fissure in attitudes of adoration. 'What we have before us here,' says Grousset, 'is a vast picture, a regular fresco in stone. This relief is a masterpiece of classic art in the breadth of its composition, the sincerity of its impulse which draws all creatures together round the beneficent waters, and its deep, fresh love of nature.'[1] A small shrine immediately to the left of the cascade contains the standing figure of Śiva. Before this temple is bowed the emaciated figure of Bhagīratha who is represented also above practising *tapas* with upraised arms. Among the sculptured animals, the monumental elephants on the right and the ascetic cat imitating the posture of Bhagīratha's penance with trustful mice playing at its feet are particularly noteworthy, as also the pair of deer which look on the scene 'from the mouth of a cave opposite, on the left hand side, with the life-like action of the stag scratching his nose with his hind foot'. More amazing still in its masterly realism is the detached family of monkeys sculptured in the round

[1] Grousset, *India* (English translation), p. 230.

'with the male picking vermin off the female while she suckles her two little ones'.

There are altogether ten *maṇḍapas* of the Mahāmalla style on various sites on the main hill at Māmallapuram. All of them exhibit much progress from the simple style of the Mahendra caves though they still retain more or less the same general character and proportions as before. None of them is a large structure. Generally speaking the dimensions are: façade, 25 feet wide, 15-20 feet high, depth (including cella) 25 feet; pillars, 9 feet high, sides 1-2 feet at their widest; cellas, rectangular, each side 5-10 feet. The pillars are the main features. The roll cornice above them in front is decorated with *kūḍus*. Above the cornice is a parapet formed of miniature shrines alternately long and short. In the interior, pilasters and mouldings on the walls supply a suitable frame for the sculptural figures of mythological subjects. Some of the more developed pillars, like those on the exterior of the Mahishāsura *maṇḍapa* and in the façade of the Varāha *maṇḍapa*, look singularly graceful. But the two inner columns of the former, both lion pillars, are the best of the whole lot. The fluting and bands of their shafts, the graceful necking (*taḍi*), the beautiful 'melon' capitals (*kumbha*) and the lotus form (*idaḻ*) above, with the wide abacus (*palagai*), combine very well to produce the typical Pallava 'order'. Notable among the sculptures are the magnificent reliefs of the Varāha and Vāmana *avatāras*, of Sūrya, Durgā and Gajalakshmī, and two fine groups of royal figures representing Simhavishnu and Mahendravarman with their queens, all in the Varāha cave. The vivid dramatic effect and the sureness in the groups of figures characteristic of these sculptures marks other reliefs also, such as the sleep of Vishnu on the serpent Ananta, and the battle of Durgā with the buffalo demon Mahisha, both in the Mahisha *maṇḍapa*, and Krishna raising the Govardhana in the Pañca Pāndava *maṇḍapa*.

Mention must be made in passing of the existence of rock-cut *maṇḍapas* in the Pāndya country. These have not received much attention, but doubtless they were contemporary with the Pallava *maṇḍapas* and are more or less in the same style. One prominent example with sculptured scenes on its walls is found at Tirupparankunṟam, near Madura, hidden behind a good-sized medieval temple of Subrahmanya and serving as its *garbhagriha*. Other instances of temples built in front of rock-cut *maṇḍapas* are known, e.g. at Śingaperumāl-kōyil in Chingleput district. But by far the most beautiful rock-cut temple of the early Pāndyas is the Veṭṭurān Koyil at Kaḻugamalai, a 'half-finished free-standing monument' remarkable for the excellence of its sculpture and iconography.

The monolithic *rathas* popularly called the Seven Pagodas, though in the same style as the *maṇḍapas*, are obviously copies of wooden religious structures with all the details of timber work faithfully reproduced in granite. None of their interiors is finished and they do not seem ever to have been actually used. There are eight of them altogether, the southern group called after the names of Draupadī, Arjuna, Bhīma, Dharmarāja and Sahadeva, and three others in the north and north-west called Ganeśa, Piḍāri and Vaḷaiyān-kuṭṭai. The *rathas* are only of moderate size, none of them being more than 42 feet long, 35 feet broad or 40 feet high. The Draupadī *ratha* is merely a cell, a copy of a thatched structure, with its base supported by animal figures, a lion alternating with an elephant. All the other *rathas* are copies of the *vihāra* or the *caitya*. The *vihāra* type is pyramidal in shape, and the Dharmarāja is a good example of the style. It is a small square hall in the centre with pillared verandahs below and a pyramidal *śikhara* above. Its plinth has many strong mouldings and its porticos with lion pillars greatly improve the appearance. 'This type of design,' says Brown, 'is not only an effective production in itself, but it is a storehouse of pleasing forms and motifs, besides being replete with potentialities.'

The Bhīma, Sahadeva and Ganeśa *rathas* are of the *caitya* type, oblong in plan, with two or more storeys, and barrel roofs with gable ends. The Sahadeva is apsidal, a form adopted in some later Pallava and early Chola temples, the shape of the latter specially designated *gajaprishṭha* ('elephant back'). The Ganeśa is entered through a pillared portico on its long side. The oblong plan, diminishing storeys and barrel roofs with pinnacles (*kalaśas*) and gable ends of these *rathas* may well have suggested the design for the later *gōpuras*, or entrance towers of temples. All these *rathas* were most probably Śaiva in character and the figure sculpture on all of them is of the same high quality as in the *maṇḍapas*. Men and gods are sculptured in the most graceful forms, and the animal sculpture is superb. Deities have four arms, *dvārapālas* only two. For some unknown reason work on these monoliths was left incomplete, and we enter on the second phase of Pallava architecture marked entirely by structural temples in stone.

These structural temples again fall into two groups—the Rājasimha group (*c.* 700-800), and the Nandivarman group (800-900). There are six examples of the former: three at Māmallapuram (the Shore, Īśvara and Mukunda temples), one at Panamalai (South Arcot district), and the temples of Kailāsanātha and Vaikuṇṭhaperumāl at Kānchipuram. The earliest of them was doubtless the Shore temple (Pl. VIIIa). Its excellent workmanship is proved by its having withstood, in a very exposed position, the action of wind and sea and the shifting sands of the shore. The plan of the temple is somewhat unusual. Its cella faces the sea and is located almost at the water's edge. The usual adjuncts to the temple had therefore to be accommodated in its rear. A massive enclosing wall surrounds the central building and entry into the open courtyard is obtained from the west. Two additional shrines were attached as an afterthought to the western end of the main shrine, one of which has a smaller *vimāna* and presents the appearance at first sight of being the main entrance. These additions go far to account for the unusual, though by no means unpleasing, appearance of the Shore temple with its two *vimānas.* Clearly the buildings in this temple are a logical development from the Dharmarāja *ratha*, allowance being made for the change from the rock-cut to the structural technique. At the same time there is a marked attempt, particularly in the treatment of the *vimānas*, to leave the idea of the *vihāra* behind and evolve a lighter and more rhythmic tower. The lion motif, particularly, in the pilasters becomes more developed, and in the Shore temple, as Brown remarks, 'this heraldic lion, erect and holding up a Dravidian capital, projects from every angle, and is also introduced at intervals around the lower part of the entire building'. The outer enclosure contained a system of shallow cisterns holding water brought by conduits, any overflow being led into the sea. The parapet of the imposing surrounding wall was crowned by figures of couchant bulls and all round the exterior there were boldly carved lion pilasters at close intervals. The richly ornamented doorway on the west led into a *maṇḍapa* of which only the foundations remain.

Not long after the Shore temple came the Kailāsanātha at Kānchipuram built mostly in the reign of Rājasimha though the actual completion of the structure owed something to his son Mahendravarman and his queen Rangapatākā. In its original form, the temple consisted of a sanctuary with its pyramidal *vimāna* and a detached pillared hall or *maṇḍapa* in front, the whole enclosed in a rectangular courtyard by a high wall composed of cells. The *maṇḍapa* and the sanctuary were joined together centuries later by an intermediate *ardhamaṇḍapa* which has spoiled the total effect. The sanctum and the *vimāna* conform to the type of the Dharmarāja *ratha* except for the subsidiary shrines. These are seven in number, one at each angle of the sanctum and one in the middle of each free side, and they add greatly to the beauty of the whole. All the main features of the Pallava style are assembled together in this temple in a very fascinating way. The cells in the interior of the enclosing wall which bear traces of painting, 'the design of the wall itself with its parapet of cupolas', the sturdy pillars of the *maṇḍapa* and the constant repetition of the lion pilaster, all fit into the scheme admirably. The *vimāna* is a further development from that of the Shore temple and is at once substantial and well-proportioned. The entrance to the courtyard is by means of small openings on the sides of a large subsidiary temple, the Mahendravarmeśvara, built in such a manner as to suggest the beginnings of the *gōpuram*. The builders of the Kailāsanātha temple would seem to have exercised some thought in selecting their building materials as its foundations are of granite and able to carry a great weight, while sandstone was used for the sculptured superstructure. The action of time has rendered many repairs necessary and these have not always been effected with discrimination.

Perhaps the most mature example of Pallava architecture, however, is the Vaikuṇṭhaperumāl (Pl. VIIIb). Slightly larger than the Kailāsanātha, its principal parts—cloisters, portico, and sanctum—are no longer separate buildings but are amalgamated into a well-articulated structure. The sanctum is a square with sides of nearly 90 feet, and its front is carried forward 28 feet on the east to provide the portico. The whole is enclosed by a high outer wall which is decorated outside with simple and effective ornamental motifs, while inside it are the open ambulatory and the cloisters with a colonnade of lion pillars and sculptures inscribed with the leading events of Pallava history. The portico is a square with sides of 21½ feet, its ceiling supported on eight pillars. A vestibule leads from it to the rectangular cella over which rises the *vimāna*. This *vimāna* is square in plan with sides of 47 feet and reaches a height of 60 feet from the ground. It has four storeys, 'each with a passage round its exterior, a cella in the centre, and a corridor encircling two of these for circumambulation'.

The second group of Pallava structural temples, the Nandivarman group, mostly consist of small temples and in no way form an advance on the achievements of the previous age. The principal examples are the Mukteśvara and Matangeśvara at Kānchipuram, the Vāḍāmallīśvara at Oragadam, near Chingleput, the temple of Vīraṭṭāneśvara at Tiruttaṇi near Arkonam, and the Paraśurāmeśvara at Guḍimallam (near Renigunta). Perhaps the earliest in the group are the two temples at Kānchipuram, which both have porticos supported on two pillars at the entrance. The other four temples of this group are all apsidal in character, possibly based on the example of the Sahadeva *ratha* at Māmallapuram. These modest structures are witnesses to the decline of Pallava power. To the Pallavas, however, belongs the credit of having kept up and developed the traditions of Amarāvatī and transmitted them to lands beyond the seas where in course of time there arose vast monuments which threw even the splendid achievements of the mother country into the shade.

The Cholas were the inheritors and continuers of the Pallava traditions in temple construction. They built numberless stone temples throughout their kingdom, but to the end of the tenth century the buildings were not very large. Unlike the great imperial designs of the early eleventh century, they imply limited resources and local developments. The district of Pudukkōṭṭai contains an unusually large number of early Chola monuments, in a good state of preservation, which give a very good idea of the stages by which later Pallava architecture grew into the Chola style proper. Among them, the Vijayālaya-Choleśvara at Nārttāmalai has the first claim on our attention. This temple was most likely built in the time of Vijayālaya, the first Chola ruler of the period. It faces west, and is one of the finest examples of the early Chola style. It has the unusual arrangement of a circular cella within a square *prākāra*. Above the cella and *prākāra* rises the *vimāna* in four diminishing storeys of which the three lower ones are square and the uppermost circular, the whole surmounted by a dome-shaped *śikhara* with a round *kalaśa* on top. There is an enclosed *maṇḍapa* in front. The external walls are adorned with ornamental pilasters with characteristic features of the Chola ‘ order ’. There are no niches in the walls and a frieze of *bhūtas* is carved below the curved cornice at the top, the cornice itself being decorated at intervals with *kūḍus* containing human heads or animal figures, while at the corner the decoration takes the form of very pleasing scroll work. Above the cornice is another frieze of lions (*vyālas*), changing at the corners into the form of a *makara* head. The parapet over the ceiling carries miniature shrines (*pañjarams*), which are square in plan at the corners and rectangular elsewhere. The *pañjarams* are also repeated in the lower storeys of the *vimāna*. The pillars in the *maṇḍapa* in front are still of the Pallava style, square at the base and top and octagonal in the middle. The corbels carrying the roll ornamentation have a slightly raised, plain, medium band. Over the main entrance is an elegantly carved floral design, and on either side of it are two *dvārapālas* inside niches 5 feet high facing forwards, but with their bodies half-turned towards the entrance, one leg crossed over the other. They have only two arms, as in Pallava monuments. Round the main temple in an open yard are seven small sub-shrines, all facing inwards, all built of stone and resembling the main temple in essential features. This arrangement of seven or eight sub-shrines round the main temple was typical of the early Chola period. The Bālasubrahmanya temple of Kaṇṇanūr (Pudukkoṭṭai), built in the reign of Āditya I, is another temple in the same style in which, however, elephants take the place of *nandis* at the four corners of the roof of the shrines and below the *śikhara* in the *vimāna*, the elephant being the vehicle of Subrahmanya.

The beautiful little temple of Nāgeśvara at Kumbakonam is more or less of the same period and style, but its most remarkable feature is the sculptures found in the niches on its outer walls. The central niche on each side of the cella enshrines the usual deity—Ardhanārī on the west, Brahmā on the north, Dakshiṇāmūrti on the south—but the others carry almost life-size sculptures of men and women in such high relief as to appear almost in the round; they are in graceful attitudes and are undoubtedly portraits either of donors to the temple or contemporary princes and princesses. There are other sculptures of Purāṇic scenes in somewhat low relief in small squares on the plinth below the pilasters of the walls of the cella, which remind one of the art of the goldsmith or of the carver in wood.

The next stage of evolution is best represented by the temple of Koranganātha at Śrīnivāsanallūr (Trichinopoly district), built in the reign of Parāntaka I. The temple has a total length of 50 feet, the cella being a square of 25 feet and the *maṇḍapa* in front a rectangle 25 feet by 20 feet. The height of the *śikhara* is 50 feet. The interior is a small hall with four pillars, and a vestibule and passage beyond lead to the cella, a square chamber of 12 feet. As in the other examples already noticed, there is in this moderate-sized temple a general simplification in its parts, an avoidance of excess in ornamental details combined with an appreciation of the value of plain surfaces. The lion motif disappears from the pillars though it is reproduced in friezes at suitable stages. The interior pillars are typical of the Chola 'order'. In the words of Brown, 'two changes from the Pallava type of order are discernible, one relating to the capital itself, the other to the abacus above. In the capital a neck moulding has been introduced where it joins on to the shaft, thus appropriating to itself a segment of the upper part of the shaft, and adding another member to the lower part of the capital in the form of a vessel or pot (*kalaśa*). As to the abacus, the *palagai* or "plank" is much expanded, so that, combined with the flower shape (*idal*) underneath, it becomes the most striking element in the order.' The central niches outside the walls of the cella enshrine the usual deities: Dakshiṇāmūrti on the south seated beneath a tree with devotees, lions, and *gaṇas* on either side, a standing Vishnu on the west, and a standing Brahmā on the north. Other niches contain standing figures which may be portraits. All the sculptures are in very high relief and of fine workmanship.

The Mūvarkōil ('Temple of the Three',) in Koḍumbāḷūr (Pudukkōṭṭai) is another early Chola temple-complex notable alike for the fineness of its architecture and the beauty of its sculptures. These three *vimānas* forming the central shrines amidst a group of sub-shrines were built in the second half of the tenth century by Bhūti Vikramakesari, a feudatory of Chola Parāntaka II. A big monastery in charge of the Kālāmukha preceptor Mallikārjuna was attached to them. The three central shrines are all 21 feet square at the base. They are separated from one another by about 10 feet and stand on a north-south line and face west.

The central and southern shrines are intact, but of the northern only the moulded basement remains. Each of these shrines had an *ardhamaṇḍapa*, about 18 feet square. Common to all the three and at a distance of 8 feet from the edge of the *ardhamaṇḍapas* was a *mahāmaṇḍapa*, 91 feet north to south by 41 feet east to west. In front of the *mahāmaṇḍapa*, placed centrally at a distance of less than 2 feet, was a small *nandi* shrine, a square with sides of a little over 11 feet. Midway between the *nandi* shrine and the main entrance is a plinth 5 feet 9 inches square—either the *balipīṭha* or *dhvajastambha*. Around the whole group was a covered cloister with fifteen sub-shrines of slightly varying dimensions but all miniatures of the main shrines. The fifteen sub-shrines are distributed as follows: two on either side of the main entrance of the western wall, four each on the inside of the northern and southern walls, and three on the eastern wall behind the main shrines. The outer enclosure was a massive stone wall 3 feet 4 inches thick with an entrance *gōpura* on the western side which must once have been a fair-sized structure, though smaller than the principal *vimānas*. The doorway below is 4 feet 6 inches wide. There was another entrance 4 feet wide on the north-east corner leading down a flight of steps to a circular stone well 10 feet in diameter just outside the wall. The three principal shrines have been conceived as *padmakośas*, one of the lowest mouldings in the basement simulating the petals of a full-blown lotus. The other architectural features are the same as in other temples, only more finely wrought. The frieze of *gaṇas* below the cornice has been made particularly interesting by the variety which the craftsman has introduced into the attitudes, actions and countenances of its members. Noteworthy among the sculptures on the walls of the *vimāna*, or on loose-lying slabs, are several forms of Śiva such as Ardhanārī, Vīṇādhara Dakshiṇāmūrti, Gajāri, Andhakāsura Samhāramūrti, Kirātamūrti, Gangādhara, Harihara, Umāprasādana, Chandraśekhara and Kālāri, besides Chandra, Sūrya, Umā, Jyeshṭhā, Saptamātrikas and Mohinī.

Temple building received great impetus from the conquests and the genius of Rājarāja I and his son Rājendra. In the early years of Rājarāja, many temples larger than the specimens so far described, but still of moderate size, sprang up in different parts of his growing empire. One of the most remarkable—unique for the wealth and detail of its sculpture—was the Tiruvālīśvaram temple at Brahmadeśam in the Tinnevelly district. Its *garbhagriha* is square; the *yāli* frieze on the plinth consists of the full figures of the animal, not of the bust alone as elsewhere. The *gaṇa* frieze below the cornice is very well composed and shows figures in different dance poses or otherwise engaged in merriment; some have comic features, like lion- or monkey-faces and pot bellies, and the whole scene of dancing, mockery and music is very humorously portrayed. The entire cornice is elaborately embellished by designs of foliage and creepers in the spaces between the *kūḍus* which are themselves highly ornate arches surmounted by *simhamukhas* ('lion faces'). The first storey of the *vimāna* carries a number of fine sculptures of the greatest interest for the iconography of the period. On the southern side there is the figure of Naṭarāja in the centre with Vrishabhārūḍha and Gangādhara on the proper left, and Vīrabhadra and Devī on the proper right. On the western side, the centre is taken by Lingodbhava flanked by Vishnu and Brahmā. To the proper left are Kālārimūrti and Kirātamūrti and on the other side Yogadakshiṇāmūrti and Umāsahita. Gajāri occupies the centre on the northern side with Chandeśānugraha and Sukhāsanamūrti on the proper right, and Somāskanda and an unidentified figure on the left. The eastern side is hidden by the thick brick terrace over the *ardhamaṇḍapa* put up in modern times. The second storey of the *vimāna* reproduces on a reduced scale the ornamental features of the exterior of the *garbhagriha* including the friezes of *gaṇas* and *yālis* and the cornice. On the top of the second storey are placed four magnificent recumbent bulls, very life-like, one at each corner and facing outwards. In the centre rises an octagonal plinth with the *grīvā* and the domical eight-ribbed *śikhara* above. The *grīvā* has niches at the cardinal points bearing figures of a Vyākhyā-dakshiṇāmūrti on the south, Yoganarasimha on the west, Brahmā on the north, and Indra on the east. Over the highly ornate *śikhara* are the *mahāpadma* and *paṭṭika* with the *stūpi* above. The *ardhamaṇḍapa* in front of the temple is coeval with it, but the *mahāmaṇḍapa* was a later addition perhaps of the reign of Rājendra I, while the shrine of the goddess is later still, probably dating from the thirteenth century. The Uttara Kailāsa shrine at Tiruvadi (Tanjore district), the Vaidyanātha temple at Tirumalavāḍi (Trichinopoly district), the twin temples to Śiva and Vishnu at Dādāpuram (South Arcot district), and Śivadevāle No. 2 at Polonnaruva

(Ceylon) are some of the more notable among the many small temples of Rājarāja's reign, though none of them approaches Tiruvālīśvaram from the standpoint of sculpture.

The maturity of Chola architecture found expression in the two magnificent temples of Tanjore and Gangaikondaśōḷapuram. The superb Śiva temple of Tanjore, completed about 1009 (Pl. IX), is a fitting memorial to the material achievements of the time of Rājarāja. The largest and the tallest of all Indian temples, it is a masterpiece constituting the high-water mark of South Indian architecture. The *vimāna*, the *ardhamaṇḍapa*, *mahāmaṇḍapa*, and the large *nandi* pavilion in front are all aligned in the centre of a spacious walled enclosure, 500 feet by 250 feet, with a *gōpura* gateway in front on the east. On the inner side of the high enclosing wall runs a pillared corridor connecting together a number of sub-shrines raised at the cardinal points and at intervals along the four sides. A second *gōpura* in front of the first forms the gateway of a second and outer enclosure. The main feature of the whole scheme is the grand *vimāna* towering to a height of nearly 200 feet over the *garbhagriha* in the west and dominating everything in its vicinity. Its great dignity is due to the simplicity of its parts—the 'square vertical base, the tall tapering body and over all the graceful domical finial'. The vertical base is a square with sides 82 feet long rising perpendicularly to a height of 50 feet. Above it is the pyramidal body mounting up in thirteen diminishing tiers, the width at the apex being equal to one-third of its base. 'On the square platform thus formed stands the cupola, the inward curve of its neck producing a pleasing break in the otherwise rigid outlines of the composition, while the bulbous dome poised like a light but substantial globe is a fitting finish to its soaring character.' The lowest vertical portion is divided into two storeys by a massive cornice, the only striking horizontal feature of the *vimāna*. The walls above and below this cornice are adorned with ranges of pilasters combined with several ornamental devices and dividing the wall-space into a number of elegantly proportioned compartments. The middle of each compartment is occupied by a niche containing a sculptured figure-subject of high quality. In the tapering section the horizontal lines of the diminishing tiers intersect vertical disposition of the ornamental shrines and thus produce an 'architectural texture of great beauty'. Lastly, the rounded cupola with its winged niches on all four sides relieves 'the severity of the outline just where this is required'.

The cella is a 45-foot square inside with a narrow circumambulatory passage 9 feet wide around it. The inner walls of this passage contain fine frescoes coeval with the temple (Frontispiece) but overlaid by later tempera work of the Nāyak rulers of Tanjore. The cella enshrines an enormous *lingam* originally called Rājarājeś-vara and now known as Brihadīśvara. Its height with its pedestal occupies the space of both the storeys. In front of the cella is a transept reached by flights of steps on the south and north, and the walls of the *garbhagriha* and *ardhamaṇḍapa* on either side are adorned with pilasters and large niches, the same as the outer walls of the shrine. The entrance to the shrine-chamber is guarded by two large *dvārapālas* in niches. The roof of the transept is supported by two rows of four piers each. In front of the transept is the *ardhamaṇḍapa* (also a two-storeyed structure) on the same plinth with the same type of pilasters and niches. Then comes the *mahāmaṇḍapa* with rows of pillars along the middle and aisles on either side. In front of the *mahāmaṇḍapa* is another transept reached by flights of steps on the north and south. The relatively small *maṇḍapa* added to this with another flight of steps in front is a very late accretion. Some yards away in front is the *nandi-maṇḍapa* containing one of the largest monolithic bulls known in South India. The outer walls of the *ardhamaṇḍapa* contain niches carrying sculptures of gods and goddesses of considerable iconographic and artistic interest. The whole temple from the heavily moulded parts of its high basement to its finial is a magnificent example of solidity combined with proportion and grace of form.

The temple of Gangaikondaśōḷapuram, the creation of Rājarāja's son Rājendra, was evidently meant to excel its predecessor in every way. The town which once surrounded it, as also the large lake of fresh water that once adorned the neighbourhood of the Chola capital, have now disappeared, and this fine temple therefore stands in the solitude of the wilderness except for the mud huts of a small village nearby. Erected about 1030, only two decades after the temple of Tanjore and in much the same style, the greater elaboration in its appearance attests the more affluent state of the Chola empire under Rājendra. It is larger in plan though not so tall, the *vimāna* being 100 feet square at the base and 186 feet high.

The temple, which forms a large rectangle 340 feet long and 110 feet wide, occupies the middle of an immense walled enclosure partly designed for defensive purposes, as may be seen from a substantial bastion at the south-east angle and a smaller one on the west. Its main entrance is on the east, next to which is the *mahāmaṇḍapa*, a rather low building 175 feet by 95 feet with over 150 pillars of ordinary design. These pillars are arranged in colonnades on a solid platform 4 feet high which is divided by a wide passage or aisle down the centre while a narrower passage on the same level is carried round the hall. Between the *mahāmaṇḍapa* and the sanctuary is a transept with doorways to the north and south, 'both deeply recessed side entrances approached from outside by flights of steps'. As in Tanjore, there are in the transept two rows of massive square piers, eight in all.

The *vimāna* has the same construction as in Tanjore but the number of tiers making up the pyramidal body is only eight as against thirteen in Tanjore. The most important difference lies in the introduction of curves in the place of the strong straight lines of the Tanjore *vimāna*. The pyramidal body is slightly concave in its outline at its angles while the sides are curved to produce a somewhat convex outline. These curves enrich the beauty of form of the *vimāna* though they detract from its stateliness and power. Of the two *vimānas* considered together Brown observes: 'Each is the final and absolute vision of its creator made manifest through the medium of structural form, the one symbolizing conscious might, the other sub-conscious grace. But both dictated by that "divinity which has seized the soul".'

The scheme of decoration and sculpture on the outside of the walls is also the same as in Tanjore, but the style is more ornate. The Chaṇḍēśvara shrine to the north of the *vimāna* is a small structure of the same style and period as the main temple. The separate temple of the goddess, a medium-sized structure with a *vimāna* following the Tanjore model more closely, appears to have been built not long after the main shrine.

The Chola style continued to flourish for a century longer and expressed itself in a very large number of temples all of which cannot be mentioned here. But two large temples deserve particular mention as being almost worthy of comparison with the two largest specimens described above. They are the temple of Airāvateśvara at Dārāsuram (Tanjore district), a magnificent structure typical of the stage of architectural development reached in the age of Rājarāja II, and the Kampahareśvara at Tribhuvanam near Kumbakonam which has survived intact as built by Kulottunga III though with a few later accretions by way of subsidiary structures. The architecture and sculpture of both these temples have many features in common with those of their predecessors.

The Chola period is also remarkable for its sculptures and bronzes, many of which are masterpieces. The Tanjore inscriptions mention a number of bronzes in groups illustrating the sacred legends of Śaivism but they have all disappeared. Among existing specimens in the various museums of the world and in the temples of South India may be seen many fine figures of Śiva in his various forms, Brahmā, the seven mothers, Vishnu and his consorts Lakshmī (Pl. XI) and Bhūdevī, Rāma and Sītā with their attendants, the Śaiva saints—the figures of Sambandar being most numerous among them, the infant Krishna dancing on the serpent Kāliya, and many other subjects. The statues often compare most favourably with the finest of the stone sculptures of the various schools mentioned above. Though conforming generally to iconographic conventions established by long tradition, the sculptor worked in great freedom in the eleventh and twelfth centuries and his productions show classic grace, grandeur, and perfect taste. This art is seen at its best in the numerous images of the Divine Dancer, Naṭarāja (Pl. X). 'Whether he be surrounded or not by the flaming aureole of the *tiruvāśi* (*prabhāmaṇḍala*)—the circle of the world which he both fills and oversteps—the King of the Dance is all rhythm and exaltation. The tambourine which he sounds with one of his right hands draws all creatures into this rhythmic motion and they dance in his company. The conventionalized locks of flying hair and the blown scarfs tell of the speed of this universal movement, which crystallizes matter and reduces it to powder in turn. One of his left hands holds the fire which animates and devours the worlds in this cosmic whirl. One of the god's feet is crushing a Titan, for "this dance is danced upon the bodies of the dead", yet one of the right hands is making the gesture of reassurance (*abhayamudrā*), so true it is that, seen from the cosmic point of view and *sub specie aeternitatis*, the very cruelty of this universal determinism is kindly, as the generative principle of the future. And, indeed, on more than one of our bronzes, the King of the Dance wears a broad smile. He smiles at death and at life, at pain and at joy alike, or rather, if we may be allowed so to express it, his smile is both death and life, both joy and pain. . . . From this lofty point of view, in fact, all things fall into their place, finding their explanation and logical compulsion. Here art is the faithful interpreter of the philosophical concept. The plastic beauty of rhythm is no more than the expression of an ideal rhythm. The very multiplicity of arms, puzzling as it may seem at first sight, is subject in turn to an inward law, each pair remaining a model of elegance in itself, so that the whole being of the Naṭarāja thrills with a magnificent harmony in his terrible joy. And as though to stress the point that the dance of the divine actor is indeed a sport, (*līlā*)—the sport of life and death, the sport of creation and destruction, at once infinite and purposeless—the first of the left hands hangs limply from the arm in the careless gesture of the *gajahasta* (hand as the elephant's trunk). And lastly as we look at the back view of the statue, are not the steadiness of these shoulders which uphold the world, and the majesty of this Jove-like torso, as it were a symbol of the stability and immutability of substance, while the gyration of the legs in its dizzy speed would seem to symbolize the vortex of phenomena?'[1]

Under the Pāndyas the builders began to divert their attention from the central shrine to the outlying portions of the temple. They sought to emphasize the sanctity of the shrine by making the entrances to the enclosures containing it into vast towered gateways of imposing size and appearance, and thus the *gōpuras* came to form immense piles and provided a basis for a wealth of sculptural embellishments. Generally the two lowest storeys of the *gōpura* are vertical and built of solid stone masonry, a stable foundation for the high pyramidal superstructure of brick and plaster. These *gōpuras* are some of them firm and rigid in their contours with straight sloping sides while others have somewhat curved and concave outlines imparting to them an impressive upward sweep. In the latter class the sculpture is of a more florid character. The pillar also underwent a further evolution under the Pāndyas: the *idaḻ* became more pronounced with a scalloped edge, the corbel was moulded into a pendant or drop, and the *palagai* increased in width. Pāndya architecture generally spent

[1] Grousset, *India* (English translation), pp. 252-3.

itself in embellishing existing temples by adding outer *maṇḍapas*, additional sub-shrines and *gōpuras*, rather than in building entire temples. One of the early examples of the Pāndya *gōpura* is that in the second enclosure wall of the temple of Jambukeśvara on the island of Śrīrangam, a twelfth-century structure, still retaining many features of the Chola style. Later and more typical Pāndya *gōpuras* are the Sundara Pāndya *gōpura* also at Jambukeśvara and the eastern *gōpura* of the temple of Chidambaram, both mid-thirteenth century. In Pāndya art, in general, is seen an attempt to produce a more elegant effect by an increase of decorative detail which may be taken to mark the transition from the restrained maturity of Chola architecture to ' the exquisite though extravagant productions of Vijayanagar'.

Mention must also be made of two Jaina monuments of particular interest at Śravana Belgola, both creations of Chāmundarāya, the minister of the Ganga king Rācamalla IV. One of them is the Chāmundarāya *basadi*, the largest and finest of a number of Jaina temples on the side of the Chandragiri hill. It measures 70 feet in length together with the portico on its eastern front, and its width is 36 feet. It must have been built originally about A.D. 980 although in its present form the structure is typical of Chola architecture of the early twelfth century. The other monument is the stupendous monolithic image of Gommaṭa, son of the first Tīrthankara, rising to a height of 56 feet on the hill known as Indrabeṭṭa. This colossus, carved about A.D. 983, represents the ascetic standing entirely nude and absorbed in meditation with ant-hills rising at his feet and plants winding themselves about his limbs. Two similar but smaller statues, also monoliths, were made in Kanara, one over 40 feet high at Kārkala in 1432, and the other at Yēnūr, about 35 feet high, in 1604. One feature common to Jaina temples of the South is the *mānastambha* standing in front of the temple on a wide square base of several moulded steps. The column is generally square in the lower part but becomes circular above and bears ' shallow flutes crossed by lateral bands at regular intervals '. The capital is generally a fluted vase supporting an elaborate superstructure carried on an abacus supported by figures of rampant gryphons. Some of these free-standing pillars are over 50 feet in height and are in themselves impressive works of art.

The temples built in the western Deccan under the Chālukyas of Kalyāni developed features which received their most mature expression in the architecture of the Hoysala temples in Mysore. These temples often had their principal entrances not at the front but at the sides, and the decoration of their external walls with architectural motifs dividing the wall into well-proportioned areas tended to be singularly graceful and restrained, while their *vimānas* were a compromise between the plain, stepped storeys of the early Chālukyas and the closely moulded tiers of the Hoysala style. The pillars were turned on lathes and had a pronounced knife-edge very considerably projected below the capital. The doorways, both at the outer entrance and of the shrine-chamber, were very elaborately carved with fine detail and finish. The Navalinga (Nine Lingas) and Kalleśvara temples at Kukkanur near Gadag are perhaps the earliest examples of this style and possibly date from the close of the tenth century, though they still bear resemblances to the early Chālukyan group of Aihole and Pattadakal. From among the numerous other examples of this style spread over the entire area of the Chālukyan empire, the temples of Kāśi-viśveśvara at Lakkundi, of Mahadevā at Ittagi and of Mallikārjuna at Kuruvatti may be mentioned as the most typical.

The builders of Hoysala temples invariably used a dark stone of much finer grain than the large unwieldy blocks of sandstone used by the early Chālukyas. The change of material made it possible for the masonry of the Mysore temples to be better finished and the sculptures to be carved in more minute and exquisite detail. In general, the Hoysala temple comprises a central structure surrounded by walls containing a number of cells with a pillared verandah or cloister in front. The main building contained the cella with a vestibule in front known as *sukhanāsi* and connecting with a pillared hall (*navaranga*). In front of this there was often an open pillared pavilion, the *mukha-maṇḍapa*. In many cases, the Hoysala temples are not single but double, having all essential parts duplicated; indeed they are frequently even built in triplicate, quadruplicate, and, occasionally, even quintuplicate. Another notable feature was the star shape of the external walls of the main shrine, set on a high platform, the sides of which project or recede with lines and angles parallel to those of the building it supports. The platform is much wider than the temple, leaving a flat surface all round to serve as the *pradakshiṇapatha* for which there is no provision inside. The general treatment of wall surfaces is marked by a large number of horizontal friezes imposed upon one another. The walls of the *vimāna* are divided into three horizontal divisions while those of the pillared hall have only two; but a wide continuous cornice binds the two parts of the structure together. In both, a high and almost vertical basement, 9 or 10 feet high, (Pl. XIII) is made up of a number of sculptured animal friezes running right round the building. The lowest band is usually a procession of elephants; the next, of horsemen. Then, after another band of spiral foliage, and on a level with the eye, is a wider frieze depicting a succession of Purāṇic scenes executed with great effect and a considerable wealth of detail. Above this is a border of *yāḷis* with spirals of foliage issuing from their mouths, and crowning all is a running frieze of *hamsas*. The basement of the pillared hall is terminated above by a 'sloping seat-back' (*āsana*) above which rise the external pillars of the hall with their moulded shafts at regular intervals, the spaces between the columns being filled by perforated stone screens.

The three horizontal divisions of the *vimāna* are even more ornate than the two of the hall. The basement, which is continuous with that of the hall, is just the same. Above it, the broad space corresponding to that taken up by the pillars and screens of the hall is adorned with ornate niches containing images of gods under foliated canopies, each one so elaborately chiselled (and often signed by the sculptor) as to constitute a more or less distinct work of art (Pl. XII). The rich effect of all this statuary is enhanced by the star shape of the structure which produces vertical planes like facets and provides an abundant variety of light and shade. The *śikhara* separated by the wide projecting cornice from the body of the temple below keeps the stellate formation, but its vertical lines are balanced by horizontal mouldings so that the whole tower appears as an orderly succession of diminishing tiers terminating in a low finial having the shape of a parasol at its apex. Miniature shrines and niches adorn each of these tiers.

The shape of the pillar and its capital was another remarkable feature of this style. The shaft is a monolith fashioned into beautiful shapes by being turned on a lathe, the base being left square. A sloping bracket-stone was set above the capital, to which it was fixed by sockets. These brackets, also monolithic, carried carvings of fine images with leafy aureoles known as *madanakai* figures.

Their high finish rivals that of the figures in the niches of the *vimāna.*

These Hoysala temples, though basically developments of the South Indian style, represent an art which applies to stone the technique of the ivory worker or the goldsmith (Pl. XII, XIII). The wealth of jewellery borne by many of the figures, the variety of head-dresses and other details are well calculated to give a fair idea of the social life of the times. A very typical and complete example of the style is the Keśava temple at Somanāthapur twenty miles from Seringapatam. It is a triple shrine in the shape of a cross, 87 feet by 83 feet, with only one entrance on the east, set within a rectangular courtyard surrounded by sixty-four cells, the whole enclosure measuring 215 feet by 177 feet. 'So well balanced and finely proportioned are its parts that no element obtrudes or is out of place, and although the three stellate towers are only 30 feet high they are fully in accord with the rest of the building.'

A larger and earlier example is furnished by a group of temples at Belūr dating from about 1117 of which the temple of Chennakeśava is the centre. Its superstructure is now missing but clearly when complete it must have been a work of surpassing beauty. It has three entrances, one on each of the free sides of the pillared hall, 'approached by a flight of steps flanked by a pagoda-like shrine, the last a useful note of architectural emphasis'. On the main pillars of the hall and its recessed ceiling the sculptor has bestowed the largest amount of attention. The hall is 92 feet by 78 feet and the total number of pillars is forty-six. All of them, except the four in the central bay, are of different design so that the variety and complexity of the whole is astonishing. Each pillar must have been the handiwork of a separate artist and his assistants, an arrangement which set the masters of the art to compete with one another in the production of their finest work.

The temple of Hoysaleśvara at Halebid was perhaps the highest achievement of the school though its present ruined condition—for it lacks the whole of its superstructure—renders it difficult to realize this. This grand temple was designed and erected by Kedaroja, the master-builder of Narasimha I, under the supervision of Ketamalla, chief officer of the public works. It is a double temple, two complete structures exactly alike built side by side and connected by their side transepts. Each measures

112 feet in length and about 100 feet in width. The infinite wealth of sculpture over the exterior of this temple makes it one of the most remarkable monuments of the World and an unrivalled 'repository of religious thought expressed in plastic form'.

In the kingdom of Kalinga (Orissa) many temples were built from the ninth to the thirteenth century in the North Indian style. Bhuvaneśvar contains the main group, numbering over thirty. Within fifty miles of it are two of the largest and most important monuments of the locality, the temple of Jagannāth at Puri and that of the Sun at Konarak. There is also a small group in the south of Mukhalingam on the coast of the Ganjam district. The Mukhalingam series may well be taken to count among the earliest examples and to date from the ninth century, if not earlier, as it contains architectural features bringing it into unmistakable relation with the early Chālukyan temples of the Deccan. The most striking example in the group is the Mukhalingeśvara, comprising five shrines—a central sanctuary with four minor shrines one at each corner. In its decorative features the temple shows traces of both Chālukya and Gupta influences.

In Orissa the sanctum (usually a square building) is called *deul*, and the assembly hall in front of it bears the name *jagamohan*. In larger temples there are two other parts, the *naṭmandir* or dancing hall in front of the *jagamohan*, and the *bhogmandir* in front of the *naṭmandir*—all aligned on one axis. These halls stood on a plinth and were invariably of one storey comprising a cubical portion below with a pyramidal roof above. Pillars are conspicuous by their absence here. In larger halls where support was necessary to sustain the weight of the pyramidal roof four solid piers were introduced, 'one at each corner of a four-square system of roof-beams'. Indeed one chief characteristic of the Orissan temple is the plain treatment of the interior in striking contrast with the profusely ornamented surfaces of the exterior.

The temple of Paraśurāmeśvar and the Vaital *deul* at Bhuvaneśvar are two early examples of the period 750-900. They are of great interest as throwing light on the origins and affiliations of the style. The former has a *deul* and *jagamohan* with an overall length of 48 feet, and the *śikhara* over the *deul* is 44 feet high. The hall is a low rectangular structure with a double roof, plain, massive eaves, a doorway on each of its three free sides, and two rows of three pillars each in the interior supporting the ceiling of the nave which was higher than that of the aisles. The original *deul* must have fallen into decay and been rebuilt later, as is evident from the joint between it and the hall, and from the difference in the character of the sculpture on the walls of the two buildings. The shape of the *śikhara* is rather thick-set and rudimentary. Two stone grilles, one on each side of the doorway on the west, contain representations of young dancers and musicians with their instruments, a work of considerable artistic merit. Large blocks of stone were employed in the construction with no mortar or other cementing material. While this feature and some others connect the temple with early Chālukya temples at Aihole, the pilasters with vase and foliage capitals and other ornamental modes would seem to be derived from Gupta art.

The Vaital *deul* is notable for its barrel-roofed *śikhara*, its small supplementary shrines at the corners of its *jagamohan* (making it virtually a nascent *pañcāyatana* shrine), and for the well-balanced arrangement of all its parts. A small structure measuring only 18 feet by 25 with a height of 35 feet, it is a very pleasing blend of well-marked Southern and Northern forms.

The second period, from 900-1100, is represented by the small temple of Mukteśvar (975) on the outskirts of Bhuvaneśvar, and by the two very large temples of Lingarāja at Bhuvaneśvar (1000) and the Jagannāth at Puri (1100). The Mukteśvar registers a considerable advance on the earlier period and is one of the few temples of the region containing sculptured decorations in the interior. The Lingarāja (Pl. XIV) occupies the centre of a large quadrangle 520 feet by 465 feet enclosed by a high and massive wall with a platform inside making for easy defence when necessary. Within the enclosure are many small shrines, replicas of the central temple. The Lingarāja has all the parts of a large temple though the *naṭmandir* and the *bhogmandir* were later additions. The most striking feature of the temple is the great *śikhara* over the *deul* which dominates the whole town by its height (125 feet) and volume. The plastic decoration of its external walls is of absorbing interest and gives ample evidence of the fertile invention of the artists.

The construction of the Jagannāth at Puri was begun about 1100 by Anantavarman Chodaganga but was not completed till much later. It is built on the same plan as the Lingarāja and consists of four parts in one alignment. The extreme length is 310 feet and the width 80 feet. The tower is nearly 200 feet high. As it stands on an eminence, the temple with its soaring *śikhara* is an imposing landmark for many miles around. Except for its impressive proportions this temple is no improvement on the Lingarāja, of which it is a close imitation. The action of sea air has rendered extensive renovations necessary from time to time and these have also detracted from the original appearance of the structure. The *naṭmandir* is a large square with a side of 80 feet, and its ceiling is borne on 16 pillars in four rows of four each, the one real example of a pillared hall in Orissa. There are some 30 to 40 minor shrines round the main temple and the whole group is enclosed within three concentric walls, known as 'the three garlands', with gateways in the centre of each side. These gateways are substantial structures with pyramidal roofs and bear no resemblance to the *gōpura* of South India.

The third and last period (1100-1250) of the Orissan style is represented by a number of medium-sized temples, all remarkable for the richness and finish of their appearance. There are at least a dozen at Bhuvaneśvar, most having only the two essential parts, the *deul* and the *jagamohan*. One striking example, the Anantavāsudeva, also has the *naṭmandir* and *bhogmandir* as later additions. This gives the temple a total length of 125 feet with a breadth of 40 feet, and a tower of 68 feet. As the whole structure is built on a substantial plinth, it presents a very impressive effect. Another temple, the Rājarāni, has its *deul* completed but not its *jagamohan*, but the unfinished condition of the latter gives a fair idea of the technical methods followed by the sculptors of the time. The completed *deul* is very refined in its curves, contours, and in the disposition of decoration on the tower, and may almost be said to have started a new mode in the embellishment of *śikharas* which was carried further in the temples of Khajurāho in Central India. The *deul* of the Rājarāni temple is placed diagonally to the hall in its front, a rather unusual arrangement for Orissa.

But undoubtedly the greatest achievement of the period was the temple of the Sun at Konarak, some twenty miles from Puri along the sea-coast in a north-easterly direction. Built by king Narasimhadeva (1238-63), the ruined mass of this temple, popularly known as the Black Pagoda, is a prominent landmark in the locality. It may be doubted if it was ever quite completed as it seems that the foundations began to give way before the heavy superstructure was finished. 'The conception of this temple,' says Brown, 'was that of a genius, but its colossal grandeur outstripped the means of execution. . . . It was however a magnificent failure, for without unduly straining the imagination, it is possible to see, even in its ruin, that it was one of the finest architectural efforts the Indian master-mason ever made.' The whole temple is fashioned like a wheeled chariot being drawn by the seven horses of the Sun. There are twelve giant wheels each nearly 10 feet high on either side of the immense plinth while the wide flight of steps in the front is flanked by seven richly caparisoned horses 'rearing and straining in their harness as they strive to drag its great bulk along'. The *naṭmandir* was a separate structure with a pyramidal roof on a high square plinth in front of the temple and reproducing all its main features on a smaller scale. Round it were a number of supplementary shrines and other accessories all enclosed within a courtyard 875 feet by 540 feet with pyramidal gateways on three of its sides. The immense surfaces of the walls of the temple and its accessories are decorated with many sculptured forms—some of outstanding beauty, but others of a crudely erotic character. Only the *jagamohan*, a square hall 100 feet long with a stepped pyramidal roof 100 feet high, remains in a tolerable state of preservation. Notable among the subsidiary structures is the ornate temple of Rāmachandra in the south-western portion of the enclosure. Many colossal groups of sculptures, some of them superb works of art intended to occupy salient positions in the structure, are lying loose on the ground (Pl. XV). Among them are two spirited war-horses and the statues of Sūrya and of Gangā. The decorations on the walls of the main temple include every motif and subject known to the Indian mind, carved with minute precision. It has at its basis a frame of vertical and horizontal courses which combine to produce an astonishingly beautiful impression.

A variation of the Northern style flourished in the north-western part of the Deccan from the eleventh to the thirteenth centuries. The most striking feature in this Deccani type of temple is the design of the *śikhara* which has a well-marked vertical band carried from the lower cornice right up to the finial at each of its angles. The space between these bands is filled in with rows of small replicas of the *śikhara* itself, each one supported on a pedestal of suitable size. This principle of using miniatures of the entire structure as decorations on its sides is applied in other parts of the temple also with generally very pleasing results. In the larger examples the sanctum is laid out on a diagonal arrangement; and the shaping of the walls also undergoes a marked elaboration by means of projections and recesses of the wall-surfaces—sometimes carried to excess. Horizontal mouldings, many of them with a knife-edged section named *kani*, break the vertical effect of the treatment of the wall-surface. The pillars were generally lathe-turned, had *kani* moulding, and were richly carved throughout, though sometimes the lower third was left simply as a plain square prism. Even the largest of these Deccani temples does not exceed 80 feet in length, but they are all very well proportioned, the unit furnishing the proportion of the various parts being the height of the monolithic pillar in the interior.

One of the earliest temples and perhaps the finest in this group is that of Ambarnāth in the Thāna district of Bombay. Erected about 1060 in a delightful situation, by the side of a long deep pool, the temple is covered with intricate decoration of a lavish but tasteful design. The two essential parts of the temple are both set diagonally astride the axis making an attractive plan 90 feet long by 75 feet in width. A series of vertical projections and recesses break up the sides and multiply the shadows and lights. There are three doorways, one on each of the free angles of the assembly-hall. There is much excellent carving in the panels of the ceiling and its shallow domes, but the pillars of the main hall, especially the four columns in the centre, are particularly elaborately decorated with conventional designs and figure subjects. A smaller but beautiful replica of Ambarnāth is found at Balsane in Khandesh in the midst of a number of other temples probably built over a period of more than a century. One of these is almost an exact copy of a rock-cut *vihāra*. The Gondeśvara temple (first half of the twelfth century) at Sinnar (Nāsik district) is a *pañcāyatana*, the main temple being surrounded by four smaller supplementary shrines in the same style, all upon a moulded, stepped platform measuring 125 feet by 95 feet. The main shrine occupies the centre of the platform with a *nandi* pavilion in front. There is a falling off in the quality of the sculpture which seems to indicate a decline in technique.

In the latter half of the thirteenth and early fourteenth century were built a number of temples marked by their heavy proportions and a scarcity of external figure sculpture. They are generally referred to as in the Hemadpanti style—Hemādri, or Hemadpant, as we have seen, being a minister of the last Yādava rulers of Devagiri and reputed to be the builder of many religious edifices. Examples of this style are not confined to the Deccan but extend to Madhya Pradesh (the Berars) also.

Under Vijayanagar, South Indian art attained a certain fullness and freedom of rich expression in keeping with the general consciousness of the great task of the empire, namely the preservation and development of all that remained of Hinduism against the onslaughts of Islam. In this period, temples became very elaborate both in structure and organization; even old temples were amplified by the addition of pillared halls, pavilions and other subordinate structures. The most characteristic of such additions is the *kalyāṇa-maṇḍapa*, generally put on the left in the courtyard of the temple as we enter it from the east. This is a very ornate pillared pavilion with a raised platform in the centre 'for the reception of the deity and his consort at the annual celebration of their marriage ceremony'. The goddesses invariably came to have separate shrines of their own, a development of which the beginnings go back to the late Chola period. Another feature was the so-called 'thousand-pillared *maṇḍapa*', a huge hall with many rows of pillars. In fact the varied and complicated treatment of the pillar was perhaps the most striking feature of the Vijayanagar style. The shaft becomes just a core round which is grouped a vast amount of statuary of great size and sculptured in the round, 'having as its most conspicuous element a furiously rearing horse, rampant hippogryph or upraised animal of a supernatural kind'—the whole of it, pillar and sculptures, being carved out of a single block of stone (Pl. XVI). Another type shows a cluster of miniature pillars encircling the central column, and so carved sometimes as to give out, when struck, the seven separate notes of Indian music. There were also other modes of treatment, but all pillars had ornamental brackets as part of their capitals, and below the bracket a pendant which was elaborated in this period into an inverted lotus-bud. The tall entrance towers or *gōpuras*, evolved under the Pāndyas, continued in this period also.

Buildings in the Vijayanagar style are distributed throughout the country south of the Tungabhadra, but the finest and most characteristic group is to be found in the deserted city of Vijayanagar itself. The principal temples here are the Viṭṭhala and the Hazāra Rāma but there are also others of interest.

The Viṭṭhala is by far the most ornate temple. Begun in the time of Devarāya II, if not earlier, its construction was continued even in the reign of Achyuta Rāya, but was never entirely finished. The rectangular courtyard, 500 feet by 310 feet, with cloisters on the interior with a triple row of pillars, surrounds the temple. There are three entrances with *gōpuras*, those on the east and south being more important. The main temple occupies the centre and there are five other structures mostly of the nature of pillared halls within the enclosure. The main temple is dedicated to Vishnu as Viṭṭhala. It is a long (230 feet), low structure aligned from east to west, its height being only 25 feet. It comprises three distinct sections, the *mahāmaṇḍapa*, an open pillared hall in front, an *ardhamaṇḍapa*, a similar closed hall in the middle, and the *garbhagriha* in the rear. The *mahāmaṇḍapa* is impressive with its deeply recessed sides measuring 100 feet at its greatest length and breadth. It stands on a moulded plinth 5 feet high, with flights of steps guarded by elephants on its three free sides. A very wide double-curved eave surmounted by turrets of brickwork is its other notable feature. There are fifty-six pillars inside, each twelve feet high. Forty of them are disposed at regular intervals to form an aisle round the hall's outer edge, and the remaining sixteen provide an oblong passage in the centre. The pillars are variants of the types generally described above and exhibit an amazing exuberance of the most ornate and vigorous carving. The rest of the temple is a unified structure, rectangular in shape, 135 feet by 67 feet, and its external walls are embellished with the usual arrangement of pilasters, niches and canopies. Besides the entrance from the *mahāmaṇḍapa* on the east, the *ardhamaṇḍapa* has two side-entrances 'each having steps and a pillared porch of some size'. Its interior is a square with sides 55 feet long, with a square dais at the centre and one pillar at each of its corners. The other pillars are disposed to form an aisle near the perimeter. The *vimāna* is 75 feet long and 72 feet wide and includes a *pradakshiṇa* path on the same level as the outer courtyard. This is entered by flights of steps descending on either side of the vestibule connecting the *garbhagriha* with the *ardhamaṇḍapa*. Of the remaining structures, the *kalyāṇa-maṇḍapa*, as may be expected, throws the rest into the shade by the excellence of its statuary, although it is little more than half the size of the *mahāmaṇḍapa*. Near the *kalyāṇamaṇḍapa* and facing the entrance to the *mahāmaṇḍapa* is the *ratha* or chariot of the god. Its base and principal storey are carved out of a single block of granite with movable wheels, the superstructure of brick having disappeared. Similar stone cars are found in other temples of the period, for example at Tāḍpatri and Tiruvālūr.

The Hazāra Rāma temple, most probably the work of Virūpāksha II, is a more modest but perfectly finished example of this style. Besides the main temple there are a shrine for the goddess, a *kalyāṇamaṇḍapa* and other subsidiary temples all enclosed in a courtyard by a wall 24 feet high. The enclosure is entered by means of a well-proportioned flat-roofed porch on the east, which leads to the assembly-hall with a group of four huge blackstone pillars, one at each corner of a central square. These pillars are of unusual design, cubes alternating with fluted cylinders in their shafts, all richly carved. There are two other entrances with porches to the hall—one on each side—leading to the courtyard. The *vimāna* with its lower storey of stone and the pyramidal superstructure of brick, now much decayed, is impressive though it is less than 50 feet in height. The inner walls of the temple are decorated in relief with scenes from the *Rāmāyaṇa*.

Some secular buildings within the citadel of Vijayanagar of which the lower portions have escaped the fury of its destroyers deserve a passing notice. Two of these impressive basements stand out above many others—the King's Audience Hall and the Throne Platform (or House of Victory, as it is sometimes called because it was intended to commemorate Krishnadeva Rāya's conquest of Orissa). These buildings go far to show that the encomiums bestowed on the architecture of the city by many foreign travellers were fully justified. Both terraces must have been surmounted by pillared pavilions with pyramidal roofs, several storeys high. The Audience Hall was a hall of a hundred pillars, ten rows of ten pillars each. The pillars evidently had square bases, cylindrical shafts and bracket capitals. The basement, in three spacious diminishing stages one above the other with fine flights of steps and sides, was decorated by broad, bold mouldings and courses in conformity with the monumental character of the whole structure. The Throne Platform is also in three diminishing stages, square in plan, the lowest tier having sides of 132 feet and the highest sides of 78 feet. The highest stage of the platform is decorated by extremely beautiful mouldings in stone while the two lower stages are more or less plain masonry plinths, carrying, however, bands of figures and animals of an entertaining character in low relief.

In the rest of the empire Vellore, Kumbakonam, Kānchipuram, Tāḍpatri, and Śrīrangam are justly celebrated for their temples in the style of this period. The *kalyāṇamaṇḍapa* of the temple at Vellore is considered to be the most beautiful structure of its kind, and its *gōpura* is typical of the style of the century. The temple of Mārgasakheśvara at Virinchipuram (North Arcot district) is also remarkable for the exuberant treatment of its *kalyāṇamaṇḍapa*. The Ekāmranātha and the Varadarāja temples at Kānchipuram contain pavilions of remarkable size, the pillars of which are notable even in this period for their 'bizarre grouping of imaginative statuary'. Two *gōpuras* of the temple of Rāmeśvara at Tāḍpatri are remarkable for their rich and exquisite carvings in the whole of the perpendicular part usually left comparatively plain. 'These carvings', says Fergusson, 'are in better taste than anything else in this style.' Lastly, the so-called 'horse court' or Śeshagirimaṇḍapa at Śrīrangam contains a 'colonnade of furiously fighting steeds each rearing up to a height of nearly nine feet, the whole executed in a technique so emphatic as to be not like stone but hardened steel' (Brown).

The last stages of Vijayanagar architecture are rightly known as the Madura style as they found most encouragement from the Nāyaks of Madura. To some extent it was a revival and continuation of the building methods of the Pāndyas, which often took the shape of enlarging older temples by adding new parts to them. We may note in particular the provision of additional *prākāras* by means of concentric outer enclosure walls, each *prākāra* wall having generally four *gōpuras* at the cardinal points, and enclosing important adjuncts to the temple like a hall of a thousand pillars or a sacred tank. Śrīrangam, for instance, has seven such concentric rectangular enclosures. There is a tendency to multiply the pillars wherever possible, and some of them begin to bear on their shafts more than life-size statues of deities or donors.

Among the more important temples of this period may be named those of Madura, Śrīrangam and Jambukeśvara, Tiruvālūr, Rāmeśvaram, Chidambaram, Tinnevelly, Tiruvaṇṇāmalai and

Śrīvilliputtūr. The temple of Madura is, perhaps, the most typical of them, most of it having been built at one time. It is a double temple, one dedicated to Sundareśvara and the other to his consort Mīnākshī. These two shrines take the largest space inside the main enclosure, an area 850 feet by 725 within a high wall, with four large *gōpuras* towards the centre of each of its four sides. The main entrance is on the east and communicates with a beautiful pillared avenue 200 feet long and nearly 100 feet wide. This leads to a smaller *gōpura*, the eastern entrance to the second *prākāra*—a rectangle 420 feet by 310, with a *gōpura* in the middle of each of its sides smaller than the outer *gōpura*. Most of this second enclosure is roofed in, while a part of the northern side is open. Within there is a smaller covered court, 250 feet by 160 feet, entered by only one gateway from the east. It is outside this entrance that a very elaborate grouping of pillars, in some ways the most impressive part of the scheme, is found. Within the last enclosure is the main temple with the usual three compartments, the cella being surmounted by a *śikhara* which projects above the flat roof covering the whole of this part of the temple. All the corridors and halls in these enclosures have long colonnades of pillars in the characteristic style of the period offering vistas in all directions. The sanctuary of Mīnākshī is an enclosure attached to the southern side of the main temple and somewhat to its rear, and is a smaller replica of the main temple, roughly half its size. It measures 225 feet by 150 feet and is entered by two *gōpuras*, a relatively small one on the east and a larger one on the west. As in the adjacent Śiva temple, the *śikhara* of the sanctum rises above the flat roof of the temple. In front of the temple of Mīnākshī is the Tank of Golden Lilies (Pl. XVII), a reservoir 165 feet by 120 feet, surrounded by steps and a pillared portico on the sides. Its picturesque appearance is enhanced by the background of the southern *gōpura*, over 150 feet high, which is reflected on its surface. Near the north-east corner of the tank, a fair-sized *gōpura* marks a processional passage from outside to the Mīnākshī temple, and constitutes an independent entrance to that shrine. The Hall of a Thousand Pillars in the north-east angle of the outer *prākāra* covers an area 240 feet by 250 feet, and its front which faces south lies alongside of the wide, pillared approach to the main temple. Its interior is symmetrical in the arrangement of the pillars and includes a central aisle leading up to a small shrine of Sabhāpati at its northern end. The sculptures on the pillars, says Fergusson, ' surpass those of any other hall of its class I am acquainted with '. Outside the main enclosure but in axial alignment with the eastern *gōpura* and separated from it by a street, is the *Pudumaṇḍapam* known also as ' Tirumalai's choultry '. This is a large open hall 350 feet by 105 feet, divided longitudinally into a nave and two aisles by four rows of pillars, all very elaborately carved. The pillars towards the centre of the hall bear life-size statues of the Nāyak kings of Madura, the latest being that of Tirumalai, the builder of the *maṇḍapa*.

The additions made by the Nāyaks of Madura to the Ranganātha temple of Śrīrangam contributed in no small measure to make it by far the largest of South Indian temples. The outermost *prākāra* is a rectangle, 2,880 feet by 2,475. There are no fewer than six other *prākāras* within, making in all seven concentric enclosures round the shrine in the centre. The three outer enclosures are as much parts of the surrounding town as of the temple, and are remarkable only for some of their *gōpuras*. Of the two incomplete *gōpuras* on the outermost wall, that on the south or main approach would, if it had been finished according to plan, have attained a height of nearly 300 feet. The temple proper may be taken to begin at the fourth court of which the outer wall measures 1,235 feet by 849 feet, and has *gōpuras* on the north, south and east, the last being the finest and largest in the whole scheme. Near this *gōpura* at the north-eastern angle of the fourth enclosure is the Hall of a Thousand Pillars, 500 feet by 160 feet. The celebrated ' horse-court ' is also in this enclosure. The next or third enclosure has *gōpuras* on the north and the south, but the latter opening into the fine pillared *garuḍamaṇḍapa* is the main entrance. This enclosure contains two tanks named after the Sun and the Moon. The second enclosure is a covered court occupied mainly by pillared halls with a long processional passage on the western side. It has two entrances, from north and south. Within is the innermost enclosure with its entrance on the south side, its sides being 240 feet by 181 feet. The sanctuary is a circular chamber set within a square compartment and surrounded by a larger rectangular chamber; its position is indicated by its golden domical *vimāna* projecting above the flat roof.

The temple of Rāmeśvaram, planned and constructed on a unitary plan like that at Madura, is remarkable for its impressive pillared corridors which completely surround it besides forming avenues leading up to it. These passages vary in width from 17 to 21 feet and have a height of about 25 feet. Their total length is calculated to be about 3,000 feet.

The art of casting bronzes which began to be practised on an extensive scale under the Cholas continued to flourish under the rulers of Vijayanagar and their feudatories. The subjects of sculpture and the mode of treatment continued to be the same as before, but this period is remarkable for some actual life-size portraits which have survived, like those of Krishnadeva Rāya and his two wives, of Venkata I, and others of doubtful identity, all in the Tirupati temple. Mention may also be made of a small stone statue in the round of Krishnadeva Rāya in a niche in the doorway below the northern *gōpura* of the temple at Chidambaram which he built in 1520.

We may conclude with a brief sketch of the architecture of the Bāhmanī kingdom and its successors. In general the model of Delhi architecture was followed here even after the political bond with Delhi was snapped in 1347. No provincial style of Muslim architecture in India was less influenced by the surrounding indigenous styles than the art of the Bāhmanī kingdom. From the beginning of the fifteenth century, however, other and more remote influences began to come into play. The Bāhmanī rulers were generous patrons of art, science and learning, and their court was as attractive to poets, scholars and artists as their army was to soldiers of fortune. Influences from the military architecture of Europe and the civil architecture of Persia come more into evidence here than in any other contemporary style of India. The Jami Masjid of Gulbarga is known to be the work of Persian architects. Others like the Chand Minar at Daulatabad (1435) and the college of Mahmud Gawan at Bidar (1472) are also dominantly Persian, and must have been the work mostly of architects and craftsmen from that country. Other structures show Persian inspiration in a more partial and indirect form. Towards the end of the fifteenth century, however, the Deccan reasserted itself and the influence of pre-Muslim styles appears strongly in the architecture of Bijapur on which Indian artists were employed in considerable numbers.

Only two monuments can be ascribed with confidence to the period from 1294 to 1347—the Jami Masjid at Daulatabad (*c.* 1315) and the Deval Mosque at Bodhan of the reign of Muhammad Tughlak. But both are only adaptations of Hindu shrines and have no real bearing on the history of Islamic art. There was much sound work during this period on the fortification of strongholds, as at Daulatabad; but the history of military architecture has not yet been properly studied, and it is difficult to discriminate clearly between the work of successive periods or even between Hindu and Muslim. In Daulatabad (Pl. XVIII), for instance, Yādava, Tughlak and Bāhmanī work met and combined. The inner citadel stands on an isolated rock 600 feet high. The outer wall is 2¾ miles in perimeter and in between the two there are three inner walls, all loop-holed and battlemented and furnished with fortified gateways, outworks and bastions, and so arranged that the maximum of fire could be concentrated on an assailant. In addition, a moat below the glacis surrounded the outer wall. The Bāhmanīs did much for military architecture as they had powerful enemies on all sides. Among the more important fortresses are Ellichpur, Gawilgarh and Narnala in the north of Berar; Mahur, in Adilabad district, which served to keep in check the highland chieftains of Satpura and the wild tribes beyond the Wardha river; Parenda, Nāldurg, Panhala and Gulbarga itself in the west; Bidar in the centre; Wārangal and Golconda towards the east; and Mudgal and Raichur in the south-west corner. Some of these were taken over from conquered Hindu states but so transformed as to retain little of their original character. Raichur, for instance, was built in 1294 by a Hindu chieftain and Mudgal was once the seat of local Yādava governors. Bidar has walls 50 feet high and three miles in circumference, provided with battlements, bastions and outworks, all solidly constructed, and protected further by a triple ditch hewn out of solid rock. Parenda, a smaller fort traditionally ascribed to Mahmud Gawan, is remarkable for the singular efficiency of its defences. It is a clear case of imitation from European models in military engineering probably due to foreigners, Turks and others, in Bāhmanī service. But the architectural style is essentially local and 'combines sincerity of purpose with an innate sense for the decorative' (Marshall).

The capital cities of Gulbarga and Bidar were the centres of the civil architecture of the Bāhmanīs. In the former are two groups of royal tombs—one near the south gate of the fort and the other to the east of the town. They fall into two patterns:

single tombs, 'simple square chambers crowned with battlements and corner turrets and roofed by a single dome, the whole standing on a low square plinth'; and double tombs which are merely duplications of the single ones. In the treatment of details, changes are traceable from reign to reign. First, Sultan Hasan's tomb is typical of the Tughlak style of Delhi. So also are the tombs of Muhammad Shah, Mujahid, and Daud. In that of Ghiyyas-ud-din, at the close of the fourteenth century, Hindu craftsmanship begins to appear in the carvings of the prayer niche. A generation later, the splendid mausoleum of Firuz Shah and his family, measuring externally 153 feet by 76 feet, bears witness to the growing strength of this Hindu influence as well as to the new preference for Persian ornament, the former on the outside and the latter in the shining plaster and painted decorations of the interior recalling the rich designs of Persian book-binding and embroidery.

At Gulbarga, Muhammad Shah built two mosques: the earlier and smaller one is now the Shah Bazar Masjid, austere in the simplicity of its style, imitating the Tughlak architecture of Firuz Shah's reign at Delhi. The other, the famous Jami Masjid (1367) within the fort has stilted domes and narrow entrances typical of the Persian style, but otherwise belonging more to Delhi than to Persia. The squat arches of its cloisters, appearing here for the first time, become henceforth a familiar feature of Deccan architecture. The treatment of its courtyard is unique, for instead of being left open to the sky as usual it 'is covered in by 63 small domes carried on arched bays, the cloisters at the sides being roofed with corresponding vaults, and light and air being admitted to the interior through open archways in their outer walls'. The building measures 216 feet by 176 feet overall and has four shapely domes at its four corners. A fifth and larger one dominating the whole is raised on a square clerestory above the prayer chamber. The dignified simplicity and grandeur of the structure place it in the front rank of such buildings and account for its undoubted influence in the subsequent development of the style.

Bidar comes up from the time of Ahmad Shah Wali (1422-35). Here are two separate groups of tombs, one of later Bāhmanī kings and the other of Barid Shahi. The former number twelve and resemble the Gulbarga tombs though 'their scale is larger, their domes loftier and more bulbous and their façades adorned with a greater multiplicity of arched recesses or screened windows'. The finest of them is that of Ahmad himself which has its interior decorated with brilliantly coloured paintings in the Persian style and bands of Kufic and other inscriptions worked out in letters of gold on a ground of deep blue or vermilion. Persianization is carried further in the Chand Minar at Daulatabad of the time of Ala-ud-din Ahmad Shah (1436-58), and in the tomb of that emperor, of which the façade is covered with enamel tiles in various shades of blue. But the Madrasa of Gawan in Bidar (1472) is the most remarkable building in the Persian style (Pl. XX). Three storeys in height with towering minarets at its two front corners, it covers an area of 205 feet by 180 feet. 'In it were a mosque, library, lecture halls, professors' quarters and students' cubicles ranged about an open courtyard, a hundred feet this way and that. The mosque and library were to the front of the building on either side of the entrance; the lofty lecture rooms (which rose to the full height of the three storeys) in the middle of the other sides; and the professors' rooms in the corners —all planned for convenience and comfort and amply provided with light and air.' The corner towers are like the Chand Minar in form and the whole front façade between them was emblazoned with a glittering surface of encaustic tile work, 'which with its chevron patterning and deep bold bands of sacred texts, would challenge comparison with anything of its kind in Persia'.

The Adil Shahi rulers of Bijapur made it one of the most magnificent cities in the whole of India. Coming into existence to meet the real need of a large town to serve as a fortified centre of administration, it had all the constituents of a state capital—palaces, mosques, tombs, mint and gateways. The material used in construction, the local trap, gives the whole city a sombre and monotonous look, a striking contrast with the cities in red sandstone and white marble of contemporary Mughal architecture.

The Jami Masjid begun by Adil Shah I about 1565 is one of the first buildings of importance and illustrates the style in its formation. 'Never quite finished, it still lacks the frontage of the courtyard. The arcaded prayer hall has five aisles supported on massive piers and with its fine dome is very impressive. Ornament has been sparingly used and the surfaces are finished with a coat of fine plaster which time has mellowed to a pleasant creamy tint. The central bay, however, is embellished with the most gorgeous array of patterns in colour and gold, work of a later hand which is not in keeping with the austere refinement of the rest. The Ibrahim Rauza, built at the end of the sixteenth century, is a highly ornate structure on a large scale. It consists of the tomb of Sultan Ibrahim II and its mosque, both on a raised terrace inside a walled enclosure, and may claim to rival the finest buildings of the Mughals. The tomb is the more important structure and its artistic finish, with carved decorations by local craftsmen, leaves nothing to be desired.

The versatility of the Bijapur workman is seen in the contrast between the majestic proportions and breadth of treatment of the Gol Gumbaz, the tomb of Muhammad Adil Shah (Pl. XIX), and 'the exquisite detail of the miniature Mihtar Mahal'. The former, the most striking monument in the city, is a *tour de force*. Its dome is one of the largest of its kind and covers an area of no less than 18,000 square feet. Under Muhammad (1627-56), Bijapur reached the height of its power and this monument is its expression. The scheme of the Gol Gumbaz includes 'a mosque, a gateway and musicians' gallery, a hostel and other annexes essential to a royal tomb, all disposed within an extensive walled enclosure'. It is doubtful if the entire scheme was completed. The tomb chamber is one of the largest single cells ever constructed—'a hall of noble proportions'. Externally, apart from the vast size of the dome, 'the most arresting features are the octagonal turrets which project at each angle' and the heavy bracketed cornice below the parapet. Only three sunken arches relieve the wall-space between, and something seems to have been left incomplete here. The arrangement of the arches supporting the dome forms a skilful and artistic solution of a difficult problem of construction, that of gaining a circular platform for the dome from the square sides of the walls. The only other example of its kind was constructed at Cordova 600 years earlier.

The Mihtar Mahal (1620) is not a palace as its name implies but an ornamental gateway to the courtyard of a mosque. It is a tall graceful building with an upper storey consisting of an assembly-room. 'Above this again is an open terrace surrounded by a high wall with oriel windows and a perforated parapet. On each side of the façade are two slender ornamental minarets... but it is the projecting balcony window filling the entire space between that is the most striking feature. It is thrown out from the wall on a series of closely set carved brackets, and the wide eaves-board is supported by struts of stone so finely wrought with the chisel as to have every appearance of wood.' The delicate prettiness of the whole structure is unrivalled.

A few examples of secular Hindu architecture showing strong Islamic influence may also be noticed. The Lotus Mahal, a garden palace of Vijayanagar built about 1575, employs recessed and foliated arches of the Lodi type together with a pyramidal roof built up in tiers after the manner of the *śikhara* of a southern temple. The large palace in the fort at Chandragiri (early seventeenth century) presents a magnificent façade combining the same features with very pleasant results. On the other hand the palace of Tirumalai Nāyaka at Madura (*c.* 1645), in which some European influence can also be traced in addition, is imposing by its large dimensions, but lacks satisfactory co-ordination of the architectural features drawn from different sources.

BIBLIOGRAPHY

PERCY BROWN: *Indian Architecture*, Vols. I and II (Bombay, no date)

Cambridge History of India, Vols. III and IV (Cambridge, 1937)

A. K. COOMARASWAMY: *History of Indian and Indonesian Art* (New York, 1927)

J. FERGUSSON: *History of Indian and Eastern Architecture*, Vols. I and II (London, 1910)

R. GROUSSET (tr. C. A. PHILLIPS): *India* ('The Civilizations of the East' Series) (London, 1932)

Indian Archaeology Annual Review (Arch. Survey of India)

G. JOUVEAU-DUBREUIL: *Archéologie du Sud de l'Inde* (Paris, 1914)

A. U. POPE AND P. ACKERMAN: *A Survey of Persian Art* (London, 1938)

K. R. SRINIVASAN: Art and Architecture in S. India, ch. xxiii in *Mauryas and Satavahanas*, ed. K. A. N. Sastri (Calcutta, 1957)

—: The Pallava Architecture of S. India, *Ancient India* No. 14 (1958)

—: *Cave Temples of the Pallavas* (New Delhi, 1964)

INDEX

(*In references to Ch. XIV* LITERATURE *only the names of authors have been indexed not their works.*)

D